The LaTeX Companion

Michel Goossens
CN Division, CERN, Geneva, Switzerland

Frank Mittelbach
LaTeX3 Project Coordinator, Mainz, Germany

Alexander Samarin
ISO, Geneva, Switzerland

ADDISON-WESLEY PUBLISHING COMPANY

Reading, Massachusetts • Menlo Park, California • New York
Don Mills, Ontario • Wokingham, England • Amsterdam • Bonn
Sydney • Signapore • Tokyo • Madrid • San Juan • Milan • Paris

Many of the designations used by the manufacturers and sellers to distinguish their products are claimed as trademarks. Where those designations appear in this book, and Addison-Wesley was aware of a trademark claim, the designations have been printed in initial caps or all caps.

The procedures and applications presented in this book have been included for their instructional value. They have been tested with care but are not guaranteed for any particular purpose. The publisher does not offer any warranties or representations, nor does it accept any liabilities with respect to the programs or applications.

Library of Congress Cataloging-in-Publication Data

```
Goossens Michel.
    The LaTeX companion / by Michel Goossens, Frank Mittelbach
        p.      cm.
    Includes bibliographical references (p.) and index.
    ISBN 0-201-54199-8
    1. LaTeX (Computer file)   2. Computerized typesetting.
 I. Mittelbach, Frank.   II. Samarin, Alexander.   III. Title.
 Z253.4.L38666   1993
 686.2'2544536--dc20                                     93-23150
                                                             CIP
```

Reproduced by Addison-Wesley from camera-ready copy supplied by the authors.

TO OUR WIVES
ALBINA, CHRISTEL, AND TATIANA
AND SONS
ALEXEI, ANDREI, ARNO, NICOLAS, AND ROMAN
FOR THEIR PATIENCE AND UNDERSTANDING.

Preface

LaTeX is a generic typesetting system that uses TeX as its formatting engine. This companion is a detailed guide through the visible and not-so-visible beauties of LaTeX. As such, it is a comprehensive treatise of those points not fully discussed in Leslie Lamport's LaTeX: *A Document Preparation System* (henceforth referred to as the LaTeX book) [49]. Extensions to basic LaTeX, as described in that book, are discussed, so that the LaTeX book, together with this companion, provide a ready reference to the full functionality of the LaTeX system.

Due to its flexibility, ease of use, and professional typographic quality, LaTeX is presently used in almost all areas of science and the humanities. Unlike many word processors, LaTeX (and its underlying formatting engine TeX) comes free of charge and is not linked to any particular computer architecture or operating system. Since LaTeX source files are plain text files, it is possible to ship them, and the packages referenced, from any computer to any other computer in the world (over electronic networks or via normal mail). The recipient will be able to obtain a final output copy identical to the one generated at the sender's site, independently of the hardware used. Thus members of groups, geographically spread over several sites in different countries, or even on different continents, can now work together in composing complex documents where different parts can be dealt with by different individuals, and then brought together without problems. Moreover, the use of electronic manuscripts has the potential to speed up the publication of papers by publishers.

LaTeX is not difficult to learn and a beginner can benefit from the system after reading through the first few chapters of Lamport's LaTeX book, the basic reference on LaTeX. After some experience, you will probably have to solve some more advanced problems whose solution cannot be found directly in that book. If you are one of those users who would like to know how LaTeX can be extended to create the nicest documents possible without becoming a (LA)TEX guru[1], then this book is for you.

You will be guided, step by step, through the various important areas of LATEX and be shown the links that exist between them. The structure of a LATEX document, the basic formatting tools, and the layout of the page are all dealt with in great detail. A sufficient library of packages in the area of floats, graphics, tables, PostScript, and multi-language support are presented in a convenient way. This book is the first volume to include all of the important LATEX tools, such as: up-to-date descriptions of version 2 of the New Font Selection Scheme (NFSS2), the $\mathcal{A}_{\mathcal{M}}S$-LATEX mathematics extensions, the epic and eepic extensions to LATEX's picture environment, and the *MakeIndex* and BIBTEX programs for producing and controlling the generation of indices and bibliographic references. Finally, an overview of ways to define new commands and environments, lengths, boxes, general lists, etc., as well as ways of facilitating the handling of these objects, complete the picture.

All three of us have been involved for several years in the support and development of LATEX applications in various professional environments and countries. We have taught the secrets of LATEX to many different audiences, and have been listening to the user community by following the discussions in the text processing related news groups and at TEX conferences. This has allowed us to gather a coherent view of a vast collection of subjects, which, we think, you might need one day if you want to fully exploit the richness and strengths of the LATEX system. Note, however, that this book is not a replacement for, but a companion to, the LATEX book. You are assumed to have read the first part of that book, and in any case, it should be considered a reference for precise and full description of the LATEX commands.

To make the presented information even more complete and useful, our readers are kindly invited to send their comments, suggestions, or remarks to any one of the authors. We shall be glad to correct any remaining mistakes or oversights in a future edition, and are open to suggestions for improvements or the inclusion of important developments that we may have overlooked.

LATEX 2$_\varepsilon$—The New LATEX Release

Over the years many extensions have been developed for LATEX with one unfortunate result: incompatible LATEX formats came into use at different sites. Thus, to process documents from various places, a site maintainer was forced to keep LATEX (with and without NFSS), SLITEX, $\mathcal{A}_{\mathcal{M}}S$-LATEX, and so on. In addition, when looking at a source file it was not always clear what format the document was written for.

---

[1] A (LA)TEX guru is a person knowing the internals of both LATEX and primitive TEX by heart. In this book we use the logo (LA)TEX whenever we refer to both TEX and LATEX.

To put an end to this unsatisfactory situation a new LATEX release was announced for fall 1993 that brings all such extensions back under a single format and thus prevents the proliferation of mutually incompatible dialects of LATEX 2.09. With LATEX2$_\varepsilon$ the new font selection will be standard and style files like amstex (formerly $\mathcal{A}_{\mathcal{M}}S$-LATEX format) or slides (formerly SLiTEX format) will become extension packages, all working with the same base format. The introduction of a new release also made it possible to add a small number of often-requested features (like an extended version of \newcommand). All the new possibilities are described in this book, thus allowing you to make full use of the new LATEX release.

To make it easy to distinguish between old LATEX 2.09 sources and new sources (making use of new features), the first command in a LATEX document was changed from \documentstyle to \documentclass, thus enabling the software to automatically detect an old source file and switch to compatibility mode if necessary.

The LATEX3 Project

LATEX is presently being rewritten under the coordination of one of the authors (Frank Mittelbach), Chris Rowley and Rainer Schöpf. This endeavor is called the LATEX3 Project [57]. A lot of the functionality described in this book as extensions to basic LATEX will be available in that system: as part of the kernel, or in one of the extension packages. To help funding, half of the royalties from this book will go directly to the LATEX3 Project. Therefore, when buying this book, you not only obtain a handy, complete, and up-to-date reference to many important and useful packages available with LATEX today, but you also actively contribute to making LATEX more powerful and user-friendly in the future.

Acknowledgments

We first of all wish to thank Peter Gordon, our editor at Addison-Wesley, who not only made this book possible, but through his constant encouragement kept us on the right track. His suggestions and ideas made the companion richer, both in content and in form. We also wish to acknowledge Marsha Finley, of *Superscript* Editorial Production Services, for the efficiency with which she helped us with the practical aspects relating to the preparation of this book. Helen Goldstein, associate editor at Addison-Wesley, was always ready to advise us whenever we asked.

We gratefully recognize all of our many colleagues in the (LA)TEX world who developed the packages, not only those described here, but also the hundreds of others, which help users typeset their documents better and faster. Without the continuous effort of all these enthusiasts, LATEX would not be the magnificent and flexible tool it is today. We hope we have done some justice to them by mentioning, when first describing a given package, the original author and/or other major contributors, as far as this information was known to us.

We are especially indebted to Johannes Braams, David Carlisle, Michael Downes, Sebastian Rahtz, and Rainer Schöpf for their careful reading of the manuscript. Their numerous comments, suggestions, corrections, and hints have substantially improved the quality of the text. Roger Woolnough proofread an early version of the manuscript, Silvio Levy the chapter on NFSS. Finally we want to express our gratitude to CERN for allowing us to use its computer facilities for preparing the compuscript.

How to Read This Book

The titles of the various chapters should convey relatively clearly the subject area addressed in each case. In principle, all chapters can be read more or less independently and, if necessary, pointers are given to where complementary information can be found in other parts of the book.

Chapter 1	gives a short introduction to the LaTeX system.
Chapter 2	discusses generic and document-oriented markup.
Chapter 3	describes LaTeX's basic typesetting commands.
Chapter 4	explains which tools are available to globally define the visual layout of the pages of a document by using pagestyles.
Chapter 5	shows how to assemble material into columns and rows with the extended tabular and array environments, and their multipage equivalents—supertabular and longtable.
Chapter 6	provides a general treatment of floating material.
Chapter 7	discusses in detail LaTeX's New Font Selection Scheme (NFSS2) and presents its various user commands. It is shown how to add new fonts, both in math and text mode.
Chapter 8	reviews the amstex package, which adds many powerful typesetting commands in the field of mathematics.
Chapter 9	looks at the problem of using LaTeX in the multi-language or non-English environment. The babel system and other language-specific packages are described.
Chapter 10	addresses the field of device-independent graphics showing how the epic, eepic and other packages extend the possibilities of LaTeX's basic picture environment.

Chapter 11	shows how the PostScript page description language not only can turn LaTeX into a full-blown graphics utility, but also how it makes it possible, via the NFSS, for a user to choose a font from amongst hundreds of font families, available as PostScript Type 1 outlines.
Chapter 12	tackles the problems associated with preparing an index. The program *MakeIndex* is described in detail.
Chapter 13	surveys how LaTeX's companion program BIBTEX tries to solve problems related to maintaining bibliographic data bases. Various existing bibliographic styles are discussed and the format of the BIBTEX language used in the style files is presented in detail, allowing the user to customize an existing style.
Chapter 14	shows how to document LaTeX files using the doc package and its companion program DOCSTRIP.
Appendix A	first reviews how to handle and manipulate the basic LaTeX programming structures. The extensions introduced by the calc package in the field of arithmetic operations, and extended control structures added to LaTeX2_ε are discussed.[2]
Appendix B	explains how to get the files described in this book from the various TEX archives or from the TEX Users Groups.

In order to make the examples as independent as possible from basic TEX, extensive use has been made of the packages calc and ifthen, which are described in the appendices A.4 and A.5. You should study the extensions to LaTeX, introduced in these packages, if you want to understand how many of the examples in this book function in detail.

Many examples make use of new features in LaTeX2_ε; especially font changes for text are all done in LaTeX2_ε style, i.e., with the commands shown in table 7.2 on page 171. Abbreviated forms, like {\bf word} are normally not used, since they are style defined commands and may or may not be available for all classes of documents.

While it is certainly possible to make good use of most parts of this book within a LaTeX 2.09 environment (the event of LaTeX2_ε happened after 90% of the book was finished) we suggest that you upgrade to the new version as soon as possible so that the worldwide community of LaTeX users again speaks a single language. As said above, LaTeX2_ε is able to identify and process old documents written for LaTeX 2.09. However, packages written or updated for LaTeX2_ε will not run with the old system.

---

[2]In LaTeX 2.09 programming structures like if-then-else were made available in the package ifthen; in LaTeX2_ε this package is extended and enhanced.

Typographic Conventions

As explained in the discussion about the links between content and form or generic and layout markup, it is essential that the presentation of the material conveys immediately its function in the framework of the text. Therefore, we present below the typographic conventions used in this book.

LaTeX command and environment names are in monospaced type (for example, `\caption`, `enumerate`, `\begin{tabular}`), while names of package and class files are in sans-serif type (e.g., article).

The syntax of LaTeX constructs is presented inside a rectangular box. Command arguments are shown in italic type.

```
\commandname{arg1}{arg2}{arg3}
```

Lines containing examples with LaTeX commands are indented and are typeset in a monospaced type at a size somewhat smaller than that of the main text.

```
\chapter{Title of the Chapter}
\section{Section Title}
Some text...
```

When it is important to show the result of a series of commands, then the input and output are shown side by side as follows:

The right column shows the input text to be treated by LaTeX. In the left column one sees the result after typesetting.

```
The right column shows the input text to
be treated by \LaTeX{}. In the left column
one sees the result after typesetting.
```

For large examples, where the input and output cannot be shown conveniently alongside one another, the following layout is used:

Input text

```
This is a wide line, whose input commands and output result
cannot be shown nicely in two columns.
```

This is a wide line, whose input commands and output result cannot be shown nicely in two columns.

Output text

Cross-references to page numbers where a given subject is treated in Leslie Lamport's LaTeX book are shown in the margin in parentheses and are preceded by a calligraphic $\mathcal{L}$, as seen here. They correspond to the page numbers as they

($\mathcal{L}$ 4)

were in the first edition that described LaTeX 2.09; all differences to LaTeX 2_ε are noted in this book.

Commands to be typed by the user on a computer terminal are shown in monospaced type and are underlined, e.g.: <u>This is user input</u>.

Using All Those Packages

In this book we describe over 150 packages and options that extend or modify LaTeX's basic possibilities. In order to show their action, we (in principle) have to load them all at the same time. For various reasons that is impractical, if not impossible. Indeed many packages, like program, use up a lot of counters, and TeX only allows a total of 256 counters. Therefore, when you hit this limit you must reduce the number of files you load simultaneously. In the production of this book we used a different strategy: we prepared some of the examples as separate files and included them as Encapsulated PostScript. Moreover, we used the package hackalloc. It redefines the allocation primitive so that *all* allocation becomes group-local. This means that by loading packages only when they are needed inside a brace group, the counter and length variables will be deallocated when you exit from the group. This procedure, however, can have some side effects, and should only be used with great care. However, we used most of the packages together, with the result that we had to recompile TeX several times during the preparation of this book. One of the log files produced during the last steps of the preparation showed the following summary:

```
Here is how much of TeX's memory you used:
 9692 strings out of 16716
 118315 string characters out of 133654
 236569 words of memory out of 262141
 8131 multiletter control sequences out of 9500
 81058 words of font info for 228 fonts, out of 90000 for 255
 20 hyphenation exceptions out of 607
 34i,23n,41p,509b,1403s stack positions out of 300i,40n,60p,3000b,4000s
Output written on companion.dvi (555 pages, 2008780 bytes).
```

As you can see, we nearly reached the font limit (which cannot be raised further) because of the many fonts shown in chapter 7, and the usage for strings, characters, main memory, and control sequences is probably much higher than in any LaTeX run you ever made. This is not surprising given that the whole book is produced in a single LaTeX run with all those packages working together to produce the examples.

Even when you do not reach a limit of the kind mentioned above, there are other interference effects between different packages. For instance, some extensions such as french make some characters active (i.e., some characters act as though they were control sequences). Problems may result when such a character is then encountered in another package. This means that not all of the packages described in this book can be used together. Sometimes you can solve the problem by loading problematic packages as one of the last \usepackage declarations. Also, some packages make the @ character active (e.g., amstex), and this can have nasty consequences if you load other packages that use the @ character.

As a rule of thumb, if you observe some odd behavior when you add a package to an existing list of packages, which seemed to work nicely together before, there might be a compatibility problem. Try loading the new file at the end, and if that does not work, take out each of the other files one by one. In this way you might find the file or files that are responsible for the problem.

Contents

List of Tables

List of Figures

CHAPTER 1

Introduction

LaTeX is not just a system for typesetting mathematics. Its applications span the one-page memorandums, business or personal letters, newsletters, articles about exact sciences and developments in the humanities, and full-scale book and reference works on all topics. Nowadays, versions of LaTeX exist for practically every large mainframe, workstation, or personal computer. To better understand why this happened, the first section of this chapter looks back at the origins of TeX and LaTeX, and then asks where to go next. The second section gives an overview of the LaTeX system as a whole. This orientation should help the reader to clearly understand the rôle of the various components and files created by LaTeX. The important difference between generic and visual markup is the subject of the next sections. The advantages of the generic approach are explained in the context of the separation of the content and form of a document, and it is emphasized that documents should be built on the generic principle as much as possible. When, for the sake of clarity, it proves necessary to use visual markup, the latter should be classified into categories whose definitions are grouped at the beginning of the document and then used locally. This practice guarantees consistency and ease of use.

1.1   A Short History of TeX and LaTeX

1.1.1   In the Beginning There Was TeX

In May 1977, Donald Knuth of Stanford University [38] started work on a text-processing system which is now known as TeX and METAFONT [39–43]. In the foreword of the TeX book [39] Knuth writes: "TeX [is] a new typesetting system intended for the creation of beautiful books—and especially for books that contain a lot of mathematics. By preparing a manuscript in TEX format, you will be telling a computer exactly how the manuscript is to be transformed into pages whose typographic quality is comparable to that of the world's finest printers."

TEX has become popular with thousands of scientists because it can be used for transforming any kind of writing into articles, reports, proposals, books, poetry, and other formats in a way that can be specified completely by the writer through a rich language of commands. The companion program METAFONT allows the design of typefaces to be used to print the output pages.

TEX is particularly useful when the document contains mathematical formulae or when book-like quality appearance is desired. Moreover, it is a portable system, running on a wide range of computer platforms, from micros to mainframes, and its behavior is identical on all machines, a fact extremely important in the scientific and technical community. Related to this portability is TEX's printing device independence, so that a document can be printed on anything from a CRT screen, a medium-resolution dot matrix or laser printer, to a professional high-resolution phototypesetter.

Because of these qualities, and since it is available in the public domain, TEX has become the *de facto* standard text-processing system in many academic departments and research laboratories, whilst it also gains momentum in the professional publishing world as a printing engine. It is available on every conceivable computer platform, from IBM PC-like personal computers and Macintoshes, via UNIX and VMS workstations, to supercomputers like the Cray. In addition, excellent previewers are available that run on most workstations and other graphic displays.

In his foreword to *TEX and METAFONT, New Directions in Typesetting* [37] Gordon Bell wrote over ten years ago that "Don Knuth's Tau Epsilon Chi (TEX) is potentially the most significant invention in typesetting in this century. It introduces a standard language in computer typography and in terms of importance could rank near the introduction of the Gutenberg press."

Recently, Donald Knuth officially announced that TEX would not undergo any further development [47] in the interest of stability.

1.1.2   Then Leslie Lamport Developed LATEX

At the beginning of the 1980s, Leslie Lamport started work on a document preparation system called LATEX, based on the TEX formatter. The system adds a level of abstraction to the plain TEX commands and lets the user concentrate on the structure of a document rather than on formatting details. A few high-level commands allow the user to easily compose most documents. You do not have to worry about typography. Such details are left to the document designer who has the task of providing style files for every application.

LaTeX's functionality, in conjunction with a few auxiliary programs, includes the generation of indices, bibliographies, cross-references, and tables of contents, and the inclusion of figures—features that are lacking in basic TeX.

1.1.3   With LaTeX toward the Year 2000?

Since the number of TeX and especially LaTeX users has grown to many thousands in the last few years, LaTeX has spread into areas for which it is not necessarily optimized (law texts, critical editions of classic authors, poetry, side-by-side multi-language editions, newsletters, to name a few). Recent issues of *TUGboat*, the journal of the TeX Users Group, have carried a number of articles about the shortcomings of TeX, LaTeX and their associated programs [55, 59, 61, 88, 91].

After a meeting with Leslie Lamport at the 1989 TeX Users Group meeting in Stanford, Frank Mittelbach, Chris Rowley, and Rainer Schöpf started work on a reimplementation and extension of LaTeX, the so-called LaTeX3 Project [57]. The main idea is to build an optimized and efficient kernel with basic commands complemented by various packages that will handle functionality in specific areas (like tables, pictures, and mathematics). The new system will provide a complete reimplementation of the style file user interface, making it easier to develop and maintain one's own styles.

In March 1992 at the German DANTE TeX Users meeting in Hamburg a discussion group, NTS, for "The New Typesetting System," was set up to discuss and coordinate areas where TeX should be extended to provide the functionality needed for creating "masterpieces of the Publishing Art" [81].

1.2   LaTeX and Its Components

This section introduces the basic principles of the LaTeX environment, and describes briefly the various files and programs, about which an informed LaTeX user should know. More details can be found in an article by Joachim Schrod, "The Components of TeX" [76].

1.2.1   How Does LaTeX Work?

LaTeX reads and writes several files and you should have a clear understanding of their function. Figure 1.1 on the next page shows schematically the flow of information in a LaTeX run and presents a list of the various files needed.

The most important file in any LaTeX run is the input source file. It is a plain text file, usually prepared with a text editor, and in general has the extension .tex. Files containing structure and layout definitions (extensions .cls, .sty) are usually stored in some standard directories. LaTeX is distributed with five standard document classes, namely, article, report, book, slides, and letter.

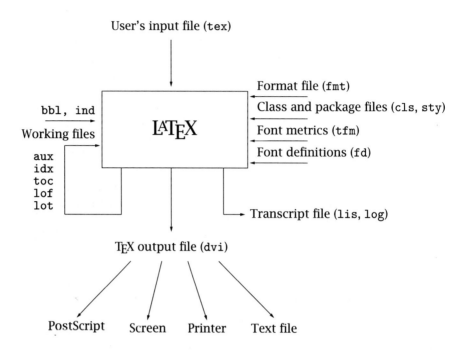

Figure 1.1: Overview of the main files needed by TEX and LATEX

These basic document classes can be further customized by specifying one or more class options or using additional packages like those described in this book. The dimensions of the characters for fonts used by TEX are called *font metrics* and are encoded in .tfm files (for TEX font metrics). For each font used in a document there must be a .tfm file describing height, depth, and width as well as kerning information for every character. TEX only uses these character boxes in its line-breaking algorithm when composing paragraphs. TEX hyphenates words automatically using a language-independent trie-algorithm [53]. For each language, a different set of word-breaking hyphenation patterns can be specified when a format (extension .fmt) file is generated. The LATEX format (usually called lplain.fmt or latex.fmt) mainly contains a precompiled image of all LATEX commands, and the .tfm information for the several preloaded fonts. The correspondence between internal font names and external font files is stored in font-definition files (extension .fd).

The output from LATEX is a set of files. One of them (extension .dvi) contains a representation of the formatted text where the type and position on the page are specified for each character to be output. These .dvi files specify only font names—they do not contain the actual character images. TEX positions its (character) boxes with a resolution better than a thousandth of an inch, so that the output file generated by TEX can be effectively considered *device independent*, hence the name .dvi. To visualize the result the .dvi file must be transformed by a "dvi driver" into the desired output format (e.g., PostScript).

For every run, LaTeX generates a transcript file that usually has the extension .log or .lis but may have others (or even none at all), depending on the operating system. This file contains information, most of which also appears on the screen, such as the names of the files read, the numbers of the pages processed, warning and error messages, and other pertinent data.

Other LATEX output files contain information about cross-referencing (extension .aux), table of contents (extension .toc), list of figures (extension .lof), and list of tables (extension .lot). They are used in a subsequent LATEX run to produce particular elements of the document.

A file with extension .idx contains all indexed items. They can be sorted by a program like *MakeIndex*, which was written by Pehong Chen and Michael Harrison. *MakeIndex* reads the .idx file that contains the index entries and the corresponding page numbers, sorts these items, unifies them, and writes them as LATEX input into a file (extension .ind). Index style information can be specified in an .ist file. Messages created by *MakeIndex* are written to the .ilg file (see chapter 12 for more details).

BIBTEX (see chapter 13) is a program written by Oren Patashnik for the preparation of bibliographies. BIBTEX handles reference data bases collected in .bib files. LATEX writes information about the references required in a document into its .aux file(s); the latter are then read by BIBTEX, which generates a sorted bibliography in a .bbl file. The .bbl file is used by LATEX in a subsequent run. The kind of sorting and the format of the "cite keys" are defined by *bibliography styles*, specified in .bst files. The messages generated by BIBTEX are written to a .blg transcript file.

1.2.2 Output Processors (dvi Drivers)

Once the document has been successfully processed by TEX, you will probably want to see the result. Several options are open, namely:

- Generate a high-quality (greater than 1000 dpi) copy on paper. In this case the .dvi file is translated into dots on a film via a dedicated driver or PostScript is generated.

- Generate a medium-quality (300 dpi) copy on paper. Different dvi drivers, specific to a given printing device, can be used. More and more often, PostScript is becoming the obvious choice.

- The contents (text and graphics) can be visualized on a computer graphics screen, where utilities like xdvi (on X Window System) can be used. Again, PostScript previewers can use the latter language for looking at the information in the document.

- The contents may be viewable on a "dumb" character-only terminal. Graphics cannot be shown in this case, but the text is formatted in columns narrow enough to fit nicely on screen less than 80 columns wide. This kind of documentation is often used for bundling computer program descriptions with the code.

It is clear from the above that the PostScript language plays an important rôle in the process of document visualization. METAFONT sources (.mf) exist for all Computer Modern and LATEX fonts, and thus bitmap images (.pk) can be generated for any kind of printer. PostScript Type 1 renderings of the Computer Modern, LATEX, American Mathematical Society, and Euler fonts also exist and are commercially available from Blue Sky Research and Y&Y. Moreover, Adobe and other type foundries offer a vast choice of fonts, which can be used with LATEX (see section 11.9). This means that you can decide what is the best (and most pleasing) way to present the information in your document.

1.3 The Concept of Generic Markup

1.3.1 What Is Generic Markup?

Originally, markup was the annotation of manuscripts by a copyeditor telling the typesetter how to format the manuscript. It consisted of handwritten notes such as: "*Set this heading in 12-point Helvetica Italic on a 10-point text body, justified on a 22-pica slug with indents of 1 em on the left and none on the right.*"

With the introduction of computers, these remarks could be coded electronically using a special coding system. Each phototypesetter had its own proprietary "language," called markup language by analogy with the old manual system. Since many typesetting companies also provided a "keyboarding" service, the markup source of the documents to be typeset was always the same and the lack of compatibility was not an issue. When, however, authors and clients of typesetting companies started to type their own manuscripts this situation created problems. They could only do the typing if they knew in advance the markup format of their typesetting vendor. If they typed on their own system, it was likely that the markup format of their document would be incompatible with that of the typesetter.

The situation only got worse when people started using computers for document preparation. As in the case of phototypesetting systems, documents were coded with *specific* markup commands. These are low-level formatting commands such as "carriage return," "center the following text," and "go to the next page." A document containing the following specific markup (SCRIPT [31]):

```
.pa ;.sp 2 ;.ce ;.bd
Title of chapter
.sp
```

can only be converted to other typesetting systems at great cost. Another example of specific markup (plain TEX) is:

```
\vfill\eject\begingroup\bf\obeylines\vskip 20pt
\hfil TITLE OF CHAPTER
\vskip 10pt\endgroup\bigskip
```

A movement was started to create a standard markup language, which all typesetting vendors would be persuaded to accept as input. It would be the typesetter's problem to translate this language into the language of their own photocomposition machines. This markup language was a generic markup language. Generic markup means adding information to the text indicating the logical components of a document such as paragraphs, headings, and footnotes. The formatting (visual representation) associated with a component is decoupled from its function (position) in the (hierarchical) structure of the text.

LaTeX is, to a large extent, an example of a "generic markup language" (GML). Thanks to the class file mechanism, the visual style of the various document elements are described in a single place outside of the source document itself.

Building on the pioneering GML work by Charles Goldfarb and also taking into account ideas of Brian Reid's Scribe system, the International Standards Organization developed the SGML (Standard Generalized Markup Language) standard (ISO 8879), which was published in 1986. SGML is a markup language for representing documents in an exchangeable format. SGML is intended "for publishing in its broadest definition, ranging from single medium conventional publishing to multimedia data base publishing. SGML can also be used in office document processing when the benefits of human readability and interchange with publishing systems are required." [34] For an introduction to SGML, see [27,92]. SGML is a meta-language. That is, it specifies the rules by which an infinite variety of markup languages can be created. SGML should not concern itself with the formatting of marked-up documents, i.e., there should be *no* "layout" tags in SGML, like "new page," "new line," or "rule." Instead, these layout-oriented features are properties of certain format components. For example, a heading of level 1 may, in a given layout style, be starting a new page, or a rule may be used to separate a heading from the body of a memo.

As a practical typesetting tool, authored by a scientist, LaTeX combines and balances the advantages of high-level generic characteristics à la SGML, with layout specific support. The class file mechanism makes it possible to produce the same source document in different layouts, while enough bells and whistles are available to fine-tune important documents for producing the highest quality.

1.3.2 Advantages of Generic Markup

The use of a consistent layout throughout a document helps the reader understand the various visual clues associated with a given component. It also allows the document to be reused for producing online documentation, or eases the automatic extraction of information via predefined keywords.

One should also bear in mind the fact that typography is a creative skill, requiring a level of experience and craftsmanship that is rarely found in the untrained layman. Therefore the development of a new style is better left to specialist designers, and casual users should restrict themselves mostly to *small* and *consistent* modifications of an already existing style. Extreme care should be taken not to upset the subtle visual balance between the various document elements.

1.3.3 Separation of Content and Form

In order to ensure that all logical document elements receive the same typographical treatment throughout the document, you should define new document elements in a generic way in the document preamble. By this means you can be sure that the same presentation will be used everywhere to flag the element in question.

As an example, when writing a reference manual you might want to have every occurrence of a command typeset in a given font, and entered in the index automatically. Or you might choose to put the description of a command with its parameters in a shaded box, always in an identical way. You might even contemplate giving a certain presentation form to your `tabular` material. Therefore, it is best to define a corresponding style for your `tabular` environment in the document preamble. Similar considerations apply for lists, headings, and so on. Definitions of (and possible later changes) need only be made in one place in the preamble, and they will propagate automatically to your complete document.

Another advantage of using generic commands is that it is extremely simple to apply a different style just by selecting a different class in the `\documentclass` or specifying additional options to the `\documentclass` and `\usepackage` commands (see section 2.1 on page 11).

1.4 Necessity of Layout Markup

Notwithstanding all the benefits of generic markup, as discussed above, in the final preparation of your document you will sometimes need to overrule the decisions made by TeX.

An example is the representation of data in a `tabular` environment where the clarity of the layout of the data in the table can contribute substantially to a better understanding of the presentation. Moreover, when the final version of a document is being readied, it frequently occurs that the author has to insert line and page breaks in some strategic places.

1.4.1 Pitfalls of Layout Markup

As already pointed out, it is not good practice to make certain layout markup decisions inside the text of a document. It is much better to define a new LaTeX environment, like `Ctab` for a centered `tabular` environment, if that is what is generally desired. Similarly, local font changes inside an environment should be limited and the generic nature of the use of a given font should be formalized by defining a corresponding specific new environment or command. Otherwise, any change in the presentation of your material results in an enormous amount of manual labor—you have to find and modify every instance of your layout markup.

You should also not misuse generic structural commands to obtain a given visual effect. For example, the sectioning commands like `\paragraph` should *not* be used to get the first few words in a paragraph in bold face. Sectioning commands have a structural function inside a document (see section 2.3.1 on page 20) and using them to customize the local layout might generate some surprises when you switch to a different implementation of the same class structures—like seeing some of your paragraphs getting preceded by numbers! You are better off defining a dedicated command like `\Boldtext` or `\Boldpar` to obtain the desired effect.

1.4.2   When to Use Layout Markup

When preparing the final form of a document you will find that it is often necessary to intervene locally at the micro-level to obtain a certain visual effect. Nevertheless it is always preferable to hide as much as possible the layout markup
behind the generic markup. You can do this, for example, by building into the
generic commands facilities for checking the space left on the page, for calculating the width of certain text strings, and so on.

CHAPTER 2

The Structure of a LaTeX Document

As explained earlier it is important to separate the form and structure of a document. In this chapter we show how this general principle is implemented in LaTeX.

The first section of this chapter shows how document class files, packages, options, and preamble commands can affect the structure and layout of a document.[1] The logical subdivisions of a document are discussed in general, before explaining in more detail how sectioning commands and their arguments define a hierarchical structure, how they generate numbers for titles, and how they produce running heads and feet. Different ways of typesetting section titles are presented with the help of examples. It is also shown how the information that is written to the table of contents can be controlled and how the look of this table, as well as that of the lists of tables and figures, can be customized. The final section introduces LaTeX commands for managing cross-references and their scoping rules.

2.1 The Structure of a Source File

You can use LaTeX for several purposes, like writing an article or a letter, or producing your overhead slides. Clearly, documents for different purposes may

---

[1] Compared to LaTeX 2.09, in LaTeX 2_ε the general structure of the source file has been reorganized and enhanced. Older documents will be treated automatically using a compatibility mode.

```
\documentclass[twocolumn,a4paper]{article}
\usepackage{multicol}
\usepackage[german,french]{babel}
\addtolength{\textheight}{2cm}
\begin{document}
```

Figure 2.1: An example of a document preamble

The class of this document is article. The layout is influenced with the formatting request twocolumn (typeset in two columns) and the option a4paper (paper to print on is A4). The first \usepackage declaration informs LaTeX that this document contains commands and structures provided by the package multicol. We also use the babel package with the options german (support for German language) and french (support for French language). Finally, for this document the default height of the text body was enlarged by two centimeters.

need different logical structures, i.e., different commands and environments. We say that a document belongs to a *class* of documents having the same general structure (but not necessarily the same typographical appearance). You specify the class your document belongs to by starting your LaTeX file with a \documentclass command, where the mandatory parameter specifies the name of the *document class*. The document class defines the available logical commands and environments (for example, \chapter in the report class) as well as a default formatting for those elements. An optional argument allows you to modify the formatting of those elements by supplying a list of *class options*. For example, 11pt is an option recognized by most document classes that instructs LaTeX to choose eleven point as the basic document type size.

Many LaTeX commands described in this book are not specific to a single class but can be used with several classes. A collection of such commands is called a package and you inform LaTeX about your use of certain packages in your document by placing one or more \usepackage commands after \documentclass.

Just like the \documentclass declaration, the \usepackage declaration has a mandatory argument that is the name of the package and an optional argument that can contain a list of *package options* that modify the behavior of the package.

The document classes and the packages are realized in external files with the extension .cls and .sty, respectively.[2] Code for class options is sometimes stored in files (in this case with the extension .clo) but is normally directly specified in the class or package file. See appendix A for more information on

---

[2]In LaTeX 2.09 "style files" had the extension .sty. Since nearly all such style files for LaTeX 2.09 can be used without modifications as packages in LaTeX 2ε, .sty was chosen as the extension for packages in LaTeX 2ε.

declaring options. However, in case of options, the file name can differ from the option name, for example, the option 11pt might be related to `art11.clo` when used in the article class and to `bk11.clo` inside the book class.

Commands between the `\documentclass` command and `\begin{document}` are in the so-called *document preamble*. All style parameters must be defined in that area, either in package or class files or directly in your document *before* the `\begin{document}` command, which sets the values for some of the global parameters; an example is shown in figure 2.1 on the facing page.

As a rule, nonstandard LaTeX package files contain general modifications or improvements[3] with respect to standard LaTeX, while commands in the preamble define changes for the current document.

Thus, if you want to modify the layout of your document you have several possibilities:

- change the standard settings for parameters in a class file by options defined for that class;

- add one or more packages to your document and make use of them;

- change the standard settings for parameters in a package file by options defined for that package;

- define your own local packages containing special parameter settings and load them with `\usepackage` after the package or class they are supposed to modify (this is explained in the next section), and

- make last minute adjustments inside the preamble.

And if you want to get deeper into LaTeX's internals, you can, of course, define your own general purpose packages that can be manipulated with options. For this you will find additional information in appendix A.

2.1.1   Processing of Options and Packages

The algorithm in LaTeX2_ε used to process the options of `\documentclass` and `\usepackage` is more powerful than the mechanism that handled options in the LaTeX 2.09 `\documentstyle` command. There is a clear distinction between declared options (of a class or package) and general purpose package files.[4]

---

[3]A lot of them have become de facto standards and are described in this book. This does not mean, however, that packages that are not described in this book are necessarily less important or useful, of inferior quality, or that they should not be used. We merely concentrated on a few of the more established ones and for the others we chose to explain what functionality is possible in a given area.

[4]In LaTeX 2.09 the options of the `\documentstyle` command were a mixture of declared options (executed directly) and undeclared options (which resulted in a `.sty` file to be read after the `\documentstyle` command finished processing). In LaTeX2_ε this is now cleanly separated.

The latter have to be specified using the \usepackage command. Think of options as properties of the whole document (when used in \documentclass) or as properties of individual packages (if specified in \usepackage).

You can only specify options in a \usepackage command if these options are declared by the package. Otherwise, you will receive an error message, informing you that your specified option is unknown to the package in question. Options to the \documentclass are handled slightly differently. If a specified option is not declared by the class it will assumed to be a "global option."

All options to \documentclass (declared and global ones) are automatically passed as class options to all \usepackage declarations. Thus, if a package file loaded with a \usepackage declaration recognizes (i.e., declares) some of the class options it can take appropriate actions; otherwise, the class options will be ignored while processing that package. Since all options have to be defined inside the class or package file their action is under the control of the class or package (it can be anything from setting internal switches to reading an external file). For this reason their order in the optional argument of \documentclass or \usepackage is irrelevant.

If you want to use several packages, all taking the same options (for example, none), it is possible to load them all with a single \usepackage command by specifying the package names as a comma separated list in the mandatory argument, e.g.:

```
\usepackage[german]{babel}
\usepackage[german]{varioref}
\usepackage{multicol}
\usepackage{epic}
```

is equivalent to

```
\usepackage[german]{babel,varioref}
\usepackage{multicol,epic}
```

By specifying german as a global option this can be further shortened to

```
\documentclass[german]{book}
\usepackage{babel,varioref,multicol,epic}
```

since then german will be passed to all packages specified and thus will be processed by those packages that declare it.

Finally, when the \begin{document} is reached, all global options are checked to see whether they have been used by any package; if not, you will get an error message. The reason for the error is usually a spelling mistake in your option name or the removal of a \usepackage command loading a package that used this option.

Therefore, if you want to make some modifications to a document class or a package (for example, parameter changes or redefinitions of some commands), you should put the relevant code into a separate file with the extension .sty. Then load this file with a \usepackage command after the package whose behavior you wish to modify (or the document class if your modifications concern class issues). Such a local package file should contain one special declaration at the beginning which tells LaTeX 2_ε for which distribution (release) it was originally written, namely:

```
\NeedsTeXFormat{format}[release]
```

The *format* must be the string LaTeX2e. If the optional *release* argument is specified it should contain the release date of your LaTeX 2_ε distribution in the form YYYY/MM/DD. For example

```
\NeedsTeXFormat{LaTeX2e}[1994/02/01]
```

would specify the LaTeX 2_ε release distributed on the first of February 1994 (LaTeX 2_ε is distributed twice a year on fixed dates). The purpose of this command is the detection of obsolete releases of LaTeX 2_ε. If, for example, your package makes use of a command that had a bug in the 1994/02/01 release and that was corrected in the 1994/08/01 release, a specification of 1994/08/01 in the optional argument of \NeedsTeXFormat will output a warning if your package is used with an older LaTeX 2_ε release. A newer release date is accepted without a warning.

The other way to modify the layout is by placing the relevant code directly into the preamble of your document. However, there is one important TeXnical difference between commands inside package or class files and commands in the preamble: LaTeX has many *internal* commands that you cannot type inside your document without special precautions. These internal commands have names containing the @ character. It must be recalled that nonalphabetic characters cannot normally appear in the name of LaTeX commands. (Apart from about two dozen commands, which have two-character names composed of a backslash (\) followed by a single non-letter, all other command names consist of a \ symbol followed by one or more letters.) Yet, when executing commands in a package file, LaTeX considers the @ as a letter. This allows package files to work smoothly with these internal commands while they cannot be used as such in the document preamble.

($\mathcal{L}$ 150)

Nevertheless, you can work with internal commands in the preamble by bracketing the area where the @ should be considered as a letter inside \makeatletter and \makeatother commands. As an example, let us consider the command that instructs LaTeX to reset some counter whenever some other counter is incremented (the internal command \@addtoreset). Thus, when using the article document class, you can number equations within sections by writing the code shown below into your preamble.

```
\documentclass{article}
...
\makeatletter   % '@' is now a normal "letter" for TeX
\@addtoreset{equation}{section}
\makeatother    % '@' is restored as a "non-letter" character for TeX
\begin{document}
  ......
```

As explained above, inside a package file the @ is considered a normal letter and can be used in command names. Therefore you should be careful *never* to use the \makeatletter and \makeatother commands inside package files.

2.1.2   Splitting the Source File into Parts

(ℒ 76,188) LaTeX source documents can be conveniently split into several parts by using \include commands. Moreover, documents can be reformatted piecewise by specifying as arguments of an \includeonly command only those files LaTeX has to reprocess. For the other files that are specified in \include statements, the counter information (page, chapter, table, figure, equation,...) will be read from the corresponding .aux files as long as they have been generated during a previous run. For instance in the case shown in figure 2.2 the user only wants to reprocess files chap1.tex and appen1.tex.

Beware that LaTeX only issues a warning message like "No file xxx.tex" when it cannot find a file specified in an \include statement, not an error message, and continues processing.

If the information in the .aux files is up-to-date, it is possible to process only part of a document and have all counters, cross-references, and pages correct in the reformatted part. However, if one of the counters (including the

```
\documentclass{book}         % the document class ''book''
\includeonly{chap1,appen1}   % only include chap1 and appen1
\begin{document}
\include{chap1}              % input chap1.tex
\include{chap2}              % input chap2.tex
\include{chap3}              % input chap3.tex
\include{appen1}             % input appen1.tex
\include{appen2}             % input appen2.tex
\end{document}
```

Figure 2.2: Structuring a LaTeX document

page number for cross-references) changes in the reprocessed part, then the complete document might have to be rerun to get the index, table of contents, and bibliographic references consistently correct.

Therefore, while it is certainly an advantage to split a larger document into smaller parts and to work on more manageable files with a text editor, partial reformatting should only be used with great care and when still in the developing stage for one or more chapters. However, when a final and completely correct copy is needed, the only safe procedure is to reprocess the complete document. If the document is too large to process in a single run, you should \include each section *in the correct sequence.*

2.1.3 Combining Several Files

When sending a LaTeX document to some other person you may have to send local or uncommon package files (e.g., your private modifications to some packages) along with the source. In such cases it is often helpful if you can put all the information required to process the document into a single file.

For this, LaTeX offers you the environment `filecontents`. This environment takes one argument, the name of a file; its body should consist of the contents of this file. It is only allowed to appear before a \documentclass declaration.

If LaTeX encounters such an environment it will check whether it can find the mentioned file name. If not, it will write the body of the environment verbatim into a file in the current directory and inform you about this action. On the other hand, if a file with that name was found by LaTeX it will inform you that it has ignored this instance of the `filecontents` environment because the file is already provided.

To get a list of (nearly) all files used in your document, specify the command \listfiles in the preamble.

2.2 Logical Structure

The standard LaTeX classes contain commands and environments to define the different hierarchical structural units of a document (e.g., chapters, sections, appendices). Each such command defines a nesting level inside a hierarchy and each structural unit belongs to some level.

A typical document (like an article) consists of a title, some sections with probably a multilevel nested substructure, and a list of references. To describe such a structure the title-generating command \maketitle, the sectioning commands such as \section and \subsection, and the `thebibliography` environment are used (figure 2.3 on the following page). The commands should be correctly nested. Thus, a \subsection command should only be issued after a previous \section.

(L 23,157)

```
\documentclass{article}  % the standard class ``article''
\begin{document}
\maketitle
\section{...}
\section{...}
   \subsection{...}
        \subsubsection{...}
\section{...}
\begin{thebibliography}  ...  \end{thebibliography}
\end{document}
```

Figure 2.3: The hierarchical structure of a simple LaTeX document
This example shows the nesting structure of a LaTeX document. In the case of
the article class no \chapter command is available.

Longer works (like reports, manuals, and books) start with more complex title information, are subdivided into chapters (and parts), provide cross-reference
information (table of contents, list of figures, list of tables, and indices) and probably have appendices. In such a document you can easily distinguish the *front
matter*, *body* and *back matter* (figure 2.4 on the next page).

(*L* 157)   In the front matter the so-called *starred form* of the \section sectioning
command is used normally. This form suppresses the numbering of a head-
ing. Sectional units with fixed names, such as "Introduction," "Index," and
"Preface," are usually not numbered. In the standard classes, the commands
\tableofcontents, \listoftables, \listoffigures, and the theindex and
thebibliography environments internally invoke the command (\section or
\chapter) using their starred form.

2.3 Sectioning Commands

Standard LaTeX provides the set of sectioning commands shown in table 2.1 on
page 20. The \chapter command defines level zero of the hierarchical structure
of a document, the \section level one, and so on, whereas the optional \part
command defines the level minus one (or zero in classes that do not define
\chapter). Not all of these commands are defined in all document classes:
the article class does not have \chapter and the letter class does not support
sectioning commands at all. It is also possible for a package to define further
sectioning commands, allowing either additional levels or variants for already
supported levels.

```
\documentclass{book} % the standard class ''book''
\begin{document}
%-------------------- front matter of the document
\maketitle
    \section*{...}      % e.g. section named like ''Preface''
\tableofcontents        % chapter with the table of contents
\listoffigures          % chapter with the list of figures
\listoftables           % chapter with the list of tables
%-------------------- body of the document
\part{...}
\chapter{...}
    \section{...}
\chapter{...}
\part{...}
%-------------------- back matter of the document
\appendix               % following chapters are appendices
\chapter{...}
\chapter{...}
\begin{thebibliography}   \end{thebibliography}
\begin{theindex}          \end{theindex}
\end{document}
```

Figure 2.4: The hierarchical structure of a complex LaTeX document
The more complex example shown here subdivides the document into front
matter, body and back matter. Each of these contains lower level document
elements, like the table of contents in the front matter, chapter, sections and
subsections in the body, and appendices, an index and a bibliography in the back
matter.

Generally the sectioning commands automatically perform one or more of
the following typesetting actions:

- produce the heading number reflecting the hierarchical level;

- store the heading as an entry for a table of contents (into the `.toc` file);

- save the contents of the heading to be (perhaps) used in a running head
  and/or foot; and

- format the heading.

All sectioning commands have a common syntax as shown in table 2.2 on the
next page. The starred form (e.g., \section*{...}) suppresses the numbering   (£ 23,157)

\part (book and report)	level -1	\part (article)	level 0
\chapter	level 0	\section	level 1
\subsection	level 2	\subsubsection	level 3
\paragraph	level 4	\subparagraph	level 5

Table 2.1: LaTeX's standard sectioning commands

form	numbering	.toc	running h/f
\section{title}	yes	title	title
\section[toc_entry]{title}	yes	toc_entry	toc_entry
\section*{title}	no	no	no

Table 2.2: Syntax of the sectioning commands

for a title. The optional argument is used when the text string for the table of contents and the running head and/or foot is different from the printed title.

The remaining part of this section will discuss how the appearance of section headings can be modified. You will learn how to define a command like \section that has the above syntax, produces a table of contents entry if desired, but has a thick rule above its heading text or uses a normal-sized *italic* font rather than a large **bold** one.

First there are some examples on how to change the numbering of headings. Further examples demonstrate how to enter information about headings into the table of contents. Finally, changes to the general layout of headings are discussed, showing what LaTeX offers to define them.

2.3.1 Numbering Headings

To support numbering, LaTeX uses a counter for each sectional unit and composes the heading number from these counters.

Perhaps the change desired most often concerning the numbering of titles is to alter the nesting level up to which a number should be produced. This is controlled by a counter named secnumdepth, which holds the highest level with numbered headings. For example, some documents have none of their headings numbered. Instead of always using the starred form of the sectioning commands, it is more convenient to set the counter secnumdepth to -2 in the document preamble. The advantage of this method is that an entry in the table of contents can still be produced, and that arguments from the sectioning

(£ 157,160)

```
\newcounter{part}                       % (-1)  parts
\newcounter{chapter}                     % (0)   chapters
\newcounter{section}[chapter]            % (1)   sections
\newcounter{subsection}[section]         % (2)   subsections
\newcounter{subsubsection}[subsection]%  (3)   subsubsections
\newcounter{paragraph}[subsubsection]  % (4)   paragraphs
\newcounter{subparagraph}[paragraph]   % (5)   subparagraphs
```

Figure 2.5: Numbering the section headings

commands can produce information in running headings. As discussed above, these features are suppressed in the starred form.

To number all headings down to \subparagraph or whatever the deepest sectioning level for the given class is called, the following declaration is certainly sufficient.

```
\setcounter{secnumdepth}{10}
```

Finally, using the \addtocounter command gives an easy way of numbering a few more or less levels without worrying about the level numbers of the corresponding sectioning commands. For example, if you find that you need one more level with numbers you can just add

```
\addtocounter{secnumdepth}{1}
```

in the preamble of your document.

Every sectioning command has an associated counter, which by convention has the same name as the sectioning command (e.g., the command \subsection goes together with the counter subsection). This counter holds the current number for the given sectioning command. Thus, in the report class, the commands \chapter, \section, \subsection, and so on represent the hierarchical structure of the document and a counter like subsection keeps track of the number of \subsections used inside the current \section. Normally, when a counter at a given hierarchical level is stepped, then all lower level counters (i.e., those with higher level numbers) are reset. So, for example, the report class file contains the definitions shown in figure 2.5.

These commands declare the various counters. The level one (section) counter is reset when the level zero (chapter) counter is stepped, and similarly the level two (subsection) counter is reset whenever the level one (section) counter is stepped. The same mechanism is used down to the \subparagraph command. Note that in the standard classes the part counter is completely decoupled from the other counters, and has no influence on the lower level sectioning commands. This means that \chapters in the book or report class or \sections in article will be numbered consecutively even if a \part command intervenes. Changing this is simple, you just have to replace the corresponding definition of the chapter counter, e.g.,

```
\newcounter{chapter}[part]
```

The behavior of an already existing counter can be changed with the command \@addtoreset, e.g.,

```
\@addtoreset{chapter}{part}
```

Remember that this instruction should only be issued inside an option file or in the document preamble between \makeatletter and \makeatother commands, as explained in section 2.1.1.

(£ 92)

Every counter in LaTeX, including the sectioning counters, has an associated command constructed by prefixing the counter name with \the, which generates a typeset representation of the counter in question. In case of the sectioning commands this representation form is used to produce the full number associated with the commands, as in the following definitions:

```
\renewcommand{\thechapter}{\arabic{chapter}}
\renewcommand{\thesection}{\thechapter.\arabic{section}}
\renewcommand{\thesubsection}{\thesection.\arabic{subsection}}
```

In the above example \thesubsection produces an arabic number representation of the subsection counter prefixed by the command \thesection and a dot. This kind of recursive definition eases modifications to the counter representations since changes do not need to be made in more than one place. If, for example, you want to number chapters using capital letters, you can redefine the command \thechapter:

D.7   A Different Looking Section

Due to the default definitions not only the numbers on chapters change; but lower-level sectioning commands also show this representation of the chapter number.

```
\renewcommand{\thechapter}{\Alph{chapter}}
\section{A Different Looking Section}
Due to the default definitions not only the
numbers on chapters change; but lower-level
sectioning commands also show this
representation of the chapter number.
```

Thus by changing the counter representation commands it is possible to change the number displayed by a sectioning command. However, the representation of the number cannot be changed arbitrarily by this method. Suppose you want to produce a section heading with the number surrounded by a box.

Given the above examples one straightforward approach would be to redefine \thesection, e.g.,

```
\renewcommand{\thesection}{\fbox{\thechapter.\arabic{section}}}
```

But this is not correct, as one sees when trying to reference such a section.

| 4.7 | A mistake

Referencing a section in this format produces a funny result which we can see looking at section | 4.7 |. We get a boxed reference.

```
\renewcommand{\thesection}
        {\fbox{\thechapter.\arabic{section}}}
\section{A mistake}\label{wrong}
Referencing a section in this format
produces a funny result which we can see
looking at section~\ref{wrong}.
We get a boxed reference.
```

In other words, the counter representation commands are also used by LaTeX's cross-referencing mechanism (the \label, \ref commands, see section 2.5). Therefore, we can only make small changes to the counter representation commands so that their use in the \ref command still makes sense. To produce the box around the heading number without spoiling the output of a \ref we have to redefine LaTeX's internal command \@seccntformat, which is responsible for typesetting the counter part of a section title. The default definition of \@seccntformat typesets the \the representation of the section counter (i.e., in the example above it uses the \thesection command), followed by a fixed horizontal space of 1em. Thus to correct the problem, rewrite the above example as follows.

| 4.7 | This is correct

Referencing a section using this definition generates the correct result for the section reference 4.7.

```
\makeatletter
\renewcommand{\@seccntformat}[1]{\fbox
    {\csname the#1\endcsname}\hspace{0.5em}}
\makeatother
\section{This is correct}\label{sec:OK}
Referencing a section using this
definition generates the correct result
for the section reference~\ref{sec:OK}.
```

You can see that the framed box around the number in the section heading is now only defined in the \@seccntformat command, and hence the reference labels come out correctly[5]. Also note that we reduced the space between the box and the text to 0.5em (instead of the default 1em). The definition of

---

[5]The command \@seccntformat takes as argument the section level identifier, which is appended to the \the prefix to generate the presentation form needed via the \csname, \endcsname command constructor. In our example, the \@seccntformat command is called with the section argument and thus the replacement text \fbox{\csname thesection\endcsname\hspace{0.5em}} is generated. See the TeX book for more details about the \csname command.

\@seccntformat applies to all headings defined with the \@startsection command (which is described in the next section). Therefore, if you wish to use different definitions of \@seccntformat for different headings you must put the appropriate code into every heading definition.

2.3.2 Formatting Headings

LATEX provides a generic command called \@startsection, which can be used to define a wide variety of heading layouts. To define or change a sectioning command one should find out whether \@startsection can do the job. If the desired layout is not achievable that way then \secdef can be used to produce sectioning formats with arbitrary layout.

Headings can be loosely subdivided into two major groups: display and run-in headings. A display heading is a heading which is separated by a vertical space from the preceding and the following text—most headings in this book are of this type.

A run-in heading is characterized by a vertical separation from the preceding text, but the text following the title continues on the same line as the heading itself, only separated from the latter by a horizontal space.

Run-in headings. The present example shows what a run-in heading looks like. Text in the paragraph following the heading continues on the same line as the heading.

```
\paragraph{Run-in headings.}
The present example shows what a run-in
heading looks like. Text in the paragraph
following the heading continues on the
same line as the heading.
```

The \@startsection Command

The generic command \@startsection allows both types of headings to be defined. Its syntax and argument description is as follows:

\@startsection{*name*}{*level*}{*indent*}{*beforeskip*}{*afterskip*}{*style*}

---

name   This is the name of the sectioning command being defined, without the preceding backslash—for example, to define a command named \section, the word section should be specified.

level   This is a number, denoting the depth level of the sectioning command. This level is used to decide if the sectioning command gets a number (if the level is less or equal to secnumdepth, see section 2.3.1 on page 20) or shows up in the table of contents (if the value is less or equal to tocdepth, see section 2.4.1 on page 32). It should therefore reflect the position in the command hierarchy of sectioning commands, where the outermost sectioning command has level zero.[6]

---

[6]In the book and report classes, the \part command actually has level −1 (see figure 2.5).

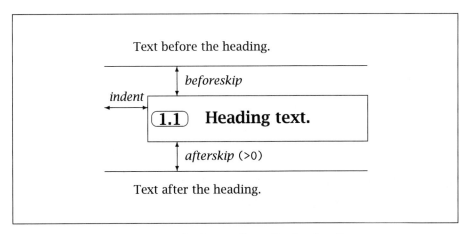

Figure 2.6: The layout for a display heading

indent The indentation of the heading with respect to the left margin. By making the value negative, the heading will start in the outer margin. Making it positive will indent all lines of the heading by this amount.

beforeskip The absolute value of this parameter defines the space to be left in front of the heading. If the parameter is negative, then the indentation of the paragraph following the heading is suppressed. This dimension is a rubber length, i.e., it can take a stretch and shrink component. Note that LaTeX starts a new paragraph before the heading, so that additionally the value of \parskip is added to the space in front.

afterskip This is the space to be left following a heading. It is the vertical space after a display heading or the horizontal space after a run-in heading. The sign of *afterskip* controls whether a display (*afterskip* $\geq$ 0) or run-in heading (*afterskip* $<$ 0) is produced. Note that in the first case a new paragraph is started so that the value of \parskip is added to the space after the heading. An unpleasant side effect of this parameter coupling is that it is impossible to define a display heading with an effective "after space" of less than \parskip using the \@startsection command. When you try to compensate for a positive \parskip value by using a negative *afterskip*, you change the display heading into a run-in heading.

style This is the style of the heading text. This argument can take any instruction that influences the typesetting of text, e.g., \Large, \bfseries or \raggedright (see the examples below).

Figures 2.6 and 2.7 on the following page show these parameters graphically in the case of display and run-in headings respectively.

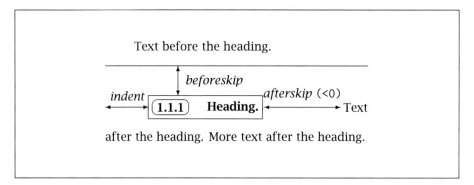

Figure 2.7: The layout for a run-in heading

We shall now show how these arguments are used in practice to define new sectioning commands. Let us suppose that you want to change the \section command of a class like report to look roughly like this:

... some text above.

4.6.3 This Is an Example of a Section Heading

The heading is set in normal-sized italic and the separation from the preceding text is exactly one baseline. The separation from the text following is half a baseline and this text is not indented.

```
\ldots\ some text above.
\subsection{This Is an Example of a
            Section Heading}
The heading is set in normal-sized italic
and the separation from the preceding text
is exactly one baseline. The separation
from the text following is half a baseline
and this text is not indented.
```

In this case the following redefinition is needed:

```
\renewcommand{\subsection}{\@startsection
    {subsection}%                           % the name
    {2}%                                     % the level
    {0mm}%                                   % the indent
    {-\baselineskip}%                        % the beforeskip
    {0.5\baselineskip}%                      % the afterskip
    {\normalfont\normalsize\itshape}}%       % the style
```

The first argument is subsection, the name of the sectioning command. In the sectional hierarchy, subsection is at level two. The third argument is 0mm since the heading should start at the left margin. The absolute value of the fourth argument specifies that a distance equal to one baseline must be left in front of the heading and, since the parameter is negative, the indentation of the paragraph following the heading should be suppressed. The absolute value of the fifth parameter (*afterskip*) specifies that a distance equal to half a baseline must be left following the heading and, since the parameter is positive, a display heading has to be produced. Finally, according to the sixth parameter, the heading should be typeset in an italic font using a size equal to the normal document type size.

It is important to note that within the definition every unnecessary space was suppressed by putting a percent sign after every right brace in the second argument of \renewcommand. Besides the fact that unnecessary spaces in a definition take up memory they sometimes find their way into the document and produce funny results.

Another layout, which is sometimes found in fiction books, is given by the following definition:

```
\renewcommand{\section}{\@startsection
    {section}%                          % the name
    {1}%                                % the level
    {1em}%                              % the indent
    {\baselineskip}%                    % the beforeskip
    {-\fontdimen2\font                  % the afterskip
      plus -\fontdimen3\font
      minus -\fontdimen4\font}%
    {\normalfont\normalsize\scshape}}%  % the style
```

This defines a run-in heading using small capitals. The space definition for the horizontal *afterskip* deserves an explanation: it is the value of the stretchable space between words taken from the current font, negated to make a run-in heading. Details about \fontdimens can be found in section 7.7.2 on page 200. The result will be something like:

... some text above.

THE MAN started to run away from the truck. He saw that he was followed by

```
\ldots\ some text above.
\section{The man}
started to run away from the truck. He
saw that he was followed by
```

Of course, for such a layout one should turn off numbering of the headings by setting secnumdepth to −1.

Which commands can be used for setting the styles of the heading texts by using the *style* argument of the \@startsection command? Apart from the font changing directives (see chapter 7) few instructions can be used here. A \centering command produces a centered display heading and a \raggedright declaration makes the text left justified. The usage of \raggedleft is possible, but may give somewhat strange results. You can also use \hrule\medskip, \newpage, or similar commands that introduce local changes. The examples in figure 2.8 on the next page show the results of various possible definitions for the *style* argument.

In the standard LaTeX document classes, words in long section headings can be hyphenated. If this is not wanted, then hyphenation can be turned off locally

4.6.3   This is a Section Heading

The style is specified by \centering\itshape commands.

4.6.4   This is a Section Heading

The style is specified by \raggedright\itshape commands.

4.6.5   This is a Section Heading

The style is specified by \raggedleft\itshape commands.

4.6.6   This is a Section Heading

The style is specified by \hrule\medskip\itshape commands.

```
\Csubsection{This is a Section Heading}
The style is specified by
\verb!\centering\itshape! commands.

\Lsubsection{This is a Section Heading}
The style is specified by
\verb!\raggedright\itshape! commands.

\Rsubsection{This is a Section Heading}
The style is specified by
\verb!\raggedleft\itshape! commands.

\Hsubsection{This is a Section Heading}
The style is specified by
\verb!\hrule\medskip\itshape! commands.
```

Figure 2.8: Changing the style of a heading

By changing the *style* argument of the \@startsection command, various effects can be achieved.

by defining and using a command like \nohyphens[7] in the *style* part of the \@startsection command. Another problem is that, if the user tries to advise TeX on how to split the heading over a few lines using the "~" symbol or the \\ command, then side effects may result when formatting the table of contents. In this case the simplest solution is to repeat the heading text without the specific markup in the optional parameter of the sectioning command.

Finally, a few words about the suppression of the indentation for the first paragraph after a display heading. Standard LaTeX document classes, following (American) English typographic tradition, suppress the indentation in this case. All first paragraphs after a display heading can be indented by specifying the package indentfirst (David Carlisle).

The \secdef Command

The highest-level sectioning commands \part and \chapter produce their titles without using \@startsection. In a similar way, you can construct your own sectioning commands without limitations. You must, however, follow a few conventions to allow LaTeX to take all the necessary typesetting actions when executing them.

The command \secdef can help you when defining such commands by providing an easy interface to the three possible forms of section headings, as shown in figure 2.9 on the facing page in the case of the \part command.

---

[7] \newcommand{\nohyphens}{\hyphenpenalty=10000\exhyphenpenalty=10000\relax}

With the definition \newcommand{\part}{\secdef\cmda\cmdb} the
following actions take place:

\part{*title*}	will invoke	\cmda[*title*]{*title*}
\part[*toc_entry*]{*title*}	will invoke	\cmda[*toc_entry*]{*title*}
\part*{*title*}	will invoke	\cmdb{*title*}

Figure 2.9: Conventions for the \secdef command

The commands you will have to provide are a (re)definition of \part and
a definition of the commands labeled \cmda or \cmdb respectively. Note that
\cmda has an optional argument containing the text to be entered in the table of
contents .toc file, while the second (mandatory) argument, as well as the single
argument to \cmdb, specifies the heading text to be typeset. In the schematic
example below, the extended functionality of LATEX 2$_\varepsilon$'s \newcommand is used. It
allows the definition of an optional argument; see also section A.1.1.

```
\renewcommand{\part}{ ... \secdef \cmda \cmdb }
\newcommand{\cmda}[2][default]{ ... }
\newcommand{\cmdb}[1]{ ... }
```

An explicit example is a simplified variant of \appendix. This redefines the
\section command to produce headings for appendices (by invoking either the
\Appendix or \sAppendix command), changing the presentation of the section
counter and resetting it to zero. The modified \section command also starts a
new page, sets a special format for the first page (see chapter 4), prohibits floats
from appearing at the top of the first page, and suppresses the indentation of
the first paragraph in a section.

```
\renewcommand{\appendix}{%
    \renewcommand{\section}{%              Redefinition of \section
        \newpage\thispagestyle{plain}%
        \secdef\Appendix\sAppendix}%
    \setcounter{section}{0}%
    \renewcommand{\thesection}{\Alph{section}}%
}
```

In the definition below you can see how \Appendix advances the section counter
using the \refstepcounter command (the latter also resets all subsidiary counters and defines the "current reference string," see section 2.5). It writes a line
into the .toc file with the \addcontentsline command, performs the formatting of the heading title, and saves the title for running heads and/or feet by

calling \sectionmark.

```
\newcommand{\Appendix}[2][?]{%    Complex form
    \refstepcounter{section}%
    \addcontentsline{toc}{appendix}%
        {\protect\numberline{\appendixname~\thesection} #1}%
    {\flushright\large\bfseries\appendixname\ \thesection\par
     \nohyphens\centering#2\par}%
    \sectionmark{#1}\vspace{\baselineskip}}
```

The \sAppendix command (starred form) only performs the formatting.

```
\newcommand{\sAppendix}[1]{%              Simplified (starred) form
        {\flushright\large\bfseries\appendixname\par
         \nohyphens\centering#1\par}%
    \vspace{\baselineskip}}
```

Applying these definitions will produce the following output:

Appendix A
The List of all Commands

Then follows the text of the first section in the appendix. Some more text in the appendix. Some more text in the appendix.

```
\appendix
\section{The List of all Commands}
```

```
Then follows the text of the first section
in the appendix.  Some more text in the
appendix.  Some more text in the appendix.
```

Do not forget that the example shown above represents only a simplified version of a redefined \section command. We did, among other things, not take into account the secnumdepth counter, which contains the numbering threshold. You might also have to foresee code dealing with various types of document formats, like one- and two-column output, or one- and two-sided printing (see chapter 4).

2.3.3 Changing Fixed Heading Texts

Some of the standard heading commands produce fixed texts, for example \chapter produces the string "Chapter" in front of the user supplied text. Similarly some environments generate headings with fixed texts. For example, by default the abstract environment displays the word "Abstract" above the text of the abstract supplied by the user. Earlier versions of LaTeX had these strings hard-coded inside the system so that it was rather difficult to change them. The present LaTeX has these strings replaced by command sequences (see table 2.3 on the next page) so that you can easily customize them to obtain your favorite names. This is shown in the example below, where the default name "Abstract," as defined in the article class, is replaced by the word "Summary."

Command	Default text
\contentsname	Contents
\listfigurename	List of Figures
\listtablename	List of Tables
\bibname	Bibliography
\indexname	Index
\chaptername	Chapter
\appendixname	Appendix
\partname	Part
\abstractname	Abstract

Table 2.3: Commands holding fixed texts for section headings

Summary

This book describes how to modify the appearance of documents produced with LaTeX.

```
\renewcommand{\abstractname}{Summary}
\begin{abstract}
 This book describes how to modify the
 appearance of documents produced with
 \LaTeX.
\end{abstract}
```

The standard LaTeX class files define a few more strings. See section 9.2, especially table 9.2 on page 267, for a full list and a discussion of the Babel system, which provides translations of these strings in over twenty languages.

2.4   Structure of the Table of Contents

A *table of contents* is a special list with the titles of the section units specifying the page numbers where each section starts. This list can be rather complicated if many units of several nesting levels are included, and it should be formatted carefully because it plays an important rôle as a navigation aid for the reader.   (£ 70,158)

Similar lists exist containing reference information about the floating elements in a document, namely, the *list of tables* and the *list of figures*. The structure of these lists is simpler, since their contents, the captions of the floating elements, are all on the same level.

Standard LaTeX can automatically create these three contents lists. By default,   (£ 186)
LaTeX enters text generated by one of the arguments of the sectioning commands into the .toc file. Similarly, LaTeX maintains two more files, one for the list of figures (.lof) and one for the list of tables (.lot), which contain the text specified as the argument of the \caption command for figures and tables.

The information written into these files during a previous LaTeX run is read   (£ 158)

and typeset (normally at the beginning of a document) during a subsequent
LaTeX run by invoking the commands: \tableofcontents, \listoffigures and
\listoftables.

To generate these cross-reference tables, it is always necessary to run LaTeX
at least twice, once to collect the relevant information, and a second time to
read back the information and typeset it in the correct place in the document.
Because of the additional material to be typeset in the second run, the cross-
referencing information may change, thus making a further LaTeX run necessary.
This is one of the reasons for the tradition of using different page-numbering
systems for the front matter and the main text: in the days of hand typesetting
any additional iteration made the final product much more expensive.

The following sections will discuss how to typeset and generate these contents lists. It will also be shown how information can be entered directly into
one of these standard files, or even how to open and write into a supplementary
file completely under user control.

2.4.1   Typesetting a Contents List

As discussed above, contents lists consist of entries of different types, corresponding to the structural units that they represent. Apart from these standard
entries, these lists may contain any commands. A standard entry is specified by
the command:

\contentsline{*type*}{*text*}{*page*}

The parameters are:

type   type of the entry, e.g., section, or figure;

text   actual text as specified in the argument of the sectioning or \caption
commands; and

page   page number.

A piece of code that generates the table of contents corresponding to part of a
book is shown in figure 2.10 on the facing page.

Note that section numbers are entered as a parameter of the \numberline
command to allow formatting with the proper indentation. It is also possible
for the user to create a table of contents by hand with the help of the command
\contentsline.

To format an entry in the table of contents files, standard LaTeX makes use
of the following command:

\@dottedtocline{*level*}{*indent*}{*numwidth*}{*text*}{*page*}

The last two parameters coincide with those of \contentsline, since the

---

Input text

```
\contentsline {section}
    {\numberline {2.4}Structure of the Table of Contents}{31}
\contentsline {subsection}
    {\numberline {2.4.1}Typesetting a Contents List}{32}
\contentsline {subsection}
    {\numberline {2.4.2}Entering Information into the Contents Files}{35}
```

2.4   Structure of the Table of Contents   31
   2.4.1   Typesetting a Contents List   32
   2.4.2   Entering Information into the Contents Files   35

Output text

Figure 2.10: Generating table of contents entries

latter itself usually invokes a `\@dottedtocline` command. The other parameters are the following:

level   The nesting level of an entry. This parameter allows the user to control how many nesting levels will be displayed. Levels greater than the value of counter `tocdepth` will not appear in the table of contents.

indent   This is total indentation from the left margin.

numwidth   The width of the box that contains the number if *text* has a `\numberline` command. This is also the amount of extra indentation added to the second and later lines of a multiple line entry.

Additionally, the command `\@dottedtocline` uses the following formatting parameters, which specify the visual appearance of all entries:

`\@pnumwidth`   The width of the box in which the page number is set.

`\@tocrmarg`   The indentation of the right margin for all but the last line of multiple line entries. Dimension, but changed with `\renewcommand`!

`\@dotsep`   The separation between dots, in `mu` (math units).[8] It is a pure number (like `1.7` or `2`). By making this number large enough you can get rid of the dots altogether. Changed with `\renewcommand` as well!

A pictorial representation of the effects described is shown in figure 2.11 on the next page. The field identified by *numwidth* contains a left justified section number, if any. You can achieve the proper indentation for nested entries by varying the settings of *indent* and *numwidth*.

---

[8]There are 18 `mu` units to an `em`, where the latter is taken from the `\fontdimen2` of the math symbol font `symbols`. See section 7.7.2 for more information about `\fontdimens`.

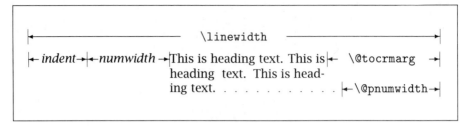

Figure 2.11: Parameters defining the layout of a contents file

The command \contentsline is implemented to take its first argument *type*, and then use it to call the corresponding \l@*type* command, which does the actual typesetting. One separate command for each of the types must be defined in the style file. For example, in the report class one finds the following definitions:

```
\newcommand{\l@section}{\@dottedtocline{1}{1.5em}{2.3em}}
\newcommand{\l@subsection}{\@dottedtocline{2}{3.8em}{3.2em}}
\newcommand{\l@subsubsection}{\@dottedtocline{3}{7.0em}{4.1em}}
\newcommand{\l@paragraph}{\@dottedtocline{4}{10em}{5em}}
\newcommand{\l@subparagraph}{\@dottedtocline{5}{12em}{6em}}
\newcommand{\l@figure}{\@dottedtocline{1}{1.5em}{2.3em}}
\newcommand{\l@table}{\l@figure}
```

By defining \l@*type* to call \@dottedtocline and specifying three arguments (*level*, *indent* and *numwidth*) the remaining arguments, *text* and *page*, of \contentsline will be picked up by \@dottedtocline as arguments four and five.

Note that some section levels build their table of contents entries in a somewhat more complicated way, so that the standard document classes have definitions for \l@part and \l@chapter that do not use \@dottedtocline. Generally they use a set of specific formatting commands, perhaps omitting ellipses and typesetting in a larger font. A possible example is shown below:

II   Part   **1**

1   Chapter   **2**
   1.1   Section   3
       1.1.1   Subsection . . .   4
              Subsection
              without number   5
     Unnumbered subsection .   6

```
\contentsline{part}{\numberline{II}Part}{1}
\contentsline{chapter}{\numberline{1}Chapter}{2}
\contentsline{section}%
    {\numberline{1.1}Section}{3}
\contentsline{subsection}%
    {\numberline{1.1.1}Subsection}{4}
\contentsline{subsection}%
    {\numberline{}Subsection without number}{5}
\contentsline{subsection}%
    {Unnumbered subsection}{6}
```

The level down to which the heading information is displayed in the table of (£ 160)
contents is controlled by the counter `tocdepth`. It can be changed, for example,
with the declaration:

```
\setcounter{tocdepth}{2}
```

In this case sectional heading information down to the second level (i.e., part,
chapter, and section) will be shown.

2.4.2   Entering Information into the Contents Files

LaTeX offers two commands to enter information directly into a contents file: (£ 159)

`\addtocontents{`*file*`}{`*text*`}   \addcontentsline{`*file*`}{`*type*`}{`*text*`}`

---

file   The extension of the contents file, usually `.toc`, `.lof`, or `.lot`.

type   The type of the entry. For the `.toc` file the *type* is normally the same as
the heading according to whose format an entry must be typeset. For the
`.lof` or `.lot` files, `figure` or `table` is specified.

text   The actual information to be written to the *file* mentioned. LaTeX commands should be protected by `\protect` to delay expansion.

The `\addtocontents` command does not contain a *type* parameter and is
intended to enter *user-specific* formatting information. For example, if you want
to generate additional spacing in the middle of a table of contents, the following
command can be issued:

```
\addtocontents{toc}{\protect\vspace{2ex}}
```

The `\addcontentsline` instruction is usually invoked *automatically* by the
document sectioning commands, or by the `\caption` commands. If the entry
contains numbered text, then `\numberline` must be used to separate the section
number (*number*) from the rest of the text for the entry (*heading*) in the *text*
parameter:

```
\protect\numberline{number}heading
```

For example, a `\caption` command inside a `figure` environment saves the
text annotating the figure as follows:

```
\addcontentsline{lof}{figure}%
    {\protect\numberline{\thefigure}captioned text}
```

Sometimes `\addcontentsline` is used in the source to complement the actions of standard LaTeX. For instance, in the case of the starred form of the

section commands, no information is written to the .toc file. So if you do not want a heading number (starred form) but an entry in the .toc file you can write something like:

```
\chapter*{Foreword}
\addcontentsline{toc}{chapter}{\numberline{}Foreword}
```

This produces an indented "chapter" entry in the table of contents, leaving the space where the chapter number would go free. Omitting the \numberline command would typeset the word "Foreword" flush left instead.

2.4.3 Defining a New TOC-Like File

If you want to make a list comprising all the examples in a book, you need to create a new contents file, and then make use of the facilities described above. First, two new commands must be defined: \listofexamples will read the information written to the .xmp file (see below) and typeset it at the point in the document where the command is called. The second command, \ecaption, associates a caption with each environment and writes its argument to the .xmp contents file. The \listofexamples command invokes \@starttoc{*xxx*} which reads the external file (with the extension *xxx*) and then reopens it for writing. This command is also used by the commands \tableofcontents, \listoffigures, and \listoftables. The supplementary file could be given an extension such as xmp. A command like \chapter*{List of examples} can be put just in front of \listofexamples to produce a title and, if desired, a command \addcontentsline can signal the presence of this list to the reader by entering it into the .toc file.

The actual typesetting of the individual entries in the .xmp file is controlled by \l@example. In the example below, the captions are typeset as paragraphs followed by an italicized page number.

```
\newcommand{\listofexamples}{\@starttoc{xmp}}
\newcommand{\ecaption}[1]{\addcontentsline{xmp}{example}{#1}}
\newcommand{\l@example}[2]{\par\noindent#1 {\itshape #2}}
```

You can also look at section 6.3 on page 146, where in the case of floats, the command \listof will generate a list of floats of the type specified as its argument.

2.4.4 Multiple Tables of Contents

The minitoc package, initially written by Nigel Ward and Dan Jurafsky and completely redesigned by Jean-Pierre Drucbert, creates a mini-table of contents (a "minitoc") at the beginning of each chapter with the book or report classes.

\dominitoc	must be put just in front of \tableofcontents, to initialize the minitoc system (Mandatory).
\faketableofcontents	this command replaces \tableofcontents when you want minitocs but no table of contents.
\minitoc	this command must be put right after each \chapter command where a minitoc is desired.
minitocdepth	a LaTeX counter that indicates how many levels of headings will be displayed in the minitoc (default value is 2).
\mtcindent	the length of the left/right indentation of the minitoc (default value is 24pt).
\mtcfont	command defining the font that is used for the minitoc entries (The default definition is a small roman font.

Table 2.4: A summary of the minitoc parameters

The mini-table of contents will appear at the beginning of a chapter, after the \chapter command. The parameters that govern the use of this package are discussed in table 2.4.

For each mini-table, an auxiliary file with extension .mtc<N>, where <N> is the chapter number, will be created.[9]

By default, these mini-tables contain only references to sections and subsections. The minitocdepth counter, similar to tocdepth, allows the user to modify this behavior.

As the minitoc takes up room on the first page(s) of a chapter, it will alter the page numbering. Therefore, three runs normally are needed to get correct information in the mini-table of contents.

To turn off the \minitoc commands, merely replace the package minitoc with minitocoff on your \usepackage command. This assures that all \minitoc commands will be ignored.

An example of the use of the minitoc package is given in figure 2.12 on the next page, where we put the global tocdepth counter to one, so that only section titles will be shown in the table of contents of the document (you can see the result in the upper left part of figure 2.13 on page 39). The depth counter for the mini-tables, minitocdepth, is put equal to two, so that section and subsection titles appear in each such table (as seen in the remaining five pictures in figure 2.13 on page 39). The text of the chapter starts immediately after the end of the mini-table.

---

[9]Because of the special extensions this package will not work without modifications on MS-DOS or MS-Windows, or more exactly, on any operating system that does not allow long file extensions.

```
\documentclass{book}
\usepackage{times}
\usepackage{minitoc}
\setcounter{tocdepth}{1}              % depth of table of contents
\setlength{\mtcindent}{24pt}          % indentation of minitocs, default
\renewcommand{\mtcfont}{\small\rm}    % font for minitocs, default
\setcounter{minitocdepth}{2}          % depth for minitoc
\begin{document}
\dominitoc                            % generate minitocs
\tableofcontents                      % generate global table of contents
\chapter{Afghanistan}
\minitoc                              % minitoc after first chapter title

\section{Afghanistan Geography}

\subsection{Total area}
    647,500 km2
\subsection{Land area}
    647,500 km2


    ..... continuation of chapter 1


\chapter{Albania}
\minitoc                              % minitoc after second chapter title
\section{Albania Geography}

\subsection{Total area}
    28,750 km2
\subsection{Land area}
    27,400 km2


    ..... continuation of chapter 2
```

Figure 2.12: Mini-table of contents—input example

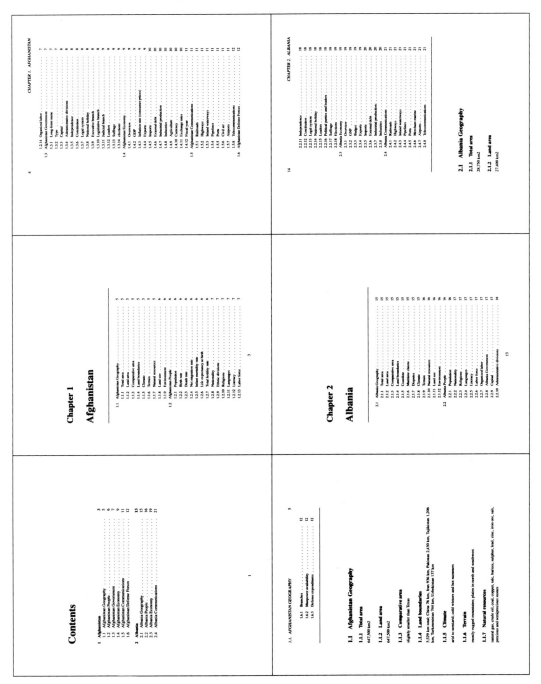

Figure 2.13: Mini-table of contents—output example

2.5 Managing References

LATEX has commands that make it easy to manage references in a document. In particular, it supports *cross-references* (internal references between elements within a document), *bibliographic* citations (references to external documents), and *indexing* of selected words or expressions. Indexing facilities will be discussed in chapter 12, and bibliographic citations in chapter 13.

To allow cross-referencing of elements inside a document, you should assign a "key" (consisting of a string of letters, digits, and punctuation) to the given structural element and then use that key to refer to that element elsewhere.

`\label{`*key_string*`}`   `\ref{`*key_string*`}`   `\pageref{`*key_string*`}`

(£ 71,186)   The `\label` command assigns key *key_string* to the current element of the document. `\ref` typesets a string, identifying the given element—such as the section, equation, or figure number depending on the type of structural element that was active when the `\label` command was issued. The `\pageref` command typesets the number of the page where the `\label` command was given. The key strings should of course be unique, and as a simple aid it can be useful to prefix them with a string identifying the structural element in question: `sec` might represent sectional units, `fig` would identify figures, and so on.

A reference of this subsection looks like: "see section 2.5 on page 40".

```
A reference of this subsection\label{sec:this}
looks like:  ``see section~\ref{sec:this}
on page~\pageref{sec:this}''.
```

For building cross-reference labels, the "currently active" structural element of a document is determined in the following way. The sectioning commands (`\chapter`, `\section`, ...), the environments `equation`, `figure`, `table`, and the `theorem` family, as well as the various levels of the `enumerate` environment, and `\footnote` set the *current reference string*, which contains the number generated by LATEX for the given element. This reference string is usually set at the beginning of an element and reset when the scope of the element is exited.

Notable exceptions to this rule are the `table` and `figure` environments where the reference string is defined by the `\caption` commands. This allows several `\caption` and `\label` pairs inside one environment. As it is the `\caption` directive that generates the number, the corresponding `\label` command must *follow* the `\caption` command in question otherwise an incorrect number will be generated. This is shown clearly in the following example, where only the labels 'fig:in2' and 'fig:in3' are placed correctly to generate the needed reference numbers for the figures. In the case of 'fig:in4' it is seen that environments (in this case `center`) limit the scope of references, since we obtain the number of the current section, rather than the number of the figure.

Text before is referenced as '2.5'.

| ... figure body ... |

Figure 4.14: Caption First

| ... figure body ... |

Figure 4.15: Caption Second

The labels are: 'before' (2.5), 'fig:in1' (2.5), 'fig:in2' (4.14), 'fig:in3' (4.15), 'fig:in4' (2.5), 'after' (2.5).

```
\label{sec:before}
Text before is referenced as '\ref{sec:before}'.
\label{before}
\begin{figure}[H]              \label{fig:in1}
    \begin{center}
        \fbox{\ldots{} figure body \ldots}
        \caption{Caption First}\label{fig:in2}

        \fbox{\ldots{} figure body \ldots}
        \caption{Caption Second}\label{fig:in3}
    \end{center}                \label{fig:in4}
\end{figure}
\label{sec:after}
\raggedright
The labels are: 'before' (\ref{sec:before}),
'fig:in1' (\ref{fig:in1}), 'fig:in2' (\ref{fig:in2}),
'fig:in3' (\ref{fig:in3}), 'fig:in4' (\ref{fig:in4}),
'after' (\ref{sec:after}).
```

For each *key_string* declared with `\label{`*key_string*`}`, LaTeX records the current reference string and the page number. Thus, multiple `\label` commands (with different key identifiers *key_string*) inside the same sectional unit will generate an identical reference string but, possibly, different page numbers.

2.5.1 varioref—More Flexible Cross-References

In many cases it is helpful, when referring to a figure or table, to put both a `\ref` and a `\pageref` command into the document, especially when there are one or more pages between the reference and the object. Therefore, some people use a command like

```
\newcommand{\fullref}[1]{\ref{#1} on page~\pageref{#1}}
```

to reduce the number of keystrokes necessary to make a complete reference. But since one never knows where the referenced object finally falls, this method can result in a citation to the current page, which is disturbing and should therefore be avoided. The package varioref, written by Frank Mittelbach, tries to solve that problem.

The User Interface

| `\vref{`*key_string*`}` |

`\vref` will produce a `\ref` only when reference and `\label` are on the same page. It will also create one of the strings: "on the facing page," "on the preceding page," or "on the following page" (if label and reference differ by one). It will produce both \ref and \pageref when the difference is larger. The word "facing" is used when label and reference both fall onto a double spread. However, if a special page numbering scheme is used instead of the usual arabic numbering (for example, \pagenumbering{roman}) then there will be no distinction between one or many pages off.

> \vpageref [*samepage*] [*otherpage*] {*key_string*}

Sometimes you may only want to refer to a page number. In that case a reference should be suppressed if you are citing the current page. For this purpose the \vpageref command is defined. It produces the same strings as \vref except that it does not start with a \ref, and it produces the string saved in \reftextcurrent if label and reference fall onto the same page.

Defining \reftextcurrent to produce something like "on this page" ensures that

```
... see the diagram \vpageref{ex:foo} which shows ...
```

does not come out as "... see the diagram which shows ...", which could be misleading.

You can put a space in front of \vpageref; it will be ignored if the command does not create any text at all. If some text is added, an appropriate unbreakable space is automatically placed in front of the text.

In fact, \vpageref allows even more control by using its two optional arguments. The first one specifies the text to be used if label and reference fall on the same page. This is helpful when both are close together, so that they may or may not be separated by a page break. In such a case, you will usually know whether the reference comes before or after the label so that you can code something like:

```
... see the diagram \vpageref[above]{ex:foo} which shows ...
```

The resultant text will be: "... see the diagram above which shows ...", when both are on the same page, or "... see the diagram on the page before which shows ..." (or something similar, depending on the settings of the \reftext..before and \reftext..after commands, see below) if they are separated by a page break. Note, however, that, if you use \vpageref with the optional argument to refer to a figure or table, depending on the float placement parameters, the float may show up at the top of the current page and therefore before the reference, even if it follows it in the source file.[10]

---

[10]To ensure that a floating object always follows its place in the source use the option flafter which is described in section 6.2.

Maybe you even prefer to say "... see the above diagram" when diagram and reference fall onto the same page, i.e., reverse the word order compared to our previous example. In fact, in some languages the word order automatically changes in that case. To allow for this variation the second optional argument *otherpage* can be used. It specifies the text preceding the generated reference if object and reference do not fall on the same page. Thus, one would write

```
... see the \vpageref[above diagram][diagram]{ex:foo} which shows ...
```

to achieve the desired effect.

Language Support

The package supports the options defined by the babel system (see section 9.2); thus a declaration like

```
\usepackage[german]{varioref}
```

will produce texts suitable for the German language. To allow further customization, the generated text strings are all defined via macros (which will be predefined by the language options).

Backward references use \reftextbefore if the label is on the preceding page but invisible, and \reftextfacebefore if it is on the facing page (that is, if the current page number is odd).

Similarly, \reftextafter is used when the label comes on the next page but one has to turn the page, and \reftextfaceafter if it is on the next, but facing page. These four strings can be redefined with \renewcommand.

Finally, the string corresponding to \reftextfaraway is used whenever label and reference differ by more than one, or when they are nonnumeric. This macro is a bit different because it takes one argument, the symbolic reference string, so that you can make use of \pageref in its replacement text. For instance, if you wanted to use your macros in German language documents you would say something like:

```
\renewcommand{\reftextfaraway}[1]{auf Seite~\pageref{#1}}
```

To allow some random variation in the generated strings you can use the command \reftextvario inside the string macros.

`\reftextvario{`*variationa*`}{`*variationb*`}`

This command takes two arguments and selects one or the other for printing depending on the number of \vref or \vpageref commands already encountered in the document.

As an example, the default definitions of the various macros described in this section are shown below.

```
\newcommand{\reftextfaceafter}
        {on the \reftextvario{facing}{next} page}
\newcommand{\reftextfacebefore}
        {on the \reftextvario{facing}{preceding} page}
\newcommand{\reftextafter}
        {on the \reftextvario{following}{next} page}
\newcommand{\reftextbefore}
        {on the \reftextvario{preceding page}{page before}}
\newcommand{\reftextcurrent}
        {on \reftextvario{this}{the current} page}
\newcommand{\reftextfaraway}[1]{on page~\pageref{#1}}
```

Thus, if you want to customize the package according to your own preferences, just write appropriate redefinitions of the above commands in a file with the extension .sty (e.g., vrflocal.sty). If you also put \RequirePackage{varioref} (see A.3 on page 460) at the beginning of this file, then your local package will automatically load the varioref package.

A Few Warnings

Defining commands, like the ones described above, pose some interesting problems. Suppose, for example, that a generated text like "on the next page" gets broken across pages. If this happens, it is very difficult to find an acceptable algorithmic solution and, in fact, this situation can even result in a document that will always change from one state to another (i.e., inserting one string, finding that this is wrong, inserting another string on the next run which makes the first string correct again, inserting ...). The current implementation of the package varioref considers the end of the generated string as being relevant. For example,

table 5 on the current ⟨*page break*⟩ page

would be true if table 5 were on the page containing the word "page," not the one containing the word "current." However, this is not completely satisfactory, and in some cases may actually result in a possible loop (where LaTeX is requesting an additional run over and over again). Therefore all such situations will produce a LaTeX error message so that you may inspect the problem and perhaps decide to use a \ref command in that place.

Also, be aware of the potential problems that can result from using \reftextvario: if you reference the same object several times in nearby places the change in wording every second time will look strange.

A final warning: every use of \vref internally generates two macro names. As a result, you may run out of name space or main memory if you make heavy use of this command on a small TeX installation. For this reason the command

\fullref is also provided. It can be used whenever you are sure that label and reference cannot fall on nearby pages.

2.5.2 References to External Documents

David Carlisle, using earlier work of Jean-Pierre Drucbert, developed a package xr, which implements a system for external references.

If, for instance, a document needs to refer to sections of another document, say other.tex, then you can specify the xr package in the main file and give the command \externaldocument{other} in the preamble.

Then you can use \ref and \pageref to refer to anything that has been defined with a \label command in either other.tex or your main document. You may declare any number of such external documents.

If any of the external documents, or the main document, uses the same \label, then a conflict will occur because the label has been multiply defined. To overcome this problem \externaldocument has an optional argument. If you declare \externaldocument[A-]{other}, then all references from the file other.tex are prefixed by A-. So, for instance, if a section in the file other.tex had a \label{intro}, then this could be referenced with \ref{A-intro}. The prefix need not be A-; it can be any string chosen to ensure that all the labels imported from external files are unique. Note, however, that if one of the packages you are using declares certain active characters (like : in French or " in German) then these characters should not be used inside \label commands. Similarly, you should not use them in the optional argument to \externaldocument.

CHAPTER 3

Basic Formatting Tools

The way information is presented visually can influence, to a large extent, the message as it is understood by the reader. Therefore, it is important that you use the best possible tools available to convey the precise meaning of your words. It must, however, be emphasized that visual presentation forms should aid the reader in understanding the text, and should not distract his or her attention. Therefore, visual consistency and uniform conventions for the visual clues are a must, and the way given structural elements are highlighted should be the same throughout a document. This constraint is most easily implemented by defining a specific command or environment for each document element that has to be treated specially and grouping the commands and environments in a package file or in the document preamble. In this way, by using exclusively these commands, you can be sure of a consistent presentation form.

The present chapter explains various ways for highlighting parts of a document. Section one looks at how short text fragments or paragraphs can be made to stand out. The second section deals with LaTeX lists. First the various parameters and commands controlling the standard LaTeX lists, `enumerate`, `itemize`, and `description`, are discussed. Then the general `list` environment is introduced and you will learn how to build custom layouts by varying the values of the parameters controlling the `list` environment. Typesetting texts verbatim is the subject of the third section. Various ways of presenting "typed" texts (like computer listings), with or without expansion of tabs, are discussed. The fourth section looks at the different kind of "notes," such as footnotes, marginal notes, and endnotes, while section five presents a package that makes it easy to typeset text in multiple columns. The chapter concludes with a discussion of a package that allows some kind of version control.

3.1 Phrases and Paragraphs

Parts of a text can be highlighted by choosing a visual appearance different from the one used for the main text. Parameters which can be customized are font shape and weight (see section 7.3.1 on page 165). Text can also be underlined, or the spacing between letters can be varied. The means for performing the latter two operations will be discussed in this section.

Two methods for modifying the appearance of a paragraph will be introduced and you will also learn how to create ragged-right text and how to modulate the inter-line distance inside paragraphs.

3.1.1 letterspace—Changing Inter-Letter Spacing

The package letterspace (by Philip Taylor) introduces the \letterspace command, which allows changing the width of a piece of text by changing the spaces between letters and between words (the latter is called *tracking*). The desired width can also be specified as a function of the natural width of the box containing the text by using the \naturalwidth parameter, as shown in the example below.

The first line shows a slightly compressed text, the second line is typeset at its natural width, and the third line is expanded by 10%. Lines four and five show the text spread out uniformly over half the line and the full line, respectively.

```
Time for good men                    \letterspace to .9\naturalwidth
Time for good men (natural size)                    {Time for good men}
Time for good men                    \letterspace {Time for good men (natural size)}
Time  for  good  men                 \letterspace to 1.1\naturalwidth
T i m e    f o r    g o o d    m e n                 {Time for good men}
                                     \letterspace to .5\linewidth{Time for good men}
                                     \letterspace to   \linewidth{Time for good men}
```

This \letterspace command should be used only with great care, since it changes the "grey" level of the text, and will disturb the reader. Its use should be restricted to situations where you need to compensate for shortcomings in a font's original widths, for example, if you want to obtain special effects or modulate the number of characters that fit on a line by adapting the density of the type. It can be very useful for creating nicer looking titles, since text at larger font sizes looks better with a looser tracking. It can also be used as a way for highlighting phrases. For instance, in the example below we use the \letterspace command to space out the title and to highlight the word "void" in the text, by spacing out its first three letters.

The first day

In the beginning God created the heaven and the earth. Now the earth was unformed and v o i d, and darkness was upon the face of the deep; and the spirit of God hovered over the face of the waters.

```
\centering\mbox{\Large\textbf{\letterspace to
              1.3\naturalwidth{The first day}}}
\begin{quotation}
In the beginning God created the heaven and the
earth. Now the earth was unformed and \letterspace
to 1.7\naturalwidth{voi}d, and darkness was upon
the face of the deep; and the spirit of God
hovered over the face of the waters.
\end{quotation}
```

3.1.2   ulem—**Emphasize via Underline**

LaTeX encourages the use of the \emph command and the \em declaration   (£ 16–18)
for marking emphasis, rather than explicit font changing declarations, like
\bfseries or \itshape.[1] The package ulem (by Donald Arseneau) redefines
the \emph command to use underlining, rather than italics. It does allow line
breaks, and even primitive hyphenation, within the underlined text. Every word
is typeset in an underlined box, so automatic hyphenation is normally disabled,
but explicit discretionary hyphens (\-) can still be used. The underlines continue
between words and stretch just like ordinary spaces do. Since spaces delimit
words, there may be some difficulty with syntactical spaces (e.g., "2.3 pt").
Some effort is made to handle such spaces. If problems occur you might try
enclosing the offending command in braces, since everything inside braces is
put inside an \mbox. Thus, braces will suppress stretching and line breaks in the
text they enclose. Note that nested emphasis constructs are not always treated
correctly by this package (see the gymnastics below to get the inter-word spaces
correct by putting each nested word separately inside an \emph expression).

No, I did <u>not</u> act in the movie *The Persecution and Assassination of Jean-Paul Marat, as performed by the Inmates of the Asylum of Charenton under the Direction of the Marquis de Sade!* But I <u>did</u> see it.

```
No, I did \emph{not} act in the movie
\emph{\emph{The} \emph{Persecution} \emph{and}
\emph{Assassination} \emph{of} \emph{Jean-Paul}
\emph{Marat}, as performed  by the Inmates of
the Asylum of Charenton under the Direc\-tion of
the Marquis de~Sade!} But I \emph{did} see it.
```

You can turn this feature off and on by using \normalem and \ULforem. The
next example shows which other variations are possible.

Just underlining (<u>under-line</u>),
a wavy underline (under-wave),
a line through text (~~strike out~~),
crossing out text (cross out, X out),

```
Just underlining (\uline{under-line}), \\
a wavy underline (\uwave{under-wave}), \\
a line through text (\sout{strike out}),   \\
crossing out text (\xout{cross out, X out}),
```

---

[1] See chapter 7 for the new font commands introduced in LaTeX2ε.

They are "optional features" and by default their definitions in the package file are commented out, so you have to activate them by hand.

3.1.3 xspace—Gentle Spacing after a Macro

The small package xspace (by David Carlisle) defines the \xspace command, which should be used at the end of a macro designed to be used mainly for text. It adds a space unless the macro is followed by certain punctuation characters.

\xspace saves you from having to type \␣ or {} after most occurrences of a macro name in text. However, if either of these constructs follows \xspace, a space is not added by \xspace. This means that it is safe to add \xspace to the end of an existing macro without making too many changes in your document. Possible candidates for \xspace are commands for abbreviations like "e.g.," and "i.e.,".

```
\newcommand{\eg}{e.g.,\xspace}
\newcommand{\ie}{i.e.,\xspace}
\newcommand{\etc}{etc.\@\xspace}
```

Notice the use of the \@ command to generate the right kind of space. If used to the right of a punctuation character it prevents extra space from being added: the dot will not be regarded as an end of sentence symbol. Using it on the left forces LATEX to interpret the dot as an end of sentence symbol.

(£ 14,154)

Sometimes \xspace may make a wrong decision and add a space when it is not required. In such cases, follow the macro with {}, as this has the effect of suppressing the space.

The United States of America has 50 states. Great Britain, the United States of America and Canada have close cultural links.

```
\newcommand{\USA}{United States of
                  America\xspace}
\newcommand{\GB}{Great Britain\xspace}
The \USA has 50 states.\\ \GB, the \USA and
Canada have close cultural links.
```

3.1.4 Paragraph Justification

(£ 111–2)

In some documents, paragraphs are not aligned at the right margin (like in this paragraph). The LATEX flushleft environment typesets an enclosed paragraph in this way. But the paragraph typesetting parameters have no universal effect, because most environments (such as minipage, tabular, and the list family) and commands (like \parbox, \footnote, and \caption) restore the alignment of paragraphs. That is, they set the \rightskip distance to zero. To put ragged right text inside such environments and commands you can issue the command \setlength{\rightskip}{0pt plus 1fil} within their scope. Inside `list`-like environments another rubber length, `\@rightskip`, is used instead of `\rightskip`.

   In the following example, which uses the `minipage` environment internally, we redefine `\rightskip` to obtain the desired effect. Note that we only allow `\rightskip` to be stretchable to a maximum of 2 cm, in order to limit the possible white space at the right of the page.

In the beginning God created the heaven and the earth. Now the earth was unformed and void, and darkness was upon the face of the deep; and the spirit of God hovered over the face of the waters.	`\setlength{\rightskip}{0pt plus 2cm}`
	`In the beginning God created the heaven and the`
	`earth. Now the earth was unformed and void, and`
	`darkness was upon the face of the deep; and the`
	`spirit of God hovered over the face of the`
	`waters.`

   Other ways of typesetting paragraphs are flush right and centered, with the `flushright` and `center` environments respectively. In these cases the line breaks are usually indicated with the `\\` command, whereas for ragged right text (the `flushleft` environment discussed above) you can let LaTeX do the line breaking itself.

   The three environments discussed in this section work by changing declarations that control how TeX typesets paragraphs. These declarations are also available as LaTeX commands, as shown in the following table of correspondence.   *(L 112)*

environment:	center	flushleft	flushright
command:	`\centering`	`\raggedright`	`\raggedleft`

   These commands, which do not start a new paragraph unlike the corresponding environments, can be used inside other environments and in a parbox, in particular, to control the alignment inside the p columns of an `array` or `tabular` environment. Note, however, that certain precautions should be taken in this case, as discussed on page 108, where the command `\PreserveBackslash` is introduced.

   The inter-word spacing in a justified paragraph (the white space between individual words) is controlled by several TeX parameters—the most important ones are `\tolerance` and `\emergencystretch`. By setting them suitably for your document you can prevent most or all of the "Overfull box" messages without any manual line breaks. `\tolerance` is a measure for how much the inter-word space in a paragraph is allowed to diverge from its optimum value.[2] This command is a TeX (not LaTeX) counter and therefore it has an uncommon assignment syntax, e.g., `\tolerance=500`. Lower values makes TeX try harder to stay near the optimum; higher values allow for loose typesetting. The default value is often 200. When TeX is unable to stay in the given tolerance you will find overfull boxes in your output (i.e., lines sticking out into the margin like this).

---

[2]The optimum is font defined: see section 7.7.2 on page 201.

By enlarging the value of \tolerance TEX will also consider poorer but still acceptable line breaks, instead of turning the problem over to you for manual intervention. Sensible values are between 50 and 9999—do not use 10000 or higher: this allows TEX to produce arbitrary bad lines (like   this   one). If you really need fully automated line breaking, it is better to set the length parameter \emergencystretch to a positive value. If TEX cannot break a paragraph without producing overfull boxes (due to the setting of \tolerance) and \emergencystretch is positive, it will add this length as stretchable space to every line, thereby accepting line breaking solutions that have been rejected before. As a result you may get some underfull box messages because all the lines are now set in a loose measure, but this will still look better than a single horrible line in the middle of an otherwise perfectly typeset paragraph.

LATEX has two predefined commands influencing the above parameters: \fussy, which is the default; and \sloppy, which allows for relatively bad lines. \sloppy is automatically applied by LATEX in some situations (e.g., when type-setting \marginpar arguments or p columns in a tabular environment) where perfect line breaking is seldom possible due to the narrow measure.

3.1.5   doublespace—Changing Inter-Line Spacing

(£ 94,155)   The \baselineskip is TEX's parameter for defining the *leading* (normal ver-tical distance) between consecutive baselines. Standard LATEX defines a lead-ing approximately 20% larger than the design size of the font (see section 7.6.1 on page 188). Because it is not recommended to change the setting of \baselineskip directly, LATEX provides the \baselinestretch command to al-low changing the \baselineskip at all sizes globally.

Note that after issuing the \renewcommand{\baselinestretch}{1.5} com-mand, the leading will not increase immediately. A font size changing command (like \small, \Large, etc.) should be executed to make the new value come into effect.

The package doublespace (by Stephen Page) defines the spacing environ-ment. The parameter *coef* is the value of the \baselinestretch for the text enclosed by the environment.

\begin{spacing}{*coef*} ... *text* ... \end{spacing}

In the example in figure 3.1 on the facing page the coefficient "2" produces a leading larger than the "double spacing" required for some publications. In this case the leading is increased twice—once by \baselineskip (where TEX already adds about 20% space between baselines) and a second time by setting \baselinestretch. "Double spacing" means that the vertical distance between baselines is about twice as large as the font size. Since \baselinestretch refers

In the beginning God created the heaven and the earth. Now the earth was unformed and void, and darkness was upon the face of the deep; and the spirit of God hovered over the face of the waters.

```
\begin{spacing}{2}
In the beginning God created the
heaven and the earth. Now the earth was
unformed and void, and darkness was upon
the face of the deep; and the spirit of
God hovered over the face of the waters.
\end{spacing}
```

Figure 3.1: Spaced-out paragraphs

spacing	10pt	11pt	12pt
one and one-half	1.25	1.21	1.24
double	1.67	1.62	1.66

Table 3.1: Effective \baselinestretch values for different font sizes

to the ratio between the desired distance and the \baselineskip, the values of \baselinestretch for different document base font sizes (and at two different optical spacings) can be calculated and are presented in table 3.1.

3.1.6   picinpar—Typeset a Paragraph with a Rectangular Hole

The package picinpar (by Friedhelm Sowa based on earlier work by Alan Hoenig) allows "windows" to be typeset inside paragraphs. The basic environment is window, which has two variants figwindow and tabwindow. These will also provide figure and table captions, respectively. The figwindow environment is similar to the wrapfigure environment described in section 6.4.2. As explained there, you should be careful when mixing figwindow and normal figure environments, since the latter can slip past the non-floating figwindow environments, and thus out-of-sequence figure numbers may result.

```
\begin{window} [nl,align,material,explanation]
```

nl   Number of lines before the window starts;

align   Alignment of the window inside the paragraph (*l*, the default value, for left, *c* for centered, and *r* for right adjusted);

material   Material to be shown in the window;

In this case we center a word printed verti-
cally inside the para- |H| graph. It is not dif-
ficult to understand |e| that tables can also
be easily included |l| with the tabwindow
environment. |l| When a paragraph
ends, like here, and |o| the window is not
yet finished, then it just continues past the
paragraph boundary, right into the next one(s).

```
\begin{window}[1,c,%
    {\fbox{\shortstack{H\\e\\l\\l\\o}}},{}]
In this case we center a word printed
vertically inside the paragraph. It is not
difficult to understand that tables can also
be easily included with the \texttt{tabwindow}
environment.\par When a paragraph ends, like
here, and the window is not yet finished, then
it just continues past the paragraph boundary,
right into the next one(s).
\end{window}
```

Figure 3.2: A "window" in a paragraph

explanation Explanatory text about the contents in the window (e.g., the caption
for figwindow and tabwindow.

Figure 3.2 shows how you can introduce a window in the middle of a paragraph. Notice the use of the \shortstack command to put the letters on top of
each other.

A figure or a table can also be included inside a paragraph. An example is
shown in figure 3.4 on the next page where we put a map of Great Britain at
the right side of the paragraph. The figwindow environment also typesets the
caption specified.

3.1.7 shapepar—Typeset a Paragraph with a Specified Shape

The package file shapepar (by Donald Arseneau) defines the command
\shapepar, which typesets paragraphs of a specified shape. The total size is
adjusted automatically so that the entire shape is filled with text. The paragraph to be typeset should not contain any display math or \vadjust material,
which includes \vspace commands. The paragraph is repeatedly formatted until its size and shape are right. As this is a slow process, this package is mainly
intended for cards, invitations—not for whole books!

The command \shapepar must be used at the beginning of a paragraph, and
it applies to the entire paragraph.

\shapepar{*shape_spec*} paragraph material

The parameter *shape_spec* gives a description of the shape for the paragraph. The syntax rules for specifying this shape are very specific, and

Is this a dagger which I see before me, The handle toward my hand? Come, let me clutch thee. I have thee not, and yet I see thee still. Art thou not, fatal vision, sensible To feeling as to sight? or art thou but A dagger of the mind, a false creation, Proceeding from the heat-oppressed brain? I see thee yet, in form as palpable As this which now I draw. Thou marshall'st me the way that I was going; And such an in-strument I was to use. Mine eyes are made the fools o' the other senses, Or else worth all the rest; I see thee still, And on thy blade and dudgeon gouts of blood, Which was not so before. (*Macbeth*, Act II, Scene 1).

Figure 3.3: United Kingdom

```
\begin{figwindow}[3,r,%
  {\fbox{\epsfig{file=ukmap.eps,width=27mm}}},%
              {United Kingdom}]
Is this a dagger which I see before me, The
handle toward my hand? Come, let me clutch
thee. I have thee not, and yet I see thee
still.  Art thou not, fatal vision, sensible
To feeling as to sight?  or art thou but A
dagger of the mind, a false creation,
Proceeding from the heat-oppressed brain?  I
see thee yet, in form as palpable As this
which now I draw.  Thou marshall'st me the way
that I was going; And such an instrument I was
to use.  Mine eyes are made the fools o' the
other senses, Or else worth all the rest; I
see thee still, And on thy blade and dudgeon
gouts of blood, Which was not so before.
(\emph{Macbeth}, Act II, Scene 1).
\end{figwindow}
```

Figure 3.4: A paragraph embedded figure

those interested should consult the package file itself. There exist four predefined shapes, three of which have also an associated predefined command \diamondpar, \squarepar and \heartpar. Their effect is shown below:

◇
Infan-
dum, regina,
iubes renovare do-
lorem, Troianas ut opes
et lamentabile regnum cruerint
Danai; quaeque ipse miserrima vidi, et
quorum pars magna fui. Quis talia fando Myrmidonum Dolopumve aut duri miles Ulixi temperet a
lacrimis? Et iam nox umida caelo praecipitat, suadentque cadentia sidera somnos. Sed si tantus
amor casus cognoscere nostros et breviter
Troiae supremum audire laborem,
quamquam animus memi-
nisse horret, luctuque
refugit,   in-
cipiam.
◇

\diamondpar{Infandum, regina,...}

Infandum, regina, iubes renovare dolorem, Troianas ut opes et lamentabile regnum cruerint Danai; quaeque ipse miserrima vidi, et quorum pars magna fui. Quis talia fando Myrmidonum Dolopumve aut duri miles Ulixi temperet a lacrimis? Et iam nox umida caelo praecipitat, suadentque cadentia sidera somnos. Sed si tantus amor casus cognoscere nostros et breviter Troiae supremum audire laborem, quamquam animus meminisse horret, luctuque refugit, incipiam.

\squarepar{Infandum, regina,...}

Infandum,   regina,
iubes renovare do-   lorem, Troianas ut
opes et   lamentabile   regnum cruerint Danai;
quaeque ipse miserrima vidi, et quorum pars
magna fui.   Quis talia fando Myrmidonum
Dolopumve aut duri miles Ulixi temperet a
lacrimis?   Et iam nox umida caelo praecipitat, suadentque cadentia sidera somnos.
Sed si tantus amor casus cognoscere
nostros et breviter Troiae supremum
audire laborem, quamquam animus   meminisse   horret,
luctuque   refugit,
incipiam.
♡

Infandum, regina, iubes renovare dolorem, Troianas ut opes et
lamentabile regnum cruerint Danai;
quaeque ipse miserrima vidi, et quorum
pars magna fui.   Quis talia fando
Myrmidonum   Dolopumve aut
duri   miles   Ulixi temperet
a lacrimis? Et   iam nox umida
caelo praecipi-   tat, suadentque
cadentia sidera   somnos.   Sed
si tantus amor   casus cognoscere
nostros et breviter Troiae supremum audire laborem, quamquam
animus meminisse horret, luctuque   refugit,   incipiam.

`\heartpar{Infandum, regina,...}`   `\shapepar\nutshape{Infandum, regina,...}`

3.2   List Structures

Lists are a very general LaTeX construct and are used to build many of LaTeX's display-like environments. LaTeX's standard list environments, `enumerate`, `itemize`, and `description`, are discussed in the next section, where we also show how they can be customized. The general list environment is discussed in section 3.2.2.

3.2.1   Modifying the Standard Lists

It is relatively easy to customize the three standard LaTeX list environments, and the three sections below will look at each of these environments in turn. Changes to the default definitions of these environments can be made globally by redefining certain list-defining parameters in the document preamble, or they can be kept local.

Customizing the `enumerate` List Environment

(£ 26,165–6)   LaTeX's enumerated (numbered) list environment `enumerate` is characterized by the commands and representation forms shown in table 3.2 on the facing page. The first row shows the names of the counter used for numbering the four possible levels of the list. The second and third rows are the commands giving the representation of the counters and their default definition in the standard LaTeX class files. Rows four, five, and six contain the commands, the default definition, and an example of the actual enumeration string printed by the list.

A reference to a numbered list element is constructed using the `\theenumi`, `\theenumii`, and other similar commands, prefixed by the commands `\p@enumi`, `\p@enumii`, etc., respectively. The last three rows in the table show the com-

	First level	Second level	Third level	Fourth level
counter	`enumi`	`enumii`	`enumiii`	`enumiv`
representation	`\theenumi`	`\theenumii`	`\theenumiii`	`\theenumiv`
default definition	`\arabic{enumi}`	`\alph{enumii}`	`\roman{enumiii}`	`\Alph{enumiv}`
label field	`\labelenumi`	`\labelenumii`	`\labelenumiii`	`\labelenumiv`
default form	`\theenumi.`	`(\theenumii)`	`\theenumiii.`	`\theenumiv.`
numbering example	1., 2.	(a), (b)	i., ii.	A., B.
prefix	`\p@enumi`	`\p@enumii`	`\p@enumiii`	`\p@enumiv`
default definition	`{}`	`\theenumi`	`\theenumi(\theenumii)`	`\p@enumiii\theenumiii`
reference example	1, 2	1a, 2b	1(a)i, 2(b)ii	1(a)iA, 2(b)iiB

Table 3.2: Commands controlling an `enumerate` list environment

mand, its default definition, and an example for the representation of references. It is important that you are careful to take into account the definitions of both the representation and reference building commands to get the references correct.

We can now create several kinds of numbered description lists simply by applying what we have just learned.

Our first example redefines the first and second level counters to use capital Roman digits and Latin characters. The visual representation should be the value of the counter followed by a dot. The default value of table 3.2 is used for the reference prefix command `\p@enumi`.

I. **Introduction**

    A. **Applications**
Motivation for research and applications related to the subject.

    B. **Organization**
Explain organization of the report, what is included, and what is not.

II. **Literature Survey**

III. **Proposed Research**

q1=I-A q2=I-B q3=II q4=III

```
\makeatletter
\renewcommand{\theenumi}{\Roman{enumi}}
\renewcommand{\labelenumi}{\theenumi.}
\renewcommand{\theenumii}{\Alph{enumii}}
\renewcommand{\labelenumii}{\theenumii.}
\renewcommand{\p@enumii}{\theenumi--}
\makeatother
\begin{enumerate} \item \textbf{Introduction}
  \begin{enumerate}
    \item \textbf{Applications}  \newline
      Motivation for research and applications
      related to the subject.        \label{q1}
    \item \textbf{Organization}  \newline
      Explain organization of the report, what
      is included, and what is not. \label{q2}
  \end{enumerate}
  \item \textbf{Literature Survey}  \label{q3}
  \item \textbf{Proposed Research}  \label{q4}
\end{enumerate}
q1=\ref{q1} q2=\ref{q2} q3=\ref{q3} q4=\ref{q4}
```

You can also decorate an enumerate field by adding something to the label field. In the example below, we have chosen the paragraph sign (§) as a prefix for each label of the first level list elements.

§1. text inside list, more text inside list, text inside list,

§2. text inside list, more text inside list, text inside list,

§3. text inside list, more text inside list, text inside list, more text inside list.

w1=1 w2=2

```
\renewcommand{\labelenumi}{\S\theenumi.}
\begin{enumerate}
\item text inside list, more text inside list,
      text inside list, \label{w1}
\item text inside list, more text inside list,
      text inside list, \label{w2}
\item text inside list, more text inside list,
      text inside list, more text inside list.
\end{enumerate}
w1=\ref{w1}   w2=\ref{w2}
```

You might even want to select different markers for consecutive labels. For instance, in the following example, characters from the PostScript font Zapf-Dingbats are used. In this case there is no straightforward way for automatically making the \ref commands produce the correct references. You can, however, use the dingautolist environment defined in the package file pifont, which is part of the PSNFSS system (see section 11.9.3 on page 335). Note also that we have used the calc package for doing the addition inside the \setcounter command (see section A.4 on page 468).

① text inside list, more text inside list, text inside list, more text inside list;

② text inside list, more text inside list, text inside list, more text inside list;

③ text inside list, more text inside list, text inside list, more text inside list.

```
\newcounter{local}\renewcommand{\labelenumi}
    {\setcounter{local}{171+\value{enumi}}%
    \ding{\value{local}}}
\begin{enumerate}
\item text inside list, more text inside list,
      text inside list, more text inside list;
\item text inside list, more text inside list,
      text inside list, more text inside list;
\item text inside list, more text inside list,
      text inside list, more text inside list.
\end{enumerate}
```

Finally, for those who do not want to get involved in customizing these commands themselves, there exists a package enumerate (by David Carlisle), which redefines the enumerate environment with an optional argument specifying the style in which the counter has to be printed. This argument can contain any one of the tokens A, a, I, i, or 1 for typesetting the value of the counter using (respectively) the \Alph, \alph, \Roman, \roman, or \arabic styles.

Moreover, you can put any LaTeX expression in the argument; however the tokens A, a, I, i, or 1 must be specified inside a {} group if they should not be interpreted in the above manner.

	First level	Second level	Third level	Fourth level
Commands	\labelitemi	\labelitemii	\labelitemiii	\labelitemiv
Definition	\m@th\bullet	\bfseries --	\m@th\ast	\m@th\cdot
Representation	•	–	*	.

Table 3.3: Commands controlling an `itemize` list

The internal command `\m@th` in the above settings locally sets the value of the `\mathsurround` parameter to zero (extra space around in-line formulas). `\m@th` should be called whenever math mode is entered for non-math purposes to avoid extra spaces in cases where `\mathsurround` was made positive by the document class file.

The cross-reference commands `\label` and `\ref` can be used as with the standard `enumerate` environment. Note, however, that with this package the `\ref` command only produces the chosen representation of the counter value— not the whole label. It prints the value in the same style as `\item`, as determined by the presence of one of the tokens A, a, I, i, or 1 in the optional argument.

EX i. text item one level one. More text item one level one

EX ii. text item two level one.

    example a) text item one level two. More text item one level two

    example b) text item two level two.

A-1 text item one level one for list two.

A-2 text item two level one for list two.

This is how list entries are referenced: 'i', 'iia' and '1' or more fully 'EX i.' and 'A-1'.

```
\begin{enumerate}[EX i.]
\item text item one level one.
  More text item one level one     \label{LA}
\item text  item two level one.
  \begin{enumerate}[{example} a)]
  \item text item one level two.
    More text item one level two \label{LB}
  \item text  item two level two.
  \end{enumerate}
\end{enumerate}
\begin{enumerate}[{A}-1]
\item text item one level one for list two.
                                   \label{LC}
\item text item two level one for list two.
\end{enumerate}
This is how list entries are referenced:
'\ref{LA}', '\ref{LB}' and '\ref{LC}' or
more fully 'EX~\ref{LA}.' and 'A-\ref{LC}'.
```

Customizing the `itemize` List Environment

For a simple unnumbered `itemize` list, the labels are defined by the commands shown in table 3.3. *(£ 26,165–6)*

    To create a list with different labels, you can redefine the label-generating command. You can make that change local for one list, as in the example below, or you can make it global by putting the `\labelitemi` redefinition in the document preamble. The following simple list is a standard `itemize` list with a marker from the PostScript ZapfDingbats font (see section 11.9.3 on page 335) for the first level label:

☞ Text of the first item in the list.

☞ Text of the first sentence in the second item of the list. And the second sentence.

☞ This sentence in the text of the third item of the list.

```
\newenvironment{MYitemize}{%
    \renewcommand{\labelitemi}{\ding{43}}%
         \begin{itemize}}{\end{itemize}}
\begin{MYitemize}
\item Text of the first item in the list.
\item Text of the first sentence in the second
         item of the list. And the second sentence.
\item This sentence in the text of the third
         item of the list.
\end{MYitemize}
```

Customizing the `description` List Environment

(*£* 26,165–6)   Using the `description` environment you can change the `\descriptionlabel` command that generates the label. In the following example the font for type-setting the labels is changed from bold to sans serif.

A. text inside list, text inside list, text inside list, more text inside list;

B. text inside list, text inside list, text inside list, more text inside list;

C. text inside list, text inside list, text inside list, more text inside list.

```
\renewcommand{\descriptionlabel}[1]%
             {\hspace{\labelsep}\textsf{#1}}
\begin{description}
\item[A.] text inside list,  text inside list,
         text inside list, more text inside list;
\item[B.] text inside list,  text inside list,
         text inside list, more text inside list;
\item[C.] text inside list,  text inside list,
         text inside list, more text inside list.
\end{description}
```

The standard LaTeX class files set the starting point of the label box in a `description` environment a distance of `\labelsep` to the left of the left margin of the enclosing environment, so that the `\descriptionlabel` command in the example above first adds a value of `\labelsep` to start the label aligned with the left margin.

3.2.2   Making Your Own Lists

(*£* 112,166–8)   Lists are generated by the generic environment `list`:

> `\begin{list}{`*default_label*`}{`*decls*`}` *item_list* `\end{list}`

The parameter *default_label* is the text to be used as a label when an `\item` command is issued without an optional argument. The parameter *decls* sets up the different geometrical parameters of the `list` environment (see figure 3.5 on the following page). That figure also shows the default values for those parameters. The parameters can all be redefined with the help of the `\setlength` or `\addtolength` commands.

Several LATEX environments are defined with the help of `list` (for example, `quote`, `quotation`, `center`, `flushleft`, and `flushright`). Note that these environments have only one item, and the `\item[]` command is specified in the environment definition.

As an example, we can consider the `quote` environment whose definition gives it the same left and right margins. The simple variant `Quote`, shown below, is identical to `quote` apart from the double quote symbols added around the text. Note the special precautions, which must be taken to eliminate undesirable white space in front of (`\ignorespaces`) and following (`\unskip`) the text.

... text before.

> "Some quoted text, more quoted text.
> Some quoted text, more quoted text."

Text following ...

```
\newenvironment{Quote}% Definition of Quote
    {\begin{list}{}{%
        \setlength{\rightmargin}{\leftmargin}}
            \item[]``\ignorespaces}
    {\unskip''\end{list}}
\ldots\ text before.
\begin{Quote}
    Some quoted text, more quoted text.
    Some quoted text, more quoted text.
\end{Quote}
Text following \ldots
```

General lists are often used for documenting computer commands or program functions. For instance, in the following examples `entry` and its variants are used. In each case the name of the topic being described is entered as the parameter of the `\item` command.

Description: Returns from a function. If issued at top-level, the interpreter simply terminates, just as if end of input had been reached.

Errors: None.

Return values:
Any arguments in effect are passed back to the caller.

```
\begin{entry}
\item[Description]
 Returns from a function.  If issued at
 top-level, the interpreter simply terminates,
 just as if end of input had been reached.
\item[Errors]    None.
\item[Return values]\mbox{}\\
          Any arguments in effect
          are passed back to the caller.
\end{entry}
```

This example shows a typical problem with description-like lists when the text in the label (*term*) is wider than the width of the label. Standard LATEX lets the text of the term continue into the text of the *description* part. This is normally

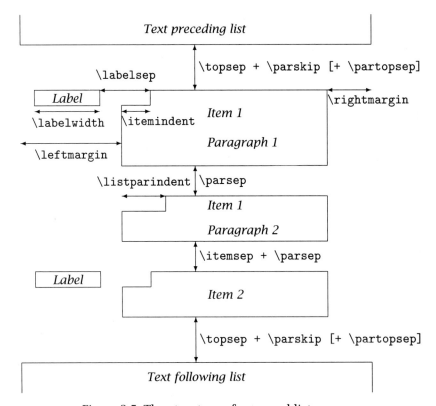

Figure 3.5: The structure of a general list

Vertical lengths

All the vertical spaces below are rubber lengths with a value depending on the type size and the level of the list.

\topsep   space between first item and preceding paragraph.

\partopsep   extra space added to \topsep when environment starts a new paragraph.

\itemsep   space between successive items.

\parsep   space between paragraphs within an item.

Horizontal lengths

\leftmargin   space between left margin of enclosing environment (or of page if top level list) and left margin of this list. Must be nonnegative. Its value depends on the list level.

\rightmargin   similar to \leftmargin but for the right margin. Its value is usually 0pt.

\listparindent   extra indentation at beginning of every paragraph of a list except the one started by \item. Can be negative, but is usually 0pt.

\itemindent   extra indentation added to the horizontal indentation of the text part of the first line of an item. It is with respect to this reference point that the starting position of the label is calculated by subtracting the values of \labelsep and \labelwidth. Its value is usually 0pt.

\labelwidth   the nominal width of the box containing the label. If the natural width of the label is ≤\labelwidth, then the label is typeset flush right inside a box of width \labelwidth. Otherwise, a box of the natural width is employed, which causes an indentation of the text on that line.

\labelsep   the space between the end of the label box and the text of the first item. Its default value is 0.5em.

not desired, and to improve the visual appearance of the list we have started the description part on the next line. A new line was forced by putting an empty box on the same line, followed by the '\\' command.

In the previous example, the \makelabel command (a command with one argument defining the layout of the \item label) and the two geometrical parameters (\labelwidth and \leftmargin) were redefined, as shown below.[3]

```
\newcommand{\entrylabel}[1]{\mbox{\textsf{#1:}}\hfil}
\newenvironment{entry}
   {\begin{list}{}%
         {\renewcommand{\makelabel}{\entrylabel}%
          \setlength{\labelwidth}{35pt}%
          \setlength{\leftmargin}{\labelwidth+\labelsep}%
         }%
   }%
   {\end{list}}
```

In the remaining part of this section various possibilities for controlling the width and mutual positioning of the term and description parts will be investigated. One method for accomplishing this is to change the width of the label. The environment is declared with an argument specifying the desired width of the label field (normally chosen to be the widest term entry). Note the redefinition of the \makelabel command where you specify how the label will be typeset. As this redefinition is put inside the definition of the Ventry environment, the argument placeholder character # must be escaped to ## to signal LaTeX that you are referring to the argument of the \makelabel command, and not to the argument of the outer environment.

Description:	Returns from a function. If issued at top-level, the interpreter simply terminates, just as if end of input had been reached.
Errors:	None.
Return values:	Any arguments in effect are passed back to the caller.

```
\begin{Ventry}{Return values}
\item[Description]
 Returns from a function.  If issued
 at top-level, the interpreter
 simply terminates, just as if end
 of input had been reached.
\item[Errors]    None.
\item[Return values] Any arguments
 in effect are passed back to the
 caller.
\end{Ventry}
```

---

[3]In this and some of the following examples, we have used the package calc and extended control structures of LaTeX2$_\varepsilon$ (see appendix A, sections A.4 and A.5).

The `Ventry` environment is defined by:

```
\newenvironment{Ventry}[1]%
   {\begin{list}{}{\renewcommand{\makelabel}[1]{\textsf{##1:}\hfil}%
      \settowidth{\labelwidth}{\textsf{#1:}}%
      \setlength{\leftmargin}{\labelwidth+\labelsep}}}%
   {\end{list}}
```

However, several lists with varying widths for the label field on the same page might look typographically unacceptable. Evaluating the width of the term is another possibility. If it is wider than `\labelwidth`, an additional empty box is appended with the effect that the description part starts on a new line. This matches the conventional method for displaying options in UNIX manuals.

```
\newlength{\Mylen}
\newcommand{\Lentrylabel}[1]{%
  \settowidth{\Mylen}{\textsf{#1:}}%
  \ifthenelse{\lengthtest{\Mylen > \labelwidth}}%
      {\parbox[b]{\labelwidth}%            term > labelwidth
         {\makebox[0pt][l]{\textsf{#1:}}\\}}%
      {\textsf{#1:}}%                      term < labelwidth
  \hfil\relax}
\newenvironment{Lentry}
   {\renewcommand{\entrylabel}{\Lentrylabel}%
    \begin{entry}}
   {\end{entry}}
```

As the last line in the definition above shows, the `Lentry` environment is defined in terms of the `entry` environment. The label generating command `\entrylabel` is now replaced by the `\Lentrylabel` command. The latter first sets the length variable `\Mylen` equal to the width of the label. It then compares that length with `\labelwidth`. If the label is smaller than `\labelwidth`, then it is typeset on the same line as the description term; otherwise it is typeset in a zero width box with the material sticking out to the right as far as needed (forcing a new line) so that the description term starts one line lower.

Description:
> Returns from a function. If issued at top-level, the interpreter simply terminates, just as if end of input had been reached.

Errors: None.

Return values:
> Any arguments in effect are passed back to the caller.

```
\begin{Lentry}
\item[Description]
  Returns from a function.  If issued at
  top-level, the interpreter simply terminates,
  just as if end of input had been reached.
\item[Errors]    None.
\item[Return values] Any arguments in effect
  are passed back to the caller.
\end{Lentry}
```

Yet another possibility is to allow multiline labels.

Description:	Returns from a function. If issued at top-level, the interpreter simply terminates, just as if end of input had been reached.
Errors:	None.
Return values:	Any arguments in effect are passed back to the caller.

```
\begin{Mentry}
\item[Description]
  Returns from a function.  If issued at
  top-level, the interpreter simply terminates,
  just as if end of input had been reached.
\item[Errors]    None.
\item[Return\\values] Any arguments in effect
  are passed back to the caller.
\end{Mentry}
```

In this example we, once more, use the `entry` environment as a basis, but this time the command `\Mentrylabel` replaces the `\entrylabel` command. The idea here is that large labels may be split over several lines. Certain precautions have to be taken to allow hyphenation of the first word in a paragraph, and therefore the `\hspace{0pt}` command is introduced in the definition. The material gets typeset inside a paragraph box of the correct width `\labelwidth`, which is then top aligned and left adjusted into a box that is itself placed inside a box with a height of 1 ex and no depth. In this way, LATEX does not realize that the material extends below the first line.

```
\newcommand{\Mentrylabel}[1]%
   {\raisebox{0pt}[1ex][0pt]{\makebox[\labelwidth][l]%
       {\parbox[t]{\labelwidth}{\hspace{0pt}\textsf{#1:}}}}}
\newenvironment{Mentry}%
   {\renewcommand{\entrylabel}{\Mentrylabel}\begin{entry}}%
   {\end{entry}}
```

An environment with an automatically incremented counter can be created by including a `\usecounter` command in the declaration of the `list` environment. This function is demonstrated with the `Notes` environment, which produces a sequence of notes. In this case, the first parameter of the `list` environment is used to provide the automatically generated text for the term part.

```
\newcounter{notes}
\newenvironment{Notes}%
   {\begin{list}{\textsc{Note} \arabic{notes}. }{\usecounter{notes}%
        \setlength{\labelsep}{0pt}\setlength{\leftmargin}{0pt}%
        \setlength{\labelwidth}{0pt}%
        \setlength{\listparindent}{0pt}}}%
   {\end{list}}
```

After declaring the `notes` counter, the default label of the `Notes` environment is defined to consist of the word NOTES in small caps, followed by the value of the `notes` counter, using as its representation an arabic number followed by a dot.

NOTE 1. This is the text of the first note item. Some more text for the first note item.

NOTE 2. This is the text of the second note item. Some more text for the second note item.

```
\begin{Notes}
\item This is the text of the first note item.
      Some more text for the first note item.
\item This is the text of the second note item.
      Some more text for the second note item.
\end{Notes}
```

3.3 Simulating Typed Text

It is often necessary to display information verbatim, i.e., "as entered at the terminal." However, to guide the reader it might be useful to highlight certain textual strings in a particular way. This calls for the ability to use other LaTeX commands inside "verbatim" texts. The present section describes packages which make this easier.

3.3.1 alltt—A Verbatim-Like Environment

The package alltt (by Leslie Lamport) defines the `alltt` environment. This acts like a verbatim environment except that backslash '\' and the braces '{' and '}' retain their usual meaning. Thus, other commands and environments can appear inside an `alltt` environment, as shown in figure 3.6 on the next page.

3.3.2 verbatim—A Style for Literal Text

The package verbatim (by Rainer Schöpf) reimplements the LaTeX environments `verbatim` and `verbatim*`. One of its major advantages is that it allows arbitrarily long verbatim texts. It also provides a `comment` environment that skips all text between the commands `\begin{comment}` and `\end{comment}`. Moreover, it contains a redefinition of LaTeX's `\verb` command, which is better at detecting the omission of the closing delimiter.

The package also provides hooks to implement user extensions for defining customized verbatim-like environments. A few such extensions are realized in the package moreverb, described in the next section.

3.3.3 moreverb—More Verbatim-Like Commands and Environments

The package file moreverb (by Angus Duggan) is based on the verbatim package discussed above. It provides some interesting predefined verbatim-like com-

```
One can have font changes, like:          \begin{alltt}
emphasized text.                           One can have font changes, like:
                                           {\em{}emphasized text\/}.

A line of special characters # $ % ^ & ~ _
                                           A line of special characters # $ % ^ & ~ _

Insert text from a file "foo.tex" by typing
'\input{foo}'. Beware that                 Insert text from a file "foo.tex" by typing
"return" starts a new line, so if foo.tex  '\(\backslash\)input\{foo\}'. Beware that
ends with a "return" you can wind up with  "return" starts a new line, so if foo.tex
an extra blank line if you are not careful. ends with a "return" you can wind up with
                                           an extra blank line if you are not careful.

The user can do mathematics too by typing
\(...\) or \[...\]. Remember               The user can do mathematics too by typing
that '$' just produces a dollar sign.      \verb!\(...\)! or \verb!\[...\]!. Remember
The same is true for the other special     that '$' just produces a dollar sign.
characters '^', '_' inside math mode:       The same is true for the other special
use \sp as in a²,                          characters '^', '_' inside math mode:
use \sb as in a₂.                          use \(\backslash\)sp as in \(a\sp{2}\),
                                           use \(\backslash\)sb as in \(a\sb{2}\).
                                           \end{alltt}
```

Figure 3.6: Verbatim-like `alltt` environment

mands for writing to and reading from files as well as several environments for the production of listings.

> \begin{verbatimwrite}{*filename*}

The `verbatimwrite` environment (originally written by Rainer Schöpf) writes its contents to a file *filename*. At the right-hand side we show the original file (tabs are shown as ▷), while at the left-hand side we show the tabs expanded.

```
*       *       *       *          \begin{verbatimwrite}{ testtab.out}
Top level                          *▷*▷*▷*
        One level up               Top level
                Level two          ▷One level up
        Embedded        tab        ▷▷Level two
                                   ▷Embedded▷tab
                                   \end{verbatimwrite}
```

> \begin{verbatimtab}[*tabstop*]

The `verbatimtab` environment allows *tab* characters (shown as ▷) to be expanded properly to a number of space characters. (Remember that standard

LATEX considers tab characters as single spaces.) The distance between tab stops can be specified by an optional argument. By default the distance between tab stops is set to eight space characters.

```
12345678901234567890123456789 0123456
                                                \begin{verbatimtab}
                                                12345678901234567890123456789 0123456
|       one       two       three     four      \end{verbatimtab}


|   one two three    four                        \begin{verbatimtab}
                                                |▷one▷two▷three▷four
                                                \end{verbatimtab}

                                                \begin{verbatimtab}[4]
                                                |▷one▷two▷three▷four
                                                \end{verbatimtab}
```

```
\verbatiminput [tabstop] {filename}
```

The command \verbatimtabinput will input the file *filename* given as the mandatory argument. The distance between tab stops can be specified by giving an optional argument *tabstop*. Note that in the example below the text has a distance of four spaces between tab stops, whereas at the beginning of the section, when file testtab.out was written, the distance was equal to the default (eight spaces).

```
*   *   *   *
Top level                                       \verbatimtabinput[4]{testtab.out}
    One level up
        Level two
    Embedded    tab
```

The boxedverbatim environment can be used to make verbatim text stand out by surrounding it with a box.

```
┌─────────────────────────────────────┐
│ The boxedverbatim environment        │        \begin{boxedverbatim}
│ puts a                               │        The boxedverbatim environment
│ frame around the                     │        puts a
│ verbatim environment.                │        frame around the
│                                      │        verbatim environment.
└─────────────────────────────────────┘        \end{boxedverbatim}
```

An environment similar to the alltt environment described in section 3.3.1 on page 66 is called verbatimcmd. An example is shown below.

```
The verbatimcmd environment can be used      \begin{verbatimcmd}
to include commands                           The verbatimcmd environment can be used
in LaTeX verbatim environments. Note          to include {\normalfont\itshape{}commands}
that spaces after commands are                in \LaTeX verbatim environments. Note
significant, so empty groups {}               that spaces after commands are
should be used to separate words.             significant, so empty groups \{\}
Otherwise, you will find                      should be used to separate words.
 strange spaces in                            Otherwise, you will find
your output.                                  {\normalfont\itshape strange} spaces in
                                              your output.
And some display math
                                              And some display math \[a\sp{b}\sb{c}d\]
             a^{b_c d}                        \end{verbatimcmd}
```

```
\begin{listing}[step]{firstline} ... \end{listing}
\begin{listing*}[step]{firstline}... \end{listing*}
```

The `listing` environment is like a `verbatim` environment, but with each line numbered. The starred version `listing*` shows a blank character as ␣ . An optional argument *step* specifies the step between numbered lines (default value is 1), and the required argument *firstline* is the number of the first line. If the user specifies *step* as "1," then all lines will be numbered. The `listing` environment below is invoked by the command `\begin{listing}[2]{3}`, which will number each second line starting at number "3."

```
    The listing environment numbers       \begin{listing}[2]{3}
4   the lines in it. It takes an           The listing environment numbers
    optional argument, which is the        the lines in it. It takes an
6   step between numbered lines (line      optional argument, which is the
    1 is always numbered if present),      step between numbered lines (line
8   and a required argument, which is      1 is always numbered if present),
    the starting line.                     and a required argument, which is
                                           the starting line.
                                           \end{listing}
```

```
\begin{listingcont} ... \end{listingcont}
\begin{listingcont*}... \end{listingcont*}
```

The `listingcont(*)` environment (example on the following page) continues where the previous `listing(*)` environment left off. The non-starred versions of these environments expand tabs using a default tab width of eight characters while the starred versions do not handle tabs.

```
10   This listingcont environment            \begin{listingcont}
     continues where the previous listing    This listingcont environment
12   environment left off.                    continues where the previous listing
     Both the listing and listingcont         environment left off.
14   environments expand tabs ''     ''       Both the listing and listingcont
     with a default tab width of 8.           environments expand tabs ''▷''
                                              with a default tab width of 8.
                                              \end{listingcont}
```

> `\listinginput [step] {firstline}{filename}`

The `\listinginput` command allows a file *filename* to be read as a listing. Numbering begins with the first line at *firstline* and then proceeds in steps of *step*.

As an example, the file `testtab.out`, written by the `verbatimwrite` environment as shown at the beginning of the present section, can be read (and listed) with the command `\listinginput{1}{testtab.out}`.

```
1    *       *       *       *
2    Top level
3            One level up
4                    Level two
5            Embedded         tab
```

3.4   Footnotes, Endnotes, and Marginals

LATEX has facilities to typeset "inserted" text, such as marginal notes, footnotes, figures, and tables. The present section looks more closely at different kinds of notes, while chapter 6 on page 141 describes floats in more detail.

3.4.1   Customizing Footnotes

Footnotes in LATEX are usually simple to use and provide a quite powerful mechanism to typeset material at the bottom of a page.[4] This material can consist of several paragraphs and can include lists, inline or display mathematics, tabular material, and so on.

(£ 91,156)   LATEX offers several parameters to customize footnotes. They are shown schematically in figure 3.7 on the next page.

(£ 99,195)   A sharp distinction is made between footnotes in the main text and footnotes inside a `minipage` environment. The former are numbered using the `footnote` counter, while inside a `minipage` the `\footnote` command is redefined to use

---

[4]An interesting and complete discussion of this subject appeared in the French TEX Users' Group magazine *Cahiers GUTenberg* [5, 62].

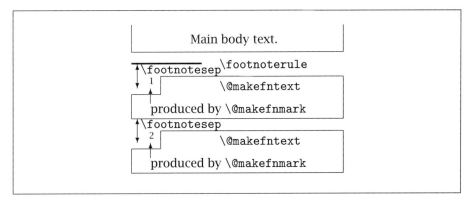

Figure 3.7: Schematic layout of footnotes

the mpfootnote counter. Thus the representation of the footnote mark is obtained by the \thefootnote or the \thempfootnote command depending on the context. By default it is an arabic number in text and a lowercase letter inside a minipage environment. You can redefine this to get a different representation by specifying, for example, for main text footnotes:

text text text*   text text text text† text

*The first
†The second

```
\renewcommand{\thefootnote}{\fnsymbol{footnote}}
text text text\footnote{The first}
text text text text\footnote{The second} text
```

Footnotes produced with the \footnote command inside a minipage environment use the mpfootnote counter and are typeset at the bottom of the parbox produced by the minipage. However, if you use the \footnotemark command in a minipage it will produce a footnote mark in the same style and sequence as the main text footnotes—i.e., stepping the footnote counter and using the \thefootnote command for the representation. This behavior allows you to produce a footnote inside your minipage that is typeset in sequence with the main text footnotes at the bottom of the page: you place a \footnotemark inside the minipage and the corresponding \footnotetext after it.

Footnotes in a minipage are numbered using lowercase letters.[a]
This text references a footnote at the bottom of the page.[5]

[a]Inside minipage

```
\begin{minipage}{\linewidth}
Footnotes in a minipage are numbered using
lowercase letters.\footnote{Inside minipage}
\par This text references a footnote at the
bottom of the page.\footnotemark
\end{minipage}\footnotetext{At bottom of page}
```

In the article class, footnotes are numbered sequentially throughout the

[5]At bottom of page

document. In report and book footnotes are numbered inside chapters. You can change this by using the \@addtoreset command (see section 2.3.1). However, do not try to number your footnotes within pages with the help of this mechanism. Since LaTeX is looking ahead while producing the final pages your footnotes would most certainly be numbered incorrectly. To number footnotes per page you can use the package footnpag (by Joachim Schrod). To manage the footnote numbers, this package writes information to an auxiliary file, with name "*jobname*.fot." You must therefore run LaTeX at least twice to ensure that all footnotes get the correct numbers. Also, in this implementation, the optional argument of \footnote is no longer available; but this seems to be a small disadvantage, since you should not have to use this argument with this layout style anyway.

The \@makefnmark command generates the footnote marker from the \@thefnmark command, which holds the current footnote's mark, created by \thefootnote or supplied by you through the optional argument of the \footnote command. The default definition is the superscript mark:

```
\renewcommand{\@makefnmark}{\mbox{$^{\@thefnmark}$}}
```

The appearance of the standard footnote can be changed by customizing the parameters shown in figure 3.7 on the preceding page and described below:

\footnotesize The font size used inside footnotes (see also table 7.1 on page 170).

\footnotesep The height of a strut placed at the beginning of every footnote. If it is greater than the \baselineskip used for \footnotesize, then additional vertical space will be inserted above each footnote. See section A.2.3 for more information about struts.

\skip\footins A low-level TeX command that defines the space between the main text and the start of the footnotes. You can change its value with the \setlength or \addtolength commands by putting \skip\footins into the first argument, e.g.,

```
\addtolength{\skip\footins}{3mm}
```

\footnoterule A macro to draw the rule separating footnotes from the main text. It is executed right after the vertical space of \skip\footins. It should take zero vertical space, i.e., it should use a negative skip to compensate for any positive space it occupies, for example:

```
\renewcommand{footnoterule}{\vspace*{-3pt}%
  \rule{.4\columnwidth}{0.4pt}\vspace*{2.6pt}}
```

You can also construct a fancier "rule," e.g., one consisting of a series of dots:

```
\renewcommand{footnoterule}{\vspace*{-3pt}%
    \qquad\dotfill\qquad\vspace*{2.6pt}}
```

The `\footnote` command executes `\@makefntext` inside a `\parbox`, with a width of `\columnwidth`. The default version looks something like:

```
\newcommand{\@makefntext}[1]%
    {\noindent\makebox[1.8em][r]{\@makefnmark}#1}
```

A more complicated variant could use a `list` environment. Each footnote is typeset as a list with one item.

```
\renewcommand{\@makefntext}[1]{\setlength{\parindent}{0pt}%
  \begin{list}{}{\setlength{\labelwidth}{1.5em}%
    \setlength{\leftmargin}{\labelwidth}%
    \setlength{\labelsep}{3pt}\setlength{\itemsep}{0pt}%
    \setlength{\parsep}{0pt}\setlength{\topsep}{0pt}%
    \footnotesize}\item[\hfill\@makefnmark]#1%
  \end{list}}
```

LaTeX does not allow you to use another `\footnote` command inside a `\footnote`, as is common in some disciplines, but you can use the `\footnotemark` command inside the first footnote and then put the text of the footnote's footnote as the argument of a `\footnotetext` command.

What if you want to reference a given footnote? For this you can use LaTeX's normal `\label` and `\ref` mechanism, although you may want to define your own command to typeset the reference in a special way, for instance:

This is some text.[1]
... as shown in footnote (1) on page 73,...

```
\newcommand{\fnref}[1]{~(\ref{#1})}
This is some text.\footnote{Text inside
referenced footnote\label{fn:myfoot}.}\par
... as shown in footnote\fnref{fn:myfoot} on
page~\pageref{fn:myfoot},...
```

[1] Text inside referenced footnote.

Standard LaTeX does not allow you to construct footnotes inside tabular material. In section 5.6.2 we shall show several ways of tackling that problem.

The package fnpara (by Dominik Wujastyk and Chris Rowley) completely changes the presentation[6] of footnotes. With this package, footnotes are typeset[7] as run-in paragraphs, instead of being stacked one on top of another. It is suitable for texts, such as critical editions, that contain many short footnotes.[8]

---

[6] This is an example of a footnote typeset as a run-in paragraph.   [7] This is another example of a footnote typeset as a run-in paragraph.   [8] See, e.g., the EDMAC system [51] for examples of what kind of footnotes and endnotes are common in critical editions.

3.4.2 Marginal Notes

> \marginpar [*left-text*] {*right-text*}

(£ 61,178) The \marginpar command generates a marginal note. This command type-sets the text given as an argument in the margin, the first line at the same height as the line in the main text where the \marginpar command occurs. When only the mandatory argument *right-text* is specified, then the text goes to the right margin for one-sided printing; to the outside margin for two-sided printing; and to the nearest margin for two-column formatting. When you specify an optional argument, then it is used for the left margin, while the second (mandatory) argument is used for the right.

There are a few important things to understand when using marginal notes. Firstly, the \marginpar command does not start a paragraph, that is, if it is used before the first word of a paragraph, the vertical alignment may not match the beginning of the paragraph. Secondly, if the margin is narrow, and the words are long (as in German), you may have to precede the first word by a \hspace{0pt} command to allow hyphenation of the first word. These two potential problems can be eased by defining a command \marginlabel{*text*}, which starts with an empty box \mbox{}, typesets a marginal note ragged left, and adds a \hspace{0pt} in front of the argument.

\marginlabel uses the outside margin for notes.

```
\newcommand{\marginlabel}[1]
   {\mbox{}\marginpar{\raggedleft\hspace{0pt}#1}}
```

By default, in one-sided printing the marginal notes go on the outside margin. These defaults can be changed by the following declarations:

\reversemarginpar marginal notes go into the opposite margin with respect to the default one;

\normalmarginpar marginal notes go into the default margin.

As explained in table 4.2 on page 87, there are three parameters to define the style of marginal notes: \marginparwidth, \marginparsep, and \marginparpush.

3.4.3 Endnotes

Scholarly works usually group notes at the end of each chapter or at the end of the document. These are called endnotes. Endnotes are not supported in standard LaTeX, but they can be created in several ways.

The package endnotes (by John Lavagnino) typesets endnotes in a way similar to footnotes. It uses an extra external file, with extension .ent, to hold the text of the endnotes. This file can be deleted after the run since a new version is generated each time.

To include the contents of the file in the document, commands like the following could be issued:

```
\newpage\begingroup
\setlength{\parindent}{0pt}\setlength{\parskip}{2ex}
\renewcommand{\enotesize}{\normalsize}
\theendnotes\endgroup
```

These commands start a new page, open a group to limit the redefinitions of the parameters and commands, redefine some paragraph parameters, and set the font size for the endnotes (\enotesize). Then the command \theendnotes will typeset the endnotes accumulated in memory at that point in the text. Finally the group is ended, so that the redefinitions remain localized.

With this package you can output your footnotes as endnotes by simply giving the command:

```
\renewcommand{\footnote}{\endnote}
```

The user interface for endnotes is very similar to the one for footnotes after substituting the word "foot" for "end." The following example shows the principle of the use of endnotes, where you save text in memory with the \endnote command, and then typeset all accumulated text material at a point in the document controlled by the user.

This is simple text.[1] This is simple text.[2]
Some more text.[3]

Notes
[1] The first endnote.
[2] The second endnote.
[3] And the third endnote.

This is some more simple text.

```
This is simple text.\endnote{The first endnote.}
This is simple text.\endnote{The second endnote.}
Some more text.\endnote{And the third endnote.}

\theendnotes \bigskip  % output endnotes here
This is some more simple text.
```

3.5 Using Multiple Columns

Standard LaTeX offers the possibility of typesetting text in one- or two-column mode, but you cannot mix both on one page.

The package multicol (written by Frank Mittelbach) defines the environment multicols, which allows switching between different multicolumn layouts on the same page. When using the twocolumn option, you have the choice of putting your footnotes in the right column only; this is achieved with the ftnright package (also by Frank Mittelbach).

3.5.1   multicol—A Flexible Way to Handle Multiple Columns

(£ 82,162)

With standard LATEX it is possible to produce documents with one or two columns (twocolumn). However, it is impossible to produce only parts of a page in two-column format since the commands \twocolumn and \onecolumn always start a fresh page. Additionally, the columns are never balanced. This sometimes results in a slightly weird distribution of the material.

The multicol package solves these problems by defining an environment, multicols, with the following properties:

- It can create an arbitrary number of columns (up to ten), which can fill several pages.

- When the environment ends, the columns on the last page will be balanced so that they are all of nearly equal length.

- The environment can be used inside other environments such as figure or minipage where it will produce a box containing the text distributed into the requested number of columns. This means that you no longer need to hand-format your layout in cases like these.

- Between individual columns, vertical rules of user defined widths can be inserted.

- The formatting can be customized globally or for individual environments.

3.5.2   Typesetting in Columns

```
\begin{multicols}{columns}[preface][skip]
```

Normally you can start the environment simply by specifying the number of desired columns.

Here is some text to be distributed over several columns. If the columns	are very narrow try typesetting ragged right.

```
\begin{multicols}{2}
  Here is some text to be distributed over
  several columns. If the columns are very
  narrow try typesetting ragged right.
\end{multicols}
```

However, you may be interested in prefixing the multicolumn text with a bit of single-column material. This can be achieved with the optional argument *preface*. LATEX will try to keep the *preface* and the start of the multicolumn text on the same page.

Some advice

Here is some text to be distributed over several columns. If the columns │ are very narrow try typesetting ragged right.

```
\begin{multicols}{2}
        [\section*{Some advice}]
    Here is some text to be distributed over
    several columns. If the columns are very
    narrow try typesetting ragged right.
\end{multicols}
```

The `multicols` environment starts a new page if there is not enough free space left on the current page. This is controlled by a global parameter. However, when using the *preface* argument the default setting for this parameter may be too small. In this case you can either change the *global* default (see below) or adjust the value for the *current* environment by using the second optional *skip* as follows:

```
\begin{multicols}{3}
        [\section*{Index}]
        [7cm]
    Text Text Text Text ...
\end{multicols}
```

This would start a new page if there were less than 7cm free space.

3.5.3 Customizing the `multicols` Environment

The `multicols` environment recognizes several parameters that can control formatting. Their meaning is described in the following sections. The default values can be found in table 3.4 (dimensions) and table 3.5 (counters) on the next page. If not stated otherwise, all changes to the parameters have to be placed before the start of the environment for which they should apply.

Free Space

The `multicols` environment first checks whether the amount of free space left on the page is at least equal to \premulticols or to the value of the optional argument *skip*, when it is specified. If the requested space is not available, a \newpage is issued. Similar action is taken when the end of the environment is reached, this time using the length parameter \postmulticols. Before and after the environment, a vertical space of length \multicolsep is placed.

Column Width and Separation

The column width inside the `multicols` environment will automatically be calculated using the number of requested columns and the current value of \linewidth. Between every two columns a space of \columnsep is left.

\premulticols	50.0pt
\postmulticols	20.0pt
\multicolsep	12.0pt plus 4.0pt minus 3.0pt
\columnsep	10.0pt
\columnseprule	0.0pt

Table 3.4: Length parameters used by `multicols`

collectmore	0
unbalance	0
columnbadness	10001
finalcolumnbadness	9999
tracingmulticols	0

Table 3.5: Counters used by `multicols`

Vertical Lines

Between every two columns, a rule of width \columnseprule is placed. If this parameter is set to 0pt, the rule is suppressed.

Here is some text to be distributed over several columns. In this example ragged right typesetting is used.

```
\setlength{\columnseprule}{0pt}
\begin{multicols}{3}
  \raggedright
  Here is some text to be distributed
  over several columns. In this example
  ragged right typesetting is used.
\end{multicols}
```

If you choose a rule width larger than the column separation, the rule will overprint the column text.

Column Formatting

By default (the \flushcolumns setting), the multicols environment tries to keep all columns the same length by stretching the available vertical space inside the columns. If you specify \raggedcolumns the surplus space will instead be placed at the bottom of each column.

At the end of the environment, the remaining text will be balanced to produce columns of equal length. If you wish to place more text in the left columns you can advance the counter unbalance. This will add space to the rightmost column. The counter unbalance determines the number of additional lines that should be put into the leftmost column. It will automatically be restored to zero at the end of multicols.

Here is some	columns. In	used.
text to be	this example	
distributed	ragged right	
over several	typesetting is	

```
\begin{multicols}{3} \raggedright
  Here is some text to be distributed
  over several columns. In this example
  ragged right typesetting is used.
  \setcounter{unbalance}{1}
\end{multicols}
```

Column balancing is further controlled by the two counters columnbadness and finalcolumnbadness. Whenever LaTeX is constructing boxes (such as a column) it will compute a badness value expressing the quality of the box. Thereby, a zero value is optimal, and a value of 10000 is infinitely bad in LaTeX's eyes.[9] While balancing, the algorithm compares the badness of possible solutions and, if any column except the last one has a badness higher than columnbadness, the solution is ignored. When the algorithm finally finds a solution it looks at the badness in the last column and if this is larger than finalcolumnbadness it will typeset this column with the excess space placed at the bottom allowing it to come out short. You can trace the algorithm by setting the counter tracingmulticols to a positive value (higher values give more tracing information).

3.5.4   Floats and Footnotes in multicol

Floats (for example figures and tables) are only partially supported within multicols. You can use star forms of the float environments, i.e., requesting floats that span all columns. Column floats and \marginpars, however, are not supported.

Footnotes are typeset (full width) on the bottom of the page, and not under individual columns. Under certain circumstances a footnote may not fall on the same page as its reference in the text. If this is a possibility, multicols will produce a warning. In that case, you should check the page in question and if the footnote reference and footnote text really are on different pages, you will have to resolve the problem locally by issuing a \pagebreak command in a strategic place. The reason for this behavior is that multicols has to look ahead to assemble material and may not be able to use all material gathered later on. The amount of look ahead is controlled by the collectmore counter.

---

[9]If the box turns out to be overfull the badness value is set to 100000, to mark this special case.

3.5.5 ftnright—**Right Footnotes in a Two-Column Environment**

It is sometimes desirable to group all footnotes in a two-column document at the bottom of the right column. This can be achieved by specifying the ftnright package (by Frank Mittelbach). The effect of this package is shown in figure 3.8 on the facing page—the first page of the original documentation of the ftnright implementation. It is clearly shown how the various footnotes collect in the lower part of the right-hand column.

The main idea for the ftnright package is to assemble the footnotes of all columns on a page and place them all together at the bottom of the right column. Allowing for enough space between footnotes and text and, in addition, setting the footnotes in smaller type.[10] Furthermore, the footnote markers are placed at the baseline instead of raising them as superscripts.[11]

This package can be used together with most other class files for LATEX. Of course, the ftnright package will only take effect with a document using a two-column layout specified with the twocolumn option on the \documentclass command. In most cases, it is best to use ftnright as the very last package to make sure that its settings are not overwritten by other options.

It is unfortunate that LATEX 2.09 had no provisions to make such changes without overwriting internal routines. The ftnright package uses the values of \textheight and \skip\footins (the space between text and footnotes). The values used are the ones current when ftnright is read. You can change both of them in the preamble of your document by calling the macro \preparefootins afterwards to reinitialize the footnote algorithm, for example:

```
\setlength{\skip\footins}{8pt}
\addtolength{\textheight}{1in}
\preparefootins
```

Once the ftnright package is updated for LATEX2_ε this will not be necessary any longer because within LATEX2_ε it is possible to make use of a hook at the \begin{document} command where execution of \preparefootins could be forced internally.

3.6 Simple Version Control

With the comment environment (provided by the verbatim package) it is possible to ignore some passages in the document during the formatting process. The

---

[10]Some journals use the same size for footnotes and text, which sometimes makes it difficult to distinguish footnote and main text.

[11]Of course, this is only done for the mark preceding the footnote text and not the one used within the main text, where a raised number or symbol set in smaller type will help to keep the flow of thoughts uninterrupted.

Footnotes in a multi-column layout*

Frank Mittelbach

August 10, 1991

1 Introduction

The placement of footnotes in a multi-column layout always bothered me. The approach taken by LaTeX (i.e., placing the footnotes separately under each column) might be all right if nearly no footnotes are present. But it looks clumsy when both columns contain footnotes, especially when they occupy different amounts of space.

In the multi-column style option [5], I used page-wide footnotes at the bottom of the page, but again the result doesn't look very pleasant since short footnotes produce undesired gaps of white space. Of course, the main goal of this style option was a balancing algorithm for columns which would allow switching between different numbers of columns on the same page. With this feature, the natural place for footnotes seems to be the bottom of the page[1] but looking at some of the results it seems best to avoid footnotes in such a layout entirely.

Another possibility is to turn footnotes into endnotes, i.e., printing them at the end of every chapter or the end of the entire document. But I assume everyone who has ever read a book using such a layout will agree with me, that it is a pain to search back and forth, so that the reader is tempted to ignore the endnotes entirely.

When I wrote the article about "Future extensions of TeX" [6] I was again dissatisfied with the outcome of the footnotes, and since this article should show certain aspects of high quality typesetting, I decided to give the footnote problem a try and modified the LaTeX output routine for this purpose. The layout I used was inspired by the yearbook of the Gutenberg Gesellschaft Mainz [1]. Later on, I found that it is also recommended by Jan White [9]. On the layout of footnotes I also consulted books by Jan Tschichold [8] and Manfred Simoneit [7], books, I would recommend to everyone being able to read German texts.

1.1 Description of the new layout

The result of this effort is presented in this paper and the reader can judge for himself whether it was successful or not.[2] The main idea for this layout is to assemble the footnotes of all columns on a page and place them all together at the bottom of the right column. Allowing for enough space between footnotes and text, and in addition, setting the footnotes in smaller type[3] I decided that one could omit the footnote separator rule which is used in most publications prepared with TeX.[4] Furthermore, I decided to place the footnote markers[5] at the baseline instead of raising them as superscripts.[6]

All in all, I think this generates a neat layout, and surprisingly enough, the necessary changes to the LaTeX output routine are nevertheless astonishingly simple.

1.2 The use of the style option

This style option might be used together with any other style option for LaTeX which does not change the three internals changed by `ftnright.sty`.[7] In most cases, it is best to use this style option as the very last option in the `\documentstyle` command to make sure that its settings are not overwritten by other options.[8]

---

*. The LaTeX style option `ftnright` which is described in this article has the version number v1.0d dated 92/06/19. The documentation was last revised on 92/06/19.

1. You can not use column footnotes at the bottom, since the number of columns can differ on one page.

2. Please note, that this option only changed the placement of footnotes. Since this article also makes use of the doc option [4], that assigns tiny numbers to code lines sprinkled throughout the text, the resulting design is not perfect.

3. The standard layout in *TUGboat* uses the same size for footnotes and text, giving the footnotes, in my opinion, much too much prominence.

4. People who prefer the rule can add it by redefining the command `\footnoterule` [2, p. 156]. Please, note, that this command should occupy no space, so that a negative space should be used to compensate for the width of the rule used.

5. The tiny numbers or symbols, e.g., the '5' in front of this footnote.

6. Of course, this is only done for the mark preceeding the footnote text and not the one used within the main text where a raised number or symbol set in smaller type will help to keep the flow of thoughts, uninterrupted.

7. These are the macros `\@startcolumn`, `\@makecol` and `\@outputdblcol` as we will see below. Of course, the option will take only effect with a document style using a twocolumn layout (like `ltugboat`) or when the user additionally specifies `twocolumn` as a document style option in the `\documentstyle` command.

8. The `ltugboat` option (which is currently set up as a style option instead of a document style option which it actually is) will overwrite

1

Figure 3.8: The placement of text and footnotes with the ftnright package

version package discussed in the remainder of this chapter goes one step further by allowing you some elementary version control.

The version package (by Stephen Bellantoni) defines environments and commands to provide some kind of version control with LaTeX.

To use this facility you should issue, somewhere near the beginning of the document, commands to set up the version control tag environments, as follows:

```
\includeversion{tagname}
```

The material bracketed inside a *tagname* environment has to be processed (typeset) by LaTeX in a normal way.

```
\excludeversion{tagname}
```

The material bracketed inside a *tagname* environment must be ignored (not typeset) by LaTeX.

tag is a name chosen by the user. As many version control environments as needed can be defined in this way by the user. For example:

The answer is YES.
```
\includeversion{YES}\excludeversion{NO}
The answer is
\begin{NO}NO.\end{NO}%
\begin{YES}YES.\end{YES}
```

The version package also defines a comment environment whose material, by default, is ignored. This behavior can, however, be redefined by issuing the command \includeversion{comment}.

AB
A Ignored by default. B
```
A\begin{comment} Normally ignored.
  \end{comment}B
```

```
\includeversion{comment}
A\begin{comment} Ignored by default.
  \end{comment}B
```

CHAPTER 4

The Layout of the Page

The text of a document usually occupies a rectangular area on the paper—the so-called *body* of the text. Above the body there is a *running header* and below the body a *running footer*. They can consist of one or more lines containing the page number; information about the current chapter, section, time, and date; and possibly other markers. The fields to the left and the right of the body are called the *margins*. Usually they are left blank, but small pieces of text, like remarks or annotations, so-called *marginal notes*, can appear there.

The size, shape and position of these fields on the output medium (paper or screen) and the contents of the running headers and footers are called the *page layout*. In this chapter we will see how to specify different layouts. Often a single document requires several different page layouts. For instance, the layout of the first page of a chapter, which carries the chapter title, is generally different from the other pages in that chapter.

The standard LaTeX document classes allow document formatting for recto-verso (*two-sided*) printing. There exist some differences between the layouts for one- and two-sided printing. In the first case the margins on odd- and even-numbered pages are equal, while in the second case care should be taken that the texts on both sides of the paper overlap. Generally one talks about the *inner* and *outer* margins. For two-sided printing, inner means the left margin on odd-numbered pages and the right margin on even-numbered ones, while for one-sided printing, inner always indicates the left margin. In a book spread, odd-numbered pages are those on the right-hand side.

4.1   Geometrical Dimensions of the Layout

(£ 163)

The dimensional parameters controlling the page layout are described below and are shown schematically in figure 4.1 on the next page.

\textheight	Height of the body (without header and footer).
\textwidth	Width of the body.
\columnsep	Width of space between columns of text in multicolumn mode.
\columnseprule	Width of a vertical line separating the two adjacent columns in multicolumn output (default 0pt, i.e., no visible rule).
\columnwidth	Width of single column in multicolumn mode. Calculated by LATEX from \textwidth and \columnsep as appropriate.
\linewidth	Width of the current text line. Usually equals \columnwidth but might get different values in environments that change the margins.
\evensidemargin	For two-sided printing, the extra space added at the left of even-numbered pages.
\oddsidemargin	For two-sided printing, the extra space added at the left of odd-numbered pages, else the extra space added at the left of all pages.
\footskip	Vertical distance separating the baseline of the last line of text and the baseline of the footer.
\headheight	Height of the header.
\headsep	Vertical separation between header and body.
\topmargin	Extra vertical space added at the top of the header.
\marginparpush	Minimal vertical space between two successive marginal notes (not shown in the figure).
\marginparsep	Horizontal space between body and marginal notes.
\marginparwidth	Width of marginal notes.

The default values for these parameters are presented in table 4.2 on page 87. In the LATEX 2$_\varepsilon$ release two additional parameters describing the physical page are available:

\paperheight	Height of the paper to print on.
\paperwidth	Width of the paper to print on.

By default these parameters are set to values corresponding to US-letter paper size in the four standard classes. Most of the other layout parameters in LATEX 2$_\varepsilon$ class files are specified in terms of the physical page size so that they automatically change when \paperwidth or \paperheight is modified at the beginning of the class file. Changing them in the preamble of your document does not have this effect, since by that time, the values for the other parameters are already calculated.

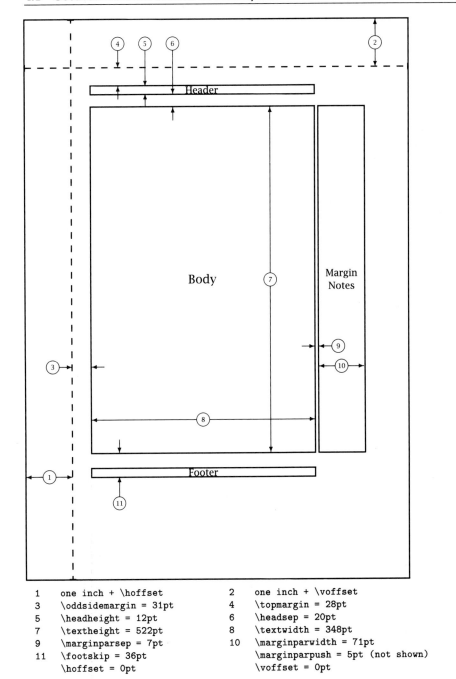

1	one inch + \hoffset	2	one inch + \voffset
3	\oddsidemargin = 31pt	4	\topmargin = 28pt
5	\headheight = 12pt	6	\headsep = 20pt
7	\textheight = 522pt	8	\textwidth = 348pt
9	\marginparsep = 7pt	10	\marginparwidth = 71pt
11	\footskip = 36pt		\marginparpush = 5pt (not shown)
	\hoffset = 0pt		\voffset = 0pt

Figure 4.1: The page layout for *The LATEX Companion*
A picture similar to this can be produced by the command \layout, which is defined in the package file layout (by Kent McPherson). The real sizes are shown reduced by a factor of two.

letterpaper	$8^1/_2 \times$	11	inches		
legalpaper	$8^1/_2 \times$	14	inches		
executivepaper	$7^1/_4 \times 10^1/_2$		inches		
a4paper	$\approx 8^1/_4 \times 11^3/_4$		inches	210×297	mm
a5paper	$\approx 5^7/_8 \times 8^1/_4$		inches	148×210	mm
b5paper	$\approx 7 \times 9^7/_8$		inches	176×250	mm

Table 4.1: Standard paper-size options in LATEX 2_ε

To ease the adjustments necessary to print on different paper, the LATEX 2_ε class files support a number of options that set those parameters to the physical size of the requested paper as well as adjusting the other parameters (like \textheight) that depend on them. The list of paper-size options supported by the standard classes is shown in table 4.1. Thus to print on A4 paper you can simply specify

```
\documentclass[a4paper]{article}
```

Additional or different options may be available for other classes but there seems to be little point in providing, say, an a0paper option for book that would produce incredibly wide text lines.

Standard-conforming dvi-drivers place the reference point for TEX one-inch down and to the right of the upper left-hand corner of the paper. These one-inch offsets are called *driver margins*. The reference point can be shifted by redefining the lengths \hoffset and \voffset. By default their values are zero. In general, the values of these parameters should never be changed. They provide, however, a convenient way to shift the complete page image (body, header, footer, and marginal notes) on the output plane without disturbing the layout. The driver margins are inherited from TEX, and are not needed in LATEX's parameterization of the page layout. A change to \topmargin shifts the complete text vertically, while changes to \oddsidemargin and \evensidemargin shift it horizontally. To simplify calculations, you can "subtract out" the driver margins by setting \hoffset and \voffset to -1in, and consider the reference point to be at the upper left-hand corner of the paper.

Note that some dvi-drivers introduce their own shifts in the placement of the text on paper. To make sure that the reference point is properly positioned, you can run the test file testpage.tex (by Leslie Lamport, with modifications by Stephen Gildea) through LATEX and the dvi-driver in question. The resulting output page will show the position of the reference point with respect to the edges of the paper. For LATEX 2_ε this file was rewritten by Rainer Schöpf to interactively support the standard paper size options.

parameter	two-sided printing			one-sided printing		
	10pt	11pt	12pt	10pt	11pt	12pt
\oddsidemargin	44pt	36pt	21pt	63pt	54pt	39pt
\evensidemargin	82pt	74pt	59pt	63pt	54pt	39pt
\marginparwidth	107pt	100pt	85pt	90pt	83pt	68pt
\marginparsep	11pt	10pt	10pt		*ditto*	
\marginparpush	5pt	5pt	7pt		*ditto*	
\topmargin	27pt	27pt	27pt		*ditto*	
\headheight	12pt	12pt	12pt		*ditto*	
\headsep	25pt	25pt	25pt		*ditto*	
\footskip	30pt	30pt	30pt		*ditto*	
\textheight	43	38	36		*ditto*	
		$\times$\baselineskip				
\textwidth	345pt	360pt	390pt		*ditto*	
\columnsep	10pt	10pt	10pt		*ditto*	
\columnseprule	0pt	0pt	0pt		*ditto*	

Table 4.2: Default values for the page layout parameters (letterpaper)
These values are identical for the three standard LaTeX document classes (article, book, and report). If a different paper-size option is selected the values may change.

4.2   Changing the Layout

When you want to redefine the values of one or more of the page layout parameters, the \setlength or \addtolength commands should be used. Nevertheless, it is recommended that these parameters be changed only in a class or package file and/or in the document preamble.

Initially, it is advisable to use TeX's \baselineskip parameter for setting vertical distances. This parameter is the distance between the baselines of two consecutive lines of text set in the "normal" document type size inside a paragraph. \baselineskip may be considered to be the height of one line of text. Therefore, the following setting always means "two lines of text."

```
\normalsize                          % set normal \baselineskip
\setlength{\headheight}{2\baselineskip} % Height of heading
```

To guarantee that \baselineskip is set properly, first invoke \normalsize to select the type size corresponding to the document base size.

Sometimes it is convenient to calculate the page layout parameters according to given typographic rules. For example, the requirement "the text should contain 50 lines" can be expressed using the command given below. It is assumed that the height of all (except one) lines is \baselineskip and the height of the top line of the text body is \topskip (this is TEX's \baselineskip length parameter for the first line with a default value of 10pt). Note that in the examples in this chapter the LATEX package calc (which simplifies the calculational notation) and the extended control structures of LATEX 2$_\varepsilon$ are used (see appendix A, sections A.4 and A.5).

```
\setlength{\textheight}{\baselineskip*49+\topskip}
```

A requirement like "the height of the body should be 198mm" can be met in a similar way, and the calculation is shown below. First calculate the number of lines that the body of the desired size can contain. To evaluate the number of lines, you should divide one dimension by another to obtain the integer part. Yet, TEX is unable to perform this kind of operation directly, and therefore the dimensions are first assigned to counters. Note that the latter assignment takes place with a high precision since sp units are used internally.

```
\setlength{\textheight}%                 % subtract top line
        {198mm-\topskip}                 %   from desired size
\newcounter{tempc}                       % 1st temporary counter
\setcounter{tempc}{\textheight}          % assign counter 1
\newcounter{tempcc}                      % 2nd temporary counter
\setcounter{tempcc}{\baselineskip}       % assign counter 2
\setcounter{tempc}%                       % divide counters
        {\value{tempc}/\value{tempcc}}
\setlength{\textheight}{\baselineskip*\value{tempc}+\topskip}
```

The value of the vertical distance, \topmargin, can also be customized. As an example, suppose you want to set this margin so that the space above the text body is two times smaller than the space below the text body. The following calculation shows how to determine the needed value in the case of A4-sized paper (the paper height is 297mm).

```
\setlength{\topmargin}%
    {(297mm-\textheight)/3 - 1in - \headheight -\headsep}
```

4.2.1 Page Layout Packages

Because the original LATEX class files are based on American page sizes, European users have developed several packages that adapt the page layout parameters for metric sizes. Examples of such packages are a4 (which generates rather small pages), a4dutch (by Johannes Braams and Nico Poppelier), which is well documented, and a4wide (by Jean-François Lamy), which produces somewhat longer lines. Often, there exist locally developed files under such names as well. For A5-sized pages one has the package files a5 and a5comb (by Mario Wolczko). Volker Kuhlmann, on the other hand, took another approach in his package vpage, where he provides commands to set the margins for all kinds of metric and American paper sizes. To use this package you must first select a paper size with \setpapersize[*orient*]{*size*}, where *size* can be Afour, Bfive, USletter, and many more, while the optional parameter *orient* specifies the orientation (portrait, the default, or landscape). You can even specify your own paper size if you want. The page margins are set with the command

> \setmargins{*leftmargin*}{*topmargin*}{*textwidth*}{*textheight*}%
> {*headheight*}{*headsep*}{*footheight*}{*footskip*}

or with

> \setmarginsrb{*leftmargin*}{*topmargin*}{*rightmargin*}{*bottommargin*}%
> {*headheight*}{*headsep*}{*footheight*}{*footskip*}

If you are using USlegal paper, and you want all margins equal to 1 inch and no headers and footers, then you can say:

```
\setpapersize{USlegal}
\setmarginsrb{1in}{1in}{1in}{1in}{0pt}{0mm}{0pt}{0mm}
```

In general, when changing the page layout you should take into account some elementary rules of legibility (see, e.g., [75]). Studies of printed material in the English language have shown that a line should not contain more than ten to twelve words, which corresponds to not more than 60 to 70 characters per line.

The number of lines on a page depends on the type size being used. The code below shows one way of calculating a \textheight that depends on the document base size (the internal LaTeX variable \@ptsize holds the number 0, 1, or 2 for the base font sizes 10pt, 11pt, and 12pt respectively).

```
\ifthenelse{\@ptsize = 0}%      10-point typeface as base size
  {\setlength{\textheight}{53\baselineskip}}{}
\ifthenelse{\@ptsize = 1}%      11-point typeface as base size
  {\setlength{\textheight}{46\baselineskip}}{}
\ifthenelse{\@ptsize = 2}%      12-point typeface as base size
  {\setlength{\textheight}{42\baselineskip}}{}
\addtolength{\textheight}{\topskip}
```

Another important parameter is the amount of white space surrounding the text. As printed documents are likely to be bound, enough white space should be left in the inner margin of the text to allow for this. If \oddsidemargin is fixed, then the calculation of \evensidemargin for two-sided printing is based on the following relationship:

```
width_of_paper =
    (1in+\hoffset)*2+\oddsidemargin+\textwidth+\evensidemargin
```

Two-sided printing is turned on by specifying the two side class option, which sets Boolean register @twoside to true. A calculation of the horizontal page layout parameters, showing how to take into account the document base size and one- or two-sided printing, is as follows:

```
\ifthenelse{\@ptsize = 0}%          10-points typeface as base size
    {\setlength{\textwidth}{5.00in}%
     \setlength{\marginparwidth}{1.00in}%
     \ifthenelse{\boolean{@twoside}}%
         {\setlength{\oddsidemargin}{0.55in}%        two-sided
          \setlength{\evensidemargin}{0.75in}%
         }
         {\setlength{\oddsidemargin}{0.55in}%        one-sided
          \setlength{\evensidemargin}{0.55in}%
         }
    }{}
```

Similarly, when there are a lot of marginal notes in a document, it is worthwhile changing the layout to increase the margins. As an example, the a4dutch package defines a command \WideMargins. This macro modifies the geometrical parameters in such a way that the width reserved for marginal notes is set to 1.5 inches by decreasing the width of the text body.

4.2.2 Typesetting Pages in Landscape Mode

Usually one considers the longer side of the paper to be the vertical orientation (so-called *portrait* orientation). For some documents, such as slides or tables, it is better to use the other (*landscape*) orientation, where the longer side is horizontally oriented. Modern printers and dvi-drivers usually allow printing in both orientations.

The landscape and portrait orientations require different page layouts. Although you should refrain from making changes to the geometrical page layout parameters after the \begin{document} command, it is still possible to change these parameters between pages. This facility is exploited by the package portland (by Hubert Partl) with commands for switching between portrait and landscape mode.

```
\portrait      \landscape
```

The first command (re)sets the page layout to the initial portrait orientation values (i.e., the values at \begin{document}). The second command sets the page layout so that the horizontal and vertical dimensions are interchanged with respect to their initial values. The total body area remains unchanged. Apart from changing the page layout, both commands issue a \clearpage, which terminates the current page and sets a few internal LATEX dimensions. This package also defines two environments, portrait and landscape, which can be used instead of the above commands. The package file requires some customization in that you need to supply the height of the paper being used as the parameter \paperheight. The default is the height of A4 paper.[1] If you use a dvi-driver that allows mixing portrait and landscape modes in the same run (for example, dvips), it is worth adding the relevant \special commands just after the \clearpage commands to get the various pages printed correctly.

If you only want to switch between landscape and portrait mode for the text, without affecting the running head and feet, then you can use David Carlisle's package lscape, which also defines a landscape environment that rotates the pages in its scope through 90 degrees. In this case, you might not have to worry about having to enter the \special commands yourself, since this package uses Tomas Rokicki's rotate package and requires his dvi-driver dvips (see section 11.2).

4.3 Page Styles

While the dimensions remain the same for almost all pages of a document, the format of the running headers and footers (*page style*) may change in the course of a document. The page style is selected by two commands: ($\mathcal{L}$ 161)

```
\pagestyle{style}      \thispagestyle{style}
```

The first command sets the page style of the current and succeeding pages to *style*; the second is similar, but for the current page only.

LATEX's standard page styles are:

empty   Both the header and footer are empty.

plain   The header is empty and the footer contains the page number.

headings   The header contains information determined by the document class and the page number; the footer is empty.

myheadings Similar to headings, but the header can be controlled by the user.

---

[1] Once this package is updated for LATEX2_ε it should be able to directly use the \paperheight and \paperwidth parameters supplied by the class files.

The first two are used in the standard classes. Usually for the title page, a command \thispagestyle{empty} is issued. For the first page of major sectioning commands (like \part or \chapter, but also \maketitle) the standard LaTeX class files issue a \thispagestyle{plain} command. This means that when you specify a pagestyle{empty} command at the beginning of your document, you will still get page numbers on the page where a \chapter or \maketitle command is issued. To get the intended behavior, you must follow each such command with a thispagestyle{empty} command or redefine the plain style to empty, i.e., \let\ps@plain=\ps@empty.

In small or medium-size documents sophisticated switching of page styles is not necessary. Usually the page style is selected in the document class. But for larger documents, such as books, you should take into account typographic tradition. For example, the front matter normally has roman page numbers while the body of the document carries arabic page numbers; parts and chapters should start on an (odd-numbered) right-hand page, and so on.

The page number is controlled by the counter page.

\pagenumbering{*style*}

This command resets the counter to 1 and redefines the command \thepage to *style*{page}. Ready-to-use page counter styles are: Alph, alph, Roman, roman, and arabic (see section A.1.3).

\clearpage   \cleardoublepage

(£ 192)   Both of these commands terminate the current paragraph and page. In two-sided printing \cleardoublepage also makes sure the next page is a right-hand (odd-numbered) one. As an example, the structure of this book, as far as page styles is concerned, is shown schematically in figure 4.2 on the facing page. Note the definition of the \clearemptydoublepage command, which generates a completely blank page, without any page markers, when needed.

4.3.1 Writing New Page Styles

The formatting commands associated with each *style* argument of the \pagestyle command are controlled by defining a corresponding macro \ps@*style*. These macros, in turn, define internal LaTeX commands, which format the running headers and footers.

\@oddhead   For two-sided printing it generates the header for the odd-numbered pages, otherwise it generates the header for all pages.

\@oddfoot   For two-sided printing it generates the footer for the odd-numbered pages, otherwise it generates the footer for all pages.

```
\documentclass[...]{companion}  %%% class file sets the default page style
...
\newcommand{\clearemptydoublepage}{\newpage{\pagestyle{empty}\cleardoublepage}}
\begin{document}
% ================== Front matter ============================
\title{The \LaTeX{} companion}
\author{...}
\pagenumbering{roman}    % page numbers are roman digits
\maketitle               % title page uses "empty" page style
\include{ch0}            % copyright page uses "empty" page style
\clearemptydoublepage
\tableofcontents         % the first page uses "empty" page style
\clearemptydoublepage    % go to odd numbered page
% ==================== Body of the document ====================
\pagenumbering{arabic}  % page numbers are arabic digits
\include{ch1}            % first page uses "empty" page style
\clearemptydoublepage    % go to odd numbered page
\include{ch2}
\clearemptydoublepage    % go to odd numbered page
...
% ================== Appendices =============================
...                      % special page style for index
```

Figure 4.2: Page styles used in *The LaTeX Companion*

\@evenhead   For two-sided printing it generates the header of the even-numbered pages.

\@evenfoot   For two-sided printing it generates the footer of the even-numbered pages.

The definition of the plain page style, producing only a centered page number in the footer, is equivalent to:

```
\newcommand{\ps@plain}{%
    \renewcommand{\@oddhead}{}%              empty
    \renewcommand{\@evenhead}{}%             empty
    \renewcommand{\@evenfoot}{\hfil\textrm{\thepage}\hfil}%
    \renewcommand{\@oddfoot}{\@evenfoot}}
```

The usage of section titles in running headers or footers is certainly a problem. Sectioning commands allow the capture of (part of the) titles by invoking the commands \chaptermark, \sectionmark, and so on. These commands can be defined to do nothing or to do proper formatting. For instance, in the book class these commands are defined (approximately) as follows:

```
\renewcommand{\chaptermark}[1]{\markboth{\chaptername\
                                    \thechapter. #1}{}}
\renewcommand{\sectionmark}[1]{\markright{\thesection. #1}}
```

In the case of a chapter, the word "Chapter" (or its equivalent in a given language, see table 9.2 on page 267 in section 9.2) followed by the sequence number of the chapter (stored in counter chapter) and the contents of (a short version of) the chapter title will be stored in \chaptermark. For a section, the section number (stored in the counter section) followed by the contents of (a short version of) the section title will be stored in \sectionmark.

Traditionally a running header or footer contains the most recent second-level title (e.g., section title) on the current page. Generally, you cannot simply save and enter sectioning titles into a running header or footer. Due to the asynchronous nature of TEX's page breaking algorithm, it is not possible to know beforehand which sectioning command will appear on the page just before the page break occurs. TEX solves this problem with its *markers* mechanism: the user puts markers inside the text and, before writing (shipping out) the current page to the .dvi file, TEX's output routine determines which are the first and last markers on the current page.

| \markboth{*left_head*}{*right_head*}   \markright{*right_head*} |

(*L* 161–2)

These two LATEX commands are for setting markers at a given point in the text. The first command sets a pair of left and right markers. Usually this command is invoked immediately following a sectioning command. The second command also sets a pair of markers, but it only changes the right one, leaving the other untouched. This command is invoked immediately after a sectioning command.

| \leftmark   \rightmark |

These two commands contain the current settings for the left and right markers as defined by LATEX's output routine from the various \markboth and \markright commands for the page being shipped out. \leftmark contains the *left_head* argument of the last \markboth command before the end of the page. \rightmark contains the *right_head* argument of the first \markright or \markboth on the page, if one exists; otherwise it contains the one most recently defined.

The marking commands work reasonably well for right markers "numbered within" left markers (for example, when the left marker is changed by a \chapter command and the right marker is changed by a \section command). However,

```
                                        marker pair     printer markers
                                                        left      right
\markboth{L1}{}                         {L1}{}
\newpage%     ----page break ----                       L1
\markright{R1.1}                        {L1}{R1.1}
\markboth{L2}{}                         {L2}{}
\markright{R2.1}                        {L2}{R2.1}
\newpage%     ----page break ---                        L2        R1.1
\markright{R2.2}                        {L2}{R2.2}
\markright{R2.3}                        {L2}{R2.3}
\markright{R2.4}                        {L2}{R2.4}
\newpage%     ----page break ----                       L2        R2.2
\markboth{L3}{}                         {L3}{}
\markright{R3.1}                        {L3}{R3.1}
\newpage%     ----page break ----                       L3
\newpage%     ----page break ----                       L3        R3.1
\markright{R3.2}                        {L3}{R3.2}
\markboth{L4}{}                         {L4}{}
\markboth{L5}{}                         {L5}{}
\newpage%     ----page break ----                       L5        R3.2
\markright{R5.1}                        {L5}{R5.1}
\end{document}                                          L5        R5.1
```

Figure 4.3: Schematic overview of how LATEX's marker mechanism works

it produces somewhat anomalous results if a \markboth command is preceded by some other mark command on the same page—see the page receiving L5 R3.2 in Figure 4.3. This figure shows schematically which left and right markers are generated for the pages being shipped out.

In the headings page style the sectioning commands set the page headers automatically by using \markboth and \markright, as shown in table 4.3 on the next page.

The standard page style myheadings is similar to headings, but it allows the user to customize a header by defining the commands \markboth and \markright described above. It also provides a way to control capturing titles from other sectional units like table of contents, list of figures, and index. In fact the commands (\tableofcontents, \listoffigures, and \listoftables) and the environments (thebibliography and theindex) use the \chapter* command, which does not invoke \chaptermark, but issues a \@mkboth command. The page style headings defines \@mkboth as \markboth, while the page style myheadings defines \@mkboth to do nothing and leaves the decision to the user.

Printing style	Command	Document class	
		book, report	article
two-sided printing	\markboth[a]	\chapter	\section
	\markright	\section	\subsection
one-sided printing	\markright	\chapter	\section

[a] Specifies an empty right marker (see figure 4.3 on the preceding page)

Table 4.3: Page style defining commands in LaTeX

4.3.2 Customizing Page Styles with fancyheadings

The package fancyheadings (by Piet van Oostrum) allows easy customization of page headers and footers. It provides the following functions:

- three-part headers and footers;
- rules in header and footer;
- headers and footers wider than \textwidth;
- multiline headers and footers;
- separate headers and footers for even and odd pages;
- separate headers and footers for chapter pages.

To use this page style, a command \pagestyle{fancy} must be given. The latter must be issued after any changes to \textwidth.

The following commands supply the information for the six fields in the footer and the header for layout fancy as shown in figure 4.4 on the next page.

```
\lhead[LH-even]{LH-odd}    \lfoot[LF-even]{LF-odd}
\chead[CH-even]{CH-odd}    \cfoot[CF-even]{CF-odd}
\rhead[RH-even]{RH-odd}    \rfoot[RF-even]{RF-odd}
```

The information in the L-fields will be left adjusted, that in the C-fields centered, and that in the R-fields right adjusted.

The thickness of the rules below the header and above the footer is controlled by the length parameters \headrulewidth (default 0.4pt) and \footrulewidth (default 0pt). A thickness of 0pt makes a rule invisible. More complicated changes are possible by redefining the \headrule and/or \footrule commands.

The headers and footers are typeset in a box of width \headwidth, which is by default set equal to the value of \textwidth. The box can be made wider (or narrower) by using the \setlength command to specify \headwidth. The headers and footers will stick out of the page on the same side as marginal notes. For example, to span marginal notes, add both \marginparsep and \marginparwidth to \headwidth (see figure 4.6 on page 99).

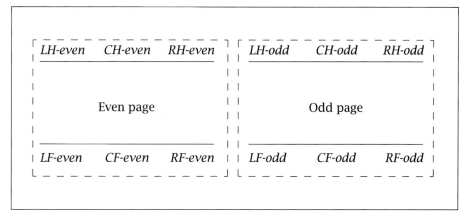

Figure 4.4: The page layout parameters for the fancyheadings package

Each of the six fields is set in an appropriate parbox, so you can use multi-line material with the \\ command. Extra space can be added by \vspace commands. Note that in this case the lengths \headheight or \footskip will probably have to be increased.

Some LaTeX commands, like \chapter, use a \thispagestyle command to automatically switch to the plain page style, thus overriding the page style currently in effect. To customize such pages use the fancyplain page style. This page style sets up fancy for normal pages and in addition redefines the page style plain to also use the page style fancy with the following modifications. The rules' thickness is defined by \plainheadrulewidth and \plainfootrulewidth, which both default to 0pt. The six fields can be defined separately for plain and normal pages by using the \fancyplain command:

```
\fancyplain{plain_value}{normal_value}
```

This command can be used inside both the optional and mandatory arguments of the \..head and \..foot commands defined above. For example,

```
\lhead[\fancyplain{F1}{F2}]{\fancyplain{F3}{F4}}
```

shows the specification for the left header field \lhead in a two-sided document. In this case, F1 is the specification for an even-numbered plain page; F2 for an even-numbered normal page; F3 for an odd-numbered plain page; and F4 for an odd-numbered normal page.

The default settings for the parameters are the following:

```
\headrulewidth          0.4pt       \footrulewidth          0pt
\plainheadrulewidth     0pt         \plainfootrulewidth     0pt
```

```
 _____          _____
| \rightmark    \leftmark |  | \leftmark    \rightmark |
|_____ |  |_____ |
|                         |  |                         |
|                         |  |                         |
|        Even page        |  |        Odd page         |
|                         |  |                         |
|                         |  |                         |
|        \thepage         |  |        \thepage         |
|_____|  |_____|
```

Figure 4.5: The default page layout with the fancyheadings package

The default layout is a slanted running header and a footer containing the page number:

```
\lhead[\fancyplain{}{\sl\rightmark}]{\fancyplain{}{\sl\leftmark}}
\rhead[\fancyplain{}{\sl\leftmark}]{\fancyplain{}{\sl\rightmark}}
\cfoot{\rm\thepage}
\chead{}\lfoot{}\rfoot{}
```

Plain output pages have an empty head and carry only the page number in the center of the footer, while normal pages have a centered page number in the footer and markers in the header, as shown in figure 4.5.

To illustrate the more advanced possibilities of the fancyheadings package, you can consider a layout that has two lines containing the section and the subsection titles in the lower right-hand corner of the page. In this case, you should specify something like:

```
\documentclass{book}
\usepackage{fancyheadings}
\pagestyle{fancy}
\renewcommand{\sectionmark}[1]{\markboth{#1}{}}
\renewcommand{\subsectionmark}[1]{\markright{#1}}
\rfoot{\leftmark\\\rightmark}
..... % further preamble commands
\begin{document}
```

As a final example, figure 4.6 on the facing page shows the definitions for a page style similar to the one used by Leslie Lamport for his LaTeX book.

```
\documentclass{book}
\usepackage{fancyheadings}
\pagestyle{fancyplain}
\addtolength{\headwidth}{\marginparsep}
\addtolength{\headwidth}{\marginparwidth}
%        remember chapter title
\renewcommand{\chaptermark}[1]%
                {\markboth{#1}{}}
%        section number and title
\renewcommand{\sectionmark}[1]%
                {\markright{\thesection\ #1}}
\lhead[\fancyplain{}{\bfseries\thepage}]%
       {\fancyplain{}{\bfseries\rightmark}}
\rhead[\fancyplain{}{\bfseries\leftmark}]%
       {\fancyplain{}{\bfseries\thepage}}
\cfoot{}
```

Figure 4.6: Running header/footer settings for the LaTeX book

4.4   Visual Formatting

As mentioned in the introduction, the final stage of an important production often needs some hand-formatting to avoid some bad page breaks. For this purpose standard LaTeX offers you the \pagebreak, \nopagebreak, \newpage and \clearpage commands as well as the \samepage declaration, although the latter is considered obsolete in LaTeX2ε. (With the \samepage declaration together with a suitable number of \nobreak commands you can request that a certain portion of your document should be kept together. Unfortunately, the results are often not satisfactory; in particular, LaTeX will never make a page larger than its nominal height (\textheight) but rather moves everything in the scope of the \samepage declaration to the next page. The LaTeX2ε command \enlargethispage* described below offers you an alternative here.)

(£ 90,190)

It is common in book production to "run" a certain number of pages (normally double spreads) short or long to avoid bad page breaks later on. This means that the nominal height of the pages is reduced or enlarged by a certain amount, for example, a \baselineskip. To support this practice, LaTeX2ε offers the command

```
\enlargethispage{size}
```

If, for example, you want to enlarge or reduce the size of some pages by one additional line of text, you would define

```
\newcommand{\longpage}{\enlargethispage{\baselineskip}}
\newcommand{\shortpage}{\enlargethispage{-\baselineskip}}
```

and use those commands between two paragraphs on the pages in question.[2]

\enlargethispage enlarges the \textheight for the current page but otherwise does not change the formatting parameters. Thus, if \flushbottom is in force the text will fill the \textheight for the page in question, if necessary by enlarging or shrinking vertical space within the page. This way, the above definitions add or remove exactly one line of text from a page while keeping the positions of the other lines. This is important to give a uniform appearance.

$\boxed{\texttt{\textbackslash enlargethispage*\{\textit{size}\}}}$

The companion command \enlargethispage* also enlarges or reduces the page height, but this time the resulting final page will be squeezed as much as possible (i.e., depending on the available white space on the page). This can be helpful if you wish to keep a certain portion of your document together on one page, even if it makes the page slightly too long. (Otherwise, just use the minipage environment.) The trick is to request a large enough amount of extra space and then place an explicit page break where you want the page break to happen, e.g.:

```
\enlargethispage*{100cm}        % absurd request
\begin{center}
 \begin{tabular}{llll}          % slightly too long
   ....                         % tabular
 \end{tabular}
\end{center}
\pagebreak                      % forced page break
```

From the description above it is clear that both commands should be used only in the final part of the production, since any later alterations in the document (adding or removing a single word, if you are unlucky) can make your hand-formatting obsolete—resulting in ugly-looking pages.

---

[2]Due to the many examples in this book, we had to use this trick a few times to avoid half-empty pages. For example, the double spread on pages 70–71 is enlarged by one \baselineskip.

CHAPTER 5

Tabular Material

Data is often most efficiently presented in tabular form. TeX uses powerful primitives for arranging material in rows and columns. Since, however, they only implement a low-level, formatting-oriented functionality, several macro packages have been developed that build upon those primitives to provide a higher-level command language and a more user-friendly interface.

In LaTeX, tables are most conveniently constructed with the `tabular` or `array` environments, although in some cases the `tabbing` environment might prove useful.

After a short look at the `tabbing` environment, the extensions to LaTeX's basic `tabular` and `array` environments provided by the `array` package are described. The latter package offers an increased functionality, especially in the area of a more flexible positioning of paragraph material, a better control of inter-column and inter-row spacing, and the possibility of defining new preamble specifiers. Combining the strengths of the `array` and `tabularx` packages, you will be able to construct complex tables in a simple way.

The next sections deal with the problem of multipage tables. Two environments, `supertabular` and `longtable`, will split a table automatically when a page is full, or when the user instructs LaTeX to go to a new page.

The following sections deal with packages that can be used in combination with those already described. In particular: `delarray` automatically calculates the height of delimiters around tabular material, `dcolumn` makes it easy to align numbers on the decimal separator, and `hhline` specifies the way horizontal or vertical rules interact.

The final section gives some practical advice and shows a series of interesting complex examples typeset with the tools described in this chapter.

Mathematically oriented readers should consult the chapter on advanced mathematics, especially section 8.5, which discusses the alignment structures for equations, and study the examples starting on page 244. And for those of you having access to a PostScript output device, many more possibilities for manipulating tabular material are available (see section 11.4.1).

5.1   Comparing the `tabbing` and `tabular` Environments

LaTeX has two families of environments that allow material to be lined up in columns—namely, the `tabbing` environment, and the `tabular` and `array` environments. The main differences between the two kinds of environment are:

- The `tabbing` environment is not as general as the `tabular` environment. It can only be typeset as a separate paragraph, while a `tabular` can be placed anywhere in the text or inside mathematics.
- The `tabbing` environment can be broken between pages, while the standard `tabular` environment cannot.
- With the `tabbing` environment the user must specify the position of each tab stop explicitly, while for the `tabular` environment LaTeX can automatically determine the width of the columns.
- It is simpler to change the typesetting of the material inside a `tabbing` environment, so that it is somewhat easier to typeset computer programs this way.
- `tabbing` environments cannot be nested, while `tabular` environments can, thus allowing complex alignments to be realized.

Sometimes it is convenient to put one or more `tabular` or `tabbing` environments inside a floating element (see chapter 6) like a `table` environment. This is useful if you want to keep tabular material together and to allow text to flow around that material. Be careful, however, not to confuse the `tabular` and `table` environments, since the former allows material to be aligned in columns, while the latter is a logical document element identifying its contents as belonging together and allowing it to be floated jointly. In particular, one `table` environment can contain several `tabular` environments. Tabular material that is longer than one page can be typeset with the `longtable` or `supertabular` environments, described in section 5.4.

5.2   Using the `tabbing` Environment

(£ 62–3,179–82)   This section deals with some of the lesser known features of the `tabbing` environment. First it must be realized that formatting is under the complete control of the user. Somewhat unexpectedly, when moving to a given tab stop, you will always end up at the exact horizontal position where it was defined, independently of where the current point is. This means that the current point can move backwards and overwrite previous text.

Be aware that the usual LaTeX commands for making accents—\', \' and \=—are redefined inside the `tabbing` environment. The accents are available by typing \a', \a' and \a= instead. The \- command, which normally signals a possible hyphenation point, is also redefined, but this is not important since the lines in a `tabbing` environment are never broken.

The scope of commands in rows is usually limited to the region between tab stops.

A style parameter \tabbingsep, used together with the \' command, allows text to be typeset at a given distance flush right from the previous tab stop. Its default value is set equal to \labelsep, which in turn is usually 5pt.

There exist a few common ways to define tab stops: using a line to be typeset, or explicitly specifying the skip to the next tab stop.

The next example shows a wrong choice for the pattern on the first line, since the first column on the second line is longer than the one specified. The last line redefines the tab position and shows the different uses of the backquote.

confused embrouillé *confused mind* esprit trouble
confusiondéconfiture

conjecturehypothèse   (from Greek)

```
\begin{tabbing}
\textbf{confused} \= embrouill\a'e \=
   \em confused mind \= esprit trouble \kill
\textbf{confused} \> embrouill\a'e \>
   \em confused mind\> esprit trouble  \\
\textbf{confusion}\> d\a'econfiture        \\[3mm]
\textbf{conjecture}\=hypoth\a'ese
                       \'(from Greek)\\
\end{tabbing}
```

The `tabbing` environment is most useful for aligning information into columns whose width is constant and known. The following is from table A.1 on page 449.

pc   Pica = 12pt   ⌐⌐
cc   Cicero = 12dd   ⌐⌐
cm   Centimeter = 10mm   ⌐——⌐

```
\newcommand{\Rivpt}{\rule{.4pt}{4pt}}
\begin{tabbing}
dd\quad \= \hspace{.55\linewidth} \= \kill
pc     \> Pica = 12pt
   \> \makebox[1pc]{\Rivpt\hrulefill\Rivpt} \\
cc     \> Cicero  = 12dd
   \> \makebox[1cc]{\Rivpt\hrulefill\Rivpt} \\
cm     \> Centimeter = 10mm
   \> \makebox[1cm]{\Rivpt\hrulefill\Rivpt} \\
\end{tabbing}
```

5.2.1　The `program` Environment

The `program` package file (by Martin Ward) is a complex example of what can be done with a `tabbing` environment. It can help you typeset computer program sections, and is especially optimized for Pascal code. The package defines the `program` and `programbox` environments, and commands for keywords and emphasized (bold) letters. The latter commands, which are used to represent program fragments, have one argument that produces a subscript index.

Inside a `program` environment newlines are significant. Each line is in math mode, hence spaces in the input file are not significant. A \\ command causes a line break in the output.

The `programbox` environment typesets a program in a LaTeX box. This is useful for keeping a piece of code on one page or for typesetting small programs in running text.

Below is a complete Pascal program. It is an example of the notation used for procedures and functions. Note the \mbox command for introducing text in the output and the \rcomment command for generating flush right comments.

A fast exponentiation procedure:
begin for
$\qquad i := 1 \text{ } \underline{\text{to}} \text{ } 10 \text{ } \underline{\text{step}} \text{ } 1 \text{ } \underline{\text{do}}$
$\qquad expt(2, i);$
$\qquad newline() \text{ } \underline{\text{od}}$
where　　　　　A comment flush to the right margin
proc $expt(x, n) \equiv$
$\quad z := 1;$
$\quad \underline{\text{do}} \text{ } \underline{\text{if}} \text{ } n = 0 \text{ } \underline{\text{then}} \text{ } \underline{\text{exit}} \text{ } \underline{\text{fi}};$
$\quad\quad \underline{\text{do}} \text{ } \underline{\text{if}} \text{ } odd(n) \text{ } \underline{\text{then}} \text{ } \underline{\text{exit}} \text{ } \underline{\text{fi}};$
$\quad\quad\quad n := n/2; \text{ } x := x * x \text{ } \underline{\text{od}};$
$\quad\quad n := n - 1; \text{ } z := z * x \text{ } \underline{\text{od}};$
$\quad\quad print(z).$
end

```
\begin{programbox}
\mbox{A fast exponentiation procedure:}
\BEGIN %
  \FOR i:=1 \TO 10 \STEP 1 \DO
    |expt|(2,i); \\ |newline|() \OD
\WHERE  \rcomment{A comment flush to the right margin}
\PROC |expt|(x,n) \BODY
      z:=1;
    \DO \IF n=0 \THEN \EXIT \FI;
        \DO \IF |odd|(n) \THEN \EXIT \FI;
            n:=n/2; x:=x*x \OD;
        n:=n-1; z:=z*x \OD;
      |print|(z) \ENDPROC
\END
\end{programbox}
```

5.3　array—Extending the `tabular` Environments

In general, when tables of any degree of complexity are required, it is usually easier to consider the `tabular`-like environments defined by LaTeX. These environments align material horizontally in rows and vertically in columns.

\begin{array}[*pos*]{*cols*}	*rows*	\end{array}
\begin{tabular}[*pos*]{*cols*}	*rows*	\end{tabular}
\begin{tabular*}{*width*}[*pos*]{*cols*}	*rows*	\end{tabular*}

Unchanged options	
l	Left adjusted column.
c	Centered adjusted column.
r	Right adjusted column.
p{*width*}	Equivalent to \parbox[t]{*width*}.
@{*decl.*}	Suppresses inter-column space and inserts *decl.* instead.
Changed option	
|	Inserts a vertical line. The distance between two columns will be enlarged by the width of the line in contrast to the original definition of LaTeX.
New options	
m{*width*}	Defines a column of width *width*. Every entry will be centered vertically in proportion to the rest of the line. It is somewhat like \parbox{*width*}.
b{*width*}	Coincides with \parbox[b]{*width*}.
>{*decl.*}	Can be used before an l, r, c, p, m or b option. It inserts *decl.* directly in front of the entry of the column.
<{*decl.*}	Can be used after an l, r, c, p{..}, m{..} or b{..} option. It inserts *decl.* right after the entry of the column.
!{*decl.*}	Can be used anywhere and corresponds with the | option. The difference is that *decl.* is inserted instead of a vertical line, so this option doesn't suppress the normally inserted space between columns in contrast to @{...}.

Table 5.1: The preamble options in the array package

Over the years several extensions have been made to the `tabular` environ-   (ℒ 63–5,182–5)
ment family, as described in the LaTeX book. The remaining part of this chapter
will explore the added functionality of the `array` package (developed by Frank
Mittelbach, with contributions from David Carlisle).

Table 5.1 shows the various options possible in the *cols* preamble declaration
of the environments in the `tabular` family.

5.3.1 Examples of Preamble Commands

If you would like to use a special font, such as \bfseries in a flushed left
column, you can write >{\bfseries}l. You no longer have to start every entry
of the column with \bfseries.

A	**B**	*C*
100	**10**	*1*

```
\begin{tabular}{| >{\large}c | >{\large\bfseries}l
                     | >{\large\itshape}c |}
\hline A & B & C\\\hline 100 & 10 & 1 \\\hline
\end{tabular}
```

Notice the use of the \extrarowheight declaration in the second example below. It adds a vertical space of 4pt above each row.[1]

A	**B**	*C*
100	**10**	*1*

```
\setlength{\extrarowheight}{4pt}
\begin{tabular}{| >{\large}c | >{\large\bfseries}l
                     | >{\large\itshape}c |}
\hline A & B & C\\\hline 100 & 10 & 1 \\\hline
\end{tabular}
```

The difference between the three paragraph building options p (the paragraph box is aligned at the top), m (the paragraph box is aligned in the center), and b (the paragraph box is aligned at the bottom) is shown schematically in the following examples.

1 1 1 1	2 2 2 2	3 3 3 3
1 1 1 1	2 2 2 2	
1 1 1 1		

```
\begin{tabular}{|p{1cm}|p{1cm}|p{1cm}|}
\hline 1 1 1 1 1 1 1 1 1 1 1 1 &
         2 2 2 2 2 2 2 2           & 3 3 3 3  \\ \hline
\end{tabular}
```

1 1 1 1		
1 1 1 1	2 2 2 2	3 3 3 3
1 1 1 1	2 2 2 2	

```
\begin{tabular}{|m{1cm}|m{1cm}|m{1cm}|}
\hline 1 1 1 1 1 1 1 1 1 1 1 1 &
         2 2 2 2 2 2 2 2           & 3 3 3 3  \\ \hline
\end{tabular}
```

1 1 1 1		
1 1 1 1	2 2 2 2	
1 1 1 1	2 2 2 2	3 3 3 3

```
\begin{tabular}{|b{1cm}|b{1cm}|b{1cm}|}
\hline 1 1 1 1 1 1 1 1 1 1 1 1 &
         2 2 2 2 2 2 2 2           & 3 3 3 3  \\ \hline
\end{tabular}
```

In columns, which have been generated with p, m, or b, the default value of \parindent is 0pt. This can be changed with the \setlength command, for instance: >{\setlength{\parindent}{1cm}{p{...}.

---

[1]In fact the effect of \extrarowheight will only be visible if the sum of its value, added to the product \baselineskip×\arraystretch (see section 5.3.2), is larger than the actual height of the cell, or more precisely, in the case of m or b, the height of the *first row* of the cell.

1 2 3 4 5 6	1 2 3 4 5 6 7 8
7 8 9 0 1 2 3 4	9 0 1 2 3 4 5 6
5 6 7 8 9 0	7 8 9 0

```
\begin{tabular}
  {|>{\setlength{\parindent}{5mm}}p{2cm}|p{2cm}|}
\hline 1 2 3 4 5 6 7 8 9 0 1 2 3 4 5 6 7 8 9 0 &
  1 2 3 4 5 6 7 8 9 0 1 2 3 4 5 6 7 8 9 0 \\ \hline
\end{tabular}
```

The < option was originally developed for the following application:
`>{$}c<{$}` generates a column in math mode in a `tabular` environment. The
use of this type of preamble in an `array` environment results in a column in LR
mode because the additional $'s cancel the existing $'s.

$10!^{10!}$	a big number
10^{-999}	a small number

```
\setlength{\extrarowheight}{2pt}
\[  \begin{array}{|l|>{$}l<{$}|}    \hline
    10!^{10!}          & a big number    \\
    10^{-999}          & a small number \\
  \hline  \end{array}    \]
```

There is an important difference between `r@{\hspace{5mm}}l` and
`r!{\hspace{5mm}}l`. In the former case the inter-column space is *exactly equal*
to 5mm. In the latter case a space of 5mm is *added* to the inter-column space
(`\arraycolsep` or `\tabcolsep` depending on the environment used).

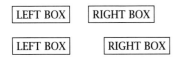

```
\begin{tabular}{r@{\hspace{5mm}}l}
  \fbox{LEFT BOX} & \fbox{RIGHT BOX}
\end{tabular}
\par \vspace{\baselineskip} \par
\begin{tabular}{r!{\hspace{5mm}}l}
  \fbox{LEFT BOX} & \fbox{RIGHT BOX}
\end{tabular}
```

Variable Width Vertical Rules

Variable width vertical rules can also be constructed with the help of a `!{decl}`
declaration and the basic TEX command `\vrule` with a width argument. This
command is used since it automatically fills the height of the column, whereas
for LATEX's `\rule` command an explicit height must be specified.

A	B	C
100	10	1

```
\begin{tabular}{|c!{\vrule width 3pt}c|c|}
\hline
A   & B & C  \\ \hline
100 & 10 & 1  \\ \hline
\end{tabular}
```

Typesetting Narrow Columns

When you have a narrow column, you must not only make sure that the first word can be hyphenated (see page 65) but that short texts are also easier to typeset in ragged right mode (without being aligned at the right margin). This is obtained by preceding the material with a `\raggedright` command (see section 3.1.4). Since this environment redefines the line-breaking command \\, we must store the row-ending \\ command of the `tabular` or `array` environments. Therefore, we define the command `\PreserveBackslash`, which will reset the \\ command to its correct value.

```
\newcommand{\PreserveBackslash}[1]{\let\temp=\\#1\let\\=\temp}
```

As shown in the example below, we can now typeset material inside a `tabular` environment ragged right, ragged left, or centered and still have control of the line breaks. We also show that the first word is now, indeed, hyphenated correctly, although in the case of Dutch, we helped TeX a little by choosing the possible hyphenation points ourselves. Note also the hyphenation of the accented French word "Possibilités," while the second French word "espérances" is not hyphenated. The reason is that in the first case the hyphenation point lies before the accent, while in the latter case it falls after.

Supercon- ciousness is a long word	Possibil- ités et espérances	Mogelijk- heden en hoop
Ragged left text in column one	Centered text in column two	Ragged right text in column three

```
\let\PBS=\PreserveBackslash %shorthand
\begin{tabular}%
     {|>{\PBS\raggedleft\hspace{0pt}}p{14mm}%
      |>{\PBS\centering\hspace{0pt}}p{14mm}%
      |>{\PBS\raggedright\hspace{0pt}}p{14mm}|}
\hline
  Superconciousness is a long word     &
  Possibilit\'es et esp\'erances       &
  Moge\-lijk\-heden en hoop               \\ \hline
  Ragged left text in column one       &
  Centered text    in column two       &
  Ragged right text in  column three   \\ \hline
\end{tabular}
```

Controlling the Horizontal Separation between Columns

The way the `tabular` environment handles the width of columns, the separation between column separators and column contents, and the various rules will be studied using a series of examples.

When there are no vertical rules, the use of `@{}` specifiers will eliminate the horizontal space between columns. The table content is of the form:

```
\begin{tabular}{...} %%%%% <---- Part which varies
  BOXES & BOXES \\    BOXES & BOXES  \\
\end{tabular}
```

The varying `tabular` preamble is shown at the right in each case.

BOXES BOXES BOXES BOXES	`{ll}`
BOXES BOXES BOXES BOXES	`{@{}ll@{}}`
BOXESBOXES BOXESBOXES	`{@{}l@{}l@{}}`

When there are vertical bars, you can control the space both in front and following the vertical column separator. To show the behavior induced by the presence of horizontal rules, the latter have also been added in the following example.

```
\begin{tabular}{...} %%%%% <---- Part which varies
                    \hline
   BOXES & BOXES  \\ \hline
   BOXES & BOXES  \\ \hline
\end{tabular}
```

BOXES | BOXES BOXES | BOXES	`{|l|l|}`
BOXES | BOXES BOXES | BOXES	`{|@{}l|l@{}|}`
BOXES| BOXES BOXES| BOXES	`{|@{}l@{}|l@{}|}`
BOXESBOXES BOXESBOXES	`{|@{}l@{}|@{}l@{}|}`

Adding one more degree of complexity, the following series of examples shows how the `tabular` environment treats double rules.

```
\begin{tabular}{...} %%%%% <---- Part which varies
  \hline\hline
   BOXES & BOXES  \\    \hline\hline
   BOXES & BOXES  \\    \hline\hline
\end{tabular}
```

BOXES || BOXES BOXES || BOXES	`{||l||l||}`

BOXES ‖ BOXES	`{||@{}l||l@{}||}`
BOXES ‖ BOXES	
BOXES‖ BOXES	`{||@{}l@{}||l@{}||}`
BOXES‖ BOXES	
BOXES BOXES	`{||@{}l@{}||@{}l@{}||}`
BOXES BOXES	
BOXESBOXES	`{|@{}|@{}l@{}|@{}|@{}l@{}|@{}|}`
BOXESBOXES	

In general, when you want to eliminate all spacing between columns, it is more straightforward to redefine the \arraycolsep and \tabcolsep lengths. Moreover, the last example shows a misuse of the @{...} qualifier, since to control the width between the double vertical (and at the same time horizontal) bars, the \doublerulesep parameter should be redefined.

5.3.2 Style Parameters

(£ 185)
The visual appearance of the tabular-like environments can be controlled by various style parameters. These parameters can be changed using the \setlength or \addtolength commands anywhere in the document. Their scope can be general or local. In the latter case the scope should be explicitly delimited by braces or another environment.

\arraycolsep Half the width of the horizontal space between columns in an array environment (default value 5pt).

\tabcolsep Half the width of the horizontal space between columns in a tabular environment (default value 6pt).

\arrayrulewidth The width of the vertical rule that separates columns (if a | is specified in the environment preamble) or by the rules created by \hline, \cline, or \vline (default value 0.4pt). When using the array package, this width is taken into account when calculating the width of the table (standard LaTeX sets the rules in such a way that they do not affect the final width of the table).

\doublerulesep The width of the space between lines created by two successive || characters in the environment preamble, or by two successive \hline commands (default value 2pt).

\arraystretch Fraction with which the normal inter-row space is multiplied, for example a value of 1.5 would move the rows 50% further apart. This is set with \renewcommand (default value 1.0).

`\extrarowheight` Extra parameter introduced in the array package. Its value
is added to the normal height of every row of the table while the depth
remains the same. This is important for tables with horizontal lines because
it is often necessary to fine-tune the distance between those lines and the
contents of the table (default value 0pt).

Environment TabularC below shows how these style parameters are used to
generate a table with a given number of equal-width columns and a total width
for the table equal to `\linewidth`. Use is made of the calc package, discussed
in section A.4. We also use the command `\PreserveBackslash`, defined on
page 108. Our environment, TabularC, takes the number of columns as its
argument. This number, let us call it x, is used to calculate the actual width of
each column by subtracting two x times the column separation and $(x + 1)$ times
the width of the rules from the width of the line. The remaining distance is
divided by x to obtain the length of a single column. The contents of the column
are centered, the \\ command is restored, and hyphenation of the first word is
allowed.

```
\let\PBS=\PreserveBackslash
\newlength{\tmplength}
\newenvironment{TabularC}[1]
   {%
    \setlength{\tmplength}{\linewidth/(#1)
                   - \tabcolsep*2
                   - \arrayrulewidth*(#1+1)/(#1)}%
    \par\begin{tabular*}{\linewidth}%
                 {*{#1}{|>{\PBS\centering\hspace{0pt}}%
                 p{\the\tmplength}}|}%
   }
   {\end{tabular*}\par}
```

Applying this definition gives the following result:

Material in column one	column two	This is column three
Column one again	and column two	This is column three
Once more column one	column two	Last time column three

```
\begin{TabularC}{3}
\hline
Material in column one & column two
          & This is column three        \\ \hline
Column one  again      & and column two
          & This is column three        \\ \hline
Once more column one   & column two
          & Last time column three      \\ \hline
\end{TabularC}
```

It is equally simple to construct environments for other column configura-
tions. If you feel a little uncomfortable with all these commands and parameters,

then you can use the `tabularx` environment, which makes this sort of calculation for you. (See section 5.3.5 and table 5.2 on page 116 for a comparison.)

5.3.3   Defining New Column Specifiers

If you have a one-off column in a table, then it is handy to be able to type:

>*{some declarations}*c<*{some more decls}*

Yet it becomes rather verbose if you often use columns of this form. Therefore, for repetitive use of a given type of column specifier, the following command has been defined to specify a new type of column:

```
\newcolumntype{col}[narg]{decl}
```

Here, *col* is a one-letter specifier to identify the new type of column inside a preamble, *narg* is an optional parameter, giving the number of arguments this specifier takes, and *decl* are legal declarations, for example:

\newcolumntype{x}{>*{some declarations}*c<*{some more decls}*}

The newly defined x column specifier can then be used in the preamble arguments of all `array` or `tabular` environments in which one needs columns of this form.

Quite often you may need math-mode and LR-mode columns inside a `tabular` or `array` environment. Thus, you can define:

```
\newcolumntype{C}{>{$}c<{$}}
\newcolumntype{L}{>{$}l<{$}}
\newcolumntype{R}{>{$}r<{$}}
```

From now on you can use C to get centered LR-mode in an `array`, or centered math-mode in a `tabular`.

Note that \newcolumntype takes the same first optional argument as \newcommand, which declares the number of arguments of the column specifier being defined. However, the current implementation does not support the extended syntax of \newcommand introduced in LATEX 2_ε.

A rather different use of the \newcolumntype command takes advantage of the fact that the replacement text in \newcolumntype may refer to more than one column. Suppose that a document contains a lot of `tabular` environments that require the same preamble, and you wish to experiment with different preambles. You can define:

```
\newcolumntype{Z}{clr}
\begin{tabular}{Z}
```

```
  . . .
\end{tabular}
```

The replacement text in a \newcolumntype command can be any of the primitives of array, or any new letter defined in another \newcolumntype command.

To display a list of all currently active \newcolumntype definitions on the terminal use the \showcols command in the preamble.

5.3.4 Some Peculiarities of the array Implementation

Error messages generated when parsing the column specification refer to the preamble argument *after* it has been rewritten by the \newcolumntype system, not to the preamble entered by the user.

The use of \extracolsep is subjected to the restrictions that there can be at most one \extracolsep command per @ or ! expression and the command must be directly entered into the @ expression, not as part of a macro definition. Thus \newcommand{\ef}{\extracolsep{\fill}} ... @{\ef} does not work with this package, but \newcolumntype{e}{@{\extracolsep{\fill}}} could be used instead.

5.3.5 tabularx—Automatic Calculation of the Column Widths

The package tabularx (by David Carlisle) implements a version of the `tabular*` environment in which the widths of certain columns are calculated automatically depending on the total width of the table. The columns, whose widths are automatically calculated, are denoted in the preamble by the X qualifier. The latter column specification will be converted to p{*some value*} once the correct column width has been calculated.

The next table, which contains the titles of Shakespeare's comedies, has been declared with \begin{tabularx}{100mm}{|X|X|X|}.

The Two Gentlemen of Verona	The Taming of the Shrew	The Comedy of Errors
Love's Labour's Lost	A Midsummer Night's Dream	The Merchant of Venice
The Merry Wives of Windsor	Much Ado About Nothing	As You Like It
Twelfth Night	Troilus and Cressida	Measure for Measure
All's Well That Ends Well	Pericles Prince of Tyre	The Winter's Tale
Cymbeline	The Tempest	

Changing the declaration to `\begin{tabularx}{\linewidth}{|X|X|X|}`
will produce the following table layout:

The Two Gentlemen of Verona	The Taming of the Shrew	The Comedy of Errors
Love's Labour's Lost	A Midsummer Night's Dream	The Merchant of Venice
The Merry Wives of Windsor	Much Ado About Nothing	As You Like It
Twelfth Night	Troilus and Cressida	Measure for Measure
All's Well That Ends Well	Pericles Prince of Tyre	The Winter's Tale
Cymbeline	The Tempest	

Commands Used to Typeset the X Columns

By default the X specification is turned into p{*some value*}. Such narrow columns
often require a special format, which may be achieved using the > syntax. Thus
you may give a specification like `>{\small}X`. Another format which is useful in narrow columns is ragged right. However, LaTeX's `\raggedright` macro
redefines `\\` in a way that conflicts with its use in a `tabular` or `array` environment (see also the discussion of the command `\PreserveBackslash` on
page 108). For this reason, the command `\arraybackslash` is defined in
the `tabularx` package. It may be used after a `\raggedright`, `\raggedleft`,
or `\centering` declaration. The result is that a `tabularx` preamble may
specify `>{\raggedright\arraybackslash}X`. This specification is saved with:
`\newcolumntype{Y}{>{\small\raggedright\arraybackslash}X}`. You may
then use Y as a `tabularx` preamble argument.

The X columns are set using the p column, which corresponds to `\parbox[t]`.
You may want to set the columns with, for example, an m column corresponding
to `\parbox[c]`. It is impossible to change the column type using the > syntax, so
another system is provided. The command `\tabularxcolumn` can be defined as a
macro, with one argument, which expands to the `tabular` preamble specification
to be used for X henceforth. The supplied argument when the command is
executed determines the actual column width.

The default definition is `\newcommand{\tabularxcolumn}[1]{p{#1}}`. A
possible alternative definition is

```
\renewcommand{\tabularxcolumn}[1]{>{\small}m{#1}}
```

Column Widths

Normally, all X columns in a single table are set to the same width. It is nevertheless possible to make `tabularx` set them to different widths. A preamble like
`{>{\setlength{\hsize}{.5\hsize}}X>{\setlength{\hsize}{1.5\hsize}}X}`

specifies two columns; the second will be three times as wide as the first. However, when using this method the following two rules should be obeyed:

- The sum of the widths of all X columns should remain unchanged. In the above example, the new widths should add up to that of two standard X columns.

- \multicolumn entries that cross any X column should not be used.

Superconciousness is a long word	Mogelijkheden en hoop
Some text in column one	A somewhat longer text in column two

```
\tracingtabularx
\begin{tabularx}{\linewidth}%
    {|>{\setlength{\hsize}{.8\hsize}}X|%
     >{\setlength{\hsize}{1.2\hsize}}X|}
Superconciousness is a long word  &
Moge\-lijk\-heden en hoop             \\
Some text in column one           &
A somewhat longer text in  column two \\
\end{tabularx}
```

Differences between tabularx **and** tabular*

Both the tabular* (standard LATEX) and the tabularx environments take the same arguments, to produce a table of a specified width. The main differences are:

- tabularx modifies the widths of the *columns*, whereas tabular* modifies the widths of the inter-column *spaces*.

- tabular and tabular* environments may be nested with no restriction. However, if one tabularx environment occurs inside another, then the inner one *must* be enclosed within { }.

- The body of the tabularx environment is, in fact, the argument to a command, and there are certain restrictions: the commands \verb and \verb* may be used, but they may treat spaces incorrectly, and the argument cannot contain a % or an unmatched { or }.

- tabular* uses a primitive capability of TEX to modify the inter-column space of an alignment. tabularx has to set the table several times as it searches for the best column widths, and is therefore much slower. Also, the fact that the body is expanded several times may break certain TEX constructs.

Table 5.2 on the following page shows a comparison of the tabularx environment with the TabularC environment described in section 5.3.2.

```
\begin{TabularC}{4}                                                              \hline
Material in column one      & column two          &
This is column three       & column four                          \\
Material in column one  again & and column two    &
This is column three       & column four                          \\
Once more column one       & column two          &
column three               & \hfill column four                   \\\hline
\end{TabularC}

\begin{tabularx}{\linewidth}{|X|X|X|X|}                                          \hline
      . . . . . same contents . . . . .
                                                                                 \hline
\end{tabularx}

\newcolumntype{Y}{>{\centering\arraybackslash}X}%
\begin{tabularx}{\linewidth}{|Y|Y|Y|Y|}                                          \hline
      . . . . . same contents . . . . .
                                                                                 \hline
\end{tabularx}
```

Material in column one	column two	This is column three	column four
Material in column one again	and column two	This is column three	column four
Once more column one	column two	column three	column four

Material in column one	column two	This is column three	column four
Material in column one again	and column two	This is column three	column four
Once more column one	column two	column three	column four

Material in column one	column two	This is column three	column four
Material in column one again	and column two	This is column three	column four
Once more column one	column two	column three	column four

Table 5.2: Comparing the `TabularC` and `tabularx` environments

As seen above, the `TabularC` and the `tabularx` environments can both do the job of typesetting the layout you want. David Carlisle, the author of the `tabularx` package, remarks nevertheless, "If the user is happy with doing TeX arithmetic, then in a situation where the column width can be pre-calculated, the `TabularC` method is much better as it avoids the problem of multiple expansion (which is used in the tabularx package). `tabularx` is mainly of benefit when some of the columns are 'c' type columns, so that the width of the 'p' columns cannot be pre-calculated, as they depend on the table entries."

Tracing the Output on the Terminal

```
\tracingtabularx
```

If this declaration is made, say in the document preamble, then all following `tabularx` environments will print information about column widths as they repeatedly reset the tables to find the correct widths. For instance, in the case of the last example we got the following output.

```
Target width: \linewidth  = 204.0pt.
    Table Width     Column Width     X Columns
    433.19998pt     204.0pt             3
    203.99998pt     89.40001pt          2
Reached target.
```

5.3.6 delarray—Specifying Delimiters Surrounding an Array

A useful extension to the array package when dealing with delimiters can be found in the package file **delarray** (by David Carlisle). It lets the user specify the delimiters, which must surround the whole environment by providing implicit `\left \right` pairs around the array construct.

$$\begin{pmatrix} A & B \\ C & D \end{pmatrix}$$

```
\[
    \begin{array}({cc})
        A & B  \\  C & D
    \end{array}
\]
```

Any delimiter may surround the preamble. Plain TeX or $\mathcal{A}_{\mathcal{M}}\mathcal{S}$-TeX users may recognize the following environments (see also sections 8.4.1 and 8.4.2):

```
\newcolumntype{L}{>{$}l<{$}}
\newenvironment{Cases}{\begin{array}\{{lL}.}{\end{array}}
\newenvironment{Matrix}{\begin{array}|{*{20}{c}}|}{\end{array}}
\newenvironment{Pmatrix}{\begin{array}({*{20}{c}})}{\end{array}}
```

$$|x| = \begin{cases} x, & \text{if } x \geq 0; \\ -x, & \text{otherwise.} \end{cases}$$

```
\[
    |x| = \begin{Cases}
            x,& if $x\ge0$; \\[2mm]
            -x,& otherwise.  \\
          \end{Cases}
\]
```

$$a = \begin{vmatrix} x-\lambda & 1 & 0 \\ 0 & x-\lambda & 1 \\ 0 & 0 & x-\lambda \end{vmatrix}^2.$$

```
\[  a = {\begin{Matrix}
            x-\lambda & 1 & 0 \\
            0 & x-\lambda & 1 \\
            0 & 0 & x-\lambda \\
        \end{Matrix}
    }^2.
\]
```

$$A = \begin{pmatrix} x-\lambda & 1 & 0 \\ 0 & x-\lambda & 1 \\ 0 & 0 & x-\lambda \end{pmatrix}.$$

```
\[  A = \begin{Pmatrix}
            x-\lambda & 1 & 0 \\
            0 & x-\lambda & 1 \\
            0 & 0 & x-\lambda \\
        \end{Pmatrix}.
\]
```

This feature is especially useful if the [t] or [b] arguments are also used. In these cases the result is not equivalent to surrounding the environment by \left...\right, as can be seen by comparing the following examples:

$$\begin{pmatrix} 1 \\ 2 \\ 3 \end{pmatrix}\begin{pmatrix} 1 \\ 2 \\ 3 \end{pmatrix}\begin{pmatrix} 1 \\ 2 \\ 3 \end{pmatrix}$$

```
\[  \begin{array}[t]({c})1\\2\\3\end{array}
    \begin{array}[c]({c})1\\2\\3\end{array}
    \begin{array}[b]({c})1\\2\\3\end{array}
\]
```

$$\begin{pmatrix} 1 \\ 2 \\ 3 \end{pmatrix}\begin{pmatrix} 1 \\ 2 \\ 3 \end{pmatrix}\begin{pmatrix} 1 \\ 2 \\ 3 \end{pmatrix}$$

```
\[  \left(
        \begin{array}[t]{c}1\\2\\3\end{array}
    \right)
    \left(
        \begin{array}[c]{c}1\\2\\3\end{array}
    \right)
    \left(
        \begin{array}[b]{c}1\\2\\3\end{array}
    \right)                                          \]
```

5.4 Multipage Tabular Material

With Leslie Lamport's original implementation, a tabular environment must always fit on one page. If the tabular becomes too large the text overwrites the page's bottom margin, and you get an Overfull \vbox message.

Two package files are available to construct tables longer than one page, supertab and longtable. They have a similar functionality, but, for an elementary use, the former's commands are perhaps more intuitive. If you want, however, to have a finer control on the width of the table, then the latter package has to be used. The next sections will review each of them in turn, and finally show, using a more complex example, the difference between the two approaches.

5.4.1 supertab—Making Multipage Tabulars

The package supertab (original by Theo Jurriens, revised by Johannes Braams) defines the environment supertabular. It uses the tabular environment internally, but it evaluates the used space every time it encounters a \\ command. If the tabular reaches the value of \textheight it automatically inserts an \end{tabular} command, starts a new page, and inserts the table head on the new page continuing the tabular. This means that the width of the columns, and hence the complete table, can vary on consecutive pages.

The new commands introduced with supertabular are:

\tablehead{...}	defines the contents of the tabular head, except the first when \tablefirsthead is defined. The argument can contain full rows (ended by \\) as well as inter-row material like \hline.
\tablefirsthead{...}	defines the contents of the first occurrence of the tabular head. This command, which is optional, should be used when the head text on the first page is different from the one specified with \tablehead.
\tabletail{...}	defines material to be inserted at the end of each page, but the last if \tablelasttail is defined.
\tablelasttail{...}	defines material to be inserted at the end of the supertabular. This command, which is optional, should be used when the tail text on the last page is different from the one specified with \tabletail.
\topcaption{...} \bottomcaption{...} \tablecaption{...}	provides a caption for the \supertabular, either at the top or at the bottom of the table. When \tablecaption is used the caption will be placed at the default location, which is at the top.

Inside a supertabular environment new lines are defined as usual by \\ commands. All column definition commands can be used, including @{...} and p{...}. You can, however, not use the optional positioning arguments, like t and b, which can be specified with \begin{tabular} or \begin{tabular*}.

Table 1: Surats of the Holy Koran

001	The Opening	002	The Cow
003	The Family Of Imran	004	Women
005	The Food	006	The Cattle
007	The Elevated Places	008	The Spoils Of War
009	Repentance	010	Yunus
011	Hud	012	Yusuf
013	The Thunder	014	Ibrahim
015	The Rock	016	The Bee
017	The Israelites	018	The Cave
019	Marium	020	TaHa
021	The Prophets	022	The Pilgrimage
023	The Believers	024	The Light
025	The Criterion	026	The Poets
027	The Ant	028	The Narrative
029	The Spider	030	The Romans
031	Luqman	032	The Adoration
033	The Allies	034	Saba
035	The Originator	036	Ya Seen
037	The Rangers	038	Suad
039	The Companies	040	The Believer
041	HaMim	042	The Counsel
043	The Embellishment	044	The Evident Smoke
045	The Kneeling	046	The Sandhills
047	Muhammad	048	The Victory
049	The Chambers	050	Qaf
051	The Scatterers	052	The Mountain
053	The Star	054	The Moon
055	The Beneficient	056	The Great Event
057	The Iron	058	The Pleading One
059	The Banishment	060	The Examined One

061	The Ranks	062	Friday
063	The Hypocrites	064	Loss And Gain
065	The Divorce	066	The Prohibition
067	The Kingdom	068	The Pen
069	The Sure Calamity	070	The Ways Of Ascent
071	Nuh	072	The Jinn
073	The Wrapped Up	074	The Clothed One
075	The Resurrection	076	The Man
077	The Emissaries	078	The Great Event
079	Those Who Pull Out	080	He Frowned
081	The Covering Up	082	The Cleaving Asunder
083	The Defrauders	084	The Bursting Asunder
085	The Mansions Of The Stars	086	The Night-Comer
087	The Most High	088	The Overwhelming Calamity
089	The Daybreak	090	The City
091	The Sun	092	The Night
093	The Early Hours	094	The Expansion
095	The Fig	096	The Clot
097	The Majesty	098	The Clear Evidence
099	The Shaking	100	The Assaulters
101	The Terrible Calamity	102	The Multiplication Of Wealth And Children
103	Time	104	The Slanderer
105	The Elephant	106	The Qureaish
107	The Daily Necessaries	108	The Heavenly Fountain
109	The Unbelievers	110	The Help
111	The Flame	112	The Unity
113	The Dawn	114	The Men

Table 5.3: The Surats of the Holy Koran (`supertabular`)

Example of the `supertabular` Environment

The first example (table 5.3) has a simple layout, and building the multipage table is easy in this case. Note the change of the width of the table between the first and second pages (left- and right-hand side of picture). The commands used to obtain the given layout are shown below.

```
\tablecaption{Surats of the Holy Koran}
\tablehead{\hline}
\tabletail{\hline}
\begin{supertabular}{|cl|cl|}
001 & The Opening          & 002 & The Cow     \\
003 & The Family Of Imran  & 004 & Women       \\
 ....
113 & The Dawn             & 114 & The Men     \\
\end{supertabular}
```

Example of the `supertabular*` Environment

The width of a supertabular can be fixed to a given width, such as the width of the text, \textwidth, as in table 5.4 on the facing page. Compared to table 5.3

Table 1: Surats of the Holy Koran			
Nb. and name of Surat		Nb. and name of Surat	
001	The Opening	002	The Cow
003	The Family Of Imran	004	Women
005	The Food	006	The Cattle
007	The Elevated Places	008	The Spoils Of War
009	Repentance	010	Yunus
011	Hud	012	Yusuf
013	The Thunder	014	Ibrahim
015	The Rock	016	The Bee
017	The Israelites	018	The Cave
019	Marium	020	TaHa
021	The Prophets	022	The Pilgrimage
023	The Believers	024	The Light
025	The Criterion	026	The Poets
027	The Ant	028	The Narrative
029	The Spider	030	The Romans
031	Luqman	032	The Adoration
033	The Allies	034	Saba
035	The Originator	036	Ya Seen
037	The Rangers	038	Suad
039	The Companies	040	The Believer
041	HaMim	042	The Counsel
043	The Embellishment	044	The Evident Smoke
045	The Kneeling	046	The Sandhills
047	Muhammad	048	The Victory
049	The Chambers	050	Qaf
051	The Scatterers	052	The Mountain
053	The Star	054	The Moon
055	The Beneficient	056	The Great Event
		continued on next page	

continued from previous page			
Nb. and name of Surat		Nb. and name of Surat	
057	The Iron	058	The Pleading One
059	The Banishment	060	The Examined One
061	The Ranks	062	Friday
063	The Hypocrites	064	Loss And Gain
065	The Divorce	066	The Prohibition
067	The Kingdom	068	The Pen
069	The Sure Calamity	070	The Ways Of Ascent
071	Nuh	072	The Jinn
073	The Wrapped Up	074	The Clothed One
075	The Resurrection	076	The Man
077	The Emissaries	078	The Great Event
079	Those Who Pull Out	080	He Frowned
081	The Covering Up	082	The Cleaving Asunder
083	The Defrauders	084	The Bursting Asunder
085	The Mansions Of The Stars	086	The Night-Comer
087	The Most High	088	The Overwhelming Calamity
089	The Daybreak	090	The City
091	The Sun	092	The Night
093	The Early Hours	094	The Expansion
095	The Fig	096	The Clot
097	The Majesty	098	The Clear Evidence
099	The Shaking	100	The Assaulters
101	The Terrible Calamity	102	The Multiplication Of Wealth And Children
103	Time	104	The Slanderer
105	The Elephant	106	The Qureaish
107	The Daily Necessaries	108	The Heavenly Fountain
109	The Unbelievers	110	The Help
111	The Flame	112	The Unity
113	The Dawn	114	The Men

Table 5.4: The Surats of the Holy Koran (`supertabular*`)

information has also been added at the top and bottom of each page, and a rubber (stretch) space has been introduced between the two last columns. Note the different spacings between these columns on the first (left) and second (right) page. In this case, the commands to obtain the given layout are the following:

```
\tablecaption{Surats of the Holy Koran}
\tablefirsthead{\hline \multicolumn{2}{|l|}{Nb. and name of Surat}
            & \multicolumn{2}{|l|}{Nb. and name of Surat}\\\hline}
\tablehead{\hline \multicolumn{4}{|l|}%
                  {\small\slshape continued from previous page}\\
         \hline  \multicolumn{2}{|l|}{Nb. and name of Surat}
          & \multicolumn{2}{l|}{Nb. and name of Surat} \\ \hline}
\tabletail{\hline\multicolumn{4}{|r|}%
                  {\small\slshape continued on next page}\\\hline}
\tablelasttail{\hline}
\begin{supertabular*}{\textwidth}%
      {|cl@{\hspace*{2mm}\extracolsep{\fill}}|c@{\extracolsep{1mm}}l|}
 001 & The Opening         & 002 & The Cow               \\
 003 & The Family Of Imran & 004 & Women                 \\
   ....
 113 & The Dawn            & 114 & The Men               \\
```

Known Problems

- When a float occurs on the same page as the start of a supertabular, unexpected results can occur. When the float is defined on the same page, you might end up with the first part of the supertabular on a page of its own. When the list of unprocessed floats is not empty it will be made empty by the first part of the supertabular (if the latter is split across pages) because it calls \clearpage.

- The supertabular environment should not be used *inside* a floating environment such as table as this will result in TeX trying to put the whole supertabular on *one* page.

- Sometimes you might still end up with overfull \vbox messages. These cases are described in the (documented version of the) package file.

5.4.2 longtable—Sophisticated Multipage Tabulars

As pointed out at the beginning of this section, for more complex long tables, where you want to control the width of the table across page boundaries, the package longtable (by David Carlisle) should be considered. As with the supertabular environment, it also shares some features with the table environment. In particular it uses the same counter, table, and has a similar \caption command. The \listoftables command lists tables produced by either the table or longtable environments.

The main difference between the supertabular and longtable environments is that the latter saves the information about the width of each longtable environment in the auxiliary .aux file, and uses this information on a subsequent run to know the widest width needed for the table in question. Thus it can construct the table with the adequate width. This feature has to be activated with the \setlongtables command. Note, however, that when one more longtable environment is added in the middle of a previous sequence, all subsequent tables will have the wrong width because the information read will be for the wrong table (the numbering will be one unit off). Problems also happen when, for one of the tables, the widest entry is shortened. As longtable always saves the widest width needed for a given table, it will never be able to reduce the size in the .aux file, so the table will always come out too wide. The only possibility in this case is to rerun your file through LaTeX without the command \setlongtables to get rid of the wrong values in the .aux files, and then to run LaTeX twice more with \setlongtables to get the correct values. Since longtable uses LaTeX's page-breaking algorithm, the page breaks will not be affected by the precise width of the columns in the longtable fragments. Therefore, you should not worry about the fact that the table fragments have different widths, and should not use the \setlongtables command unless your document is ready and you want to print a final version.

Surats of the Holy Koran			
001	The Opening	002	The Cow
003	The Family Of Imran	004	Women
005	The Food	006	The Cattle
007	The Elevated Places	008	The Spoils Of War
009	Repentance	010	Yunus
011	Hud	012	Yusuf
013	The Thunder	014	Ibrahim
015	The Rock	016	The Bee
017	The Israelites	018	The Cave
019	Marium	020	TaHa
021	The Prophets	022	The Pilgrimage
023	The Believers	024	The Light
025	The Criterion	026	The Poets
027	The Ant	028	The Narrative
029	The Spider	030	The Romans
031	Luqman	032	The Adoration
033	The Allies	034	Saba
035	The Originator	036	Ya Seen
037	The Rangers	038	Suad
039	The Companies	040	The Believer
041	HaMim	042	The Counsel
043	The Embellishment	044	The Evident Smoke
045	The Kneeling	046	The Sandhills
047	Muhammad	048	The Victory
049	The Chambers	050	Qaf
051	The Scatterers	052	The Mountain
053	The Star	054	The Moon
055	The Beneficent	056	The Great Event
057	The Iron	058	The Pleading One

Surats of the Holy Koran			
059	The Banishment	060	The Examined One
061	The Ranks	062	Friday
063	The Hypocrites	064	Loss And Gain
065	The Divorce	066	The Prohibition
067	The Kingdom	068	The Pen
069	The Sure Calamity	070	The Ways Of Ascent
071	Nuh	072	The Jinn
073	The Wrapped Up	074	The Clothed One
075	The Resurrection	076	The Man
077	The Emissaries	078	The Great Event
079	Those Who Pull Out	080	He Frowned
081	The Covering Up	082	The Cleaving Asunder
083	The Defrauders	084	The Bursting Asunder
085	The Mansions Of The Stars	086	The Night-Comer
087	The Most High	088	The Overwhelming Calamity
089	The Daybreak	090	The City
091	The Sun	092	The Night
093	The Early Hours	094	The Expansion
095	The Fig	096	The Clot
097	The Majesty	098	The Clear Evidence
099	The Shaking	100	The Assaulters
101	The Terrible Calamity	102	The Multiplication Of Wealth And Children
103	Time	104	The Slanderer
105	The Elephant	106	The Qureaish
107	The Daily Necessaries	108	The Heavenly Fountain
109	The Unbelievers	110	The Help
111	The Flame	112	The Unity
113	The Dawn	114	The Men

Table 5.5: The Surats of the Holy Koran (`longtable`)

In order to make the difference clear, the first example given with supertabular (table 5.3 on page 120) is repeated here, but using `longtable` (table 5.5). Since, in this case, we have activated the \setlongtables command, you can see that the width of the table is identical on both pages (the left and right parts of the picture). The commands that were utilized to generate the table are shown below.

```
\setlongtables
\begin{longtable}{|cl|cl|}
\caption*{Surats of the Holy Koran}                    \\
\hline
\endhead
\hline
\endfoot
001 & The Opening          &  002 & The Cow    \\
 ....
113 & The Dawn             & 114 & The Men     \\
\end{longtable}
```

The commands controlling the global formatting of the longtable environment are grouped in table 5.6 on the next page.

The `longtable` environment will never break a row in the middle (this is

Parameters (default values are shown in parentheses)		
\LTleft	(\fill)	Glue to the left of the table.
\LTright	(\fill)	Glue to the right of the table.
\LTpre	(\bigskipamount)	Glue before the table.
\LTpost	(\bigskipamount)	Glue after the table.
\LTchunksize	(20)	Number of rows per chunk (TeX counter).
\LTcapwidth	(4in)	Width of parbox containing the caption.
Setlongtables		
\setlongtables		Use column widths from the previous run.
Optional arguments to \begin{longtable}		
none		Position as specified by \LTleft and \LTright, usually center.
[c]		Center the table.
[l]		Place the table flush left.
[r]		Place the table flush right.
Commands available inside longtable		
\endhead		Rows appearing at top of every page.
\endfirsthead		Rows appearing at top of first page.
\endfoot		Rows appearing at bottom of every page.
\endlastfoot		Rows appearing at bottom of last page.
\kill		Row is "killed" (not typeset), but it is used in calculating the widths.
\caption{*foo*}		Caption "Table *xx*: foo," with a "foo" entry in the list of tables.
\caption[*bar*]{*foo*}		Caption "Table *xx*: foo," with a "bar" entry in the list of tables.
\caption[]{*foo*}		Caption "Table *xx*: foo," with no entry in the list of tables.
\caption*{*foo*}		Caption "foo," with no entry in the list of tables.
\newpage		Forces a page break.

Table 5.6: A summary of longtable commands

important for paragraph cells with p, m, and b specifiers). You can use footnotes and \newpage commands inside the longtable environment.

Table 5.6 gives an overview of the various parameters and commands controlling the longtable environment. For instance, the commands \endhead and \endfirsthead specify the text to appear on top of the table sections on all pages and on the first page (compare this with the commands \tablehead and \tablefirsthead for the supertabular environment described in section 5.4.1), while the commands \endfoot and \endlastfoot specify what is to appear at the bottom of the table sections (compare with the `supertabular` commands `\tabletail` and `\tablelasttail`).

We shall now discuss some of the other parameters and commands.

`\setcounter{LTchunksize}{`*nrows*`}`

In order that TₑX can set multipage tables, it is necessary to break them up into smaller chunks so that TₑX does not have to keep everything in memory at one time. By default `longtable` uses a value of 20 rows per chunk. This can be changed with a command such as `\setcounter{LTchunksize}{10}`. These chunks do not affect page breaking. When TₑX has a lot of memory available `\LTchunksize` can be put to a big number, making TₑX run faster. Note that `\LTchunksize` must be at least as large as the number of rows in each of the head or foot sections.

`\setlongtables`

When the `\setlongtables` command is given before a table starts, LATₑX uses the information about the width of the table collected in a previous run. As already stated in the discussion above, this command should only be used when your document is complete and only cosmetic changes remain.

`\caption[`*short title*`]{`*full title*`}`

The `\caption` command and its variant `\caption*` are essentially equivalent to writing a special `\multicolumn` entry

`\multicolumn{`*n*`}{c}{\parbox{\LTcapwidth}{...}}`

where *n* is the number of columns of the table. The width of the caption can be controlled by redefining the parameter `\LTcapwidth`. That is, you can write `\setlength{\LTcapwidth}{`*width*`}` in the document preamble. The default value is `4in`. As with the `\caption` command in the `figure` and `table` environments, the optional argument specifies the text to appear in the list of tables if this is different from the text to appear in the caption.

When captions on later pages should be different from those on the first page, place the `\caption` command with the full text in the first heading, and put a subsidiary caption using `\caption[ ]` in the main heading, since (in this case) no entry is made in the list of tables. Alternatively, if the table number should not be repeated each time, you can use the `\caption*` command. As with the `table` environment, cross-referencing the table in the text is possible with the `\label` command.

By default, `longtable` centers the tables (for example, `\LTleft` and `\LTright` are both `\fill`). Any length can be specified for these two parameters, but at least one of them should be a rubber length so that it fills up the width of the page, unless rubber lengths are added between the columns using the `\extracolsep` command. For instance, a table can be set flush left using the definitions:

```
\setlength{\LTleft}{0pt}
\setlength{\LTright}{\fill}
```

or just by specifying `\begin{longtable}[l]`.

You can use the `\LTleft` and `\LTright` parameters also to typeset a multipage table filling the full width of the page; for instance, the equivalent to

```
\begin{supertabular*}{\textwidth}{l@{\extracolsep{\fill}}l}
```

similar to the code discussed on page 121 for table 5.4 is

```
\setlength{\LTleft}{0pt}
\setlength{\LTright}{0pt}
\begin{longtable}{l@{\extracolsep{\fill}}l}
```

In general if `\LTleft` and `\LTright` are fixed lengths, the table will be set to the width of

```
\textwidth - \LTleft - LTright
```

5.4.3 A Final Comparison

Table 5.7 on the next page shows the result of typesetting a multipage table spread over three pages (page boundaries are schematically represented by the thin lines). The differences between the `supertabular` and `longtable` environments can clearly be seen. Using identical input data, you can see that the top line, corresponding to `supertabular`, typesets the contents on a page by page basis resulting in a varying width for the table sections. The `longtable` environment, on the other hand, uses the widest entry in the table to give the complete table the same width across page boundaries. Another difference is that the pages generated by `supertabular` tend to be shorter than the "standard" pages of the document. This is due to the fact that `supertabular` uses its own page-breaking algorithm. `longtable` uses LaTeX's standard page-breaking, so that in this case there is no variation in the length of the page. As a user you must decide whether the little increased complexity of `longtable` is important for presenting your data. Table 5.8 on page 128 shows that the table declarations are, in both cases, quite similar.

Table 9: Codes of the languages of the world (supertabular)

	Languages codes (ISO 639:1988)				
code	language	code	language	code	language
aa	Afar	ab	Abkhazian	af	Afrikaans
am	Amharic	ar	Arabic	as	Assamese
ay	Aymara	az	Azerbaijani		
ba	Bashkir	be	Byelorussian	bg	Bulgarian
bh	Bihari	bi	Bislama	bn	Bengali; Bangla
bo	Tibetan	br	Breton		
ca	Catalan	co	Corsican	cs	Czech
cy	Welch				
da	Danish	de	German	dz	Bhutani
el	Greek	en	English	eo	Esperanto
es	Spanish	et	Estonian	eu	Basque
fa	Persian	fi	Finnish	fj	Fiji
fo	Faeroese	fr	French	fy	Frisian
ga	Irish	gd	Scots Gaelic	gl	Galician
gn	Guarani	gu	Gujarati		
ha	Hausa	hi	Hindi	hr	Croatian
hu	Hungarian	hy	Armenian		
ia	Interlingua	ie	Interlingue	ik	Inupiak
in	Indonesian	is	Icelandic		

continued on next page

continued from previous page

code	language	code	language	code	language
ia	Interlingua	ie	Interlingue	ik	Inupiak
in	Indonesian	is	Icelandic	it	Italian
iw	Hebrew				
ja	Japanese	ji	Yiddish	jw	Javanese
ka	Georgian	kk	Kazakh	kl	Greenlandic
km	Cambodian	kn	Kannada	ko	Korean
ks	Kashmiri	ku	Kurdish	ky	Kirghiz
la	Latin	ln	Lingala	lo	Laothian
lt	Lithuanian	lv	Latvian, Lettish		
mg	Malagasy	mi	Maori	mk	Macedonian
ml	Malayalam	mn	Mongolian	mo	Moldavian
mr	Marathi	ms	Malay	mt	Maltese
my	Burmese				
na	Nauru	ne	Nepali	nl	Dutch
no	Norwegian				
oc	Occitan	om	(Afan) Oromo	or	Oriya
pa	Punjabi	pl	Polish	ps	Pashto, Pushto
pt	Portuguese				
qu	Quechua				

continued on next page

continued from previous page

code	language	code	language	code	language
rm	Rhaeto-Romance	rn	Kirundi	ro	Romanian
ru	Russian	rw	Kinyarwanda		
sa	Sanskrit	sd	Sindhi	sg	Sangro
sh	Serbo-Croatian	si	Singhalese	sk	Slovak
sl	Slovenian	sm	Samoan	sn	Shona
so	Somali	sq	Albanian	sr	Serbian
ss	Siswati	st	Sesotho	su	Sudanese
sv	Swedish	sw	Swahili		
ta	Tamil	te	Telugu	tg	Tajik
th	Thai	ti	Tigrinya	tk	Turkmen
tl	Tagalog	tn	Setswana	to	Tonga
tr	Turkish	ts	Tsonga	tt	Tatar
tw	Twi				
uk	Ukrainian	ur	Urdu	uz	Uzbek
vi	Vietnamese	vo	Volapuk		
wo	Wolof				
xh	Xhosa				
yo	Yoruba				
zh	Chinese	zu	Zulu		

Table 10: Codes of the languages of the world (longtable)

	Language codes (ISO 639:1988)				
code	language	code	language	code	language
aa	Afar	ab	Abkhazian	af	Afrikaans
am	Amharic	ar	Arabic	as	Assamese
ay	Aymara	az	Azerbaijani		
ba	Bashkir	be	Byelorussian	bg	Bulgarian
bh	Bihari	bi	Bislama	bn	Bengali; Bangla
bo	Tibetan	br	Breton		
ca	Catalan	co	Corsican	cs	Czech
cy	Welch				
da	Danish	de	German	dz	Bhutani
el	Greek	en	English	eo	Esperanto
es	Spanish	et	Estonian	eu	Basque
fa	Persian	fi	Finnish	fj	Fiji
fo	Faeroese	fr	French	fy	Frisian
ga	Irish	gd	Scots Gaelic	gl	Galician
gn	Guarani	gu	Gujarati		
ha	Hausa	hi	Hindi	hr	Croatian
hu	Hungarian	hy	Armenian		
ia	Interlingua	ie	Interlingue	ik	Inupiak
in	Indonesian	is	Icelandic	it	Italian

continued on next page

continued from previous page

code	language	code	language	code	language
iw	Hebrew				
ja	Japanese	ji	Yiddish	jw	Javanese
ka	Georgian	kk	Kazakh	kl	Greenlandic
km	Cambodian	kn	Kannada	ko	Korean
ks	Kashmiri	ku	Kurdish	ky	Kirghiz
la	Latin	ln	Lingala	lo	Laothian
lt	Lithuanian	lv	Latvian, Lettish		
mg	Malagasy	mi	Maori	mk	Macedonian
ml	Malayalam	mn	Mongolian	mo	Moldavian
mr	Marathi	ms	Malay	mt	Maltese
my	Burmese				
na	Nauru	ne	Nepali	nl	Dutch
no	Norwegian				
oc	Occitan	om	(Afan) Oromo	or	Oriya
pa	Punjabi	pl	Polish	ps	Pashto, Pushto
pt	Portuguese				
qu	Quechua				
rm	Rhaeto-Romance	rn	Kirundi	ro	Romanian
ru	Russian	rw	Kinyarwanda		
sa	Sanskrit	sd	Sindhi	sg	Sangro
sh	Serbo-Croatian	si	Singhalese	sk	Slovak

continued on next page

continued from previous page

code	language	code	language	code	language
sl	Slovenian	sm	Samoan	sn	Shona
so	Somali	sq	Albanian	sr	Serbian
ss	Siswati	st	Sesotho	su	Sudanese
sv	Swedish	sw	Swahili		
ta	Tamil	te	Telugu	tg	Tajik
th	Thai	ti	Tigrinya	tk	Turkmen
tl	Tagalog	tn	Setswana	to	Tonga
tr	Turkish	ts	Tsonga	tt	Tatar
tw	Twi				
uk	Ukrainian	ur	Urdu	uz	Uzbek
vi	Vietnamese	vo	Volapuk		
wo	Wolof				
xh	Xhosa				
yo	Yoruba				
zh	Chinese	zu	Zulu		

Table 5.7: A comparison of the `longtable` and `supertabular` environments

Declaration for the supertabular case

```
\tablefirsthead{\hline \multicolumn{6}{|c|}{Languages codes (ISO 639:1988)}\\
            code & language & code & language & code & language     \\\hline}
\tablehead{\hline \multicolumn{6}{|l|}{\small\slshape
                                continued from previous page} \\\hline
            code & language & code & language & code & language     \\\hline}
\tabletail{\hline\multicolumn{6}{|r|}{\small\slshape continued on next page}
                                                                    \\\hline}
\tablelasttail{\hline}
\topcaption{Codes of the languages of the world (supertabular)}
\begin{center}
\begin{supertabular}{|*{3}{cl}|}
\ttfamily aa &  Afar     &  \ttfamily ab &  Abkhazian   &  & ............
.................................................................
\ttfamily zh &  Chinese  &  \ttfamily zu &  Zulu          &   &  \\
\end{supertabular}
\end{center}
```

Declaration for the longtable case

```
\setlongtables
\begin{longtable}[c]{|*{3}{cl}|}
\caption{Codes of the languages of the world (longtable)}
\\ \hline
\multicolumn{6}{|c|}{Language codes (ISO 639:1988)}                  \\
        code & language & code & language & code & language     \\ \hline
\endfirsthead
\hline
\multicolumn{6}{|l|}{\small\slshape continued from previous page} \\ \hline
        code & language & code & language & code & language     \\ \hline
\endhead
\hline\multicolumn{6}{|r|}{\small\sl continued on next page}      \\ \hline
\endfoot
\hline
\endlastfoot
\ttfamily aa &  Afar     &  \ttfamily ab &  Abkhazian   &  & ............
.................................................................
\ttfamily zh &  Chinese  &  \ttfamily zu &  Zulu          &   &  \\
\end{longtable}
```

Table 5.8: A comparison of the table declarations for longtable and supertabular

5.5 Bells and Whistles

Two further package files, working nicely together with the environments described earlier, are introduced in this section. The first makes it easier to align decimal numbers inside a column, while the other introduces a larger choice for the possible combinations of vertical and horizontal lines inside `tabular`-like environments.

5.5.1 dcolumn—Defining Column Alignments

The package file dcolumn (by David Carlisle) proposes a system for defining columns of entries in `array` or `tabular`, which are to be aligned on a "decimal point." Entries with no decimal part, no integer part, and blank entries are also dealt with correctly.

The package defines a "Decimal" column specifier, D, with three arguments.

| D{*inputsep*}{*outputsep*}{*decimal places*} |

inputsep A single character, used as separator in the .tex file (for example, "." or ",").

outputsep The separator to be used in the output. It can be the same as the first argument, but may be any math-mode expression, such as \cdot.

decimal places The maximum number of decimal places in the column. If this is negative, any number of decimal places is allowed in the column, and all entries will be centered on the separator. Note that this can cause a column to be too wide (see the first two columns in the example below).

If you do not want to use all three entries in the preamble, you can customize the preamble specifiers using \newcolumntype as demonstrated below.

```
\newcolumntype{d}[1]{D{.}{\cdot}{#1}}
```

The newly defined "d" specifier takes a single argument specifying the number of decimal places. The decimal separator in the .tex input file is the normal dot ".", while the output file uses the math mode "·".

```
\newcolumntype{.}{D{.}{.}{-1}}
```

In this case the "." specifier has no arguments; the normal dot is used in both input and output, and the typeset entries should be centered on the dot.

```
\newcolumntype{,}{D{,}{,}{2}}
```

The "," specifier defined here uses the comma "," as a decimal separator in both input and output, and the typeset column should have (at most) two decimal places after the comma.

    These definitions are used in the following example, where it can be noted that the first column, with its negative value for *decimal places* (signaling that the decimal point should be in the center of the column) is wider than the second column, although they both contain the same input material.

1·2	1·2	1.2	1,2
1·23	1·23	12.5	300,2
1121·2	1121·2	861.20	674,29
184	184	10	69
·4	·4		,4
		.4	

```
\begin{tabular}{|d{-1}|d{2}|.|.,|}
   1.2   & 1.2   &1.2      &1,2      \\
   1.23  & 1.23  &12.5     &300,2  \\
   1121.2& 1121.2&861.20   &674,29 \\
   184   & 184   &10       &69       \\
   .4    & .4    &         &,4       \\
         &       &.4       &         
\end{tabular}
```

($\mathcal{L}$ 182)   The following is a variant of an example in the LaTeX book.

GG&A Hoofed Stock			
	Price		
Year	low–high	Comments	Other
1971	97–245	Bad year for farmers in the West.	23,45
72	245–245	Light trading due to a heavy winter.	435,23
73	245–2001	No gnus was very good gnus this year.	387,56

```
\newcolumntype{+}{D{/}{\mbox{--}}{4}}
% Separator will be a / and ,
\begin{tabular}{|r||+|p{2cm}|,|}   \hline
\multicolumn{4}{|c|}{GG\&A Hoofed Stock}
   \\ \hline\hline
& \multicolumn{1}{c|}{Price}& &
   \\ \cline{2-2} \multicolumn{1}{|c||}{Year}
& \mbox{low}/\mbox{high}
& \multicolumn{1}{c}{Comments}
& \multicolumn{1}{c|}{Other}     \\ \hline
1971 & 97/245  &Bad year for farmers in
      the West. & 23,45          \\ \hline
  72 &245/245  &Light trading due to a
      heavy winter.   & 435,23\\ \hline
  73 &245/2001 &No gnus was very good
      gnus this year. & 387,56\\ \hline
\end{tabular}
```

5.5.2   hhline—Combining Horizontal and Vertical Lines

The hhline package file (by David Carlisle) introduces the command \hhline, which behaves like \hline except for its interaction with vertical lines.

\hhline{*decl*}

    The declaration *decl* consists of a list of tokens with the following meanings:

=   A double \hline the width of a column.

-   A single \hline the width of a column.

~   A column without \hline, i.e., a space the width of a column.

| A \vline that "cuts" through a double (or single) \hline.

:   A \vline that is broken by a double \hline.

A double \hline segment between two \vlines.

t   The top rule of a double \hline segment.

b   The bottom rule of a double \hline segment.

*   *{3}{==#} expands to ==#==#==#, as in the * form for the preamble.

If a double \vline is specified (|| or ::), then the \hlines produced by \hhline are broken. To obtain the effect of an \hline "cutting through" the double \vline, use a #.

The tokens t and b can be used between two vertical rules. For instance, |tb| produces the same lines as #, but is much less efficient. The main use for these are to make constructions like |t: (top left corner) and :b| (bottom right corner).

If \hhline is used to make a single \hline, then the argument should only contain the tokens "-", "~", and "|" (and * expressions).

An example using most of these features is:

```
\setlength{\arrayrulewidth}{.8pt}
\begin{tabular}{||cc||c|c||}
                \hhline{|t:==:t:==:t|}
a & b & c & d \\ \hhline{|:==:|~|~||}
1 & 2 & 3 & 4 \\ \hhline{#==#~|=#}
i & j & k & l \\ \hhline{||--||--||}
w & x & y & z \\ \hhline{|b:==:b:==:b|}
\end{tabular}
```

The lines produced by \hline consist of a single (TEX primitive) \hrule. The lines produced by \hhline are made up of lots of small line segments. TEX will place these very accurately in the .dvi file, but the dvi driver used to view or print the output might not line up the segments exactly. If this effect causes a problem you can try increasing \arrayrulewidth to reduce the effect.

5.6 Applications

The following examples involve somewhat more complex placement require-ments, allowing advanced functions such as the provision of nested tables. Here, we will put to work many of the features described in this chapter.

5.6.1   Hyphenation in Narrow Columns

TeX does not hyphenate the first word in a paragraph, so very narrow cells can produce overflows. This is corrected by starting the text with \hspace{0pt}.

<table>
<tr><td>Characteristics</td><td>Char-
acteris-
tics</td><td>

```
\fbox{\parbox{11mm}{Characteristics}}
\hfill
\fbox{\parbox{11mm}%
        {\hspace{0pt}Characteristics}}
```

</td></tr>
</table>

5.6.2   Footnotes in Tabular Material

As already stated in section 3.4.1 footnotes appearing inside tabular material are not typeset by standard LaTeX. Only the tabularx and longtable environments, discussed earlier, will treat footnotes correctly.

As you generally want your "table notes" to appear just below the table, you will have to tackle the problem yourself by managing the note marks and by, for instance, using \multicolumn commands at the bottom of your tabular environment to contain your table notes.

You can also put your tabular or array environment inside a minipage environment, since in that case footnotes are typeset just following that environment. Note the redefinition of \thefootnote that allows us to make use of the \footnotemark command inside the minipage environment. Without this redefinition \footnotemark would have generated a footnote mark in the style of the footnotes for the main page, as explained in section 3.4.1.

PostScript type 1 fonts	
Courier[a]	cour, courb, courbi, couri
Charter[b]	bchb, bchbi, bchr, bchri
Nimbus[c]	unmr, unmrs
URW Antiqua[c]	uaqrrc
URW Grotesk[c]	ugqp
Utopia[d]	putb, putbi, putr, putri

[a]Donated by IBM.
[b]Donated by Bitstream.
[c]Donated by URW GmbH.
[d]Donated by Adobe.

```
\begin{minipage}{\linewidth}
\renewcommand{\thefootnote}{\thempfootnote}
\begin{tabular}{ll}
\multicolumn{2}{c}{\bfseries PostScript
                type 1 fonts}  \\
Courier\footnote{Donated by IBM.}
     & cour, courb, courbi, couri    \\
Charter\footnote{Donated by Bitstream.}
     & bchb, bchbi, bchr, bchri      \\
Nimbus\footnote{Donated by URW GmbH.}
     & unmr, unmrs                   \\
URW Antiqua\footnotemark[\value{mpfootnote}]
     & uaqrrc                        \\
URW Grotesk\footnotemark[\value{mpfootnote}]
     & ugqp                          \\
Utopia\footnote{Donated by Adobe.}
     & putb, putbi, putr, putri
\end{tabular}
\end{minipage}
```

Of course this approach does not automatically limit the width of the footnotes to the width of the table, so a little iteration with the `minipage` width argument might be necessary.

Another way to typeset table notes is with the package threeparttable by Donald Arseneau. This package has the advantage that it indicates unambiguously that you are dealing with notes inside tables and, moreover, it gives you full control of the actual reference marks and offers the possibility of having a caption for your tabular material. In this sense, the threeparttable environment is similar to the nonfloating `table` environment setup described in section 6.3.1.

Table 5.9: **PostScript type 1 fonts**

Courier[a]	cour, courb, courbi, couri
Charter[b]	bchb, bchbi, bchr, bchri
Nimbus[c]	unmr, unmrs
URW Antiqua[c]	uaqrrc
URW Grotesk[c]	ugqp
Utopia[d]	putb, putbi, putr, putri

[a]Donated by IBM.
[b]Donated by Bitstream.
[c]Donated by URW GmbH.
[d]Donated by Adobe.

```
\begin{threeparttable}
\caption[Example of a \nxLenv{threeparttable}
    environment]{\textbf{PostScript type 1 fonts}}
\begin{tabular}{@{}ll@{}}
Courier\tnote{a} & cour, courb, courbi, couri  \\
Charter\tnote{b} & bchb, bchbi, bchr, bchri    \\
Nimbus\tnote{c}  & unmr, unmrs                 \\
URW Antiqua\tnote{c} & uaqrrc                  \\
URW Grotesk\tnote{c} & ugqp                    \\
Utopia\tnote{d}      & putb, putbi, putr, putri\\
\end{tabular}
\begin{tablenotes}
\item[a] Donated by IBM.
\item[b] Donated by Bitstream.
\item[c] Donated by URW GmbH.
\item[d] Donated by Adobe.
\end{tablenotes}
\end{threeparttable}
```

5.6.3 Managing Tables with Wide Entries

Sometimes it is necessary to balance white space in narrow columns uniformly over the complete width of the table. For instance, the following table has a rather wide first row, followed by a series of narrow columns.

this-is-a-rather-long-row		
C1	C2	C3
2.1	2.2	2.3
3.1	3.2	3.3

```
\begin{tabular}{ccc}
\multicolumn{3}{c}{this-is-a-rather-long-row}\\
C1 &C2 &C3 \\ 2.1&2.2&2.3 \\ 3.1&3.2&3.3
\end{tabular}
```

You can put some rubber length in front of each column with the help of the `\extracolsep` command. The actual value of the rubber length is not important, as long as it can shrink enough to just fill the needed space. In this case you must of course specify a total width for the table.

this-is-a-rather-long-row		
C1	C2	C3
2.1	2.2	2.3
3.1	3.2	3.3

```
\begin{tabular*}{\linewidth}%
         {!{\extracolsep{4in minus 4in}}ccc}
\multicolumn{3}{c}{this-is-a-rather-long-row}\\
C1 &C2 &C3 \\ 2.1&2.2&2.3 \\ 3.1&3.2&3.3
\end{tabular*}
```

In the preceding example we did not have a lot of success, since the entries are spread out too much. We can, however, precalculate the width of the wide entry and specify it as the total width of the `tabular*`.

this-is-a-rather-long-row		
C1	C2	C3
2.1	2.2	2.3
3.1	3.2	3.3

```
\newlength{\Mylen}
\settowidth{\Mylen}{this-is-a-rather-long-row}
\begin{tabular*}{\Mylen}%
         {!{\extracolsep{4in minus 4in}}ccc}
\multicolumn{3}{c}{this-is-a-rather-long-row}\\
C1 &C2 &C3 \\ 2.1&2.2&2.3 \\ 3.1&3.2&3.3
\end{tabular*}
```

The result is already quite acceptable, but to achieve correct alignment we need to take into account the column separation (`\tabcolsep`) on both sides of an entry. We can obtain an even better alignment by adequately choosing the column alignments and inter-column spaces.

this-is-a-rather-long-row		
C1	C2	C3
2.1	2.2	2.3
3.1	3.2	3.3

```
\settowidth{\Mylen}{this-is-a-rather-long-row}
\addtolength{\Mylen}{2\tabcolsep}
\begin{tabular*}{\Mylen}%
         {!{\extracolsep{4in minus 4in}}ccc}
\multicolumn{3}{c}{this-is-a-rather-long-row}\\
C1 &C2 &C3 \\ 2.1&2.2&2.3 \\ 3.1&3.2&3.3
\end{tabular*}
```

Alternatively we can suppress the inter-column spaces at the left and right of the `tabular*` by using `@{}` expressions.

this-is-a-rather-long-row		
C1	C2	C3
2.1	2.2	2.3
3.1	3.2	3.3

```
\settowidth{\Mylen}{this-is-a-rather-long-row}
\begin{tabular*}{\Mylen}%
         {@{\extracolsep{4in minus 4in}}ccc@{}}
\multicolumn{3}{@{}c@{}}{this-is-a-rather-long-row}\\
C1 &C2 &C3 \\ 2.1&2.2&2.3 \\ 3.1&3.2&3.3
\end{tabular*}
```

5.6.4 Columns Spanning Multiple Rows

You can simulate a cell spanning a few rows vertically by putting the material in a zero-height box and raising it.

100	qqq	
	A	B
20000000	10	10

```
\begin{tabular}{|c|c|c|}                    \hline
        & \multicolumn{2}{c|}{qqq}\\\cline{2-3}
\raisebox{1.5ex}[0cm][0cm]{100}
        & A          & B              \\\hline
20000000 & 10          & 10             \\\hline
\end{tabular}
```

multirow—**Vertical Alignment in Tables**

The package file multirow (unknown author) automates the procedure of constructing tables with columns spanning several rows by defining a \multirow command. Fine-tuning is possible by specifying optional arguments. This can be useful when any of the spanned rows are unusually large, if \strut's are used asymetrically about the centerline of spanned rows, or when descenders are not taken into account correctly. In these cases the vertical centering may not come out right, and the fixup argument *vmove* can then be used to introduce vertical shifts by hand.

> \multirow{*nrow*}[*njot*]{*width*}[*vmove*]{*contents*}

Inside array, this command is somewhat less useful since the lines have an extra \jot of space (a length, by default equal to 3pt, which is used for opening up displays), which \multirow does not account for. Fixing this (in general) is almost impossible, but a semiautomatic fix is to set the length parameter \bigstrutjot to \jot, and then use the second argument *njot* of \multirow with a value equal to half the number of rows spanned.

You have some ability to control the formatting within cells. Just before the text to be typeset is expanded, the \multirowsetup macro is executed to set up any special environment. Initially, \multirowsetup contains just \raggedright, but it can be redefined with \renewcommand.

The \multirow command works in one or more columns, as shown in the example below.

	C2a		C4a
Text in	C2b	Text in	C4b
column 1	C2c	column 3	C4c
	C2d		C4d

```
\begin{tabular}{|l|l|l|l|}   \hline
\multirow{4}{14mm}{Text in column 1}
    & C2a & \multirow{4}{14mm}%
            {Text in column 3}
                    & C4a       \\
    & C2b &         & C4b       \\
    & C2c &         & C4c       \\
    & C2d &         & C4d       \\\hline
\end{tabular}
```

You are now in a position to typeset the small example shown at the beginning of this section without having to use the \raisebox command. First you must change the alignment inside the \multirow paragraph to \centering and then calculate the width of the text in the column, which is required by the \multirow command. If the column with the spanned rows has a fixed width, like in our other examples, this step is unnecessary.

100	qqq	
	A	B
20000000	10	10

```
\renewcommand{\multirowsetup}{\centering}
\newlength{\LL} \settowidth{\LL}{100}
\begin{tabular}{|c|c|c|}                    \hline
\multirow{2}{\LL}{100}&
       \multicolumn{2}{c|}{qqq}     \\\cline{2-3}
                    & A         & B     \\\hline
20000000            & 10        & 10 \\\hline
\end{tabular}
```

The effect of the optional vertical positioning parameter *vmove* can be seen below. Note the effect of the upward move by 3 mm of the lower third of the table.

Common text in column 1	Column g2a
	Column g2b
	Column g2c
	Column g2d
Common text in column 1	Column g2a
	Column g2b
	Column g2c
	Column g2d
Common text in column 1	Column g2a
	Column g2b
	Column g2c
	Column g2d

```
\begin{tabular}{|l|l|}
\hline
\multirow{4}{25mm}{Common text in column 1}
& Column g2a \\\cline{2-2} & Column g2b\\\cline{2-2}
& Column g2c \\\cline{2-2} & Column g2d\\\hline
\multirow{4}{25mm}[-3mm]{Common text in column 1}
& Column g2a \\\cline{2-2} & Column g2b\\\cline{2-2}
& Column g2c \\\cline{2-2} & Column g2d\\\hline
\multirow{4}{25mm}[3mm]{Common text in column 1}
& Column g2a \\\cline{2-2} & Column g2b\\\cline{2-2}
& Column g2c \\\cline{2-2} & Column g2d\\\hline
\end{tabular}
```

5.6.5 Tables Inside Tables

The example below shows how, with a little bit of extra effort, you can construct complex table layouts with LaTeX.

The family of tabular environments allows vertical positioning with respect to the baseline of the text in which the environment appears. By default the environment appears centered, but this can be changed to align with the first or last line in the environment by supplying a t or b value to the optional position argument. However, this does not work when the first or last element in the

environment is a \hline command—in that case the environment is aligned at
the horizontal rule.

Tables with no versus tables
hline
commands
used.

| with some |
| hline |
| commands |

```
Tables
\begin{tabular}[t]{l}
  with no\\ hline \\ commands \\ used
\end{tabular} versus tables
\begin{tabular}[t]{|l|}
  \hline
  with some \\ hline \\ commands \\
  \hline
\end{tabular} used.
```

To achieve proper alignments in such a case you can make use of two special versions of \hline, which can be defined in a package file. The variable
\@arstrutbox is a strut corresponding to the material in a cell of the table.

```
\newlength{\backup} \newlength{\extratabsurround}
\newcommand\firsthline{\multicolumn{1}{c}{\global\backup\ht\@arstrutbox
   \global\advance\backup\dp\@arstrutbox
%%%% Done locally to get restored to correct value for backup in \\
   \advance\backup\extratabsurround
%%%% This will give some extratab space above the line
   \rule{0pt}{\backup}}\\[-\backup]\hline}
%%%% this will provide for the same space below
\newcommand\lasthline{\hline\multicolumn{1}{c}{}
   \global\backup-\ht\@arstrutbox            %%%% this time globally
   \global\advance\backup\extratabsurround\\[\backup]}
```

Using \firsthline and \lasthline will cure the problem, and the tables will
align properly as long as their first or last line does not contain extremely large
objects.

Tables with no versus tables
line
commands
used.

| with some |
| line |
| commands |

```
Tables
\begin{tabular}[t]{l}
  with no\\ line \\ commands \\ used
\end{tabular} versus tables
\begin{tabular}[t]{|l|}
  \firsthline
  with some \\ line    \\ commands \\
  \lasthline
\end{tabular} used.
```

The implementation of these two commands contains an extra dimension,
which is called \extratabsurround, to add some additional space at the top and

the bottom of such an environment. This is helpful for properly aligning nested tabular material, as shown in the following example:

name	*telephone*

John	*day* *telephone*
	Wed 5554434
	Mon *time* *telephone*
	     8-10 5520104
	     1-5 2425588

Martin	*telephone* *instructions* 3356677 Mary should answer forwarded message.
Peter	*month* *telephone* Sep-May 5554434 Jun No telephone Jul-Aug 2211456
James	*telephone* *instructions* No telephone Use P.O. Box 007 NY.

This example was produced by the following input:

```
\setlength{\extratabsurround}{2pt}

\begin{tabular}{|cc|}                                        \hline
\textit{name} & \textit{telephone}                  \\\hline\hline
    John &
      \begin{tabular}[t]{|cc|}                         \firsthline
      \textit{day} & \multicolumn{1}{c|}{\textit{telephone}}
                                                     \\\hline\hline
      Wed & 5554434                                      \\\hline
      Mon &
        \begin{tabular}[t]{|cc|}                       \firsthline
        \textit{time} & \textit{telephone}       \\\hline\hline
        8--10 & 5520104 \\ 1--5 & 2425588           \\\lasthline
        \end{tabular}                               \\\lasthline
    \end{tabular}                                        \\\hline
Martin    &
```

```
    \begin{tabular}[t]{|cp{4.5cm}|}                        \firsthline
    \textit{telephone} & \multicolumn{1}{c|}{\textit{instructions}}
                                                            \\\hline\hline
    3356677 & Mary should answer forwarded message.    \\\lasthline
    \end{tabular}                                           \\\hline
  Peter   &
    \begin{tabular}[t]{|cl|}                               \firsthline
    \textit{month} &\multicolumn{1}{c|}{\itshape telephone}
                                                            \\\hline\hline
    Sep--May & 5554434  \\  Jun & No telephone  \\
    Jul--Aug & 2211456  \\                                 \lasthline
    \end{tabular}                                           \\\hline
  James   &
    \begin{tabular}[t]{|cl|}                               \firsthline
    \textit{telephone} & \multicolumn{1}{c|}{\itshape instructions}
                                                            \\\hline\hline
    No telephone &  Use P.O. Box 007 NY.            \\\lasthline
    \end{tabular}                                     \\\lasthline
\end{tabular}
```

5.6.6 Two More Examples

The LaTeX code below shows how you can combine various techniques and packages described earlier in this chapter. We have used the package tabularx to generate a twelve-column table with columns 3 to 12 of equal width. We used the package multirow to generate the stub head, "Prefix," which spans two rows in column 1. In order to position the stub head properly, we must calculate the width of the title beforehand.

```
\setlength{\tabcolsep}{1mm}
\newlength{\Tl}\settowidth{\Tl}{Prefix}
\newcommand{\T}[1]{$10^{#1}$}
\begin{tabularx}{\linewidth}{|l|l|*{10}{>{\small}X|}}   \hline
\multicolumn{12}{|c|}{\textbf{Prefixes used in the SI system of units}}  \\\hline
\multicolumn{2}{|c|}{Factor} &
\T{24} &\T{21} &\T{18} &\T{15} &\T{12} &\T{9} &\T{6} &\T{3} &\T{2} &\T{ }\\\cline{1-2}
\multirow{2}{\Tl}{Prefix}&Name    &
yotta &zetta &exa    &peta    &tera    &giga  &mega  &kilo  &hecto &deca \\
                &Symbol &
Y       &Z      &E      &P       &T       &G     &M     &k     &h     &da    \\\hline
\multirow{2}{\Tl}{Prefix}&Symbol &
y       &z      &a      &f       &p       &n     &$\mu$ &m     &c     &d     \\
                &Name   &
yocto &zepto &atto   &femto   &pico    &nano  &micro &milli &centi &deci \\\cline{1-2}
\multicolumn{2}{|c|}{Factor} &
\T{-24}&\T{-21}&\T{-18}&\T{-15}&\T{-12}&\T{-9}&\T{-6}&\T{-3}&\T{-2}&\T{-1}\\\hline
\end{tabularx}
```

Prefixes used in the SI system of units										
Factor		10^{24}	10^{21}	10^{18}	10^{15}	10^{12}	10^{9}	10^{6}	10^{3}	10^{2}	10
Prefix	Name	yotta	zetta	exa	peta	tera	giga	mega	kilo	hecto	deca
Prefix	Symbol	Y	Z	E	P	T	G	M	k	h	da
Prefix	Symbol	y	z	a	f	p	n	μ	m	c	d
Prefix	Name	yocto	zepto	atto	femto	pico	nano	micro	milli	centi	deci
Factor		10^{-24}	10^{-21}	10^{-18}	10^{-15}	10^{-12}	10^{-9}	10^{-6}	10^{-3}	10^{-2}	10^{-1}

You can use various other LATEX environments inside a `tabular` environment, as the following example shows.

A picture environment (see page 281)

```
\fbox{\begin{picture}(12,6.3)
    \bezier{200}(2.00,6.00)
    (7.00,6.00)(9.00,3.00)
  ....
\end{picture}}
```

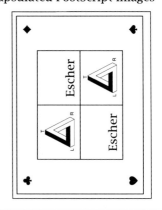

A rotated object (`turn` environment, see figure 11.7 on page 323)

```
\fbox{\begin{turn}{-45}
\fbox{\parbox[b]{13mm}{A b C d E f G h
                I j K l M n P q R}}
      \end{turn}}
```

A rotated `tabular` (see section 11.4.1) with Encapsulated PostScript images

```
\fbox{\begin{turn}{-90}
\begin{tabular}{|ccc|}           \hline
$\clubsuit$& &$\diamondsuit$ \\
&\begin{tabular}{|c|c|}           \hline
 \epsfig{file=Escher.eps,width=10mm}
              & Escher      \\\hline
 Escher &
 \epsfig{file=Escher.eps,width=10mm}
                          \\\hline
 \end{tabular} &           \\
&\heartsuit$ &  & $\spadesuit$\\\hline
\end{tabular}
\end{turn}}
```

CHAPTER 6

Mastering Floats

Documents would be easier to read if all the material that belongs together were never split between pages. However, this is often technically impossible and TeX will, by default, split textual material between two pages to avoid partially filled pages. Nevertheless, when this is not desired (as with figures and tables), the material must be "floated" to a convenient place, such as the bottom or the top of the current or next page, to prevent half-empty pages.

By default, LaTeX provides two floating environments, `figure` and `table`,   (£ 59,60,176–78) whose style parameters are described in section 6.1. Sometimes you may need environments for floating other kinds of objects like computer listings, which are examined in section 6.3. Section 6.4 discusses a few floating environments and subfigures, while section 6.5 explains how to customize captions.

6.1 Understanding Float Parameters

Floats are often problematical in the present version of LaTeX, since the system was developed at a time when the amount of graphical material in a document was considerably less than it is now. Therefore, placing floats (tables and figures) works relatively well as long as the space they occupy is not too large compared with the space taken up by the text. If, however, a lot of floating material is present (lots of pictures or tables) then it is often the case that all material from a certain point onwards floats to the end of the document. If this effect is not desired, you can issue from time to time a `\clearpage` command, which will print all unprocessed floats. You can also try to fine-tune the float style parameters for a given document or use a package which allows you to always

(ℒ 176–78)

print a table or figure where it appears in the document. In the list below "float" stands for a table or a figure and a "float page" is a page that contains only floats and no text. Changes to the parameters will only take effect on the next page (not the current one).

topnumber   Counter specifying maximum number of floats allowed at top of page (the default number is 2). Change with the \setcounter command.

bottomnumber   Counter specifying maximum number of floats allowed at bottom of page (the default number is 1). This can be changed with the \setcounter command.

totalnumber   Counter specifying maximum number of floats allowed on a single page (the default number is 3). This can be changed with \setcounter.

\topfraction   Maximum fraction of the page that can be occupied by floats at the top of the page (e.g., 0.2 means 20% can be floats; the default value is 0.7). This can be changed with \renewcommand.

\bottomfraction   Maximum fraction of the page that can be occupied by floats at the bottom of the page (the default value is 0.3). This can be changed with \renewcommand.

\textfraction   Minimum fraction of a normal page that must be occupied by text (the default value is 0.2). This can be changed with \renewcommand.

\floatpagefraction   Minimum fraction of a float page that must be occupied by floats, thus limiting the amount of blank space allowed on a float page (the default value is 0.5). This can be changed with \renewcommand.

dbltopnumber   Analog of topnumber for double-column floats in two-column style (the default number is 2). This can be changed with the \setcounter command.

\dbltopfraction   Analog of \topfraction for double-column floats on a two-column page (the default value is 0.7). This can be changed with \renewcommand.

\dblfloatpagefraction   Analog of \floatpagefraction for a float page of double-column floats (the default value is 0.5). This can be changed with \renewcommand.

\floatsep   Rubber length specifying the vertical space added between floats appearing at the top or the bottom of a page (default 12pt plus 2pt minus 2pt for 10pt and 11pt document sizes, and 14pt plus 2pt minus 4pt for 12pt document sizes). This can be changed with \setlength.

\textfloatsep   Rubber length specifying the vertical space added between floats, appearing at the top or the bottom of a page, and the text (default 20pt plus 2pt minus 4pt). This can be changed with \setlength.

\intextsep Rubber length specifying the vertical space added below and above a float that is positioned in the middle of text when the h option is given (the default is similar to \floatsep). This can be changed with \setlength.

\dblfloatsep Rubber length which is the analog of \floatsep for double-width floats on a two-column page (the default is like \floatsep). This can be changed with \setlength.

\dbltextfloatsep Rubber length which is the analog of \textfloatsep for double-width floats on a two-column page. (The default is like \textfloatsep on a text page, but it is 8pt plus 2fil on a page that contains only floats.) This can be changed with \setlength.

\topfigrule Command to place a rule or something else between floats at the top of the page and the text. It is executed right before placing the \textfloatsep that separates the floats from the text. Just like the \footnoterule it must not occupy any vertical space.

\botfigrule Same as \topfigrule, but put after the \textfloatsep skip separating text from the floats at bottom of page.

\dblfigrule Similar to \topfigrule, but for double-column floats.

Changing the values of the above parameters lets you modify the behavior of LaTeX's algorithm for placing floats. But for getting better results, you should be aware of the subtle dependencies between the parameters.

If you use the default values in a document you will observe that, with many floats, the formatted document will contain several float pages—pages containing only floats. Often there is a lot of white space on such pages, for example, you may see a page with a single float on it, occupying only half of the possible space, so that it would look better if LaTeX had filled the remaining space with text. The reason for this behavior is that the algorithm is designed to try placing as many dangling floats as possible after the end of every page. The procedure creates as many float pages as it can until there are no more floats to fill a float page. This float page production is controlled by the parameter \floatpagefraction, which specifies the minimum fraction of the page that must be occupied by float(s)—by default, half the page. Since in the standard settings every float is allowed to go on a float page (the default specifier is tbp), this setting means that every float that is a tiny bit larger than half the page is allowed to go on a float page by itself. Thus by enlarging its value you can prevents half-empty float pages. $(\mathcal{L}\ 176)$

However, enlarging the value of \floatpagefraction makes it harder to produce float pages and, as a result, some floats may get deferred, which then in turn prevents other floats from being placed. For this reason it is often better to specify explicitly the allowed placements (for example, by saying \begin{figure}[tb]) for the float producing the problem.

Another common reason for ending up with all floats at the end of your chapter is the use of the bottom placement specifier, [b]. This means that the only acceptable place is at the bottom of a page, and if your float happens to be larger than \bottomfraction (which is by default quite small) then this float cannot be placed. This will also prevent all floats of the same type from being placed. The same happens if only [h] or [t] is specified and the float is too large for the remainder of the page or too large to fit \topfraction.

In calculating these fractions, LaTeX will take into account the separation (i.e., \textfloatsep) between floats and main text. By enlarging this value, you automatically reduce the maximum size a float is allowed to have to be placeable at the top or bottom of the page.

In general, whenever a lot of your floats end up at the end of the chapter, look at the first of them to see if their placement specifiers are preventing them from being properly placed.

6.2   Improved Float Control

The float placement algorithm prefers to put floats at the top of the page, even if this means placing them before the actual reference. This is not always acceptable but there is no easy cure for this problem short of substantially changing LaTeX's algorithm. This is done in the **flafter** package (by Frank Mittelbach) which ensures that floats never come before their reference.

Sometimes, however, less drastic solutions might be preferred. For example, if the float belongs to a section that starts in the middle of a page but the float is positioned at the top of the page, it will look as if the float belongs to the previous section. Thus you might want to forbid this behavior while still allowing floats to be placed on the top of the page in other situations. For this LaTeX 2_ε offers you the following command.

> \suppressfloats[*placement*]

The optional argument *placement* can be either t or b. If the command \suppressfloats is placed somewhere in the document, then on this page any following floats for the areas specified by *placement* are deferred to a later page. If no *placement* parameter is given all further floats on this page are deferred. Thus, if you want to prevent floats from moving backward over section boundaries you can define your section commands in the following way:

```
\newcommand{\section}{\suppressfloats[t]%
                \@startsection{section}{..}{..}{..} ...
                }
```

Possible arguments to \@startsection are discussed in section 2.3.2.

Another way to influence the placement of floats in LaTeX 2_ε is to specify a ! in conjunction with the placement specifiers h, t, b. The placement of floats on float pages is not affected. This means that for this float alone, restrictions given by the settings of the parameters described before (e.g., \textfraction) are ignored. Thus, such a float can be placed in the designated areas as long as neither of the following two restrictions is violated:

- the float fits on the current page, i.e., its height plus the material already contributed to the page does not exceed \textheight;
- there are no deferred floats of the same type.

All other restrictions normally active (such as the number of floats allowed on a page, etc.) are ignored. For example, if you specify [!b] this float can be placed on the bottom of the page even if it is larger than the maximum size specified by \bottomfraction. Also, any \suppressfloats commands are ignoreed whilst processing this float.

Please remember that the order of the given specifiers is irrelevant and that all specifiers should be given at most once. For example, [bt] is the same as [tb] and thus does *not* instruct LATEX to try to place the float at the bottom and only then try to place it on the top. LATEX always uses the following order of tests until an allowed placement is found.

1. If ! is specified, ignore most restrictions as described above and continue.
2. If h is specified, try to place the float at the exact position. If this fails and no other position was specified, change the specifier to t (for a possible placement on the next page).
3. If t is specified, try to place it on the top of the current page.
4. If b is specified, try to place it on the bottom of the current page.
5. If p is specified, try to place it on a float page (or float column) when the current page (or column) has ended.
6. Stages 3 and 4 are repeated if necessary at the beginning of each subsequent page, followed by 5 at its end.

The afterpage package (by David Carlisle) implements a command \afterpage that causes the commands specified in its argument to be expanded after the current page is output.

This package can be used in the situations described below.

- Sometimes LATEX's float positioning mechanism gets overloaded, and all floating figures and tables drift to the end of the document. You may flush out all the unprocessed floats by issuing a \clearpage command, but this has the effect of making the current page end prematurely. The present package allows you to issue the command \afterpage{\clearpage}. This will let the current page be filled with text (as usual), but then a \clearpage command will flush out all the floats before the next text page begins.
- With the multipage longtable environment (see section 5.4.2), you can experience problems when typesetting the text surrounding the long table,

and it might be interesting to "float" the `longtable`. However, since the latter can be several pages long, it might prove impossible to hold them in memory and float them in the way that the `table` environment is floated. Nevertheless, if the table is in a separate file, say `ltfile.tex`, you can now use one of:

```
\afterpage{\clearpage\input{ltfile}}
\afterpage{\clearpage\input{ltfile}\clearpage}
```

The first form lets text appear on the same page at the end of the `longtable`, and the second ensures that the surrounding text starts again on a new page.

- You can also combine `\afterpage` with the float package and the [H] placement specifier, as explained at the end of section 6.3.

Note that the `\afterpage` command does not work in twocolumn mode.

6.3 float—Creating New Float Types

The float package (by Anselm Lingnau) improves the interface for defining floating objects such as figures and tables in LATEX. It adds the notion of a "float style" that governs the appearance of floats. New kinds of floats may be defined using a `\newfloat` command.

`\newfloat{`*type*`}{`*placement*`}{`*ext*`}[`*within*`]`

The `\newfloat` command takes four arguments, three obligatory and one optional with the following meaning:

type The "type" of the new class of floats, like `program` or `algorithm`. After the appropriate `\newfloat`, commands such as `\begin{program}` or `\end{algorithm*}` will be available.

placement The default placement parameters for the given class of floats. They are, like in standard LATEX: t, b, p, and h for `top`, `bottom`, `page`, and `here`, respectively. On top of that, there is a new type, H, which does not really correspond to a float, since it means: put it "here" and nowhere else. Note, however, that the H specifier is special and, because of implementation details cannot be used in the second argument to `\newfloat`. In other words, you cannot define a new float class that is placed by default "here."

ext The file name extension of an auxiliary file for the list of figures (or whatever). LATEX writes the captions to this file.

within This (optional) argument determines whether floats of this class will be numbered within some sectional unit of the document. For example, if *within* is equal to `chapter`, the floats will be numbered within chapters. (In standard LaTeX, this happens with figures and tables in the report and book document classes.)

> \floatstyle{*style*}

The \floatstyle command sets a default float style. This will be used for all the floats that are subsequently defined using \newfloat, until another \floatstyle command appears. See \restylefloat below for redefining the style of the figure and table floats. The \floatstyle command takes one argument: the name of a float style, such as \floatstyle{ruled}. Specifying a string that does not name a valid float style produces an error message. The *style* argument can be one of the following:

plain   This is the float style that LaTeX normally applies to its floats, i.e., nothing in particular. The only difference is that the caption comes out below the body of the float, regardless of where it is given in the text.

boxed   The body of the float is surrounded by a box. The caption is printed below that box.

ruled   This float style is patterned after the table style of *Concrete Mathematics* [22]. The caption is printed at the top of the float, surrounded by rules; another rule finishes off the float.

> \floatname{*float*}{*floatname*}

The \floatname command defines the name that LaTeX uses in the caption of a float, that is, "Figure" for a figure and so on. For example, \floatname{program}{Program}. By default, the \newfloat command sets the float name to its argument *type* if no other name was specified afterwards.

> \floatplacement{*float*}{*placement*}

The \floatplacement command defines the default placement specifier for the given float class, for example, \floatplacement{figure}{tp}.

> \restylefloat{*float*}

A \restylefloat command is necessary to change styles for the standard float types, figure and table. Since these aren't usually defined by \newfloat, they do not have a style associated with them. Thus, to typeset tables using the ruled float style, you would have to say:

```
\floatstyle{ruled}
\restylefloat{table}
```

This document shows some of the possibilities of float.sty for floating objects.

Program 1.2.1 A simple C++ Program.

```
#include <stream.h>
main(int argc,char #argv[])// get arguments
{
    double sum = 0        // declare variable
    for (int i = 1; i < argc; i++)
       sum += atof(argv[i]); // convert args
    cout << "average=" << sum/argc;
}
```

$$\frac{\sin z}{z} = 1 - \frac{z^2}{3!} + \frac{z^4}{5!} \cdots$$

$$\cos z = 1 - \frac{z^2}{2!} + \frac{z^4}{4!} \cdots$$

Algorithm 1: Trigonometric Expansions.

```
\documentclass{article}
\usepackage{float,times}
\thispagestyle{empty}
\floatstyle{ruled}
\newfloat{Program}{thp}{lop}[section]
\floatstyle{boxed}
\newfloat{algorithm}{thp}{loa}
\floatname{algorithm}{Algorithm}
\begin{document}
This document shows some of the
possibilities of \texttt{float.sty}
for floating objects.
\begin{Program}
\begin{verbatim}
#include <stdio.h>
int main(int argc, char **argv)
{ int i;
   for (i = 0; i < argc; ++i)
     printf("argv[%d] = %s\n", i, argv[i]);
   return 0;                          }
\end{verbatim}
\caption{The  program.}
\end{Program}
...
```

Figure 6.1: Defining two "nonstandard" floats—Program and algorithm

This command also lets you change style for floats that were defined via \newfloat, although this is, typographically speaking, not a good idea.

> \listof{*type*}{*title*}

The \listof command produces a list of all the floats of a given class. The first parameter, *type*, specifies the type of the float as given in the \newfloat command. The second argument, *title*, determines the text of the title that will be used to head the list of the information associated with the float elements, as specified by the \caption commands. The \listof command is analogous to the built-in LaTeX commands \listoffigures and \listoftables.

Figure 6.1 is an example of the definition of two "nonstandard" floats—Program and algorithm.

6.3.1 I Want My Float "Here"!

Sometimes you will find that LaTeX's float placement specifiers are too restrictive. You may want to place a float exactly at the spot where it occurs in the input file, that is, you do not want it to float at all. It is a common misunderstanding that specifying [h] means "here and nowhere else." Actually, that specifier only directs LaTeX to *try* to place the float at the current position. If there is not enough room left on the page or if an in-line placement is forbidden because of the settings of the style parameters (see section 6.1) then LaTeX ignores this request and tries to place the float according to any other specifier given. Thus, if [ht] is specified, it means that the float will appear on the top of some later page if it does not fit onto the current one. This can happen quite often if the floats you try to place in the middle of your text are moderately large and are thus likely to fall into positions where there is not enough space on the page for them. By ignoring an h and trying other placement specifiers, LaTeX avoids overly empty pages that would otherwise arise in such situations. However, in some cases you might prefer to leave large gaps on your pages, and for this reason the package **float** provides you with an [H] specifier that means "put the float here"—period.

If there is not enough space left on the current page, the float will be printed at the top of the next page together with whatever follows, even if there is still room left on the current page. It is up to you to place your H floats in such a way so that you do not obtain large patches of white space at the bottom of a page. When you mix standard and [H] placement parameters, a float with a [t] specifier (for example) that appears before one with an [H] specifier in the input file might be incorrectly positioned after the latter in the typeset output, so that—for instance—figure 4 would precede figure 3.

Note that the [H] specifier cannot be used in conjunction with the other placement specifiers. Consequently, a combination like [Hht] would be illegal. [H] also cannot be used as the default placement specifier for a whole class of floats. To summarize, all the float placement specifiers are shown together in the following example of an H table.

t	Top of page	b	Bottom of page
p	Page of floats	h	Here, if possible
H	Here, always		

Table 6.1: Float placement specifiers of the **float** package

```
\begin{table}[H]
\begin{tabular}{*2{>{\ttfamily}cl}}
  t & Top of page   & b & Bottom of page  \\
  p & Page of floats  & h & Here, if possible \\
  H & Here, always
\end{tabular}
\caption{Float placement specifiers
         of the \nxLpack{float} package}
\end{table}
```

Another important point is that, by default, the **float** package does not modify the standard `figure` and `table` environments (unlike David Carlisle's now obsolete here package). Thus, if you want to use the [H] qualifier with these environments, you must first issue `\restylefloat{figure}` and/or `\restylefloat{table}` commands.

Together with the `afterpage` package described in section 6.2, you can get an even finer control on the placement of your floats. Indeed, in some cases, although you specify the placement parameter as [H], you do not really mean "at this point," but "somewhere close." You can achieve this using the `\afterpage` command as follows:

```
\afterpage{\clearpage\begin{figure}[H]...\end{figure}}
```

This ensures that the figure is at the top of the next page. It also solves the sequencing problem, described above, since `\clearpage` stops any other figures from drifting past the [H] figure.

6.4 Different Kinds of Floating Environments

6.4.1 floatfig—Narrow Floating Figures

The floatfig package file (by Thomas J. Reid [71]) sets floating figures that do not fill the full width of the page.

```
\begin{floatingfigure}{width}
```

If the width of such figures is only part of the page width, text lines can be set beside the figures. The floatfig package is fully compatible with LaTeX's standard `figure` facility:

1. Floating figures and standard figures may be requested in any sequence.
2. Floating figures can be captioned like standard figures.
3. Captioned floating figures are inserted in the list of figures, which may be printed by the standard `\listoffigures` command.

The `floatingfigure` environment can only be used in vertical mode, i.e., between paragraphs. The floating figure will be set as soon as possible after its request has been encountered. That means that LaTeX will test whether there is enough vertical space on the current page. If the answer is negative, the figure moves to the next page. Floating figures are set alternately: i.e., on the right side of odd-numbered pages and on the left side of even-numbered pages. Figure 6.2 on the next page shows how the `floatingfigure` environment is used.

Note that the floatfig package may not be combined with the twocolumn option and that the floating figure will never appear in a paragraph that starts at the top of a page.

---

1   Aeneid Book One

ARMA virumque cano, Troiae qui primus ab oris Italiam, fato profugus, Laviniaque venit litora, multum ille et terris iactatus et alto vi superum saevae memorem Iunonis ob iram; multa quoque et bello passus, dum conderet urbem, inferretque deos Latio, genus unde Latinum, Albanique patres, atque altae moenia Romae.

Musa, mihi causas memora, quo numine laeso, quidve dolens, regina deum tot volvere casus insignem pietate virum, tot adire labores impulerit. Tantaene animis caelestibus irae?

Urbs antiqua fuit, Tyrii tenuere coloni, Karthago, Italiam contra Tiberinaque longe ostia, dives opum studiisque asperrima belli; quam Iuno fertur terris magis omnibus unam posthabita coluisse Samo; hic illius arma, hic currus fuit; hoc regnum dea gentibus esse, si qua fata sinant, iam tum tenditque fovetque. Progeniem sed enim Troiano a sanguine duci audierat, Tyrias olim quae verteret arces; hinc populum late regem belloque superbum venturum excidio

Figure 1: The Mediterranean area

Libyae: sic volvere Parcas. Id metuens, veterisque memor Saturnia belli, prima quod ad Troiam pro caris gesserat Argis— necdum etiam causae irarum saevique dolores exciderant animo: manet alta mente repostum iudicium Paridis spretaeque iniuria formae, et genus invisum, et rapti Ganymedis honores. His accensa super, iactatos aequore toto Troas, reliquias Danaum atque immitis Achilli, arcebat longe Latio, multosque per annos errabant, acti fatis, maria omnia circum. Tantae molis erat Romanam condere gentem!

Vix e conspectu Siculae telluris in altum vela dabant laeti, et spumas salis aere ruebant, cum Iuno, aeternum servans sub pectore volnus, haec secum: 'Mene incepto desistere victam, nec posse Italia Teucrorum avertere regem? Quippe vetor fatis. Pallasne exurere classem Argivom atque ipsos potuit submergere ponto, unius ob noxam et furias Aiacis Oilei? Ipsa,

Float-fig. 2

Figure 2: Caption of the second narrow floating figure

Iovis rapidum iaculata e nubibus ignem, disiecitque rates evertitque aequora ventis, illum expirantem transfixo pectore flammas turbine corripuit scopuloque infixit acuto. Ast ego, quae divom incedo regina, Iovisque et soror et coniunx, una cum gente tot annos bella gero! Et quisquam numen Iunonis adoret praeterea, aut supplex aris imponet honorem?'

Talia flammato secum dea corde volutans nimborum in patriam, loca feta furentibus

1

```
\documentclass{article}
\usepackage{floatfig,epsfig}
\begin{document}
\initfloatingfigs
\section{Aeneid Book One}
\textsc{Arma} virumque cano, ...
..., atque altae moenia Romae.
\par
\begin{floatingfigure}{6cm}
\mbox{\epsfig{file=Mediterranean.eps}}
\caption{The Mediterranean area}
\end{floatingfigure}
\quad Musa, mihi causas ...
...erat Romanam condere gentem!
\par
\begin{floatingfigure}{7cm}
\fbox{\parbox{66mm}{\rule[-2cm]{0mm}{4cm}%
\hfil        Float-fig. 2}}
\caption{Caption of the second narrow
floating figure}
\end{floatingfigure}
\quad Vix e conspectu Siculae telluris
in altum  ....
\end{document}
```

Figure 6.2: An example with a narrow floating figure

6.4.2 wrapfig—**Wrapping Text around a Figure**

The package file wrapfig (by Donald Arseneau) defines the wrapfigure environment. This environment allows a figure to be placed manually at the side of the page and wraps text around it.

`\begin{wrapfigure}[`*nlines*`]{`*placement*`}{`*width*`}`

The wrapfigure environment takes two mandatory and one optional argument with the following meaning:

nlines   (optional argument) defining the number of narrow lines. Each display equation counts as three lines.

placement   horizontal placement (l for left and r for right).

width   width of the figure.

The paragraph below, which is illustrated in figure 6.3, is preceded with the following commands:

```
\begin{wrapfigure}{r}{3in}
\begin{boxit}
  \begin{center} This is a ``wrapfigure.'' \end{center}
  \caption{A wrapfigure example}
\end{boxit}
\end{wrapfigure}
%%
wrapfigure is a different type of \emph{nonfloating} figure...
```

wrapfigure is a different type of *nonfloating* figure environment for LaTeX. A figure of the specified width will appear on either the left or right of the page. LaTeX

> This is a "wrapfigure."
>
> Figure 6.3: A wrapfigure example

will try to wrap text around the figure leaving a gap of \columnsep by producing a number of short lines of text. The number of short lines is based upon the height of the figure plus the length \intextsep. You can override this guess by specifying the optional argument.

Note that wrapfigure should not be used inside another environment (e.g., list), but it does work in twocolumn page layout. Since it does not float, it may be out of sequence with floated figures.

LaTeX will not move a wrapfigure to its optimum place, so it is up to you to position it in the best fashion. Wrapfigures should be positioned just before printing your *final copy*, since any changes to the document can ruin their careful positioning. Here are some rules for good placement:

- The environment should be placed so as to not run over a page boundary.

- Only ordinary text should have to flow past the figure but not a section title. Equations are acceptable if they fit.

- It is convenient to give \begin{wrapfigure} just after a paragraph has ended. If you want to start in the middle of a paragraph, the environment must be placed between two words where there is a natural line break.

6.4.3   subfigure—**Figures inside Figures**

The subfigure package (by Steven Cochran) allows the creation of subfigures, each with its own caption, and it allows an optional global caption under the figure as a whole.

```
\begin{figure}
\centering
\mbox{\subfigure[Big]{\epsfig{figure=elephant.eps,width=.30\textwidth}}\quad
      \subfigure[Medium]{\epsfig{figure=elephant.eps,width=.25\textwidth}}\quad
      \subfigure[Small]{\epsfig{figure=elephant.eps,width=.20\textwidth}}}
\caption{Three subfigures}
\label{fig:subfigures}
\end{figure}
```

(a) Big   (b) Medium   (c) Small

Figure 6.4: Three subfigures

The figure is horizontally centered with \subfigtopskip (default value 10pt) of vertical space added above and \subfigcapskip (default value 10pt) of vertical space added below, followed by the caption. The subfigure is followed by another \subfigtopskip of vertical space added at the bottom.

If a caption is specified between square brackets (including a null caption, []) then the subfigure is labeled with a counter supplied by the macro \thesubfigure (defined by default as (\alph{subfigure})\space}, yielding: "(a) ," "(b) ," etc. If desired, this macro can be redefined. The counter used for labeling the subfigures is subfigure and is incremented for each subfigure regardless of whether a caption was printed.

Figure 6.4 shows how three pictures can be aligned horizontally with a tabular environment. Each subfigure has its own caption, plus the figure as a whole has its global caption. The figure can be referenced in the text through the key specified on the \label command.

6.4.4 endfloat—Place Figures and Tables at the End

Some journals require figures and tables to be separated from the text and grouped at the end of a document. They may also want a list of figures and tables to precede them.

The endfloat package file (by James Darrell McCauley) puts figures and tables by themselves at the end of an article into a section named Figures or Tables.

The list of tables and figures produced at the end of a document can be turned off by putting \nofiglist and \notablist in the preamble.

Notes are left in the text. Thus "[Figure 4 about here.]" indicates approximately where the float would have normally appeared. These notes can be turned off by putting a \nomarkersintext command in the preamble of the document. The text of the notes, which is defined via the strings \figureplace and \tableplace, can be changed with \renewcommand. The default definitions are the following:

```
\newcommand{\figureplace}{% For figures
  \begin{center}[\figurename~\thepostfig\ about here.]\end{center}}
\newcommand{\tableplace}{%  For tables
  \begin{center}[\tablename~\theposttbl\  about here.]\end{center}}
```

The endfloat package file creates two extra files with the extensions .fff and .ttt. If you use this package you may need an extra LaTeX run to resolve changed cross-references due to float movements.

6.5   Customizing Your Captions

When you want to explain what is shown in your floating environment (figure or table in standard LaTeX), you normally use \caption. The \caption command is only defined inside a float environment and, apart from typesetting the text you specify and putting it in the list of figures or tables, it also increments the counter associated with the float in question. The command has the following syntax:

```
\caption[short text]{long text}
```

The optional argument *short text* goes into the list of figures or tables. If only the mandatory argument *long text* is specified then it is the latter that is used in those lists. If the caption is longer than one line, you are strongly advised to use the optional argument to provide a short and informative description of your float. Otherwise, the list of figures and tables will become unreadable and it will be difficult to locate the necessary information.

Internally, \caption invokes the command:

```
\@makecaption{numb}{text}
```

The number for the caption, *numb*, is generated internally depending on the type of float. The argument *text* is the text to be typeset. The default definition for the part doing the typesetting for a caption is something like:

```
\newcommand{\@makecaption}[2]{% #1 is e.g. Figure 1, #2 is caption text
   \vspace{10pt}\sbox{\tempbox}{#1: #2}%
   \ifthenelse{\lengthtest{\wd\tempbox > \linewidth}%
     { #1: #2\par}% More than one line
     {\begin{center}#1: #2\end{center}}%
}
```

After an initial skip of 10pt, the material is typeset in a temporary box
`\tempbox`, and its width is compared to the line width. If the material fits on
one line then the text is centered; if the material does not fit on a line, it will be
typeset as a paragraph with a width equal to the line width.

You can, of course, define other ways of formatting your captions, and
you can even supply different commands for making captions for each of the
different types of floats. For example, the command `\@makefigcaption` can be
used instead of `\@makecaption` to format the captions for a `figure` environment.

```
\newcommand{\@makefigcaption}[2]{....}
\renewcommand{\figure}
     {\let\@makecaption\@makefigcaption\@float{figure}}
```

As an example of a different way of formatting captions, the package
hangcaption (by David Jones) defines `\isucaption` (a variant of the `\caption`
command), which produces captions with a hanging indentation. If the caption
is less than a full line, it will be centered. The length variable `\captionwidth` can
be set to control the width of the caption. The interesting part of the definition,
which can be compared to the code above, is:

```
\newcommand{\@isucaption}[2]{% #1 is e.g. Figure 1, #2 is caption text
  \par\vspace{10pt}\sbox{\tempbox}{#1: #2}%
  \ifthenelse{\lengthtest{\wd\tempbox > \linewidth}%      <> 1 line?
   {\sbox{\tempbox}{#1:\ }%                    Measure text of part 1
    \addtolength{\captionwidth}{-\wd\tempbox} % Subtract from width
    \mbox{#1:\ }\parbox[t]{\captionwidth}{#2}}}%    place two boxes
     {\begin{center}#1: #2\end{center}}%            One line only
}
```

ς

CHAPTER 7

Font Selection

7.1 Introduction to NFSS

(LA)TEX as a typesetting system does half of the job of producing the desired result: from the user's input it calculates positions for characters on a page. But it has only a primitive knowledge about such characters, which it basically regards as black boxes having a width, height, and depth. This information is stored in external files, one for each font, that are called TEX font metric or .tfm files.

The character shapes that correspond to such a .tfm file come into play at a later stage, after (LA)TEX has produced its .dvi file. The character placement information in the .dvi file and the information about the character shapes present in the .pk file or in outline descriptions (e.g., PostScript) are combined by a driver program that produces the image on the output medium. Usually you need one driver program for every output medium—e.g., for screen representation, low resolution laser printer, etc.

When TEX was developed in 1979, only a dozen fonts were set up for use with TEX: the 'Almost Computer Modern' fonts, also developed by Donald Knuth. Since only these fonts were available, a straightforward approach for accessing them was used: a few control sequences were defined that changed from one external font to another.

This situation had not greatly changed much five years later by the time LATEX was first released. Only the names of the fonts supplied with (LA)TEX had changed, from 'Almost Computer Modern' to 'Computer Modern' (which are almost the same as the 'Almost Computer Modern'). So it was quite natural that LATEX's font selection scheme followed the plain TEX concept with the addition of size-changing commands that allowed typesetting in ten predefined sizes.

As a result LaTeX's font selection was far from general. For instance, when defining a heading command to produce a bolder font (by using a `\bf` command in its definition), the use of, say, `\sf` (for a sans serif font) inside such a heading did not produce a bold sans serif font but rather a medium weight sans serif font (the bold attribute was ignored). Similarly, when, say, `\bf` was used inside emphasized text, the result was not a bold italic font, as normally desired, but rather a plain roman bold font.

This behavior was caused by the fact that all the font-changing commands, like `\bf`, referred to a fixed external font and so, rather than requesting an attribute change of the current font, they replaced the current font with another. Of course, LaTeX enhanced the plain TeX mechanism to a certain extent by providing a set of size-changing commands, yet the underlying concept of the original release had a major drawback: the correspondence tables were hard-wired into LaTeX, so that changing the fonts was a difficult if not impossible task.

Since that time, low-priced laser printers have become available and with them a large number of font families from the PostScript world and other worlds. Also the number of fonts in METAFONT source format (freely available to every (LA)TeX installation) increased drastically. But, unfortunately, there was no easy and standard method of integrating these new fonts into LaTeX—typesetting with LaTeX meant typesetting in Computer Modern on almost all installations. Of course, individual fonts could be loaded using the `\newfont` command, but this capability cannot be called integration: it requires a great deal of user intervention, since such additional fonts do not change size under the control of size commands, and it does not allow a whole document to be typeset in a different font family.

(£ 116,200)

There have been a few efforts to integrate other fonts into LaTeX, but this was done by exchanging one hard-wired font table with another, thus making the resultant LaTeX variant as inflexible as the original one, and only forced the use of a different set of fonts.

This unsatisfactory situation finally was changed with the release of the New Font Selection Scheme (NFSS) [58, 60] in 1989 written by Frank Mittelbach and Rainer Schöpf, which became widely known after it was successfully used in $\mathcal{A}_{\mathcal{M}}S$-LaTeX (see chapter 8). This system contains a generic concept for varying font attributes individually and integrating new font families easily into an existing LaTeX system.

The concept is based on five attributes that can be defined independently to access different fonts, font characteristics, or font families. In order to realize the concept, some of the LaTeX commands were redefined and some new commands were added.

Later on, a prototype version for scalable fonts was coded by Mark Purtill. Starting from his work, Frank Mittelbach designed and implemented NFSS2 integrating work by Sebastian Rahtz (on PostScript fonts) and several others.

The following sections describe release 2 of NFSS, which was completed at the end of 1992. This release is now part of LaTeX2$_\varepsilon$, and, as far as the user interface is concerned, is intended for integration into LaTeX3.

Since the concepts used by NFSS completely differ from the way fonts were handled in (LA)TeX previously, we start by discussing font characteristics in general and introduce the major attributes used in NFSS for orthogonal font switching. We then describe the use of the high-level interface—i.e., the commands a user normally has to deal with. This includes commands used in normal text (section 7.3), special features for use in mathematical formulas (section 7.4), and an overview of the packages available with NFSS (section 7.5). The next part of this chapter concerns the low-level interfaces that are useful when defining complex new commands and that are important when new fonts are to be made available in LaTeX. Finally we discuss all warning and error messages in section 7.8.

7.2 Understanding Font Characteristics

There are many design principles that divide fonts into individual overlapping classes. Knowledge of these characteristics often proves helpful when deciding which font family to use in a special context.

7.2.1 Monospaced and Proportional Fonts

Fonts can be either monospaced or proportionally spaced. In a monospaced font, each individual character takes up the same horizontal space regardless of its shape. In contrast, characters in a proportionally spaced font take up different amounts of space depending on the shape of the character (see figure 7.1). You can see that the 'i' of the monospaced font occupies the same space as the 'm,' while it is noticeably narrower in the proportional font. As a result, proportional fonts (also called typographical fonts) normally allow more words to be placed on a page and are more readable than monospaced fonts. The extra spaces around individual characters of monospaced fonts make it more difficult for

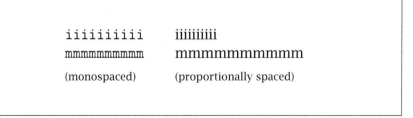

Figure 7.1: Major font characteristics

$$\boxed{\qquad \text{A} \quad \text{A} \qquad \text{n} \quad \text{n} \qquad}$$

Figure 7.2: Comparison of serifed and sans serif letters

the eyes to recognize word boundaries and thus make monospaced text less readable.

However, monospaced fonts do have uses. Within the proper context, they enhance the quality of the printed document. For example, in tables or computer listings where proper alignment of information is important, a monospaced font is a natural choice. In computer science books, it is common to display computer programs in a monospaced font to make them easily distinguishable from surrounding explanations.

But the use of monospaced fonts goes beyond marking portions of a document as special. One can even consider choosing a monospaced font as the base font for a complete document. Such a font has the flavor of the manual or electric typewriter engine; it looks handmade when used with unjustified paragraphs and therefore may be better suited to certain situations than a more professional-looking typographical font. Private letters are good candidates for monospaced type because the result looks more personalized. Keep in mind, however, that monospaced fonts look very poor when lines are justified. (See section 3.1.4 to learn how to turn off justification.)

7.2.2   Serifed and Sans Serif Fonts

Another useful classification is the presence or absence of serifs. Serifs are the tiny horizontal strokes at the extremities of character shapes (see figure 7.2). Originally serifs were produced by the chisel, when roman capitals were engraved into stone. For this reason, serifed fonts are often referred to as "roman" fonts.

Serifed fonts traditionally have been used for long texts because, it was argued, they are more readable. It was long thought that serifed letters give the eyes more clues for identification. This is certainly true if only parts of the characters are visible, but for fully visible text recent research has shown that reading speed is not substantially affected by the absence of serifs [75].

7.2.3   Font Families and Their Attributes

Besides the crude classifications of serifed vs. sans serif and monospaced vs. proportional, fonts are grouped into font families. Members of a font family share common design principles and are distinguished by variations in size, weight, width, and shape.

```
A   B   C   a   b   c   x   y   z
A   B   C   a   b   c   x   y   z
A   B   C   a   b   c   x   y   z
```

Figure 7.3: Comparison between upright and italic shapes

The first line shows letters from the Computer Modern Serif family in upright shape, and the third line shows the same letters in italic shape. For better comparison, the second line gives the italic letters without the usual slant—i.e., the letters are artificially shown in an upright position.

Font Shapes

An important attribute when classifying a member of a font family is its shape. Of course, sometimes it is a matter of personal judgment whether a set of fonts with different shapes constitutes a single family or several. For example, Donald Knuth called his collection of 31 Computer Modern fonts a family [22, 45], yet they form a meta-family of many families in the traditional sense.[1]

Although there is no uniform naming convention for font shapes, this is unimportant as long as one sticks to one particular scheme within NFSS.

Nearly every font family has one shape called the "upright" shape.[2] For example, in the font family used in this book (Lucida Bright), the font that you are now reading is in the upright shape.

Another important shape that is present in most families is the "italic" shape, which looks *like this* in the Lucida Bright family. Italic characters are slanted to the right and the individual letters generally are drawn differently from their upright counterparts, as shown in figure 7.3.

Font families without serifs often lack a proper italic shape; instead they have a "slanted" shape in which the characters slant to the right but are otherwise identical to their upright counterparts. The terms "sloped" and "oblique" are also commonly used for this shape.

Another common variant is the "small caps" shape, in which the lowercase letters are represented as capitals with a reduced height, as shown in figure 7.4.

---

[1]METAFONT, as a design tool, allows the production of completely different fonts from the same source description, so it is not surprising that in 1989 another family was created [45] based on the sources for the Computer Modern fonts. This family, Concrete Roman, was obtained merely by varying some METAFONT parameters in the source files; but since the result was so different, Knuth this time decided to give the family a different name.

[2]Sometimes you will also hear the term "roman" shape. This is due to the fact that until recently typesetting was nearly always done using serifed fonts. Thus, "roman" was considered to be the opposite of "italic" by many people. So be aware that in some books this term actually refers to the upright shape and not to a serifed font family.

EXAMPLE EXAMPLE EXAMPLE
(Normal Capitals)   (Small Caps)   (Faked Small Caps)

Figure 7.4: Comparison between caps and small caps

If such a shape is not available for a specific family, typographers sometimes use upright capitals from smaller sizes,[3] but this practice does not produce the same quality as a well designed small caps font. Real small caps have different widths and weight than capital letters from the same font that have been reduced to the height of designed small caps (you can clearly see that the strokes in the faked capitals in figure 7.4 are much too thin).

There are a few other, less important shapes. Some families contain fonts where the inner parts of the letters are drawn in a special fashion, most importantly perhaps the "outline" shapes, in which the inner parts of the letters are kept empty. For display purposes, some families also contain fonts that could be classified as "shaded"—i.e., where the letters appear three-dimensional. Examples are shown in figure 7.5 on the next page.

Special variants of the Computer Modern meta-family have been produced by setting the METAFONT parameters to special values. For example, there is "upright italic," a shape in which the individual letters are drawn in italic fashion but without the usual slant (see the second line in figure 7.3 on the preceding page). This shape was devised basically for showing the abilities of METAFONT as a tool for meta-design, but some users might take a fancy to such an unusual shape.

Weight and Width

Fonts of a certain shape within a family may differ in "weight." This characteristic refers to the thickness of the strokes used to draw the individual shapes. Once again, the commonly used names are not completely uniform, but it is relatively easy to arrive at a consistent classification. Some font manufacturers, for example, call the font weights intended to be used for normal text "book," while others call them "medium." For thin strokes the name "light" is common, while thicker strokes are usually called "bold." In larger font families, finer distinctions are often necessary, so that we sometimes find a range starting with "ultra light," going through "extra light," "light," "semi light," etc., and ending

---

[3]A good rule of thumb is using capitals from a font that is about half a point larger than the x-height of the original font. See in section 7.7.2 on page 201 for a way to determine the x-height of any font used with TeX.

Figure 7.5: Outline and shaded shapes

with "ultra bold" at the other end. On the other hand, often only a few weights are present in a family. For example, the Computer Modern Roman family has only two weights, "medium" and "**bold**." Another equally important attribute of a font is its "width"—i.e., the amount of expansion or contraction with respect to the normal or medium width in the family. Computer Modern Roman has bold fonts in "**medium width**" and "**extended width**." One application for condensed fonts is in marginal notes. Some typesetting systems can even condense fonts automatically to fit a given measure—e.g., to exactly fill a particular line in a heading. This capability is not directly possible with (LA)TEX, but in any case the results are often aesthetically questionable.

Font Sizes

Font sizes are traditionally measured in printer points (pt). There are 72.27 points to an inch. The font size is not an absolute measure of any particular characteristic; rather, it is just a value chosen by the font designer to guide the user. For example, in a 10pt font, letters of the alphabet are usually less then 10pt tall, and only characters like parentheses have approximately this height.

Two fonts of the same size may not blend well with one another because the appearance of a font depends on many factors, such as the height of the lowercase letters (the so-called x-height), the depth of the descenders (the part of the letters below the baseline, as in the letter q), etc.

In the (LA)TEX world, fonts are often available in sizes that are powers of 1.2, i.e., in a geometric progression [39, p.17]. This arrangement was chosen because it makes it easy to produce an enlarged master copy that later can be photographically reduced, thereby effectively enlarging the final output resolution. For example, if an A5 brochure is to be produced, one could print it with magnification of $1.44 \approx \sqrt{2}$ on A4 paper. Photographic reduction from the 300 dpi (dots per inch) output of a normal laser printer would produce an effective output resolution of 432 dpi and thus would give higher quality than is normally possible with such a laser printer.

However, this geometric ratio scheme used by (LA)TEX fonts produced with the METAFONT program is not common in the professional world, where the

---

Ten point type is different from magnified five point type

Figure 7.6: Scaled and designed fonts

point sizes usually found are 7, 8, 9, 10, 11, 12, 14, 16, 18, 20, 24, 30, and 36. But not all fonts are available in all these sizes, and sometimes additional sizes are offered—e.g., so-called display sizes for large headings and tiny sizes for subscripts and superscripts.

Note that the use of magnified or reduced fonts instead of fonts designed for a specific size is usually less than satisfactory, because to the human eye fonts do not scale in a linear fashion. The characters in handcrafted fonts of larger sizes usually are narrower than fonts magnified from a smaller size of the same family. While it is acceptable to scale fonts within a small size range, if necessary, one should use fonts designed for the desired size whenever possible. The difference between fonts scaled to a particular size and those designed for that size is shown in figure 7.6.

7.2.4   Encoding Schemes

To access a character from a font in a computer typesetting program, you need a way to specify that character in the input source. This point may seem trivial, since you can just type the 'A' on the keyboard when you want to get a typeset 'A' in the output, but what should you do to get a Spanish open-question mark (¿)? This character is certainly not found on many computer keyboards. In (LA)TEX, as in many other computer programs, this problem is solved by associating the characters in a font with numbers in the range of 0-255. Such a mapping is called a codepage or an encoding scheme. To illustrate what happens if we use a font with an encoding not suitable for our input, here is the the first sentence of this section again:

То аццесс а чарацтер фром а фонт ин а цомпутер тыпесеттинг програм, ыоу неед а щаы то специфы тхат чарацтер ин тхе инпут соурце.

The result is an interesting puzzle, but nothing that we want to see in ordinary documents.

There are several methods in (LA)TEX to access characters in the current font. The most common method is to put a visible ASCII character into the source document, which is then translated into the glyph in the current font that is associated with that ASCII character number in the encoding of the font. For the fonts commonly used in (LA)TEX, the positions of the letters of the Latin alphabet in the encoding are identical with their ASCII positions, so by typing an 'a' into the source document we get an 'a' in the output, rather than, say, '⊣.' But this mapping is not necessarily used for non-letters, as demonstrated by the input '<|>,' which comes out as '¡—¿' in the standard (LA)TEX encoding. More details and a table of the internally used encodings are given in sections 7.3.4 and 7.6.1.

7.3 Using Fonts in Text

When writing a LATEX document, appropriate fonts are normally chosen automatically by the logical tags used to structure the document. For example, the font attributes for a section heading, such as large size and bold weight, are defined by the document class and are applied when a \section command is used, so that you seldom need to specify font attributes yourself.

However, occasionally it becomes necessary to specify font attributes directly. One common reason is the desire to change the overall font attributes, by choosing, for example, a different font family for the main text. This alteration often can be done by simply specifying an appropriate package. Some packages for this purpose are described in section 7.5, others are given in section 11.9.

Another use for explicit font attributes can be to mark certain portions of the document as special—e.g., to denote examples, acronyms, company names, etc. For example, in this book, names of packages are formatted in a sans serif font. This formatting could be achieved by surrounding the names with \textsf{..}, but it is much better to define a new command (say, \Lpack) for this purpose so that additional information is added to the source document. By defining individual commands for logically different things—even those that are currently being set in the same way—you will make it easier to change things consistently later.

Last, but not least, in some cases you may wish to override a decision taken by the document class: you might want to typeset a table in a smaller size to make it fit on a page. This desire is legitimate, since document classes can format documents automatically only to a certain extent. Hand-formatting—like the insertion of page breaks, etc.—is thus often necessary for the final version. But explicit formatting makes further use of the document (if changes are made) difficult and error prone. Therefore, as with all visual formatting commands, you should try to minimize the direct use of font-changing commands in a document.

7.3.1 Standard NFSS Font Commands

The font used for the main text of a document is the "main font" or "normal font." It is automatically selected at the beginning of the document and also automatically selected in certain situations, such as in footnotes, figures, etc. Certain logical tags, like section headings, automatically switch to a different typeface or size, depending on the document class. These changes happen behind the scenes, and the only action necessary by the author is to introduce the correct logical markup in the document. However, sometimes you want to highlight individual parts of the text, by choosing an appropriate typeface for it; this can be done with the commands described below.

Most font change commands come in two forms: as a command with one argument, such as `\textbf{...}`, and as a declaration form, for example `\bfseries`. The declarations do not take arguments but rather instruct LaTeX that from now on (up to the end of the current group of braces or environments) it should behave in a special way. Thus, you should not write something like `\bfseries{...}`, as this would make everything bold from this point on to the end of the next environment.

To change the fonts for individual words or short phases within your document you should make use of the font commands with one argument, while declaration forms are often better in the definition of new environments or commands. For longer passages in your document, you can also use the environment form of the declaration (the declaration name without the preceding backslash) as shown in the following example:

Some words in this sentence are **typeset in bold** letters.

```
Some words in this sentence are
\begin{bfseries}typeset in bold\end{bfseries}
letters.
```

A detailed comparison of command form and declaration form and their advantages and disadvantages in special situations is given in section 7.3.3.

The Main Document Font

To switch to the main document font you can use the command `\textnormal` or the declaration `\normalfont`. They are usually only used in the definition of commands or environments when it is important to define commands that always typeset in the same font regardless of surrounding conditions. For example, the command to produce the command names in this book looks roughly like

```
\newcommand{\Lcs}[1]{{\normalfont\ttfamily\bslash#1}%
                \index{#1@{\normalfont\ttfamily\bslash#1}}}}
```

avoiding the command names coming out like `\this` in certain places.

Standard Font Families

By default, LaTeX maintains three font families that can be selected with short command sequences. These families are a serif text font, accessed with the command `\textrm`, a sans serif text font, accessed by `\textsf`, and a typewriter font (usually monospaced), accessed by \texttt. The declaration forms of these commands are \rmfamily, \sffamily, and \ttfamily, respectively.

The names of the external font families accessed by these commands depend on the document class but can be changed by packages or in the preamble (see section 7.3.5). As an installation default, the serif font is Computer Modern Roman, the sans serif font is Computer Modern Sans, and the typewriter font is Computer Modern Typewriter. If you used a different setup, take care to define these default families so that the fonts can be mixed freely without visual clashes. You must also make sure that the external fonts exist in the correct resolution for the output device.

In this book, the serif font family is Lucida Bright, the sans serif family is Lucida Sans and the typewriter family is Computer Modern Typewriter. These have been chosen by simply adding the package lucidbrb.[4]

In most document classes, the serif font, accessed by \textrm, is also the main font of the document, so the command \textrm is not used often. But if a document designer has chosen a sans serif font as the main typeface, then \textrm would be the alternative font family.

Standard Font Series

Another attribute of a typeface that can be changed is the *series*. In NFSS the series is a combination of two attributes: width and weight (boldness). NFSS provides two commands for changing the series: \textmd and \textbf; the corresponding declarations are \mdseries and \bfseries. The first command will select a font with medium values for the width and the weight, while the latter will switch to a bolder series. The actual values will depend on the document class and its options or subsequent packages. As a default for the Computer Modern families, \textbf will switch to a bold extended version of the current typeface, while \textmd will return to the medium width and medium weight version of the current typeface.

If finer control over the series attribute is desired, it is best to define additional high-level commands using the lower-level \fontseries declaration described in section 7.6.1. Some packages that make large font families available for use with LATEX sometimes provide such extra commands.

Standard Font Shapes

A third font attribute that may be changed independently of the others is the *shape* of the current typeface. The default shape for most documents is the upright shape which can be accessed, if necessary, with the command \textup or the declaration \upshape.

---

[4]To get Computer Modern Typewriter as the typewriter family we additionally redefined \ttdefault to produce cmtt; see section 7.3.5 for more details on changing the default text fonts.

Probably the most important commands for changing the shape are `\textit` and `\textsc`, which switch to an *italic* or CAPS AND SMALL CAPS font shape. The corresponding declarations are `\itshape` and `\scshape`.

An alternative to `\textit` is the `\textsl` command (its declaration form is `\slshape`), which switches to the slanted shape. Often a font family only contains either an italic or a slanted shape, but Computer Modern Roman contains both.

At the point where one switches from slanted to upright, the characters usually come too close together, especially if the last slanted character has an ascender. The proper amount of extra white space that should be added at this boundary is called the "italic correction." The value of this adjustment depends on the individual character shape and is therefore stored in the `.tfm` file. The italic correction will be automatically added by the font commands with

(*£ 17*)   arguments but must be inserted manually using `\/` when declarations are used. For an upright font, the italic correction of the characters is usually zero or very small, but there are some exceptions. (In Computer Modern, to typeset a bold 'f' in quotes, you should say '`{\bfseries f\/}`' or '`\textbf{f}`', lest you get a bold 'f' in some fonts.) In slanted or italic fonts the italic correction is usually positive, with the actual value depending on the shape of the character. Thus the correct usage of shape-changing declarations that switch to slanted shapes is:

When switching back from *italic* or *slanted* shapes to an upright font one should add the *italic correction*, except when a small punctuation character follows.

```
\raggedright
When switching back from {\itshape italic\/} or
{\slshape slanted\/} shapes to an upright font one
should add the {\itshape italic correction}, except
when a small punctuation character follows.
```

If you use the command forms with one argument instead, the italic correction is automatically added. See the further discussion of this topic in section 7.3.3.

Small capitals are sometimes used in headings or to format names. For the latter case you can, for example, define the command `\names` with one of the following definitions:

```
\newcommand{\names}[1]{\textsc{#1}}
```

or, using declarations,

```
\newcommand{\names}[1]{{\normalfont\scshape #1}}
```

The first definition simply switches to the desired shape, while the second form first resets all font attributes to their default. Which one should be used depends on the available fonts and on the type of document. If Computer Modern is being used, only the serif family contains a small caps shape, so the second definition might be preferred in certain applications because it will use small caps even in a `\sffamily` context. The first command would result in a request for a medium series small caps shaped font in the Computer Modern Sans family. Because this font is not available, NFSS would try to find a substitute by first changing the shape attribute to its default, with the result that you would not get small caps. (See section 7.6.3 for further information about substitutions.)

Another interesting use of the `\scshape` declaration is in the definition of an acronym tag in the following way:

```
\newcommand{\acro}[1]{{\scshape\lowercase{#1}}}
```

This definition makes use of the TeX primitive `\lowercase` that changes all characters within its argument (or more exactly, only the characters that do not belong to command names) to lowercase. As a result, all characters in the argument of `\acro` will be changed to lowercase and therefore typeset with small capitals.

Another slightly special shape command available in LaTeX is the `\emph` command. This command denotes emphasis in normal text; the corresponding declaration is `\em`. Traditionally, emphasized words in text are set in italic; if emphasis is desired in an already italicized portion of the text, one usually returns to the upright font. The `\emph` command supports this convention by switching to the `\itshape` shape if the current font is upright, and to the `\upshape` if the current font is already slanted (i.e., if the shape is `\itshape` or `\slshape`). Thus the user does not have to worry about the current state of the text when using the `\emph` command or the `\em` declaration.

(£ 16,38)

Nevertheless, one has to be careful about the proper *use of italic corrections on both ends of the emphasized text.* It is therefore better to use the `\emph` command, which *automatically* takes care of the italic correction on both sides.

```
{\em Nevertheless, one has to be careful about
the\/ {\em proper\/} use of italic corrections
on both ends of the emphasized text}.  It is
therefore better to use the \verb=\emph= command,
which \emph{automatically} takes care of the
italic correction on both sides.
```

Note that underlining for emphasis is considered bad practice in the publishing world. Underlining is only used when the output device can't do highlighting in another way—for example, when using a typewriter. But section 3.1.2 discusses a package that changes `\em` to produce underlining.

Standard Font Sizes

LaTeX has ten size change declarations (see table 7.1 on the following page). Since size changes are normally used only in the definition of commands, they have no corresponding command forms with one argument. The names of the declarations have been retained in NFSS, but their functionality has changed slightly. In NFSS a size change command changes only the size of the current font and all other attributes stay the same; while in the old font selection scheme

(£ 115,200)

\tiny	Size	\normalsize	Size	\huge	Size
\scriptsize	Size	\large	Size	\Huge	Size
\footnotesize	Size	\Large	Size		
\small	Size	\LARGE	Size		

Table 7.1: The standard size-changing commands

of LaTeX 2.09 a size change command also automatically switched to the main document font.

In both LaTeX 2_ε and old LaTeX the size selected by these commands depends on the settings in the document class file and possibly on options (e.g., 11pt) to it. In general, \normalsize corresponds to the main size of the document, and the size change commands form an ordered sequence starting with \tiny as the smallest up to \Huge as the largest size. Sometimes more than one command refers to the same real size; for example, when a large \normalsize is chosen, \Huge can be the same as \huge. But the order is always honored.

Unfortunately, there is currently no relative size change command in LaTeX— e.g., there is no command for requesting a size 2pt larger than the current one.

7.3.2 Combining Standard Font Commands

As already shown, the standard font-changing commands and declarations can be combined. The result is the selection of a typeface that matches the combination of all font attributes. For example:

One can typeset a text **in a large sans serif bold typeface.**

```
One can typeset a text {\sffamily\bfseries
\large in a large sans serif bold typeface.}
```

What happens behind the scenes is that the \sffamily command switches to the sans serif default family, then \bfseries switches to the default bold series in this family, and \large finally selects a large size with all other font attributes unchanged. Font metric files (i.e., .tfm files) are loaded for all intermediate typefaces, even if these fonts are never used. In the preceding example, they would be 'sans serif medium 10pt' after the \sffamily, then 'sans serif bold extended 10pt' after the \bfseries, then 'sans serif bold extended 14pt,' which is the font that is then finally used. Thus such high-level commands can force NFSS to unnecessarily load fonts that are never used. This normally does not matter, except for a small loss of processing speed when such a combination is used for the first time. However, if you have many different combinations of this type, you should consider defining them in terms of the primitive font-changing declarations (see section 7.6).

Command	*Corresponds to*	*Action*
\textrm{...}	{\rmfamily...}	Typeset text in roman family
\textsf{...}	{\sffamily...}	Typeset text in sans serif family
\texttt{...}	{\ttfamily...}	Typeset text in typewriter family
\textmd{...}	{\mdseries...}	Typeset text in medium series
\textbf{...}	{\bfseries...}	Typeset text in **bold** series
\textup{...}	{\upshape...}	Typeset text in upright shape
\textit{...}	{\itshape...}	Typeset text in *italic* shape
\textsl{...}	{\slshape...}	Typeset text in *slanted* shape
\textsc{...}	{\scshape...}	Typeset text in SMALL CAPS shape
\emph{...}	{\em...}	Typeset text *emphasized*
\textnormal{..}	{\normalfont..}	Typeset text in the document font

Table 7.2: Font-changing commands and declarations

The font-changing commands with arguments all start with \text... (except
for the \emph command) to emphasize that they are for use in normal text and
to be easily memorizable. They automatically take care of any necessary italic
correction on either side of the argument.

7.3.3   Font Commands versus Declarations

We have already seen some examples of font commands that have arguments and
change font attributes. Using such commands instead of the declarative forms
has the advantage of consistency with other LaTeX structures. These commands
are intended for typesetting short pieces of text in a specific family, series, or
shape. Table 7.2 shows the effect of all such commands. A further advantage
of using these commands is that they automatically take care of any necessary
italic correction on either side of their argument.

Thus, when using such commands, one does not have to worry about for-
getting the italic correction when changing fonts. Only in very few situations is
this additional space wrong; for example, most typographers recommend omitting the italic correction if a small punctuation character, like a comma, directly
follows the font change. Since the amount of correction required is partly a
matter of taste, you can define in what situations the italic correction should
be suppressed. This is done by specifying the characters that should cancel a
preceding italic correction in the list \nocorrlist.[5] The default definition for
this command is

```
\newcommand{\nocorrlist}{,.}
```

---

[5]Any package that changes the \catcode of a character inside \nocorrlist must redeclare the
list. Otherwise the changed character will no longer be recognized by the suppression algorithm.

It is best to declare the most often used characters first, because this will make the processing slightly faster.

In addition to the global customization it is possible to suppress the italic correction in individual instances. For this, the command \nocorr is provided. Note that you have to put \nocorr on the left or right end inside the argument of the \text... commands, depending on which side of the text you wish to suppress the italic correction.

When using the NFSS high-level commands, the proper *use of italic corrections is automatically taken care of.* Only *sometimes* one has to help LaTeX by adding a \nocorr command.

```
\emph{When using the \NFSS{} high-level commands,
the \emph{proper} use of italic corrections is
automatically taken care of}. Only
\emph{sometimes} one has to help \LaTeX{} by
adding a \verb=\nocorr= command.
```

In contrast, the use of the declaration forms is often more appropriate when you define your own commands or environments.

- **This environment produces boldface items.**
- **It is defined in terms of LaTeX's** itemize **environment and NFSS declarations.**

```
\newenvironment{bfitemize}
  {\begin{itemize}\normalfont\bfseries}
  {\end{itemize}}
\begin{bfitemize}
\item This environment produces boldface items.
\item It is defined in terms of \LaTeX's
  \texttt{itemize} environment and NFSS
  declarations.
\end{bfitemize}
```

7.3.4 Accessing All Characters of a Font

(£ 40)

Sometimes it is impossible to enter a character directly from the keyboard, even though the character exists in the font. Therefore, many useful characters are accessible via command names like \ss or \AE, which produce 'ß' and 'Æ'. Other characters are implicitly generated from sequences of letters (this is a property of fonts) like ffi, which produces 'ffi,' and ---, which produces '—' in the standard TeX fonts.

(£ 200)

In addition, there is the command \symbol, which allows you to access any character in a font by giving its number in the current encoding scheme as either a decimal, octal (preceded by '), or hexadecimal (preceded by ") number.

In the Cork font encoding (T1), characters like Þ, §, and ␣ are included and can be accessed with the \symbol command.

```
In the Cork font encoding (\texttt{T1}),
characters like \symbol{"DE}, \symbol{'237},
and \symbol{32} are included and can be
accessed with the \verb=\symbol= command.
```

The numbers corresponding to the characters in any font can be obtained by using the program nfssfont.tex, described in section 7.5.5.

Hook	Default value	Description
\encodingdefault	OT1	Encoding scheme for 'main font'
\familydefault	\rmdefault	Family selected for 'main font'
\seriesdefault	m	Series selected for 'main font'
\shapedefault	n	Shape selected for 'main font'
\rmdefault	cmr	Family selected by \rmfamily and \textrm
\sfdefault	cmss	Family selected by \sffamily and \textsf
\ttdefault	cmtt	Family selected by \ttfamily and \texttt
\bfdefault	bx	Series selected by \bfseries and \textbf
\mddefault	m	Series selected by \mdseries and \textmd
\itdefault	it	Shape selected by \itshape and \textit
\sldefault	sl	Shape selected by \slshape and \textsl
\scdefault	sc	Shape selected by \scshape and \textsc
\updefault	n	Shape selected by \upshape and \textup

Table 7.3: Font attribute hooks

For easy access to "old-style numerals," e.g., 1982, NFSS provides the command \oldstylenums, which can be used in text and within formulas. In its argument you should place the digits that you want to typeset as nonaligning digits. If used in text, spaces in the argument are honored, but you should not try to put characters other than digits into it or the results will be unpredictable.

7.3.5   Changing the Default Text Fonts

To make it easier to modify the overall appearance of a document, NFSS provides a set of built-in hooks that modify the behavior of the high-level font-changing commands discussed in the previous sections. These hooks are shown in table 7.3. The values of these hooks can be set in package files or in the preamble of a document by using \renewcommand. Suitable values for these commands can be found by looking through the font tables in this chapter.

For example, by writing in the preamble

```
\renewcommand{\familydefault}{cmss}
```

a whole document would come out in Computer Modern Sans, because this redefinition changes the font family for the main font used by NFSS. More exactly, the main document font is determined by the values of \encodingdefault, \familydefault, \seriesdefault, and \shapedefault. Thus, you have to make sure that these commands are defined in such a way that their combination points to an existing font shape in NFSS internal tables.

The default value stored in \encodingdefault currently is OT1, which means that NFSS assumes that most fonts use the original TeX encoding. A new standard, called the Cork encoding (see section 7.5.1), is expected to supplant the original TeX encoding. At that point, the default value of \encodingdefault will be changed to T1. See also section 7.6.1 for more information on encoding schemes.

Another example, this time involving a series-changing command, would be to define \bfdefault to produce b so that the \bfseries command will use **bold** instead of **bold extended**, which is the default under Computer Modern. However, there is some risk in using such a setting since, for example, in Computer Modern only the Roman family has bold variants with a medium width. Computer Modern Typewriter and Computer Modern Sans only have bold extended variants. Thus, without further adjustments, a request for, say, a bold sans serif font (i.e., \sffamily\bfseries), would force NFSS to try font substitution, and finally select a medium-weight font. (But this outcome can be avoided, as explained in section 7.7.2, by specifying that the bold extended variants of the sans family should serve as substitutes for the bold medium ones.)

Example in which some default values are changed can be found in the chapter about PostScript (section 11.9).

The initial setting of \familydefault means that changing only \rmdefault will also change \familydefault to the new value as long as no special setting for \familydefault is defined. However, if \familydefault gets changed \rmdefault is not affected.

7.3.6 LaTeX 2.09 Font Commands

The two-letter font commands used in LaTeX 2.09, like \bf, are no longer defined by LaTeX 2ε directly. Instead, they are defined in the LaTeX 2ε class files. For compatibility reasons the standard classes provide definitions for these commands that emulate their behavior in LaTeX 2.09. However, it is legitimate for you to redefine them in a package or in the preamble according to your personal taste, something you should not do with basic NFSS commands like \bfseries.

7.4 Using Fonts in Math

Unlike the situation in text, automatic changes in font shapes are generally not desired in math formulas. For mathematicians, individual shapes convey specific information: for example, bold upright letters may represent vectors. If the characters in a formula were to change because of surrounding conditions, the result would be incorrect. For this reason handling of fonts in mathematical formulas is different than in text.

Characters in a formula can be loosely put into two classes: symbols and alphabet characters (including digits). Internally, (LA)TEX distinguishes between eight types of math characters (to account for appropriate spacing), but for the user the division into two classes is generally enough.

Some symbols like = can be entered directly from the keyboard, but the bulk of them must be entered via a control sequence—e.g., \leq stands for ≤. The other main group of characters in a formula, the alphabet characters, are entered normally directly from the keyboard.

Over two hundred symbols are predefined in a standard (LA)TEX system, thus allowing the user to typeset almost any desired formula. These symbols are scattered over several fonts, but they are accessed in such a way that the user does not to have to be aware of their internal representation. If ever necessary, further symbol fonts can be made accessible in a similar way; see section 7.7.6.

The most important difference between symbols and alphabet characters is that symbols always have the same graphical representation within one formula, while it is possible for the user to change the appearance of the alphabet characters. We will call the commands that change the appearance of alphabet characters in a formula "math alphabet identifiers" and the fonts associated with these commands "math alphabets." These alphabet identifiers are independent of surrounding font commands outside the formula, so that a formula does not change if it is placed (for example) inside a theorem environment whose text is, by default, typeset in italics. This behavior is very important, since character shapes in a mathematical formula carry a meaning that must not change because the formula is typeset in a different place in a document.

Some people used to the old method of font selection may be surprised by the fact that commands like \bfseries cannot be used in formulas. This is the price we have to pay for the greater flexibility in choosing text font attributes—a flexibility that we do not want in a formula. We therefore need a different mechanism (math alphabet identifiers) for changing the typeface of certain alphabet characters in complicated formulas.

7.4.1 Special Math Alphabet Identifiers

One alphabet and a huge number of symbols are not sufficient for mathematicians to express their thoughts. They tend to use every available typeface to denote special concepts. Besides the use of foreign alphabets like Greek letters, which usually are accessed as symbols—\alpha, \beta, etc.—we find sans serif letters for matrices, bold serif letters for vectors, and Fraktur fonts for groups, ideals, or fields. Others use calligraphical shapes to denote sets. The conventions are endless, and—even more importantly—they differ from one discipline to another. For this reason NFSS makes it possible to declare new math alphabet identifiers and associate them with any desired font shape group instead of relying only upon a predefined set that cannot be extended. These identifiers are special commands for use in a formula that typeset any alphabet character

Command	*Example*	
\mathcal	$\mathcal{A}=a$	$\mathcal{A} = a$
\mathrm	max_i	max_i
\mathbf	$\sum x = \mathbf{v}$	$\sum x = \mathbf{v}$
\mathsf	G_1^2	G_1^2
\mathtt	$\mathtt{W}(a)$	$\mathtt{W}(a)$
\mathnormal	$\mathnormal{abc}=abc$	$abc = abc$
\mathit	$differ\neq\mathit{differ}$	$differ \neq \mathit{differ}$

Table 7.4: Predefined math alphabet identifiers in NFSS

As the last lines show, the letters used in formulas are taken by default from the math alphabet \mathnormal. In contrast, the letters produced by \mathit have different spacing; thus this alphabet could be used to provide full-word variable names, which are common in some disciplines.

in their argument in a specific typeface. (Symbols cannot be changed in this way.) It is possible for these identifiers to use different typefaces in different formulas, as we will see in section 7.4.3, but within one formula they always select the same typeface regardless of surrounding conditions.

Predefined Alphabet Identifiers

New math alphabet identifiers can be defined according to the user's needs, but NFSS already has a few built in. These identifiers are shown in table 7.4.

In NFSS math alphabet identifiers are commands with one argument, usually a single letter or a single word to be typeset in a special font, e.g.,

Therefore G can be computed as

(7.1)
$$G = \mathcal{A} + \sum_{i=1}^{n} \mathcal{B}_i$$

```
Therefore $\mathsf{G}$ can be computed as
\begin{equation}
    \mathsf{G} = \mathcal{A} +
                 \sum_{i=1}^{n} \mathcal{B}_{i}
\end{equation}
```

This procedure differs from the way font commands were used before in LaTeX 2.09, where commands like \rm would cause font changes (..{\rm A}..). (For the most important two-letter font-changing commands like \rm, \sf, \bf, \it, and \tt the old syntax is still supported in the standard classes and for the others you can force the old behavior by specifying the package oldlfont; see section 7.5.5. However, we suggest that you refrain from using such commands in new documents.)

As already mentioned, another difference between the old font selection scheme and NFSS is that text font declarations are no longer allowed in formulas, since they only change some characteristic of the current font rather

than switching to specific fonts. Thus, if you write {\bfseries..} instead of
\mathbf{..} in a formula, NFSS will produce an error message.

The command names for the math alphabet identifier are chosen to be descriptive rather than simple to type—i.e., they all start with \math. Therefore,
if you use the commands more than occasionally in your document, consider
defining some abbreviations in the preamble, for example

```
\newcommand{\mrm}{\mathrm}
```

You may wonder what the default math alphabet is—i.e., from what alphabet
the alphabet characters are selected if you do not specify an alphabet identifier
explicitly, as in the formula $x = 123$. The answer is that there is no single
default math alphabet. The (LA)TEX system can be set up so that alphabet characters are fetched from different alphabets as long as the user has not explicitly
asked for a specific one, and this is normally the case, as the following example
shows.

		`\begin{align}`
(7.2)	$x = 12345$	`x` &= `12345` `\\`
(7.3)	$x = 12345$	`\mathrm{x}` &= `\mathrm{12345}` `\\`
(7.4)	$x = 12345$	`\mathnormal{x}` &= `\mathnormal{12345}`
		`\end{align}`

As you can see, \mathrm does not change the digits and \mathnormal
does not change the letters, thus the default for digits in the normal setup
is the math alphabet associated with \mathrm and the default for letters is the
one associated with \mathnormal.[6] This behavior can be controlled with the
\DeclareMathSymbol command, which is explained in section 7.7.6.

Defining New Alphabet Identifiers

New math alphabet identifiers are defined with the \DeclareMathAlphabet command. Suppose that you want to make a slanted sans serif typeface available as
a math alphabet. First you decide on a new command name, such as \mathsfsl,
that should be used to select your math alphabet. Then you consult the font
tables in this chapter (starting on page 181) to find a suitable font shape group
to assign to this alphabet identifier. You will find that there is, for example, the
Computer Modern Sans family, consisting of a medium series with upright and
slanted shapes. If you decide to use the slanted shape of this family, you tell
NFSS by adding the following line to your preamble or package file:

```
\DeclareMathAlphabet{\mathsfsl}{OT1}{cmss}{m}{sl}
```

---

[6]With the default setup of LATEX2ε using Computer Modern math fonts, \mathnormal will
produce old style numerals, not the italic ones shown in the example, where Lucida is used.

More formally, \DeclareMathAlphabet has four arguments besides the identifier: the encoding scheme, the family, the series, and the shape of the font to be used. Now your alphabet identifier is ready for use in a formula: it will always switch to Computer Modern Sans medium slanted.

We demonstrate this with the formula

(7.5)
$$\sum A_i = a \tan \beta$$

```
We demonstrate this with the formula
\begin{equation}
  \sum \mathsfsl{A}_{i} = a \tan \beta
\end{equation}
```

It is also possible to redefine an existing math alphabet identifier in a package file or in the preamble of your document. For example, the declaration

```
\DeclareMathAlphabet{\mathsf}{OT1}{pss}{m}{n}
```

will override the default settings for the \mathsf alphabet identifier. After that, \mathsf will switch to Pandora Sans in your formulas.

7.4.2   Text Font Commands in Math

As mentioned previously, text font declarations like \rmfamily cannot be used in math. However, the font-changing commands with arguments—e.g., \textrm— can be used in both text and math. You can use these commands to temporarily exit the math context and typeset some text in the midst of your formula that logically belongs to the text surrounding the formula. Note that the font used to typeset this text will depend on surrounding conditions—i.e., it will pick up the current values of encoding, family, series, and shape, as in the next example.

The result will be

$$x = 10 \text{ **and thus** } y = 12$$

```
\sffamily The result will be
\[  x = 10
   \textbf{ and thus }
   y = 12 \]
```

As you see the Sans family was retained and the series was changed to bold. Perhaps more useful is the \text command, provided by the amstext package, which picks up the current values of encoding, family, series, and shape without changing any of them (see section 8.3.12).

7.4.3   Mathematical Formula Versions

Besides allowing parts of a formula to be changed by using math alphabet identifiers, NFSS also lets you change the appearance of a formula as a whole. Formulas are typeset in a certain "math version," and you can switch between math versions outside of math mode by using the command \mathversion, thereby changing the overall layout of the following formulas.

NFSS knows about two math versions called "normal" and "bold." Additional ones can be provided in special packages. For example, the concrete package (see section 7.5.1) sets up a math version called "euler" to typeset formulas in the same way as it was done in the book *Concrete Mathematics* [22].

As the name indicates, \mathversion{normal} is the default. In contrast, the bold version will produce bolder alphabet characters and symbols. The following example shows the same formula first in the normal and then in the bold math version.[7]

(7.6)
$$\sum_{j=1}^{z} j = \frac{z(z+1)}{2}$$

```
\begin{equation}
   \sum_{j=1}^{z} j = \frac{z(z+1)}{2}
\end{equation}
\mathversion{bold}
\begin{equation}
   \sum_{j=1}^{z} j = \frac{z(z+1)}{2}
\end{equation}
```

(7.7)
$$\sum_{j=1}^{z} \boldsymbol{j} = \frac{z(z+1)}{2}$$

Using \mathversion might be suitable in certain situations like headings, but remember that changing the version means changing the appearance (and perhaps the meaning) of the whole formula. If you want to darken only some symbols or characters within one formula, you should not change the \mathversion. Instead, you should use the \mathbf alphabet identifier for characters and/or use the command \boldsymbol provided in the package amsbsy; see section 8.2.1 and table 8.1 on page 218.

If you change the math version with the \mathversion command, NFSS looks in its internal tables to find out where to go to fetch all the symbols for this new math version. It also may change all or some of the math alphabet identifiers and associate them with other font shapes in this version.

But what happens to any math alphabet identifiers that you have defined yourself, like the \mathsfsl in the earlier example? As long as you only declared them using \DeclareMathAlphabet, they will stay the same in every math version.

If the math alphabet identifier is to produce a different font in a special math version, you must inform NFSS by using the \SetMathAlphabet command. For example, in the default setup the \mathsf alphabet identifier is defined to be:

```
\DeclareMathAlphabet{\mathsf}{OT1}{cmss}{m}{n}
\SetMathAlphabet{\mathsf}{bold}{OT1}{cmss}{bx}{n}
```

The first line means that the default for \mathsf in all math versions is Computer Modern Sans medium, and the second line states that in the bold math version

---

[7]For historical reasons NFSS has two additional commands to switch to its standard math versions: \boldmath and \unboldmath.

the font Computer Modern Sans bold extended should be used instead.

From the previous example, you can see that \SetMathAlphabet takes six arguments: the first is the name of the math alphabet identifier, the second is the math version name for which you are defining a special setup, and the other four are the encoding, family, series, and shape name you are associating it with.

As noted earlier, it is possible to redefine an existing math alphabet identifier using \DeclareMathAlphabet. If you do this, all previous \SetMathAlphabet declarations for this identifier are removed from the internal tables of NFSS so that it will come out the same in all math versions unless you add new \SetMathAlphabet declarations for this identifier.

7.5   Standard Packages

Several packages are distributed with NFSS and are described in this section. Many others can be obtained from various electronic archives or from TEX organizations; you will find information on them in appendix B. Also, all of the font families described below are freely available as METAFONT source code.

7.5.1   Providing New Text Fonts

One of the important advantages of using NFSS is the ease with which new fonts for use in the main text can be integrated. Besides the Computer Modern families, which are used by default, one can easily use other font families by adding the appropriate package after the \documentclass command. Of course, for successful processing and printing the corresponding font files (e.g., the .tfm and .pk files) must be installed on the system.

The DC Fonts

At the TEX Users conference in Cork (1990), a standard encoding for text fonts (T1) was developed that contains many diacritical characters (see table 9.1 on page 261) and allows typesetting in over thirty languages. At the University of Bochum (under the direction of Norbert Schwarz) the Computer Modern font families were then reimplemented, and additional characters were designed, so that the resulting fonts completely conform to this encoding scheme. Currently these fonts are released under the name DC fonts; the final version will be called "EC fonts." Their use is highly recommended, and we hope that most other font families will soon be available in this encoding scheme.

By specifying the package t1enc after the \documentclass command, the Cork encoding (T1) is made the default encoding. Consequently, instead of using Computer Modern in OT1 encoding, LATEX uses the DC fonts. PostScript fonts can also be used with the Cork encoding; see section 11.10.

family	series	shape(s)	Example of typeface
Computer Modern Roman (T1, OT1)			
cmr	m	n, it, sl, sc, u	Computer Roman small caps
cmr	bx	n, it, sl	*Comp. Mod. Roman bold extended italic*
cmr	b	n	**Computer Modern Roman bold upright**
Computer Modern Sans (T1, OT1)			
cmss	m	n, sl	Computer Modern Sans slanted
cmss	bx	n	**Computer Modern Sans bold extended**
cmss	sbc	n	Computer Modern Sans semibold condensed
Computer Modern Typewriter (T1, OT1)			
cmtt	m	n, it, sl, sc	Computer Modern Typewriter italic
Computer Modern Fibonacci (T1, OT1)			
cmfib	m	n	Computer Modern Fibonacci
Computer Modern Funny Roman (T1, OT1)			
cmfr	m	n, it	Computer Modern Funny Roman
Computer Modern Dunhill (T1, OT1)			
cmdh	m	n	Computer Modern Dunhill

Table 7.5: NFSS classification of the Computer Modern fonts

The Concrete Fonts

For the text of the book *Concrete Mathematics* [22], Donald Knuth designed a new typeface, to go with the Euler mathematics fonts designed by Hermann Zapf. This font family, called "Concrete Roman," was created from the Computer Modern METAFONT sources by supplying different parameter settings. Thus, starting from the work done for the DC fonts, it was relatively easy to create Concrete Roman fonts with the Cork encoding; a suitable set of METAFONT driver files is part of the NFSS distribution. The fonts available in these families are shown in table 7.6 on the following page.

To access these font families in normal text it is best to use the package beton (by Frank Jensen), which also takes care of small but important typographical details, like slightly enlarging the \baselineskip value.

There is also the package concrete that, in addition to setting up Concrete Roman for text, defines a new math version named euler. This file, together with its documentation, can serve as a template for people who want to define their own combination of text and math fonts.

family	series	shape(s)	Example of the typeface
Concrete Roman (T1, OT1)			
ccr	m	n, sc	Concrete Roman medium
ccr	c	sl	*Concrete Roman condensed slanted*
Concrete Math (OML)			
ccm	m	it	*Concrete Math.* α Ω

Table 7.6: The Concrete families

family	series	shape(s)	Example of the typeface
Pandora Roman (OT1)			
panr	m	n, sl	Pandora Roman medium
panr	b	n	**Pandora Roman bold**
Pandora Sans (OT1)			
pss	m	n, sl	*Pandora Sans medium slanted*
pss	b	n	**Pandora Sans bold**

Table 7.7: The Pandora families

The Pandora Fonts

The Pandora families designed by Nazeen N. Billawala consists of the **Pandora Roman** family and Pandora Sans family [11, 12]. The complete set of variants is shown in table 7.7. Unfortunately, both families are currently available only in the traditional TeX encoding (OT1). To use Pandora as the main text it is best to load the pandora package after the \documentclass command.

Typesetting with Old German Fonts

There is a set of beautiful fonts for typesetting in 𝕲𝖔𝖙𝖍𝖎𝖘𝖈𝖍, 𝖆𝖑𝖘𝖔 𝖈𝖆𝖑𝖑𝖊𝖉 𝕿𝖊𝖝𝖙𝖚𝖗 (Gothisch, also called Textur), 𝕾𝖈𝖍𝖜𝖆𝖇𝖆𝖈𝖍𝖊𝖗 (Schwabacher), and 𝕱𝖗𝖆𝖐𝖙𝖚𝖗 (Fraktur) designed after traditional typefaces by Yannis Haralambous [25]. The collection also contains a font for initials that is shown in figure 7.7 on the facing page.

   To access these fonts, use the package oldgerm after the \documentclass command. This package defines the commands \gothfamily, \frakfamily, and

Figure 7.7: The Initial font `yinit` by Yannis Haralambous
This font is set up as family `yinit`, series `m`, shape `n`, and encoding `U`.

family	series	shape(s)	Example of the typeface
Gothic (U)			
ygoth	m	n	𝔜𝔞𝔫𝔫𝔦𝔰 𝔊𝔬𝔱𝔥𝔦𝔠
Fraktur (U)			
yfrak	m	n	𝔜𝔞𝔫𝔫𝔦𝔰 𝔉𝔯𝔞𝔨𝔱𝔲𝔯
Schwabacher (U)			
yswab	m	n	𝔜𝔞𝔫𝔫𝔦𝔰 𝔖𝔠𝔥𝔴𝔞𝔟𝔞𝔠𝔥𝔢𝔯

Table 7.8: The Old German text font families
Because these fonts contain many ligatures, necessary for traditional typesetting, and therefore do not follow any standard encoding, they are set up for NFSS with U encoding.

`\swabfamily` to switch to the corresponding font families. Since these families only consist of one shape in one series, commands like `\bfseries` or `\itshape` have no effect when typesetting in these families. However, size-changing commands are honored. In addition, the package defines the corresponding font commands with arguments—that is, `\textgoth`, `\textfrak`, and `\textswab`.

7.5.2   Providing New Math Fonts

The Euler Fonts

As mentioned above, Hermann Zapf designed a beautiful set of fonts for mathematics—upright characters with a handwritten flavor—named after the famous mathematician Leonhard Euler. These fonts can be accessed by specifying the package euler. This package does not provide an additional math

family	series	shape(s)	Example of the typeface
Euler Roman (U)			
eur	m	n	Euler Roman medium
eur	b	n	**Euler Roman bold**
Euler Script (U)			
eus	m	n	$\mathcal{EULER\ SCRIPT}$
Euler Fraktur (U)			
euf	m	n	$\mathfrak{Euler\ Fraktur}$

Table 7.9: The Euler math families

The fonts in the current distribution of the Euler math families, unfortunately, are available only in encoding schemes that differ from all other encoding schemes for mathematics. As a result, you need to redeclare several math symbols if these fonts are used (this is done by the package euler). For this reason, the fonts are assigned the encoding U until they have been reencoded.

version; instead it modifies the normal and the bold math versions so that they produce characters from these font families.

If only the $\mathcal{SCRIPT}$ alphabet of the Euler fonts is of interest, you can use the euscript package, which makes this math alphabet available under the name \EuScript.

To access the $\mathfrak{Euler\ Fraktur}$ fonts in formulas, use the package eufrak, which defines the math alphabet \EuFrak for you. The complete set of fonts in these families is shown in table 7.9.

latexsym—**Providing LaTeX Symbols**

Eleven math symbols provided by LaTeX 2.09 are no longer defined in the base setup of NFSS. These are

$$\mho \quad \Join \quad \Box \quad \Diamond \quad \leadsto$$
$$\sqsubset \quad \sqsupset \quad \lhd \quad \unlhd \quad \rhd \quad \unrhd$$

| \mho | $\mho$ | \Join | $\Join$ | \Box | $\Box$ | \Diamond | $\Diamond$ | \leadsto | $\leadsto$ |
| \sqsubset | $\sqsubset$ | \sqsupset | $\sqsupset$ | \lhd | $\lhd$ | \unlhd | $\unlhd$ | \rhd | $\rhd$ | \unrhd | $\unrhd$ |

If you want to use these symbols specify the latexsym package in your document. Alternatively, these symbols are made available if you load the amsfonts or the amssymb package; see also section 8.6.5.

Special Math Extension Fonts

Normally the font used for large mathematical symbols is available in only one size. This is usually sufficient, since most of the characters included are available in several different sizes in this font and (LA)TEX is specially equipped to automatically chose the best fitting size. However, when a document requires a lot of mathematics in large sizes—e.g., in headings—the selected symbols may appear to be too small. In this case, you can use the package exscale, which provides for using different math extension fonts.

If this package is used, you need scaled versions of the cmex10 font in the sizes 10.95pt, 12pt, 14.4pt, 17.28pt, 20.74pt, and 24.88pt. Additionally, cmex variants for the sizes 7pt to 9pt are necessary. These fonts are part of the AMS font package and can be found on many servers.

7.5.3 slides—**Producing Overhead Slides**

For producing overhead slides with the original font selection, it was necessary to use a special LATEX variant called SLITEX, since a completely different set of fonts was necessary. However, nowadays the same effect can be achieved simply by using the document class slides, which provides basically the same functionality as the original SLITEX program.

(£ 131–38)

There are several advantages to this NFSS class: you do not need a special precompiled format file and you are able to choose special fonts for your slides simply by selecting appropriate packages. For example, if you have the PostScript Times family, you can produce slides using this family by saying

```
\documentclass{slides}
\usepackage{times}
```

7.5.4 **Processing Older Documents**

oldlfont—LATEX 2.09 Compatibility

As we have seen, NFSS—and thus LATEX 2_ε—differs from LATEX 2.09 in several ways in the treatment of font commands. This difference is most noticeable in math formulas where commands like \bfseries are not supported. Nevertheless, it is very simple to typeset older documents with NFSS.

If you only want to reprint a document, LATEX 2_ε will see the \documentstyle command and automatically switch to compatibility mode emulating the old font selection mechanism of LATEX 2.09 as described in the first edition of the LATEX book. Alternatively, you can add the package oldlfont after the \documentclass command. If you do so, all old font-selecting commands will be defined, font-changing commands cancel each other and all these commands can be used in mathematical formulas.

Some authors may have used internally defined font commands like `\twlrm` or `\nintt` in their documents. Such commands now generate an error message, because they are no longer defined (not even in compatibility mode). One reason they are not supported is that they were never available at all installations. To process a document containing such explicit font-changing commands you have to define them in the preamble using the commands described in section 7.6. For example, for the above commands, it would be sufficient to add the definitions

```
\newcommand{\twlrm}{\fontsize{12}{14pt}\normalfont\rmfamily}
\newcommand{\nintt} {\fontsize{9}{11pt}\normalfont\ttfamily}
```

to the preamble.

Reusing parts of documents also is very simple: just paste them into the new document and watch what happens. There is a good chance that NFSS will happily process the old document fragment and, if not, it will explicitly inform you about the places where you have to change your source.

newlfont—**NFSS1 Compatibility**

In the first release of NFSS, the two-letter font-changing commands were redefined to modify individual attributes only—e.g., `\sf` or `\it` behaved just like the NFSS2 commands `\sffamily` and `\itshape`. If you prefer this behavior for the shorthands, just load the package newlfont after the `\documentclass` command.

7.5.5   Special Packages for NFSS

syntonly—**Checking Syntax Only**

The package syntonly implements the `\syntaxonly` declaration for LaTeX. This command can then be used in the preamble to run a document through LaTeX for syntax checking (without getting any output), which goes about four times as fast as normally.

tracefnt—**Tracing NFSS**

The package tracefnt can be used to detect problems in the font selection system. This package supports several options that allow you to customize the amount of information displayed by NFSS on the screen and in the transcript file.

errorshow   This option suppresses all warnings and information messages on the terminal; they will be written to the transcript file only. Only real errors will be shown. Since warnings about font substitutions and so on can mean that the final result will be incorrect, you should carefully study the transcript file before printing an important publication.

warningshow When this option is specified warnings and errors are shown on the terminal. This setting gives you the same amount of information as LaTeX2_ε does without the tracefnt package loaded.

infoshow This is the default when you load the tracefnt package. Extra information, which is normally only written to the transcript file, is now also displayed on your terminal.

debugshow This option additionally shows information about changes of text font and the restoration of such fonts after a group. Be careful when you turn on this option because it can produce very large transcript files that fill up your disk space.

In addition to these "standard tracing" options[8] the package tracefnt supports the following options:

pausing This option turns all warning messages into errors to help detecting the detection of problems in important publications.

loading This option shows the loading of external fonts. However, if the format or document class you use has already loaded some fonts then these will not be shown by this option.

The Program nfssfont

Within the NFSS distribution is a LaTeX file called nfssfont.tex that can be used to test new fonts, produce font tables showing all characters, etc. This file is an adaption of the program testfont.tex originally written by Donald Knuth. When you run this file through LaTeX, you will be asked to enter the name of the font to test. Your answer should be the external font name without any extension—e.g., cmr10 (Computer Modern Roman 10pt) or yinit (Yannis Haralambous' Initial font). You are then requested to enter a command. Probably the most important one is \table, which will produce a font chart like the one on page 207. To switch to a new test font, type \init; to finish the test, type \bye or \stop; and to learn about all the other possible tests (at the moment basically still tailored for OT1 encoding), type \help.

7.6 The Low-Level Interface

While the high-level font commands are intended for use in a document, the low-level commands are mainly for defining new commands in packages, or in the preamble of a document; see also section 7.6.4. To make the best use of such font commands, it is helpful to understand the internal organization of fonts in the New Font Selection Scheme.

---

[8]It is suggested that package writers who support tracing of their packages use these four standard names if applicable.

One goal of NFSS is to allow rational font selection, with algorithms guided by the principles of generic markup. For this purpose, it would be desirable to allow independent changes for as many font attributes as possible. On the other hand, font families in real life normally contain only a subset of the imaginable font attribute combinations. Therefore, allowing independent changes in too many attributes results in too many combinations for which no real (external) font is available and a default has to be substituted.

NFSS internally keeps track of five independent font attributes: the "current encoding," the "current family," the "current series," the "current shape," and the "current size." The encoding attribute was introduced in NFSS release 2 after it became clear that real support of multiple languages would be possible only by maintaining the character-encoding scheme independently of the other font attributes.

The values of these attributes determine the font currently in use. NFSS also maintains a large set of tables used to associate attribute combinations with external fonts (i.e., .tfm files that contain the information necessary for (LA)TEX to do its job). Font selection inside NFSS is then done in two steps:

- Some or all attributes are changed using the low-level commands \fontencoding, \fontfamily, \fontseries, \fontshape, and \fontsize.

- The font corresponding to this new setting is selected by calling the \selectfont command.

The second step comprises several actions. NFSS first checks whether or not the font corresponding to the desired attribute settings is already known to the system (i.e., the .tfm file is already loaded) and, if so, this font is selected. If not, the internal tables are searched to find the external font name associated with this setting. If such a font name can be found, the corresponding .tfm file is read into memory and afterward the font is selected for typesetting. If this process is not successful NFSS tries to find an alternative font as explained in section 7.6.3.

7.6.1 Setting Individual Font Attributes

Every font attribute has one command to change its current value. All of these commands will accept more or less any character string as an argument, but only a few values make sense. These values are not hard-wired into the NFSS system—they are only conventions set up in the internal tables. The following sections introduce the naming conventions used in the standard setup of NFSS, but anyone can change this setup by adding new font declarations to the internal tables. Obviously, anybody setting up new fonts for use with NFSS should try to obey these conventions whenever possible, since only a consistent naming convention can guarantee that appropriate fonts are selected in a generically marked-up document.

If you want to select a specific font using this interface—say, Computer Modern Dunhill bold condensed italic 14pt—a knowledge of the interface conventions alone is not enough, since there does not exist an external font for every combination of attribute values. You could try your luck by specifying something like the following set of commands

```
\fontencoding{OT1}\fontfamily{cmdh}\fontseries{bc}\fontshape{it}%
\fontsize{14}{16pt}\selectfont
```

which would be correct according to the naming conventions, as we will see in the following sections. But since this attribute combination does not correspond to a real font, NFSS would have to substitute a different font. The substitution mechanism may choose a font that is quite different from the one desired, so you should consult the font tables to see if the desired combination is available. (See section 7.6.3 for more details on the substitution process.) Every installation should have a local guide telling you exactly what fonts are available.

Choosing the Font Family

The font family is selected with the command `\fontfamily`. Its argument is a character string that refers to a font family declared in the internal tables. The character string was defined when these tables were set up and is usually a short letter sequence—for example, `cmr` for the Computer Modern Roman family. The family names should not be longer than five letters, because they will be combined with possibly three more letters to form a file name, which on some systems can have at most eight letters.

Choosing the Font Series

The series attribute is changed with the `\fontseries` command. The series combines weight and width in its argument; in other words, it is not possible to change the width of the current font independently of its weight. This arrangement was chosen because it is hardly ever necessary to change weight or width individually. On the contrary, a change in weight (say, to bold) often is accompanied by a change in width (say, to extended) in the designer's specification. This is not too surprising, since weight changes alter the horizontal appearance of the letters and thus call for adjustment in the expansion (i.e., the width) to produce a well-balanced look.

In the naming conventions for the argument for the `\fontseries` command the names for both the weight and the width are abbreviated so that each combination is unique. The conventions are shown in table 7.10 on the following page. These classifications are combined in the argument to `\fontseries`; however, any instance of `m` (standing for medium in weight or width) is dropped, except when both weight and width are medium. The latter case is abbreviated with a single `m`. For example, bold expanded would be `bx`, whereas medium expanded would be `x` and bold medium would be `b`.

Weight Classes			*Width Classes*		
Ultra Light	ul		Ultra Condensed	50%	uc
Extra Light	el		Extra Condensed	62.5%	ec
Light	l		Condensed	75%	c
Semi Light	sl		Semi Condensed	87.5%	sc
Medium (normal)	m		Medium	100%	m
Semi Bold	sb		Semi Expanded	112.5%	sx
Bold	b		Expanded	125%	x
Extra Bold	eb		Extra Expanded	150%	ex
Ultra Bold	ub		Ultra Expanded	200%	ux

Table 7.10: Weight and width classification of fonts

The percent values are derived from [30]. To combine the abbreviations in the \fontseries command, weight is used first and any instance of medium (m) is dropped except when weight and width are both medium. In this case, a single m is used.

Choosing the Font Shape

To change the shape attribute the \fontshape command is used. Again, for the standard shapes one- and two-letter abbreviations are used; these are shown in table 7.11 on the next page.

Choosing the Font Size

The font size is changed with the \fontsize{⟨*size*⟩}{⟨*skip*⟩} command. This is the only font attribute command that takes two arguments: the ⟨*size*⟩ to switch to and the baseline ⟨*skip*⟩ (the distance from baseline to baseline for this size). Font sizes are normally measured in points, so by convention the unit is omitted. The same is true for the second argument. However, if the baseline skip should be a rubber length—that is, if it contains plus or minus—you have to specify a unit. Thus, a valid size change could be requested by

```
\fontsize{14.4}{17}\selectfont
```

Even if such a request is valid in principle, no corresponding external font may exist in this size. In this case, NFSS would try to find a nearby size if its internal tables allow for size correction or would report an error if not.

If you use fonts existing in arbitrary sizes, (for example, PostScript fonts) you can, of course, select any size you want, e.g.:

```
\fontsize{1in}{1.2in}\selectfont Happy Birthday
```

Abbreviation	Description
n	upright (or normal) shape
it	*italic shape*
sl	*slanted or oblique shape*
sc	SMALL CAPS SHAPE
ui	*upright italic shape*
ol	OUTLINE shape

Table 7.11: Classification of font shapes

The standard abbreviations of the shapes for use in the \fontshape command are shown here using the Computer Modern Roman family as an example. The outline shape was generated by applying the METAFONT code presented in [26].

will produce a birthday poster line with letters in one inch size. However, there is one problem with using arbitrary sizes: since NFSS doesn't know for sure whether or not you are going to use formulas in the requested size, it sets up all fonts used in formulas for the new size. For arbitrary size, this usually means that it has to calculate the font sizes for use in subscripts and subsubscripts etc. In turn, this probably means that it has to load a lot of new fonts—something you can tell by looking at the transcript file. For this reason it is possible that you finally hit some internal limit if you have too many different size requests in your document. If this happens, you should tell NFSS what sizes to load for formulas using the \DeclareMathSizes declaration, rather than letting it use its own algorithm. See section 7.7.6 for more information on how to do this.

Choosing the Encoding

A change of encoding is performed with the command \fontencoding, where the argument is the internal name for the desired encoding. This name must be known to NFSS, either as one of the predefined encodings shown in table 7.12 on the following page or as declared with the \DeclareFontEncoding command (see section 7.7.4).

NFSS is based on the assumption that most (or, better, all) fonts for text are available in the same encoding as long as they are used to typeset in the same language. In other words, encoding changes only should become necessary if one is switching from one language to another. For example, an environment for typesetting in Cyrillic could be defined with

Some text по русски embedded

```
\newenvironment{Cyr}
        {\fontencoding{OT2}\fontfamily{cmr}\selectfont}{}
    Some text \begin{Cyr}po russki\end{Cyr} embedded
```

where OT2 specifies the University of Washington Cyrillic encoding. For this to work the encoding must be declared in the preamble or a package file.

Encoding	Description	Declared by
T1	TeX text Cork encoding	NFSS
OT1	TeX text as defined by Donald Knuth	NFSS
OML	TeX math text (italic) as defined by Donald Knuth	NFSS
OMS	TeX math symbol as defined by Donald Knuth	NFSS
OMX	TeX math extended symbol as defined by Donald Knuth	NFSS
U	Unknown encoding (for arbitrary rubbish)	NFSS
L..	Local encoding (for private encodings)	—

Table 7.12: The standard encodings used in NFSS

We hope that most of these encoding schemes will be superseded by standards defined by the TeX user groups so that in the future a change of encoding will be necessary only if one is switching from one language to another. For this reason, the names of most encodings start with O to emphasize that they are old and *obsolete*.

7.6.2 Setting Several Font Attributes

When designing page styles (see 4.3) or layout-oriented commands, you often want to select a particular font—that is, you need to specify values for all attributes. For this task NFSS provides the command \usefont, which takes four arguments: the encoding, family, series, and shape. The command updates those attributes and then calls \selectfont. If you also want to specify the size and baseline skip, place a \fontsize command in front of it, e.g.,

```
\fontsize{14}{16pt}\usefont{OT1}{cmdh}{bc}{it}
```

which would produce the same result as the hypothetical example from page 189.

Besides \usefont, NFSS also provides you with the \DeclareFixedFont declaration that can be used to define new commands that switch to a completely fixed font. Such commands are extremely fast since they do not have to look up any internal tables. They are therefore very useful in command definitions that have to switch back and forth between fixed fonts. For example, in the doc package (see chapter 14) the code-line numbers are typeset using the following definitions:

```
\DeclareFixedFont{\CodelineFont}{\encodingdefault}{\familydefault}
                {\seriesdefault}{\shapedefault}{7pt}
\newcommand{\theCodelineNo}{\CodelineFont\arabic{CodelineNo}}
```

As you can see from the example, \DeclareFixedFont has six arguments: the name of the command to be defined followed by the five font attributes used by

NFSS. Instead of supplying fixed values (except for the size), the built-in hooks that describe the main document font are used (see also section 7.3.5). Thus, in the example above \CodelineFont still depends on the overall layout for the document (via the settings of \encodingdefault, etc.). However, once the definition is carried out its meaning is frozen.

7.6.3 Automatic Substitution of Fonts

Whenever a font change request cannot be carried out because the combination is not known to NFSS, the system tries to recover by using a font with similar attributes. Here is what happens: If the combination of encoding scheme, family, series, and shape is not declared (see section 7.7.2), NFSS tries to find a known combination by first changing the shape attribute to a default. If the resulting combination is still unknown, it tries changing the series to a default. As a last resort it changes the family to a default value. Finally the internal table entry is looked up to find the requested size. For example, if you ask for \ttfamily\bfseries\itshape—i.e., for a typewriter font in a bold series and italic shape (which usually does not exist)—then you will get a typewriter font in medium series and upright shape, since NFSS first resets the shape before changing the series. If you prefer a typewriter font with italic shape in such a situation you have to announce your intention to NFSS using the sub function, which is explained on page 198.

The encoding scheme is never changed by the substitution process, because any alteration could produce wrong characters in the output. Recall that the encoding scheme defines how to interpret the input characters while the other attributes define how the output should look. It would be catastrophic if, say, a £ sign were changed into a $ sign on an invoice just because the software tried to be clever.

Thus every encoding scheme must have a default family, series, and shape, and at least the combination consisting of the encoding scheme together with the corresponding defaults must have a definition inside NFSS, as explained in section 7.7.4.

7.6.4 Using Low-Level Commands in the Document

The low-level font commands described in the preceding sections are intended to be used in the definition of higher-level commands, either in class or package files or in the document preamble.

Whenever possible, you should avoid using the low-level commands directly in a document if you can use high-level font commands like \textsf instead. The reason is that the low-level commands are very precise instructions to switch to a particular font, while the high-level commands can be customized using packages or declarations in the preamble. Suppose, for example, that you have selected Computer Modern Sans in your document using `\fontfamily{cmss}\selectfont`. If you later decide to typeset the whole document with PostScript fonts—say, Times—applying a package unfortunately would change only those parts of the document that do not contain `\fontfamily` commands.

7.7 Setting Up New Fonts

7.7.1 Overview

Setting up new fonts for use with NFSS basically means filling the internal tables of NFSS with the information necessary for later associating a font request in a document with the external `.tfm` file containing character information used by (LA)TEX. Thus the tables are responsible for associating with

```
\fontencoding{OT1}\fontfamily{cmdh}\fontseries{m}\fontshape{n}%
\fontsize{10}{12pt}\selectfont
```

the external `.tfm` file `cmdunh10.tfm`. To add new fonts, you need to reverse this process. For every new external font you have to ask yourself five questions:

1. What is the font's encoding scheme—i.e., which characters are in what positions?
2. What is its family name?
3. What is its series (weight and width)?
4. What is its shape?
5. What is its size?

The answers to the above questions will provide the information necessary to classify your external font according to the NFSS conventions, as described in section 7.6. The next few sections discuss how to enter new fonts into the NFSS tables so that they can be used in the main text. You normally need this information if you want to make use of new fonts—e.g., if you want to write a short package file for accessing a new font family. Later sections discuss more complicated concepts that come into play if you want to use, for example, special fonts for math instead of the standard ones.

7.7.2 Declaring New Font Families and Font Shape Groups

Each family/encoding combination has to be made known to NFSS through the command `\DeclareFontFamily`. This command has three arguments. The first two are the encoding scheme and the family name. The third is usually empty, but it may contain special options for font loading and is explained on page 200.

Thus, if you want to introduce a new family—say, Computer Modern Dunhill with the old TeX encoding scheme—you would write

```
\DeclareFontFamily{OT1}{cmdh}{}
```

A font family normally consists of many individual fonts. Instead of announcing each family member individually to NFSS, you have to combine fonts that differ only in size and declare them as a group.

Such a group is entered into the internal tables of NFSS with the `\DeclareFontShape` command, which has six arguments. The first four are the encoding scheme, the family name, the series name, and the shape name under which you want to access these fonts later on. The fifth argument is a list of sizes and external font names, given in a special format that we discuss below. The sixth argument is normally empty; its use is explained on page 200.

We will first show a few examples and introduce terminology; then we will discuss all the features in detail.

As an example, an NFSS table entry for Computer Modern Dunhill medium (series) upright (shape) in the encoding scheme "TeX text" could be entered as

```
\DeclareFontShape{OT1}{cmdh}{m}{n}{ <10> cmdunh10 }{}
```

assuming that there is only one external font for size 10pt available. If you also have this font available at 12pt, the declaration would be

```
\DeclareFontShape{OT1}{cmdh}{m}{n}{ <10> <12>cmdunh10 }{}
```

If the external font is available in all possible sizes (as is the case with Type 1 PostScript (outline) fonts, or when the driver program is able to generate fonts on demand by calling METAFONT), the declaration becomes very simple. For example, Times Roman bold (series) upright (shape) in the "Cork text" encoding scheme could be entered as

```
\DeclareFontShape{T1}{times}{b}{n}{ <-> pstimb }{}
```

The above example declares a size range with two open ends (no sizes specified to the left and the right of the -). As a result, the same external `.tfm` file (`pstimb`) is used for all sizes and is scaled to the desired size. If you have more than one `.tfm` file for a PostScript font—say, `pstim` for text sizes and `psdtim` for display sizes—the declaration would be

```
\DeclareFontShape{T1}{times}{m}{n}{ <-12> pstim <12-> psdtim }{}
```

in which case the `.tfm` file `pstim` would be used for sizes less than 12pt and `psdtim` for all sizes greater than or equal to 12pt.

The preceding examples show that the fifth argument of the command \DeclareFontShape consists of size specifications surrounded by angle brackets (i.e., <...>) intermixed with loading information for the individual sizes (e.g., font names). The part inside the angle brackets is called the "size info" and the part following the closing angle bracket is called the "font info." The font info is further structured into a "size function" (often empty) and its arguments; we discuss this case below. Within the arguments of \DeclareFontShape blanks are ignored to help make the entries more readable. In the unusual event that a real space has to be entered, you can use the command \space.

Simple Sizes and Size Ranges

The size infos—i.e., the parts between the angle brackets in the fifth argument to \DeclareFontShape—can be divided into "simple sizes" and "size ranges." A simple size is given by a single (decimal) number, like <10> or <14.4>, and in principle can have any positive value. However, since the number represents a font size measured in points, you probably won't find values less than 4 or higher than 120. A size range is given by two simple sizes separated by a hyphen, to indicate a range of font sizes that share the same font info. The lower boundary (i.e., the size to the left of the hyphen) is included in the range, while the upper boundary is excluded. For example, <5-10> denotes sizes greater than or equal to 5pt and less than 10pt. You can leave out the number on either side of the hyphen in a size range, with the obvious interpretation: <-> stands for all possible sizes, <-10> stands for all sizes less than 10pt, and <12-> for all sizes greater than or equal to 12pt.

Often several simple sizes have the same font info, in which case a convenient shorthand is to omit all but the last font infos, e.g.,

```
\DeclareFontShape{OT1}{panr}{m}{n}{ <5> <6> <7> <8> <9> <10>
            <10.95> <12> <14.4> <17.28> <20.74> <24.88> pan10 }{}
```

This example declares the font Pandora medium Roman as being available in several sizes, all of them produced by scaling from the same design size.

Size Functions

As noted earlier, the font info (the string after the closing angle bracket) is further structured into a size function and its argument. If there is a * in the font info string, everything to the left of it forms the function name and everything to the right is the argument. If there is no asterisk, as in all of the examples so far, the whole string is regarded as the argument and the function name is "empty."

Based on the size requested by the user and the information in the \DeclareFontShape command, size functions produce the specification necessary for NFSS to find the external font and load it at the right size. They are also responsible for informing the user about anything special that happens. For example, some functions differ only in whether or not they issue a warning. This capability allows the system maintainer to set up NFSS in the way best suited for the particular site.

The name of a size function consists of zero or more letters. Some of the size functions can take two arguments, one optional and one mandatory. Such an optional argument has to be enclosed in square brackets. For example, the specification

```
<-> s * [0.9] cmfib8
```

would select, for all possible sizes (we have the range 0 to ∞), the size function s with the optional argument 0.9 and the mandatory argument cmfib8.

The size specification in \DeclareFontShape are inspected in the order they are specified. When a size info matches the requested user size, the corresponding size function is executed. If this process yields a valid font no further entries are inspected. Otherwise the search is continued with the next entry.

The standard size functions are listed below. The documentation accompanying NFSS describes how to define additional functions if this should ever become necessary.

The "empty" Function   Because the empty function is used most often, it has the shortest possible name. (Every table entry takes up a small bit of internal memory, so the syntax chosen tries to find a balance between a perfect user interface and compactness of storage.) The empty function loads the font info exactly at the requested size if it is a simple size. If there is a size range and the size requested by the user falls into the range, it loads the font exactly at the user size.

For example, if the user requested 14.4, then the specification

```
<-> panr10
```

would load the .tfm file panr10.tfm at 14.4 pt. Since this font was designed for 10pt (it is the Pandora Roman font at 10pt), all the values in the .tfm file are scaled by a factor of 1.44.

Sometimes one wants to load a font at a slightly larger or smaller size than the one requested by the user. This adjustment may be necessary when fonts from one family appear to be too large compared to fonts from other families used in the same document. For this purpose the empty size function allows an optional argument to represent a scale factor that, if present, is multiplied by the requested size to yield the actual size to be loaded. Thus,

```
<-> [0.95] helvetica
```

would always load the font Helvetica at 95 percent of the requested size. If the optional argument is used, the empty size function will issue a warning to alert the user that a font is not loaded at its intended size.

The "s" Function   The s function has the same functionality as the empty function, but does not produce warnings (the s means silence). Writing

```
\DeclareFontShape{T1}{times}{b}{n}{ <-> s * [0.9] pstimb }{}
```

avoids all the messages that would be written on the terminal if the empty function were used. Messages are still written to the transcript file so that you can find out what fonts have been used if something goes wrong.

The "gen" Function   Often the external font names are built by appending the font size to a string that represents the typeface—e.g., cmtt8, cmtt9, and cmtt10 are the external names for the fonts Computer Modern Typewriter in 8, 9, and 10pt. If font names are organized in such a scheme, you can make use of the gen function to shorten the entry. This function combines the font info and the requested size to generate (hence gen) the external font names so that you can write

```
<8> <9> <10> gen * cmtt
```

as a shorthand for

```
<8> cmtt8 <9> cmtt9 <10> cmtt10
```

thereby saving eight characters in the internal tables of NFSS. This function combines both parts literally, so do not use it with decimal sizes like 14.4. Also ensure that the digits in the external font name really represent the design size (for example, cmr17 is actually Computer Modern Roman at 17.28pt).

Otherwise the gen function behaves like the empty function—i.e., the optional argument, if given, represents a scale factor and, if used, generates an information message.

The "sgen" Function   The sgen function is the silent variant of the gen function. It writes any message only to the transcript file.

The "sub" Function   Another important size function is the sub function, used to substitute a different font shape group if no external font exists for the current font shape group. In this case the argument is not an external font name but a different family, series, and shape combination separated by slashes (the encoding will not change for reasons explained before). For example, the Computer Modern Sans family has no italic shape, only a slanted shape. Thus it makes sense to declare the slanted shape as a substitute for the italic one by defining

```
\DeclareFontShape{OT1}{cmss}{m}{it}{ <-> sub * cmss/m/sl }{}
```

Without this declaration, the automatic substitution mechanism of NFSS (see section 7.6.3) would substitute the default shape, Computer Modern Sans upright.

Besides the substitution of complete font shape groups, there are other good uses for the sub function:

```
\DeclareFontShape{OT1}{cmss}{m}{sl}{ <-8> sub * cmss/m/n
   <8> cmssi8  <9> cmssi9  <10><10.95> cmssi10  <12><14.4> cmssi12
   <17.28><20.74><24.88> cmssi17 }{}
```

This declaration means that for sizes below 8pt NFSS should look in the font shape declaration for OT1/cmss/m/n. Such substitutions can be chained. People familiar with the standard font distribution know that there is no Computer Modern Sans font smaller than 8pt, so the substituted font shape group will probably contain another substitution entry. Nevertheless using this device has the advantage that when you get an additional font you have to change only one font shape group declaration—other declarations that use this one benefit automatically.

The size function sub generates an information message on the terminal about the substitution. If you want to prevent this message, use the ssub function instead.

The "ssub" Function   The ssub function has the same functionality as the sub function, but does not produces on-screen warnings (the first s means silence).

The "subf" Function   The subf function is a cross between the empty function and sub in that it loads fonts in the same way as the empty function but produces a warning that this was done as a substitution because the requested font shape is not available. Thus you can use this function to substitute some external fonts without the need to declare a separate font shape group for them, as in the case of the sub function.

The "ssubf" Function   This is the silent variant of the subf; it writes its messages only to the transcript file.

The "fixed" Function   This function disregards the requested size and instead loads the external font given as an argument. If present, the optional argument denotes the size (in points) at which the font will be loaded. Thus this function allows you to specify size ranges for which one font in some fixed size will be loaded.

The "sfixed" Function   Once more, `sfixed` is a silent variant. This function is used, for example, to load the font containing the large math symbols, which is often only available in one size.

Font-Loading Options

As already mentioned, you need to declare each family using the command `\DeclareFontFamily`. The argument to this command, as well as the sixth argument to `\DeclareFontShape`, can be used to specify special operations that are carried out when a font is loaded. In this way, you can change parameters which are associated with a font as a whole.

For every external font (LA)TEX maintains, besides the information about each character, a set of global dimensions and other values associated with each font. For example, every font has its own "hyphen character," the character that is inserted automatically when (LA)TEX hyphenates a word. Another example is the normal width and the stretchability of a blank space between words (the "inter-word space"), again a value maintained for every font and changed whenever (LA)TEX switches to a new font. By changing these values when a font is loaded, special effects can be achieved.

Normally changes apply to a whole family; for example, you may want to prohibit hyphenation for all words typeset in the typewriter family. In this case, the third argument of `\DeclareFontFamily` should be used. If the changes should only apply to a specific font shape group, you have to use the sixth argument of `\DeclareFontShape`. In other words, when a font is loaded, NFSS first applies the argument of `\DeclareFontFamily` and then the sixth argument of `\DeclareFontShape`, so that it can override the load options specified for the whole family if necessary.

Below we study the information that can be set in this way (unfortunately, not everything is changeable) and discuss some useful examples. This part of the interface addresses very low-level commands of TEX. Since it is so specialized, no effort was made to make the interface more LATEX-like. Therefore the methods for assigning integers and dimensions to variables are somewhat unusual.

By `\hyphenchar\font=`⟨*number*⟩ (LA)TEX denotes the character that is inserted as the hyphen when a word is hyphenated. The ⟨*number*⟩ represents the position of this character within the encoding scheme. The default is the value of `\defaulthyphenchar`, which is 45, representing the position of the - character in most encoding schemes. If this number is set to −1, hyphenation is suppressed. Thus, by declaring

```
\DeclareFontFamily{OT1}{cmtt}{\hyphenchar\font=-1}
```

you can suppress hyphenation for all fonts in the `cmtt` family with the encoding scheme OT1. Fonts with the Cork encoding have an alternate hyphen character in position 127, so that you can set, for example

```
\DeclareFontFamily{T1}{dcmr}{\hyphenchar\font=127}
```

This makes the hyphen character inserted by (LA)TEX different from the compound-word dash entered in words like "so-called." (LA)TEX does not hyphenate words that already contain explicit hyphen characters (except just after the hyphen) which can be a real problem in languages where the average word length is much larger than in English. With the above setting this problem can be solved.

Every (LA)TEX font has an associated set of dimensions, changed by assignments of the form `\fontdimen`⟨*number*⟩`\font=`⟨*dimen*⟩, in which ⟨*number*⟩ is the reference number for the dimension and ⟨*dimen*⟩ is the value to be assigned. The default values are taken from the `.tfm` file when the font is loaded. Each font has at least seven such dimensions:

`\fontdimen1` specifies the slant per point of the characters. If the value is zero, the font is upright.

`\fontdimen2` specifies the normal width of a space used between words (interword space).

`\fontdimen3` specifies the additional stretchability of the inter-word space—i.e., the extra amount of white space that (LA)TEX is allowed to add to the space between words to produce justified lines in a paragraph. In an emergency (LA)TEX may add more space than this allowed value; in that case an "underfull box" will be reported.

`\fontdimen4` specifies the allowed shrinkability of the inter-word space—i.e., the amount of space that (LA)TEX is allowed to subtract from the normal inter-word space (`\fontdimen2`) to produce justified lines in a paragraph. (LA)TEX will never shrink the inter-word space below this minimum.

`\fontdimen5` is the so-called x-height of the font. It defines the font-oriented dimension 1 ex.

`\fontdimen6` is the so-called quad width. It defines the font-oriented dimension 1 em.

`\fontdimen7` specifies the amount of extra space added after end-of-sentence periods when `\nonfrenchspacing` is in force.

When changing the inter-word spacing associated with a font, you cannot use an absolute value because such a value must be usable for all sizes within one font shape group. You therefore have to define the value by using some other parameter that depends on the font. You could say, for example

```
\DeclareFontShape{OT1}{cmr}{m}{n}{...}
   {\fontdimen2\font=.7\fontdimen2\font}
```

This declaration reduces the normal inter-word space to 70 percent of its original value. In a similar manner, the stretchability and shrinkability could be changed.

Some fonts used in formulas need more than seven font dimensions. These are the symbol fonts called "`symbols`" and "`largesymbols`"; see section 7.7.6. TeX will not typeset a formula if these symbol fonts have fewer then 22 and 13 `\fontdimen` parameters, respectively. The values of these parameters are used to position the characters in a math formula. Explaining the meaning of every such `\fontdimen` parameter goes beyond the scope of this book; details can be found in appendix G of the TeXbook [39].

One unfortunate optimization is built into the TeX system: TeX loads every `.tfm` file only once at one size. It is therefore not possible to define one NFSS font shape group (with the `\DeclareFontShape` command) to load some external font—say, `cmtt10`—and use another `\DeclareFontShape` command to load the same external font, this time changing some of the `\fontdimen` parameters or some other parameter associated with the font. Trying to do this changes the values for both font shape groups.

Suppose, for example, that you try to define a font shape with tight spacing by making the inter-word space smaller—e.g., saying

```
\DeclareFontShape{T1}{times}{m}{n}{ <-> pstim }{}
\DeclareFontShape{T1}{times}{c}{n}{ <-> pstim }
                 {\fontdimen2\font=.7\fontdimen2\font}
```

This declaration would not work. The inter-word spacing for the medium shape would change when the tight shape was loaded to the values specified there, and this result is not what you wanted. The best way to solve this problem is to define a virtual font that contains the same characters as the original font, differing only in the settings of the font dimensions (see also section 9.1.1).

7.7.3 Modifying Font Families and Font Shape Groups

If you need a nonstandard font shape group declaration for a particular document, just place your private declaration in a package or the preamble of your document. This will overwrite any existing declaration for the font shape combination. Note, however, that the use of `\DeclareFontFamily` prevents a later loading of the corresponding `.fd` file (see section 7.7.5). Also your new declaration has no effect on fonts already loaded.

7.7.4 Declaring New Encoding Schemes

Font changes that involve alterations in the encoding scheme require certain precautions. For example, in the Cork encoding, most accented letters have their own glyphs, whereas in the traditional TeX text encoding, accented letters have

to be generated from accents and letters using the \accent primitive. (It is desirable to have glyphs for accented letters rather than using the \accent primitive
because, among other things, the former approach allows correct hyphenation.)
If the two approaches have to be mixed, perhaps because a font is only available
in one of the encodings, you need to change the definitions of commands like
\", so that they behave differently depending on the font.

For these reasons, every encoding scheme has to be formally introduced to
NFSS using the \DeclareFontEncoding command, which takes three arguments.
The first argument is the name of the encoding under which you access it using
the \fontencoding command. See table 7.12 on page 192 for the list of standard
encoding schemes and their internal NFSS names.

The second argument contains any code (such as definitions) to be executed every time NFSS switches from one encoding to another using the
\fontencoding command. The final argument contains code to be used whenever the font is accessed as a mathematical alphabet. Thus these arguments
can be used to redefine commands that depend on the positions of characters
in the encoding. To avoid spurious spaces in the output (coming from extra
spaces in such arguments) the space character is ignored within them. In the
unlikely event that you need spaces in a definition in one of the arguments, use
the \space command.

The starting letters T, O, and M are reserved for standard encodings and
should not be used when you define your private encodings. For this purpose
you should choose names starting with L for "local." This practice ensures that
files using official encodings are portable. The NFSS maintainers will add new
standard encodings to the NFSS documentation.

Also, as we saw in section 7.6.3 on font substitution, the default values
for family, series, and shape may need to be different for different encodings.
For this, NFSS provides the command \DeclareFontSubstitution, which again
takes the encoding as the first argument. The next three arguments are the
default values (associated with this encoding) for family, series, and shape for
use in the automatic substitution process, as explained in section 7.6.3.

7.7.5   Internal File Organization

Font families can be declared when a format file is generated or in the document
preamble, or they can be loaded on demand when a font change command
in the document requests a combination that so far has been unused. The
first option takes up internal memory in every LaTeX run, even if the font is
not used, while the second and the third possibilities take a little more time
during document formatting, since the font definitions have to be read in during
processing time. Nevertheless, it is preferable to use the latter solution for most
font shape groups, because it allows you to typeset a wide variety of documents
with a single LaTeX format.

When the format is generated, LATEX will read a file named `fontdef.ltx`, which should contain the font family definitions normally used in documents. All other font family definitions should be declared in external files loaded on request: either package files or font definition (`.fd`) files (see below).

If you place font family definitions in a package file you must explicitly load this package after the `\documentclass` command. But there is a third possibility: whenever NFSS gets a request for a font family `foo` in an encoding scheme `BAR` and it has no knowledge about this combination, it will try to load a file `BARfoo.fd`. If this file exists, it is supposed to contain font shape group definitions for family `foo` in encoding scheme `BAR`—that is, declarations of the form

```
\DeclareFontFamily{BAR}{foo}{..}
\DeclareFontShape{BAR}{foo}{..}{..}{..}{..}
    ...
\endinput
```

In this way it is possible to declare a huge number of font families for the NFSS system without filling valuable internal memory with information that is almost never used. Unfortunately, this feature is not fully available on (LA)TEX systems that use different search paths for the commands `\input` and `\openin`. On such systems the `.fd` feature can be activated at installation time by supplying NFSS with a full path denoting the directories containing all the `.fd` files. As a result, however, local `.fd` files—those stored in the current directory—may not be usable on such systems. This is currently the case for some VMS installations, but we hope that this restriction will be lifted in the near future.

To summarize, each `.fd` file should contain all font definitions for one font family in one encoding scheme. It should consist of one or more `\DeclareFontShape` declarations and exactly one `\DeclareFontFamily` declaration. Other definitions should not appear in such a file, except perhaps for `\typeout` commands informing the user about the font loading. As an alternative to the `\typeout` command, you can use the plain TEX command `\wlog`, which writes its argument only into the transcript file. Detailed information in the transcript file should be generated by all `.fd` files that are used in production, because looking at this transcript will help to locate errors by providing information about the files and their version used in a particular job. If `\typeout` or `\wlog` commands are used, it is important to know that spaces and empty lines in a `.fd` file are ignored. Thus you have to use the command `\space` in the argument to `\typeout` or `\wlog` to obtain a blank space on the screen and the transcript file.

New encoding schemes cannot be introduced via the `.fd` mechanism. NFSS will reject any request to switch to an encoding scheme that was not declared in `fontdef.ltx` or in a package file.

7.7.6   Declaring New Fonts for Use in Math

Specifying Font Sizes

For every text size NFSS maintains three sizes that are used to typeset formulae (see also section 8.9.1). These are the size in which to typeset most of the symbols (selected by \textstyle or \displaystyle), the size for first order sub- and superscripts (\scriptstyle), and the size for higher order sub- and superscripts (\scriptscriptstyle). If you switch to a new text size, for which the corresponding math sizes are not yet known, NFSS tries to calculate them as fractions of the text size. Instead of letting NFSS do the calculation you might want to specify the correct values yourself by using \DeclareMathSizes. This declaration takes four aguments: the outer text sizes and the three math sizes for this text size. For example, the class file for *The LaTeX Companion* contains settings like

```
\DeclareMathSizes{14}{14}{10}{7}      \DeclareMathSizes{36}{}{}{}
```

The first declaration defines the math sizes for the 14pt heading size to be 14pt, 10pt, and 7pt, respectively. With the second declaration (the size for the chapter headings) we inform NFSS that no math sizes are necessary for 36pt text size. This avoids the unnecessary loading of more than thirty additional fonts which would have made it impossible to process *The LaTeX Companion* with all its examples as a single document. However, you should be careful with disabling math sizes, because if some formula is typeset in such a size after all, it will be typeset in whatever math sizes are still in effect from an earlier text size.

Adding New Symbol Fonts

We have already seen how to use math alphabet commands to produce letters with special shapes in a formula. We now discuss how to add fonts containing special symbols and how to make such symbols accessible in formulas. Such fonts are called "symbol fonts."

The process of adding new symbol fonts is similar to declaring a new math alphabet identifier: \DeclareSymbolFont defines the defaults for all math versions, and \SetSymbolFont overrides the defaults for a particular version.

The math symbol fonts are accessed via a symbolic name that is a string of letters. If, for example, you want to install the AMS fonts msbm10, shown in table 7.8 on page 207, you first have to make the typeface known to NFSS using the declarations described in the previous sections. These instructions would look like

```
\DeclareFontFamily{U}{msb}{}
\DeclareFontShape{U}{msb}{m}{n}{ <5> <6> <7> <8> <9> gen * msbm
        <10> <10.95> <12> <14.4> <17.28> <20.74> <24.88> msbm10}{}
```

Type	Meaning	Example	Type	Meaning	Example
\mathord	Ordinary	/	\mathop	Large operator	\sum
\mathbin	Binary operator	+	\mathrel	Relation	=
\mathopen	Opening	(	\mathclose	Closing	)
\mathpunct	Punctuation	,	\mathalpha	Alphabet character	A

Table 7.13: The math symbol types

in your package file. In fact, only the \DeclareFontEncoding declaration must be in the package or class file; the other two can be placed in a .fd file. Then you have to declare that symbol font for all math versions by issuing the command

```
\DeclareSymbolFont{AMSb}{U}{msb}{m}{n}
```

which makes the font shape group U/msb/m/n available as a symbol font under the symbolic name AMSb. If there were a bold series in this font family (unfortunately there is not), you could then change the setup for the bold math version by saying

```
\SetSymbolFont{AMSb}{bold}{U}{msb}{b}{n}
```

After taking care of the font declarations, you can make use of this symbol font in math mode. But how do you tell NFSS that $a\lessdot b$ should produce $a < b$, for example? For this, you have to introduce your own symbol names to NFSS, using \DeclareMathSymbol. For example, \lessdot would be declared using

```
\DeclareMathSymbol{\lessdot}{\mathbin}{AMSb}{"6C}
```

The first argument to \DeclareMathSymbol is your chosen command name. Instead of a command name you can also use a single character in the first argument. For example, the euler package has several declarations of the form

```
\DeclareMathSymbol{0}{\mathalpha}{letters}{"30}
```

that specify where to fetch the digits from.

The second argument is one of the commands shown in table 7.13 and describes the nature of the symbol—whether it is a binary operator, a relation, etc. This information is used by (LA)TEX to leave the correct amount of space around the symbol when it is encountered in a formula. Incidentally, except for \mathalpha, these commands can be used directly in math formulas as functions with one argument, in which case they space their (possibly complex) argument as if it were of the corresponding type.

Test of msbm7 on December 1,1993 at 2129

	´0	´1	´2	´3	´4	´5	´6	´7	
´00x	≨	≩	≰	≱	≮	≯	⊀	⊁	˝0x
´01x	⪇	⪈	⋦	⋧	⪕	⪖	⋨	⋩	
´02x	⋨	⋩	≨	≩	⪉	⪊	⪵	⪶	˝1x
´03x	⪹	⪺	⪍	⪎	≁	≆	/	\	
´04x	⊊	⊋	⊈	⊉	⊊	⊋	⊊	⊋	˝2x
´05x	⊊	⊋	⊄	⊅	∦	⊬	′	″	
´06x	↚	↛	⇍	⇏	⊭	⊬	⊮	⊯	˝3x
´07x	↤	↦	⇤	⇥	⇹	↔	∗	∅	
´10x	∄	A	B	C	D	E	F	G	˝4x
´11x	H	I	J	K	L	M	N	O	
´12x	P	Q	R	S	T	U	V	W	˝5x
´13x	X	Y	Z	⌢	⌢	⌢	⌢		
´14x	⅃	Ɔ					℧	ð	˝6x
´15x	≊	⊐	⊒	⌐	<	>	⋉	⋊	
´16x	∣	∥	∖	∼	≈	≅	≊	⪿	˝7x
´17x	⌢	⌢	Ⅎ	ϰ	k	ℏ	ℏ	϶	
	˝8	˝9	˝A	˝B	˝C	˝D	˝E	˝F	

Figure 7.8: Output of the **nfssfont.tex** program for the font `msbm7`

In the third argument you name the symbol font from which the symbol should be fetched—that is, the symbolic name introduced with the `\DeclareSymbolFont` command. The fourth argument gives the symbol's position in the font encoding, either as a decimal, octal, or hexadecimal value. Octal (base 8) and hexadecimal (base 16) numbers are preceded by ' and ", respectively. If you look at figure 7.8, you can easily determine the positions of all glyphs in this font. Such tables can be printed using the LaTeX program nfssfont, which is part of the NFSS distribution; see the section on page 187.

Since `\DeclareMathSymbol` is used to specify a position in some symbol font, it is important that all external fonts associated with this symbol font via the `\DeclareSymbolFont` and the `\SetSymbolFont` commands have the same character in that position. The simplest way to ensure this uniformity is to use only fonts with the same encoding (unless it is the U encoding, since this means unknown and thus may differ from font to font).

If you look again at the font chart for `msbm7`, you will notice that this font contains so-called "blackboard bold" letters, e.g., $\mathbb{ABC}$. If you want to use these letters as a math alphabet, you can define them using `\DeclareMathAlphabet`, but since this symbol font is already firmly present, it is better to use a shortcut:

```
\DeclareSymbolFontAlphabet{\Bbb}{AMSb}
```

That is, you give the name of your math alphabet identifier and the symbolic name of the previously declared symbol font.

An important reason not to duplicate symbol fonts is that there is an upper limit of sixteen for the number of math fonts that can be active at any given time in (LA)TEX. In calculating this limit, each symbol font counts; math alphabets count only if they are actually used in the document, and they count locally in each math version. Thus, if eight symbol fonts are declared, you can use up to eight (possibly different) math alphabet identifiers within every version.

To summarize: for introducing new symbol fonts you only need to issue a few `\DeclareFont...` declarations and a possibly large number of `\DeclareMathSymbol` commands; so adding such fonts is best done in a package file.

Introducing New Math Versions

We've already mentioned that the standard setup predeclares two math versions, normal and bold. If you want to introduce additional versions, you have to use the declaration `\DeclareMathVersion`. This declaration has one argument, the name of the new math version. All symbol fonts and all math alphabets previously declared are automatically available in this math version; the default fonts are assigned to them—i.e., the fonts you have specified with `\DeclareMathAlphabet` or `\DeclareSymbolFont`.

You can then change the setup for your new version by issuing appropriate `\Set...` commands, as shown in the previous sections for the bold math version. Again, the introduction of a new math version is normally done in a package file.

Changing the Symbol Font Setup

Besides adding new symbol fonts to access additional symbols, the commands we have just seen also can be used to change an existing setup. This capability is of interest if you like to use special fonts in some or all math versions.

The default settings in NFSS are:

```
\DeclareMathVersion{normal}   \DeclareMathVersion{bold}
\DeclareSymbolFont{operators}      {OT1}{cmr}{m} {n}
```

```
\SetSymbolFont    {operators}{bold}{OT1}{cmr}{bx}{n}
\DeclareSymbolFont{letters}         {OML}{cmm}{m}{it}
\SetSymbolFont    {letters}  {bold}{OML}{cmm}{b}{it}
\DeclareSymbolFont{symbols}{OMS}{cmsy}{m}{n}
\DeclareSymbolFont{largesymbols}{OMX}{cmex}{m}{n}
```

In the standard setup, digits and text produced by "log-like operators" such as \log and \max are taken from the symbol font called operators. To change this situation so that these elements agree with the main text font—say Computer Modern Sans rather than Computer Modern Roman—you can say

```
\SetSymbolFont{operators}{normal}{OT1}{cmss}{m} {n}
\SetSymbolFont{operators}{bold}   {OT1}{cmss}{bx}{n}
```

Symbol fonts with the names symbols and largesymbols play a unique rôle in TeX and for this reason need a special number of \fontdimen parameters attached to them. Thus, only specially prepared fonts can be used for these two symbol fonts. In principle it is possible to add such parameters to any font at loading time by using the third parameter of \DeclareFontFamily or the sixth parameter of \DeclareFontShape. Information on the special parameters for these symbol fonts can be found in appendix G of [39].

7.7.7 The Order of Declaration

NFSS forces you to give all declarations in a specific order so that it can check whether or not you have specified all necessary information. If you declare objects in the wrong order, NFSS will complain. Here are the dependencies that you have to obey:

- \DeclareFontFamily checks that the encoding scheme was previously declared with \DeclareFontEncoding.

- \DeclareFontShape checks that the font family is declared to be available in the requested encoding (\DeclareFontFamily).

- \DeclareSymbolFont checks that the encoding scheme is valid.

- \SetSymbolFont additionally ensures that the requested math version is already declared (\DeclareMathVersion) and that the requested symbol font is already declared (\DeclareSymbolFont).

- \DeclareSymbolFontAlphabet checks that the command name for the alphabet identifier can be used and that the symbol font was previously declared.

- \DeclareMathAlphabet checks that the chosen command name can be used and that the encoding scheme is already declared.

- \SetMathAlphabet checks that the alphabet identifier was previously declared with \DeclareMathAlphabet or \DeclareSymbolFontAlphabet and that the math version and the encoding scheme are already known.

- \DeclareMathSymbol makes sure that the command name can be used (that is, is either undefined or was previously declared to be a math symbol) and that the symbol font was previously declared.

- Finally, when the \begin{document} command is reached, NFSS makes some additional checks, like verifying that substitution defaults for every encoding scheme point to known font shape group declarations.

7.8   Warning and Error Messages

The most striking difference between the old font selection and NFSS is probably the appearance of overfull box messages. For example, earlier drafts of this book produced messages like

```
Overfull \hbox (14.13165pt too wide) in paragraph at lines 775--775
[]\OT1/cmtt/m/n/8 oldlfont.sty       {\errmessage{The package
'oldlfont' does not make sense if you[]
```

As you can see, the message shows the overfull box text with internal font representations, such as \OT1/cmtt/m/n/8, which in NFSS are considerably longer and more detailed and which clearly show the encoding, family, series, and shape of the font in question. The old LaTeX probably would have displayed something like \\ptt\@viiipt in this case (indeed, with two backslashes), but the NFSS display is more informative. However, if such overfull boxes contain formula material, the result unfortunately becomes nearly unreadable, since in a formula nearly every character is taken from a special font. For example,

```
Overfull \hbox (10.01093pt too wide) detected at line 23
$\OML/cmm/m/it/10 A \OMS/cmsy/m/n/10 ^^T [][] \OML/cmm/m/it/10 x$
```

is the symbolic representation that (LA)TEX would display for the simple formula

$$A \leq \textstyle\sum_{i=1}^{n} x$$

$$\verb|$A\leq\sum_{i=1}^n x$|$$

In such a case it is better to check the line number in your source (in this case 23) to find the offending text.

The following alphabetical list describes the remaining warning and error messages issued by NFSS and explains their most likely causes. The warning messages are usually prefixed with the string Warning: or Info:. The error messages either identify themselves as LaTeX errors or, if they should occur only in an improperly set up system, as TeX errors.

`Calculating math sizes for size` ⟨*text size*⟩
  NFSS has to guess the correct font sizes for subscripts and superscripts because it could not find the information for the current ⟨*text size*⟩ in its internal tables. This message usually is followed by several font size correction warnings because NFSS's initial guess is seldom successful. This situation can arise when you select an uncommon size using the `\fontsize` command; see also section 7.7.6.

`Checking defaults for` ⟨*cdp*⟩/⟨*font shape*⟩
  This message is written in the transcript file when NFSS is verifying that the substitution defaults for the encoding ⟨*cdp*⟩ are sensible. It is followed either by `...okay` or by an error message. In the latter case, the ⟨*font shape*⟩ group specified with `\DeclareFontEncoding` is unknown to NFSS.

`Command` ⟨*name*⟩ `already defined`
  NFSS issues this message when you have tried to declare a command that already has a meaning. Your declaration is ignored and you have to choose a different name.

`Command` ⟨*name*⟩ `invalid in math mode`
  This is either a warning or an error message that means you have used a command in math mode that should only be used in normal text. In case of an error message, use `h` to get further help.

`Command` ⟨*name*⟩ `not defined as a math alphabet`
  This error is issued when you try to use `\SetMathAlphabet` on a ⟨*name*⟩ that was not previously declared with `\DeclareMathAlphabet` or `\DeclareSymbolFontAlphabet` to be a math alphabet identifier.

`Command \tracingfonts not provided`
  You have specified `\tracingfonts=...` in the preamble of your document but removed the tracefnt package from the document. This is just a friendly warning that can be ignored.

`Corrupted NFSS tables`
  You will get this message when NFSS has tried some font substitution and detected a loop. If `\DeclareErrorFont` was set up correctly, you can continue, but this error always should be brought to the attention of your system maintainer.[9]

`Encoding` ⟨*name*⟩ `has changed to` ⟨*new name*⟩ `for` `...`
  This warning is issued when in the declaration of a symbol font different

---

[9]The declaration `\DeclareErrorFont` is used during installation and points to a font that should be used when everything else fails. See the installation description of NFSS for more details.

encoding schemes have been used in different math versions. This may mean that the \DeclareMathSymbol commands for this symbol font are not valid in all math versions.

Encoding scheme ⟨*name*⟩ unknown

The encoding scheme ⟨*name*⟩ you have specified in a declaration or in \fontencoding is not known to the system. You either forgot to declare it using \DeclareFontEncoding or you misspelled its name.

External font ⟨*name*⟩ loaded for size ⟨*size*⟩

NFSS has ignored your request to load some font shape at size ⟨*size*⟩ and has loaded the external font ⟨*name*⟩ instead. (This message is generated by the size function fixed.)

FontDef file: ⟨*name*⟩ ...

You will find such a message in your transcript file of the (IA)TEX run. ⟨*name*⟩ is the name of a font definition file that was loaded. Such files contain font shape group declarations and are described in section 7.7.5.

Font family ⟨*cdp*⟩+⟨*family*⟩ unknown

You tried to declare a font shape group with \DeclareFontShape without first declaring the font ⟨*family*⟩ as being available in the encoding ⟨*cdp*⟩ using \DeclareFontFamily.

Font ⟨*name*⟩ not found

The internal tables of NFSS have been corrupted and it was unable to find the external font ⟨*name*⟩.

Font shape ⟨*font shape*⟩ in size ⟨*size*⟩ not available

This message is issued by NFSS when it tries to select a font but finds that the requested combination is not available. Depending on the contents of the internal tables, it will then issue one of the following additional messages:

external font ⟨*name*⟩ used

NFSS has selected the external font ⟨*name*⟩ in that particular situation and does not know to which font shape group it belongs. (This message is generated by the size function subf.)

size ⟨*size*⟩ substituted

NFSS has selected the correct shape, but since the requested size is not available NFSS has chosen the nearby size ⟨*size*⟩. This action is taken automatically if none of the simple sizes or size ranges in the ⟨*font shape*⟩ group declaration match.

shape ⟨*font shape*⟩ tried

NFSS has selected a different ⟨*font shape*⟩ group because the requested one is not available for the requested ⟨*size*⟩. (This message is generated by the size function sub.)

`Font shape ⟨`*font shape*`⟩ will be scaled to size ⟨`*size*`⟩`
> NFSS informs you that it has loaded your requested font by scaling it to the desired size. This action keeps (LA)TEX happy, but to print a document containing scaled fonts your printer driver must have these fonts in the correct size or must be able to scale them automatically.

`Font shape ⟨`*font shape*`⟩ undefined. Using '⟨`*other shape*`⟩' instead`
> This information is given after NFSS has decided which substitution shape it is going to use.

`Font shape ⟨`*font shape*`⟩ not found`
> This error message is issued when there is something very wrong with a \DeclareFontShape declaration—e.g., if it does not contain any size specifications. Check the setup for the font shape group in question.

`Math alphabet identifier ⟨`*id*`⟩ is undefined in math version ⟨`*name*`⟩`
> You have tried to use the math alphabet identifier ⟨*id*⟩ in a math version (⟨*name*⟩) for which it was not set up. Add an additional \SetMathAlphabet declaration to the preamble of your document to assign a font shape group for this alphabet identifier.

`Math version ⟨`*name*`⟩ is not defined`
> You tried to assign a math alphabet or a symbol font to a math version that is unknown to NFSS. You either misspelled its name or you forgot to declare this version (perhaps you have to add some package file). It is also possible that the math version you selected with \mathversion is not known to the system.

`*** NFSS release 1 command ⟨`*name*`⟩ found`
> This comes either as a warning or as an error message. NFSS has encountered the command ⟨*name*⟩, which is no longer valid in release 2. In most cases NFSS will be able to recover by substituting the corresponding release 2 command, but in any case, you should update the file that contains the offending command.

`No declaration for shape ⟨`*font shape*`⟩`
> The sub or ssub size function used in a \DeclareFontShape command points to a substitution shape that is unknown to NFSS.

`Overwriting ⟨`*something*`⟩ in version ⟨`*name*`⟩ ...`
> A declaration, like \SetSymbolFont or \DeclareMathAlphabet, has changed the assignment of font shapes to ⟨*something*⟩ (a symbol font or a math alphabet) in the math version ⟨*name*⟩.

`Redeclaring math alphabet ⟨`*name*`⟩`
> A \DeclareMathAlphabet or \DeclareSymbolFontAlphabet command was issued to declare ⟨*name*⟩, which was already defined to be a math alphabet identifier. The new declaration overrides all previous settings for ⟨*name*⟩.

`Redeclaring math symbol` ⟨*name*⟩
> The command ⟨*name*⟩ was already declared as a math symbol and your declaration overrides the old definition.

`Redeclaring math version` ⟨*name*⟩
> You issued a \DeclareMathVersion command for a version that was already declared. The new declaration overrides all previous settings for this version with the default values.

`Redeclaring symbol font` ⟨*name*⟩
> You issued a \DeclareSymbolFont command for a symbol font that was previously declared. The new declaration overrides the symbol font in all math versions.

`Size substitutions with differences up to` ⟨*size*⟩ `have occured`
> This message will appear at the end of the run in case NFSS selected at least one significantly different size because the requested size was not available. The ⟨*size*⟩ is the maximum deviation that was needed.

`Some font shapes were not available, defaults substituted`
> This message will appear at the end of the run in case NFSS had to use automatic font substitution for some font shapes.

`Symbol font` ⟨*name*⟩ `is not defined`
> You tried to make use of the symbol font ⟨*name*⟩, for example within a \DeclareMathSymbol command, without declaring it first with a \DeclareSymbolFont declaration.

`This NFSS system isn't set up properly`
> If this error occurs, then NFSS has detected a mistake while trying to verify the font substitution tables. In this case either a \DeclareFontSubstitution or \DeclareErrorFont declaration is corrupted. Type h for additional information and inform your system maintainer. If you are the system maintainer, read section 7.7.4.

`Try loading font information for` ⟨*cdp*⟩`+`⟨*family*⟩
> You will find such messages in the transcript file whenever NFSS tries to load a .fd file for the encoding/family combination ⟨*cdp*⟩/⟨*family*⟩.

`Undefined font size function` ⟨*name*⟩
> A size function used in \DeclareFontShape was misspelled. Check the entry or tell your system maintainer.

`*** Use` ⟨*command*⟩ `for` ⟨*old command*⟩ `***`
> Your source contains ⟨*old command*⟩, which is considered obsolete in NFSS release 2.

CHAPTER **8**

Higher Mathematics

Basic LaTeX offers a high level of mathematical typesetting capabilities. However, when complex equations or other mathematical constructs have to be input repeatedly, it is up to you to define new commands or environments to ease the burden of typing. The American Mathematical Society (AMS), recognizing that fact, has sponsored the development of extensions to TeX, known as $\mathcal{AMS}$-TeX. They make the preparation of mathematical compuscripts less time-consuming and the copy more consistent.

Recently these extensions were ported to LaTeX. It is, however, important to distinguish between the original, non-LaTeX implementation of $\mathcal{AMS}$-TeX and the modified form of it that constitutes the LaTeX package amstex, popularly known as the $\mathcal{AMS}$-LaTeX distribution [95]. A sans serif font will be used to denote the LaTeX package amstex [95], and the standard $\mathcal{AMS}$-TeX logo will be used for the original non-LaTeX version.

8.1   The $\mathcal{AMS}$-LaTeX Project

$\mathcal{AMS}$-TeX was originally released for general use in 1982. Its main strength is that it facilitates mathematical typesetting, while producing output that satisfies the high standards of mathematical publishing. It provides a predefined set of natural commands such as `\matrix` and `\text` that make complicated mathematics reasonably convenient to type. These commands incorporate the typesetting experience and standards of the American Mathematical Society, to handle problematic possibilities, such as matrices within matrices or a word of text within a subscript, without burdening the user.

$\mathcal{AMS}$-TEX, unlike LATEX, does not have certain features that are very convenient for authors—automatic numbering that adjusts to addition or deletion of material being the primary one. Nor does it have the laborsaving abilities of LATEX for preparing indexes, bibliographies, tables, or simple diagrams. These features are such a convenience for authors that the use of LATEX spread rapidly in the mid-1980s (a reasonably mature version of LATEX was available by the end of 1983), and the American Mathematical Society began to be asked by its authors to accept electronic submissions in LATEX.

Thus, the $\mathcal{AMS}$-LATEX project came into being in 1987 and three years later $\mathcal{AMS}$-LATEX version 1.0 was released. The conversion of $\mathcal{AMS}$-TEX's mathematical capabilities to LATEX, and the integration with the NFSS, were done by Frank Mittelbach and Rainer Schöpf, working as consultants to the AMS, with assistance from Michael Downes of the AMS technical support staff.

To use the $\mathcal{AMS}$-LATEX developments you should load the amstex package with a \usepackage command.

8.2   Fonts and Symbols in Formulae

8.2.1   Names of Math Font Commands

The list of math font commands specific to the amstex package is shown in table 8.1 on page 218, where for each case an example is shown. In addition, the math font commands of table 7.4 on page 176 can be used.

In the amstex package, \boldsymbol is to be used for individual bold math symbols and bold Greek letters—everything in math except for letters (where one would use \mathbf). For example, to obtain a bold ∞, $+$, π, or $\mathbf{0}$, you can use the commands \boldsymbol{\infty}, \boldsymbol{+}, \boldsymbol{\pi}, or \boldsymbol{0}.

Since \boldsymbol takes a lot of typing, you can introduce new commands for bold symbols to be used frequently:

$$B_\infty + \pi B_1 \sim \mathbf{B}_\infty + \pi\mathbf{B}_1$$

```
\newcommand{\bpi}{\boldsymbol{\pi}}
\newcommand{\binfty}{\boldsymbol{\infty}}
\[ B_\infty + \pi B_1 \sim
   \mathbf{B}_{\binfty} \boldsymbol{+}
   \bpi \mathbf{B}_{\boldsymbol{1}}
\]
```

For those math symbols where the command \boldsymbol has no effect because the bold version of the symbol does not exist in the currently available fonts, there exists a command "Poor man's bold" (\pmb), which simulates bold by typesetting several copies of the symbol with slight offsets. This procedure must be used for the extension and large operator symbols from the \cmex font, as well as the $\mathcal{A}_{\mathcal{M}}\mathcal{S}$ extra math symbols from the \msam and \msbm fonts.

$$\frac{\partial w}{\partial u} \left| \frac{\partial u}{\partial v} \right.$$

```
\[ \frac{\partial w}{\partial u}
   \pmb{\Bigg\vert}
   \frac{\partial u}{\partial v} \]
```

With large operators and extension symbols (for example, $\sum$ and $\prod$) \pmb does not currently work very well because the proper spacing and treatment of limits is not preserved. Therefore, the TEX operator \mathop needs to be used (see table 7.13 on page 206).

$$\sum_{j<P} \prod_\lambda \lambda R(r_i) \qquad \sum_{x_j} \prod_\lambda \lambda R(x_j)$$

```
\[ \sum_{j<P}
   \prod_\lambda \lambda R(r_i) \qquad
   \mathop{\pmb{\sum}}_{x_j}
   \mathop{\pmb{\prod}}_\lambda \lambda R(x_j)
\]
```

To make an entire math formula bold (or as much of it as possible, depending on the available fonts), use \boldmath preceding the formula.

The sequence \mathbf{\hat{A}} produces a bold accent character over the A. However, combinations like \mathcal{\hat{A}} will not work in ordinary LATEX because the \mathcal font does not have its own accents. In the amstex package the font change commands are defined in such a way that accent characters will be taken from the \mathrm font if they are not available in the current font (in addition to the \mathcal font, the \Bbb and \frak fonts don't contain accents).

8.2.2 Mathematical Symbols

Tables 8.3 on the next page to 8.12 on page 220 review the mathematical symbols available in standard LATEX. You can put a slash through a LATEX symbol by preceding it with the \not command, for instance.

$u \not< v$ or $a \notin \mathbf{A}$

($\mathcal{L}$ 42–47)

($\mathcal{L}$ 44)

```
$u \not< v$ or $a \not\in \mathbf{A}$
```

Tables 8.13 on page 220 to 8.20 on page 222 show the extra math symbols of the $\mathcal{A}_{\mathcal{M}}\mathcal{S}$-Fonts, which are automatically available when you specify the amssymb package. However, if you want to define only some of them (perhaps because your TEX installation has insufficient memory to define all the symbol names), you can use the amsfonts package and the \DeclareMathSymbol command, which is explained in section 7.7.6.

\Bbb	Blackboard bold alphabet, e.g., $\Bbb{NQRZ}$ gives: $\mathbb{NQRZ}$.
\boldsymbol	Used to obtain bold numbers and other nonalphabetic symbols, as well as bold Greek letters.
\frak	Euler Fraktur alphabet, e.g., $\frak{E}=\frak{mc}^2$ gives: $\mathfrak{E} = \mathfrak{mc}^2$.
\pmb	"Poor man's bold," used for math symbols when bold versions don't exist in the available fonts, e.g., $\pmb{\oint}$ gives: $\oint$ and $\pmb{\triangle}$ gives: $\triangle$.
\text	Produce normal text with correct text-spacing in the current font used outside math, e.g., $E=mc^2\quad\text{(Einstein)}$ gives: $E = mc^2$ (Einstein).

Table 8.1: Font commands available in mathematics with the amstex package

$\hat{a}$	\hat{a}	$\acute{a}$	\acute{a}	$\bar{a}$	\bar{a}	$\dot{a}$	\dot{a}	$\breve{a}$	\breve{a}
$\check{a}$	\check{a}	$\grave{a}$	\grave{a}	$\vec{a}$	\vec{a}	$\ddot{a}$	\ddot{a}	$\tilde{a}$	\tilde{a}

Table 8.2: Math mode accents

α	\alpha	β	\beta	γ	\gamma	δ	\delta
ϵ	\epsilon	ε	\varepsilon	ζ	\zeta	η	\eta
θ	\theta	ϑ	\vartheta	ι	\iota	κ	\kappa
λ	\lambda	μ	\mu	ν	\nu	ξ	\xi
o	o	π	\pi	ϖ	\varpi	ρ	\rho
ϱ	\varrho	σ	\sigma	ς	\varsigma	τ	\tau
υ	\upsilon	ϕ	\phi	φ	\varphi	χ	\chi
ψ	\psi	ω	\omega				
Γ	\Gamma	Δ	\Delta	Θ	\Theta	Λ	\Lambda
Ξ	\Xi	Π	\Pi	Σ	\Sigma	Υ	\Upsilon
Φ	\Phi	Ψ	\Psi	Ω	\Omega		

Table 8.3: Greek letters

$\pm$	\pm	$\cap$	\cap	$\diamond$	\diamond	$\oplus$	\oplus
$\mp$	\mp	$\cup$	\cup	$\triangle$	\bigtriangleup	$\ominus$	\ominus
$\times$	\times	$\uplus$	\uplus	$\bigtriangledown$	\bigtriangledown	$\otimes$	\otimes
$\div$	\div	$\sqcap$	\sqcap	$\triangleleft$	\triangleleft	$\oslash$	\oslash
$\ast$	\ast	$\sqcup$	\sqcup	$\triangleright$	\triangleright	$\odot$	\odot
$\star$	\star	$\vee$	\vee	$\lhd^a$	\lhd^a	$\bigcirc$	\bigcirc
$\circ$	\circ	$\wedge$	\wedge	$\rhd^a$	\rhd^a	$\dagger$	\dagger
$\bullet$	\bullet	$\setminus$	\setminus	$\unlhd^a$	\unlhd^a	$\ddagger$	\ddagger
$\cdot$	\cdot	$\wr$	\wr	$\unrhd^a$	\unrhd^a	$\amalg$	\amalg

[a] Not predefined in NFSS. Use the latexsym or amssymb package.

Table 8.4: Binary operation symbols

$\leq$	`\leq\le`	$\geq$	`\geq`	$\equiv$	`\equiv`	$\models$	`\models`	$\prec$	`\prec`
$\succ$	`\succ`	$\sim$	`\sim`	$\perp$	`\perp`	$\preceq$	`\preceq`	$\succeq$	`\succeq`
$\preccurlyeq$	`\simeq`	$\mid$	`\mid`	$\ll$	`\ll`	$\gg$	`\gg`	$\asymp$	`\asymp`
$\parallel$	`\parallel`	$\subset$	`\subset`	$\supset$	`\supset`	$\approx$	`\approx`	$\bowtie$	`\bowtie`
$\subseteq$	`\subseteq`	$\supseteq$	`\supseteq`	$\cong$	`\cong`	$\Join$	`\Join`	$\sqsubset$	`\sqsubset`
$\sqsupset$	`\sqsupset`	$\neq$	`\neq`	$\smile$	`\smile`	$\sqsubseteq$	`\sqsubseteq`	$\sqsupseteq$	`\sqsupseteq`
$\doteq$	`\doteq`	$\frown$	`\frown`	$\in$	`\in`	$\ni$	`\ni`	$\propto$	`\propto`
$=$	`=`	$\vdash$	`\vdash`	$\dashv$	`\dashv`	$<$	`<`	$>$	`>`

Table 8.5: Relation symbols

$\leftarrow$	`\leftarrow`	$\longleftarrow$	`\longleftarrow`	$\uparrow$	`\uparrow`
$\Leftarrow$	`\Leftarrow`	$\Longleftarrow$	`\Longleftarrow`	$\Uparrow$	`\Uparrow`
$\rightarrow$	`\rightarrow`	$\longrightarrow$	`\longrightarrow`	$\downarrow$	`\downarrow`
$\Rightarrow$	`\Rightarrow`	$\Longrightarrow$	`\Longrightarrow`	$\Downarrow$	`\Downarrow`
$\leftrightarrow$	`\leftrightarrow`	$\longleftrightarrow$	`\longleftrightarrow`	$\updownarrow$	`\updownarrow`
$\Leftrightarrow$	`\Leftrightarrow`	$\Longleftrightarrow$	`\Longleftrightarrow`	$\Updownarrow$	`\Updownarrow`
$\mapsto$	`\mapsto`	$\longmapsto$	`\longmapsto`	$\nearrow$	`\nearrow`
$\hookleftarrow$	`\hookleftarrow`	$\hookrightarrow$	`\hookrightarrow`	$\searrow$	`\searrow`
$\leftharpoonup$	`\leftharpoonup`	$\rightharpoonup$	`\rightharpoonup`	$\swarrow$	`\swarrow`
$\leftharpoondown$	`\leftharpoondown`	$\rightharpoondown$	`\rightharpoondown`	$\nwarrow$	`\nwarrow`

Table 8.6: Arrow symbols

$\ldots$	`\ldots`	$\cdots$	`\cdots`	$\vdots$	`\vdots`	$\ddots$	`\ddots`	$\aleph$	`\aleph`
$\prime$	`\prime`	$\forall$	`\forall`	∞	`\infty`	$\hbar$	`\hbar`	$\emptyset$	`\emptyset`
$\exists$	`\exists`	∇	`\nabla`	$\surd$	`\surd`	$\Box$	`\Box`[a]	$\triangle$	`\triangle`
$\Diamond$	`\Diamond`[a]	$\imath$	`\imath`	$\jmath$	`\jmath`	ℓ	`\ell`	$\neg$	`\neg`
$\top$	`\top`	$\flat$	`\flat`	$\natural$	`\natural`	$\sharp$	`\sharp`	$\wp$	`\wp`
$\bot$	`\bot`	$\clubsuit$	`\clubsuit`	$\diamondsuit$	`\diamondsuit`	$\heartsuit$	`\heartsuit`	$\spadesuit$	`\spadesuit`
$\mho$	`\mho`[a]	$\Re$	`\Re`	$\Im$	`\Im`	$\angle$	`\angle`	∂	`\partial`

[a] Not predefined in NFSS. Use the latexsym or amssymb package.

Table 8.7: Miscellaneous symbols

$\sum$	`\sum`	$\prod$	`\prod`	$\coprod$	`\coprod`	$\int$	`\int`	$\oint$	`\oint`
$\bigcap$	`\bigcap`	$\bigcup$	`\bigcup`	$\bigsqcup$	`\bigsqcup`	$\bigvee$	`\bigvee`	$\bigwedge$	`\bigwedge`
$\bigodot$	`\bigodot`	$\bigotimes$	`\bigotimes`	$\bigoplus$	`\bigoplus`	$\biguplus$	`\biguplus`		

Table 8.8: Variable-sized symbols

\arccos	\cos	\csc	\exp	\ker	\limsup	\min	\sinh
\arcsin	\cosh	\deg	\gcd	\lg	\ln	\Pr	\sup
\arctan	\cot	\det	\hom	\lim	\log	\sec	\tan
\arg	\coth	\dim	\inf	\liminf	\max	\sin	\tanh

Table 8.9: Log-like symbols

↑	\uparrow	⇑	\Uparrow	↓	\downarrow	⇓	\Downarrow
{	\{	}	\}	↕	\updownarrow	⇕	\Updownarrow
⌊	\lfloor	⌋	\rfloor	⌈	\lceil	⌉	\rceil
⟨	\langle	⟩	\rangle	/	/	\	\backslash
|	|	‖	\\|				

Table 8.10: Delimiters

⎱	\rmoustache	⎰	\lmoustache	⎱	\rgroup	⎰	\lgroup
⎥	\arrowvert	‖	\Arrowvert	⎪	\bracevert		

Table 8.11: Large delimiters

$\widetilde{abc}$	\widetilde{abc}	$\widehat{abc}$	\widehat{abc}
$\overleftarrow{abc}$	\overleftarrow{abc}	$\overrightarrow{abc}$	\overrightarrow{abc}
$\overline{abc}$	\overline{abc}	$\underline{abc}$	\underline{abc}
$\overbrace{abc}$	\overbrace{abc}	$\underbrace{abc}$	\underbrace{abc}
$\sqrt{abc}$	\sqrt{abc}	$\sqrt[n]{abc}$	\sqrt[n]{abc}
f'	f'	$\frac{abc}{xyz}$	\frac{abc}{xyz}

Table 8.12: LaTeX math constructs

$Ϝ$	\digamma	$\varkappa$	\varkappa	ℶ	\beth	ℸ	\daleth	ℷ	\gimel

Table 8.13: AMS Greek and Hebrew (available with amssymb package)

⌜	\ulcorner	⌝	\urcorner	⌞	\llcorner	⌟	\lrcorner

Table 8.14: AMS delimiters (available with amssymb package)

⇢	\dashrightarrow	⇠	\dashleftarrow	⇇	\leftleftarrows
⇆	\leftrightarrows	⇐	\Lleftarrow	↞	\twoheadleftarrow
↢	\leftarrowtail	↫	\looparrowleft	⇋	\leftrightharpoons
↶	\curvearrowleft	↺	\circlearrowleft	↰	\Lsh
⇈	\upuparrows	↿	\upharpoonleft	⇂	\downharpoonleft
⊸	\multimap	↭	\leftrightsquigarrow	⇉	\rightrightarrows
⇄	\rightleftarrows	⇉	\rightrightarrows	⇄	\rightleftarrows
↠	\twoheadrightarrow	↣	\rightarrowtail	↬	\looparrowright
⇌	\rightleftharpoons	↷	\curvearrowright	↻	\circlearrowright
↱	\Rsh	⇊	\downdownarrows	↾	\upharpoonright
⇃	\downharpoonright	⇝	\rightsquigarrow		

Table 8.15: AMS arrows (available with amssymb package)

↚	\nleftarrow	↛	\nrightarrow	⇍	\nLeftarrow
⇏	\nRightarrow	↮	\nleftrightarrow	⇎	\nLeftrightarrow

Table 8.16: AMS negated arrows (available with amssymb package)

≦	\leqq	⩽	\leqslant	⪕	\eqslantless
≲	\lesssim	⪅	\lessapprox	≊	\approxeq
⋖	\lessdot	⋘	\lll	≶	\lessgtr
⋚	\lesseqgtr	⪋	\lesseqqgtr	≑	\doteqdot
≓	\risingdotseq	≒	\fallingdotseq	∽	\backsim
⋍	\backsimeq	⊆	\subseteqq	⋐	\Subset
⊏	\sqsubset	≼	\preccurlyeq	⋞	\curlyeqprec
≾	\precsim	⪷	\precapprox	◁	\vartriangleleft
⊴	\trianglelefteq	⊨	\vDash	⊪	\Vvdash
⌣	\smallsmile	⌢	\smallfrown	≏	\bumpeq
≎	\Bumpeq	≧	\geqq	⩾	\geqslant
⪖	\eqslantgtr	≳	\gtrsim	⪆	\gtrapprox
⋗	\gtrdot	⋙	\ggg	≷	\gtrless
⋛	\gtreqless	⪌	\gtreqqless	≖	\eqcirc
≗	\circeq	≜	\triangleq	∼	\thicksim
≈	\thickapprox	⊇	\supseteqq	⋑	\Supset
⊐	\sqsupset	≽	\succcurlyeq	⋟	\curlyeqsucc
≿	\succsim	⪸	\succapprox	▷	\vartriangleright
⊵	\trianglerighteq	⊩	\Vdash	∣	\shortmid
∥	\shortparallel	≬	\between	⋔	\pitchfork
∝	\varpropto	◀	\blacktriangleleft	∴	\therefore
϶	\backepsilon	▶	\blacktriangleright	∵	\because

Table 8.17: AMS binary relations (available with amssymb package)

≮	\nless	≰	\nleq	⪇	\nleqslant
≨	\nleqq	≨	\lneq	⪇	\lneqq
⪇	\lvertneqq	⪅	\lnsim	⪉	\lnapprox
⊀	\nprec	⋠	\npreceq	⪵	\precnsim
⪹	\precnapprox	≁	\nsim	∤	\nshortmid
∤	\nmid	⊬	\nvdash	⊭	\nvDash
⋪	\ntriangleleft	⋬	\ntrianglelefteq	⊈	\nsubseteq
⊊	\subsetneq	⊊	\varsubsetneq	⊊	\subsetneqq
⊊	\varsubsetneqq	≯	\ngtr	≱	\ngeq
⪈	\ngeqslant	≩	\ngeqq	⪈	\gneq
≩	\gneqq	⪈	\gvertneqq	⪊	\gnsim
⪊	\gnapprox	⊁	\nsucc	⋡	\nsucceq
⪶	\succnsim	⪺	\succnapprox	≇	\ncong
∦	\nshortparallel	∦	\nparallel	⊭	\nvDash
⊮	\nVDash	⋫	\ntriangleright	⋭	\ntrianglerighteq
⊉	\nsupseteq	⊋	\nsupseteqq	⊋	\supsetneq
⊋	\varsupsetneq	⊋	\supsetneqq	⊋	\varsupsetneqq

Table 8.18: AMS negated binary relations (available with amssymb package)

∔	\dotplus	∖	\smallsetminus	⋒	\Cap
⋓	\Cup	⊼	\barwedge	⊻	\veebar
⊼	\doublebarwedge	⊟	\boxminus	⊠	\boxtimes
⊡	\boxdot	⊞	\boxplus	⊛	\divideontimes
⋉	\ltimes	⋊	\rtimes	⋋	\leftthreetimes
⋌	\rightthreetimes	⋏	\curlywedge	⋎	\curlyvee
⊖	\circleddash	⊛	\circledast	⊚	\circledcirc
·	\centerdot	⊺	\intercal		

Table 8.19: AMS binary operators (available with amssymb package)

ℏ	\hbar	ℏ	\hslash	△	\vartriangle
▽	\triangledown	□	\square	◇	\lozenge
Ⓢ	\circledS	∠	\angle	∡	\measuredangle
∄	\nexists	℧	\mho	⅁	\Finv[a]
⅁	\Game[a]	𝕜	\Bbbk[a]	‵	\backprime
∅	\varnothing	▲	\blacktriangle	▼	\blacktriangledown
■	\blacksquare	◆	\blacklozenge	★	\bigstar
∢	\sphericalangle	∁	\complement	ð	\eth
╱	\diagup[a]	╲	\diagdown[a]		

[a] Not defined in old releases of the amssymb package; define with the \DeclareMathSymbol command.

Table 8.20: AMS miscellaneous (available with amssymb package)

8.3   Compound Symbols, Delimiters, and Operators

This section[1] presents the math commands that are available through the amstex package, which supplements LaTeX in the area of compound symbols, large delimiters, etc. In the examples, amstex's alignment environments are used. In principle a detailed understanding of how they work is not necessary at this stage, but an interested reader can turn to section 8.5 for more information.

8.3.1   Multiple Integral Signs

\iint, \iiint, and \iiiint give multiple integral signs, with the spacing between them nicely adjusted, in both text and display style. \idotsint gives two integral signs with dots between them.

(8.1)
$$\iint\limits_V \mu(u, v)\, du\, dv$$

(8.2)
$$\iiint\limits_V \mu(u, v, w)\, du\, dv\, dw$$

(8.3)
$$\iiiint\limits_V \mu(t, u, v, w)\, dt\, du\, dv\, dw$$

(8.4)
$$\int \cdots \int\limits_V \mu(u_1, \dots, u_k)$$

```
\begin{gather}
\iint\limits_V \mu(u,v)\,du\,dv                   \\
\iiint\limits_V \mu(u,v,w)\,du\,dv\,dw            \\
\iiiint\limits_V \mu(t,u,v,w)\,dt\,du\,dv\,dw\\
\idotsint\limits_V \mu(u_1,\dots,u_k)
\end{gather}
```

8.3.2   Over and Under Arrows

Some extra over and under arrow operations are available. (In standard LaTeX one has \overrightarrow and \overleftarrow.)

$$\overrightarrow{\psi_\delta(t) E_t h} = \psi_\delta(t) E_t \overrightarrow{h}$$
$$\overleftarrow{\psi_\delta(t) E_t h} = \psi_\delta(t) E_t \overleftarrow{h}$$
$$\overleftrightarrow{\psi_\delta(t) E_t h} = \psi_\delta(t) E_t \overleftrightarrow{h}$$

```
\begin{align*}
  \overrightarrow{\psi_\delta(t) E_t h}        &
=\underrightarrow{\psi_\delta(t) E_t h}        \\
  \overleftarrow{\psi_\delta(t) E_t h}         &
=\underleftarrow{\psi_\delta(t) E_t h}         \\
  \overleftrightarrow{\psi_\delta(t) E_t h}    &
=\underleftrightarrow{\psi_\delta(t) E_t h}
\end{align*}
```

They all scale properly in subscript sizes.

$\int_{\overrightarrow{uv}} vt\, dt$

```
$ \int_{\overrightarrow{uv}} vt\,dt $
```

---

[1] Some material in this and the following sections is reprinted from the electronic document testart.tex with permission of the American Mathematical Society.

8.3.3 Dots

Ellipsis dots should almost always be typed as \dots. Positioning (on the base-line or centered) is automatically selected according to whatever follows the \dots. If the next character is a plus sign, the dots will be centered; if it's a comma, they will be on the baseline. These default dot placements provided by the amstex package can be changed if different conventions are wanted.

If the dots fall at the end of a math formula, the next character will be something like \end or \) or \$, which does not give any information about how to place the dots. If that is the case, you must help by using \dotsc for "dots with commas," or \dotsb for "dots with binary operators/relations," or \dotsm for "multiplication dots," or \dotsi for "dots with integrals." In the example below, low dots are produced in the first instance and centered dots in the others, with the spacing on either side of the dots nicely adjusted.

A series $H_1, H_2, \ldots$, a regional sum $H_1 + H_2 + \cdots$, an orthogonal product $H_1 H_2 \cdots$, and an infinite integral

$$\int_{H_1} \int_{H_2} \cdots$$

```
A series $H_1,H_2,\dotsc$,
a regional sum $H_1+H_2+\dotsb$, an
orthogonal product $H_1H_2\dotsm$, and
an infinite integral
\[\int_{H_1}\int_{H_2}\dotsi\]
```

8.3.4 Accents in Math

The following accent commands automatically position double accents correctly:

$$\acute{\acute{A}} \qquad \bar{\bar{B}} \qquad \check{\check{C}} \qquad \check{D}$$
$$\ddot{\ddot{E}} \qquad \dot{\dot{F}} \qquad \grave{\grave{G}} \qquad \hat{\hat{H}}$$
$$\tilde{\tilde{I}} \qquad \vec{\vec{J}}$$

```
\begin{gather*}
\Acute{\Acute{A}} \qquad\Bar{\Bar{B}} \qquad
\Breve{\Breve{C}} \qquad\Check{\Check{D}}    \\
\Ddot{\Ddot{E}}    \qquad\Dot{\Dot{F}} \qquad
\Grave{\Grave{G}} \qquad\Hat{\Hat{H}}        \\
\Tilde{\Tilde{I}} \qquad\Vec{\Vec{J}}
\end{gather*}
```

This double accent operation is complicated and tends to slow down the processing of a LaTeX file. If the document contains many double accents, you can use \accentedsymbol in the preamble of the document to help speed things up. It stores the result of the double accent command in a box register for quick retrieval. \accentedsymbol is used like \newcommand:

This is a double hat $\hat{\hat{A}}$ and this $\dot{\bar{\delta}}$ a delta with a bar and a dot.

```
\accentedsymbol{\Ahathat}{\Hat{\Hat A}}
\accentedsymbol{\dbardot}{\Dot{\Bar \delta}}
This is a double hat \(\Ahathat\) and this
\(\dbardot\) a delta with a bar and a dot.
```

8.3.5 Superscripted Accents

Some accents have a wide form: typing $\widehat{xy}, \widetilde{xy}$ produces $\widehat{xy}, \widetilde{xy}$. Because these wide accents have a certain maximum size, extremely long expressions are better handled by a different notation: $(AmBD)^{\hat{}}$ instead of $\widehat{AmBD}$. amstex has the following control sequences to achieve this easily:

(8.5)	$(AmBD)^{\hat{}}$	$(AmBD)^{\vee}$	
(8.6)	$(AmBD)^{\sim}$	$(AmBD)^{\cdot}$	
(8.7)	$(AmBD)^{\cdot\cdot}$	$(AmBD)^{\cdot\cdot\cdot}$	
(8.8)		$(AmBD)^{\smile}$	

```
\begin{gather}
(AmBD)\sphat    \qquad (AmBD)\spcheck \\
(AmBD)\sptilde \qquad (AmBD)\spdot    \\
(AmBD)\spddot  \qquad(AmBD)\spdddot  \\
(AmBD)\spbreve
\end{gather}
```

8.3.6 Dot Accents

\dddot and \ddddot are available to produce tripled and quadrupled dot accents in addition to the \dot and \ddot accents already available in LaTeX:

$\dddot{Q}$ $\ddddot{R}$

```
$   \dddot{Q}  \qquad  \ddddot{R}  $
```

8.3.7 Roots

In ordinary LaTeX the placement of root indices is sometimes not good. With amstex the commands \leftroot and \uproot allow the adjustment of the position of the root. Positive arguments to these commands will move the root index to the left and up respectively, while a negative argument will move them right and down. The units of increment are quite small, which is useful for such adjustments. In the example below, the root index β is moved 2 units to the left and 4 units up.

$\sqrt[\beta]{k}$ $\sqrt[\beta]{k}$

```
\[ \sqrt[\beta]{k} \qquad
   \sqrt[\leftroot{2}\uproot{4}\beta]{k} \]
```

8.3.8 Boxed Formulae

The command \boxed puts a box around its argument, similar to \fbox, except that the contents are in math mode:

$\boxed{W_t - F \subseteq V(P_i) \subseteq W_t}$

```
\[ \boxed{W_t - F \subseteq
          V(P_i)  \subseteq W_t} \]
```

8.3.9 Extensible Arrows

`@>>>` and `@<<<` produce arrows that extend automatically to accommodate unusually wide subscripts or superscripts. The text of the subscript or superscript is typed in between the > or < symbols.

$$F \times \triangle[n-1] \xrightarrow[\partial_0\alpha(b)]{} E^{\partial_0 b}$$

```
\[ F\times\triangle[n-1]
    @>>{\partial_0\alpha(b)}>E^{\partial_0b} \]
```

See also section 8.4.4 on commutative diagrams. For keyboards without < and > keys, `@)))` and `@(((` are available as synonyms.

8.3.10 \overset, \underset, **and** \sideset

LaTeX provides \stackrel for placing a superscript above a binary relation. amstex introduces somewhat more general commands, \overset and \underset. These can be used to place one symbol above or below another symbol, independently of whether it is a relation or something else. The input \overset{*}{X} will place a superscript-size $*$ above the X; \underset performs the parallel operation that one would expect.

$$\overset{*}{X} \qquad \underset{*}{X} \qquad \overset{a}{\underset{b}{X}}$$

```
\[ \overset{*}{X}              \qquad
   \underset{*}{X}             \qquad
   \overset{a}{\underset{b}{X}}     \]
```

There is also a command called \sideset that serves a rather special purpose: it puts symbols in the subscript and superscript positions of large operator symbols such as $\sum$ and $\prod$. A prime example is the case when you want to put a prime on a sum symbol. If there are no limits above or below the sum, you could just use \nolimits:

(8.9)
$$\sum{}' E_n.$$

```
\begin{equation}
   \sum\nolimits' E_n.
\end{equation}
```

But if you want not only the prime but also limits on the sum symbol, things are not so easy. Suppose you want to add a prime on the sum symbol in an expression, like

(8.10)
$$\sum_{n<k,\; n \text{ odd}} nE_n$$

```
\begin{equation}
   \sum_{n<k,\;n\ \mathrm{odd}}nE_n
\end{equation}
```

then you can use \sideset like this: \sideset{}{'}\sum_{...}nE_n. The extra pair of empty braces is explained by the fact that \sideset has the capability of putting an extra symbol or symbols at each corner of a large operator.

$$
{}^*_*\prod^*_*{}_k \qquad \sideset{}'_{0\le i\le m} E_i\beta x
$$

```
\[
\sideset{_*^*}{_*^*}\prod_k          \qquad
\sideset{}{'}\sum_{0\le i\le m} E_i\beta x
\]
```

8.3.11 The \smash Command

The plain TEX command \smash retains the contents of a box but annihilates its height and depth. The amstex package introduces the optional arguments t and b with the \smash command. \smash[t]{...} annihilates only the top of the box contents, retaining the bottom part, while \smash[b]{...} annihilates the bottom part and keeps the top.

$$
X_j = (1/\sqrt{\lambda_j})X_j' \qquad X_j = (1/\sqrt{\lambda_j})X_j'
$$

```
\[ X_j=(1/\sqrt{\smash[b]{\lambda_j}})X_j'
\qquad
X_j=(1/\sqrt{\lambda_j})X_j'                      \]
```

The previous example shows how the \smash command was used to limit the depth of the radical, which otherwise extends to encompass the depth of the subscript (right-hand side of the formula).

8.3.12 The \text Command

The main use of the \text command, which is also available separately with the amstext package, is for words or phrases in a display. It is similar to the LATEX command \mbox in its effects, but has a couple of advantages. If you would like a word or phrase of text in a subscript, you can type

```
..._{\text{word or phrase}}
```

which, apart from having a more descriptive name, is also slightly easier to enter than the equivalent \mbox, since the correct size is automatically chosen:

```
..._{\mbox{\scriptsize word or phrase}}
```

$$
\mathbf{y} = \mathbf{y}' \quad \text{if and only if} \quad y_k' = \delta_k y_{\tau(k)}
$$

```
\[ \mathbf{y}=\mathbf{y}'           \quad
\text{if and only if}               \quad
y'_k=\delta_k y_{\tau(k)}           \]
```

8.3.13 Operator Names

Math functions such as log, sin, and lim are traditionally set in roman type to help avoid confusion with single math variables, set in math italic. The more common ones have predefined names: \log, \sin, \lim, and so forth (see table 8.9 on page 220). New ones, however, come up all the time in mathematical papers. The amstex package provides \operatorname and \operatornamewithlimits for producing new function names that will have the same typographical treatment. For instance, \operatorname{xxx} produces xxx in the proper font and automatically adds proper spacing on either side when necessary, so that you get *A* xxx *B* instead of *AxxxB*. If you use a particular operator name often, you can save some typing and make the LaTeX file more readable by defining an abbreviation, for example (the \: commands add some space; see table 8.21 on page 242):

Input text

```
\newcommand{\meas}{\operatorname{meas}}
\begin{align*}
\|f\|_\infty                                            = &
  \operatornamewithlimits{ess\,sup}_{x\in R^n}|f(x)|              \\
\meas_1\{u\in R_+^1\:f^*(u)>\alpha\}                     = &
  \meas_n\{x\in R^n\:|f(x)|\geq\alpha\} \qquad \forall\alpha>0.
\end{align*}
```

$$\|f\|_\infty = \operatorname*{ess\,sup}_{x\in R^n} |f(x)|$$
$$\operatorname{meas}_1\{u \in R_+^1 \, f^*(u) > \alpha\} = \operatorname{meas}_n\{x \in R^n \, |f(x)| \geq \alpha\} \qquad \forall \alpha > 0.$$

Output text

You can use \operatornamewithlimits just like \operatorname; the only difference is the placement of subscripts and superscripts, as seen in the example above.

With amstex the following operators are predefined: \varlimsup, \varliminf, \varinjlim, and \varprojlim. Here's what they look like in use:

$$\tag{8.11} \varlimsup_{n\to\infty} Q(u_n, u_n - u^{\#}) \leq 0$$
$$\tag{8.12} \varliminf_{n\to\infty} |a_{n+1}| / |a_n| = 0$$
$$\tag{8.13} \varprojlim (m_i^\lambda \cdot)^* \leq 0$$
$$\tag{8.14} \varliminf_{p\in S(A)} A_p \leq 0$$

```
\begin{gather}
\varlimsup_{n\rightarrow\infty}
  \mathcal{Q}(u_n,u_n-u^{\#}) \le 0                       \\
\varliminf_{n\rightarrow\infty}
  \left|a_{n+1}\right|/\left|a_n\right| = 0               \\
\varinjlim (m_i^\lambda\cdot)^* \le 0                     \\
\varprojlim_{p\in S(A)}A_p \le 0
\end{gather}
```

8.3.14   \mod **and Its Relatives**

Commands \mod, \bmod, \pmod, and \pod are provided to deal with the rather special spacing conventions of "mod" notation. \bmod and \pmod are available in LaTeX, but with amstex the spacing of \pmod will adjust to a smaller value if it is used in a nondisplay formula. \mod and \pod are variants of \pmod preferred by some authors; \mod omits the parentheses, whereas \pod omits the "mod" and retains the parentheses.

(8.15) $u \equiv v + 1 \pmod{n^2}$

(8.16) $u \equiv v + 1 \mod n^2$

(8.17) $u \equiv v + 1 \ (n^2)$

```
\begin{align}
  u & \equiv v + 1 \pmod{n^2}   \\
  u & \equiv v + 1 \mod{n^2}    \\
  u & \equiv v + 1 \pod{n^2}
\end{align}
```

8.3.15   **Fractions and Related Constructions**

In addition to \frac (available in LaTeX), amstex provides \dfrac and \tfrac as convenient abbreviations for {\displaystyle\frac ... } and {\textstyle\frac ... }. Furthermore, the thickness of the fraction line can be varied, using an optional argument of the \frac command.

| \frac[*dimension*]{...}{...} |

$$\frac{M(y + u) - M(y) - CM(y)u}{\|u\|}$$

```
\[
  \frac[1.3pt]{M(y+u)-M(y)-CM(y)u}{\|u\|}
\]
```

The \fracwithdelims command allows the delimiters around the fraction to be specified.

| \fracwithdelims{*left delimiter*}{*right delimiter*}[*dimension*]{...}{...} |

$$\left[\frac{M(y + u) - M(y) - CM(y)u}{\|u\|}\right]$$

```
\[
  \fracwithdelims[]{M(y+u)-M(y)-CM(y)u}{\|u\|}
\]
```

For binomial expressions such as $\binom{n}{k}$ amstex defines the commands \binom, \dbinom, and \tbinom. \binom is an abbreviation for \fracwithdelims(){0pt}.

The commands \dbinom and \tbinom are shorthands similar to \dfrac and \tfrac described above.

(8.18)
$$\sum_{\gamma \in \Gamma_C} I_\gamma = 2^k - \binom{k}{1} 2^{k-1} + \binom{k}{2} 2^{k-2}$$
$$+ \cdots + (-1)^l \binom{k}{l} 2^{k-l} + \cdots + (-1)^k$$
$$= (2-1)^k = 1$$

```
\begin{equation}
\begin{split}
\sum_{\gamma\in\Gamma_C} I_\gamma
     &=2^k-\binom{k}{1}2^{k-1}+
                           \binom{k}{2}2^{k-2}\\
     &\quad+\dots+(-1)^l\binom{k}{l}2^{k-l}
                            +\dots+(-1)^k\\
     &=(2-1)^k=1
\end{split}
\end{equation}
```

8.3.16   Continued Fractions

A continued fraction can be obtained as follows:

(8.19)
$$\cfrac{1}{\sqrt{2} + \cfrac{1}{\sqrt{3} + \cfrac{1}{\sqrt{4} + \cfrac{1}{\sqrt{5} + \cfrac{1}{\sqrt{6} + \cdots}}}}}$$

```
\begin{equation}
\cfrac{1}{\sqrt{2}+
  \cfrac{1}{\sqrt{3}+
    \cfrac{1}{\sqrt{4}+
      \cfrac{1}{\sqrt{5}+
        \cfrac{1}{\sqrt{6}+\dotsb
}}}}}
\end{equation}
```

Left or right positioning of any of the numerators is achieved by using \lcfrac or \rcfrac instead of \cfrac.

8.3.17   Big-g-g-g Delimiters

In order to better control the sizes of math delimiters, basic TeX introduces four commands \big, \Big, \bigg and \Bigg, which produce ever larger versions of the delimiter specified as parameter. These commands can be used with any of the delimiters that can follow the \left or \right command (see tables 8.10, 8.11, and 8.14 on page 220). Moreover, for each of the four commands above, three variants exist for use as an opening symbol (e.g., \bigl), as a binary relation (e.g., \Bigm), or as a closing symbol (e.g., \Biggr).[2] Whereas, with basic

---

[2] See table 7.13 on page 206 for a discussion of the various math symbol types.

TEX, the sizes of these delimiters are fixed, with the amstex package the sizes adapt to the size of the surrounding material.

$$\left(\mathbf{E}_y \int_0^{t_\varepsilon} L_{x,y^x(s)} \varphi(x)\, ds \right)$$

```
\[ \biggl(\mathbf{E}_{y}\int_0^{t_\varepsilon}
    L_{x,y^x(s)}\varphi(x)\,ds \biggr)
\]
\begin{Large}
\[ \biggl(\mathbf{E}_{y}\int_0^{t_\varepsilon}
    L_{x,y^x(s)}\varphi(x)\,ds \biggr)       \]
\end{Large}
```

$$\left(\mathbf{E}_y \int_0^{t_\varepsilon} L_{x,y^x(s)} \varphi(x)\, ds \right)$$

8.4 Matrix-Like Environments and Commutative Diagrams

8.4.1 The cases Environment

"Case" constructions can be produced using the cases environment.

(8.20)

$$P_{r-j} = \begin{cases} 0 & \text{if } r-j \text{ is odd,} \\ r!\,(-1)^{(r-j)/2} & \text{if } r-j \text{ is even.} \end{cases}$$

```
\begin{equation}
P_{r-j}=
   \begin{cases}
     0& \text{if $r-j$ is odd},\\
     r!\,(-1)^{(r-j)/2}& \text{if $r-j$ is even}.
   \end{cases}
\end{equation}
```

Notice the use of \text and the embedded math.

8.4.2 The Matrix Environments

The matrix environments are similar to LaTeX's array, except they do not have an argument specifying the format of the columns. Instead, a default format is provided: up to 10 centered columns. The examples below show how to use the matrix environments matrix, pmatrix, bmatrix, vmatrix, and Vmatrix:

$$\begin{matrix} 0 & 1 \\ 1 & 0 \end{matrix} \begin{pmatrix} 0 & -i \\ i & 0 \end{pmatrix} \begin{bmatrix} 1 & 0 \\ 0 & -1 \end{bmatrix}$$
$$\begin{vmatrix} a & b \\ c & d \end{vmatrix} \begin{Vmatrix} 1 & 0 \\ 0 & 1 \end{Vmatrix}$$

```
\begin{gather*}
\begin{matrix} 0 & 1 \\ 1 & 0\end{matrix} \quad
\begin{pmatrix}0 &-i \\ i & 0\end{pmatrix}\quad
\begin{bmatrix}1 & 0 \\ 0 &-1\end{bmatrix}\\
\begin{vmatrix}a & b \\ c & d\end{vmatrix}\quad
\begin{Vmatrix}1 & 0 \\ 0 & 1\end{Vmatrix}
\end{gather*}
```

The maximum number of columns is determined by the counter MaxMatrixCols, which you can change using LaTeX's standard counter commands. For example, suppose you have a large matrix with 19 or 20 columns, then you can do something like this:

```
\begin{equation}
\setcounter{MaxMatrixCols}{20}
A=\begin{pmatrix}
...&...&...&...&...&...&...&...&...&...&...&...  ...  \\
   ...  \\
   ...
\end{pmatrix}
\end{equation}
\setcounter{MaxMatrixCols}{10}
```

As counters are global in LaTeX, you might want to reset the value of MaxMatrixCols to its default value of 10 after finishing your wide matrix, since with a high value, LaTeX must work a lot harder to typeset a matrix.

To produce a small matrix suitable for use in text, use the smallmatrix environment.

To show the effect of the matrix on surrounding lines inside a paragraph, we put it here: $\left(\begin{smallmatrix} a & b \\ c & d \end{smallmatrix}\right)$ and follow it with enough text to ensure that there is at least one full line below the matrix.

```
To show the effect of the matrix on surrounding
lines inside a paragraph, we put it here:
\begin{math}
  \left( \begin{smallmatrix}
       a&b\\ c&d
    \end{smallmatrix} \right)
\end{math}
and follow it with enough text to ensure that
there is at least one full line below the matrix.
```

A row of dots in a matrix, spanning a given number of columns, can be obtained with the command:

\hdotsfor[*spacing-factor*]{*number*}

The spacing of the dots can be varied by using the optional parameter *spacing-factor*, for example, \hdotsfor[1.5]{3}. The number in square brackets multiplies the spacing between the dots; the normal value is one.

```
                              Input text
\[ W(\Phi)= \begin{Vmatrix}
   \dfrac\varphi{(\varphi_1,\varepsilon_1)}          &0&\dots&0\\
   \dfrac{\varphi k_{n2}}{(\varphi_2,\varepsilon_1)}&
   \dfrac\varphi{(\varphi_2,\varepsilon_2)}          &\dots&0  \\
   \hdotsfor{5}                                                 \\
   \dfrac{\varphi k_{n1}}{(\varphi_n,\varepsilon_1)}&
   \dfrac{\varphi k_{n2}}{(\varphi_n,\varepsilon_2)}&\dots&
   \dfrac{\varphi k_{n\,n-1}}{(\varphi_n,\varepsilon_{n-1})}&
   \dfrac{\varphi}{(\varphi_n,\varepsilon_n)}
\end{Vmatrix}\]
```

$$W(\Phi) = \begin{Vmatrix} \dfrac{\varphi}{(\varphi_1,\varepsilon_1)} & 0 & \cdots & 0 \\ \dfrac{\varphi k_{n2}}{(\varphi_2,\varepsilon_1)} & \dfrac{\varphi}{(\varphi_2,\varepsilon_2)} & \cdots & 0 \\ \hdotsfor{5} \\ \dfrac{\varphi k_{n1}}{(\varphi_n,\varepsilon_1)} & \dfrac{\varphi k_{n2}}{(\varphi_n,\varepsilon_2)} & \cdots & \dfrac{\varphi k_{n\,n-1}}{(\varphi_n,\varepsilon_{n-1})} & \dfrac{\varphi}{(\varphi_n,\varepsilon_n)} \end{Vmatrix}$$

Output text

8.4.3 The Sb and Sp Environments

The Sb and Sp environments can be used to typeset several lines as a subscript or superscript, using \\ as the row delimiter. These environments can be used anywhere an ordinary subscript or superscript can be used.

(8.21) $\displaystyle\sum_{\substack{0 \le i \le m \\ 0 < j < n}} P(i,j)$

```
\begin{equation}
   \sum  \begin{Sb}
            0\le i\le m \\
            0<j<n
         \end{Sb}         P(i,j)
\end{equation}
```

8.4.4 Commutative Diagrams

The commutative diagram commands of $\mathcal{A}_{\mathcal{M}}\mathcal{S}$-TEX are not included in the amstex package, but are available as a separate package, amscd. This conserves memory for users who do not need commutative diagrams. The picture environment can be used for complex commutative diagrams, but for simple diagrams without diagonal arrows the amscd commands are more convenient.[3]

$$
\begin{array}{ccc}
S^{\mathcal{W}_\Lambda} \otimes T & \xrightarrow{j} & T \\
\downarrow & & \downarrow{\scriptstyle\mathrm{End}\,P} \\
(S \otimes T)/I & =\!=\!= & (Z \otimes T)/J
\end{array}
$$

```
\newcommand{\End}{\operatorname{End}}
\begin{equation*}
\begin{CD}
S^{{\mathcal{W}}_\Lambda}\otimes T@>j>>T\\
    @VVV                  @VV{\End P}V\\
(S\otimes T)/I        @= (Z\otimes T)/J
\end{CD}
\end{equation*}
```

A similar result, which does not look quite as good, can be produced in ordinary LATEX by:

$$
\begin{array}{ccc}
S^{\mathcal{W}_\Lambda} \otimes T & \xrightarrow{j} & T \\
\downarrow & & \downarrow{\scriptstyle\mathrm{End}\,P} \\
(S \otimes T)/I & = & (Z \otimes T)/J
\end{array}
$$

```
\[
  \begin{array}{ccc}
    S^{\mathcal{W}}_\Lambda\otimes T &
      \stackrel{j}{\longrightarrow}   &
    T                                                         \\
    \Big\downarrow                   &     &
    \Big\downarrow\vcenter{%
      \rlap{$\scriptstyle{\mathrm{End}}\,,P$}}\\
    (S\otimes T)/I                       & = &
    (Z\otimes T)/J
  \end{array}
\]
```

When using the amscd package, you will obtain longer horizontal arrows and improved spacing between elements of the diagram.

In the CD environment the commands @>>>, @<<<, @VVV, and @AAA give (respectively) right, left, down, and up arrows. For people with keyboards lacking the angle brackets the notations @))) and @(((are available as alternatives.

For the horizontal arrows, material between the first and second > or < symbols will be typeset as a superscript, and material between the second and third will be typeset as a subscript. Similarly, material between the first and second, or second and third, A's or V's of vertical arrows will be typeset as left or right "sidescripts." This was used in the first example above to place the operator "End *P*" to the right of the arrow.

---

[3]Much more extensive commutative diagram packages are Kristoffer Rose's XY-pic system [73], Paul Taylor's Commutative Diagram package [80], and the Diagram 3 system by Francis Borceux [14].

The final example again shows the use of \operatorname.

$$\text{cov}(\mathcal{L}) \longrightarrow \text{non}(\mathcal{K}) \longrightarrow \text{cf}(\mathcal{K})$$

```
\begin{equation*}
\newcommand{\add}{\operatorname{add}}
\newcommand{\cf}{\operatorname{cf}}
\newcommand{\cov}{\operatorname{cov}}
\newcommand{\non}{\operatorname{non}}
\begin{CD}
  \cov(\mathcal{L}) @>>> \non(\mathcal{K})
                    @>>> \cf(\mathcal{K})\\
  @VVV @AAA @AAA              \\
  \add(\mathcal{L}) @>>> \add(\mathcal{K})
                    @>>> \non(\mathcal{K})\\
\end{CD}
\end{equation*}
```

8.5   Alignment Structures for Equations

The amstex package defines several environments for creating multiline display equations. They perform similarly to LATEX's equation and eqnarray environments. The following structures are discussed in the next sections.

align	align*	alignment at a single place
alignat	alignat*	alignment at several places
xalignat	xxalignat	spaced-out variants of the above
equation	equation*	one-line formula
gather	gather*	combining formula without alignment
multline	multline*	multiline equation (one equation number)
split		splitting long formulas

Some of these multiline display environments allow you to align parts of the formula. In contrast to the original LATEX environments eqnarray and eqnarray*, the structures implemented by the amstex package use a different concept for marking the alignment points: while eqnarray is similar to an array environment with a {rcl} preamble and therefore uses two ampersand characters surrounding the part that should be aligned, in the amstex structures you should mark the alignment point (or points in alignat, for example) only with a single ampersand character, placing it to the left of the character that should be aligned with previous or following lines.

The amstex structures give correct spacing around the alignment points, while the eqnarray environment produces extra spaces depending on the parameter settings for array. The difference can be seen clearly in the next example, where we typeset the same equation using the equation, align, and eqnarray environments; ideally all three should produce the same result, but the eqnarray environment comes out too wide.

(8.22)	$x^2 + y^2 = z^2$	

```
\begin{equation}
  x^2+y^2  =  z^2
\end{equation}
\begin{align}
  x^2+y^2 &= z^2 \\    x^3+y^3 &< z^3
\end{align}
\begin{eqnarray}
  x^2+y^2 &=& z^2 \\ x^3+y^3 &<& z^3
\end{eqnarray}
```

(8.23) $x^2 + y^2 = z^2$

(8.24) $x^3 + y^3 < z^3$

(8.25) $x^2 + y^2 \quad = \quad z^2$

(8.26) $x^3 + y^3 \quad < \quad z^3$

8.5.1   The align Environment

The align environment is used for two or more equations when vertical alignment is desired (usually binary relations such as equal signs are aligned). The term "equation" is used rather loosely here to mean any math formula that is intended by an author to be a self-contained subdivision of the larger display, usually, but not always, containing a binary relation.

(8.27) $x^2 + y^2 = 1$

(8.28) $x = \sqrt{1 - y^2}$

```
\begin{align}
x^2  + y^2 & = 1\\
x          & = \sqrt{1-y^2}
\end{align}
```

More examples are shown in section 8.7.4 on page 248.

8.5.2   The gather Environment

Like the align environment, the gather environment is used for two or more equations, but when there is no alignment desired among them each one is centered separately between the left and right margins.

(8.29) $(a + b)^2 = a^2 + 2ab + b^2$

(8.30) $(a + b) \cdot (a - b) = a^2 - b^2$

```
\begin{gather}
(a + b)^2 = a^2 + 2ab + b^2\\
(a + b) \cdot (a - b) = a^2 - b^2
\end{gather}
```

More examples are shown in section 8.7.3 on page 248.

8.5.3 The `alignat` Environment

The `align` environment takes up the whole width of a display. If you want to have several "align"-type structures side by side, you can use an `alignat` environment. It has one required argument, for specifying the number of "align" structures. For an argument of n, the number of ampersand characters per line is $2n - 1$ (one ampersand for alignment within each align structure, and ampersands to separate the align structures from one another).

`xalignat` and `xxalignat` are forms of the `alignat` environment with added space between the component align structures. If each align structure is considered to correspond to a column, then `xalignat` has equal spacing between columns and at the margins; `xxalignat` has equal spacing between columns and zero spacing at the margins.

--------	------------------	------------------	
(8.31)	$L_1 = R_1$	$L_2 = R_2$	`\begin{alignat}{2}`
			`L_1 & = R_1 & \qquad L_2 & = R_2  \\`
(8.32)	$L_3 = R_3$	$L_4 = R_4$	`L_3 & = R_3 & \qquad L_4 & = R_4`
			`\end{alignat}`

--------	-------------	-------------	
(8.33)	$L_1 = R_1$	$L_2 = R_2$	`\begin{xalignat}{2}`
			`L_1 & = R_1 & \qquad L_2 & = R_2  \\`
(8.34)	$L_3 = R_3$	$L_4 = R_4$	`L_3 & = R_3 & \qquad L_4 & = R_4`
			`\end{xalignat}`

-------------	-------------	
$L_1 = R_1$	$L_2 = R_2$	`\begin{xxalignat}{2}`
		`L_1 & = R_1 & \qquad L_2 & = R_2  \\`
$L_3 = R_3$	$L_4 = R_4$	`L_3 & = R_3 & \qquad L_4 & = R_4`
		`\end{xxalignat}`

Note that with `xxalignat` equation numbers do not make sense, so none are generated. More examples are shown in section 8.7.6 on page 250.

8.5.4 The `multline` Environment

The `multline` environment is a variation of the `equation` environment used for equations that do not fit on a single line. The first line of a `multline` will be at the left margin and the last line at the right margin except for an indention on both sides whose amount is equal to `\multlinegap`. The value of `\multlinegap` can be changed using LaTeX's `\setlength` and `\addtolength` commands. If `multline` contains more than two lines, any lines other than the first and last will be centered individually between the margins.

<table>
<tr><td>(8.35)</td><td>First line of equation
Middle line of equation
Other middle line of equation
Last line of equation</td></tr>
</table>

```
\begin{multline}
\text{First line of equation}          \\
\text{Middle line of equation}         \\
\text{Other middle line of equation} \\
\text{Last line of equation}
\end{multline}
```

More examples are shown in section 8.7.2 on page 247.

8.5.5   The `split` Environment

Like `multline`, the `split` environment is for single equations that are too long to fit on a single line and hence must be split into multiple lines. Unlike `multline`, however, the `split` environment provides for alignment among the split lines, using an ampersand to mark alignment points, as usual. In addition (unlike the other amstex equation structures) the `split` environment provides no numbering because it is intended to be used only inside some other displayed equation structure, such as `equation`, `align`, or `gather`. These outer environments will provide the numbering.

(8.36)
$$
\begin{aligned}
(a+b)^4 &= (a+b)^2(a+b)^2 \\
&= (a^2 + 2ab + b^2)(a^2 + 2ab + b^2) \\
&= a^4 + 4a^3b + 6a^2b^2 + 4ab^3 + b^4
\end{aligned}
$$

```
\begin{equation}
\begin{split}
(a+b)^4 &=  (a+b)^2 (a+b)^2                 \\
        &=  (a^2+2ab+b^2)(a^2+2ab+b^2)   \\
        &=  a^4+4a^3b+6a^2b^2+4ab^3+b^4 \\
\end{split}
\end{equation}
```

When the ctagsplt option is specified, the equation number for the `split` environment will be centered vertically on the height of the `split`, provided there is enough room for it.

(8.37)
$$
\begin{aligned}
(a+b)^3 &= (a+b)(a+b)^2 \\
&= (a+b)(a^2 + 2ab + b^2) \\
&= a^3 + 3a^2b + 3ab^2 + b^3
\end{aligned}
$$

```
\begin{equation}
\begin{split}
(a+b)^3 &=  (a+b) (a+b)^2          \\
        &=  (a+b)(a^2+2ab+b^2)   \\
        &=  a^3+3a^2b+3ab^2+b^3 \\
\end{split}
\end{equation}
```

More examples are shown in section 8.7.1 on page 244.

8.5.6 Alignment Environments as Parts of Displays

In addition to the `split` environment, there are some other equation alignment environments that do not constitute an entire display. They are self-contained units that can be used inside other formulae, or set side by side. The environment names are: `aligned`, `gathered`, and `alignedat`. These environments take an optional argument to specify their vertical positioning with respect to the material on either side. The default alignment is centered (`[c]`), and its effect is seen in the following example.

$$x^2 + y^2 = 1$$
$$x = \sqrt{1 - y^2}$$

$$(a+b)^2 = a^2 + 2ab + b^2$$
$$(a+b) \cdot (a-b) = a^2 - b^2$$

```
\begin{equation*}
\begin{aligned}
   x^2  + y^2 & = 1                     \\
        x & = \sqrt{1-y^2}
\end{aligned}                                      \qquad
\begin{gathered}
   (a + b)^2 = a^2 + 2ab + b^2 \\
   (a + b) \cdot (a - b) = a^2 - b^2
\end{gathered}
\end{equation*}
```

The same mathematics can now be typeset using different vertical alignments for the environments.

$$x^2 + y^2 = 1$$
$$x = \sqrt{1 - y^2}$$

$$(a+b)^2 = a^2 + 2ab + b^2$$
$$(a+b) \cdot (a-b) = a^2 - b^2$$

```
\begin{equation*}
\begin{aligned}[b]
   x^2  + y^2 & = 1                     \\
        x & = \sqrt{1-y^2}
\end{aligned}                                      \qquad
\begin{gathered}[t]
   (a + b)^2 = a^2 + 2ab + b^2 \\
   (a + b) \cdot (a - b) = a^2 - b^2
\end{gathered}
\end{equation*}
```

8.5.7 Vertical Spacing and Page Breaks in Equation Structures

You can use the `\\`[*dimension*] command to get extra vertical space between lines in all the `amstex` displayed equation environments, as is usual in LaTeX. Unlike `eqnarray`, the `amstex` environments do not allow page breaks between lines, unless `\displaybreak` or `\allowdisplaybreaks` is used. The reason for this is that page breaks in such situations should receive individual attention from the author. `\displaybreak` must go before the `\\` where it is supposed to take effect. Like LaTeX's `\pagebreak`, `\displaybreak` takes an optional argument between zero and four denoting the desirability of the page break. \displaybreak[0] means "it is permissible to break here" without encouraging a break; \displaybreak with no optional argument is the same as \displaybreak[4] and forces a break.

There is also an optional argument for \allowdisplaybreaks. This command obeys the usual LaTeX scoping rules. The normal way of limiting its scope is to put {\allowdisplaybreaks at the beginning and } at the end of the desired range. Within the scope of an \allowdisplaybreaks command, the * command can be used to prohibit a page break, as usual.

8.5.8 The \intertext **Command**

The \intertext command is used for a short interjection of one or two lines of text in the middle of a display alignment. Its salient feature is the preservation of alignment, which would not be possible if you simply ended the display and then started it up again afterwards. \intertext may only appear immediately after a \\ or * command.

$$(8.38) \quad A_1 = N_0(\lambda; \Omega') - \phi(\lambda; \Omega'),$$

$$(8.39) \quad A_2 = \phi(\lambda; \Omega')\phi(\lambda; \Omega),$$

and finally

$$(8.40) \quad A_3 = \mathcal{N}(\lambda; \omega).$$

```
\begin{align}
A_1&=N_0(\lambda;\Omega') -
                \phi(\lambda;\Omega'), \\
A_2&=\phi(\lambda;\Omega')
                \phi(\lambda;\Omega),   \\
\intertext{and finally}
A_3&=\mathcal{N}(\lambda;\omega).
\end{align}
```

Here the words "and finally" fall outside the display at the left margin.

8.6 Miscellaneous

This section discusses amstex commands that have not been introduced yet, and it gives a list of the document class files that come with the $\mathcal{A}_{\mathcal{M}}\mathcal{S}$-LaTeX distribution.

8.6.1 Equation Numbers

Each environment, except for split, has both starred and unstarred forms, where the unstarred forms have automatic numbering, using LaTeX's equation counter. The number on any particular line can be suppressed by putting \notag before the \\. You can also override it with a tag of your own design using

```
\tag{label}  \tag*{label}
```

where *label* can be any arbitrary text to be used to number the equation.

The starred form, \tag*, causes the *label* to be typeset without any annotations like parentheses that might otherwise be added by the document class. \tag and \tag* can also be used in the starred versions of all the amstex alignment environments.

$$
\begin{aligned}
(8.41) \qquad & x^2 + y^2 = z^2 \\
& x^3 + y^3 = z^3 \\
(*) \qquad & x^4 + y^4 = r^4 \\
* \qquad & x^5 + y^5 = r^5 \\
(8.41') \qquad & x^6 + y^6 = r^6
\end{aligned}
$$

```
\begin{gather}
  x^2+y^2 = z^2 \label{eq:r2}      \\
  x^3+y^3 = z^3 \notag             \\
  x^4+y^4 = r^4 \tag{$*$}          \\
  x^5+y^5 = r^5 \tag*{$*$}         \\
  x^6+y^6 = r^6 \tag{\ref{eq:r2}$'$}
\end{gather}
```

Notice the use of the \label and \ref commands in the previous example to allow subnumbering of equations.

When the option righttag is specified, the equation number will be printed at the right side of the equation (by default, with amstex, it comes out at the left).

$$
\sin^2 \eta + \cos^2 \eta = 1 \qquad (8.42)
$$

```
\begin{equation}
  \sin^2\eta + \cos^2\eta = 1
\end{equation}
```

8.6.2 Resetting the Equation Counter

In LaTeX, if you want to have equations numbered within sections—that is, have equation numbers (1.1), (1.2), ... , (2.1), (2.2), ... , in sections 1, 2, and so forth—you would probably redefine \theequation:

```
\renewcommand{\theequation}{\thesection.\arabic{equation}}
```

But now you have to reset the equation number by hand at the beginning of each new section or chapter. To make this a little more convenient, amstex provides a command \numberwithin. To have equation numbering tied to section numbering, with automatic reset of the equation counter, the command is

```
\numberwithin{equation}{section}
```

As the name implies, \numberwithin can be applied to other counters besides the equation counter, but the results may not be satisfactory in all cases

Positive space			Negative space		
Abb.	ex.	Spelled out	Abb.	ex.	Spelled out
\,	$x\,x$	\thinspace	\!	xx	\negthinspace
\:	$x\:x$	\medspace		xx	\negmedspace
\;	$x\;x$	\thickspace		xx	\negthickspace
@,	xx		@!	xx	
	$x\quad x$	\quad			
	$x\qquad x$	\qquad			

Table 8.21: The mathematical spacing commands

because of potential complications. Normal LaTeX methods should be used where available, for example, in \newtheorem.[4]

To make cross-references to equations easier, an \eqref command is provided. This automatically supplies the parentheses around the equation number, and adds an italic correction before the closing parenthesis, if necessary. To refer to an equation that was labeled with the label e:baset, the usage would be \eqref{e:baset}.

8.6.3   Fine-Tuning Spacing in Math Mode

Although TeX generally does a good job of spacing elements of formulae inside mathematics, it is sometimes necessary to fine-tune the position of one or two of those elements. Therefore, the spacing commands shown in table 8.21 are provided. Both the spelled-out and abbreviated forms of these commands are robust, and they can also be used outside of math.

The commands @, and @! typeset one-tenth the space of \, and \! respectively, for extra fine-tuning where necessary.

8.6.4   A Few Points to Note

(£ 151–52)
Many of the commands added by the amstex package are fragile and will need to be \protected in commands with "moving arguments."

In amstex, the @ character has a special use in the extensible arrows @>>> and @<<< and in the math microspacing commands @, and @!. In order to get an ordinary printed @ character you should type @@ instead of @.

With the various alignment environments available in the amstex package, the eqnarray environment is no longer needed. Furthermore, since it does not prevent overlapping of the equation numbers with wide formulae, as most of the

---

[4]See also the discussion of the \@addtoreset command on page 22.

amstex alignments do, using the amstex alignments seems better. amstex reimplements the LATEX equation environment as a one-line gather environment,
and adds an unnumbered version, equation*, for symmetry. Note, however,
that the command \verb might not work in the alignment environments.

\nonumber is interchangeable with \notag; the latter seems slightly preferable, for consistency with the name \tag.

8.6.5 Options and Sub-Packages to the amstex Package

A few options are recognized by the amstex package and the classes provided
by $\mathcal{A}_{\mathcal{M}}\mathcal{S}$-LATEX.[5] They affect the positioning of math operator limits or \tags.

ctagsplt The text of the tags is vertically centered with respect to the height of
the split environment.

intlim The limits of an integral have to be placed above and below rather
than on the side of the integral symbol.

nonamelm The limits of an "operator" name have to be placed on the side rather
than above and below the operator symbol.

nosumlim The limits of a sum have to be placed on the side rather than above
and below the sum symbol.

righttag This will output equation tags on the right rather than on the left.

Also, some of the component parts of the amstex package are available
individually and can be used separately in a \usepackage command:

amsbsy defines the amstex \boldsymbol and (poor man's bold) \pmb commands.

amscd defines some commands for easing the generation of commutative
diagrams.

amsfonts defines the \frak and \Bbb commands and sets up the fonts msam
(extra math symbols A), msbm (extra math symbols B, and blackboard
bold), eufm (Euler Fraktur), extra sizes of cmmib (bold math italic and
bold lowercase Greek), and cmbsy (bold math symbols and bold script),
for use in mathematics.

amssymb defines the names of all the math symbols available with the $\mathcal{A}_{\mathcal{M}}\mathcal{S}$
fonts collection.

amstext defines the amstex \text command.

---

[5]This is only true for the LATEX 2_ε release of $\mathcal{A}_{\mathcal{M}}\mathcal{S}$-LATEX. Older versions of $\mathcal{A}_{\mathcal{M}}\mathcal{S}$-LATEX realize
these options as sub-packages.

The amsbsy, amstext, and amsfonts packages are included automatically when you use the amstex package. The other two, amssymb and amscd, can be used together with amstex if their functionality is needed.

8.6.6 $\mathcal{A}_{\mathcal{M}}\mathcal{S}$-LaTeX Document Classes

The $\mathcal{A}_{\mathcal{M}}\mathcal{S}$-LaTeX package comes with a pair of document classes called amsart and amsbook, corresponding to LaTeX's article and book. They are primarily designed to prepare manuscripts for submission to the AMS, but there is nothing to prohibit their use for other purposes. With these class files the amstex package is automatically included, so that you can start your document simply with \documentclass{amsart} or \documentclass{amsbook}.

8.7 Examples of Multiple-Line Equation Structures

On the following pages we show a lot of real-life examples of the alignment environments discussed earlier. The lines indicating the margins around the typeset examples are not part of the environments but have been added to make the marginal spacing stand out clearly.

8.7.1 The split Environment

The split environment is not an independent environment but should be used inside something else, such as equation or align.

If there is not enough room for it, the equation number for a split will be shifted to the previous line when equation numbers are on the left; the number shifts down to the next line when numbers are on the right.

When you do not want an equation number, use the equation* environment.

(8.43)

$$
\begin{aligned}
f_{h,\varepsilon}(x,y) &= \varepsilon \mathbf{E}_{x,y} \int_0^{t_\varepsilon} L_{x,y_\varepsilon(\varepsilon u)} \varphi(x) \, du \\
&= h \int L_{x,z} \varphi(x) \rho_x(dz) \\
&\quad + h[\frac{1}{t_\varepsilon}(\mathbf{E}_y \int_0^{t_\varepsilon} L_{x,y^x(s)} \varphi(x) \, ds - t_\varepsilon \int L_{x,z} \varphi(x) \rho_x(dz)) \\
&\quad + \frac{1}{t_\varepsilon}(\mathbf{E}_y \int_0^{t_\varepsilon} L_{x,y^x(s)} \varphi(x) \, ds - \mathbf{E}_{x,y} \int_0^{t_\varepsilon} L_{x,y_\varepsilon(\varepsilon s)} \varphi(x) \, ds)]
\end{aligned}
$$

This was produced by the following input (the TeX command \phantom is used to leave a space equal to the width of its argument):

```
\begin{equation}
\begin{split}
f_{h,\varepsilon}(x,y)
  &= \varepsilon \mathbf{E}_{x,y} \int_0^{t_\varepsilon}
     L_{x,y_\varepsilon(\varepsilon u)} \varphi(x) \, du        \\
  &= h \int L_{x,z} \varphi(x) \rho_x (dz)                      \\
  & \quad +h \biggl[ \frac{1}{t_\varepsilon} \biggl(
    \mathbf{E}_{y} \int_0^{t_\varepsilon} L_{x,y^x(s)} \varphi(x)\,ds
    -t_\varepsilon \int L_{x,z} \varphi(x) \rho_x(dz) \biggr) \\
  & \phantom{{=}+h\biggl[}+\frac{1}{t_\varepsilon}
    \biggl( \mathbf{E}_{y} \int_0^{t_\varepsilon} L_{x,y^x(s)}
      \varphi(x) \,ds - \mathbf{E}_{x,y} \int_0^{t_\varepsilon}
      L_{x,y_\varepsilon(\varepsilon s)}
      \varphi(x) \,ds \biggr) \biggr]                          \\
\end{split}
\end{equation}
```

If the option ctagsplt is included in the options list of the amstex package, the equation numbers for split environments will be centered vertically on the height of the split, as shown in the example below.

$$
\begin{split}
|I_2| &= \left| \int_0^T \psi(t) \left\{ u(a,t) - \int_{\gamma(t)}^a \frac{d\theta}{k(\theta,t)} \int_a^\theta c(\xi) u_t(\xi,t) \, d\xi \right\} dt \right| \\
&\le C_6 \left| \left| f \int_\Omega \left| \widetilde{S}_{a,-}^{-1,0} W_2(\Omega,\Gamma_l) \right| \right| \left| |u| \overset{\circ}{\to} W_2^{\widetilde{A}}(\Omega;\Gamma_r,T) \right| \right|.
\end{split} \tag{8.44}
$$

This is produced by the following input:

```
\begin{equation}
\begin{split}
|I_2|
  &=\left| \int_{0}^T \psi(t)
      \left\{ u(a,t)-\int_{\gamma(t)}^a \frac{d\theta}{k(\theta,t)}
             \int_{a}^\theta c(\xi)u_t(\xi,t)\,d\xi \right\} dt
    \right| \\
  &\le C_6 \left| \left|
            f\int_\Omega
              \left| \widetilde{S}^{-1,0}_{a,-} W_2(\Omega,\Gamma_1)
                \right|
              \right|
            \left|
              |u|\overset{\circ}{\to} W_2^{\widetilde{A}}
              (\Omega;\Gamma_r,T)
            \right| \right|.
\end{split}
\end{equation}
```

One further example involving `split` and `align`. To obtain unnumbered equations use the `align*` environment instead.

(8.45)

$$|I_1| = \left| \int_\Omega gRu\,d\Omega \right|$$
$$\le C_3 \left[\int_\Omega \left(\int_a^x g(x_1,t)\,d\xi \right)^2 d\Omega \right]^{1/2}$$
$$\times \left[\int_\Omega \left\{ u_x^2 + \frac{1}{k} \left(\int_a^x cu_t\,d\xi \right)^2 \right\} c\Omega \right]^{1/2}$$
$$\le C_4 \left| \left| f \left| \widetilde{S}_{a,-}^{-1,0} W_2(\Omega,\Gamma_l) \right| \right| \left| |u| \overset{\circ}{\to} W_2^{\widetilde{A}}(\Omega;\Gamma_r,T) \right| \right|.$$

(8.46)

$$|I_2| = \left| \int_0^T \psi(t) \left\{ u(a,t) - \int_{y(t)}^a \frac{d\theta}{k(\theta,t)} \int_a^\theta c(\xi) u_t(\xi,t)\,d\xi \right\} dt \right|$$
$$\le C_6 \left| \left| f \int_\Omega \left| \widetilde{S}_{a,-}^{-1,0} W_2(\Omega,\Gamma_l) \right| \right| \left| |u| \overset{\circ}{\to} W_2^{\widetilde{A}}(\Omega;\Gamma_r,T) \right| \right|.$$

The input for the above formulae is:

```
\begin{align}
\begin{split}
|I_1| &= \left| \int_\Omega gRu \,d\Omega \right|                    \\
     &\le C_3 \left[ \int_\Omega \left( \int_{a}^x
        g(x\i,t) \,d \xi \right)^2d \Omega \right]^{1/2}             \\
     &\quad\times \left[ \int_\Omega \left\{ u^2_x + \frac{1}{k}
        \left( \int_{a}^x cu_t \, d\xi \right)^2 \right\}
        c \Omega \right]^{1/2}                                      \\
     &\le C_4 \left| \left| f \left| \widetilde{S}^{-1,0}_{a,-}
        W_2(\Omega,\Gamma_l) \right| \right|
        \left| |u| \overset{\circ} \to W_2^{\widetilde{A}}
        (\Omega;\Gamma_r,T) \right| \right|.
\end{split}\label{eq:A}                                             \\
\begin{split}
|I_2| &= \left| \int_{0}^T \psi(t) \left\{ u(a,t)
        -\int_{\gamma(t)}^a \frac{d\theta}{k(\theta,t)}
        \int_{a}^\theta c(\xi) u_t(\xi,t) \,d \xi \right\} dt
        \right|                                                    \\
     &\le C_6 \left| \left| f \int_\Omega
        \left| \widetilde{S}^{-1,0}_{a,-}
        W_2(\Omega,\Gamma_l)  \right| \right|
        \left| |u| \overset{\circ} \to W_2^{\widetilde{A}}
        (\Omega;\Gamma_r,T) \right| \right|.
\end{split}
\end{align}
```

8.7.2 The `multline` Environment

Numbered version:

$$(8.47) \quad \int_a^b \{ \int_a^b [f(x)^2 g(y)^2 + f(y)^2 g(x)^2] - 2f(x)g(x)f(y)g(y)\, dx \}\, dy$$
$$= \int_a^b \{ g(y)^2 \int_a^b f^2 + f(y)^2 \int_a^b g^2 - 2f(y)g(y) \int_a^b fg \}\, dy$$

This was obtained with the lines shown below.

```
\begin{multline}\label{eq:E}
  \int_a^b \biggl\{ \int_a^b [ f(x)^2 g(y)^2 + f(y)^2 g(x)^2 ]
  -2f(x) g(x) f(y) g(y) \,dx \biggr\} \,dy              \\
=\int_a^b \biggl\{ g(y)^2 \int_a^b f^2 + f(y)^2
  \int_a^b g^2 - 2f(y) g(y) \int_a^b fg \biggr\} \,dy
\end{multline}
```

An unnumbered version of the above is obtained with the same input, except the `multline` environment is replaced by `multline*`.

$$\int_a^b \{ \int_a^b [f(x)^2 g(y)^2 + f(y)^2 g(x)^2] - 2f(x)g(x)f(y)g(y)\, dx \}\, dy$$
$$= \int_a^b \{ g(y)^2 \int_a^b f^2 + f(y)^2 \int_a^b g^2 - 2f(y)g(y) \int_a^b fg \}\, dy$$

And now an unnumbered version numbered with a `\tag*` command.

$$[a] \quad \int_a^b \{ \int_a^b [f(x)^2 g(y)^2 + f(y)^2 g(x)^2] - 2f(x)g(x)f(y)g(y)\, dx \}\, dy$$
$$= \int_a^b \{ g(y)^2 \int_a^b f^2 + f(y)^2 \int_a^b g^2 - 2f(y)g(y) \int_a^b fg \}\, dy$$

This was generated with:

```
\begin{multline*}\tag*{[a]}   ...   \end{multline*}
```

This is the same display, but with `\multlinegap` set to zero. Notice that the space on the left of the first line does not change, because of the equation number, while the second line is pushed over to the right margin.

$$[a] \quad \int_a^b \{ \int_a^b [f(x)^2 g(y)^2 + f(y)^2 g(x)^2] - 2f(x)g(x)f(y)g(y)\, dx \}\, dy$$
$$= \int_a^b \{ g(y)^2 \int_a^b f^2 + f(y)^2 \int_a^b g^2 - 2f(y)g(y) \int_a^b fg \}\, dy$$

This was generated with:

```
{\setlength{\multlinegap}{0pt}
\begin{multline*}\tag*{[a]}  ...  \end{multline*}}
```

8.7.3   The gather Environment

Numbered version with \notag on the second line:

$$
\begin{gather}
(8.48) \qquad D(a,r) \equiv \{z \in \mathbf{C}: |z-a| < r\}, \\
\operatorname{seg}(a,r) \equiv \{z \in \mathbf{C}: \Im z = \Im a, \ |z-a| < r\}, \\
(8.49) \qquad c(e,\theta,r) \equiv \{(x,y) \in \mathbf{C}: |x-e| < y\tan\theta, \ 0 < y < r\}, \\
(8.50) \qquad C(E,\theta,r) \equiv \bigcup_{e \in E} c(e,\theta,r).
\end{gather}
$$

This was generated with:

```
\begin{gather}
  D(a,r) \equiv \{ z \in \mathbf{C}: |z-a|<r \},          \\
  \operatorname{seg}(a,r) \equiv \{ z \in \mathbf{C}:
     \Im z = \Im a, \ |z-a|<r\},                     \notag \\
  c(e,\theta,r) \equiv \{ (x,y) \in \mathbf{C}:
     |x-e|<y \tan \theta, \  0<y<r \},                    \\
  C(E,\theta,r) \equiv \bigcup_{e \in E}c(e,\theta,r).
\end{gather}
```

8.7.4   The align Environment

Numbered version:

$$
\begin{align}
(8.51) \qquad \gamma_x(t) &= (\cos tu + \sin tx, v), \\
(8.52) \qquad \gamma_y(t) &= (u, \cos tv + \sin ty), \\
(8.53) \qquad \gamma_z(t) &= \left(\cos tu + \frac{\alpha}{\beta}\sin tv, -\frac{\beta}{\alpha}\sin tu + \cos tv\right).
\end{align}
$$

This was produced using the following input:

```
\begin{align}
  \gamma_x(t) &= (\cos tu + \sin tx, v),                   \\
  \gamma_y(t) &= (u, \cos tv + \sin ty),                   \\
  \gamma_z(t) &= \left( \cos tu + \frac\alpha\beta \sin tv,
                 - \frac\beta\alpha \sin tu + \cos tv \right).
\end{align}
```

Unnumbered version:

$$\begin{aligned}
\gamma_x(t) &= (\cos tu + \sin tx, v), \\
\gamma_y(t) &= (u, \cos tv + \sin ty), \\
\gamma_z(t) &= \left(\cos tu + \frac{\alpha}{\beta}\sin tv, -\frac{\beta}{\alpha}\sin tu + \cos tv\right).
\end{aligned}$$

This was generated using the following construct:

```
\begin{align*}   ...   \end{align*}
```

8.7.5 Using the `align` and `split` Environments within `gather`

When using the `align` environment within the `gather` environment, one or the other, or both, should be unnumbered (using the `*` form), since having numbering for both the outer and inner environment would not be meaningful.

Automatically numbered `gather` with `split` and `align*`:

$$\begin{aligned}
\varphi(x, z) &= z - \gamma_{10}x - \sum_{m+n\ge2} \gamma_{mn}x^m z^n \\
&= z - Mr^{-1}x - \sum_{m+n\ge2} Mr^{-(m+n)}x^m z^n
\end{aligned}$$

$$\begin{aligned}
\zeta^0 &= (\xi^0)^2, \\
\zeta^1 &= \xi^0\xi^1
\end{aligned}$$

(8.54)

Here the `split` environment gets a number from the outer `gather` environment; numbers for individual lines of the `align*` are suppressed because of the star.

```
\begin{gather}
  \begin{split}
    \varphi(x,z)
      &= z - \gamma_{10} x - \sum_{m+n\ge2} \gamma_{mn} x^m z^n \\
      &= z - M r^{-1} x - \sum_{m+n\ge2} M r^{-(m+n)} x^m z^n
  \end{split}                                              \\[6pt]
  \begin{align*}
    \zeta^0   &= (\xi^0)^2,        \\
    \zeta^1   &= \xi^0 \xi^1
  \end{align*}
\end{gather}
```

Shown below, is the *-ed form of `gather` with the non-*-ed form of `align`.

$$\varphi(x, z) = z - y_{10}x - \sum_{m+n \geq 2} y_{mn}x^m z^n$$
$$= z - Mr^{-1}x - \sum_{m+n \geq 2} Mr^{-(m+n)}x^m z^n$$

$$(8.55) \qquad \zeta^0 = (\xi^0)^2,$$
$$(8.56) \qquad \zeta^1 = \xi^0 \xi^1$$

The latter was produced with the following construct:

```
\begin{gather*}
    \begin{split} ...\end{split}                    \\[6pt]
    \begin{align*}...\end{align*}
\end{gather*}
```

8.7.6 Using the `alignat` Environments

Numbered version:

$$(8.57) \qquad V_i = v_i - q_i v_j, \qquad X_i = x_i - q_i x_j, \qquad U_i = u_i, \qquad \text{for } i \neq j;$$
$$(8.58) \qquad V_j = v_j, \qquad X_j = x_j, \qquad U_j u_j + \sum_{i \neq j} q_i u_i.$$

This example was obtained with the commands below:

```
\begin{alignat}{3}
V_i &= v_i - q_i v_j, & \qquad X_i &= x_i - q_i x_j,
  & \qquad U_i &= u_i, \qquad \text{for $i\ne j\,$;}\label{eq:B}  \\
V_j &= v_j, & \qquad X_j &= x_j,
  & \qquad U_j & u_j + \sum_{i\ne j} q_i u_i.
\end{alignat}
```

Unnumbered version:

$$V_i = v_i - q_i v_j, \qquad X_i = x_i - q_i x_j, \qquad U_i = u_i, \qquad \text{for } i \neq j;$$
$$V_j = v_j, \qquad X_j = x_j, \qquad U_j u_j + \sum_{i \neq j} q_i u_i.$$

This was generated using the following construct:

```
\begin{alignat*}{3}   ...   \end{alignat*}
```

The most common use for `alignat` is for things like

$$
\begin{array}{lll}
(8.59) & x = y & \text{by (8.45)} \\
(8.60) & x' = y' & \text{by (8.57)} \\
(8.61) & x + x' = y + y' & \text{by Axiom 1.}
\end{array}
$$

This example was obtained with the commands below:

```
\begin{alignat}{2}
x      &= y   && \qquad \text{by (\ref{eq:A})}\label{eq:C} \\
x'     &= y'  && \qquad \text{by (\ref{eq:B})}\label{eq:D} \\
x + x' &= y+y' && \qquad \text{by Axiom 1.}
\end{alignat}
```

The expanded version, `xalignat`:

$$
\begin{array}{lll}
(8.62) & x = y & \text{by (8.59)} \\
(8.63) & x' = y' & \text{by (8.60)} \\
(8.64) & x + x' = y + y' & \text{by Axiom 1.}
\end{array}
$$

This was generated using the following construct:

```
\begin{xalignat}{2}  ...  \end{xalignat}
```

8.8   Extensions to the `theorem` Environment

The theorem package, developed by Frank Mittelbach [54], offers an extension of the LaTeX theorem mechanism by allowing the layout of theorems to be manipulated by specifying a style.

(*£* 58, 174)

In the present context the word "theorem" is used for any kind of labeled enunciations, often set off from the main text by extra space and a font change. Theorems, corollaries, conjectures, definitions, and remarks are all instances of "theorems." The header of these structures is composed of a label (such as THEOREM or REMARK) and a number, which serializes an item in the sequence of items with the same label.

Often it is necessary, in order to satisfy the requirements of different mathematics journals, to customize the layout of the theorem environment. Additionally, different formats may be needed to differentiate the "sort of theorem": e.g., remarks and definitions are set in roman, while italic is employed for main theorems.

8.8.1   Defining New Theorem Environments

As in the original LaTeX version, the command `\newtheorem` defines a new "theorem-like structure." Two required arguments name the new environment and give the text to be typeset with each instance of the new environment, while an optional argument determines how the environment is enumerated:

> `\newtheorem{`*env-name*`}{`*label-text*`}`

The above `\newtheorem` command defines the *env-name* environment and its printed name will be *label-text*. It uses its own counter.

> `\newtheorem{`*env2-name*`}[`*env-name*`]{`*label-text2*`}`

The above `\newtheorem` command defines the *env2-name* environment, and its printed name will be *label-text2*. It uses the same counter as theorem set *env-name*.

> `\newtheorem{`*env3-name*`}{`*label-text3*`}[`*section*`]`

The above variant defines the *env3-name* environment and its printed name is *label-text3*. Its counter is enumerated within the counter *section*, that is, with every new `\section` the enumeration starts again with one, and the enumeration is composed from the section number and the theorem counter itself.

> `\theoremstyle{`*style*`}`

The `\theoremstyle` command can define the layout of various, or all, theorem sets. It should be noted that any theorem set defined by `\newtheorem` is typeset in the `\theoremstyle` that is current at the time of the definition.
Thus, the following

```
\theoremstyle{break}        \newtheorem{Cor}{Corollary}
\theoremstyle{plain}        \newtheorem{Exa}{Example}[section]
```

leads to the result that the set Cor is formatted in the style break, while the set Exa and all the following ones are formatted in the style plain, unless another `\theoremstyle` follows. Since the definitions installed by `\newtheorem` are global, you can also limit `\theoremstyle` locally by grouping braces.

> `\theorembodyfont{`*font-declarations*`}`

The choice of the font for the theorem body is completely independent of the chosen `\theoremstyle`; this has proven to be very advantageous. For example,

```
{\theorembodyfont{\rmfamily}        \newtheorem{Rem}{Remark}}
```

plain	Emulates the original LATEX definition, except that additionally the parameters \theorempreskipamount and \theorempostskipamount are used.
break	In this style, the theorem header is followed by a line break.
marginbreak	The theorem number is set in the margin, and there is a line break as in break.
changebreak	Like break, but with header number and text interchanged.
change	Header number and text are interchanged, without a line break.
margin	The number is set in the left margin, without a line break.

Table 8.22: List of existing theorem styles

All styles (except plain) select \normalfont\slshape as the default for \theorembodyfont.

defines a theorem set Rem, which will be set in \rmfamily in the current layout (which in our example is plain). As with \theoremstyle, the \theorembodyfont chosen is that which is current at the time of \newtheorem. If \theorembodyfont is not specified or you define \theorembodyfont{}, then the font used will be defined by \theoremstyle.

\theoremheaderfont{*font-declarations*}

It is also possible to customize the font used for the theorem headers. This is, however, a global declaration and, therefore, there should be at most one \theoremheaderfont command in the preamble. If it is actually necessary to have different header fonts, you will have to define new theorem styles (substituting the desired font).

Two additional parameters affect the vertical space around the theorem environments: \theorempreskipamount and \theorempostskipamount define, respectively, the spacing before and after such an environment. These parameters apply to all theorem sets and can be manipulated with the ordinary length macros. They are rubber lengths, and therefore can contain plus and minus parts. These parameters are set using the \setlength command.

The commands to define theorem sets, as described in this section, can only be placed in the document preamble or in a package file.

Theorem styles, which exist to date, are shown in table 8.22

8.8.2 Examples of the Definition and Use of Theorems

Suppose that the preamble contains the declarations:

```
\theoremstyle{break}        \newtheorem{Cor}{Corollary}
\theoremstyle{plain}        \newtheorem{Exa}{Example}[section]
```

```
{\theorembodyfont{\rmfamily}  \newtheorem{Rem}{Remark}}
\theoremstyle{marginbreak}    \newtheorem{Lem}[Cor]{Lemma}
\theoremstyle{change}
\theorembodyfont{\itshape}    \newtheorem{Def}[Cor]{Definition}

\theoremheaderfont{\scshape}
```

Then the typical examples below show the typeset output resulting from their use.

COROLLARY 1
This is a sentence typeset in the theorem environment Cor.

```
\begin{Cor}
   This is a sentence typeset in the theorem
   environment \Lenv{Cor}.
\end{Cor}
```

EXAMPLE 8.8.1   *This is a sentence typeset in the theorem environment* Exa.

```
\begin{Exa}
   This is a sentence typeset in the theorem
   environment \Lenv{Exa}.
\end{Exa}
```

REMARK 1   This is a sentence typeset in the theorem environment Rem.

```
\begin{Rem}
   This is a sentence typeset in the theorem
   environment \Lenv{Rem}.
\end{Rem}
```

2   LEMMA (BEN USER)
This is a sentence typeset in the theorem environment Lem.

```
\begin{Lem}[Ben User]
   This is a sentence typeset in the theorem
   environment \Lenv{Lem}.
\end{Lem}
```

3 DEFINITION (VERY IMPRESSIVE DEFINITION)   *This is a sentence typeset in the theorem environment* Def.

```
\begin{Def}[Very impressive Definition]
   This is a sentence typeset in the theorem
   environment \Lenv{Def}.
\end{Def}
```

The last two examples show the effect of the optional argument to a theorem environment (it is typeset in parentheses right after the label).

8.8.3   Special Considerations

The theorem header and body are implemented as a single unit. This means that the \theoremheaderfont will inherit characteristics of the \theorembodyfont if the NFSS is being used. Thus, if, for example, \theorembodyfont is \itshape and \theoremheaderfont is \bfseries the font selected for the header will have the characteristics "bold extended italic." If this is not desired you should set it to something like \theoremheaderfont{\normalfont\bfseries}. That is, you should supply all the necessary font information explicitly. See chapter 7 for more details about how to do that.

8.9   Mathematical Style Parameters

This section explains how you can globally control the style of your mathematical formulae, and how you can modify the size of certain (sub)formula elements.

8.9.1   Controlling the Size of Characters

Letters and mathematical symbols sometimes get smaller when they appear in fractions, superscripts, or subscripts. In fact, TeX has eight different styles in which it can treat formulae, namely:

D, D'	\displaystyle	formulae displayed on lines by themselves
T, T'	\textstyle	formulae embedded in the text
S, S'	\scriptstyle	formulae used as super- or subscripts
SS, SS'	\scriptscriptstyle	second- and higher-order super- or subscripts

The accented symbols represent the so-called *cramped* styles, which are similar to the normal styles except that exponents are not raised so much. TeX also uses three different type sizes for mathematics, namely: text size, script size, and scriptscript size.

A formula set inside text (between a $ pair, or between \(...\)) is typeset using text style (style T). A formula on a line by itself, which is entered between \[...\], will be typeset in display style (style D). The size of the different parts of a formula can be determined according to the following scheme:

A symbol in style	will be typeset in	(example)
D, D', T, T'	text size	(text size)
S, S'	script size	(script size)
SS, SS'	scriptscript size	(scriptscript size)

The kind of style used in mathematics formulae is as follows:

style	superscript	subscript	numerator	denominator
D	S	S'	T	T'
D'	S'	S'	T'	T'
T	S	S'	S	S'
T'	S'	S'	S'	S'
S, SS	SS	SS'	SS	SS'
S', SS'	SS'	SS'	SS'	SS'

The last two columns describe the style used in the numerator or denominator of a fraction. An example of the various styles can be seen in the continued fraction below (see also section 8.3.16):

$$b^0 + \cfrac{a^1}{b_1 + \cfrac{a^2}{b_2 + \frac{a^3}{b_3}}}$$

```
\normalsize
\[ b^0 + \frac{a^1}{b_1 +
         \frac{a^2}{b_2 +
         \frac{a^3}{b_3}}}
\]
```

In the formula above the b of b^0 is in style D, with the 0 in style S; the a and b of a^1 and b_1 are in style T and T', respectively, with the exponent 1 in style S and the subscript 1 in style S'; the a and b of a^2 and b_2 are both in style S', with the exponent and subscript in style SS'; finally everything in a^3 and b_3 is in style SS'.

You can give a nicer look to the above example by deciding which style is to be used in each case. Note that to save typing, we define the abbreviation \D for the \displaystyle command.

$$b^0 + \cfrac{a^1}{b_1 + \cfrac{a^2}{b_2 + \cfrac{a^3}{b_3}}}$$

```
\newcommand{\D}{\displaystyle}
\normalsize
\[ b^0 +  \frac{a^1}{\D b_1 +
          \frac{a^2}{\D b_2 +
          \frac{a^3}{b_3}}}
\]
```

8.9.2 LaTeX Math Style Parameters

(£ 170)
Because LaTeX uses much of the mathematical machinery from TeX, we briefly describe the mathematical style parameters that LaTeX uses to typeset formulae. All these parameters are expressed as lengths, which you can redefine with the \setlength or \addtolength commands (see section A.1.4 on page 447).

(£ 82)
Moreover, two standard options, leqno and fleqn, control the numbering and alignment of formulae. The option fleqn causes formulae to be aligned on the left, a fixed distance from the left margin (see \mathindent below), instead of being centered.

The option leqno causes the formula numbers produced by the equation and eqnarray environments to appear on the left, instead of at the right. Note that LaTeX puts equation numbers at the right by default, while with the amstex package activated, they are at the left. Therefore, with amstex you have to specify the option righttag to have them at the right (see section 8.6.5 on page 243).

In the list of mathematics style parameters below, all lengths (except \jot and \arraycolsep) are rubber lengths. With the option fleqn, the four displayskip lengths are made equal to the list defining length \topsep, to which the value of \partopsep is added if the display starts a paragraph (see figure 3.5 on page 62).

\arraycolsep This gives half the width of the horizontal space between columns in an array environment (default value 5pt, see also section 5.3.2).

\jot This is the extra vertical space that is added between rows in an eqnarray or eqnarray* environment (default value 3pt).

\mathindent This defines the indentation from the left margin of displayed formulae for the fleqn option (the default value is equal to the indentation of a first level list, i.e., 2.5em, and is defined by the option fleqn).

\abovedisplayskip This specifies the extra space left above a long displayed formula, except with the option fleqn, where \topsep is used. A long formula is one that lies closer to the left margin than does the end of the preceding line (default value 12pt plus 3pt minus 9pt).

\belowdisplayskip This specifies the extra space left below a long displayed formula, except with the option fleqn, where \topsep is used (default value 12pt plus 3pt minus 9pt).

\abovedisplayshortskip This specifies the extra space left above a short displayed formula, except with the option fleqn, where \topsep is used. A short formula is one which starts to the right of where the preceding line ends (default value 0pt plus 3pt).

\belowdisplayshortskip This specifies the extra space left below a short displayed formula, except with the option fleqn, where \topsep is used (default value 7pt plus 3pt minus 4pt).

CHAPTER 9

L^AT_EX in a Multilingual Environment

This chapter starts with a short introduction to the many technical problems that must be solved in order to use (L^A)T_EX with a non-English language. The second section discusses the Babel system, which provides a convenient way for generating documents in different languages. Then, as an example of a more complex package, we have a look at the package french, developed by Bernard Gaulle. It goes a long way towards adapting the look and feel of documents to French typographic traditions.

9.1 T_EX and Non-English Languages

Due to its popularity in the academic world, T_EX spread rapidly throughout the world and is now used, not only with the different languages based on the Latin alphabet, but also with Chinese, Japanese, Korean, Coptic, Russian, Thai, Vietnamese, several Indian languages, Persian, Arabic, and Hebrew. These developments quickly made some of the limitations of T_EX2.x more evident, especially the 7-bit input character set and its inability to load hyphenation patterns for more than one language at the same time. Consequently, Donald Knuth announced at the 10th Annual Meeting of TUG in 1989 that a new version of T_EX and METAFONT would be produced to address the problems of multilingual support. These versions, T_EX3 and METAFONT2, were officially released in March 1990. Although they were a (large) step in the right direction, by themselves they do not solve all the problems associated with providing a convenient environment for using LaTeX with multiple or non-English languages.

To achieve this, TeX and its companion programs should be made truly international, and the following points should be addressed:

1. Adjust all programs to the particular language(s):

   - create proper fonts containing national symbols,
   - define standard character set encodings, and
   - generate patterns for the hyphenation algorithm.

2. Provide a translation for the document element terms, create national layouts for the standard documents, and provide TeX code to treat the language-dependent typesetting rules automatically.

3. Support the processing of multilingual (more than one language in the same document) and international (one language only, but a choice between various possibilities) documents. For instance, the sorting of indexes and bibliographic references should be performed in accordance with a given language's alphabet or collating sequence.

At the same time you should be able to conveniently edit, view, and print your documents using any given character set, and LaTeX should be able to successfully process files thus created. There exist, however, almost as many different character encoding schemes as there are languages (for example, IBM PC personal computers have dozens of code pages). In addition, there exist several international standards, such as the series ISO-8859-x [33] (see below). Therefore, some thought should be given to the question of compatibility and portability. If a document is to be reproducible in multiple environments, issues of standardization become important. In particular, sending 8-bit encoded documents via electronic mail often generates problems, since some mail gateways drop the higher order bit, thus making the document unprocessable. The mail problem will probably be solved when mailers adhere to the Multipart Internet Mail Extentions (MIME) standard, where the use of a particular encoding standard (e.g., ISO-8859-x) is explicitly declared in the mail's header. Document encoding problems will, however, only be solved when new standards, like Unicode [85] or ISO-10646 [35], are adopted by everybody.

The importance of these problems was realized by the TeX community, and at the TUG Portland meeting in July 1992 TUG's Technical Council set up the "Technical Working Group on Multiple Language Coordination" (TWGMLC), chaired by Yannis Haralambous. The goal of this group is to promote and coordinate the standardization and development of TeX related software adapted to different languages. For each language or group of languages a package has to be produced that will ease typesetting. Such a package should contain details about fonts, input conventions, hyphenation patterns, a LaTeX option file com-

	00	10	20	30	40	50	60	70	80	90	A0	B0	C0	D0	E0	F0
0	`	"	␣	0	@	P	'	p	Ă	Ř	ă	ř	À	Đ	à	ð
1	´	"	!	1	A	Q	a	q	Ą	Ś	ą	ś	Á	Ñ	á	ñ
2	ˆ	„	"	2	B	R	b	r	Ć	Š	ć	š	Â	Ò	â	ò
3	˜	«	#	3	C	S	c	s	Č	Ş	č	ş	Ã	Ó	ã	ó
4	¨	»	$	4	D	T	d	t	Ď	Ť	ď	ť	Ä	Ô	ä	ô
5	˝	–	%	5	E	U	e	u	Ě	Ţ	ě	ţ	Å	Õ	å	õ
6	˚	—	&	6	F	V	f	v	Ę	Ű	ę	ű	Æ	Ö	æ	ö
7	ˇ		'	7	G	W	g	w	Ğ	Ů	ğ	û	Ç	Œ	ç	œ
8	˘	₀	(	8	H	X	h	x	Ĺ	Ÿ	ĺ	ÿ	È	Ø	è	ø
9	¯	₁	)	9	I	Y	i	y	Ľ	Ź	ľ	ź	É	Ù	é	ù
A	˙	ȷ	*	:	J	Z	j	z	Ł	Ž	ł	ž	Ê	Ú	ê	ú
B	˛	ff	+	;	K	[	k	{	Ń	Ż	ń	ż	Ë	Û	ë	û
C	¸	fi	,	<	L	\	l	|	Ň	IJ	ň	ij	Ì	Ü	ì	ü
D	,	fl	-	=	M	]	m	}	Ŋ	İ	ŋ	ı	Í	Ý	í	ý
E	‹	ffi	.	>	N	^	n	~	Ő	đ	ő	¿	Î	Þ	î	þ
F	›	ffl	/	?	O	_	o	-	Ŕ	§	ŕ	£	Ï	SS	ï	ß

Table 9.1: The extended TEX font layout accepted at Cork in 1990

patible with the babel concept (see section 9.2), possibly a preprocessor, and of course documentation in English and the target language.

In section 7.5.1 we introduced the DC-EC fonts, which use the Cork encoding scheme, shown in table 9.1. Style files exist for mapping various input encodings to the 256-bit DC-font glyphs. For instance, the isolatin1 package translates files encoded according to ISO-8859-1 (also known as Latin-1). As an example, this package translates the input code "ab (left guillemets "«" in Latin1) into DC-code point "13 (see table 9.1) when the DC fonts are loaded, or else into the TEX command giving an approximate representation $<<$. Similar packages can be developed for other encodings, such as for the popular IBM PC International code page 850.

9.1.1   The Virtual Font Mechanism

A convenient way of constructing new fonts is with the virtual fonts mechanism [46]. Virtual fonts provide a good solution to the problem of rearranging a font, that is, they can redefine the mapping between codes and glyphs. They also allow you to construct composite characters (for instance, characters with diacritical marks) and composite fonts (combining characters from different fonts, e.g., Computer Modern Roman and lowercase Greek) without having to write special TEX macros. Virtual fonts let you use a standard input method adapted to your particular language (e.g., an ISO-8859 set, or later ISO-10646 encoding).

A virtual font needs to exist only in a logical, not necessarily in a physical, sense. TEX can do its job without knowing where the actual characters come from. It is up to the device driver, using the information in the virtual font file, to collect imaging information for the actual characters. The latter can be shifted, magnified, or combined with other characters from many different fonts. A virtual font can even make use of characters from other virtual fonts, including itself. Virtual fonts also allow convenient character substitutions for proofreading purposes when fonts designed for one output device are unavailable on another. The virtual font mechanism, thus, provides a general interface mechanism to allow switching between the myriad font layouts provided by different suppliers of typesetting equipment.

There remains, however, the problem of the portability of dvi-files. A virtual font can contain a local re-encoding of some actual fonts. The result after running TEX will be a dvi-file that is not portable. To solve this problem, dvi-files containing virtual fonts can be handled in various ways:

- Use a dvi-driver that understands virtual fonts. Examples of such drivers are dvips and the drivers from the emTEX collection.

- If the dvi-driver does not support virtual fonts, then a dvi-to-dvi conversion program (dvicopy by Peter Breitenlohner or PosTeX by Vassily Malyshev) can be used to remove the references to virtual fonts from the dvi-file and replace them with references to actual fonts. This makes the dvi-file portable.

9.2   Babel—LATEX Speaks Multiple Languages

The LATEX distribution contains a few standard document classes that are used by most users. These classes (article, report, book, and letter) have a certain American look and feel, which is not liked by everybody. Moreover, the names of the document elements, like "chapter" and "Table of Contents," come out in English by default.

The babel package by Johannes Braams [15] provides a set of option files that allow the user to choose the language in which the document has to be typeset. It has the following characteristics:

- Multiple languages can be used simultaneously.

- The hyphenation patterns, which are loaded when INITEX is run, can be defined dynamically via an external file.

- Translations for the names of document elements and commands for facilitating text input are provided for over twenty different languages.

The user interface of the system is simple. It consists of two user commands: one to select a language, and another to query what the current language is.

9.2.1 The User Interface

Any language that you use in your document should be declared on the `\usepackage` command as a language option.[1] Currently supported options are enumerated in table 9.3 on page 267. For example, the following declaration prepares for typesetting in the languages German (option german[2]) and Italian (option italian).

```
\usepackage[german,italian]{babel}
```

The last language on the `\usepackage` command line will be the default language at the beginning of the document. In the above example, the names of the document elements, the hyphenation patterns (if they were loaded for the given language when the LʌTEX format was generated with INITEX; see the discussion on page 266), and possibly the interpretation of certain language-dependent commands (such as the date) will be for Italian from the beginning of the document up to the point where you choose a different language. You can change the language with the command `\selectlanguage`, whose syntax is:

```
\selectlanguage{language}
```

For instance, if you want to switch to German, you would use the command `\selectlanguage{german}`. The process is the same for switching to other languages, as long as they have been declared at the beginning of the document on a `\usepackage` command.

When you are using more than one language, it might be necessary to know which language is active at a specific time. This can be checked by a call to the `\iflanguage` command, whose syntax is:

```
\iflanguage{language}{true-clause}{false-clause}
```

The first argument, *language*, is the name of a language; the second argument, *true-clause*, specifies which commands should be executed if *language* is the currently active language; and the third argument, *false-clause*, specifies the commands to be executed in the opposite case.

---

[1]In principle, since the language(s) in which a document is written is a global characteristic of the document in question, it makes good sense to declare it on the `\documentclass` command, e.g., `\documentclass[polish]{...}`. See section 2.1 for a detailed discussion.

[2]For compatibility with the LʌTEX 2.09 version of babel, the option germanb is also recognized by babel.

9.2.2 The german **Option**

We now discuss the german option,[3] as an example of the functionality offered by the babel system.

Apart from translating the language dependent document element names into German, the german option provides the following:

- "a is an abbreviation for \"a, which typesets ä. Umlauts can be added to the other vowels through a similar process (see figure 9.2 on page 268);
- "s for scharfes s: ß, "S gives "SS" (see figure 9.2 on page 268);
- "ck for "ck," which will become "k-k" when hyphenated;
- "ff for "ff," to be hyphenated as "ff-f," and similarly for l, m, n, p and t;
- "' or \glqq for lower and "' or \grqq for upper German quotation marks („Gänsefüßchen");
- \glq for lower and \grq for upper ‚simple quotation marks';
- "< or \flqq for left and "> or \frqq for right French quotation marks («guillemets»);
- \flq for left and \frq for right ‹simple French quotation marks›, which are used for *quotations inside quotations*;
- "| to prevent ligatures;
- "- to indicate a hyphenation point, just like \-, but hyphenation before and after the indicated point remains possible;
- "" similarly indicates a hyphenation point, but no hyphenation sign will be printed if the word is actually split;
- \dq prints the " sign.

Examples of these commands are given below.

Nachfolgend sind einige Beispiele für die Verwendung der deutschen Befehle:

Die schönste älteste Brücke
DIE SCHÖNSTE ÄLTESTE BRÜCKE
Straße oder STRASSE

„Ja, bitte!", »Nein, danke!«
„Sag' immer ‚Ja, bitte!'"
»Sag' immer ›Ja, bitte!‹«

Drucker bzw. Druk-ker
Rolladen bzw. Roll-laden
Auflage (statt Auflage)

```
Nachfolgend sind einige Beispiele f"ur
die Verwendung der deutschen Befehle:
\begin{flushleft}
Die sch"onste "alteste Br"ucke      \\
DIE SCH"ONSTE "ALTESTE BR"UCKE      \\
Stra"se oder STRA"SE               \\[3pt]
"'Ja, bitte!"', ">Nein, danke!"< \\
"'Sag' immer \glq Ja, bitte!\grq"'\\
">Sag' immer \frq Ja, bitte!\flq"<\\[3pt]
Drucker bzw.\ Druk-ker             \\
Rolladen bzw.\ Roll-laden          \\
Auf"|lage (statt Auflage)          \\
\end{flushleft}
```

---

[3]The babel option german is based on the german package [63], coordinated by DANTE and maintained by Bernd Raichle. Note that this package is incompatible with the babel system.

\selectlanguage	Output of \today command
english	31st January 1993
german	31. Januar 1993
austrian	31. Jänner 1993

Figure 9.1: Dates and dialects in babel

Differences between "dialects" of a language are also coped with, as seen in figure 9.1, which shows how dates are printed.

Figure 9.2 on page 268 shows a source file containing a text in German, which has been input using the conventions of the babel option german. Note especially the use of the LaTeX commands for creating the different tables of contents and how the figure and table caption are labeled. The result of typesetting that file is shown on the page opposite page 268, where it is seen that the names of the document elements have been translated into German ("Inhaltverzeichnis" for "Table of Contents," "Abbildung" for "Figure," etc.). You should compare these two pages with figure 9.3 on page 270 and its facing right-hand page. On those pages we show the input file and typeset result of a file equivalent to the one on page 268, but with the basic text translated into French. The same LaTeX commands are used and, in this case, by merely specifying francais instead of german on the \usepackage command, all language dependent document element names come out in French.

9.2.3   The Structure of the babel Language Style Files

The language-specific files of the babel system have to conform to a number of conventions. First they must declare the new language and then supply the language-specific information.

```
\addlanguage{language}
```

The macro \addlanguage defines the new language *language*.

```
\adddialect{dialect-name}
```

The macro \adddialect can be used when two languages can (or have to) use the same hyphenation patterns. This can be useful when you want to use a language for which no patterns are preloaded in the format. In such a case the default behavior of the babel system is to define this language as a "dialect" of the language for which the patterns were loaded as \language0.

The language-specific information is supplied by four macros.

```
\captionslang
```

The macro `\captionslang` defines the command strings that hold the texts to replace the original English texts for the name of the document elements in language *lang*. The name of these commands strings are shown in the first columns of table 9.2 on the facing page, while the the other columns show the values of these command strings for English and Czech.

> `\datelang`

The macro `\datelang` defines the command `\today` in the language *lang*, including the correct format and name of the months.

> `\extraslang`

The macro `\extraslang` contains all the extra definitions needed for the given language *lang*, such as typographic shortcuts for entering accents, umlauts, and making punctuation active. In some cases, there are variants between different user communities of the same basic language (for example, Portuguese in Brasil and Portugal, and German in Germany and Austria). Some languages have supplementary commands defined in the option file to ease the correct use of typographic conventions, for instance, Czech (for a few accents), Dutch (typographic shortcuts and hyphenation spelling rules), French (a lot of rules, shortcuts, and special formats for lists and bibliographies), German (typographic shortcuts and hyphenation spelling rules; see section 9.2.2 for examples) and Spanish (typographic conventions).

You can add your own definitions of commands that activate when a language is selected by specifying them as the argument of the `\addto` command, for instance,

```
\addto\extrasdutch{my supplementary definitions}
```

All your supplementary command definitions will become active together with those already defined in babel, when, in this case, the command `\selectlanguage{dutch}` is encountered.

> `\noextraslang`

When you are finished with language *lang*, babel should return you to the state you were in before choosing language *lang*. As mentioned above, `\extraslang` sets all the command definitions for language *lang* but at the same time saves the settings of the definitions that it changes. The command `\noextraslang` uses these stored values to restore LATEX to the state it was in before the command `\extraslang` was executed.

The hyphenation patterns for the different languages supported in a given babel configuration cannot be loaded when LATEX is run, but they must be read when the LATEX format is generated with INITEX. The babel system uses an

Command	English	Czech
\abstractname	Abstract	Abstrakt
\appendixname	Appendix	Dodatek
\bibname	Bibliography	Literatura
\ccname	cc	cc
\chaptername	Chapter	Kapitola
\contentsname	Contents	Obsah
\enclname	encl	Příloha
\figurename	Figure	Obrázek
\headpagename	Page	Strana
\headtoname	To (letter)	Komu
\indexname	Index	Index
\listfigurename	List of Figures	Seznam obrázků
\listtablename	List of Tables	Seznam tabulek
\partname	Part	Část
\prefacename	Preface	Předmluva
\seename	see	viz
\alsoseename	see also	viz též
\refname	References	Reference
\tablename	Table	Tabulka

Table 9.2: Examples of the translation of LATEX document element names in babel

The present version of babel recognizes the following options:

american (variant of english),
austrian (variant of german),
brazil (variant of portuges),

catalan,	croatian,
czech,	danish,
dutch,	english,
esperanto,	finnish,
french,	galician,
german,	italian,
magyar,	norsk,

nynorsk (variant of norsk),

polish,	portuges,
romanian,	russian,
slovak,	slovene,
spanish,	swedish,
turkish.	

(also francais and germanb)

Table 9.3: Options supported by the babel system

external file, `language.dat`, with a one line entry for each language for which hyphenation patterns are provided, to control the loading of these patterns with INITEX.

An example of a `language.dat` file is the following:

```
% Name: language.dat
% Use:  Correspondence language name - hyphenation patterns
english    ehyphen.tex    % English
german     ghyphen3.tex   % German
francais   fr8hyph.tex    % French
italian    italhyph.tex   % Italian
spanish    spanhyph.tex   % Spanish
```

The first element on each line specifies the name of the language, followed by the name of the file containing the hyphenation patterns. For each language in the file `language.dat` the command \l@*lang* is defined, i.e., \l@english, and so on. When LATEX is run for a given language *lang*, babel checks whether the command \l@*lang* is defined and, if so, loads the corresponding hyphenation patterns; otherwise, it loads the patterns for the default language 0 (the first one loaded by INITEX, i.e., English in the example above).

```
\documentclass[german]{article}% document class article and option german
\usepackage{babel}              % load babel package
\usepackage[dvips]{epsfig}      % load epsfig package and use dvips driver code
\usepackage{makeidx}            % load makeidx package
\newcommand{\DQ}[1]{\texttt{\dq#1}\enspace"#1}% Print argument preceeded by " sign
\makeindex
\begin{document}                % End of preamble and beginning of text.
\begin{center}\Large Beispiel eines Artikels in deutscher Sprache\\\today\end{center}
\tableofcontents
\listoffigures
\listoftables
\section{Eine EPS Abbildung}\index{Abschnitt}
Dieser Abschnitt zeigt, wie man eine PostScript-Abbildung\cite{bib-PS}
in ein \LaTeX{} Dokument einbinden kann.
Abbildung~\ref{Fpsfig} wurde mit dem Befehl
\verb!\epsfig{file=colorcir.eps,width=3cm}! in den Text aufgenommen.
\index{Abbildung}\index{PostScript}
\begin{figure}[hbt]
  \centering
  \begin{tabular}{c@{\qquad}c}
    \mbox{\epsfig{file=colorcir.eps,width=3cm}}&
    \mbox{\epsfig{file=tac2dim.eps,width=3cm}}}
  \end{tabular}
  \caption{Zwei EPS Bilder}\label{Fpsfig}
\end{figure}
\section{Beispiel einer Tabelle}
Die Tabelle~\ref{tab:exa} auf Seite~\pageref{tab:exa}
zeigt, wie man die Umgebung \texttt{table} gebrauchen kann.
\begin{table}[hbt]
  \centering\begin{tabular}{ccccccc}
    \DQ{a}  & \DQ{A} & \DQ{o} & \DQ{O} & \DQ{u}  & \DQ{U} & \DQ{s}
  \end{tabular}
  \caption{Eingabe der deutschen Zusatzzeichen}\label{tab:exa}\index{Tabelle}
\end{table}
\begin{thebibliography}{99}
\index{Literaturverzeichnis}
  \bibitem{bib-PS} Adobe Inc. \emph{PostScript Handbuch (2. Auflage)}
                   Addison-Wesley (Deutschland) GmbH, Bonn, 1991
\end{thebibliography}
\printindex
\index{Index}
\end{document}                % End of document.
```

Figure 9.2: Example using babel's option german (output on facing page)

Beispiel eines Artikels in deutscher Sprache

11. Oktober 1993

Inhaltsverzeichnis

Abbildungsverzeichnis

Tabellenverzeichnis

1   Eine EPS Abbildung

Dieser Abschnitt zeigt, wie man eine PostScript-Abbildung[1] in ein LaTeX Dokument einbinden kann. Abbildung 1 wurde mit dem Befehl `\epsfig{file=colorcir.eps,width=3cm}` in den Text aufgenommen.

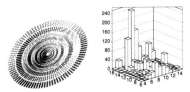

Abbildung 1: Zwei EPS Bilder

2   Beispiel einer Tabelle

Die Tabelle 1 auf Seite 1 zeigt, wie man die Umgebung `table` gebrauchen kann.

"a ä   "A Ä   "o ö   "O Ö   "u ü   "U Ü   "s ß

Tabelle 1: Eingabe der deutschen Zusatzzeichen

Literatur

[1] Adobe Inc. *PostScript Handbuch (2. Auflage)* Addison-Wesley (Deutschland) GmbH, Bonn, 1991

Index

1

```
\documentclass{article}
\usepackage[french]{babel}    % load babel package and initialize french
\usepackage[textures]{epsfig}% load epsfig package and use textures driver code
\usepackage{makeidx}          % load makeidx package
\newcommand{\Lcs}[1]{\texttt{\symbol{'134}#1}\enspace}% add \ before argument
\makeindex
\begin{document}                       % End of preamble and beginning of text.
\begin{center}\Large Exemple d'un article en fran\c{c}ais\\\today\end{center}
\tableofcontents
\listoffigures
\listoftables
\section{Une figure EPS}
\index{section}
Cette section montre comment inclure une figure PostScript\cite{bib-PS}
dans un document \LaTeX. La figure~\ref{Fpsfig}
est ins\'er\'ee dans le texte \'a l'aide de la commande
\verb+\epsfig{file=colorcir.eps,width=3cm}+.
\index{figure}\index{PostScript}
\begin{figure}[hbt]
  \centering
  \begin{tabular}{c@{\qquad}c}
    \mbox{\epsfig{file=colorcir.eps,width=3cm}}&
    \mbox{\epsfig{file=tac2dim.eps,width=3cm}}
  \end{tabular}
  \caption{Deux images EPS}\label{Fpsfig}
\end{figure}
\section{Exemple d'un tableau}
Le tableau~\ref{tab:exa} \'a la page \pageref{tab:exa}
montre l'utilisation de l'environnement \texttt{table}.
\begin{table}[hbt]
  \centering\begin{tabular}{cccccc}
    \Lcs{primo} \primo & \Lcs{secundo} \secundo & \Lcs{tertio} \tertio &
    \Lcs{quatro} \quatro & 2\Lcs{ieme}\ 2\ieme
  \end{tabular}
  \caption{Quelques commandes du paquet \texttt{francais}}\label{tab:exa}
  \index{tableau}
\end{table}
\begin{thebibliography}{99}
  \bibitem{bib-PS} Adobe Inc.
  \emph{PostScript, manuel de r\'ef\'erence (2\ieme \'edition)}
  Inter\'Editions (France), 1992 \index{r\'ef\'erences}
\end{thebibliography}
\printindex
\index{index}
\end{document}                % End of document.
```

Figure 9.3: Example using babel's option francais (output on facing page)

Exemple d'un article en français

11 octobre 1993

Table des matières

Liste des figures

Liste des tableaux

1   Une figure EPS

Cette section montre comment inclure une figure PostScript[1] dans un document LATEX. La figure 1 est insérée dans le texte à l'aide de la commande `\epsfig{file=colorcir.eps,width=3cm}`.

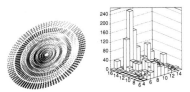

Figure 1: Deux images EPS

2   Exemple d'un tableau

Le tableau 1 à la page 1 montre l'utilisation de l'environnement `table`.

`\primo` 1ᵒ   `\secundo` 2ᵒ   `\tertio` 3ᵒ   `\quatro` 4ᵒ   2`\ieme` 2ᵉ

Tableau 1: Quelques commandes du paquet `francais`

Références

[1] Adobe Inc. *PostScript, manuel de référence (2ᵉ édition)* InterÉditions (France), 1992

Index

9.3 Implementing Typographic Rules

The babel system, presented in the previous section, does a good job of translating document element names and making text input somewhat more convenient. In this section we take a look at a second class of packages, which go one step further since they try to customize LATEX to better reflect the typographic traditions of the target language.

An example of such a package is french [21], which was developed by Bernard Gaulle. The french package does not limit itself to the translation of language dependent document element terms and the definition of abbreviations for typing accents, but it also provides several commands to more easily apply French typographical rules and adds/redefines several LATEX commands to give documents typeset with the french package a real French "look and feel."

9.3.1 Traditional French Typographic Rules

This section summarizes the most important rules for typing French texts (see the reference works [6, 32, 79]). By following these rules you will benefit most from the possibilities of the french package. However, you can force the package to try to do all the work itself—e.g., if you do not want to type the spaces before double punctuation, etc., you can specify the command \untypedspaces, which will take the correct action. Note however that such an automatic procedure might not always have the expected result.

- There must be a space:
    - in front of double punctuation (! ? : ;);
    - in front of closing "guillemets" (»);
    - in front of % and generally before units, e.g., 10 km, 1000 francs;
    - following « and of course » ; :   , . ! ?

- The guillemets (« and ») are input << and >>. No other quotation marks are normally used in French (' " ' ` ´ " „ ").

- Ellipsis dots (points de suspension) are input as three normal dots (. . .).

- Numbers have a comma between units and decimals, e.g., 3,14159.

- Latin expressions (quite common in French) are typeset in *italic* inside roman text (exception for cf., etc., and Latin words which have become part of the French vocabulary, like the word critérium).

- Some common abbreviations and the way they should be typed are:

```
c.-\`a-d. / \emph{i.e.} / p.ex. / etc. / cf. / id. / p.i. / p.o.
chap. / part. / vol. / paragr. /  R.S.V.P.  / T.S.V.P. /...
```

In fact, the distribution of the french package comes with a file `frabbrev`, containing the most important abbreviations of the French language.

- There should be no dots between the letters of abbreviations for trademarks, company names, etc., and they are normally set in small caps. The command `\lcs` deals with this case—i.e., `\lcs{RATP}` and `\lcs{SnCf}` will typeset respectively RATP and SNCF, regardless of the case in which the arguments were entered.

- Capitalized vowels carry accents.

- Only the first letter of the first word in a title should be capitalized [4].

- In a simple enumeration list, i.e., in which there is only one sentence per list element, each item should start with an en dash—and the first word should begin with a small letter and all list items, but the last one should be terminated with a semicolon.

- Last names are written in small capitals, while first names are in Roman, e.g., Donald KNUTH. The command `\fcs` is provided for this case; thus `\fcs{KNUTH}` and `\fcs{knuth}` will both typeset KNUTH.

9.3.2   Commands of the french Package

A few commands have been added to facilitate the generation of documents in French. Only a selection of the commands is given below. For more details consult the original documentation.

- `\begin{resume}` texte du résumé `\end{resume}`

- `\begin{order}`,... `\end{order}` generates an enumerated list of the type $(1^o \ldots 2^o \ldots)$;

- `\sommaire[n]` for a summary; [n] indicates the nesting level for the title;

- `\annexe` or `\annexes` for appendices;

- `\glossaire` or `\glossaires` for glossaries;

- in the main text the following commands are available:
  - `\ier` for 1er (`1\ier{}`); `\iere` for 1re (`1\iere{}`); `\ieme` for 2^e (`2\ieme{}`);
  - `\primo`, `\secundo`, `\tertio`, `\quatro` will print 1° , 2° , 3° , 4° . You can continue with the `\quando` command, e.g., `\quando={11}` giving 11° ;
  - `\fup{`*text*`}` will raise the argument *text* and print it in a smaller typeface, e.g., to write XVIe (`XVI\fup{e}`);

English input	English output	French input	French output
`ellipsis\ldots`	ellipsis ...	`points de suspension...`	points de suspension...
`123,456.789`	123,456.789	`123 456,789`	123 456,789
`semicolon;`	semicolon;	`point-virgule ;`	point-virgule;
`He said: Yes`	He said: Yes	`Il dit : oui`	Il dit: oui
`My god!`	My god!	`Mon Dieu !`	Mon Dieu!
`Why not?`	Why not?	`Pourquoi pas ?`	Pourquoi pas?
`''I say''`	"I say"	`<< Je dis >>`	« Je dis »

Table 9.4: Comparison of French and English typography

- various special commands for typesetting personal and business letters with a French "look and feel."

Depending on the exact combination of option commands specified, the french package makes various characters active, namely < ' " ' > and : ; ! ?. This makes these characters equivalent to command sequences, and their occurrence will invoke the TEX macros associated with their names. This can lead to problems if you use the french package together with other packages where these characters are used. To typeset any of these characters literally inside your text, you can use the following commands:

`\inferieura`	for	<	`\pointvirgule`	for	;
`\superieura`	for	>	`\pointexclamation`	for	!
`\lq`	for	'	`\pointinterrogation`	for	?
`\rq`	for	'	`\dittomark`	for	"
`\lqq`	for	''	`\deuxpoints`	for	:
`\rqq`	for	''			

9.3.3 Structure of the french Package

The french package consists of four distinct parts: typography (in the main text), page layout, translation of the document element terms, and supplementary command definitions. When loading the package, all four parts are activated. Each part can be turned on or off individually with the commands:

`\frenchtypography`	...	`\nofrenchtypography`
`\frenchlayout`	...	`\nofrenchlayout`
`\frenchtranslation`	...	`\nofrenchtranslation`
`\frenchmacros`	...	`\nofrenchmacros`

Some of the main differences between the way English and French texts are input, and their typographic result, are shown in table 9.4.

CHAPTER 10

Portable Graphics in LaTeX

TeX probably has the best algorithm for formatting paragraphs and building pages from them. But in this era of ever increasing information exchange, most publications do not limit themselves to text—the importance of graphical material has grown tremendously. TeX by itself does not address this issue, since it deals only with positioning (black) boxes on a page. Knuth, however, provided a hook for implementing "features" that are not available in the basic language, via the \special command. The latter command does not affect the output page being formatted, but TeX will put the material, specified as an argument in the \special command, literally at the current point in the .dvi file. It is the dvi-driver that has to interpret the received information and produce the output image accordingly.

Many articles have been devoted to how best to generate graphics with TeX, and various authors have come up with solutions, which are often very user-specific and hence unusable for the general public.

In his review article, "A Survey of TeX and Graphics" [67], Sebastian Rahtz discusses six distinct ways of producing graphics in TeX:[1]

1. ASCII drawing, such as PiCTeX [89], which provides a complete plotting language where curves are implemented by combining a very large number of small dots. For complex plots this requires a very large internal memory for the TeX program and also a lot of computing time.

2. Picture-element fonts, such as LaTeX's picture environment. Kristoffer Rose's XY-pic system [73] uses special fonts to typeset diagrams.

---

[1] See also "Portable Graphics in TeX:" [18] by Malcolm Clark.

3. Picture macro packages, mainly based on the `picture` environment or on TeX's raw line-drawing commands. Amongst others, packages exist for drawing Feynman diagrams, chemical formulae, and trees.

4. Picture fonts, where each character to be typeset is one, possibly enormous, "letter" in a font. One can use METAFONT for generating the pictures [28], or else use already existing bitmaps and transform them into a .pk file directly. Angus Duggan's `pbmtopk` program can transform a picture from one of the "pbm" (portable bitmap) formats into a .pk file format, and it assigns successive pictures to letters of the alphabet. BM2FONT converts different kinds of bitmap files to TeX fonts and writes an input file for integration of those graphics into documents [78].

5. Halftone fonts are blocks consisting of various levels of grey, which can be combined in the normal TeX way to generate pictures [17,44].

6. Graphics material can be included, using the `\special` command. This approach is by definition device dependent, since it relies on the possibilities of the `dvi`-driver and the output device. However this approach becomes more and more popular with the spread of low-cost PostScript printers and previewers. `psfrag` and `pstricks` are examples of systems using PostScript together with LaTeX. See also the discussion in chapter 11.

All these methods have their advantages and drawbacks. Although approaches 1 to 5 are portable, they suffer from a lack of flexibility, especially when artwork has to be scaled or rotated. The method of the `\special` command is only limited by the possibilities of the target language itself, and although this approach is by definition device-dependent, it allows, in the case of PostScript, the use of all commands of this rich language and the inclusion of material produced by the many packages generating output in PostScript. Such developments will be discussed in the next chapter.

This chapter mainly discusses LaTeX's built-in graphics tools, which are based on the `picture` environment, and packages that extend this environment to generate high-quality device-independent graphics. We also look at other visual effects, such as "shadow boxes," that can be produced in a portable way. By using portable utilities, you can be certain that the recipient of a document, who has the same LaTeX environment as the originator, will obtain the same output as the sender.

The first section of this chapter discusses ornaments, which can be useful to make important material stand out. The next section looks at the `picture` environment, and presents packages for drawing bar charts and arbitrary curves. Then we turn our attention to two packages, epic and eepic, which extend the `picture` environment by introducing a set of new commands. They are described in detail and examples show how they are used in practice. Finally we discuss two packages based on epic and eepic for drawing bipartite graphs and trees.

10.1 Ornaments

LaTeX boxes are reviewed briefly in section A.2. Below, we present packages that provide extensions to the usual LaTeX boxes.

10.1.1 Boxed Minipages

The `boxedminipage` environment, defined in the `boxedminipage` package (by Mario Wolczko), behaves like the standard `minipage` environment, but it is surrounded by a frame. The thickness of the rules is controlled by the `\fboxrule` and `\fboxsep` style parameters.

> This is an example of a small boxed minipage[a] which moreover has a footnote.
> _____
> [a]Very simple example

```
\begin{boxedminipage}[t]{5cm}
This is an example of a small
boxed minipage\footnote{Very simple
example} which moreover has a footnote.
\end{boxedminipage}
```

10.1.2 Shadow Boxes

The `shadow` package (by Mauro Orlandini) defines the `\shabox` command, which is similar to the LaTeX command `\fbox` except for the fact that a "shadow" is added to the bottom and the right side of the box.

Three parameters control the visual appearance of the box (defaults are given in parentheses):

`\sboxrule`   width of the lines for the frame (0.4pt);

`\sboxsep`   separation between the frame and the text (10pt);

`\sdim`   dimension of the shadow (4pt).

A standard framed box │framed text│, then a shadow box │framed text with shadow│.

A complete paragraph can be highlighted by putting it in a parbox, nested inside a framebox.

```
A standard framed box \fbox{framed text},
then a shadow box
\shabox{framed text with shadow}.
\par\bigskip
\renewcommand{\sdim}{1.5\fboxsep}
\shabox{\parbox{6cm}{%
A complete paragraph can be highlighted
by putting it in a parbox, nested
inside a \texttt{framebox}.}}
```

10.1.3   Fancy Frames

Timothy Van Zandt, in the framework of his seminar package for producing slides, developed the fancybox package. He introduces various new commands for framing information in LaTeX. In this section we only review a few of the more basic commands. More information can be found in the documentation accompanying the seminar package mentioned above.

Variants for \fbox

The fancybox package introduces four variants for the \fbox command. As with the \fbox command the distance between the box and the frame is given by the length parameter \fboxsep (default 3pt). Other parameters governing these boxes are described below.

\shadowbox

> This is a shadowbox

The line thickness is defined by \fboxrule (the same parameter as for \fbox). The width of the shadow is \shadowsize (default: 4pt).

\doublebox

> This is a doublebox

The width of the inner and outer frames are .75\fboxrule and 1.5\fboxrule, respectively. The distance between the two frames is 1.5\fboxrule plus 0.5pt.

\ovalbox

> This is an ovalbox

The width of the frame is defined by the \thinlines command, while the diameter of the corner arcs is set with a \cornersize command, which has one argument. The latter can have two forms, namely *num*, a factor which multiplies the smaller of the height or width of the box, or *dia*, a length specifying the diameter of the corner arcs (default is *num*=0.5).

\Ovalbox

> This is an Ovalbox

Similar to \ovalbox, but the thickness of the lines is controlled by the \thicklines command.

Defining Boxed Environments

To help you define boxed environments fancybox defines the Sbox environment. It is similar to the \sbox command. It saves the contents of the environment in a storage bin that can be retrieved with a \TheSbox command. Using this command you can reimplement the boxedminipage environment discussed in section 10.1.1

> An example of a boxed minipage
> defined using the Sbox command.

```
\newenvironment{Boxedminipage}%
  {\begin{Sbox}\begin{minipage}}%
  {\end{minipage}\end{Sbox}\fbox{\TheSbox}}
\begin{Boxedminipage}{5cm}
An example of a boxed minipage
defined using the Sbox command.
\end{Boxedminipage}
```

The package predefines the following boxed environments.

- `Bcenter`, `Bflushleft`, and `Bflushright` generate a boxed `center`, `flushleft`, and `flushright` environment, respectively.

- `Bitemize`, `Benumerate`, and `Bdescription` generate a boxed `itemize`, `enumerate`, and `description` environment, respectively.

- `Beqnarray` produces a boxed environment similar to `eqnarray`, but the equation number will always come out on the right. `Beqnarray*` is like `eqnarray*`, but the generated box is just large enough to hold all the equations.

For all these commands it is up to you to add a frame. An example is given below.

$$
\begin{array}{rcl}
y &=& x^2 \\
a^2 + 2ab + b^2 &=& (a+b)^2 \\
\int_0^\infty e^{-ax} dx &=& \dfrac{1}{a}
\end{array}
$$

```
\fbox{\begin{Beqnarray*}
                  y & = & x^2        \\
        a^2 + 2ab + b^2 & = & (a + b)^2 \\
\int_0^\infty e^{-ax} dx & = & \frac{1}{a}
           \end{Beqnarray*}}
    \par\bigskip
\fbox{\begin{Beqnarray}
                  y & = & x^2        \\
        a^2 + 2ab + b^2 & = & (a + b)^2 \\
\int_0^\infty e^{-ax} dx & = & \frac{1}{a}
           \end{Beqnarray}}
```

$$
\begin{array}{rcll}
y &=& x^2 & (10.1) \\
a^2 + 2ab + b^2 &=& (a+b)^2 & (10.2) \\
\int_0^\infty e^{-ax} dx &=& \dfrac{1}{a} & (10.3)
\end{array}
$$

The package also defines commands for framing a whole page, and reimplements several commands to typeset verbatim texts (see also section 3.3). In particular a framed verbatim text can be defined and used as follows.

```
\newenvironment{FramedVerb}%
  {\VerbatimEnvironment
    \begin{Sbox}\begin{minipage}{60mm}\begin{Verbatim}}%
  {\end{Verbatim}\end{minipage}\end{Sbox}
   \setlength{\fboxsep}{3mm}\fbox{\TheSbox}}
```

```
\newcommand{\Com}[1]{#1^a_b}
```

```
\begin{FramedVerb}
\newcommand{\Com}[1]{#1^a_b}
\end{FramedVerb}
```

10.2 The `picture` **Environment**

(£ 101-11)

LaTeX's basic `picture` environment can be used in many circumstances for generating simple graphics output and it is used for many line drawings in this book. The present section discusses various packages which have been developed to extend the `picture` environment.

10.2.1 Bezier Approximations

LaTeX2_ε allows the construction of quite complicated mathematical curves using the technique of approximations with Bezier splines. Note that the PostScript language also uses (third order, or cubic) Bezier curves as the basis of its curve drawing functions.

`\qbezier`[*N*](*AX,AY*)(*BX,BY*)(*CX,CY*)

The above command defines a quadratic Bezier curve, which is defined by its two end points, (*AX,AY*) and (*CX,CY*), with (*BX,BY*) as the control point. The optional parameter *N*, if present, specifies that $N + 1$ points are plotted to approximate the curve.[2] In the next example *A* and *C* are the end points and *B* is the control point; the number of plotted points is calculated automatically.

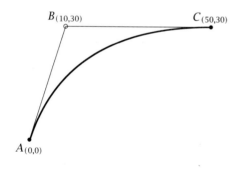

```
\setlength{\unitlength}{1mm}
\begin{picture}(50,30)(-10,10)
  \linethickness{1pt}
  \qbezier(0,0)(10,30)(50,30)
  \thinlines
  \put(0,0){\line(1,3){10}}
  \put(50,30){\line(-1,0){40}}
  \put(0,0){\circle*{1}}
  \put(0,-1){\makebox(0,0)[t]{$A_{(0,0)}$}}
  \put(10,30){\circle{1}}
  \put(10,31){\makebox(0,0)[b]{$B_{(10,30)}$}}
  \put(50,30){\circle*{1}}
  \put(50,31){\makebox(0,0)[b]{$C_{(50,30)}$}}
\end{picture}
```

---

[2]For LaTeX 2.09 Leslie Lamport's bezier package defines the command `\bezier`, with the following relation: `\bezier{N}(AX,AY)(BX,BY)(CX,CY)=\qbezier[N](AX,AY)(BX,BY)(CX,CY)`. The main difference is that the number of points required to obtain a smooth continuous curve is calculated automatically by `\qbezier`, and need no longer be specified.

Varying the number of dots and the control point has a clear effect. In the next example two curves use the default number of points the others specify the number to use.

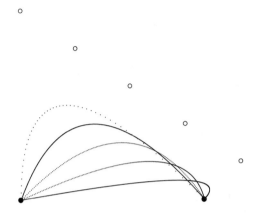

```
\setlength{\unitlength}{.5mm}
\begin{picture}(120,100)(-5,0)
  \linethickness{.5pt}
  \qbezier [50](0,0)(0,100)(100,0)
  \qbezier     (0,0)(30,80)(100,0)
  \qbezier[150](0,0)(60,60)(100,0)
  \qbezier[200](0,0)(90,40)(100,0)
  \qbezier     (0,0)(120,20)(100,0)
% mark the end points
  \put(0,0){\circle*{3}}
  \put(100,0){\circle*{3}}
% mark the control points
  \multiput(0,100)(30,-20){5}{\circle{2}}
\end{picture}
```

Finally, the code for one of the diagrams of figure 10.5 on page 295 is shown:

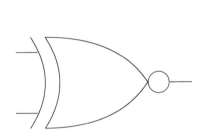

```
\setlength{\unitlength}{4mm}
\begin{picture}(12,10)(-2,0)
  \linethickness{0.4pt}
  \qbezier(2.00,6.00)(7.00,6.00)(9.00,3.00)
  \qbezier(2.00,0.00)(7.00,0.00)(9.00,3.00)
  \qbezier(2.00,6.00)(4.00,3.00)(2.00,0.00)
  \qbezier(1.00,6.00)(3.00,3.00)(1.00,0.00)
  \put(9.75,3.00){\circle{1.50}}
  \put(10.50,3.00){\line(1,0){1.50}}
  \put(0.00,5.00){\line(1,0){1.50}}
  \put(0.00,1.00){\line(1,0){1.50}}
\end{picture}
```

10.2.2   Putting Multiple Boxes

The multibox package (by Brian Hamilton Kelly) defines the following two new commands for use inside the `picture` environment:

```
\multimake(x,y)(dx,dy){n}(w,h)[pos]{text₁}{text₂}...{textₙ}
\multiframe(x,y)(dx,dy){n}(w,h)[pos]{text₁}{text₂}...{textₙ}
```

These commands set the n texts, $text_1$ to $text_n$, inside a \makebox or \framebox respectively. The first box has its lower-left corner at (x,y), and successive boxes are located at $(x+dx,y+dy)$, to $(x+(n-1)dx,y+(n-1)dy)$.

Each box has a width and a height determined by (w,h), while the optional box placement parameter *pos* is applied to all the generated texts. A simple example, in which the syntax can be compared with that of the LATEX \multiput command, is shown below:

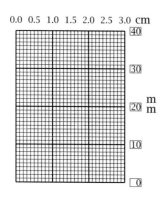

```
\setlength{\unitlength}{1mm}
\begin{picture}(40,50)(-10,0)
\linethickness{0.25mm}\scriptsize
 \multiput(0,0)(10,0){4}{\line(0,1){40}}
 \multiput(0,0)(0,10){5}{\line(1,0){30}}
\linethickness{0.1mm}
\multimake(-2,42)(5,0){8}(4,3)[b]{0.0}{0.5}%
    {1.0}{1.5}{2.0}{2.5}{3.0}{\small cm}
\multiframe(31.5,-1)(0,10){5}(3,2)[r]%
                {0}{10}{20}{30}{40}
\small
\put(36,18.5){\shortstack{m\\ m}}
\multiput(1,0)(1,0){29}{\line(0,1){40}}
\multiput(0,1)(0,1){39}{\line(1,0){30}}
\end{picture}
```

10.2.3   Drawing Binary or Ternary Trees

The trees package (by Peter Vanroose) is based exclusively on the picture environment. Another package for drawing trees is discussed in section 10.5.2. It defines macros that let you draw a (binary or ternary) tree of any size. For each internal node, you only have to specify the descending nodes, with a \branch (binary node) or \tbranch (ternary node) command.

The tree diagrams are produced inside a picture environment, and the following commands are available with the trees package:

\branchlabels{*labela*}{*labelb*}{*labelc*}

The command above specifies the label to be used for each of the branches.

\root(*x-coord, y-coord*) *rootid*.

(*x-coord, y-coord*) are the absolute coordinates of the root, identified by *rootid*, in the picture. Note that the parentheses pair, the space, and the period are obligatory.

\branch{*steepness*}{*text*}{*branchid*}:*childa,childb*.

The *steepness* parameter determines the steepness of the branches; it is an integer between 0 and 3. *text* specifies explanatory text written above the branch point. *branchid* is the identifier of the present branch, while *childa* and *childb* are the identifiers of the two children. The colon, comma, and final period are obligatory.

\tbranch{*steepness*}{*text*}{*branchid*}:*childa,childb,childc*.

This command is the same as the preceding one, except that it allows three rather than two child identifiers.

\leaf{*toptext*}{*sidetext*}{*leafid*}.

Parameters *toptext* and *sidetext* specify, respectively, text that will be written above and to the right of the current leaf, which has identifier *leafid*.

Trees are constructed with labels on the branches (default 0 and 1), and with text (its name or value) on the nodes.

An example is shown below. The (internal) identifiers (0-7), used for labeling the branches and leaves, can be replaced by anything.

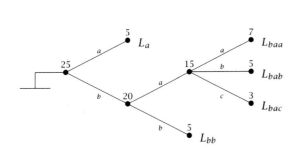

```
\setlength{\unitlength}{4pt}
\begin{picture}(50,30)
\branchlabels abc      % default is 012
\root(10,15) 0.        % root label 0
                % node 0 has children 1 and 2
\branch2{25} 0:1,2.
    \leaf{5}{$L_a$} 1. % node 1 is a leaf
\branch2{20} 2:3,7.
        % branch to node 3 goes up
        % it has a label a
    \tbranch2{15} 3:4,5,6.
            \leaf{7}{$L_{baa}$}4.
            \leaf{5}{$L_{bab}$}5.
            \leaf{3}{$L_{bac}$}6.
    \leaf{5}{$L_{bb}$}7.
\end{picture}
```

10.2.4 Drawing Bar Charts

The bar package (by Joachim Bleser and Edmund Lang) can produce bar charts and is entirely based on the picture environment. The bar diagrams are produced with the barenv environment.

Inside a `barenv` environment the following commands are available:

\bar{*height*}{*hatch-index*}[*description*]

A bar is defined by giving its *height* and the *hatch-index*—a number between 1 and 8, according to the following scheme:

| 1 | 2 | 3 | 4 | 5 | 6 | 7 | 8 |

The optional argument is a textual *description* of the bar, and is typeset according to the settings of \setnumberpos and \setstyle.

\hlineon

This command activates the background horizontal lines.

\legend{*hatch-index*}{*legend text*}

This command associates the hatch style, *hatch-index*, with the explanatory text, *legend text*.

\setdepth{*number*}

This defines the depth for a 3-D bar chart (*number* ≥ 10).

\sethspace{*fraction*}

This defines the horizontal space to be left between the bars. It is expressed as a fraction of the bar width.

\setlinestyle{*style*}

This defines the style for the horizontal background lines (activated with \hlineon). Possible values for *style* are solid and dotted.

\setnumberpos{*position*}

This defines the positioning of the description of the bar contents. Possible values for *position* are:

empty	No description is needed.
axis	The description goes under or above the x-axis.
down	The description goes under the bars.
inside	The description goes inside the bars.
outside	The description goes outside the bars.
up	The description goes on top of the bars.

`\setprecision{`*digits*`}`

This defines the number of digits to be printed after the decimal sign.

`\setstretch{`*factor*`}`

This defines the scaling factor for the vertical dimension of the chart.

`\setstyle{`*fontstyle*`}`

This defines the font characteristics.

`\setwidth{`*number*`}`

This defines the width of the bars in points.

`\setxaxis{`*origin*`}{`*end*`}{`*step*`}`

This defines the division of the x-axis. The three parameters specify the start and end values and the value of the step.

`\setxname{`*x-label*`}`

This defines the descriptive label for the x-axis.

`\setxvaluetyp{`*type*`}`

This defines the way the x-axis divisions are labeled. By default, numbers are used, but you can use the names of the days or the months. Therefore, *type* in the definition above can be either `month` or `day`. In this case the begin and end values for the x-axis specified with the `\setxaxis` command use a correspondence for the months of 1 for January, 2 for February, etc., 12 for December, 13 for January again, and so on. For the days you have the correspondence: 1 for Monday, 2 for Tuesday, etc., 7 for Sunday, 8 for Monday again, and so on. (However, in the current release of the package only the German language is supported.)

`\setyaxis[`*offset*`]{`*origin*`}{`*end*`}{`*step*`}`

This command defines the division of the y-axis. The three mandatory parameters are the same as for `\setxaxis`, while the optional argument, *offset*, specifies a value that is added to the origin and end values, but without altering the division of the axis: at the origin, at the end point, and the step size.

`\setyname{`*x-label*`}`

This defines the descriptive label for the y-axis.

The general structure of the command sequences for generating bar diagrams is the following:

```
\begin{barenv}
     Declarations
          \bar{height}{hatch-index}

               .
               .
               .

          \bar{height}{hatch-index}
     \end{barenv}
          Legend
```

Note that, since the `barenv` environment uses the `picture` environment, all commands that are valid inside the latter are also available.

10.2.5 Examples of the `barenv` Environment

The first example shows a simple bar chart generated by using the default settings of the `barenv` environment.

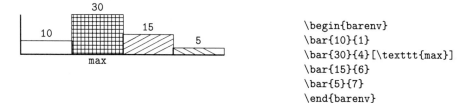

```
\begin{barenv}
\bar{10}{1}
\bar{30}{4}[\texttt{max}]
\bar{15}{6}
\bar{5}{7}
\end{barenv}
```

Axis information and a title can be added easily:

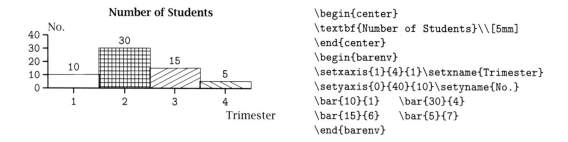

```
\begin{center}
\textbf{Number of Students}\\[5mm]
\end{center}
\begin{barenv}
\setxaxis{1}{4}{1}\setxname{Trimester}
\setyaxis{0}{40}{10}\setyname{No.}
\bar{10}{1}     \bar{30}{4}
\bar{15}{6}     \bar{5}{7}
\end{barenv}
```

Perhaps we prefer to see this information using a 3-D effect, and to make the differences more visible we stretch the y-axis. To make the trimesters more precise, we show the middle month of each.

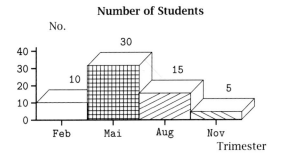

```
\begin{center}
\textbf{Number of Students}\\[5mm]
\end{center}
\begin{barenv}
\setdepth{10}% 3-D effect
\setstretch{1.4}% stretch y-dimension
\setnumberpos{up}% numbers above bars
\setxvaluetyp{month}% months on x-axis
\setxaxis{2}{12}{3}\setxname{Trimester}
\setyaxis{0}{40}{10}\setyname{No.}
\bar{10}{1} \bar{30}{4}
\bar{15}{6} \bar{5}{7}
\end{barenv}
```

If we want to emphasize changes in the number of students between trimesters, we can use the following representation.

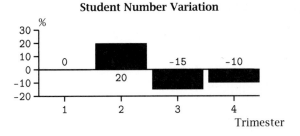

```
\begin{center}
\textbf{Student Number Variation}\\[5mm]
\end{center}
\begin{barenv}
\setxaxis{1}{4}{1}\setxname{Trimester}
\setyaxis{-20}{30}{10}\setyname{\%}
\sethspace{0.1}\setnumberpos{axis}
\bar{0}{1}      \bar{20}{8}
\bar{-15}{8}    \bar{-10}{8}
\end{barenv}
```

Our final, and most complex, example shows the variation in the price of shares for company XyZ, in two different ways. First it is illustrated as a 2-D bar chart (figure 10.1 on the following page) and then as a 3-D chart (figure 10.2 on page 289).

10.2.6   Drawing Arbitrary Curves

The curves package (by I.L. Maclaine-cross) extends LATEX's picture environment by drawing curves that superimpose small disks, whose sizes and number are tuned to optimize visual smoothness. Segments between coordinate points are approximated as parabolas. A special sub-package, curvesls, reimplements some of the more time- and space-consuming parts of the code with \special commands defined in Eberhard Mattes's emTEX for IBM PC compatibles.

The capabilities of this package include:

- A compatible replacement for the bezier package.
- The ability to adjust curve thickness between 0.5 and 15pt (0.17 and 5.2mm).

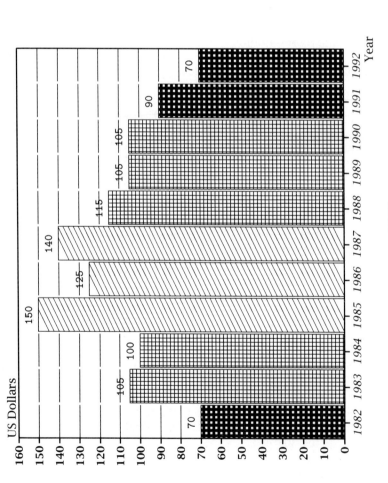

```
\begin{center}
\Large\bfseries
Share price for Company
   \textsf{XyZ}\\[6mm]
\begin{barenv}
  \setstretch{1.6}
  \setwidth{25}
  \sethspace{0.1}
  \setstyle{\bfseries}
  \setxname{Year}
  \setyname{US Dollars}
  \setstyle{\small\itshape}
  \setxaxis{1982}{1992}{1}
  \setstyle{\small\bfseries}
  \setyaxis{0}{160}{10}
  \setlinestyle{solid}
  \hlineon
  \setnumberpos{up}
  \setstyle{\small\ttfamily}
  \bar{70}{5}  \bar{105}{4}
  \bar{100}{4} \bar{150}{6}
  \bar{125}{6} \bar{140}{6}
  \bar{115}{4} \bar{105}{4}
  \bar{105}{4} \bar{90}{5}
  \bar{70}{5}
\end{barenv}
\end{center}
\par\vspace{2\baselineskip}
Yield: \legend6{Good}    \qquad
\legend4{Moderate} \qquad
  \legend5{Bad}
```

Figure 10.1: Example of a bar chart—2-D option

```
\begin{center}
\textbf{\Large Share price for
Company \textsf{XyZ}}\\[5mm]
\begin{barenv}
\setstretch{1.6}
\setnumberpos{down}
\setwidth{25}\setdepth{10}
\setstyle{\small\bfseries}
\setxname{Year}
\setyname{US Dollars}
\setstyle{\small\itshape}
\setxaxis{1982}{1992}{1}
\setstyle{\small\bfseries}
\setyaxis[10]{0}{160}{10}
\setlinestyle{dotted}
\hlineon
\setnumberpos{axis}
\bar{70}{5}    \bar{105}{4}
\bar{100}{4}   \bar{150}{6}
\bar{125}{6}   \bar{140}{6}
\bar{115}{4}   \bar{105}{4}
\bar{105}{4}   \bar{90}{5}
\bar{70}{5}
\end{barenv}
\end{center}
\par\vspace{2}\baselineskip}
Yield: \legend6{Good}    \qquad
       \legend4{Moderate} \qquad
       \legend5{Bad}
```

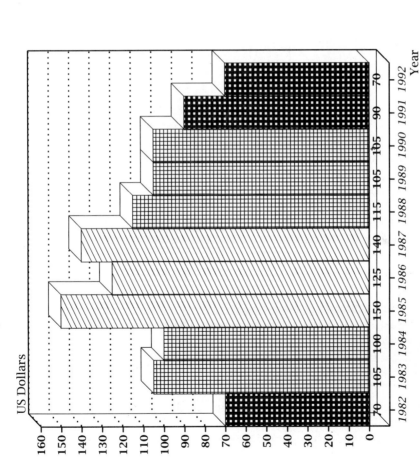

Figure 10.2: Example of a bar chart—3-D option

- Continuously sloping curves.
- Control of end slopes using \tagcurve.
- Closed curves with continuous slope using \closecurve.
- Large circles with \bigcircle and circular arcs with \arc.
- Independent scaling of curve abscissa and ordinates to fit graphs.
- Affine scaling for making arcs or circles elliptical.
- Support for symbols and dash patterns.

Curve Drawing Commands

This section reviews the more important curve drawing commands that are used in the examples below. The curves drawn consist of parabolic arcs between coordinate points, with tangents at each point parallel to the straight line through adjacent points. Segments at a curve's end points are a parabola going through the last three points.

```
\arc[nbsymb](x_1, y_1){angle}
```

This command draws a circular arc centered on the current position, starting at (x_1, y_1) and proceeding counterclockwise for *angle* degrees. The optional argument *nbsymb* specifies the number of patterns or symbols to be drawn (the default is 0).

```
\bigcircle[nbsymb]{diameter}
```

This command draws a circle with a diameter equal to *diameter* times \unitlength. The optional argument *nbsymb* is as described above.

```
\closecurve[nbsymb](x_1, y_1, x_2, y_2...x_n, y_n)
```

This command draws a closed curve with continuous tangents at all points. At least six coordinates are required. The optional argument *nbsymb* is as described above.

```
\curve[nbsymb](x_1, y_1, x_2, y_2...x_n, y_n)
```

This command draws a curve through the specified coordinates. Two pairs of coordinates generate a straight line; three pairs a parabola going through the points specified. The optional argument *nbsymb* is as described above.

```
\scaleput(x_1, y_1){pict-object}
```

This command places the picture object *pict-object* at the position (x_1, y_1). At the same time it applies an axonometric projection or rotation specified by the scale factors \xscale, \xscaley, \yscale, and \yscalex, whose initial values are 1.0, 0.0, 1.0, and 0.0, respectively.

\tagcurve [*nbsymb*] $(x_1, y_1, x_2, y_2...x_n, y_n)$

This command draws a curve without its first and last segments. If only three coordinate pairs are specified, then it draws the last segment only. The optional argument *nbsymb* is as described above.

Examples

```
\setlength{\unitlength}{0.4pt}
\linethickness{0.7mm}
\begin{picture}(400,110)(-10,0)
   \tagcurve(80,0, 0,0, 40,100, 80,0, 0,0)
   \closecurve(150,0, 190,100, 230,0)
   \curve(300,0, 340,100, 380,0)
\end{picture}
```

The following example shows an airfoil section that is often used in aerodynamics research. The \arc commands draw the leading and trailing radii. The coordinates quoted inside the first \curve command are input from aerodynamic tables and correspond to the top section of the airfoil; the second \curve command, containing two coordinate pairs, plots the flat chord at the bottom.

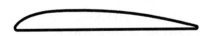

```
\newcommand{\RAFsixE}{%
   \scaleput(1.25,1.25){\arc(0,-1.25){-135}}
   \scaleput(0,0){\curve(0.36,2.13,
    1.25,3.19,2.5,4.42, 5.0,6.10 , 7.5,7.24,
    10,8.09   ,15,9.28 ,20,9.90    ,30,10.3  ,
    40,10.22  ,50,9.80 ,60,8.98    ,70,7.70  ,
    80,5.91   ,90,3.79 ,95,2.58    ,99.24,1.52)}
   \scaleput(99.24,0.76){\arc(0,-0.76){180}}
   \scaleput(0,0){\curve(1.25,0, 99.24,0)}    }
\begin{center}
  \begin{picture}(100,20)
   \RAFsixE
  \end{picture}
\end{center}
```

We can now rotate this foil using the scaling parameters described with the command \scaleput. In the example below, we choose a clockwise rotation over

an angle of 10°, so that the diagonal elements, \xscale and \yscale, correspond
to cos(10°) while the off-diagonal elements correspond to ± sin(10°).

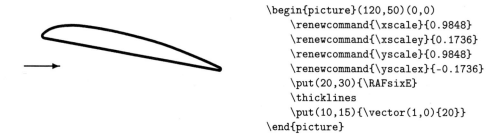

```
\begin{picture}(120,50)(0,0)
    \renewcommand{\xscale}{0.9848}
    \renewcommand{\xscaley}{0.1736}
    \renewcommand{\yscale}{0.9848}
    \renewcommand{\yscalex}{-0.1736}
    \put(20,30){\RAFsixE}
    \thicklines
    \put(10,15){\vector(1,0){20}}
\end{picture}
```

Axonometric projection is another scaling application. Circles become ellipses and circular arcs become elliptical arcs. Note that the angles for the \arc
in the example were found by trial and error.

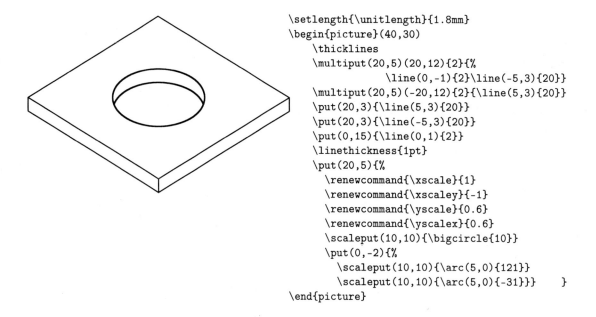

```
\setlength{\unitlength}{1.8mm}
\begin{picture}(40,30)
    \thicklines
    \multiput(20,5)(20,12){2}{%
              \line(0,-1){2}\line(-5,3){20}}
    \multiput(20,5)(-20,12){2}{\line(5,3){20}}
    \put(20,3){\line(5,3){20}}
    \put(20,3){\line(-5,3){20}}
    \put(0,15){\line(0,1){2}}
    \linethickness{1pt}
    \put(20,5){%
      \renewcommand{\xscale}{1}
      \renewcommand{\xscaley}{-1}
      \renewcommand{\yscale}{0.6}
      \renewcommand{\yscalex}{0.6}
      \scaleput(10,10){\bigcircle{10}}
      \put(0,-2){%
        \scaleput(10,10){\arc(5,0){121}}
        \scaleput(10,10){\arc(5,0){-31}}}    }
\end{picture}
```

It is quite easy to add symbols to your curves. The command \curvesymbol
defines the symbol to be used. If the value of the optional parameter *nbsymb*
on one of the curve commands is negative, then it fixes the number of symbols
per curve segment. The TEX primitive command \phantom is used for centering
the 1mm circle. The example shows the (height–distance) trajectory of an object
thrown into the air as a function of time.

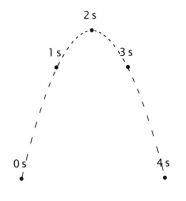

```
\thinlines
\setlength{\unitlength}{1mm}
\begin{picture}(80,46)(0,0)
% 1mm dashes interspersed with 2mm white space
  \curvedashes[1mm]{0,1,2}
  \put(10,0){\curve(0,0, 19.6,39.2, 39.2,0)}
  \curvedashes{} % reset dashes
  \newcounter{time}
  \curvesymbol{\textsf{\thetime\,s}
               \addtocounter{time}{1}}
  \put(10,4){\curve[-2](0,0, 19.6,39.2, 39.2,0)}
  \curvesymbol{\phantom{\circle*{1}}\circle*{1}}
  \put(10,0){\curve[-2](0,0, 19.6,39.2, 39.2,0)}
\end{picture}
```

10.2.7 Other Packages

In theoretical physics, the Feynman package by Michael Levine [52] has become very popular. It allows the user, via a high level command language built on top of the `picture` commands, to draw the various particle lines and vertex groups of Feynman diagrams. Figure 10.3 on the following page shows a typical picture made with this package.

A set of macros by Roswitha Haas and Kevin O'Kane [24] has been developed in the field of organic chemistry. Their ChemTEX system allows you to draw complex molecules (see figure 10.4 on page 295).

A set of circuit schematic symbols for LATEX's picture mode has been developed by Adrian Johnstone (see figure 10.5 on page 295). The set includes all basic logic gates in four orientations, FETs, power supply pins, transmission gates, capacitors, resistors and wiring T-junctions. It uses the bezier package discussed earlier.

10.3 Enhancements to the `picture` Environment—epic

The epic [66] package (by Sunil Podar) enhances the graphic capabilities of LATEX and provides a powerful high level user interface to the `picture` environment. The main aim is to reduce the amount of manual calculations required to specify the layout of *objects*. The additional epic commands allow the drawing of sophisticated pictures with less effort than was previously possible.

Most picture drawing commands require explicit specification of coordinates for every *object*. Higher level commands can, however, help to reduce the amount of coordinates that need to be manually calculated. Basically, two approaches

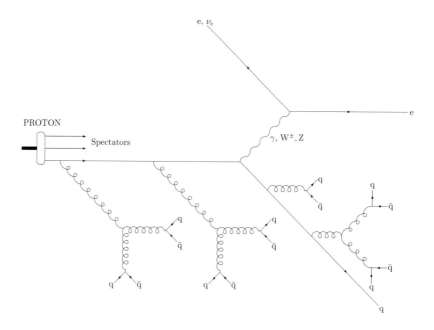

Figure 10.3: Example of a picture generated with the Feynman package

can be taken to design such commands:

- A set of objects can be selected so that the entire set can be plotted by specifying one or two coordinate pairs—the \shortstack command falls into this category.

- Commands are provided that will do most of the computations internally and require only simple coordinate pairs to be specified—the \multiput command is an example of this approach.

The obvious advantage of having commands that fall into the above categories is that, not only are they easier to specify initially, but any subsequent modification to the layout requires minimal recalculations.

The frequently used primitive command \line has severe limitations and drawbacks. Its arguments are very nonintuitive and require extensive calculations—often the thought process in writing a \line command involves:

1. calculating the coordinates of the two end points;

2. calculating the horizontal and vertical distance;

3. determining whether the desired slope is available and if not then repeating steps 1. and 2. until a satisfactory slope is achieved;

4. translating the above into an (x,y) pair for specifying a slope and a horizontal distance for specifying the length of the line.

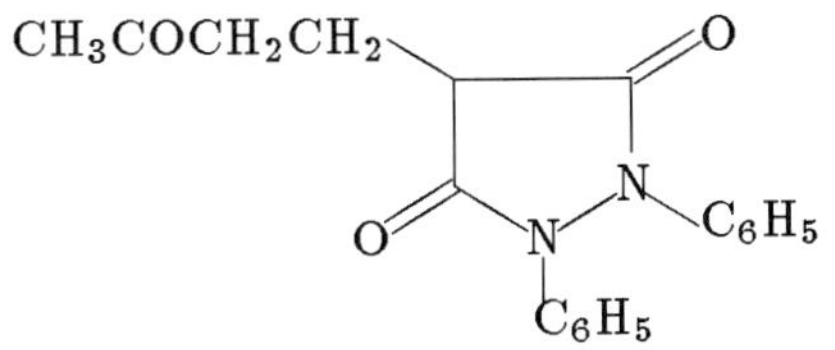

Figure 10.4: Example of chemical formula

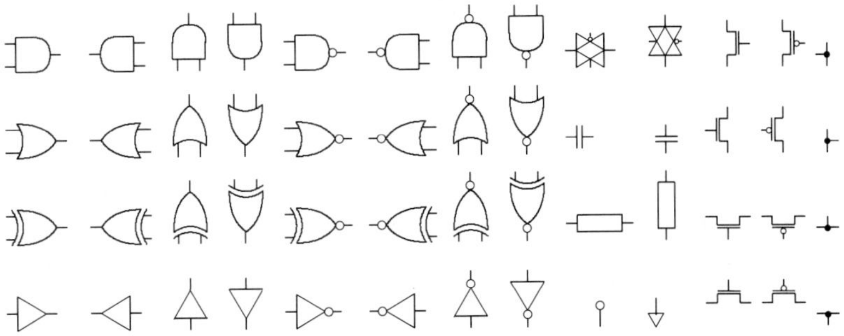

Figure 10.5: Electronic circuit symbols prepared with `picture` commands

The above mechanism is very cumbersome. Moreover, the length of the shortest line at different slopes is not the same due to the way the \line command is implemented. The epic package introduces line drawing commands that overcome these drawbacks, while at the same time providing a simpler syntax. These commands take only the coordinates of the end points, thus eliminating the other steps involved in specifying a line. On top of that a few high-level new commands are also defined. Thus, the epic package will make it possible to produce sophisticated pictures with less effort than before.

10.3.1   Description of the Commands

\multiputlist(*x,y*)(Δ*x*,Δ*y*)[*pos*]{*item1,item2,item3,...,itemN*}

This command is a variant of LATEX's \multiput command, which allows the *same* object to be placed at regularly spaced coordinates. The \multiputlist command is similar, but permits the objects to be *different*. While the \multiputlist command is executed, the objects to be put are picked up from the *list of items*, as the coordinates are incremented. (The first item goes in position one, the second item in position two, etc.) For example, you can plot numbers along the x-axis in a graph by specifying:

```
\multiputlist(0,0)(10,0){1.00,1.25,1.50,1.75,2.00}
```

The objects in the list can be virtually anything, including \makebox, \framebox, or math characters. This command enforces a certain regularity and symmetry on the layout of the various objects in a picture.

$$\backslash\texttt{matrixput}(x, y)(\Delta x_1, \Delta y_1)\{n_1\}(\Delta x_2, \Delta y_2)\{n_2\}\{object\}$$

The \matrixput command is the two-dimensional equivalent of the primitive LATEX command \multiput. It is more efficient, however, to use \matrixput than the equivalent n_1 \multiput statements. This command is especially useful for pictures where a pattern is repeated at regular intervals in two dimensions.

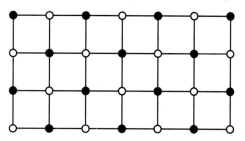

```
\setlength{\unitlength}{1mm}
\begin{picture}(62,32)(-1,-1)
\thicklines
\matrixput(0,0)(10,0){7}(0,10){4}{\circle{2}}
\matrixput(10,0)(20,0){3}(0,20){2}{\circle*{2}}
\matrixput(0,10)(20,0){4}(0,20){2}{\circle*{2}}
\matrixput(1,0)(10,0){6}(0,10){4}{\line(1,0){8}}
\matrixput(0,1)(10,0){7}(0,10){3}{\line(0,1){8}}
\end{picture}
```

$$\backslash\texttt{grid}(width,height)(\Delta width, \Delta height)[initial\text{-}X\text{-}int,initial\text{-}Y\text{-}int]$$

The \grid command makes a grid of dimensions *width* units by *height* units. Vertical lines are drawn at intervals of $\Delta width$ and horizontal lines at intervals of $\Delta height$. When the third (optional) argument is specified, then the borders of the grid will be labeled with numbers whose starting values are the integer numbers *initial-X-int* and *initial-Y-int* respectively. They will be incremented by $\Delta width$ and $\Delta height$ along the axes.

The \grid command produces a box. Therefore, it must be \put at the required coordinates, for example:

```
\put(0,0){\grid(50,100)(5,10)}
\put(0,0){\tiny \grid(100,100)(5,5)[-50,0]} % make numbers \tiny
```

Drawing Different Kinds of Lines

$$\backslash\texttt{dottedline}[dotchar]\{dotgap\}(x_1, y_1)(x_2, y_2)...(x_n, y_n)$$

The \dottedline command connects the specified points by drawing a dotted line between each pair of coordinates. At least two points must be defined. The dotted line is drawn with an inter-dot gap as specified in the second (first mandatory) argument *dotgap* (in \unitlengths). Since the number of dots to be plotted must be an integer, the inter-dot gap may not come out exactly as specified. By default, a little square (\picsquare, described below) is used as the dot, and can be changed by selecting another character, *dotchar*, using the optional argument. When the default character is used, the thickness of the dots is controlled by the currently active \thinlines, \thicklines, or \linethickness declarations. Note that some characters like "∗" in the roman font do not come out centered, although most other characters do.

```
\begin{picture}(150,15)(0,0)
\thicklines
\dottedline{2}(0,10)(70,10)
\dottedline[$\bullet$]{3}(0,5)(70,5)
\dottedline[$\diamond$]{4}(0,0)(70,0)
\end{picture}
```

```
\dashline[stretch]{dashlength}[dashdotgap](x₁,y₁)(x₂,y₂)...(xₙ,yₙ)
```

The \dashline command connects the specified points by drawing a dashed line between each pair of coordinates. At least two points must be specified. Each dash is constructed using the \dottedline command. The mandatory parameter *dashlength* determines the length of the dash, and the optional *dashdotgap* gives the gap between the dots that are used to construct the dash, both in \unitlengths. By default, a solid looking dash is constructed.

```
\begin{picture}(70,22)(0,-2)
\dashline{3}[0.7](0,18)(63,18)
\thicklines
\dashline{3}(0,13)(63,13)
\dashline[-30]{3}(0,8)(63,8)
\dashline[+15]{3}(0,4)(63,4)
\dashline[+30]{3}(0,0)(63,0)
\end{picture}
```

In the definition of the \dashline command the optional *stretch* parameter is an integer between -100 and ∞. This indicates the percentage with which the number of dashes is "stretched" or increased (*stretch* > 0) or "shrunk" or reduced (*stretch* < 0). If *stretch* is zero, the minimum number of dashes compatible with an approximate equal spacing relative to the empty space between dashes is used. The idea behind the *stretch* percentage parameter is that if several dashed lines of different lengths are being drawn, then all dashed lines with identical *stretch* values will have a similar visual appearance. The default settings for the *stretch* percentage can be changed by a \renewcommand call for the parameter \dashlinestretch:

```
\renewcommand{\dashlinestretch}{-50} % Only integers permitted
```

The argument determines the percentage (as an integer) increase or reduction that will be applied to all subsequent \dashline commands except for those where the *stretch* parameter is explicitly specified as the first optional argument.

\drawline [*stretch*] $(x_1, y_1)(x_2, y_2)...(x_n, y_n)$

The \drawline command connects the given points by drawing a line between each pair of coordinates using line segments of the closest slope available in the fonts. A minimum of two points must be specified. Since there are only a finite number of slopes available in the line segment fonts, some lines may appear jagged. A \drawline can generate a thick or thin line depending on the setting of the \thinlines or \thicklines parameters in effect; these are the only two thicknesses available for such lines. This command offers the most efficient way, in terms of memory and cpu usage, for drawing lines at arbitrary slopes. The optional *stretch* parameter is similar to the one described for the \dashline command. If *stretch* is zero, the result is the minimum number of dashes required to make the line appear solid with each dash "connected" at the ends. If *stretch* is greater than zero more dashes are used in constructing the line, giving a less jagged appearance. As with the \dashlinestretch parameter and the \dashline command, a similar parameter, \drawlinestretch, allows you to set the default value for the *stretch* percentage parameter of the \drawline command.

```
\renewcommand{\drawlinestretch}{20} % Only integers permitted
```

Commands for Drawing Multiple Curves

\jput$(x, y)${*object*}

\begin{dottedjoin} [*dotchar*] {*dotgap*}
.....   \jput commands connected internally with \dottedline
\end{dottedjoin}

\begin{dashjoin} [*stretch*] {*dashlength*} [*dashdotgap*]
.....   \jput commands connected internally with \dashline
\end{dashjoin}

\begin{drawjoin} [*stretch*]
.....   \jput commands connected internally with \drawline
\end{drawjoin}

The three environments—dottedjoin, dashjoin, and drawjoin—correspond to the three line drawing commands—\dottedline, \dashline, and \drawline. The arguments have the same meaning as for the corresponding drawing commands, and the \dashlinestretch and \drawlinestretch parameters can be used to redefine the *stretch* globally. These environments use the new command \jput (join and put), which is identical to the regular \put command of LATEX except it is inside these three environments. All *objects* put using a \jput command within the scope of any of the three environments are, in addition to being plotted, joined by lines of their respective type. Note that it is up to the user to center the objects at the plotted points.

An instance of any of the three join environments defines a separate "curve," hence every set of points belonging to different "curves" should be enclosed in separate join environments. The prime motivation for designing the join environments is for plotting graphs that use different types of curves and dissimilar lines. Figure 10.7 on page 305 shows an example.

> \picsquare

The \picsquare command generates a little square dot with its center as the reference point. The size of the square is dependent on the current setting of the \thinlines, \thicklines, or \linethickness command. Most of the epic commands that plot little dots use this command, although it has been provided primarily to be used in conjunction with the \putfile command described below.

> \putfile{*filename*}{*object*}

The \putfile command is similar to LATEX's \put command, except the x and y coordinates required by the \put command are read from an external file and the same *object* is plotted at each of those coordinates. This command is provided because TEX lacks the capability of doing floating point arithmetic, which is required if you wish to plot a parametric curve different from a straight line. The coordinates of points on such curves can easily be generated by a program in some computer language and subsequently read in by TEX. The external file must contain the (x, y) coordinate pairs, one pair per line, with a space between the two coordinates. The % is available as a comment character, but you should leave at least one space following the y entry if a comment is on the same line as data since a % masks the newline character.

For example, to plot a smooth curve along a set of coordinates, you can use the following procedure:

1. Create a file with the (x, y) coordinates of the data points, which you might call plot.data, for example.

2. If you wish, smooth the data.

3. Put the following inside a picture environment in your LATEX file.
   \putfile{plot.data}{\picsquare}

10.4   Extending the epic Package

LaTeX provides a basic but limited picture drawing capability, which is extended by commands for drawing solid lines, dotted lines, dashed lines, and new environments suitable for plotting graphs of the epic package described in the previous section.

However, epic still inherits many of the limitations of LaTeX in picture drawing. As a result, some of the functions take a long time to accomplish or the output is not very high quality.

A few years ago the pic programming language was developed to provide a "natural language" method of describing simple pictures and graphs [19]. A preprocessor, like gnu's gpic, can translate these graphics commands into output that the UNIX formatter, troff, understands. More interestingly for us, it can also generate TeX \special commands, which many dvi-driver programs support. For instance, the dvips dvi-to-PostScript translator, described in section 11.2, can interpret these commands.

The eepic [48] package, written by Conrad Kwok, is an extension of both LaTeX and epic that alleviates some of the limitations in LaTeX, epic, and gpic by generating gpic \specials using TeX commands. Because eepic is a superset of epic, you can use it to process any picture that uses epic commands and get better-looking output.

10.4.1   eepic's Extensions to LaTeX

In LaTeX, special fonts are used to draw lines and circles. Therefore, only limited functions are provided. The extensions in eepic allow users to draw lines in any slope and to draw circles in any size. However, the limitation of slopes for vectors remains the same. This means that the only slopes that can be handled are of the form x/y, where x and y are integers in the range $[-4, 4]$.

(ℒ 106)

`\line(x,y){`*length*`}`

The syntax of the \line command is the same as in LaTeX. But now x and y can be any integers acceptable to TeX. Furthermore, there is no longer a lower limit for the *length* parameter (about 3.5mm in standard LaTeX).

`\circle{`*diameter*`}`   `\circle*{`*diameter*`}`

(ℒ 107)

The syntax for drawing hollow and filled circles, \circle and \circle*, is the same as that in LaTeX. But now the *diameter* parameter can be any number acceptable to TeX and a circle with a diameter of (exactly) the specified value will be drawn.

$\boxed{\texttt{\textbackslash oval}(\textit{x-dimen,y-dimen})\{\textit{part}\}}$

The \oval command has been modified so that the maximum diameter of the quarter circles at the corners can be set to any value. This can be done by setting the variable \maxovaldiam to the desired TeX dimension (default 40pt).

10.4.2 eepic's Extensions to epic

epic generates standard dvi-files and requires the presence of only the standard LaTeX fonts. eepic as an extension to epic offers better line drawing output, faster operation, and requires less memory. It reimplements the \drawline, \dashline, and \dottedline commands (see page 296) and the corresponding join environments, dashjoin, dottedjoin, and drawjoin (see page 298).

10.4.3 New Commands with eepic

eepic introduces a number of new commands. Apart from the \path command, these commands do not have equivalents in LaTeX and epic. Please read section 10.4.4 for issues of compatibility.

$\boxed{\texttt{\textbackslash allinethickness}\{\textit{dimension}\}}$

The \allinethickness command sets the line thickness of all line drawing commands, including lines in slopes, circles, ellipses, arcs, ovals, and splines.

$\boxed{\texttt{\textbackslash Thicklines}}$

After issuing \Thicklines, the thickness of all subsequently drawn lines will be about 1.5 times greater than \thicklines.

$\boxed{\texttt{\textbackslash path}(x_1, y_1)(x_2, y_2)...(x_n, y_n)}$

The \path command is a fast version of the \drawline command. The optional *stretch* argument of the latter is not allowed and thus \path only draws solid lines. The \path command is mainly used for drawing complex paths.

$\boxed{\texttt{\textbackslash spline}(x_1, y_1)(x_2, y_2)...(x_n, y_n)}$

The \spline command draws a Chaikin's curve which passes through only the first and last point. All other points are control points only.

$\boxed{\texttt{\textbackslash ellipse}\{\textit{x-diameter}\}\{\textit{y-diameter}\} \qquad \texttt{\textbackslash ellipse*}\{\textit{x-diameter}\}\{\textit{y-diameter}\}}$

In complete analogy with the \circle and \circle* commands, the \ellipse and \ellipse* commands draw a hollow or filled ellipse using the specified *x-diameter* and *y-diameter* parameters.

\arc{*diameter*}{*start-angle*}{*end-angle*}

The \arc command draws a circular arc. The first parameter, *diameter*, is given in \unitlength. Both *start-angle* and *end-angle* are in radians; *start-angle* must lie within the interval $[0, \frac{\pi}{2}]$ and *end-angle* can be any value between *start-angle* and *start-angle* + 2π. Arcs are drawn clockwise with the angle 0 pointing to the right on the paper.

\filltype{*area-fill-type*}

The \filltype command specifies the type of area fill for the \circle* and \ellipse* commands. The instruction itself does not draw anything. It only changes the interpretation of * in the two commands specified above. Possible values for *area-fill-type* are: black (default), white, and shade, e.g., you can change the area fill type to white with \filltype{white}.

10.4.4 Compatibility

The eepic package is not necessarily available at all LaTeX sites. In order to avoid portability problems that can arise from its use, and at the same time take advantage of eepic's more precise printout, you must take the following precautions:

- Do not to use \line commands, but use \drawline instead because \line in LaTeX only supports a limited set of slopes.

- Do not use the \arc command. \spline should be used if a complex curve is really necessary.

- Avoid using solid or small inter-dot gaps in drawing long dash lines, as these need a lot of TeX memory in the original epic implementation. The \drawline command with negative stretch should be used to draw the dashed lines.

If your installation does not support eepic but you have to print your document, then you should use the eepic emulation macros defined with the eepicemu package. The extended commands are emulated in the following ways:

- Circles larger than 40pt will be drawn using \oval.
- Ellipses will be drawn using \oval.
- Splines will be approximated with \drawline

- \path will be substituted by \drawline.
- \Thicklines will be substituted by \thicklines.
- \allinethickness will be substituted by \thicklines and \linethickness.

As the eepic package redefines several commands of the epic package the eepic package declaration must follow the epic package declaration. That is,

```
\documentclass[...]{article}
\usepackage{epic}
...
\usepackage{eepic}
```

Although not strictly necessary, it is good practice to always include epic when using eepic commands. In any case, the eepic emulation package eepicemu will only work when both are specified.

10.4.5 Examples

Figure 10.6 on page 304 shows a series of power curves. You can see how the grid is used to set up the coordinate system, and how the different kind of line styles, discussed in the previous sections (dotted, plain, dashed) are used to differentiate the various curves. Each curve is identified by a label representing the fractional power used to calculate the points. Note also that the lines below the diagonal were drawn using the \thinlines command, while those in the upper part of the diagram were drawn with the \thicklines command.

Figure 10.7 on page 305 is an example of a possible real-life application. It shows the excitation (•) and threshold (◦) energies of isotopes with atomic weights around 235 (Uranium). In this case we constructed the horizontal and vertical axes using \multiputlist commands. The text along the vertical axis was printed using the \shortstack command. Finally the various data points were entered using epic's dottedjoin and dashjoin environments and their associated \jput commands (see page 298 and following).

10.5 Packages Based on epic

10.5.1 Drawing Bipartite Graphs

The eclbip package, written by Hideki Isozaka, uses the functionality of the epic package to generate bipartite graphs. A bipartite graph is a linear network in which the nodes can be partitioned into two groups, *left* and *right*, and the begin and end points of all the arcs start are in opposite groups.

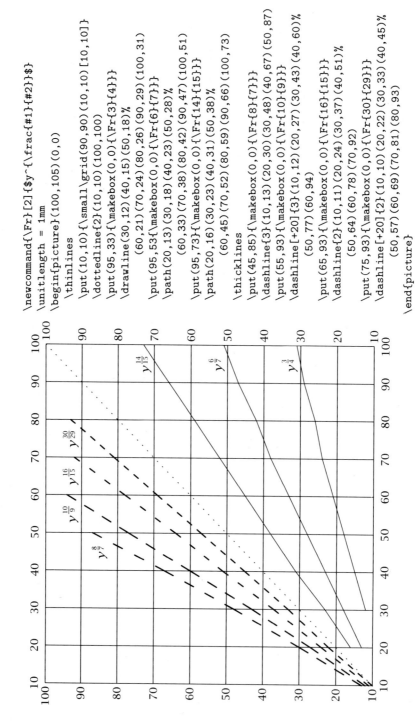

```
\newcommand{\Fr}[2]{$y^{\frac{#1}{#2}}$}
\unitlength = 1mm
\begin{picture}(100,105)(0,0)
  \thinlines
  \put(10,10){\small\grid(90,90)(10,10)[10,10]}
  \dottedline{2}(10,10)(100,100)
  \put(95,33){\makebox(0,0){\Fr{3}{4}}}
  \drawline(30,12)(40,15)(50,18)%
           (60,21)(70,24)(80,26)(90,29)(100,31)
  \put(95,53){\makebox(0,0){\Fr{6}{7}}}
  \path(20,13)(30,18)(40,23)(50,28)%
       (60,33)(70,38)(80,42)(90,47)(100,51)
  \put(95,73){\makebox(0,0){\Fr{14}{15}}}
  \path(20,16)(30,23)(40,31)(50,38)%
       (60,45)(70,52)(80,59)(90,66)(100,73)
  \thicklines
  \put(45,85){\makebox(0,0){\Fr{8}{7}}}
  \dashline{3}(10,13)(20,30)(30,48)(40,67)(50,87)
  \put(55,93){\makebox(0,0){\Fr{10}{9}}}
  \dashline[+20]{3}(10,12)(20,27)(30,43)(40,60)%
                   (50,77)(60,94)
  \put(65,93){\makebox(0,0){\Fr{16}{15}}}
  \dashline{2}(10,11)(20,24)(30,37)(40,51)%
              (50,64)(60,78)(70,92)
  \put(75,93){\makebox(0,0){\Fr{30}{29}}}
  \dashline[+20]{2}(10,10)(20,22)(30,33)(40,45)%
                   (50,57)(60,69)(70,81)(80,93)
\end{picture}
```

Figure 10.6: Line drawing commands with the epic and eepic packages

```
\newcommand{\CHo}{\makebox(0,0){$\bullet$}}
\newcommand{\CHc}{\makebox(0,0){$\circ$}}
\newcommand{\El}[2]{\makebox(0,0){${}^{#1}$#2}}
\setlength{\unitlength}{10mm}
\begin{picture}(11,9)(229,-1)
\linethickness{1pt}
\put(230,0){\vector(1,0){10}}
\put(230,0){\vector(0,1){7}}
\thicklines
\multiput(230,0)(1,0){10}{\line(0,1){.1}}
\multiput(230,0)(0,1){7}{\line(1,0){.1}}
\multiput(231,-.3)(1.,0){\El{231}{Pa},%
  \El{232}{Th},\El{233}{U}, ,\El{235}{U},%
  ,\El{237}{Np},\El{238}{U},\El{239}{Pu}}
\multiput(230.2,1)(0,1){1}{\small
  4.0,4.5,5.0,5.5,6.0,6.5}
\put(235,-.8){\makebox(0,0){Isotope}}
\put(229.6,4.){\makebox(0,0){\shortstack{%
  E\\n\\e\\r\\g\\y\\[2ex]in\\[2ex]M\\e\\V}}}
\put(234.5,7.6){\makebox(0,0){\fbox{%
  \makebox(.3,.2)[lb]{\put(.2,.06){\(\CHo}}:
    Excitation Energy\quad
  \makebox(.3,.2)[lb]{\put(.2,.06){\(\CHc}}:
    Threshold Energy}}}
\thinlines
\begin{dottedjoin}{.2}
  \jput(231,3.8){\(\CHo}\jput(232,3.2){\(\CHo}
  \jput(233,6.2){\(\CHo}\jput(235,5.8){\(\CHo}
  \jput(237,3.0){\(\CHo}\jput(238,2.8){\(\CHo}
  \jput(239,5.8){\(\CHo}
\end{dottedjoin}
\begin{dashjoin}{.2}
  \jput(231,3.0){\(\CHc}\jput(232,6.0){\(\CHc}
  \jput(233,2.2){\(\CHc}\jput(235,3.6){\(\CHc}
  \jput(237,1.4){\(\CHc}\jput(238,4.0){\(\CHc}
  \jput(239,1.0){\(\CHc}
\end{dashjoin}
\end{picture}
```

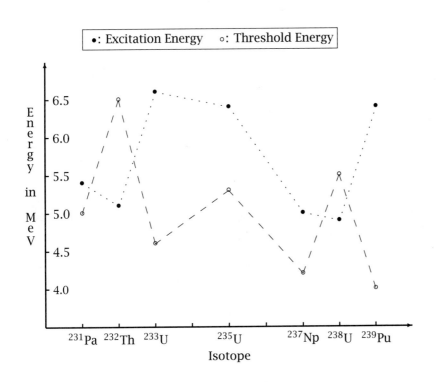

Figure 10.7: A graph made with the epic and eepic packages

A bipartite graph is drawn by using the `bipartite` environment.

```
\begin{bipartite}{leftwd}{gapwd}{rightwd}{gapht}{labelwd}
```

The `bipartite` environment has five arguments:

leftwd   Maximum width of labels in the left node group.

gapwd   Width of gap between the left node group and the right node group.

rightwd   Maximum width of labels in the right node group.

gapht   Minimum height of vertical gaps between node labels.

labelwd   Width between a node (bullet) and its label.

The commands, listed below, are available in a `bipartite` environment.

```
\leftnode[short-label]{long-label}
```

This is the label to be written on the left node. The mandatory argument, *long-label*, will be printed, while the *short-label* abbreviation can be used in the `\match` command.

```
\rightnode[short-label]{long-label}
```

This is the label for the right node. The arguments are the same as for `\leftnode`.

```
\match{leftnode}{rightnode}
```

This connects the nodes identified by *leftnode* and *rightnode*.

```
\brush{draw-command}
```

This specifies the drawing command to be used for subsequent `\draw` commands.

```
\begin{bipartite}{2cm}{1.5cm}{2cm}{3mm}{2mm}
    \leftnode{xxx} \leftnode{yyy} \leftnode{zzz}
    \rightnode{aaa}\rightnode{bbb}\rightnode{ccc}
    \match{xxx}{ccc}
\end{bipartite}
```

The use of long and short labels is shown in the next example:

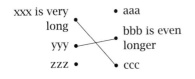

```
\begin{bipartite}{2cm}{1.5cm}{2cm}{3mm}{2mm}
  \leftnode[x]{xxx is very long}
  \leftnode{yyy} \leftnode{zzz}
  \rightnode{aaa}
  \rightnode[b]{bbb is even longer}
  \rightnode{ccc}
  \match{x}{ccc} \match{yyy}{b}
\end{bipartite}
```

You can use epic's line drawing commands (see page 296) to draw the match lines by specifying your choice as an argument to the \brush command.

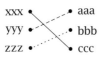

```
\begin{bipartite}{2cm}{1.5cm}{2cm}{3mm}{2mm}
  \leftnode{xxx} \leftnode{yyy} \leftnode{zzz}
  \rightnode{aaa}\rightnode{bbb}\rightnode{ccc}
  \match{xxx}{ccc}
  \brush{\dottedline{3}}    \match{zzz}{bbb}
  \brush{\dashline[50]{3}} \match{yyy}{aaa}
\end{bipartite}
```

10.5.2 Drawing Trees

The ecltree package, also written by Hideki Isozaka, uses the functions of the epic package to draw trees. Another package for drawing binary and ternary trees is described in section 10.2.3.

A tree graph can be drawn using the bundle environment.

\begin{bundle}{*topnode*}

The bundle environment has one argument, *topnode*, indicating the label of the top node.

Inside the bundle environment, the following commands are available:

\chunk[*edge-text*]{*node-text*}

The \chunk command specifies the nodes of the tree. The mandatory *node-text* argument is the label that will be used for the node, while, when present, the optional *edge-text* argument will be used to label the edge.

\drawwith{*draw-commands*}

This command controls the attributes of the edge lines. Its argument is one of the epic commands, whose description begins on page 296.

The first example shows two nested bundle environments, while the second shows the use of the optional argument for labeling the edges.

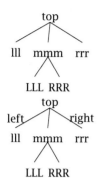

```
\begin{bundle}{top}
\chunk{lll}
\chunk{\begin{bundle}{mmm}
        \chunk{LLL} \chunk{RRR}
        \end{bundle}}
\chunk{rrr}
\end{bundle}


\begin{bundle}{top}
\chunk[left]{lll}
\chunk{\begin{bundle}{mmm}
        \chunk{LLL} \chunk{RRR}
        \end{bundle}}
\chunk[right]{rrr}
\end{bundle}
```

The line attributes are controlled with the \drawwith command. Note that the argument of the \drawwith command is evaluated when exiting the bundle environment at the \end{bundle} command. Therefore, in the example, the first \drawwith command is ignored.

```
\begin{bundle}{xxx}
 \chunk{aaa}
 \chunk{\begin{bundle}{yyy}
        \drawwith{\drawline}%Ignored
        \chunk{bbb}
        \drawwith{\dashline[50]{3}}
        \chunk{ddd}
        \end{bundle}}
 \drawwith{\dottedline{3}}
 \chunk{ccc}
\end{bundle}
```

A sequence of attributes can be specified by nesting the \drawwith commands, which are then executed in reverse order.

```
\drawwith{\drawwith{\drawwith{\dottedline{3}}}%
                    \drawline}%
            \dashline{3}}
\begin{bundle}{xxx}
 \chunk{aaa}
 \chunk{\begin{bundle}{yyy}
        \chunk{bbb} \chunk{ddd} \chunk{eee}
        \end{bundle}}
 \chunk{ccc} \chunk{fff}
\end{bundle}
```

The spacing inside a `bundle` environment is controlled by three parameters, whose values should be set before entering the `bundle` environment.

`\GapDepth`   The minimum height of gaps between adjacent nodes.

`\GapWidth`   The minimum width of gaps between adjacent nodes.

`\EdgeLabelSep`   The separation of an edge label from the lower node of the edge.

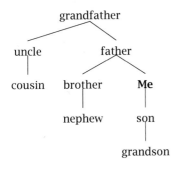

```
\setlength{\GapDepth}{5mm}
\setlength{\GapWidth}{5mm}
\begin{bundle}{grandfather}
  \chunk{\begin{bundle}{uncle}
             \chunk{cousin}
          \end{bundle}}
  \chunk{\begin{bundle}{father}
             \chunk{\begin{bundle}{brother}
                        \chunk{nephew}
                    \end{bundle}}
             \chunk{\begin{bundle}{\textbf{Me}}
                        \chunk{\begin{bundle}{son}
                                   \chunk{grandson}
                                \end{bundle}}
                     \end{bundle}}
          \end{bundle}}
\end{bundle}
```

CHAPTER 11

Using PostScript

As mentioned in the previous chapter, complex graphics expressed in PostScript commands can be included in LaTeX documents via \special commands, which are interpreted by a dvi-driver supporting the PostScript language.

This chapter first presents a short introduction to the PostScript language and then introduces dvips, one of the most popular dvi-drivers supporting PostScript. The following sections deal with how to merge graphics and text, and how to manipulate (rotate, scale, shade, and apply color) document elements by exploiting the capabilities of the PostScript language and the dvips driver. In the final section another visit to the NFSS will show how, with the help of virtual fonts, native PostScript fonts can be used with LaTeX.

11.1 The PostScript Language

11.1.1 About the Language

PostScript [1, 2, 69, 70, 74, 77] is a page description language. It provides a method for expressing the appearance of a printed page, including text, lines, and graphics. PostScript is a device- and resolution-independent programming language, which describes a complete page at a time, rather than one line at a time, like a line printer.

PostScript is a high-level programming language, which is stack-oriented and uses "reverse Polish" or postfix notation. It is a flexible language, since it includes looping constructs, procedures, and comparison operators, and it supports many data types, including reals, Booleans, arrays, strings, and complex objects such as dictionaries.

PostScript is resolution- and device-independent, that is, the software is not tied to any particular piece of hardware. The same ASCII file will print on a common 300 dots per inch (dpi) laser printer and a 2,540 dpi phototypesetter. It can also be viewed on a computer display with Display PostScript or previewers, such as ghostscript/ghostview.

Although it would be possible to compile PostScript for a given application, a PostScript file is normally interpreted in the printer, so that applications can be developed in a transparent way. Hence, most people will never come into direct contact with the language, but they should realize that they are using PostScript each time they print something on a PostScript printer.

The PostScript language features the following possibilities, which can be used in any combination:

- Arbitrary shapes can be constructed from straight lines, arcs, and cubic curves. The shapes may self-intersect and contain disconnected sections and holes.

- The painting primitives permit shapes to be outlined with lines of any thickness, filled with any color, or used as a clipping path to crop any other graphic.

- Text is fully integrated with graphics. In PostScript, text characters are treated as graphical shapes that may be operated on by any of the language's graphics operators. This is true both for type 1 fonts, where character shapes are defined by using specially encoded procedures [3], and for user defined type 3 fonts, where character shapes are defined as ordinary PostScript language procedures. At present, thousands of typefaces, including those of the world's major typesetting companies, such as Linotype, Agfa-Compugraphic, Monotype, Autologic, and Varityper, are available in PostScript form. You can download these fonts, or those of your own making, to any PostScript printer from your Mac or PC, or from a mainframe. Although bitmapped fonts can be used, generally outline fonts are preferred for the following reasons:

  - They are device- and resolution-independent.
  - They are built using a mathematical representation.
  - The use of Bezier curves provides a gain of accuracy and flexibility.
  - They are defined in a 1,000 by 1,000 coordinate system for a character 1 point in size, which can then be scaled, rotated, and skewed at will (see, e.g., figure 11.1 on page 314).

- For complex languages with many thousands of characters (e.g., Chinese and Japanese) composite type 0 fonts can be used.

- Images (such as photographs or synthetically generated images) can be sampled at any resolution and with a variety of dynamic ranges. PostScript provides facilities to control the rendering of images on the output device.

- Several color models are supported and conversion from one model to another is possible.

  - RGB or the additive *Red Green Blue* model, used with displays and film recorders.

  - HSB or the *Hue Saturation Brightness* model, where *hue* is the amount of red, green, and blue; *saturation* the amount of color and shade; and *brightness* the amount of light, dark to full color.

  - CMYK or the subtractive *Cyan Magenta Yellow Black* model, used by the printing industry.

  - CIE or the international standard, used in the graphics arts, television, and printing industries for reference.

- A general coordinate system facility supports all combinations of linear transformations, including scaling, rotation, reflection, and skewing. These transformations apply uniformly to all page elements, including text, graphical images, and sampled images.

- You can build dictionaries for color spaces, fonts, forms, images, halftones, and patterns.

- There are several compression filters available , such as JPEG and LZW.

Again, see figure 11.1 on the next page for an illustration of some of these properties.

11.1.2 What Is Encapsulated PostScript?

PostScript pictures often have to be included in text that was composed by a text formatter such as TEX. Adobe has defined the *Encapsulated PostScript* file format (EPS or EPSF), which complies with the *PostScript Document Structuring Conventions* (see appendices G and H in [2] or [87]). The EPS format defines standard rules for importing PostScript language files into different environments. EPS files should be "well behaved" in their use of certain PostScript operators, manipulation of the graphics state, interpreter stack, and global dictionaries, so that they do not interfere destructively with the page being composed by the text formatter.

Most modern graphics applications generate a conventional Encapsulated PostScript file that can be used without difficulty by LATEX. Sometimes, however, you may be confronted with a bare PostScript file that does not contain the

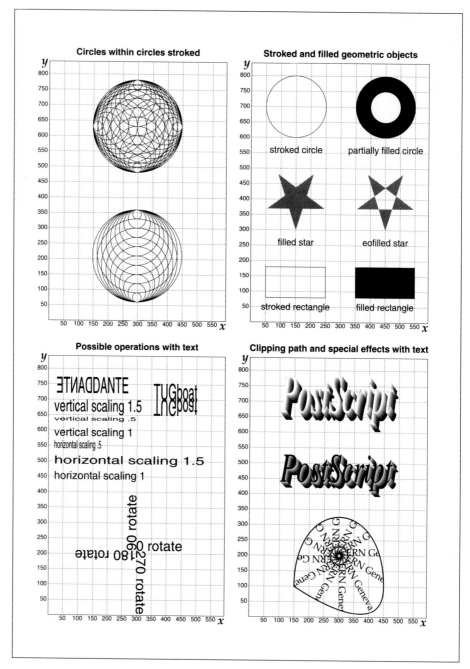

Figure 11.1: Examples of the capabilities of PostScript
The numbers on the axes and the dotted lines show the coordinate system used.

necessary information. For use with LaTeX, a PostScript file does not have to conform strictly to the structuring conventions mentioned previously. If the file is "well behaved" (see above) it is enough that the PostScript file contains the dimensions of the box occupied by the picture. These dimensions are provided to LaTeX by using the PostScript comment line %%BoundingBox, as shown below:

```
%!
%%BoundingBox: LLx LLy URx URy
```

The first line indicates that we are dealing with a nonconforming Encapsulated PostScript file. Note that the %! characters must occupy the first two columns of the line. The second line, which is the more important one for our purpose, specifies the size of the included picture in PostScript "big" points, of which there are 72 to an inch (see table A.1 on page 449). Its four parameters are the x and y coordinates of the lower left-hand corner (LLx and LLy) and the upper right-hand corner (URx and URy) of the picture. For instance, a full A4 page (210 mm by 297 mm) with zero at the lower left corner would need the following declaration:

```
%!
%%BoundingBox: 0 0 595 842
```

If the picture starts at $(100, 200)$ and is enclosed in a square of 4 inches (288 points), the statement would be:

```
%!
%%BoundingBox: 100 200 388 488
```

It is good practice to add one or two points to make sure that the complete picture will be included, because of possible rounding errors during the computations done in the interpreter.

11.2 dvips—A dvi to PostScript Converter

Most TeX documents at a particular site are designed to use the standard paper size (for example, letter size in the United States or A4 in Europe). The dvips dvi to PostScript translator, developed by Tomas Rokicki [72], defaults to these paper sizes and can be customized for the defaults at each site or on each printer. dvips supports graphics in a natural way, allowing PostScript graphics to be included and automatically scaled and positioned in a variety of ways. PostScript commands can be included literally in \special commands, but their use is to be discouraged.

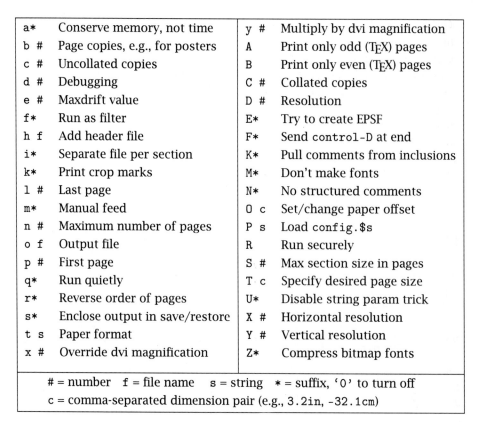

`a*`	Conserve memory, not time	`y #`	Multiply by dvi magnification
`b #`	Page copies, e.g., for posters	`A`	Print only odd (TEX) pages
`c #`	Uncollated copies	`B`	Print only even (TEX) pages
`d #`	Debugging	`C #`	Collated copies
`e #`	Maxdrift value	`D #`	Resolution
`f*`	Run as filter	`E*`	Try to create EPSF
`h f`	Add header file	`F*`	Send `control-D` at end
`i*`	Separate file per section	`K*`	Pull comments from inclusions
`k*`	Print crop marks	`M*`	Don't make fonts
`l #`	Last page	`N*`	No structured comments
`m*`	Manual feed	`O c`	Set/change paper offset
`n #`	Maximum number of pages	`P s`	Load `config.$s`
`o f`	Output file	`R`	Run securely
`p #`	First page	`S #`	Max section size in pages
`q*`	Run quietly	`T c`	Specify desired page size
`r*`	Reverse order of pages	`U*`	Disable string param trick
`s*`	Enclose output in save/restore	`X #`	Horizontal resolution
`t s`	Paper format	`Y #`	Vertical resolution
`x #`	Override dvi magnification	`Z*`	Compress bitmap fonts

# = number   f = file name   s = string   * = suffix, '0' to turn off
c = comma-separated dimension pair (e.g., 3.2in, -32.1cm)

Table 11.1: Major options of the dvips program

Missing fonts can be generated automatically if METAFONT exists on the system. If a font cannot be generated, a scaled version of the same font at a different size will be used instead, although dvips will complain about the poor esthetics of the resulting output.

One of its most important features is that dvips has virtual font support, which allows the use of native PostScript fonts with TEX (see section 11.9 for more about this). PostScript fonts are accompanied by an "Adobe font metric" (.afm) file, such as Times-Roman.afm, which describes characteristics of a given font. To use such fonts with TEX, .tfm files should be generated, which contain information about each character. The afm2tfm program, distributed with dvips, extracts the necessary information from the .afm file, and generates the .tfm and .vf files. It also allows a different encoding to be used for a PostScript font, which comes in handy in some circumstances.

The dvips driver has a plethora of command line options. Table 11.1 presents a summary of those options.

Option	Description of drivers	epsfig	rotating	changebar
ln	Digital Corp. printers (e.g., LN03)	X	–	X
dvips	Tomas Rokicki's dvips	X	X	X
dvitops	James Clark's dvitops	X	X	X
emtex	Eberhard Mattes's emTeX	X	–	X
oztex	Andrew Trevorrow's OzTeX	X	n.a.	n.a.
textures	Blue Sky Research's TEXTURES	X	X	n.a.
	Command used to specify driver:	\psfigdriver	\rotdriver	\driver
X means supported, – means not or partially supported, n.a. means not available				

Table 11.2: Overview of `dvi`-driver support for various packages

11.3   Merging Text and PostScript Graphics

In this section, a few packages, which use features of dvips and the PostScript language, will be described. In principle, some of the functions are also available with other drivers, such as dvitops, or the emTEX collections (see table 11.2). Of course, PostScript pictures will only be visible with printer drivers or previewers that support PostScript, like ghostview. Note that this powerful tool gives you a simple way to determine on your computer screen the bounding box of your PostScript pictures (see section 11.1.2). Table 11.2 shows which drivers are known to the packages and to what extent the functionality offered by the package can be implemented if a certain driver is used. Future releases of the packages might support additional drivers, thus you should consult the accompanying documentation for an up-to-date listing. The table also gives the specific command used by each package to specify the driver for which LATEX has to generate \special commands in the dvi file.

The updated version of these packages for LATEX 2ε will support the driver names as options to the package, e.g., you can write something like

```
\documentclass[..,emtex]{article}
\usepackage{epsfig}   \usepackage{changebar}
```

where epsfig and changebar will pick up the global option emtex to select the code suitable for the intended driver. Alternatively, as seen in figures 9.2 on page 268 and 9.3 on page 270 you can also specify the option on the \usepackage command itself, but since you can have only one driver processing the whole document afterwards placing the option on the \documentclass command is more economical. It is expected that under LATEX 2ε other packages that also contain driver dependent implementation parts will recognize the same option names, so that the above names (and additional ones) will become standard options for packages dealing with driver dependent code.

Currently, a package called graphics is under development for later inclusion into the standard distribution of LaTeX 2_ε. This package is intended to serve as a base for other packages offering graphic facilities, by providing graphic inclusion possibilities and graphic manipulation constructs (like rotating or scaling of boxes). Look at the documentation accompanying the LaTeX 2_ε distribution once this package is available.

The package epsfig (by Sebastian Rahtz, based on earlier work by Trevor Darrell) facilitates the inclusion of Encapsulated PostScript figures into TeX documents. It extracts the information about the bounding box of the figure from the file and positions it automatically, properly scaled according to the user's wishes on the page, leaving the proper amount of space. You can use custom characters, such as "∞" and "☻" (the latter obtained with \epsfig{file=cm.eps,height=3mm}), freely throughout your document.

> \epsfig{file=*fn*,height=*ht*,width=*wd*,clip=,angle=*degrees*,%
>   silent=,bbllx=*blx*,bblly=*bly*,bburx=*brx*,bbury=*bry*}

file   This is the file name of the Encapsulated PostScript file (you can also use the alias figure=).

height   This sets the desired height of the picture (in any of the accepted TeX units). If this parameter is not specified, then the picture will be printed with its "natural" height, i.e., the one specified on the BoundingBox line inside the PostScript file. When only the width is specified and no height, the latter is scaled in the same proportion as the width.

width   This sets the desired width of the picture (in any of the accepted TeX units). If this parameter is not specified, the picture will be printed with its "natural" width, i.e., the one specified on the BoundingBox line inside the PostScript file. When only the height is specified and no width, the latter is scaled in the same proportion as the height.

bbllx   The x-coordinate of the lower left-hand corner of the BoundingBox.

bblly   The y-coordinate of the lower left-hand corner of the BoundingBox.

bburx   The x-coordinate of the upper right-hand corner of the BoundingBox.

bbury   The y-coordinate of the upper right-hand corner of the BoundingBox.

clip   This parameter ensures that no portion of the figure will appear outside its BoundingBox. "clip=" is a switch and takes no value, but the "=" must be present.

angle   This determines the angle of rotation (in degrees counting counter-clockwise).

silent   This makes the \epsfig command work silently.

Normally, when you are dealing with Encapsulated PostScript files, you do not have to specify the BoundingBox parameters, since they are read by \epsfig in the file. Note that when you specify BoundingBox parameters in front of the

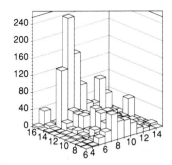

```
\begin{center}
\epsfig{file=tac2dim.eps,%
        height=4cm}
\end{center}
```

Figure 11.2: A single centered figure

`file=` specifier on the \epsfig command, then the ones inside the PostScript file are ignored. This is useful if the BoundingBox parameters are absent from the PostScript file or are wrong. This facility should not be used to obtain specific scaling or translation effects on the page. The `width` or `height` parameters should be used for those purposes. The \epsfig macro is not sensitive to white space; if you get errors due to some blanks in the argument you have an obsolete release of the package.

\psfigdriver{*driveroption*}

This command specifies the driver for which \special commands must be generated. Supported values for *driveroption* are given in the third column of table 11.2 on page 317. The default value is `dvips`. As mentioned before, the LaTeX2ε version of the package will alternatively recognize the driver name specified as a document option.

11.3.1   Simple Figures

When including an EPS picture, you would usually specify the desired height or width on the output page (if you do not specify any dimensions, the "natural" dimensions of the picture are taken, as read on the BoundingBox line in the file, corresponding to the size shown when the picture is printed separately on a PostScript printer). The lower edge of the picture will be located at the point where the command \epsfig is issued. The image will be scaled to the desired width (or height), using the same factor horizontally and vertically if one of the parameters (`height` or `width`) is specified.

Figure 11.2 shows a picture with a desired height of 4cm. It is centered by putting it in a `center` environment.

```
\psdraft              % switch to draft mode
\begin{center}
  \epsfig{file=tac2dim.eps,height=3cm}
\end{center}
\psfull               % switch back to full mode
```

Figure 11.3: A figure in draft mode

11.3.2   Draft Figures

Some PostScript figures can take quite a long time to transmit to the printer and print; for these figures a "draft" mode is available to speed printing of draft versions of the document. A figure printed in draft mode will appear as a box with the name of the figure file (figure 11.3). By specifying the option draft all figures come out in draft mode. Full processing, which is the default, can be explicitly specified with the option final. Within the document the command \psdraft will switch into draft mode, and all subsequent \epsfig commands will produce draft figures until reaching the macro \psfull, which switches out of draft mode. No \special commands are used in draft mode, so a draft document can be previewed using any dvi-driver.

11.3.3   More Complex Figure Arrangements

Figures 11.4 to 11.6 on the facing page show how to place various figures on a page using the minipage environment.

11.4   Rotating Material

The package rotating [68] (Sebastian Rahtz and Leonor Barroca) defines new environments that let you easily rotate information in LaTeX documents. The LaTeX2_ε upgrade of this package will recognize the driver names given in table 11.2 on page 317 as options. For backward compatibility the used driver can be specified using

> \rotdriver{*driveroption*}

This command specifies the driver for which \special commands must be generated. Supported values for *driveroption* are given in the fourth column of table 11.2 on page 317. The default value is dvips.

```
\noindent
\begin{minipage}[b]{.46\linewidth}
  \centering\epsfig{figure=Europe.eps,width=\linewidth}
  \caption{Pre-1991 Europe}        \label{fig:Europe}
\end{minipage}\hfill
\begin{minipage}[b]{.46\linewidth}
  \centering\epsfig{figure=CentralAmerica.eps,width=\linewidth}
  \caption{Central America}        \label{fig:CentralAmerica}
  \end{minipage}
\centering\epsfig{figure=TheWorld.eps,width=\linewidth}
\caption{A map of the world}       \label{fig:World}
```

Figure 11.4: Pre-1991 Europe

Figure 11.5: Central America

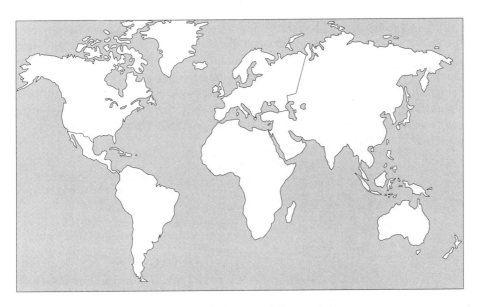

Figure 11.6: A map of the world

The `rotate` environment provides a generalized rotation environment where the text is rotated (clockwise, as is normal in PostScript) by the number of degrees specified as a parameter to the environment. However, no special arrangement is made to find space for the result.

Start here End here

```
Start here \begin{rotate}{56}
    LATEX
\end{rotate} End here
```

If the user desires LaTeX to leave space for the rotated box, the `turn` environment should be used:

Start here   End here

```
Start here \begin{turn}{-56}
    LATEX
\end{turn} End here
```

The `sideways` environment is a special case, setting the rotation to −90, and leaving the correct space for the rotated box.

Start here End here

```
Start here \begin{sideways}
    LATEX
\end{sideways} End here
```

If you have to deal with whole paragraphs of text, you will soon realize that TeX boxes are not as simple as they sometimes look: they have a height *and* a depth. Rotations are made about the point on the left-hand edge of the box that meets the baseline. The results can be unexpected, as shown in a full set of paragraph rotations in figure 11.7 on the next page. If you really want to turn a paragraph so that it appears to rotate about the *real* bottom of the TeX box, you have to adjust the box by using the (optional) placement parameters with the LaTeX commands:

Start   Continue   End

```
\newcommand{\T}{A B C D E F G H I J K
            L M N O P R S T U V W X Y Z}
Start
    \begin{turn}{-45}
        \parbox[t]{15mm}{\T}\end{turn}
Continue
    \begin{turn}{-45}
        \parbox[b]{15mm}{\T}\end{turn}
End
```

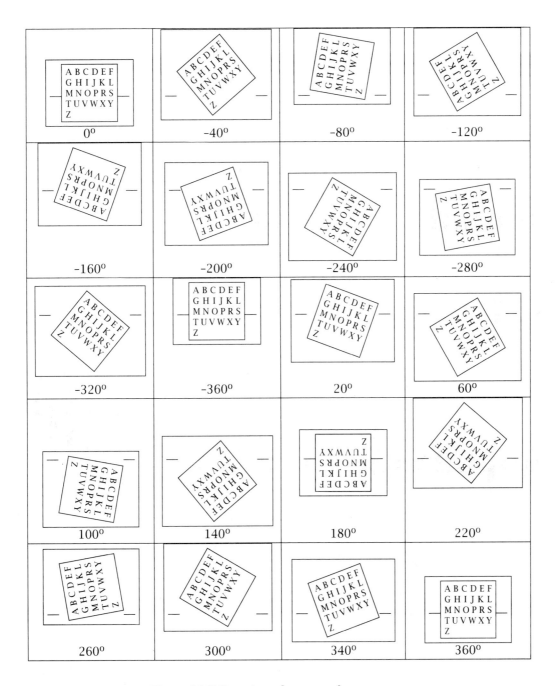

Figure 11.7: Rotation of paragraphs

11.4.1   Rotating Tabular Material

Tabular material can also be rotated in this way. The examples below show how the distance between the columns and the vertical placement of the table can be controlled by the use of zero width or zero height rules.

Column 1	Column 2	Column 3
1	2	3
4	5	6
7	8	9

```
\begin{tabular}{rrr}
\rule{0pt}{15mm}% vertical placement
\begin{rotate}{-45}Column 1\end{rotate}&
\begin{rotate}{-45}Column 2\end{rotate}&
\begin{rotate}{-45}Column 3\end{rotate}\\
\hline 1& 2& 3\\ 4& 5& 6\\ 7& 8& 9\\ \hline
\end{tabular}
```

Column 1	Column 2	Column 3
1	2	3
4	5	6
7	8	9

```
\begin{tabular}{ccc}
\begin{turn}{-45}Column 1\end{turn}&
\begin{turn}{-45}Column 2\end{turn}&
\begin{turn}{-45}Column 3\end{turn}\\
\hline 1& 2& 3\\ 4& 5& 6\\ 7& 8& 9\\ \hline
\end{tabular}
```

Column 1	Column 2	Column 3
1	2	3
4	5	6
7	8	9

```
\begin{tabular}{rrr}
\rule{0pt}{15mm}% vertical placement
\begin{rotate}{-45}Column 1\end{rotate}
\rule{.5cm}{0pt}&
\begin{rotate}{-45}Column 2\end{rotate}
\rule{.5cm}{0pt}&
\begin{rotate}{-45}Column 3\end{rotate}
\rule{.5cm}{0pt}\\
\hline 1& 2& 3\\ 4& 5& 6\\ 7& 8& 9\\ \hline
\end{tabular}
```

Rotations can be nested, as shown below.

Word	Occurrences
hello	33
goodbye	34

```
\begin{sideways}
\begin{tabular}{l@{\qquad}r}
\em Word \rule{0pt}{1in}
          & \begin{rotate}{-90}%
Occurrences\end{rotate}   \\[1mm]
\hline
hello & 33\\ goodbye & 34\\ \hline
\end{tabular}
\end{sideways}
```

ISO paper formats (mm)							
		A series		B series		C series	
	0	841×1189		1000×1414		917×1297	
	1	594×841		707×1000		648×917	
	2	420×594		500×707		458×648	
	3	297×420		353×500		324×458	
	4	210×297		250×353		229×324	
	5	148×210		176×250		162×229	
Format classes	6	105×148		125×176		114×162	
	7	74×105		88×125		81×114	
	8	52×74		62×88		57×81	

```
\renewcommand{\arraystretch}{1.2}
\setlength{\tabcolsep}{2mm}
\begin{sideways}
\begin{tabular}{|l|l*3{r@{$\times$}l}|}
                              \hline
\multicolumn{8}{|c|}{ISO paper formats (mm)}
                              \\\hline
&&\multicolumn{2}{c}{A series}
 &\multicolumn{2}{c}{B series}
 &\multicolumn{2}{c|}{C series}\\\cline{2-8}
&0&841&1189&1000&1414&917&1297 \\\cline{2-8}
&1&594&841 & 707&1000&648&917 \\\cline{2-8}
&2&420&594 & 500&707 &458&648 \\\cline{2-8}
&3&297&420 & 353&500 &324&458 \\\cline{2-8}
&4&210&297 & 250&353 &229&324 \\\cline{2-8}
&5&148&210 & 176&250 &162&229 \\\cline{2-8}
&6&105&148 & 125&176 &114&162 \\\cline{2-8}
&7& 74&105 & 88&125 & 81&114 \\\cline{2-8}
\rule{1mm}{0pt}
\begin{rotate}{-90}%
    \hspace*{8mm}Format classes%
\end{rotate}\rule{1mm}{0pt}
&8& 52&74 & 62&88 & 57&81    \\\hline
\end{tabular}
\end{sideways}
```

Table 11.3: Rotating tabular information

A more complex example is the one in table 11.3. The tabular material is rotated using the `sideways` environment. Note also the use of the `rotate` environment to generate vertically running text. As `rotate` generates a zero width box, it is surrounded by two "invisible rules" of 1mm each. These are added to the `\tabcolsep` of 2mm and give the result shown in the table. A rotated table can also be generated with the `sidewaystable` environment where both the table and the caption are rotated (see table 11.4 on the next page). The `sidewaystable` environment works on a width of `\textheight` so that when the float is rotated, it comes out the right height. This is not actually very satisfactory, since what you really want are rotated floats that occupy the space they actually use. But captions are a problem since they can precede the figure or table. As a result, they cannot be set in a box of the right width (i.e., the height of the forthcoming object), because it is not known yet. One possible solution is to make the `sidewaystable` (and its equivalent `sidewaysfigure` discussed in the next section) always fill a complete page. If that is not desired, you can construct a box of the right size and set the material and caption inside.

```
\begin{sidewaystable}
\centering
\begin{tabular}{|l|c|c|c|c|c|c|l|}
 ....
\end{tabular}
\caption[...]{....}
\label{tab:sidewaystable}
\end{sidewaystable}
```

	Study Area	Number of Sites				Accept or Reject Null Hypoth.
		To-tal	In Boundary Zone			
			Obs.	Expected		
				From	To	
Primary units	Full sample	41	31	10.3	27.0	Reject
	Sample area 1	23	16	4.3	16.7	Accept
	Sample area 2	18	15	2.8	13.7	Reject
	Rushen	13	9	1.2	10.4	Accept
	Arbory	10	7	0.6	8.8	Accept
	Marown	10	8	0.4	8.6	Accept
	Santon	8	7	0.0	7.3	Accept

Table 11.4: Rotating tabular information with the `sidewaystable` environment

It is seen that in this case the complete contents of the environment, including the caption, is rotated.

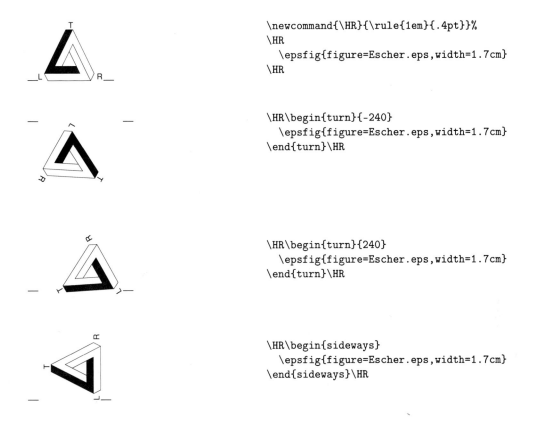

```
\newcommand{\HR}{\rule{1em}{.4pt}}%
\HR
  \epsfig{figure=Escher.eps,width=1.7cm}
\HR


\HR\begin{turn}{-240}
  \epsfig{figure=Escher.eps,width=1.7cm}
\end{turn}\HR




\HR\begin{turn}{240}
  \epsfig{figure=Escher.eps,width=1.7cm}
\end{turn}\HR




\HR\begin{sideways}
  \epsfig{figure=Escher.eps,width=1.7cm}
\end{sideways}\HR
```

Figure 11.8: A normal, turned, and sideways picture within a figure

11.4.2   Rotating a Figure

Figures can be rotated using the same commands. Figure 11.8 shows how an EPS file using the \epsfig command can be rotated at will. Note the position of the baseline, shown by the em dash rule (defined with the command \HR).

As with a table and its sidewaystable environment, it is possible to rotate the whole figure environment, including caption, by specifying a sidewaysfigure instead of a figure environment.

11.4.3   Rotated Captions Only

Sometimes it turns out that the rotation of complete figures does not give quite the right result. Therefore, it may be desirable to rotate the caption and the float contents separately within a conventional figure. The caption can be rotated separately by 90° by using the \rotcaption instead of the \caption command.

11.5   Using Revision Bars

The changebar package, adapted to PostScript by Johannes Braams, and drawing upon the earlier work of Michael Fine and Neil Winton, implements a way of indicating modifications in a LaTeX document by putting bars in the margin. This package works with most dvi-to-ps drivers, in particular dvips.

Note that, just as with cross-references and labels, you will usually need to process a document twice (and sometimes three times) to ensure that the changebars come out correctly. A warning will be issued if another pass is required.

Changebars can be nested within each other. Each nesting level can be characterized by a different thickness of the bar. They may also be nested within other environments including floats and footnotes. Changebars are applied to all the material within the "barred" environment, including floating bodies, regardless of where the floats float to. An exception to this are marginal floats. Changebars may cross page boundaries.

11.5.1   The User Interface

`\driver{driver}`

This command specifies the driver for which `\special` commands must be generated. Supported values for *driver* are given in the fifth column of table 11.2 on page 317. The default value is dvips.

`\cbstart[barwidth]`

The `\cbstart` command indicates the beginning of the region, which has to be flagged with a changebar. The optional *barwidth* parameter specifies the width with which the changebar has to be drawn. If no width is specified, the current value of the parameter is `\changebarwidth`. The latter can be redefined at any point with the `\setlength` command.

`\cbend`

The command `\cbend` indicates the end of the region where a changebar is to be used. `\cbstart` and `\cbend` can be used anywhere, but they must be correctly nested with floats and footnotes. For example, you cannot have one end of the bar inside a floating insertion and the other outside.

`\begin{changebar}`

Apart from the `\cbstart` and `\cbend` macros, a LaTeX environment changebar is defined, which has the same effect as the pair `\cbstart` and

\cbend. The advantage of using the environment whenever possible is that LaTeX will do all the work of checking the correct nesting of different environments.

\cbdelete [*barwidth*]

The \cbdelete command prints a square bar in the margin to indicate that some text was removed at that point from the document. The optional argument *barwidth* specifies the width of the bar. When no argument is specified, the current value of the \deletebarwidth parameter will be used. The latter can be redefined with the \setlength command.

This is the text in the first paragraph. This is the text in the first paragraph.

```
\cbstart
This is the text in the first paragraph.
This is the text in the first paragraph.\cbend
```

This is the text in the second paragraph. This is the text in the second paragraph.

```
This is the text in the second paragraph.
\cbdelete
This is the text in the second paragraph.
```

This is paragraph three.

This is paragraph four.

```
\begin{changebar}
This is paragraph three.\par This is paragraph four.
\end{changebar}
```

\nochangebars

The command \nochangebars disables the changebar commands.

11.5.2   Changebar Parameters

\changebarwidth

The width of the changebars is controlled with the LaTeX length parameter \changebarwidth. Its default value is 2pt. It can be changed with the \setlength command. Changing the value of \changebarwidth affects all subsequent changebars subject to the scoping rules of \setlength.

\deletebarwidth

The width of the deletebars is controlled with the LaTeX length parameter \deletebarwidth. Its default value is 4pt. It can be changed with the \setlength command. Changing the value of \deletebarwidth affects all subsequent deletebars subject to the scoping rules of \setlength.

$\boxed{\texttt{\textbackslash changebarsep}}$

The separation between the text and the changebars is determined by the value of the LaTeX length parameter \changebarsep. Its default value is 35pt.

$\boxed{\texttt{changebargrey}}$

The "blackness" of the bars can be controlled with the help of the LaTeX counter changebargrey. A command like \setcounter{changebargrey}{85} changes that value. The value of the counter is a percentage, where the value 0 yields black bars, and 100 yields white bars. Its default value is 65.

$\boxed{\texttt{outerbars}}$

The changebars will be printed in the "inside" margin of the document. This means they appear on the left side of the page. When the twoside option is in effect, the bars will be printed on the right side of even pages. This behavior can be changed by including the \outerbarstrue command in the document.

11.5.3 Deficiencies and Bugs

- There is a limit of twenty bars per page.
- This implementation has not been designed for two column printing.
- The algorithm may fail for footnotes split over multiple pages. The simplest way to circumvent this is to prevent footnotes from being split but this may give less satisfying page breaks.
- The \cbend normally gets "attached" to the token after it, rather than the one before it. This may lead to a longer bar than intended. For example, consider the sequence "word1 \cbend word2." If there is a line break between "word1" and "word2" the bar will incorrectly be extended an extra line. This particular case can be fixed with the incantation "word1\cbend{}␣word2."

11.6 Boxing and Gray Shading

The psboxit package (by Jérôme Maillot) puts a PostScript generated box behind a TeX box, which controls its position and the size. To initialize the PostScript commands of this package, the command \PScommands should be executed at the beginning of your LaTeX job.

\psboxit{*PScommands*}{*T_EX material*}

The \psboxit command gets the PostScript code that should be executed from its first argument, *PScommands*. The package defines several PostScript procedures, such as cartouche, rectcartouche, and roundedbox, for obtaining certain effects (see the examples below). The second argument, *T_EX material*, is first typeset inside a box before being subjected to the PostScript commands of *PScommands*.

-CCC— DDD — EEE -

```
--\psboxit{5 cartouche}{CCC}--%
--\psboxit{rectcartouche}{\spbox{DDD}}--%
--\psboxit{box .7 setgray fill}{\spbox{EEE}}--
```

The additional command \spbox works like \fbox, that is, it puts a box around its argument, but it does not draw the frame itself; it just adds a supplementary space equal to \fboxsep around the natural boundaries of the box. Its main purpose is to be able to construct a gray box filling the same rectangular area as its framed \fbox equivalent.

More convenient commands can be easily defined, for example:

```
\newcommand{\graybox}[1]{\psboxit{box .7 setgray fill}{\fbox{#1}}}
```

\begin{boxitpara}{*PScommands*}

The boxitpara environment lets you handle larger pieces of text.

This is the text of a paragraph. This is the text of a paragraph. This is the text of a paragraph. This is the text of a paragraph.

```
\begin{boxitpara}{box 0.7 setgray fill}
This is the text of a paragraph.
This is the text of a paragraph.
This is the text of a paragraph.
This is the text of a paragraph.
\end{boxitpara}
```

11.7 Color Output

Colors were not directly included in L^AT_EX 2.09 in the past, but dvips provides support for some color models present in the PostScript language via the use of \special commands and James Hafner's colordvi package.

For L^AT_EX 2_ε a color package is currently under development. The availability of that package will be announced via the usual channels and interested users should consult the documentation coming with it.

11.8   Overlaying Text on the Output Page

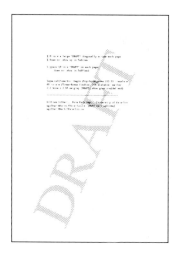

DRAFT

dvips provides several hooks, e.g., `start-hook`, `end-hook`, `bop-hook`, and `eop-hook`, for including user PostScript code at the beginning or the end of a document, or at the end of each page (see [72] for more details).

You can use this facility, for instance, to have a word or other mark printed across each page. An example is the draftcopy package, which prints the word "DRAFT" diagonally across each page.

11.9   The NFSS Revisited

By combining the possibilities of the NFSS and the virtual font mechanism, it is relatively easy to use PostScript fonts with LaTeX. dvips has the necessary machinery to permit the use of resident (in the printer) or downloadable (from disk) PostScript fonts with LaTeX.

11.9.1   Naming Those Thousands of Fonts

A font naming scheme that can be used with TeX was proposed by Karl Berry [10], provoking some discussion [56]. He tries to classify all font file names using eight alphanumeric characters, where case is not significant. This eight character limit guarantees that the same file names can be used across all computer platforms (something IBM mainframe and MS-DOS users will appreciate!). The principle of the scheme is described in table 11.5, while table 11.6 on the facing page shows the classification of the thirty-five "basic" PostScript fonts according to

F	TT	W	V	E	DD
Foundry	Typeface name	Weight	Variant	Expansion	Design Size
e.g., p=PostScript	tm=Times	b=Bold	i=Italic	c=Condensed	10=10 point

Table 11.5: Karl Berry's font file name classification scheme

Family	Series	Shape	External names
(T1, OT1)			*Serif families*
ptm	m	n, it	`Times-Roman(ptmr), Times-Italic(ptmri)`
	b	n, it	`Times-Bold(ptmb), Times-BoldItalic(ptmbi)`
ppl	m	n, it	`Palatino-Roman(pplr), Palatino-Italic(pplri)`
	b	n, it	`Palatino-Bold(pplb), Palatino-BoldItalic(pplbi)`
pnc	m	n, it	`NewCenturySchlbk-Roman(pncr), NewCenturySchlbk-Italic(pncri)`
	b	n, it	`NewCenturySchlbk-Bold(pncb), NewCenturySchlbk-BoldItalic(pncbi)`
pbk	m	n, it	`Bookman-Light(pbkl), Bookman-LightItalic(pbkli)`
	b	n, it	`Bookman-Demi(pbkd), Bookman-DemiItalic(pbkdi)`
(T1, OT1)			*Sans serif families*
phv	m	n, sl	`Helvetica(phvr), Helvetica-Oblique(phvro)`
	b	n, sl	`Helvetica-Bold(phvb), Helvetica-BoldOblique(phvbo)`
	c	n, sl	`Helvetica-Narrow(phvrrn), Helvetica-Narrow-Oblique(phvron)`
	bc	n, sl	`Helvetica-Narrow-Bold(phvbrn), Helvetica-Narrow-BoldOblique(phvbon)`
pag	m	n, sl	`AvantGarde-Book(pagk), AvantGarde-BookOblique(pagko)`
	b	n, sl	`AvantGarde-Demi(pagd), AvantGarde-DemiOblique(pagdo)`
(T1, OT1)			*Non-proportional font*
pcr	m	n, sl	`Courier(pcrr), CourierOblique(pcrro)`
	b	n, sl	`Courier-Bold(pcrb), Courier-BoldOblique(pcrbo)`
(U) [a]			*Special display fonts*
psy	m	n	`Symbol(psyr)`
pzd	m	n	`ZapfDingbats(pzdr)`
pzc	m	n	`ZapfChancery-MediumItalic(pzcmi)`

[a]Except ZapfChancery, which is available in T1 and OT1 encoding

Table 11.6: NFSS classification of the basic PostScript fonts (in parentheses—Karl Berry's file name)

the NFSS scheme. For each font the full Adobe name and, between parentheses, the corresponding short (Karl Berry) file name is given. The scheme provides a handy way to map long typeface names onto shorter equivalents, which are handled easily by dvips on the various systems where it is installed.

Most or all of the fonts in table 11.6 are present in the ROM of the common laser printers. Yet, there still are some printers (often older or cheaper models) that do not carry all of these fonts. Therefore, if portability of the printed document is important, it is wise to stick to the three basic PostScript fonts: Times-Roman, Helvetica, and Courier.

The mapping between the layout in a PostScript font and the font encoding

Style file	Sans font	Roman font	Typewriter font
times	Helvetica	Times	Courier
palatino	Helvetica	Palatino	Courier
helvet	Helvetica		
avant	AvantGarde		
newcent	AvantGarde	NewCenturySchoolbook	Courier
bookman	AvantGarde	Bookman	Courier
garamond	Optima	Garamond	Courier
basker	Univers	Baskerville	Courier
mtimes	Univers	Monotype Times	cmtt
bembo	Optima	Bembo	Courier
lucid	LucidaSans	Lucida	Courier
lucidbrb	LucidaSans	LucidaBright	LucidaSansTypewriter
lucidbry	LucidaSans	LucidaBright	LucidaSansTypewriter

Table 11.7: Fonts used by various PSNFSS packages

needed by TEX is performed using the virtual font mechanism, which dvips understands. The mapping between font names used inside TEX and external (Karl Berry) file names is controlled by the file psfonts.map. dvips searches this file to see whether fonts should be included in the document, or are resident in the printer. By simply editing this file it is, for instance, possible to use PostScript renderings of the Computer Modern family instead of the bitmap .pk images. The advantage is that your document can now be printed on any PostScript printer, independent from the resolution or the printing engine. Especially at higher resolutions, this reduces enormously the disk space needed for storing font images. The PostScript renderings of the Computer Modern fonts were produced by Blue Sky Research; Y&Y added the LATEX, AMS, and Euler fonts.

11.9.2 The PSNFSS System

The PSNFSS system, developed by Sebastian Rahtz, and based upon earlier work by Kresten Thorup and Timothy van Zandt, offers a set of files that provide a complete working setup of the NFSS2 for use with PostScript fonts. The PSNFSS system uses the Karl Berry naming scheme throughout.

In normal use you will probably only have to include one of the packages times, newcent, helvet, palatino, etc., to change the default text fonts for one or more of the roman, sans serif, and typewriter faces. Table 11.7 lists PostScript fonts that are used for each of these three categories.

In each case the font family chosen for the roman (the default font for the document text), sans serif, and typewriter fonts are shown, except for the packages helvet and avant, which only set the sans serif font to Helvetica and

AvantGarde, respectively. The packages in the upper part of the table only use fonts that are generally available in the ROM of the PostScript laser printers. The packages in the lower half of the table refer to fonts that you normally would have to buy (apart from Courier and cmtt). Note that the packages lucidbrb and lucidbry load the same Lucida-Bright font family, but the former uses the Karl Berry names for the font files, while the latter uses original names as defined in the distribution by Y&Y.

Note that math fonts will stay the same unless you have suitable fonts to load. If the Lucida Math fonts have been purchased, and appropriate metrics obtained, loading the lucmath package will remove all reference to cmr fonts in the document. Alternatively, you can purchase the Lucida Bright font set and use the lucidbrb (lucidbry) package. Another interesting package is pifont, which sets up various commands for use with the so called Pi fonts, i.e., special character fonts like ZapfDingbats or Symbols (see section 11.9.3).

11.9.3   Using the PostScript Pi Fonts

Fonts containing collections of special symbols, which you normally do not find in a text font, are called Pi fonts. One such font, the PostScript font ZapfDingbats, is available if you use the pifont package. It is part of the PSNFSS system.

The directly accessible characters of the PostScript ZapfDingbats font are shown in table 11.8 on the next page. A given character can be chosen via the \ding command. The parameter for the \ding command is an integer that specifies the character to be typeset according to the table. For example, \ding{38} gives ✆.

The dinglist environment is a special itemize list. The argument specifies the number of the character to be used as the beginning of each item.

> ➤   The first item in the list.

> ➤   The second item in the list.

> ➤   The third item in the list.

```
\begin{dinglist}{228}
\item The first item in the list.
\item The second item in the list.
\item The third item in the list.
\end{dinglist}
```

You can fill a complete line with a given character using the command \dingline, the argument once more indicating the desired character. For filling the remaining part of a line, use the command \dingfill.

✄ ✄ ✄ ✄ ✄ ✄ ✄ ✄ ✄ ✄ ✄ ✄

text text text text ➊ ➊ ➊ ➊ ➊ ➊ ➊ ➊ ➊

```
\dingline{35}
\par\medskip
text text text text \dingfill{253}
```

There also exists an environment dingautolist, which allows you to build

		32	33 ✁	34 ✂	35 ✃	36 ✄	37 ☎	38 ✆	39 ✇
40 ✈	41 ✉	42 ☛	43 ☞	44 ✌	45 ✍	46 ✎	47 ✏	48 ✐	49 ✑
50 ✒	51 ✓	52 ✔	53 ✕	54 ✖	55 ✗	56 ✘	57 ✚	58 ✚	59 ✛
60 ✜	61 ✝	62 ✞	63 ✟	64 ✠	65 ✡	66 ✢	67 ✣	68 ✤	69 ✥
70 ✦	71 ✧	72 ★	73 ✩	74 ✪	75 ✫	76 ✬	77 ✭	78 ✮	79 ✯
80 ✰	81 ✱	82 ✲	83 ✳	84 ✴	85 ✵	86 ✶	87 ✷	88 ✸	89 ✹
90 ✺	91 ✻	92 ✼	93 ✽	94 ✾	95 ✿	96 ❀	97 ❁	98 ❂	99 ❃
100 ❄	101 ❅	102 ❆	103 ❇	104 ❈	105 ❉	106 ❊	107 ❋	108 ●	109 ❍
110 ■	111 ❏	112 ❐	113 ❑	114 ❒	115 ▲	116 ▼	117 ◆	118 ❖	119 ◗
120 ❘	121 ❙	122 ❚	123 ❛	124 ❜	125 ❝	126 ❞			
	161 ❡	162 ❢	163 ❣	164 ❤	165 ❥	166 ❦	167 ❧	168 ♣	169 ♦
170 ♥	171 ♠	172 ①	173 ②	174 ③	175 ④	176 ⑤	177 ⑥	178 ⑦	179 ⑧
180 ⑨	181 ⑩	182 ❶	183 ❷	184 ❸	185 ❹	186 ❺	187 ❻	188 ❼	189 ❽
190 ❾	191 ❿	192 ➀	193 ➁	194 ➂	195 ➃	196 ➄	197 ➅	198 ➆	199 ➇
200 ➈	201 ➉	202 ➊	203 ➋	204 ➌	205 ➍	206 ➎	207 ➏	208 ➐	209 ➑
210 ➒	211 ➓	212 →	213 →	214 ↔	215 ↕	216 ➘	217 ➙	218 ➚	219 ➛
220 ➜	221 ➝	222 ➞	223 ➟	224 ➠	225 ➡	226 ➢	227 ➣	228 ➤	229 ➥
230 ➦	231 ➧	232 ➨	233 ➩	234 ➪	235 ➫	236 ➬	237 ➭	238 ➮	239 ➯
	241 ➱	242 ➲	243 ➳	244 ➴	245 ➵	246 ➶	247 ➷	248 ➸	249 ➹
250 ➺	251 ➻	252 ➼	253 ➽	254 ➾					

Table 11.8: The characters in the PostScript font ZapfDingbats

an enumerated list with a set of ZapfDingbats characters. In this case, the argument specifies the number of the first character in the list. Subsequent items will be numbered with the character following the previous one, as shown in table 11.8.

① The first item in the list.

② The second item in the list.

③ The third item in the list.

References to list items work ①, ②, ③

```
\begin{dingautolist}{192}
\item The first item in the list.
      \label{lst:zd1}
\item The second item in the list.
      \label{lst:zd2}
\item The third item in the list.
      \label{lst:zd3}
\end{dingautolist}
References to list items work
\ref{lst:zd1}, \ref{lst:zd2}, \ref{lst:zd3}
```

11.9.4   Generic Commands in the Style pifont

The pifont package has a general mechanism for coping with Pi fonts. It provides the following generic commands with, in each case, the first argument *fontname* specifying the (Karl Berry short) name of the Pi font in question (such as psy for the Symbol font, and pzd for the ZapfDingbats font; see table 11.6 on page 333).

> `\Pifont{`*fontname*`}`

This switches to the font *fontname*.

> `\Pisymbol{`*fontname*`}{`*numsym*`}`

The symbol at decimal position *numsym* is typeset in font *fontname* (compare this with the `\ding` command).

> `\Piline{`*fontname*`}{`*numsym*`}`

This typesets a full line consisting of several copies of the symbol at decimal position *numsym* in font *fontname* (compare with the `\dingline` command).

> `\Pifill{`*fontname*`}{`*numsym*`}`

The remaining part of a line is filled with several copies of the symbol at decimal position *numsym* in font *fontname* (compare with the `\dingfill` command).

> `\begin{Pilist}{`*fontname*`}{`*numsym*`}`

This defines an environment where the symbol at decimal position *numsym* in font *fontname* is used in front of each item in an itemized list (compare with the `dinglist` environment).

> `\begin{Piautolist}{`*fontname*`}{`*numsym*`}`

This defines an environment where a series of symbols starting with the symbol at decimal position *numsym* in font *fontname* is used to number the items in an enumerated list (compare this with the `dingautolist` environment).

11.9.5   The Symbol Font

Using the commands described in the previous section, it now becomes easy to access the characters in the Symbol font, shown in table 11.9 on the following page. For example, `\Pisymbol{psy}{224}` gives ◊.

							32		33	!	34	∀	35	#	36	∃	37	%	38	&	39	϶
40	(	41	)	42	*	43	+	44	,	45	−	46	.	47	/	48	0	49	1
50	2	51	3	52	4	53	5	54	6	55	7	56	8	57	9	58	:	59	;
60	<	61	=	62	>	63	?	64	≅	65	A	66	B	67	X	68	Δ	69	E
70	Φ	71	Γ	72	H	73	I	74	ϑ	75	K	76	Λ	77	M	78	N	79	O
80	Π	81	Θ	82	P	83	Σ	84	T	85	Y	86	ς	87	Ω	88	Ξ	89	Ψ
90	Z	91	[	92	∴	93	]	94	⊥	95	_	96		97	α	98	β	99	χ
100	δ	101	ε	102	φ	103	γ	104	η	105	ι	106	φ	107	κ	108	λ	109	μ
110	ν	111	o	112	π	113	θ	114	ρ	115	σ	116	τ	117	υ	118	ϖ	119	ω
120	ξ	121	ψ	122	ζ	123	{	124	|	125	}	126	~						
		161	ϒ	162	′	163	≤	164	/	165	∞	166	ƒ	167	♣	168	♦	169	♥
170	♠	171	↔	172	←	173	↑	174	→	175	↓	176	°	177	±	178	″	179	≥
180	×	181	∝	182	∂	183	•	184	÷	185	≠	186	≡	187	≈	188	…	189	|
190	—	191	↵	192	ℵ	193	ℑ	194	ℜ	195	℘	196	⊗	197	⊕	198	∅	199	∩
200	∪	201	⊃	202	⊇	203	⊄	204	⊂	205	⊆	206	∈	207	∉	208	∠	209	∇
210	®	211	©	212	™	213	∏	214	√	215	·	216	¬	217	∧	218	∨	219	⇔
220	⇐	221	⇑	222	⇒	223	⇓	224	◊	225	⟨	226	®	227	©	228	™	229	Σ
230	⌈	231	|	232	⌊	233	⌈	234	|	235	⌊	236	⌈	237	{	238	⌊	239	|
		241	⟩	242	∫	243	⌠	244	|	245	⌡	246	⌡	247	|	248	⌡	249	⌉
250	|	251	⌡	252	⌡	253	}	254	⌡										

Table 11.9: The characters in the PostScript font Symbol

a	α	b	β	c	χ	d	δ	e	ε	f	φ	g	γ	h	η	i	ι	j	φ	k	κ	l	λ	m	μ
n	ν	o	o	p	π	q	θ	r	ρ	s	σ	t	τ	u	υ	v	ϖ	w	ω	x	ξ	y	ψ	z	ζ
A	Α	B	Β	C	Χ	D	Δ	E	Ε	F	Φ	G	Γ	H	H	I	I	J	ϑ	K	K	L	Λ	M	M
N	N	O	O	P	Π	Q	Θ	R	P	S	Σ	T	T	U	Y	V	ς	W	Ω	X	Ξ	Y	Ψ	Z	Z

Table 11.10: Accessing the Greek characters in the PostScript font Symbol

When only Greek letters are desired, you can use the \Pifont command and consult the correspondence in table 11.10, for example,

ΑΛϑΑ   ωμεγα   αλφα.

```
{\Pifont{psy} ALJA\quad wmega\quad alja}.
```

You can also make a list with characters in the Symbol font, as follows:

⇒ The first item in the list.

⇒ The second item in the list.

```
\begin{Pilist}{psy}{222}
   \item The first item in the list.
   \item The second item in the list.
\end{Pilist}
```

11.9.6 Setting Up New PostScript Fonts Yourself

If you want to set up new (PostScript) fonts and create the necessary `.fd` files, you should follow the procedure explained in section 7.7. Suitable models for a large multifont installation can be found in `psfonts.fdd` (covering both old TEX encoding and EC encoding), but an `.fd` file for a single font is easy to write by hand, once you know which font encoding it uses. As an example, we shall look at the declaration file `OT1ppl.fd` for old-style TEX-encoding Palatino (OT1):

```
% Primary declarations
\DeclareFontFamily{OT1}{ppl}{}
\DeclareFontShape{OT1}{ppl}{m}{n}{<->pplr}{}
\DeclareFontShape{OT1}{ppl}{m}{it}{<->pplri}{}
\DeclareFontShape{OT1}{ppl}{b}{n}{<->pplb}{}
\DeclareFontShape{OT1}{ppl}{b}{it}{<->pplbi}{}
\DeclareFontShape{OT1}{ppl}{m}{sc}{<->pplrc}{}
\DeclareFontShape{OT1}{ppl}{m}{sl}{<->pplro}{}
% Substitutions
\DeclareFontShape{OT1}{ppl}{b}{sc}{<->sub * ppl/m/sc}{}
\DeclareFontShape{OT1}{ppl}{b}{sl}{<->sub * ppl/b/it}{}
\DeclareFontShape{OT1}{ppl}{bx}{n}{<->sub * ppl/b/n}{}
\DeclareFontShape{OT1}{ppl}{bx}{it}{<->sub * ppl/b/it}{}
\DeclareFontShape{OT1}{ppl}{bx}{sc}{<->sub * ppl/m/sc}{}
\DeclareFontShape{OT1}{ppl}{bx}{sl}{<->sub * ppl/m/sl}{}
\endinput
```

Once we declare the font family and encoding, each combination of series and style is mapped to the name of a `.tfm` file. In the case of PostScript, we do not have to worry about what sizes are available, because these fonts can be scaled to any size (hence the `<->` declarations on the `\DeclareFontShape` commands). The second part of the file sets up some substitutions for situations where there might be no font available (bold small caps, bold slanted, or bold-extended series).

If you want to create your own package that can be used in the same way as the ones provided with PSNFSS, then you should simply use the standard NFSS2 constructs. Below we show the relevant part of the file times. After declaring the sans serif (Helvetica, phv), roman (Times-Roman, ptm) and teletype (Courier, pcr) fonts we make "b" the default for bold rather than "bx."

```
% File times.sty
\renewcommand{\sfdefault}{phv}% declare sans-serif font
\renewcommand{\rmdefault}{ptm}% declare roman font
\renewcommand{\ttdefault}{pcr}% declare teletype font
\renewcommand{\bfdefault}{b}  % use bold ``b''
\endinput
```

11.9.7   Replacing All TEX Fonts with PostScript Fonts

With the help of the PSNFSS system it becomes easy to replace all TEX fonts in a document with PostScript fonts.

You can, of course, first replace the .pk versions of the Computer Modern family with their commercial type 1 equivalents, which is trivial by merely editing dvips's control file psfonts.map. In this case, your output will be printable on all PostScript devices, without loss of quality.

Another possibility is to use a font like Times-Roman for your text (using, for example, the times package). Many people still keep the Computer Modern math family, but their documents look unbalanced, since the various typographic characteristics of Times-Roman, cmsy, and cmmi are quite different (cm fonts look too light and their x-height is also different). To obtain better visual results you can try the *mathtime* font package of Michael Spivak [82]. This family of type 1 PostScript fonts have been designed specifically to typeset mathematics that blend with Times-Roman. Alan Jeffrey has developed the pstimesm package, which together with some macros by Spivak himself replace the cm math fonts with *mathtime*'s.

Another solution is to completely replace all TEX fonts with the LucidaBright and LucidaNewMath fonts, available from Y&Y [93]. These fonts were designed by Charles Bigelow and Chris Holmes and the package consists of 22 type 1 fonts with over 4,000 different characters. It includes all of the symbols needed by both LATEX and $\mathcal{A}_{\mathcal{M}}\mathcal{S}$-TEX (see tables 8.2 to 8.20 beginning on page 218), a lot of extra fonts, like a Calligraphic and Blackletter font, plus of course TEX characters. The lucidbrb (or lucidbry) package provides all the definitions for typesetting your complete document with this font family.

Figures 11.9 to 11.11 starting on page 342 show the same text typeset in the three setups described above.

11.10   DCPS—The Cork Encoding with PostScript Fonts

The Adobe PostScript fonts do not always contain all the characters that are needed to print documents in all Latin languages. In particular, most fonts lack some of the characters of the Cork scheme (table 9.1 on page 261).

The native Adobe character encoding is also different from the one used in the Cork scheme. As an example, consider the layout for the PostScript font Helvetica (shown in table 11.11). You can see that most accented characters, such as à or ü are absent since they are not encoded in the standard Adobe encoding vector [2, page 598].

To suit the Cork layout you must reencode the PostScript fonts. This is most easily done via virtual fonts. The recent versions of afm2tfm and dvips provide reencoding facilities so you can rearrange directly all accessible characters into their positions for the extended layout. The result is shown in table 11.12.

	00	10	20	30	40	50	60	70	80	90	A0	B0	C0	D0	E0	F0
0				0	@	P	`	p							—	
1			!	1	A	Q	a	q			¡	–	`		Æ	æ
2			"	2	B	R	b	r			¢	†	´			
3			#	3	C	S	c	s			£	‡	^		ª	
4			$	4	D	T	d	t			/	·	~			
5			%	5	E	U	e	u			¥		¯			ı
6			&	6	F	V	f	v			ƒ	¶	˘			
7			'	7	G	W	g	w			§	•	˙			
8			(	8	H	X	h	x			¤	‚	¨		Ł	ł
9			)	9	I	Y	i	y			'	„			Ø	ø
A			*	:	J	Z	j	z			"	"	°		Œ	œ
B			+	;	K	[	k	{			«	»	¸		º	ß
C			,	<	L	\	l					‹	…				
D			-	=	M	]	m	}			›	‰	˝			
E			.	>	N	^	n	~			fi		˛			
F			/	?	O	_	o				fl	¿	ˇ			

Table 11.11: Original Adobe font layout for the Helvetica font

	00	10	20	30	40	50	60	70	80	90	A0	B0	C0	D0	E0	F0
0	`	"	␣	0	@	P	`	p	Ă	Ř	ă	ř	À	Đ	à	ð
1	´	"	!	1	A	Q	a	q	Ą	Ś	ą	ś	Á	Ñ	á	ñ
2	ˆ	„	"	2	B	R	b	r	Ć	Š	ć	š	Â	Ò	â	ò
3	˜	«	#	3	C	S	c	s	Č	Ş	č	ş	Ã	Ó	ã	ó
4	¨	»	$	4	D	T	d	t	Ď	Ť	ď	ť	Ä	Ô	ä	ô
5	˝	–	%	5	E	U	e	u	Ě	Ţ	ě	ţ	Å	Õ	å	õ
6	˚	—	&	6	F	V	f	v	Ę	Ű	ę	ű	Æ	Ö	æ	ö
7	ˇ		'	7	G	W	g	w	Ğ	Ů	ğ	ů	Ç	Œ	ç	œ
8	˘	‰	(	8	H	X	h	x	Ĺ	Ÿ	ĺ	ÿ	È	Ø	è	ø
9	¯	¦	)	9	I	Y	i	y	Ľ	Ź	ľ	ź	É	Ù	é	ù
A	˙	ȷ	*	:	J	Z	j	z	Ł	Ž	ł	ž	Ê	Ú	ê	ú
B	˛		+	;	K	[	k	{	Ń	Ż	ń	ż	Ë	Û	ë	û
C	¸	fi	,	<	L	\	l			Ň	IJ	ň	ij	Ì	Ü	ì	ü
D	,	fl	-	=	M	]	m	}	Ŋ	İ	ŋ	ı	Í	Ý	í	ý
E	‹		.	>	N	^	n	~	Ő	đ	ő	¿	Î	Þ	î	þ
F	›		/	?	O	_	o	-	Ŕ	§	ŕ	£	Ï	SS	ï	ß

Table 11.12: DC TEX font layout with Helvetica

1   Multiple integral signs

\iiint, and \iiiint give triple and quadruple multiple signs with the intermediate spacing nicely adjusted, in text style, for example, $\iiint_A f(x,y,z)\,dx\,dy\,dz$
and $\iiiint_A f(w,x,y,z)\,dw\,dx\,dy\,dz$, as well as in display style.

$$(1) \qquad \iiint_A f(x,y,z)\,dx\,dy\,dz$$

$$(2) \qquad \iiiint_A f(w,x,y,z)\,dw\,dx\,dy\,dz$$

2   Binomial expressions

For binomial expressions such as $\binom{n}{k}$ you have the commands \binom, \dbinom,
and \tbinom. \binom is an abbreviation for \fracwithdelims(){Opt}.

$$(3) \qquad \sum_{\gamma \in \Gamma_C} I_\gamma = 2^k - \binom{k}{1} 2^{k-1} + \binom{k}{2} 2^{k-2}$$

$$+ \cdots + (-1)^l \binom{k}{l} 2^{k-l} + \cdots + (-1)^k$$

$$= (2-1)^k = 1$$

3   Split equations

The split environment provides no numbering because it is intended to be
used only inside some other displayed equation structure, such as equation,
align, or gather. These outer environments will provide the numbering.

$$(4) \qquad (a+b)^4 = (a+b)^2(a+b)^2$$

$$= (a^2 + 2ab + b^2)(a^2 + 2ab + b^2)$$

$$= a^4 + 4a^3b + 6a^2b^2 + 4ab^3 + b^4$$

Figure 11.9: Example of a page typeset with the Computer Modern fonts

1 Multiple integral signs

\iiint, and \iiiint give triple and quadruple multiple signs with the intermediate spacing nicely adjusted, in text style, for example, $\iiint_A f(x, y, z)\, dx\, dy\, dz$
and $\iiiint_A f(w, x, y, z)\, dw\, dx\, dy\, dz$, as well as in display style.

$$
(1) \qquad \iiint_A f(x, y, z)\, dx\, dy\, dz
$$

$$
(2) \qquad \iiiint_A f(w, x, y, z)\, dw\, dx\, dy\, dz
$$

2 Binomial expressions

For binomial expressions such as $\binom{n}{k}$ you have the commands \binom, \dbinom,
and \tbinom. \binom is an abbreviation for \fracwithdelims()[0pt].

$$
(3) \qquad \sum_{\gamma \in \Gamma_C} I_\gamma = 2^k - \binom{k}{1} 2^{k-1} + \binom{k}{2} 2^{k-2}
$$

$$
+ \cdots + (-1)^l \binom{k}{l} 2^{k-l} + \cdots + (-1)^k
$$

$$
= (2 - 1)^k = 1
$$

3 Split equations

The split environment provides no numbering because it is intended to be
used only inside some other displayed equation structure, such as equation,
align, or gather. These outer environments will provide the numbering.

$$
(4) \qquad (a + b)^4 = (a + b)^2 (a + b)^2
$$

$$
= (a^2 + 2ab + b^2)(a^2 + 2ab + b^2)
$$

$$
= a^4 + 4a^3 b + 6a^2 b^2 + 4ab^3 + b^4
$$

Figure 11.10: Example of a page typeset with the Mathtime fonts

1 Multiple integral signs

`\iiint`, and `\iiiint` give triple and quadruple multiple signs with the intermediate spacing nicely adjusted, in text style, for example, $\iiint_A f(x, y, z)\,dx\,dy\,dz$ and $\iiiint_A f(w, x, y, z)\,dw\,dx\,dy\,dz$, as well as in display style.

$$(1) \qquad \iiint_A f(x, y, z)\,dx\,dy\,dz$$

$$(2) \qquad \iiiint_A f(w, x, y, z)\,dw\,dx\,dy\,dz$$

2 Binomial expressions

For binomial expressions such as $\binom{n}{k}$ you have the commands `\binom`, `\dbinom`, and `\tbinom`. `\binom` is an abbreviation for `\fracwithdelims(){0pt}`.

$$(3) \qquad \sum_{y \in \Gamma_C} I_y = 2^k - \binom{k}{1} 2^{k-1} + \binom{k}{2} 2^{k-2}$$
$$+ \cdots + (-1)^l \binom{k}{l} 2^{k-l} + \cdots + (-1)^k$$
$$= (2 - 1)^k = 1$$

3 Split equations

The `split` environment provides no numbering because it is intended to be used only inside some other displayed equation structure, such as `equation`, `align`, or `gather`. These outer environments will provide the numbering.

$$(4) \qquad (a + b)^4 = (a + b)^2 (a + b)^2$$
$$= (a^2 + 2ab + b^2)(a^2 + 2ab + b^2)$$
$$= a^4 + 4a^3 b + 6a^2 b^2 + 4ab^3 + b^4$$

Figure 11.11: Example of a page typeset with the Lucida Math fonts

CHAPTER 12

Index Generation

To find a topic of interest in a large document, book, or reference work, you usually turn to the table of contents or, more often, to the index. Therefore, an index is a very important part of a document, and most users' entry point to a source of information is precisely through a pointer in the index. You should, therefore, plan an index and develop it along with the main text. For reasons of consistency, it is useful, with the technique discussed below, to use special commands in the text to always print a given keyword in the same way in the text and the index throughout the whole document.

This chapter first reviews the basic indexing commands, and explains which tools are available to help you build a well-thought-out index. The LaTeX book itself does not contain a lot of information about the syntax of the \index entries. There are, however, several articles in *TUGboat* that deal with the question of generating an index with TeX or LaTeX [7, 8, 20, 29, 83, 84, 94]. The syntax described in section 12.1 is the one recognized by *MakeIndex* [16, 50], the most generally used index preparation program. Its user interface is described in sections 12.2 and 12.3.

(*£ 77–79*)

Section 12.4 discusses the various steps of preparing an index for typesetting, presenting in some detail the formats for the input and output files read and written by *MakeIndex*. The interpretation of the input file and the format of the output file are controlled by style parameters. These parameters are described and several simple examples are given to show how changing them influences the typeset result.

The final section is devoted to the subject of multiple indexes, which will be discussed with the help of an example.

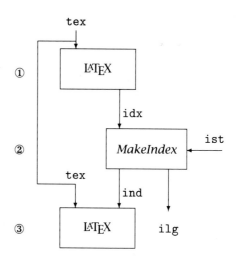

① A raw index (.idx file) is generated by running LaTeX.

② The raw index, together with some optional style information (.ist file), is used as input to the index processor, *MakeIndex*, which creates an alphabetized index (.ind file) and a transcript (.ilg file).

③ The index (.ind file) is read by LaTeX to give the final typeset result.

Figure 12.1: The sequential flow of index processing and the various auxiliary files used by LaTeX and *MakeIndex*.

The process of generating an index is schematically shown in figure 12.1. The steps for generating an index with LaTeX and *MakeIndex* are illustrated in this figure. Figure 12.2 on the next page shows, with an example, the various steps of transforming an input file into a typeset index. It also shows, in somewhat more detail, which files are involved in the index generating process. Figure 12.2(a) shows some occurrences of index commands (\index) in the document source, with corresponding pages listed on the left. Figure 12.2(b) shows a raw index .idx file generated by LaTeX. After running through the index processor *MakeIndex*, it becomes an alphabetized index .ind file with LaTeX commands specifying a particular output format (figure 12.2(c)). The typeset result after formatting with LaTeX is shown in figure 12.2(d).

LaTeX and *MakeIndex*, together, use a certain number of markup conventions to help you control the precise format of the output. In section 12.1, which describes the format of the \index command, we always use the default settings for the special characters (as described in tables 12.1 on page 358 and 12.2 on page 359) defining the interface. Section 12.4.1 will show how you can customize these characters and the generated output to suit your particular needs.

12.1 Syntax of the Index Entries

This section describes the default syntax used to generate index entries with LaTeX and *MakeIndex*. Different levels of complexity are introduced progressively, showing, for each case, the input file and the generated typeset output.

Page vi:	`\index{animal}`
Page 5:	`\index{animal}`
Page 6:	`\index{animal}`
Page 7:	`\index{animal}`
Page 11:	`\index{animalism|see{animal}}`
Page 17:	`\index{animal@\emph{animal}}`
	`\index{mammal|textbf}`
Page 26:	`\index{animal!mammal!cat}`
Page 32:	`\index{animal!insect}`

```
\indexentry{animal}{vi}
\indexentry{animal}{5}
\indexentry{animal}{6}
\indexentry{animal}{7}
\indexentry{animalism|see{animal}}{11}
\indexentry{animal@\emph{animal}}{17}
\indexentry{mammal|textbf}{17}
\indexentry{animal!mammal!cat}{26}
\indexentry{animal!insect}{32}
```

(a) The input file   (b) The `.idx` file

```
\begin{theindex}
  \item animal, vi, 5-7
    \subitem insect, 32
    \subitem mammal
      \subsubitem cat, 26
  \item \emph{animal}, 17
  \item animalism, \see{animal}{11}
  \indexspace
  \item mammal, \textbf{17}
\end{theindex}
```

animal, vi, 5-7
   insect, 32
   mammal
      cat, 26
animal, 17
animalism, *see* animal

mammal, **17**

(c) The `.ind` file   (d) The typeset output

Figure 12.2: Stepwise development of index processing

12.1.1   Simple Index Entries

Each `\index` command causes LATEX to write an entry in the `.idx` file. The following example shows some simple `\index` commands, together with the index entries that they produce. The page number refers to the page containing the text where the `\index` command appears. As shown in the example below, duplicate commands on the same page (such as `\index{stylistic}` on page 23) produce only one "23" in the index.

style, 14	Page iii:	`\index{style}`
style , 16	Page xi:	`\index{Stylist}`
style, iii, 12	Page 12:	`\index{style}`
style , 15		`\index{styles}`
style file, 34	Page 14:	`\index{ style}`
styles, 12	Page 15:	`\index{style }`
Stylist, xi	Page 16:	`\index{ style }`
stylist, 34	Page 23:	`\index{stylistic}`
stylistic, 23		`\index{stylistic}`
	Page 34:	`\index{style file}`
		`\index{stylist}`

We draw your particular attention to the way spaces are handled. Spaces inside \index commands are written literally to the output .idx file and, by default, they are treated as ordinary characters by *MakeIndex*, which places them in front of all letters. In the example above, look at the `style` entries on pages 14 and 16. The leading spaces are placed at the beginning of the index and on two different lines because the trailing blank on page 16 lengthens the string by one character. We end up with four different entries for the same term, an effect which was probably not desired. It is therefore important to eliminate such spurious spaces from the \index commands. Alternatively, you can specify the -c option when running the *MakeIndex* program. This option suppresses the effect of leading and trailing blanks (see section 12.3). Another often occurring error is that the same word is spelled inconsistently with an initial lowercase and uppercase letter (as with `Stylist` on page xi). Unless this is a design feature, such spurious double entries should be eliminated.

12.1.2   Generating Subentries

Up to three levels of index entries (main, sub, and subsub entries) are available with LATEX-*MakeIndex*. To produce such entries, the argument of the \index command should contain both the main and subentries, separated by a ! character. This character can be redefined in the *MakeIndex* style file (see table 12.1 on page 358).

box, 21
    dimensions of, 33
    parameters, 5
dimensions
    figure, 12
    rule
      height, 12
      width, 3
    table, 9

Page 3:   \index{dimensions!rule!width}
Page 5:   \index{box!parameters}
Page 9 :   \index{dimensions!table}
Page 12:   \index{dimensions!rule!height}
            \index{dimensions!figure}
Page 21:   \index{box}
Page 33:   \index{box!dimensions of}

12.1.3   Page Ranges and Cross-References

You can specify a page range by putting the command \index{...|(} at the beginning of the range and \index{...|)} at the end of the range. Page ranges should span a homogeneous numbering scheme (e.g., roman and arabic page numbers cannot fall within the same range). Note that *MakeIndex* does the right thing when both ends of a page range fall on the same page, or when an entry falls inside an active range.

You can also generate cross-reference index entries without page numbers by using the `see` encapsulator. Since the "see" entry does not print any page number, the commands \index{...|see{...}} can be placed anywhere in the input file after the \begin{document} command. For practical reasons, it is convenient to group all such cross-referencing commands in one place.

fonts	Page ii:	\index{table|(}
Computer Modern, 13–25	Page xi:	\index{table|)}
math, *see* math, fonts	Page 5:	\index{fonts!PostScript|(}
PostScript, 5		\index{fonts!PostScript|)}
table, ii–xi, 14	Page 13:	\index{fonts!Computer Modern|(}
	Page 14:	\index{table}
	Page 17:	\index{fonts!math|see{math, fonts}}
	Page 21:	\index{fonts!Computer Modern}
	Page 25:	\index{fonts!Computer Modern|)}

12.1.4   Controlling the Presentation Form

Sometimes you may want to sort an entry according to a key, while using a different visual representation for the typesetting, such as Greek letters, mathematical symbols, or specific typographic forms. This function is available with the syntax: *key@visual*, where *key* determines the alphabetical position and the string *visual* produces the typeset text of the entry.

delta, 14	Page 5:	\index{ninety-five}
δ, 23	Page 14:	\index{delta}
delta wing, 16	Page 16:	\index{delta wing}
flower, 19	Page 19:	\index{flower@\textbf{flower}}
ninety, 26	Page 23:	\index{delta@δ}
xc, 28		\index{tabular@\texttt{tabular} environment}
ninety-five, 5	Page 26:	\index{ninety}
`tabular` environment, 23	Page 28:	\index{ninety@xc}

For some indexes, certain page numbers should be formatted specially, with an italic page number (for example) indicating a primary reference, and an *n* after a page number denoting that the item appears in a footnote on that page. *MakeIndex* allows you to format an individual page number in any way you want by using the encapsulator syntax specified by the | character. What follows the | sign will "encapsulate" or enclose the page number associated with the index entry. For instance, the command \index{keyword|xxx} will produce a page number of the form \xxx{*n*}, where *n* is the page number in question. Similarly, the command \index{keyword|(xxx} will generate a page range of the form \xxx{*n-m*}.

Preexisting commands (like \textit in the example below) or user commands can be used to encapsulate the page numbers. As an example, a document containing the command definition:

```
\newcommand{\nn}[1]{#1n}
```

would yield something like:

tabular, **ii**, *21*, 22n	Page ii:	`\index{tabular|textbf}`
tabbing, *7*, *34-37*	Page 7:	`\index{tabbing}`
	Page 21:	`\index{tabular|textit}`
	Page 22	`\index{tabular|nn}`
	Page 34:	`\index{tabbing|(textit}`
	Page 37:	`\index{tabbing|)}`

The `see` encapsulator is a special case of this facility, where the `\see` command is predefined by the `makeidx` package.

12.1.5   Printing Those Special Characters

To typeset one of the characters having a special meaning to *MakeIndex* (!, ", @, or |)[1] in the index, precede it with a " character. More precisely, any character is said to be quoted if it follows an unquoted " that is not part of a \" command. The latter case is for allowing umlaut characters. Quoted !, @, ", or | characters are treated like ordinary characters, losing their special meaning. The " preceding a quoted character is deleted before the entries are alphabetized.

@ sign, 2		`\index{bar@\texttt{"|}|see{vertical bar}}`
|, *see* vertical bar	Page 1:	`\index{quote (\verb+""+)}`
exclamation (!), 4		`\index{quote@\texttt{""} sign}`
Ah!, 5	Page 2:	`\index{atsign@\texttt{"@} sign}`
Mädchen, 3	Page 3:	`\index{maedchen@M\"{a}dchen}`
quote ("), 1	Page 4:	`\index{exclamation ("!)}`
" sign, 1	Page 5:	`\index{exclamation ("!)!Ah"!}`

12.1.6   Points to Note

When an `\index` command is used directly in the text, its argument is only expanded when the index is typeset, not when the `.idx` file is written. However, when the `\index` command is contained in the argument of another command, characters with a special meaning to TeX, like \, must be properly protected against expansion. This is likely to be a problem when indexing items in a footnote, or in commands that put their argument in the text and enter it at the same time in the index (see the discussion in the next section). Even in this case, robust commands can be placed in the "@" part of an entry, as in `\index{rose@{\it rose}}`, but fragile commands must be protected with the `\protect` command.

If the index text contains commands, as in `\index{\Prog}`, it is likely that the entry is wrongly sorted since in main text this entry is sorted under the sort

---

[1] As noted earlier, other characters can be substituted for the default ones to carry a special meaning. This is explained on page 360.

key \Prog (with the special character \ as the starting sort character) regardless of the definition of the \Prog program. On the other hand, if used in some argument of another command, \Prog will expand before it is written to the .idx file and the placement in the index will then depend on the expansion of \Prog.

As with every argument of a command you need to have a matching number of braces. However, due to the feature of \index allowing special characters like % or \ in its argument if used in main text, the brace matching has an anomaly: braces in the commands \{ or \} take part in the matching. Thus you cannot write \index{\{} or something similar.

For sorting, *MakeIndex* assumes that pages numbered with roman numerals precede those numbered with arabic numerals, which in turn precede alphabetic page numbers. This precedence order can be changed (see the entry page_precedence in table 12.2 on page 359).

MakeIndex will place symbols (i.e., patterns starting with a nonalphanumeric character) before numbers, and before alphabetic entries in the output. Symbols are sorted according to their ASCII value. For word sorting, uppercase and lowercase are considered the same, but for identical words, the uppercase variant will precede the lowercase one. Numbers are sorted in numeric order. Spaces are treated as ordinary characters when alphabetizing the entries and for deciding whether two entries are the same (see also the example on page 348). Thus if "␣" denotes a space character, then the commands \index{cat}, \index{␣cat}, and \index{cat␣} produce three separate entries. All three entries look similar when printed. Similarly, \index{a␣space} and \index{a␣␣space} produce two different entries that look the same on output. It is thus important to check for such spurious spaces by being careful when splitting the argument of an \index command across lines in the input file.

The showidx package (by Leslie Lamport) can help you improve the entries in the index and locate possible problems. It shows all \index commands in the margin of the printed page. Figures 12.3 and 12.4 on page 354 show the input and generated output of a small LaTeX document, where various simple possibilities of the \index command are shown, together with the result of including the showidx package. To make the index entries consistent (see the next section), the commands \Com and \Prog were defined and used. The index generating environment theindex has been redefined to get the output on one page (see section 12.5 to see how this can be done).

12.1.7 Consistency and Index Entries

As it was pointed out in the introduction, it is very important to use the same visual representation for identical names or commands throughout a complete document, including the index. You therefore can define user commands, which always introduce similar constructs in the same way into the text and the index.

For example, you can define the command \Index, whose argument enters its argument at the same time in the text and in the index.

```
\newcommand{\Index}[1]{#1\index{#1}}
```

As explained at the beginning of the previous section, you must be careful that the argument of such a command does not contain expandable material (typically control sequences) or spurious blanks. In general for simple terms, like single words, there is no problem and this technique can be used. You can even go one step further and give a certain visual representation to the entry, for instance, typesetting in a typewriter font.

```
\newcommand{\Indextt}[1]{\texttt{#1}\index{#1@\texttt{#1}}}
```

Finally, you can group certain terms by defining commands that have a generic meaning. For instance, LaTeX commands and program names could be treated with special commands, like:

```
\newcommand{\bs}{\symbol{'134}}% print backslash
\newcommand{\Com}[1]{\texttt{\bs#1}\index{#1@\texttt{\bs#1}}}
\newcommand{\Prog}[1]{\texttt{#1}\index{#1@\texttt{#1} program}}
```

The \Com command adds a backslash to the command's name in both text and index, thus easing the work of the typist. At the same time, commands will be ordered in the index by their name, ignoring the \. The \Prog command, similarly, does not include the \texttt command in the alphabetization process, since entries like \index{\texttt{key}} and \index{key} would result in different entries in the index.

12.2 Preparing the Index

12.2.1 Generating the Raw Index

After having introduced the necessary \index commands in the document, as described in the previous section, we now want to generate the index to be included back into the LaTeX document on a subsequent run.

Therefore, if the main file of a document is main.tex, then the following changes should be made to that file:

- Include the makeidx package with an \usepackage command.

(£ 78)

- Put a \makeindex command in the document preamble.

- Put a \printindex command where the index is to appear—usually at the end, right before the \end{document} command.

You then run LATEX on the entire document, causing it to generate the file main.idx, which we shall call the .idx file.

12.2.2   Generating the Formatted Index

To generate the formatted index, you should run the *MakeIndex* program by typing the following command (main is the name of the input file):

```
makeindex main.idx
```

This produces the file main.ind, which will be called the .ind file. If *MakeIndex* generated no error messages, you can now rerun LATEX on the document and the index will appear. (You can remove the \makeindex command if you do not want to regenerate the index.) See page 356 if there are error messages.

By reading the index, you may discover additional mistakes. These should be corrected by changing the appropriate \index commands in the document and regenerating the .ind file.

An example of running *MakeIndex* is shown below, where the .idx file, main.idx, is generated by a first LATEX run on the input shown in figure 12.3 on the next page. You can clearly see that two files are written, namely the ordered .ind index file for use with LATEX main.ind and the index .ilg log file, main.ilg, which (in this case) will contain the same text as the output on the terminal. If errors are encountered then the latter file will contain the line number and error message for each error in the input stream. Figure 12.4 on the following page shows the result of the subsequent LATEX run.

```
> makeindex main
This is makeindex, portable version 2.12 [26-May-1993].
Scanning input file main.idx....done (8 entries accepted, 0 rejected).
Sorting entries....done (24 comparisons).
Generating output file main.ind....done (19 lines written, 0 warnings).
Output written in main.ind.
Transcript written in main.ilg.
```

12.3   Running the *MakeIndex* Program

In the previous section we showed examples where we ran the *MakeIndex* program using its default settings. In this section we shall first take a closer look at the *MakeIndex* program, and then discuss ways of changing its behavior.

```
\documentclass{article}
\usepackage{makeidx,showidx}
\newcommand{\bs}{\symbol{'134}}% print backslash
\newcommand{\Com}[1]{\texttt{\bs#1}%
          \index{#1@\texttt{\bs#1}}}
\newcommand{\Prog}[1]{\texttt{#1}%
          \index{#1@\texttt{#1} program}}
\begin{document}
\section{Generating an Index}
Using the \textsf{showidx} package users can
see where they define index entries.
\par Entries are entered into the index by the
\Com{index} command. More precisely, the argument
of the \Com{index} command is written literally into
the auxiliary file \texttt{idx}. Note, however, that
information is actually only written into that file
when the \Com{makeindex} command was given in the
document preamble.

\section{Preparing the Index}
In order to prepare the index for printing, the
\texttt{idx} file has to be transformed by an
external program, like \Prog{makeindex}.
This program writes the \texttt{ind} file.
\begin{verbatimcmd}
makeindex filename
\end{verbatimcmd}

\section{Printing the Index}
\index{Final production run}
During the final production run of a document the
index can be included by putting a \Com{printindex}
command at the position in the text where you want
the index to appear (normally at the end).
This command will input the \texttt{ind} file
prepared by \Prog{makeindex} and \LaTeX{} will
typeset the information.
\printindex
\end{document}
```

Figure 12.3: Example of \index commands and the showidx package. This file is run through LaTeX once, then the *MakeIndex* program is executed and LaTeX is run a second time.

---

1 Generating an Index

Using the showidx package users can see where they define index entries.

Entries are entered into the index by the \index command. More precisely, the argument of the \index command is written literally into the auxiliary file idx. Note, however, that information is actually only written into that file when the \makeindex command was given in the document preamble.

2 Preparing the Index

In order to prepare the index for printing, the idx file has to be transformed by an external program, like makeindex. This program writes the ind file.

```
makeindex filename
```

3 Printing the Index

During the final production run of a document the index can be included by putting a \printindex command at the position in the text where you want the index to appear (normally at the end). This command will input the ind file prepared by makeindex and LaTeX will typeset the information.

Index Entries

Final production run, 1

include index, 1

\index, 1

\makeindex, 1
makeindex program,
    1

\printindex, 1

(margin entries)
index@\index
index@\index
makeindex@\makeindex program
include index
Final production run
printindex@\printindex
makeindex@\makeindex program

Figure 12.4: This figure shows the index generated by the example input of figure 12.3. All index entries are shown in the margin, so that it is easy to check for errors or duplications.

12.3.1 Detailed Options of the *MakeIndex* Program

The syntax of the options of the *MakeIndex* program are described below:

```
makeindex [-ciglqr] [-o ind] [-p no] [-s sty] [-t log] [idx0 idx1 ...]
```

-c   This will enable blank compression. By default, every blank counts in the index key. The -c option ignores leading and trailing blanks and tabs and compresses intermediate ones to a single space.

-i   Use standard input (stdin) as the input file. When this option is specified and -o is not, output is written to standard output (stdout, the default output stream).

-g   Employ German word ordering in the index, following the rules given in German standard DIN 5007. In this case the normal precedence rule of *MakeIndex* for word ordering (symbols, numbers, uppercase letters, lowercase letters) is replaced by the German word ordering (symbols, lowercase letters, uppercase letters, numbers). Additionally, this option enables *MakeIndex* to recognize the German TEX commands "a, "o, "u and "s (see section 9.2.2), as ae, oe, ue and ss for sorting purposes. The quote character must be redefined in a style file (see page 360); otherwise you will get an error message and *MakeIndex* will abort. Note that not all versions of *MakeIndex* recognize this option.

-l   Use letter ordering. Default is word ordering. In word ordering, a space comes before any letter in the alphabet. In letter ordering, spaces are ignored. For example, the index terms "point in space" and "pointing" will be alphabetized differently in letter and word ordering.

-q   This is quiet mode. No messages are sent to the error output stream (stderr). By default, progress and error messages are sent to stderr as well as the transcript file. The -q option disables the stderr messages.

-r   This option disables implicit page range formation. By default, three or more successive pages are automatically abbreviated as a range (e.g., 1-5). The -r option disables it, making explicit range operators the only way to create page ranges.

-o ind   Take .ind as the output index file. By default, the file name base of the first input file idx0 concatenated with the extension .ind is used as the output file name.

-p no   Set the starting page number of the output index file to be no. This is useful when the index file is to be formatted separately. Other than pure numbers, three special cases are allowed for no: any, odd, and even. In these special cases, the starting page number is determined by retrieving the last page number from the .log file of the last LATEX run. The .log file name is determined by concatenating the file name base of the first raw index file (idx0) with the extension .log. The last source page is obtained by searching backward in the log file for the first instance of a number included in square brackets. If a page number is missing or the `log` file is not found, no attempt will be made to set the starting page number. The meaning of each of these cases follows.

any   The starting page is the last source page number plus one.

odd   The starting page is the first odd page following the last source page number.

even   The starting page is the first even page following the last source page number.

-s sty   Take `sty` as the style file. There is no default for the style file name. The environment variable `INDEXSTYLE` defines where the style file resides.

-t log   Take `.log` as the transcript file. By default, the file name base of the first input file `idx0` concatenated with the extension `.ilg` is used as the transcript file name.

12.3.2   Error Messages

MakeIndex types out on the terminal the number of lines read and written and how many errors were found. Messages that identify the error are written in the transcript file which, by default, has the extension `.ilg`. *MakeIndex* can produce error messages when it is reading the `.idx` file or when it is writing the `.ind` file. Each error message contains the nature of the error and the number of the line where the error occurs in the file. In the reading phase, the line number refers to the `.idx` file.

Errors in the Reading Phase

`Extra '!' at position ...`
> The `\index` command's argument has more than two unquoted ! characters. Perhaps some of them should be quoted.

`Extra @ at position ...`
> The `\index` command argument has two or more unquoted @ characters with no intervening !. Perhaps one of the @ characters should be quoted.

`Extra '|' at position ...`
> The `\index` command's argument has more than one unquoted | character. Perhaps the extras should be quoted.

`Illegal null field`
> The `\index` command argument does not make sense because some string is null that shouldn't be. The command `\index{!funny}` will produce this error, since it specifies a subentry "funny" with no entry. Similarly, the command `\index{@funny}` is incorrect because it specifies a null string for alphabetizing.

`Argument ... too long (max 1024)`
    The document contained an `\index` command with a very long argument.
    You probably forgot the right brace that should delimit the argument.

Other errors

MakeIndex can produce a variety of other error messages indicating that something is seriously wrong with the `.idx` file. If you get such an error, it probably means that the `.idx` file was corrupted in some way. If LaTeX did not generate any errors when it created the `.idx` file, then it is highly unlikely to have produced a bad `.idx` file. If it did, you should examine the `.idx` file to establish what went wrong.

Errors in the Writing Phase

`Unmatched range opening operator`
    An `\index{...|(}` command has no matching `\index{...|)}` command following it. The "..." in the two commands must be completely identical.

`Unmatched range closing operator`
    An `\index{...|)}` command has no matching `\index{...|(}` command preceding it.

`Extra range opening operator`
    Two `\index{...|(}` commands appear in the document with no intervening command `\index{...|)}`.

`Inconsistent page encapsulator ... within range`
    MakeIndex has been instructed to include a page range for an entry and a single page number within that range that is formatted differently—for example, by having an `\index{cat|iv}` command between an `\index{cat|(}` and an `\index{cat|)}` command.

`Conflicting entries`
    MakeIndex thinks it has been instructed to print the same page number twice in two different ways—e.g., by the command sequences `\index{lion|see{...}}` and `\index{lion}` appearing on the same page.

12.4 Customizing the Index

MakeIndex ensures that the formats of the input and output files do not have to be fixed, but they can be adapted to the needs of a specific application. To achieve this format independence, the *MakeIndex* program is driven by a style file, usually characterized with a filetype `.ist` (see also figure 12.1 on page 346). This file consists of a series of keyword/value pairs. These keywords can be

keyword	default value	description
keyword (s)	"\\indexentry"	command telling *MakeIndex* that its argument is an index entry
arg_open (c)	'{'	argument opening delimiter
arg_close (c)	'}'	argument closing delimiter
range_open (c)	'('	opening delimiter indicating beginning of explicit page range
range_close (c)	')'	closing delimiter indicating end of explicit page range
level (c)	'!'	delimiter denoting new level of subitem
actual (c)	'@'	symbol indicating that the next entry is to appear in the actual index file
encap (c)	'|'	symbol indicating that rest of argument list is to be used as encapsulating command for the page number
quote (c)	'"'	quote symbol
escape (c)	'\\'	symbol which escapes the next letter, unless its preceding letter is escape, i.e., quote is used to escape the letter which immediately follows it. But if it is preceded by escape, it does not escape anything. The two symbols quote and escape must be distinct.
page_compositor (s)	"-"	composite page delimiter

(*s*) signals an attribute of type string, (*c*) of type char

Table 12.1: Input style parameters for *MakeIndex*

divided into input and output style parameters. Table 12.1 describes the various keywords and their default values for the programming of the input file. It is in this table that you can find, for instance, how to modify the index level separator (level, with ! as default character value). On the other hand, table 12.2 on the next page describes the keywords and the defaults for steering the translation of the input information into LaTeX commands. So here you will find how to define the way the various levels are formatted (using the item series of keywords). Examples will show in more detail how these various input and output keywords can be used in practice.

12.4.1   Example of Index Style Files

In the following sections we show how, by just making a few changes to the values of the default settings of the parameters controlling the index, you can customize the index.

12.4.2   A Stand-Alone Index

The example style mybook.ist (shown below) defines a stand-alone index for a book, where stand-alone means that it can be formatted independent of the main source. This can be useful if the input text of the book is frozen (the page

keyword	default value	description
Context		
preamble (*s*)	"\\begin{theindex}\n"	preamble command preceding the index
postamble (*s*)	"\n\n\\end{theindex}\n"	postamble command following the index
Starting page		
setpage_prefix (*s*)	"\n\\setcounter{page}{"	prefix for the command setting the page
setpage_suffix (*s*)	"}\n"	suffix for the command setting the page
New group/letter		
group_skip (*s*)	"\n\n\\indexspace\n"	vertical space inserted before new group
heading_prefix (*s*)	""	prefix for heading of new letter group
heading_suffix (*s*)	""	suffix for heading of new letter group
headings_flag (*n*)	0	A value flag=0 inserts nothing between the different letter groups; a value flag>0 (<0) includes an uppercase (lowercase) instance of the symbol characterizing the new letter group, prefixed with heading_prefix and appending heading_suffix
Entry separators		
item_0 (*s*)	"\n\\item "	command to be inserted in front of level 0 entry
item_1 (*s*)	"\n \\subitem "	ditto for level 1 entry starting at level ≥ 1
item_2 (*s*)	"\n \\subsubitem "	ditto for level 2 entry starting at level ≥ 2
item_01 (*s*)	"\n \\subitem "	command before level 1 entry starting at level 0
item_12 (*s*)	"\n \\subsubitem "	ditto for level 2 entry starting at level 1
item_x1 (*s*)	"\n \\subitem "	command to be inserted in front of level 1 entry when parent level has no page numbers
item_x2 (*s*)	"\n \\subsubitem "	ditto for level 2 entry
Page delimiters		
delim_0 (*s*)	", "	entry-page number delimiter at level 0
delim_1 (*s*)	", "	ditto at level 1
delim_2 (*s*)	", "	ditto at level 2
delim_n (*s*)	", "	delimiter between different page numbers
delim_r (*s*)	"--"	designator for a page range
Page encapsulators		
encap_prefix (*s*)	"\\"	prefix to be used in front of a page encapsulator
encap_infix (*s*)	"{"	infix to be used for a page encapsulator
encap_suffix (*s*)	"}".	suffix to be used for a page encapsulator
Page precedence		
page_precedence (*s*)	"rRnaA"	page number precedence: a, A are lower-, uppercase alphabetic; n numeric; r and R lower- and uppercase roman
Line wrapping		
line_max (*n*)	72	maximum length of an output line
indent_space (*s*)	"\t\t"	indentation commands for wrapped lines
indent_length (*n*)	16	length of indentation for wrapped lines

"\n" and "\t" are a new line and a tab; (*s*) signals an attribute of type string, (*n*) of type number

Table 12.2: Output style parameters for *MakeIndex*

numbers will no longer change), and you only want to reformat the index.

```
% MakeIndex style file mybook.ist
preamble
"\\documentclass[12pt]{book}
\\begin{document}
\\begin{theindex}\n"
postamble
"\n\n\\end{theindex}
\\end{document}\n"
```

Assuming that the raw index commands are in the file `mybook.idx` then you can call *MakeIndex* specifying the style file's name:

```
makeindex  -s mybook.ist -o mybookind.tex mybook
```

The reason for using a non-default output file name is to avoid clobbering the source output (presumably `mybook.dvi`) because if the index is in file `mybook.ind`, its typeset output will also be in `mybook.dvi`, thus overwriting the original `.dvi` file.

If, moreover, you want the page numbers for the index to come out right, then you can also specify the page number where the index has to start (e.g., 181 in the example below).

```
makeindex  -s mybook.ist  -o mybookind.tex -p 181  mybook
```

MakeIndex can also read the LaTeX log file `mybook.log` to find the page number to be used for the index (see the `-p` option described on page 355).

12.4.3 Changing the "Special Characters"

The next example shows how you can change the interpretation of special characters in the input file. To do this, you must specify the new special characters in a style file (for instance, `myinchar.ist` shown below.) Using table 12.1 on page 358, in the following example we change the @ character (see page 349) to =, the sublevel indicator ! (see page 348) to >, and the quotation character " (see page 350) to ! (the default sublevel indicator).

```
% MakeIndex style file myinchar.ist
actual '='      % = instead of default @
quote '!'       % !                     "
level '>'       % >                     !
```

In the example of figure 12.5 on the next page, which should be used in conjunction with the german option of the babel package, the double quote character (") is used as a shortcut for the umlaut construct \". This shows

```
" sign, 1                Page 1:   \index{\texttt{"} sign}
= sign, 2                Page 2:   \index{\texttt{@} sign}
@ sign, 2                Page 2:   \index{\texttt{!=} sign}
Brücke, 5                Page 3:   \index{Maedchen=M\"{a}dchen}
Brücke, V                Page c:   \index{Maedchen=M"adchen}
Brücke, v                Page v:   \index{Bruecke=Br"ucke}
dimensions               Page 5:   \index{Br"ucke}
    rule                 Page V:   \index{Br\"ucke}
        width, 3         Page 3:   \index{dimensions>rule>width}
exclamation (!), 4       Page 4:   \index{exclamation (!!)}
    Ah!, 5               Page 5:   \index{exclamation (!!)>Ah!!}
Mädchen, c
Mädchen, 3
```

Figure 12.5: Example of the use of special characters with *MakeIndex*

another feature of the ordering of *MakeIndex*, namely, the constructs " and \" are considered as different entries (Br"ucke and Br\"ucke, M"adchen and M\"adchen, although in the latter case the key entry was identical, i.e., Maedchen). Therefore, it is important to use the same input convention throughout a complete document.

12.4.4 Changing the Output Format of the Index

You can also personalize the output format of the index. The first thing that we could try is to build an index with a nice big letter between each letter group. This is achieved with the style myhead.ist shown below (see table 12.2 on page 359 for more details) and gives the result shown in figure 12.6 on the next page.

```
% MakeIndex style file myhead.ist
heading_prefix  "{\\bfseries\\hfil "       % Insert in front of letter
heading_suffix  "\\hfil}\\nopagebreak\n"   % Append after letter
headings_flag    1                         % Turn on headings (uppercase)
```

You could go a bit further and right-adjust the page numbers, putting in dots between the entry and the page number to guide the eye, as shown in figure 12.7 on the following page. This can be achieved by adding the following commands.

```
% MakeIndex style file myright.ist
delim_0    "\\dotfill "
delim_1    "\\dotfill "
delim_2    "\\dotfill "
```

The LATEX command \dotfill can be replaced by fancier commands, but the principle remains the same.

```
Page 2:    {\texttt{"@} sign}
Page 3:    {dimensions!rule!width}
Page 5:    {box!parameters}
           {fonts!PostScript}
Page 9:    {dimensions!table}
Page 12:   {dimensions!rule!height}
Page 17:   {dimensions!figure}
Page 21:   {box}
           {fonts!Computer Modern}
Page 33:   {box!dimensions of}
           {rule!depth}
Page 41:   {rule!width}
Page 48:   {rule!depth}
```

Figure 12.6: Example of how you can customize the output format of an index

```
Page 2:    {\texttt{"@} sign}
Page 3:    {dimensions!rule!width}
Page 5:    {box!parameters}
           {fonts!PostScript}
Page 9:    {dimensions!table}
Page 12:   {dimensions!rule!height}
Page 17:   {dimensions!figure}
Page 21:   {box}
           {fonts!Computer Modern}
Page 33:   {box!dimensions of}
           {rule!depth}
Page 41:   {rule!width}
Page 48:   {rule!depth}
```

Figure 12.7: Adding leaders to an index

12.4.5   Treating Funny Page Numbers

As described earlier, *MakeIndex* accepts five basic kinds of page numbers: digits, upper- and lowercase alphabetic, and upper- and lowercase roman numerals. You can also build composed page numbers. The separator character for composed page numbers is controlled by the *MakeIndex* keyword `page_compositor` (the default is the hyphen character (-); see table 12.1 on page 358), while the precedence of ordering the various kinds of page numbers is given by the keyword `page_precedence` (the default is `rRnaA`; see table 12.2 on page 359).

Let us start with simple page numbers and assume the pages with numbers `ii, iv, 1, 2, 5, a, c, A, C, II`, and `IV` contain an `\index` command with the word `style`. This would be typeset in the index as shown below.

style, ii, iv, c, II, IV, C, 1, 2, 5, a, A

In this example, you can see that the c and C entries were considered as roman numerals, rather than alphabetic numbers.

This order can be changed using the `page_precedence` keyword, as shown in the style file `mypages.ist`.

```
% MakeIndex style file mypages.ist
page_precedence "rnaRA"
```

The result of running *MakeIndex* on the same index entries yields:

style, ii, iv, c, 1, 2, 5, a, II, IV, C, A

The next step you can take is to use composed page numbers in your document. The default input separator is the hyphen. Suppose you have a reference to the word `style` on the following (unsorted) series of pages: `C-3, 1-1, D-1-1, B-7, F-3-5, 2-2, D-2-3, A-1, B-5` and `A-2`. After running *MakeIndex*, the following sorted output is obtained:

style, 1-1, 2-2, A-1, A-2, B-5, B-7, C-3, D-1-1, D-2-3, F-3-5

The separator can be changed to, for example, a dot, by using the `page_compositor` keyword, shown in the style file `mypagsep.ist`.

```
% MakeIndex style file mypagsep.ist
page_compositor "."
```

The result of running *MakeIndex* on the same index entries with the "-" replaced by "." yields:

style, 1.1, 2.2, A.1, A.2, B.5, B.7, C.3, D.1.1, D.2.3, F.3.5

12.4.6   Glossary Entries

(£ 79)

LaTeX also has a \glossary command for making a glossary. The \makeglossary command produces a file with extension .glo, which is similar to the .idx file for the \index commands. LaTeX transforms the \glossary commands into \glossaryentry entries, just as it translates \index commands into \indexentry entries.

MakeIndex can also treat these glossary commands, but you must change the value for some of the style file keywords, as shown in the style file myglossary.ist.

```
% MakeIndex style file myglossary.ist
keyword    "\\glossaryentry"            % keyword for glossary entry
preamble   "\n \\begin{theglossary}\n"  % Begin glossary entries
postamble  "\n\n \\end{theglossary}\n"   % End    glossary entries
```

In addition you might have to define a suitable theglossary environment.

12.5   Modifying the Layout

(£ 77)

You can redefine the environment theindex, which by default is used to print the index. The layout of the theindex environment and the definition of the \item, \subitem, and \subsubitem commands are defined in the class files article, book, and report. In the book class you can find the following definitions:

```
\newenvironment{theindex}
            {\@restonecoltrue\if@twocolumn\@restonecolfalse\fi
             \columnseprule \z@  \columnsep 35\p@
             \twocolumn[\@makeschapterhead{\indexname}]%
             \@mkboth{\uppercase{\indexname}}{\uppercase{\indexname}}%
             \thispagestyle{plain}\parindent\z@
             \parskip\z@ \@plus .3\p@\relax
             \let\item\@idxitem}
            {\if@restonecol\onecolumn\else\clearpage\fi}
\newcommand\@idxitem   {\par\hangindent 40\p@}
\newcommand\subitem    {\par\hangindent 40\p@ \hspace*{20\p@}}
\newcommand\subsubitem{\par\hangindent 40\p@ \hspace*{30\p@}}
```

You can make an index in three rather than two columns. To do this, you can use the multicol package and the multicols environment.

```
\renewenvironment{theindex}{\newpage
   \addcontentsline{toc}{chapter}{Index Entries}%
   \pagestyle{plain}\let\item\@idxitem
   \begin{multicols}{3}[{\Large\bfseries Index Entries}]
```

```
    \par\bigskip}%          definition of \begin{theindex}
   {\end{multicols}}}%      definition of \end{theindex}
```

First, a new page is started before the index is entered as a chapter heading into the table of contents file .toc and the page style is changed to plain. Then the \item command is redefined to cope with index entries (see above), and the entries themselves are typeset in three columns using the multicols environment.

12.5.1 Multiple Indexes

A multind package (by F.W. Long) redefines the \makeindex, \index and \printindex commands to allow multiple indexes. It achieves this by using the filename of the index as supplementary argument.

```
\makeindex{indexname}
\index{indexname}{entry}
\printindex{indexname}{indextitle}
```

The first time the file shown in figure 12.8 on the next page is run through LATEX it generates the files A.idx and B.idx. These files have to be transformed into their respective .ind files by running both .idx files through *MakeIndex*.

```
> makeindex A
This is makeindex, portable version 2.12 [26-May-1993].
Scanning input file A.idx....done (5 entries accepted, 0 rejected).
Sorting entries....done (12 comparisons).
Generating output file A.ind....done (18 lines written, 0 warnings).
Output written in A.ind.
Transcript written in A.ilg.
> makeindex B
This is makeindex, portable version 2.12 [26-May-1993].
Scanning input file B.idx....done (5 entries accepted, 0 rejected).
Sorting entries....done (14 comparisons).
Generating output file B.ind....done (21 lines written, 0 warnings).
Output written in B.ind.
Transcript written in B.ilg.
```

After one more run through LATEX you will obtain the output shown in figure 12.9 on the following page. In that example we have used a redefined theindex environment similar to the one shown in section 12.5 to produce three columns instead of the standard two. The title for the indexes is generated by the second argument of the redefined \printindex command.

1 Generating more than one Index

Using the package multind users can enter information in more than one index. The commands \makeindex and \index have been modified to allow multiple indexes. In both cases the first parameter is the index name.

2 New printindex command

When you want to include the index in the document, you should run the makeindex program on each file.

```
makeindex A
makeindex B
```

A modified \printindex command lets you print multiple indexes. The first parameter is the index name, the second parameter is the index title (as printed). Some more text. The final text .

Commands and programs

\makeindex, 1
makeindex (program), 1
\index, 1
\printindex, 1

Final to index A, 1

Other stuff

multind package, 1
entry index B, 1
Final to index B, 1
index name, 1
One more to B, 1

1

Figure 12.9: Output file showing multiple indexes

```
\documentclass[12pt]{article}
\usepackage{multind}
\renewcommand[2]{\printindex}{% Redefine \printindex
  \begin{center}\textbf{\large#2}\end{center}
  \input{#1.ind}}
\makeindex{A}
\makeindex{B}
\begin{document}
\section{Generating more than one Index}

Using the package \textsf{multind}
\index{B}{multind package}%
users can enter information in more than one index.
The commands \Com{makeindex} and \Com{index} have been
modified to allow multiple indexes.
In both cases the first parameter is the index name.
\index{B}{index name}

\section{New printindex command}

When you want to include the index in the document,
you should run the \Prog{makeindex} program on each file.
\index{B}{One more to B}

\begin{verbatimcmd}
makeindex A
makeindex B
\end{verbatimcmd}

A modified \Com{printindex} command lets you print
multiple indexes.
The first parameter is the index name,
the second parameter is the index title (as printed).
Some more text\index{B}{entry index B}.
The final text
\index{A}{Final to index A}\index{B}{Final to index B}.

\printindex{A}{Commands and programs}
\printindex{B}{Other stuff}

\end{document}
```

Figure 12.8: Example input file for multiple indexes

12.5.2   A Reimplementation of the Index Commands

The index package (by David Jones) augments the possibilities of LaTeX's indexing mechanism in several areas:

1. Multiple indexes are supported.

2. A two-stage process is used for creating the raw index files (such as the default .idx file) similar to that used to create the .toc file. First the index entries are written to the .aux file, and then they are copied to the .idx file at the end of the run. In this way, if you have a large document consisting of several included files (using the \include command), you no longer lose the index if you format only part of the document with \includeonly.

3. A *variant of the \index command is introduced. In addition to entering its argument in the index, it also typesets it in the running text.

4. To simplify typing, the \shortindexingon command activates a short-hand notation. Now you can type ^{foo} for \index{foo} and _{foo} for \index*{foo}. These shorthand notations are turned off with a \shortindexingoff command. Because the underscore and hat characters have a special meaning inside math mode, this shorthand notation is unavailable there.

5. This package includes the functionality of the showidx package. The command \proofmodetrue enables the printing of index entries in the margins. You can customize the size and style of the font used in the margin with the \indexproofstyle command, which takes a font definition as argument, e.g., \renewcommand{\indexproofstyle}{\footnotesize\itshape}.

You declare new indexes with the \newindex command, while the \renewindex command is used to redefine existing indexes.

\newindex{*tag*}{*raw-ext*}{*proc-ext*}{*indexname*}

The first argument, *tag*, is a short identifier used to refer to the index. In particular the commands \index and \printindex are redefined to take an optional argument, namely the tag of the index you are referring to. If this optional argument is absent, the index with the tag "default" is used, which corresponds to the usual index. The second argument, *raw-ext*, is the extension of the raw index file where LaTeX should write the unprocessed entries for this index (for the default index this is .idx). The third argument, *proc-ext*, is the extension of the index file where LaTeX expects to find the processed index (for the default index this is .ind). The fourth argument, *indexname*, is the title that LaTeX will print at the beginning of the index.

```
\documentclass{book}
\usepackage{index}
\makeindex
\newindex{aut}{adx}{and}{Name Index}
\newindex{not}{ndx}{nnd}{List of Notation}
\shortindexingon
\proofmodetrue
\newcommand{\aindex}[1]{\index*[aut]{#1}}
\begin{document}
\tableofcontents
\newpage
\chapter{Here is a ^[aut]{chapter} title}
\section{Section header\index[aut]{section}}
\par Here is some text.\index{subject}
\par Here is \index[not]{notation}some
        more\index[not]{sin@$\sin$} text.
\par Here is some ^{more} _[not]{notation} text.
\par Here is yet more \aindex{text}.

\section{Another Section header _[aut]{section2}}

\par And here is some math: $x^1_b$.
\par Here is an ^[aut]{index} entry
        \fbox{inside an \index[not]{min@$\min$}fbox}
\par \fbox{Here is an ^[aut]{entry} in a box.}

\printindex[not]
\printindex[aut]
\printindex
\end{document}
```

Figure 12.10: Multiple indexes—input file

The commands for building the multiple indexes for the input file of figure 12.10 are shown in figure 12.11 on the facing page together with the generated transcript. It is seen that *MakeIndex* was run on each of the separate
raw index files, i.e., the standard one, then on adx, which yields the and file,
and finally on ndx, which is transformed into the nnd file. Then LaTeX is executed
again and it reads these files in the order defined by the \printindex commands
in the input file (figure 12.10). The result of the complete run is displayed in
figure 12.12 on page 370.

```
> latex multindexa.tex
This is TeX, C Version 3.141
(multindexa.tex
LaTeX Version 2.09 <25 March 1992>
(/usr/local/lib/tex/macros/book.sty
Standard Document Style 'book' <14 Jan 92>.
(/usr/local/lib/tex/macros/bk10.sty)) (index.sty
Style-Option: 'index' v3.01 <19 July 1993> (dmj))
index.sty> Writing index file multindexa.idx
index.sty> Writing index file multindexa.adx
index.sty> Writing index file multindexa.ndx
No file multindexa.aux.
No file multindexa.toc.
[1] [2]
Chapter 1.
No file multindexa.nnd.
No file multindexa.and.
No file multindexa.ind.
[3] (multindexa.aux) )
Output written on multindexa.dvi (3 pages, 1556 bytes).
Transcript written on multindexa.log.
> makeindex multindexa
This is makeindex, portable version 2.12 [26-May-1993].
Scanning input file multindexa.idx....done
        (2 entries accepted, 0 rejected).
Sorting entries...done (2 comparisons).
Generating output file multindexa.ind....done
        (9 lines written, 0 warnings).
Output written in multindexa.ind.
Transcript written in multindexa.ilg.
> makeindex -o multindexa.and multindexa.adx
This is makeindex, portable version 2.12 [26-May-1993].
Scanning input file multindexa.adx....done
        (6 entries accepted, 0 rejected).
Sorting entries...done (20 comparisons).
Generating output file multindexa.and....done
        (22 lines written, 0 warnings).
Output written in multindexa.and.
Transcript written in multindexa.ilg.
> makeindex -o multindexa.nnd multindexa.ndx
This is makeindex, portable version 2.12 [26-May-1993].
Scanning input file multindexa.ndx....done
        (4 entries accepted, 0 rejected).
Sorting entries...done (9 comparisons).
Generating output file multindexa.nnd....done
        (13 lines written, 0 warnings).
Output written in multindexa.nnd.
Transcript written in multindexa.ilg.
> latex multindexa
This is TeX, C Version 3.141
(multindexa.tex
LaTeX Version 2.09 <25 March 1992>
(/usr/local/lib/tex/macros/book.sty
Standard Document Style 'book' <14 Jan 92>.
(/usr/local/lib/tex/macros/bk10.sty)) (index.sty
Style-Option: 'index' v3.01 <19 July 1993> (dmj))
index.sty> Writing index file multindexa.idx
index.sty> Writing index file multindexa.adx
index.sty> Writing index file multindexa.ndx
(multindexa.aux) (multindexa.toc) [1] [2]
Chapter 1.
(multindexa.nnd [3] [4]) (multindexa.and [5])
(multindexa.ind [6]) (multindexa.aux) )
Output written on multindexa.dvi (6 pages, 2776 bytes).
Transcript written on multindexa.log.
```

Figure 12.11: Multiple indexes—running LaTeX and *MakeIndex*

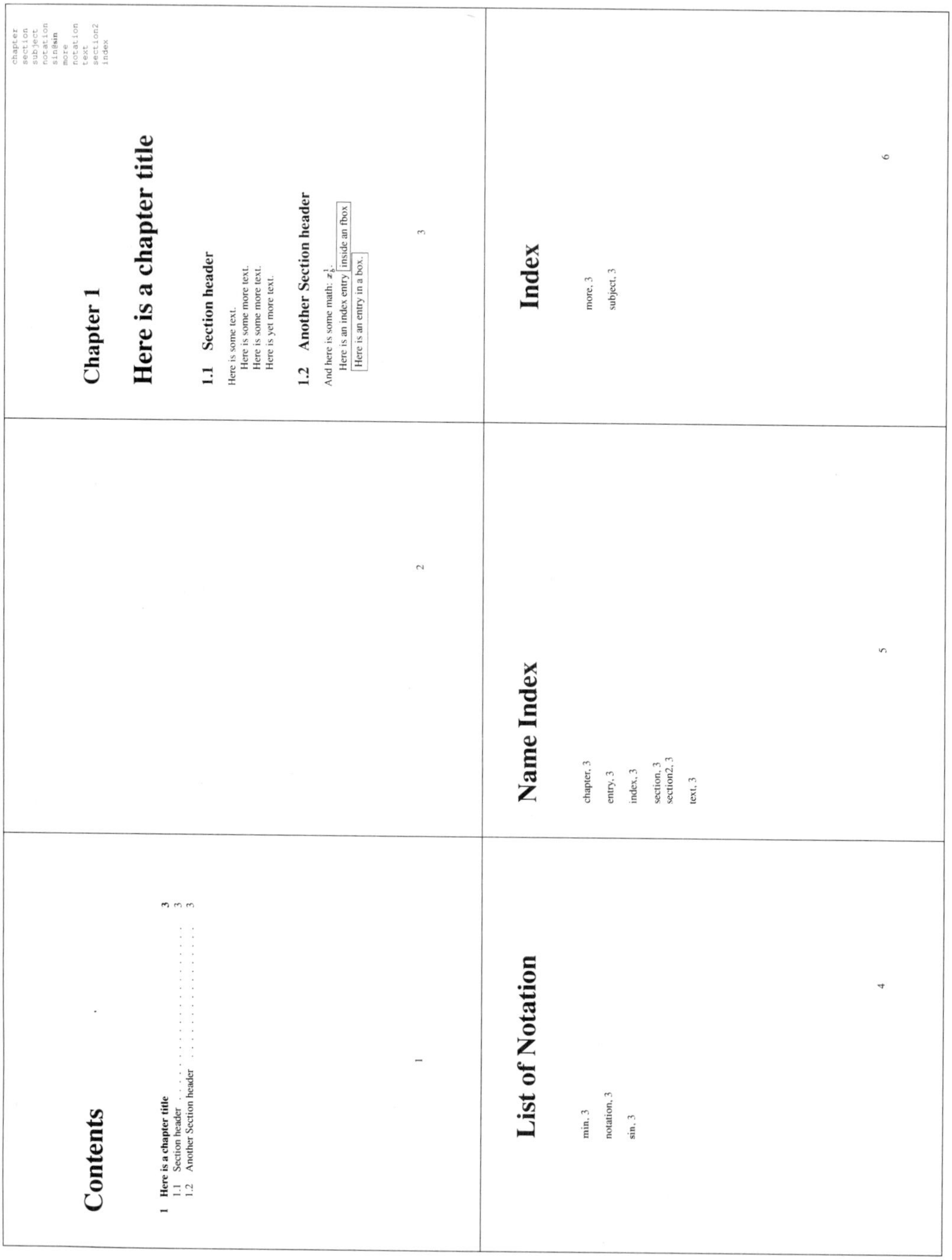

```
chapter
section
subject
notation
sinkin
more
notation
text
section2
index
```

Chapter 1

Here is a chapter title

1.1 Section header

Here is some text.
Here is some more text.
Here is some more text.
Here is yet more text.

1.2 Another Section header

And here is some math: $x_k^{\frac{1}{2}}$
Here is an index entry | inside an fbox
Here is an entry in a box.

2

3

Index

more, 3
subject, 3

Contents

1

Name Index

5

List of Notation

4

6

Figure 12.12: Multiple indexes—output example

CHAPTER 13

Bibliography Generation

While a table of contents (see section 2.4) and an index (discussed in chapter 12) make it easier to navigate through a book, the presence of bibliographic references should allow you to probe further subjects you consider interesting. To make this possible, the references should be precise and lead to the relevant work with a minimum of effort.

There exist many ways for formatting bibliographies, and different fields of scholarly activities have developed very precise rules in this area. An interesting overview can be found in the chapter on bibliographies in *The Chicago Manual of Style* [86].

Normally, authors must follow the rules laid out by their publisher. Therefore, one of the more important tasks when submitting a book or an article for publication is to generate the bibliographic reference list according to those rules.

Traditional ways of composing such lists by hand, without the systematic help of computers, are plagued with the following problems:

- Citations, particularly in a document with contributions from many authors, are hard to make consistent. Difficulties arise, such as variations in the use of full forenames versus abbreviations (with or without periods), italicization or quoting of titles, spelling "ed.," "Ed.," or "Editor," and the various forms of journal volume number.

- A bibliography laid out in one style (e.g., alphabetic by author and year) is extremely hard to convert to another (e.g., numeric citation order) if requested by a publisher.

- It is difficult to maintain one large data base of bibliographic references that can be reused in different documents.

This chapter describes one solution to the bibliography problem. It is based on LATEX and its companion program BIBTEX, written by Oren Patashnik. Over the years several dozen BIBTEX bibliography styles (see table 13.1 on page 377) have been developed, so it should not be too difficult to find or adapt a style that suits the demands of a particular publisher.

The first section describes how to include citations in the text. This is followed by an overview of how LATEX and BIBTEX work together, and a discussion of several BIBTEX styles. With the help of an example, which uses in each case an identical input file and BIBTEX data base, it is shown how easy it is to change the appearance of the citations in the text, as well as the bibliographic references themselves.

(*L* 140–47)　　　The next sections provide an updated and augmented version of appendix B in the LATEX book, which details how to construct a BIBTEX data base.

The final sections describe the format of BIBTEX's style files, giving a short overview of the commands and intrinsic functions available in them. Then the global structure of the generic style documentation file `btxbst.doc` will be explained. From that knowledge we will show you how to adapt an existing style file to the needs of a particular house style or foreign language.

13.1　Entering the Citations

(*L* 73–74)　　　Bibliographic citations inside the text of a LATEX document are flagged with the command

> `\cite[`*text*`]{`*cite_key-list*`}`

The `\cite` command associates the list of comma separated keywords in the *cite_key-list* parameter with the arguments of `\bibitem` commands inside a `thebibliography` environment, and it writes the keys into the `.aux` file. As with other LATEX identifiers, these keys are case-sensitive.

The optional parameter *text* is an additional note, which will be printed together with the text generated by the `\cite` command. When BIBTEX is not used, the citation numbers are defined by the order in which the keys appear on the `\bibitem` commands inside the `thebibliography` environment.

```
\begin{thebibliography}{widest_entry}
\bibitem[label1]{cite_key1} bibliographic information
\bibitem[label2]{cite_key2} bibliographic information
    . . .
\end{thebibliography}
```

As stated above, the association between a \cite command and one or more bibliography entries is made via the *cite_key-list* argument. The citation text, which will actually appear in the typeset text, depends on the chosen bibliographic style.

With BIBTEX (see below) you can use a variant of the \cite command: (ℒ 74)

\nocite{*cite_key-list*}

This command produces no text, but writes its argument list *cite_key-list* in the .aux file, so that the associated bibliography information will appear in the references. A command \nocite{*} includes all entries of a BIBTEX data base into the list of references.

13.1.1   Customizing the Citations

The actual formatting of the citation is controlled by the internal LATEX command, \@cite. The definitions of possible forms are (see section A.5 in appendix A for the syntax of \ifthenelse):

- References enclosed in square brackets (default format),

```
\renewcommand{\@cite}[2]{%
            [{#1\ifthenelse{\boolean{@tempswa}}{,#2}{}]}
```

- Exponent-like references,

```
\renewcommand{\@cite}[2]{%
            {$^{#1}$\ifthenelse{\boolean{@tempswa}}{,#2}{}}}
```

To understand this code you should know that LATEX sets the temporary Boolean variable \if@tempswa to the value true if you specify an optional argument on the \cite command.

The cite package (by Donald Arseneau) collapses a list of three or more consecutive numbers into a range. For example, [4,5,6,7,9,8,6] is transformed into [4-7,9,8,6]. An additional command, \citen, can be used to get the numbers (and write to the .aux file) without the brackets or further formatting. Therefore, "See also ref.~\citen{junk}." gives "See also ref. 9."

The citesort package (by Ian Green) goes one step further and sorts the numbers before collapsing them. So the previous example would become [4-9].

The overcite package (by Donald Arseneau) works like cite, but displays citations as superscript numbers with a comma and a small space between each number. Lists of three or more consecutive numbers are compressed into a number range, but it does not sort them for optimized compression. When an optional note is given, then the whole list of citations will be typeset as though cite.sty were in effect (see above). The punctuation characters (.,;:) will be moved in front of the superscript except when the \cite immediately follows a quotation, e.g., ``Transition State''\cite{Eyring}. gives "Transition State."[8]

Many of the bibliography styles discussed in the next section define supplementary commands to control the form of the citations better. In particular, the chicago package, which implements the recommendations of *The Chicago Manual of Style* [86], has the list of commands shown below:

\cite{*key*}	full author list and year,e.g.,
	(Brown 1978; Jarke, Turner, Stohl, et al. 1985)
\citeA{*key*}	only the full author list, e.g.,
	(Brown; Jarke, Turner and Stohl)
\citeN{*key*}	full author list and year, for use in text, e.g.,
	Shneiderman (1978) states that ...
\shortcite{*key*}	abbreviated author list and year
\shortciteA{*key*}	abbreviated author list
\shortciteN{*key*}	abbreviated author list and year, for use inside text
\citeyear{*key*}	year only, within parentheses

All these commands have a variant without parentheses (the same name with NP appended), for example, \citeNP.

Patrick W. Daly, the author of the makebst program (see section 13.9), has developed the natbib BIBTEX style, which must be used together with the natbib package. It implements various forms of the "author-year" citation format, like the ones seen above, and it can be used as a unique replacement for the apalike, astron, authordate series, harvard, named, and newapa BIBTEX styles, described in table 13.1 on page 377. The punctuation used inside the citations can be customized with the \bibpunct command.

13.1.2   Customizing the Bibliography Labels

(*L* 187)

The thebibliography environment is implemented as a general list. The label of a bibliography item has the following default definition:

```
\newcommand{\@biblabel}[1]{[#1]}
```

Bibliographic styles that use the name of the author(s) as citation keys, like the apalike and chicago styles, redefine the \@biblabel command as empty, because they construct their own more complex label. The indentation of the entries is controlled by the length \bibhang, which by default is 2em.

Different blocks of information, such as the authors or the title, are separated inside one \bibitem in the bibliography by \newblock commands. Normally these groups are typeset together in one paragraph. If, however, you want your bibliography to be "open," i.e., each block starts on a new line with succeeding lines inside a block indented by a length \bibindent (default 1.5em), then the openbib package should be specified.

(*L* 160)

① Run LATEX, which generates a list of \cite references in its auxiliary file, .aux.

② Run BIBTEX, which reads the auxiliary file, looks up the references in a data base (one or more .bib files), and then writes a file (the .bbl file) containing the formatted references according to the format specified in the style file (the .bst file). Warning and error messages are written to the log file (the .blg file). It should be noted that BIBTEX never reads the original LATEX source file.

③ Run LATEX again, which now reads the .bbl reference file.

④ Run LATEX a third time, resolving all references.

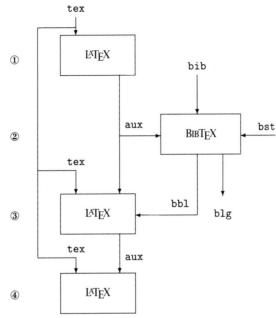

Figure 13.1: Data flow when running BIBTEX and LATEX

13.2 Using BIBTEX with LATEX

LATEX implements full cross-referencing, and a special form of this is used for bibliographical citation. The previous section showed how to specify citations in the text with the command \cite{*cite_key*}, where *key* is the keyword identifying an entry in the bibliography list environment thebibliography. This latter list can be constructed by hand for a small number of references, but it is probably more practical to read the information in a bibliography data base. In this case the same key *cite_key* should also uniquely identify an entry in that data base, so that the citation reference can be resolved when the document is processed. The procedure for running LATEX and BIBTEX is schematically shown in figure 13.1.

The precise format of a BIBTEX entry will be described in detail in section 13.5. In order to follow the discussion of the examples in the present section more easily, you should nonetheless know that the basic structure of a BIBTEX entry consists of three parts:

1. an *entry type*, e.g.: "book," "article," "inproceedings," and "phdthesis";

2. a *user-chosen keyword* identifying the publication. If you want to reference

the entry in your document, then the argument *cite_key* of the \cite command should be identical (also in case) to this keyword.

3. a *series of fields* consisting of a field identifier with its data between quotes or curly braces, e.g.: "author," "journal," and "title."

Various schemes exist for conveniently associating bibliography keywords with their entries in a data base. A popular one is the so-called Harvard system, where you take the author's surname (converted to lowercase) and the year of publication, and combine them using a colon. For example, smith:1987. Other possibilities for labeling bibliography entries are seen in figure 13.4 on page 381, which shows an example BIBTEX data base.

BIBTEX entries are read by BIBTEX in the bibliography data base (the .bib file), and the formatting of the entries is controlled by an associated bibliography style (the .bst file), which contains a set of instructions written in a stack-based language. The latter is interpreted by the BIBTEX program (see sections 13.7 and following).

BIBTEX has knowledge of what fields are required, optional, and ignored for any given entry type (see table 13.2 on page 408). It will issue warnings like "author name required" if something is missing. The style file can control the typesetting of both the citation string in the main text and the actual bibliography entry inside the thebibliography environment.

It is important to note that LATEX by itself can still compose a bibliography and cross-references in the text. Without BIBTEX, you can still produce a bibliography by providing the bibliographic entries yourself. It is also simple to manually edit the output from BIBTEX to cope with extraordinary cases. Moreover, if your document has to be self-contained, then the contents of the .bbl file can be included in the LATEX document (see the aux2bib tool described on page 392).

13.2.1 A List of BIBTEX Style Files

Various organizations or individuals have developed style files that correspond to the house style of particular journals or editing houses. Nelson Beebe has collected a large number of BIBTEX styles (see table 13.1 on the facing page). For each style he also provides an example file, which allows you to see the effect of using the given style.[1] Some of the BIBTEX styles, for instance, authordate⟨*i*⟩, jmb, and named, must be used in conjunction with their accompanying LATEX package (as indicated in table 13.1 on the next page), to obtain the desired effect.

Note that you can yourself customize a bibliography style, by making small changes to one of those in the table (see section 13.8 for a description of how this is done), or else generate your own using the makebst program (as explained in section 13.9).

---

[1] See appendix B to find out how you can obtain these files from one of the TEX archives.

Table 13.1: Selection of BibTeX style files

Style name	Description
abbrv.bst	Standard BibTeX style
abstract.bst	Modified alpha style with abstract keyword
acm.bst	Association for Computing Machinery BibTeX style
agsm.bst	Australian Government publications BibTeX style
alpha.bst	Standard BibTeX style
amsalpha.bst	alpha-like BibTeX style for $\mathcal{A}_{\mathcal{M}}S$-TeX
amsplain.bst	plain-like BibTeX style for $\mathcal{A}_{\mathcal{M}}S$-TeX (numeric labels)
annotate.bst	Modified alpha BibTeX style with annote keyword
annotation.bst	Modified plain BibTeX style with annote keyword
apa.bst	American Psychology Association
apalike.bst	Variant of apa BibTeX style
apalike.sty	LaTeX package for use with apalike.bst
apalike2.bst	Variant of apalike BibTeX style
astron.bst	Astronomy BibTeX style
authordate$i$.bst	i=[1,4]. Series of BibTeX styles producing author-date reference list.
authordate1-4.sty	LaTeX package to be used together with authordate$i$.bst
bbs.bst	Behavioral and Brain Sciences BibTeX style
cbe.bst	Council of Biology Editors BibTeX style (includes such journals as American Naturalist, Evolution, etc.)
cell.bst	Small modifications to jmb BibTeX style
dcu.bst	Design Computing Unit (Sidney University) BibTeX style
harvard.sty	LaTeX package for use with Harvard styles (agsm, dcu, kluwer)
humanbio.bst	Human Biology BibTeX style
humannat.bst	Human Nature and American Anthropologist journals
ieeetr.bst	Transactions of the Institute of Electrical and Electronic Engineers BibTeX style
is-abbrv.bst	abbrev BibTeX style with ISSN and ISBN keyword added
is-alpha.bst	alpha BibTeX style with ISSN and ISBN keyword added
is-plain.bst	plain BibTeX style with ISSN and ISBN keyword added
is-unsrt.bst	unsrt BibTeX style with ISSN and ISBN keyword added
jmb.bst	Journal of Molecular Biology style
jmb.sty	LaTeX package for use with jmb.bst
jtb.bst	Journal of Theoretical Biology BibTeX style
kluwer.bst	Kluwer Academic Publishers BibTeX style
named.bst	BibTeX style with [author(s), year] type of citation
named.sty	LaTeX package for use with named.bst
namunsrt.bst	Named variant of unsrt BibTeX style

continued on next page

continued from previous page	
Style name	*Description*
nar.bst	Nucleic Acid Research BiBTeX style
nar.sty	LaTeX package for use with nar.bst
natbib.bst	Generic BiBTeX style file implementing various "author-year" reference formats
natbib.sty	LaTeX package for use with natbib.bst
nature.bst	Nature BiBTeX style
nature.sty	LaTeX package for use with nature.bst
newapa.bst	Modification of apalike.bst
newapa.sty	LaTeX package for use with newapa.bst
phaip.bst	American Institute of Physics journals BiBTeX style
phcpc.bst	Computer Physics Communications BiBTeX style
phiaea.bst	Conferences of the International Atomic Energy Agency BiBTeX style
phjcp.bst	Journal of Computational Physics BiBTeX style
phnf.bst	Nuclear Fusion BiBTeX style
phnflet.bst	Nuclear Fusion Letters BiBTeX style
phpf.bst	Physics of Fluids BiBTeX style
phppcf.bst	Physics version of apalike BiBTeX style
phreport.bst	Internal physics reports BiBTeX style
phrmp.bst	Reviews of Modern Physics BiBTeX style
plain.bst	Standard BiBTeX style
plainyr.bst	plain BiBTeX style with primary sort by year
siam.bst	Society of Industrial and Applied Mathematics BiBTeX style
unsrt.bst	Standard BiBTeX style

13.2.2   Examples of BiBTeX Styles

The examples in this section show the effect of using different bibliography styles on identical input and bibliography files.

Figure 13.2 on the facing page shows the input file, which contains a sample of most normally occurring reference entry types. This example uses the plain bibliography style and references the BiBTeX data base bsample. Figure 13.3 on page 380 shows the whole sequence necessary to produce the final document. First LaTeX was run on this file. Next BiBTeX was run on the generated .aux file; the relevant entries were read from the data base, which can be seen *in extenso* in figure 13.4 on page 381. The actual bibliography style in which the data base entries are to be output to the .bbl file for later treatment by LaTeX is specified with the command \bibliographystyle in the source. Then LaTeX is run twice more to resolve all references.

In this case, using the "standard" BiBTeX style plain and the input file shown in figure 13.2, you would get the output shown on the left of page 382. The five other output examples shown in figures 13.5 to 13.7, starting on the right of

(*£ 74*)

```
\documentclass{article}
\pagestyle{empty}
\begin{document}
\section*{Example of Citations of Kind \texttt{plain}}

Citation of a normal book~\cite{Eijkhout:1991} and an edited
book~\cite{Roth:postscript}.
Now we cite an article written by a single~\cite{Felici:1991}
and by multiple authors~\cite{Mittelbach/Schoepf:1990}.
A reference to an article inside proceedings~\cite{Yannis:1991}.
We refer to a manual~\cite{Dynatext}
and a technical report~\cite{Knuth:WEB}.
A citation of an unpublished work~\cite{EVH:Office}.
A reference to a chapter in a book~\cite{Wood:color} and
to a PhD thesis~\cite{Liang:1983}.
An example of multiple citations~\cite{Eijkhout:1991,Roth:postscript}.

\bibliographystyle{plain}
\bibliography{bsample}
\end{document}
```

Figure 13.2: Example of a LaTeX file using BibTeX

page 382, correspond to the three remaining standard BibTeX bibliography styles and two variants and are produced by replacing the plain style in the example document and reprocessing it as explained above.

($\mathcal{L}$ 74,75)

plain   Standard BibTeX style. Entries sorted alphabetically with numeric labels.

unsrt   Standard BibTeX style. Similar to plain, but entries are printed in order of citation, rather than sorted. Numeric labels are used.

alpha   Standard BibTeX style. Similar to plain, but the labels of the entries are formed from the author's name and the year of publication.

abbrv   Standard BibTeX style. Similar to plain, but entries are more compact, since first names, month, and journal names are abbreviated.

acm   Alternative BibTeX style, used for the journals of the Association for Computing Machinery. It has the author name (surname and first name) in small caps, and numbers as labels.

apalike   Alternative BibTeX style, used by the journals of the American Psychology Association. It should be used together with the LaTeX apalike package. The bibliography entries are formatted alphabetically, last name first, each entry having a hanging indentation and no label.

```
$ latex bsample                    %%%%%%%%%% 1st run of LaTeX
This is TeX, C Version 3.141
(bsample.tex
LaTeX Version 2.09 <06 August 1993> with NFSS2
(/usr/local/lib/tex/macros/article.sty
Standard Document Style 'article' <14 Jan 92>.
(/usr/local/lib/tex/macros/art10.sty)) (bsample.aux)
LaTeX Warning: Citation 'Eijkhout:1991' on page 1 undefined on input line 9.
LaTeX Warning: Citation 'Roth:postscript' on page 1 undefined on input line 10.
LaTeX Warning: Citation 'Felici:1991' on page 1 undefined on input line 11.
LaTeX Warning: Citation 'Mittelbach/Schoepf:1990' on page 1 undefined on input line 12.
LaTeX Warning: Citation 'Yannis:1991' on page 1 undefined on input line 13.
LaTeX Warning: Citation 'Dynatext' on page 1 undefined on input line 14.
LaTeX Warning: Citation 'Knuth:WEB' on page 1 undefined on input line 15.
LaTeX Warning: Citation 'EVH:Office' on page 1 undefined on input line 16.
LaTeX Warning: Citation 'Wood:color' on page 1 undefined on input line 17.
LaTeX Warning: Citation 'Liang:1983' on page 1 undefined on input line 18.
LaTeX Warning: Citation 'Eijkhout:1991' on page 1 undefined on input line 19.
LaTeX Warning: Citation 'Roth:postscript' on page 1 undefined on input line 19
No file bsample.bbl.
[1] (bsample.aux) )
Output written on bsample.dvi (1 page, 904 bytes).
Transcript written on bsample.log.

$ bibtex bsample                   %%%%%%%%%% BibTeX run
This is BibTeX, C Version 0.99c
The top-level auxiliary file: bsample.aux
The style file: plain.bst
Database file #1: bsample.bib
Warning--empty volume in Wood:color's crossref of Roth:postscript
(There was 1 warning)

$ latex bsample                    %%%%%%%%%% 2nd run of LaTeX
This is TeX, C Version 3.141
(bsample.tex
(bsample.aux)   ...        %%%% Still unresolved citation references

$ latex bsample                    %%%%%%%%%% 3rd run of LaTeX
This is TeX, C Version 3.141
(bsample.tex (bsample.aux)  ...   %%%% Now all citation references are resolved
```

Figure 13.3: Running LaTeX with a BibTeX bibliography data base

Some BibTeX styles modify the citation and bibliography list items compared to those available with standard LaTeX. Therefore, in addition to denoting the BibTeX style with a \bibliographystyle command, a corresponding LaTeX package must also be specified using the \usepackage command. This is, for example, the case for the apalike style that we used in the last example.

```
% BiBTeX sample data base                      address    ={Stanford, CA 94305},
                                               number     ={STAN-CS-83-980},
%% bibtexfile{                                 institution ={Department of Computer
%% author  = "Michel Goossens",                            Science, Stanford University} }
%% version = "1.12",
%% date    = "15 November 1993",               @phdthesis{Liang:1983,
%% filename = "bsample.bib",                    author    ={Franklin Mark Liang},
%% address = "CN Division, CERN                  month     =jun, year = 1983,
%%            CH1211, Geneva 23                  school    ={Stanford University},
%%            Switzerland",                      address   ={Stanford, CA 94305},
%% email   = "<goossens at node cern.ch>" }     title     ={{Word Hy-phen-a-tion by
                                                            Com-pu-ter}},
@Preamble{{\input{bibnames.sty}}               note      ={Also available as Stanford
 # {\hyphenation{Post-Script Sprin-ger}}                   University, Department of
}                                                          Computer Science Report
                                                           No. STAN-CS-83-977}         }
@String{AW = {{Ad\-di\-son-Wes\-ley}}}
@String{AW:adr = {Reading, Massachusetts}}     @Article{Mittelbach/Schoepf:1990,
@String{j-TUGboat = {TUGboat}}                  author    ={Frank Mittelbach and
                                                           Rainer Sch{\"o}pf},
@manual{Dynatext,                               title     ={{The New Font Selection --- User
 key       ={Dynatext},                                     Interface to Standard \LaTeX}},
 title     ={{Dynatext, Electronic Book         journal   =j-TUGboat,
             Indexer/Browser}},                 volume    =11, number = 2,
 organization={Electronic Book                  pages     ={297--305},
             Technology Inc.},                   year      =1990                       }
 address   ={Providence, Rhode Island},
 year      =1991                       }       @Inbook{Wood:color,
                                                author    ={Pat Wood},
@Book{Eijkhout:1991,                            crossref  ={Roth:postscript},
 author    ={Victor Eijkhout},                  booktitle ={{Real World PostScript}},
 title     ={{\TeX{} by Topic, a                 title     ={PostScript Color Separation},
             \TeX}nicians Reference}},           pages     ={201--225}                 }
 publisher =AW,
 address   =AW:adr,                            @Book{Roth:postscript,
 year      =1991,                      }        editor    ={Stephen E. Roth},
                                                title     ={{Real World PostScript}},
@techreport{EVH:Office,                         publisher =AW,
 author    ={Eric van Herwijnen},               address   =AW:adr,
 title     ={{Future Office Systems             year      =1988,
             Requirements}},
 institution ={CERN DD Internal Note},          ISBN      ={0-201-06663-7}            }
 year      =1988, month = nov          }       @Inproceedings{Yannis:1991,
                                                title = {{\TeX} and those other languages},
@Article{Felici:1991,                           author= {Yannis Haralambous},
 author    ={James Felici},                      pages = {539--548},
 title     ={{PostScript versus TrueType}},      booktitle ={1991 Annual Meeting Proceedings,
 journal   ={Macworld},                                    Part 2, \TeX{} Users Group,
 volume    =8,pages={195--201},                            Twelfth Annual Meeting, Dedham,
 month     =sep, year = 1991           }                   Massachusetts, July 15--18, 1991},
                                                editor = {Hope Hamilton},
@techreport{Knuth:WEB,                          organization ={{\TeX} Users Group},
 title     ={{The \textsf{WEB} System of        year    =  {1991},
             Structured Documentation}},         address ={Providence, Rhode Island},
 month     =sep, year = 1983,                    journal =j-TUGboat,
 author    ={Donald E. Knuth},                   volume  = 12, month = dec             }
```

Figure 13.4: Example of a BIBTEX data base

This example data base file was used in the runs with the input file shown in figure 13.2 on page 379 to generate the output files shown in figures 13.5 to 13.7 beginning on page 382.

Example of citations of kind `plain`

Citation of a normal book [1] and an edited book [8]. Now we cite an article written by a single [3] and by multiple authors [7]. A reference to an article inside proceedings [4]. We refer to a manual [2] and a technical report [5]. A citation of an unpublished work [9]. A reference to a chapter in a book [10] and to a PhD thesis [6]. An example of multiple citations [1, 8].

References

[1] Victor Eijkhout. *TEX by Topic, a TEXnicians Reference.* Addison-Wesley, Reading, Massachusetts, 1991.

[2] Electronic Book Technology Inc., Providence, Rhode Island. *Dynatext, Electronic Book Indexer/Browser*, 1991.

[3] James Felici. PostScript versus TrueType. *Macworld*, 8:195–201, September 1991.

[4] Yannis Haralambous. TEX and those other languages. In Hope Hamilton, editor, *1991 Annual Meeting Proceedings, Part 2. TEX Users Group, Twelfth Annual Meeting, Dedham, Massachusetts, July 15–18, 1991*, volume 12, pages 539–548, Providence, Rhode Island, December 1991. TEX Users Group.

[5] Donald E. Knuth. The WEB System of Structured Documentation. Technical Report STAN-CS-83-980, Department of Computer Science, Stanford University, Stanford, CA 94305, September 1983.

[6] Franklin Mark Liang. *Word Hy-phen-a-tion by Com-pu-ter.* PhD thesis, Stanford University, Stanford, CA 94305, June 1983. Also available as Stanford University, Department of Computer Science Report No. STAN-CS-83-977.

[7] Frank Mittelbach and Rainer Schöpf. The New Font Selection — User Interface to Standard LATEX. *TUGboat*, 11(2):297–305, 1990.

[8] Stephen E. Roth, editor. *Real World PostScript.* Addison-Wesley, Reading, Massachusetts, 1988.

[9] Eric van Herwijnen. Future Office Systems Requirements. Technical report, CERN DD Internal Note, November 1988.

[10] Pat Wood. *PostScript Color Separation*, pages 201–225. In Roth [8], 1988.

Example of citations of kind `unsrt`

Citation of a normal book [1] and an edited book [2]. Now we cite an article written by a single [3] and by multiple authors [4]. A reference to an article inside proceedings [5]. We refer to a manual [6] and a technical report [7]. A citation of an unpublished work [8]. A reference to a chapter in a book [9] and to a PhD thesis [10]. An example of multiple citations [1, 2].

References

[1] Victor Eijkhout. *TEX by Topic, a TEXnicians Reference.* Addison-Wesley, Reading, Massachusetts, 1991.

[2] Stephen E. Roth, editor. *Real World PostScript.* Addison-Wesley, Reading, Massachusetts, 1988.

[3] James Felici. PostScript versus TrueType. *Macworld*, 8:195–201, September 1991.

[4] Frank Mittelbach and Rainer Schöpf. The New Font Selection — User Interface to Standard LATEX. *TUGboat*, 11(2):297–305, 1990.

[5] Yannis Haralambous. TEX and those other languages. In Hope Hamilton, editor, *1991 Annual Meeting Proceedings, Part 2. TEX Users Group, Twelfth Annual Meeting, Dedham, Massachusetts, July 15–18, 1991*, volume 12, pages 539–548, Providence, Rhode Island, December 1991. TEX Users Group.

[6] Electronic Book Technology Inc., Providence, Rhode Island. *Dynatext, Electronic Book Indexer/Browser*, 1991.

[7] Donald E. Knuth. The WEB System of Structured Documentation. Technical Report STAN-CS-83-980, Department of Computer Science, Stanford University, Stanford, CA 94305, September 1983.

[8] Eric van Herwijnen. Future Office Systems Requirements. Technical report, CERN DD Internal Note, November 1988.

[9] Pat Wood. *PostScript Color Separation*, pages 201–225. In Roth [2], 1988.

[10] Franklin Mark Liang. *Word Hy-phen-a-tion by Com-pu-ter.* PhD thesis, Stanford University, Stanford, CA 94305, June 1983. Also available as Stanford University, Department of Computer Science Report No. STAN-CS-83-977.

Figure 13.5: Output examples of the plain and unsrt BIBTEX styles

Example of citations of kind `alpha`

Citation of a normal book [Eij91] and an edited book [Rot88]. Now we cite an article written by a single [Fel91] and by multiple authors [MS90]. A reference to an article inside proceedings [Har91]. We refer to a manual [Dyn91] and a technical report [Knu83]. A citation of an unpublished work [vH88]. A reference to a chapter in a book [Woo88] and to a PhD thesis [Lia83]. An example of multiple citations [Eij91, Rot88].

References

[Dyn91] Electronic Book Technology Inc.. Providence, Rhode Island. *Dynatext, Electronic Book Indexer/Browser*, 1991.

[Eij91] Victor Eijkhout. *TeX by Topic, a TeXnicians Reference*. Addison-Wesley, Reading, Massachusetts, 1991.

[Fel91] James Felici. PostScript versus TrueType. *Macworld*, 8:195–201, September 1991.

[Har91] Yannis Haralambous. TeX and those other languages. In Hope Hamilton, editor, *1991 Annual Meeting Proceedings, Part 2. TeX Users Group, Twelfth Annual Meeting, Dedham, Massachusetts, July 15–18, 1991*, volume 12, pages 539–548, Providence, Rhode Island, December 1991. TeX Users Group.

[Knu83] Donald E. Knuth. The WEB System of Structured Documentation. Technical Report STAN-CS-83-980, Department of Computer Science, Stanford University, Stanford, CA 94305, September 1983.

[Lia83] Franklin Mark Liang. *Word Hy-phen-a-tion by Com-pu-ter*. PhD thesis, Stanford University, Stanford, CA 94305, June 1983. Also available as Stanford University, Department of Computer Science Report No. STAN-CS-83-977.

[MS90] Frank Mittelbach and Rainer Schöpf. The New Font Selection — User Interface to Standard LaTeX. *TUGboat*, 11(2):297–305, 1990.

[Rot88] Stephen E. Roth, editor. *Real World PostScript*. Addison-Wesley, Reading, Massachusetts, 1988.

[vH88] Eric van Herwijnen. Future Office Systems Requirements. Technical report, CERN DD Internal Note, November 1988.

[Woo88] Pat Wood. *PostScript Color Separation*, pages 201–225. In Roth [Rot88], 1988.

Example of citations of kind `abbrv`

Citation of a normal book [11] and an edited book [8]. Now we cite an article written by a single [3] and by multiple authors [7]. A reference to an article inside proceedings [4]. We refer to a manual [2] and a technical report [5]. A citation of an unpublished work [9]. A reference to a chapter in a book [10] and to a PhD thesis [6]. An example of multiple citations [1, 8].

References

[1] V. Eijkhout. *TeX by Topic, a TeXnicians Reference*. Addison-Wesley, Reading, Massachusetts, 1991.

[2] Electronic Book Technology Inc.. Providence, Rhode Island. *Dynatext, Electronic Book Indexer/Browser*, 1991.

[3] J. Felici. PostScript versus TrueType. *Macworld*, 8:195–201, Sept. 1991.

[4] Y. Haralambous. TeX and those other languages. In H. Hamilton, editor, *1991 Annual Meeting Proceedings, Part 2. TeX Users Group, Twelfth Annual Meeting, Dedham, Massachusetts. July 15–18, 1991*, volume 12, pages 539–548, Providence, Rhode Island. Dec. 1991. TeX Users Group.

[5] D. E. Knuth. The WEB System of Structured Documentation. Technical Report STAN-CS-83-980, Department of Computer Science, Stanford University, Stanford, CA 94305, Sept. 1983.

[6] F. M. Liang. *Word Hy-phen-a-tion by Com-pu-ter*. PhD thesis, Stanford University, Stanford, CA 94305, June 1983. Also available as Stanford University, Department of Computer Science Report No. STAN-CS-83-977.

[7] F. Mittelbach and R. Schöpf. The New Font Selection — User Interface to Standard LaTeX. *TUGboat*, 11(2):297–305, 1990.

[8] S. E. Roth, editor. *Real World PostScript*. Addison-Wesley, Reading, Massachusetts, 1988.

[9] E. van Herwijnen. Future Office Systems Requirements. Technical report, CERN DD Internal Note, Nov. 1988.

[10] P. Wood. *PostScript Color Separation*, pages 201–225. In Roth [8], 1988.

Figure 13.6: Output examples of the alpha and abbrv BibTeX styles

Example of citations of kind `acm`

Citation of a normal book [1] and an edited book [8]. Now we cite an article written by a single [3] and by multiple authors [4]. We refer to a manual [2] and a technical report [5]. A citation of an unpublished work [9]. A reference to a chapter in a book [10] and to a PhD thesis [6]. An example of multiple citations [1, 8].

References

[1] EIJKHOUT, V. *TeX by Topic, a TeXnicians Reference.* Addison-Wesley, Reading, Massachusetts, 1991.

[2] ELECTRONIC BOOK TECHNOLOGY INC. *Dynatext. Electronic Book Indexer/Browser.* Providence, Rhode Island, 1991.

[3] FELICI, J. PostScript versus TrueType. *Macworld 8* (Sept. 1991), 195–201.

[4] HARALAMBOUS, Y. TeX and those other languages. In *1991 Annual Meeting Proceedings, Part 2, TeX Users Group. Twelfth Annual Meeting, Dedham, Massachusetts, July 15–18, 1991* (Providence. Rhode Island, Dec. 1991), H. Hamilton, Ed., vol. 12, TeX Users Group, pp. 539–548.

[5] KNUTH, D. E. The WEB System of Structured Documentation. Tech. Rep. STAN-CS-83-980, Department of Computer Science, Stanford, CA 94305, Sept. 1983.

[6] LIANG, F. M. *Word Hy-phen-a-tion by Com-pu-ter.* PhD thesis, Stanford University, Stanford, CA 94305, June 1983. Also available as Stanford University, Department of Computer Science Report No. STAN-CS-83-977.

[7] MITTELBACH, F., AND SCHÖPF, R. The New Font Selection — User Interface to Standard LaTeX. *TUGboat 11*, 2 (1990), 297–305.

[8] ROTH, S. E., Ed. *Real World PostScript.* Addison-Wesley, Reading, Massachusetts, 1988.

[9] VAN HERWIJNEN, E. Future Office Systems Requirements. Tech. rep. CERN DD Internal Note, Nov. 1988.

[10] WOOD, P. *PostScript Color Separation.* In Roth [8], 1988, pp. 201–225.

Example of citations of kind `apalike`

Citation of a normal book (Eijkhout, 1991) and an edited book (Roth, 1988). Now we cite an article written by a single (Felici, 1991) and by multiple authors (Mittelbach and Schöpf, 1990). A reference to an article inside proceedings (Haralambous, 1991). We refer to a manual (Dynatext, 1991) and a technical report (Knuth, 1983). A citation of an unpublished work (van Herwijnen, 1988). A reference to a chapter in a book (Wood, 1988) and to a PhD thesis (Liang, 1983). An example of multiple citations (Eijkhout, 1991; Roth, 1988).

References

Dynatext (1991). *Dynatext. Electronic Book Indexer/Browser.* Electronic Book Technology Inc., Providence. Rhode Island.

Eijkhout, V. (1991). *TeX by Topic, a TeXnicians Reference.* Addison-Wesley, Reading, Massachusetts.

Felici, J. (1991). PostScript versus TrueType. *Macworld,* 8:195–201.

Haralambous, Y. (1991). TeX and those other languages. In Hamilton, H., editor, *1991 Annual Meeting Proceedings, Part 2, TeX Users Group, Twelfth Annual Meeting, Dedham, Massachusetts, July 15–18, 1991,* volume 12, pages 539–548, Providence, Rhode Island. TeX Users Group.

Knuth, D. E. (1983). The WEB System of Structured Documentation. Technical Report STAN-CS-83-980, Department of Computer Science. Stanford University, Stanford, CA 94305.

Liang, F. M. (1983). *Word Hy-phen-a-tion by Com-pu-ter.* PhD thesis, Stanford University, Stanford, CA 94305. Also available as Stanford University, Department of Computer Science Report No. STAN-CS-83-977.

Mittelbach, F. and Schöpf, R. (1990). The New Font Selection — User Interface to Standard LaTeX. *TUGboat,* 11(2):297–305.

Roth, S.E., editor (1988). *Real World PostScript.* Addison-Wesley, Reading, Massachusetts.

van Herwijnen, E. (1988). Future Office Systems Requirements. Technical report, CERN DD Internal Note.

Wood, P. (1988). *PostScript Color Separation,* pages 201–225. In (Roth, 1988).

Figure 13.7: Output examples of the acm and apalike BibTeX styles

13.3 Multiple Bibliographies in One Document

In large documents with several independent sections, in conference proceedings containing many different articles, or in a book with separate parts written by different authors, it is often necessary to have separate bibliographies for each of the units. In this section we discuss two LATEX packages, chapterbib and bibunits, that address this problem. Note that the latter package only works without modifications on UNIX.

13.3.1 The chapterbib Package

The chapterbib package (by Niel Kempson) allows multiple bibliographies in a LATEX document, including the same cited items occurring in more than one bibliography. The following restrictions apply, however:

1. The \bibliography and \bibliographystyle commands may not be used in the root file, only in files that have been included with the \include command. Bibliography commands in the root file will be ignored. Moreover, only a single \bibliography command should be present in each included file.

2. If you want to use \cite commands in the root file, then their keys must be resolved by providing a stand-alone thebibliography environment inside the root file, as shown on the example on page 387.

For demonstration purposes (in real life choosing such different styles would certainly be considered a heresy) the LATEX example in figure 13.8 on page 387 combines two different BIBTEX styles. As the BIBTEX program only handles one style at a time (i.e., allows only one \bibliographystyle command), BIBTEX must be run separately on each .aux file, bs1.aux and bs2.aux, to write the respective .bbl files, bs1.bbl and bs2.bbl, as shown below:

```
$ latex chapterbibexa              %%%% 1st run of LATEX
   ...
$ bibtex bs1                       %%%% BIBTEX run on 1st file
This is BibTeX, C Version 0.99c
The top-level auxiliary file: bs1.aux
The style file: plain.bst
Database file #1: bsample.bib
$ bibtex bs2                       %%%% BIBTEX run on 2nd file
This is BibTeX, C Version 0.99c
The top-level auxiliary file: bs2.aux
The style file: alpha.bst
Database file #1: bsample.bib
$ latex chapterbibexa              %%%% 2nd run of LATEX
   ...
```

```
$ latex chapterbibexa                    %%%% 3rd run of LaTeX
       ...
```

The final result is shown in figure 13.9 on page 388.

13.3.2   The bibunits Package

The bibunits package (by Jose Alberto Fernandez) generates separate bibliographies for different units (parts) of the text (chapters, sections, or bibunit environments). The style will separate the citations of each unit of text into a separate file to be processed by BibTeX. The global bibliography section produced by LaTeX can also appear in the document, and citations can be placed in both at the same time.

`\bibliographyunit [unit]`

This command specifies for which document unit references must be generated, i.e., *unit*=\chapter (for each chapter) or *unit*=\section (for each section). If the optional argument is not given, the command \bibliographyunit deactivates bibliography units, and the bibliography is made global for the complete document.

When \bibliographyunit is active, the \bibliographystyle and \bibliography commands specify the BibTeX files and the style to be used by default in the local units. The commands \bibliography* and \bibliographystyle* specify defaults for the given bibunit only and do not affect the global bibliography.

`\begin{bibunit} [style]`

While \bibliographyunit is not active the bibunit environment allows the creation of a bibliography unit. The optional parameter *style* specifies a style for the bibliography different from the default, if any.

`\putbib [bibtex-files]`

A \putbib command must be inserted before the end of each *unit* at the point in the text where the bibliography should be typeset. If the optional argument is absent, \putbib uses the default *bibtex-files*, if any.

With the bibunits package, you must run BibTeX for each *unit* in sequence since, for each such *unit*, there is now a corresponding file jobname.i.aux created, where i is the sequence number of the unit.

As an example, the input file shown in figure 13.10 on page 389 plus the commands given in figure 13.11 on page 390 will produce the output shown in figure 13.12 on page 391.

```
%%%%%%%%%%%%%   Root file bsamplemult.tex   %%%%%%%%%%%%%%%%
\documentclass{article}
\usepackage{chapterbib}
\begin{document}
\include{bs1}
\include{bs2}
\section*{Example of citations in the root file}
Citation of a normal book~\cite{Eijkhout:1991} in the root file.
\begin{thebibliography}{1}
\bibitem{Eijkhout:1991}
   Victor Eijkhout, \emph{\TeX{} by Topic, a
   {\TeX}nicians Reference}, Addison-Wesley (1991).
\end{thebibliography}
\end{document}

%%%%%%%%%%%%%%%%   Included file bs1.tex   %%%%%%%%%%%%%%%%

\section{Example of citations in an included chapter}
\subsection{First in plain style}
Citation of a normal book~\cite{Eijkhout:1991}
and an edited book~\cite{Roth:postscript}.
Now we cite an article written by a single~\cite{Felici:1991}
and by multiple authors~\cite{Mittelbach/Schoepf:1990}.
A reference to an article inside proceedings~\cite{Yannis:1991}.
We refer to a manual~\cite{Dynatext} and a
technical report~\cite{Knuth:WEB}.
A citation of an unpublished work~\cite{EVH:Office}.
A reference to a chapter in a book~\cite{Wood:color} and
to a PhD thesis~\cite{Liang:1983}. An example of
multiple citations~\cite{Eijkhout:1991,Roth:postscript}.
\bibliographystyle{plain}
\bibliography{bsample}

%%%%%%%%%%%%%%%%   Included file bs2.tex   %%%%%%%%%%%%%%%%

\section{Example of citations in an included chapter}
\subsection{Then in alpha style}
      ...... Same input ......
\bibliographystyle{alpha}
\bibliography{bsample}
```

Figure 13.8: A root file and two included files with separate bibliographies

1 Example of citations in an included chapter

1.1 First in plain style

Citation of a normal book [1] and an edited book [8]. Now we cite an article written by a single [3] and by multiple authors [7]. A reference to an article inside proceedings [4]. We refer to a manual [2] and a technical report [5]. A citation of an unpublished work [9]. A reference to a chapter in a book [10] and to a PhD thesis [6]. An example of multiple citations [1, 8].

References

[1] Victor Eijkhout. *TₑX by Topic, a TₑXnicians Reference*. Addison-Wesley, Reading, Massachusetts, 1991.

[2] Electronic Book Technology Inc., Providence, Rhode Island. *Dynatext. Electronic Book Indexer/Browser*, 1991.

[3] James Felici. PostScript versus TrueType. *Macworld*, 8:195–201, September 1991.

[4] Yannis Haralambous. TₑX and those other languages. In Hope Hamilton, editor, *1991 Annual Meeting Proceedings, Part 2, TₑX Users Group, Twelfth Annual Meeting, Dedham, Massachusetts, July 15–18, 1991*, volume 12, pages 539–548, Providence, Rhode Island, December 1991. TₑX Users Group.

[5] Donald E. Knuth. The WEB System of Structured Documentation. Technical Report STAN-CS-83-980, Department of Computer Science, Stanford University, Stanford, CA 94305, September 1983.

[6] Franklin Mark Liang. *Word Hy-phen-a-tion by Com-pu-ter*. PhD thesis, Stanford University, Stanford, CA 94305, June 1983. Also available as Stanford University, Department of Computer Science Report No. STAN-CS-83-977.

[7] Frank Mittelbach and Rainer Schöpf. The New Font Selection — User Interface to Standard LaTeX. *TUGboat*, 11(2):297–305, 1990.

[8] Stephen E. Roth, editor. *Real World PostScript*. Addison-Wesley, Reading, Massachusetts, 1988.

[9] Eric van Herwijnen. Future Office Systems Requirements. Technical report, CERN DD Internal Note, November 1988.

[10] Pat Wood. *PostScript Color Separation*, pages 201–225. In Roth [8], 1988.

1

2 Example of citations in an included chapter

2.1 Then in alpha style

Citation of a normal book [Eij91] and an edited book [Rot88]. Now we cite an article written by a single [Fel91] and by multiple authors [MS90]. A reference to an article inside proceedings [Har91]. We refer to a manual [Dyn91] and a technical report [Knu83]. A citation of an unpublished work [vH88]. A reference to a chapter in a book [Woo88] and to a PhD thesis [Lia83]. An example of multiple citations [Eij91, Rot88].

References

[Dyn91] Electronic Book Technology Inc., Providence, Rhode Island. *Dynatext. Electronic Book Indexer/Browser*, 1991.

[Eij91] Victor Eijkhout. *TₑX by Topic, a TₑXnicians Reference*. Addison-Wesley, Reading, Massachusetts, 1991.

[Fel91] James Felici. PostScript versus TrueType. *Macworld*, 8:195–201, September 1991.

[Har91] Yannis Haralambous. TₑX and those other languages. In Hope Hamilton, editor, *1991 Annual Meeting Proceedings, Part 2, TₑX Users Group, Twelfth Annual Meeting, Dedham, Massachusetts, July 15–18, 1991*, volume 12, pages 539–548, Providence, Rhode Island, December 1991. TₑX Users Group.

[Knu83] Donald E. Knuth. The WEB System of Structured Documentation. Technical Report STAN-CS-83-980, Department of Computer Science, Stanford University, Stanford, CA 94305, September 1983.

[Lia83] Franklin Mark Liang. *Word Hy-phen-a-tion by Com-pu-ter*. PhD thesis, Stanford University, Stanford, CA 94305, June 1983. Also available as Stanford University, Department of Computer Science Report No. STAN-CS-83-977.

[MS90] Frank Mittelbach and Rainer Schöpf. The New Font Selection — User Interface to Standard LaTeX. *TUGboat*, 11(2):297–305, 1990.

[Rot88] Stephen E. Roth, editor. *Real World PostScript*. Addison-Wesley, Reading, Massachusetts, 1988.

[vH88] Eric van Herwijnen. Future Office Systems Requirements. Technical report, CERN DD Internal Note, November 1988.

[Woo88] Pat Wood. *PostScript Color Separation*, pages 201–225. In Roth [Rot88], 1988.

2

Example of citations in the root file

Citation of a normal book [1] in the root file.

References

[1] Victor Eijkhout. *TₑX by Topic, a TₑXnicians Reference*, Addison-Wesley (1991).

3

Figure 13.9: Multiple bibliographies in one file (generated output)

These multiple pages are produced by running the input in figure 13.8 on the preceding page through LaTeX and BibTeX. You can see that each included file is treated completely independently from each other included file. Having different \bibliographystyle commands in one document is perhaps not an advisable precedure, but when BibTeX is run on each .aux file separately, different styles are possible.

```
\documentclass{article}
\usepackage{bibunits}
\begin{document}

\section{The bibunits package}
\begin{bibunit}[unsrt]%%%%%%%%%%%%%%%%%%%%%%% Start the first unit
\subsection{First in bibstyle unsrt}
Citation of a PhD thesis~\cite{Liang:1983}.
Now we cite an article written by multiple
authors~\cite{Mittelbach/Schoepf:1990}.
A reference to an article inside
proceedings~\cite{Yannis:1991}.
\putbib[bsample]
\end{bibunit}

\subsection{Let us continue in bibstyle abbrv}
\begin{bibunit}[abbrv]%%%%%%%%%%%%%%%%%%%%%%% Start the second unit
We refer to a manual~\cite{Dynatext}
and a technical report~\cite{Knuth:WEB}.
A reference to a chapter in a
book~\cite{Wood:color} and
to an edited book~\cite{Roth:postscript}.
\putbib[bsample]
\end{bibunit}

\subsection{And finish in bibstyle alpha}
\begin{bibunit}[alpha]%%%%%%%%%%%%%%%%%%%%%%% Start the third unit
Citation of a normal book~\cite{Eijkhout:1991}
of an article written by a
single~\cite{Felici:1991} author.
\putbib[bsample]
\end{bibunit}
\end{document}
```

Figure 13.10: Example input for the bibunits package

Of the two packages chapterbib and bibunits, the former is the more intuitive. You must remember, however, that units for which a separate bibliography is desired must be put in separate files and input with the \include command. The bibunits package is more powerful, but you must be careful not to lose control over the various bibliography units, which can be defined in various places. Moreover, since bibunits creates file names containing three elements jobname.i.aux, it will not work without modifications on non-UNIX systems, like MS-DOS, CMS, or VMS.

```
$ latex bibunitsexa              %%%%%%%%%%%%   1st run of LaTeX
This is TeX, Version 3.141
(bibunitsexa.tex
No file bibunitsexa.aux.   ...   %%% Unresolved references
No file bibunitsexa.1.bbl. ...   %%% Unresolved citation references
No file bibunitsexa.2.bbl. ...   %%%        ditto
No file bibunitsexa.3.bbl. ...   %%%        ditto
[1] (bibunitsexa.aux) )
Output written on bibunitsexa.dvi (1 page, 1032 bytes).
Transcript written on bibunitsexa.log.
$ bibtex bibunitsexa.1           %%%%%%%%%%%%   Run BibTeX on 1st file
This is BibTeX, C Version 0.99c
The top-level auxiliary file: bibunitsexa.1.aux
The style file: unsrt.bst
Database file #1: bsample.bib
$ bibtex bibunitsexa.2           %%%%%%%%%%%%   Run BibTeX on 2nd file
This is BibTeX, C Version 0.99c
The top-level auxiliary file: bibunitsexa.2.aux
The style file: abbrv.bst
Database file #1: bsample.bib
$ bibtex bibunitsexa.3           %%%%%%%%%%%%   Run BibTeX on 3rd file
This is BibTeX, C Version 0.99c
The top-level auxiliary file: bibunitsexa.3.aux
The style file: alpha.bst
Database file #1: bsample.bib
$ latex bibunitsexa              %%%%%%%%%%%%   2nd run of LaTeX
This is TeX, C Version 3.141
(bibunitsexa.tex
(bibunitsexa.aux)     ...
(bibunitsexa.1.bbl) ...   %%% Still unresolved citation references
(bibunitsexa.2.bbl) ...   %%%        ditto
(bibunitsexa.3.bbl) ...   %%%        ditto
[1] (bibunitsexa.aux) )
$ latex bibunitsexa              %%%%%%%%%%%%   3rd and final run of LaTeX
This is TeX, Version 3.141
(bibunitsexa.tex
    ...
(bibunitsexa.aux)
(bibunitsexa.1.bbl) (bibunitsexa.2.bbl) (bibunitsexa.3.bbl)
[1] (bibunitsexa.aux) )
Output written on bibunitsexa.dvi (1 page, 3232 bytes).
```

Figure 13.11: Running multiple bibliographies with the bibunits style
These commands are used to run the input of figure 13.10 on the preceding
page to obtain the output of figure 13.12 on the next page.

1 The bibunits package

1.1 First in bibstyle unsrt

Citation of a PhD thesis [1]. Now we cite an article written by multiple authors [2]. A reference to an article inside proceedings [3].

References

[1] Franklin Mark Liang. *Word Hy-phen-a-tion by Com-pu-ter*. PhD thesis, Stanford University, Stanford, CA 94305, June 1983. Also available as Stanford University, Department of Computer Science Report No. STAN-CS-83-977.

[2] Frank Mittelbach and Rainer Schöpf. The New Font Selection — User Interface to Standard LaTeX. *TUGboat*, 11(2):297–305, 1990.

[3] Yannis Haralambous. TeX and those other languages. In Hope Hamilton, editor, *1991 Annual Meeting Proceedings, Part 2, TeX Users Group, Twelfth Annual Meeting, Dedham, Massachusetts, July 15–18, 1991*, volume 12, pages 539–548, Providence, Rhode Island, December 1991. TeX Users Group.

1.2 Let us continue in bibstyle abbrv

We refer to a manual [1] and a technical report [2]. A reference to a chapter in a book [4] and to an edited book [3].

References

[1] Electronic Book Technology Inc., Providence, Rhode Island. *Dynatext, Electronic Book Indexer/Browser*, 1991.

[2] D. E. Knuth. The WEB System of Structured Documentation. Technical Report STAN-CS-83-980, Department of Computer Science, Stanford University, Stanford, CA 94305, Sept. 1983.

[3] S. E. Roth, editor. *Real World PostScript*. Addison-Wesley, Reading, Massachusetts, 1988.

[4] P. Wood. *PostScript Color Separation*, pages 201–225. In Roth [3], 1988.

1.3 And finish in bibstyle alpha

Citation of a normal book [Eij91] of an article written by a single [Fel91] author.

References

[Eij91] Victor Eijkhout. *TeX by Topic, a TeXnicians Reference*. Addison-Wesley, Reading, Massachusetts, 1991.

[Fel91] James Felici. PostScript versus TrueType. *Macworld*, 8:195–201, September 1991.

1

Figure 13.12: Output generated from the example of figure 13.10 on page 389

13.4   Bibliography Data Base Management Tools

A sorted listing of all entries in a BIBTEX data base is often useful for easy reference. Various tools, with more or less the same functionality, are available, and
choosing one or the other is mostly a question of taste.

First there is the LATEX package biblist by Joachim Schrod. It can create a
typeset listing of a (possibly large) BIBTEX input file. With large files, especially if
the cite keys are long, TEX's string space is often exceeded and BigTEX must be
run on the TEX file. With the biblist package, even small versions of TEX will do.

You must prepare a LATEX document using the article class and the biblist
package. Options and packages like twoside, german or a4 can be added, but
neither twocolumn nor multicol will work.

The \bibliography command must contain the names of all BIBTEX data
bases you want to print. With a \bibliographystyle command you can choose
a specific bibliography style. By default, all bibliography entries in the data
base will be output. However, if you issue explicit \nocite commands, only the
selected entries from the data bases will be printed.

The following is the input file used for generating the output of figure 13.13
on page 395.

```
\documentclass{article}
\usepackage{a4}
\usepackage{biblist}
\begin{document}
  \bibliographystyle{is-alpha}
  \bibliography{bsample}
\end{document}
```

You must run LATEX, BIBTEX, and LATEX. You do not need to run LATEX twice after
the BIBTEX run.

A series of interesting BIBTEX tools are generally available. The first set was
written (mostly) by David Kotz. These tools are available for UNIX systems, but
the ideas are quite general, so the scripts can be used as a basis for porting the
tools to other operating systems.

aux2bib   Given an .aux file, this perl script creates a portable .bib file. This is
useful when LATEX files need to be shipped elsewhere.

bibkey   This C-shell script uses the sed, egrep, and awk utilities to prepare the
list of all entries having a given keyword in their keyword field.
Usage: bibkey keyword file
Characters in the keyword parameter above that have a special meaning in
regular expressions used by either sed or egrep must be escaped with a
\ (e.g., \\ for the backslash \). Case is ignored in the search. Any valid

egrep expression is allowed, for example, a search for multiple keywords:
`bibkey 'jones|smith' foo.bib`

looktex   Entries containing a given keyword in a BIBTEX data base are listed when this C-shell script is run. It is a generalization of the bibkey script above, and all comments about that entry also apply in this case.

makebib   This C-shell script makes an exportable .bib file from a given set of .bib files and an optional list of citations.
Usage: `makebib file.bib...   [citekey]...`
The output is written to `subset.bib`. If `citekey` is not given, then all refs in the bibfile(s) are included.

printbib   This is a C-shell script that makes a .dvi file from a .bib file for handy reference. It is sorted by cite key and includes `keyword` and `abstract` fields.
Usage: `printbib bibfile...`
The file `abstract.dvi` is generated and can be run through a dvi-driver to be printed. Figure 13.14 on page 396 shows the output when running this shell script on the data base `bsample.bib` of figure 13.4 on page 381.

A second set of tools to handle BIBTEX data bases were developed by Nelson Beebe (Utah University). We give a brief description of each of them.

bibclean   This is a prettyprinter, syntax checker, and lexical analyser for BIBTEX bibliography data base files [9]. The program, which runs on UNIX, Vax/VMS and MS-DOS platforms, has many options, but in general you can just type:
`bibclean < bibfile1 bibfile2,...  > outfile`

bibextract   Extracts from a list of BIBTEX files those bibliography entries that match a pair of specified regular expressions, sending them to *stdout*, together with all `@Preamble` and `@String` commands. Two regular expressions must be specified, the first one to select `keyword` values (if this string is empty then all entries are examined), and the second one to further select from the value part of the entries which bibliography entries must be output.
For example, the following command will extract all entries containing "PostScript" in any of the fields:
`bibextract "" "PostScript" bibfile(s)>new-bibfile`
while the next command will only extract those entries containing the same string but with `Adobe` in the author or organization fields:
`bibextract "author|organization" "Adobe" bibfile(s) >new-bibfile`

citefind.sh and citetags.sh   Sometimes you have to extract the entries effectively referenced in your publication from several large BIBTEX data bases. The Bourne shell scripts citefind.sh and citetags.sh use the awk and sed tools to accomplish that task. First citetags.sh extracts the BIBTEX citation tags from the LATEX source or .aux files and sends them to the standard output *stdout*, where citefind.sh picks them up and tries to find the given keys in the .bib styles specified. It then writes the resulting new bibliography file to *stdout*, for instance

```
citetags.sh *.aux | citefind.sh - mybib1.bib mybib2.bib > newbib.bib
```

bibsort.sh As citefind.sh outputs the citation information in the order in which it was found in the .bib files, it might be worthwhile, for ease of reference by a human reader, to sort the entries using the bibsort.sh shell script. This script uses the sort program internally, so it also will honor most command switches of the latter utility.

bibview Those with access to an X-window graphics terminal can use the bibview program to manipulate BIBTEX data bases more easily using an X-window interface.

Nelson Beebe maintains a large number of BIBTEX data bases related to TEX, graphics, and a series of styles, which we already mentioned in table 13.1 on page 377. His most interesting .bib data bases, as far as TEX is concerned, are texbook1.bib and texbook2.bib (books about TEX, METAFONT and friends), gut.bib (the contents of the French *Cahiers Gutenberg* journal), komoedie.bib (the contents of the German *Die TEXnische Komödie* journal), texgraph.bib (about how to make TEX and graphics work together), texjourn.bib (a list of journals accepting TEX as input), tugboat.bib (listing all the articles in *TUGboat*), type.bib (containing a list of articles and book about typography), and standard.bib (listing software standards).

Nelson Beebe also developed the bibmods and showtags packages. You can see how these packages are used and what kind of output they generate by looking at figure 13.15 on page 397, which corresponds to running the input file below through the LATEX-BIBTEX suite of programs using the example data base of figure 13.4 on page 381.

```
\documentclass[twocolumn]{article}

%%%% Using the bibmods and showtags packages %%%%%
\usepackage{bibmods}
\usepackage{bibnames}
\usepackage{showtags}

\begin{document}
  \nocite{*}
  \bibliographystyle{is-alpha}
  \bibliography{bsample}
\end{document}
```

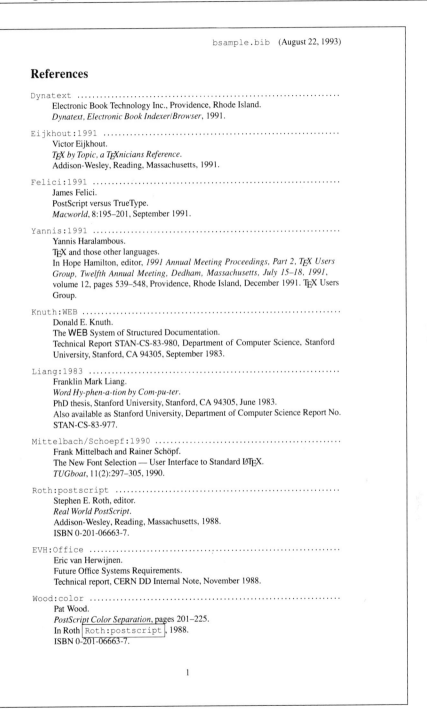

Figure 13.13: List of entries in `bsample.bib` using biblist

Bibliography files
bsample
August 22, 1993

References

[Dynatext] Electronic Book Technology Inc., Providence, Rhode Island. *Dynatext, Electronic Book Indexer/Browser*, 1991.

[EVH:Office] Eric van Herwijnen. Future Office Systems Requirements. Technical report, CERN DD Internal Note, November 1988.

[Eijkhout:1991] Victor Eijkhout. *TEX by Topic, a TEXnicians Reference*. Addison-Wesley, Reading, Massachusetts, 1991.

[Felici:1991] James Felici. PostScript versus TrueType. *Macworld*, 8:195–201, September 1991.

[Knuth:WEB] Donald E. Knuth. The WEB System of Structured Documentation. Technical Report STAN-CS-83-980, Department of Computer Science, Stanford University, Stanford, CA 94305, September 1983.

[Liang:1983] Franklin Mark Liang. *Word Hy-phen-a-tion by Com-pu-ter*. PhD thesis, Stanford University, Stanford, CA 94305, June 1983. Also available as Stanford University, Department of Computer Science Report No. STAN-CS-83-977.

[Mittelbach/Schoepf:1990] Frank Mittelbach and Rainer Schöpf. The New Font Selection — User Interface to Standard LATEX. *TUGboat*, 11(2):297–305, 1990.

[Roth:postscript] Stephen E. Roth, editor. *Real World PostScript*. Addison-Wesley, Reading, Massachusetts, 1988.

[Wood:color] Pat Wood. *PostScript Color Separation*, pages 201–225. In Roth [?], 1988.

[Yannis:1991] Yannis Haralambous. TEX and those other languages. In Hope Hamilton, editor, *1991 Annual Meeting Proceedings, Part 2, TEX Users Group, Twelfth Annual Meeting, Dedham, Massachusetts, July 15–18, 1991*, volume 12, pages 539–548, Providence, Rhode Island, December 1991. TEX Users Group.

1

Figure 13.14: List of entries in `bsample.bib` using the `printbib` command

References

Dynatext

[Dyn91] Electronic Book Technology Inc., Providence, Rhode Island. *Dynatext, Electronic Book Indexer/Browser*, 1991.

Eijkhout:1991

[Eij91] Victor Eijkhout. *T_EX by Topic, a T_EXnicians Reference*. Addison-Wesley, Reading, Massachusetts, 1991.

Felici:1991

[Fel91] James Felici. PostScript versus TrueType. *Macworld*, 8:195–201, September 1991.

Yannis:1991

[Har91] Yannis Haralambous. T_EX and those other languages. In Hope Hamilton, editor, *1991 Annual Meeting Proceedings, Part 2, T_EX Users Group, Twelfth Annual Meeting, Dedham, Massachusetts, July 15–18, 1991*, volume 12, pages 539–548, Providence, Rhode Island, December 1991. T_EX Users Group.

Knuth:WEB

[Knu83] Donald E. Knuth. The WEB System of Structured Documentation. Technical Report STAN-CS-83-980, Department of Computer Science, Stanford University, Stanford, CA 94305, September 1983.

Liang:1983

[Lia83] Franklin Mark Liang. *Word Hyphen-a-tion by Com-pu-ter*. PhD thesis, Stanford University, Stanford, CA 94305, June 1983. Also available as Stanford University, Department of Computer Science Report No. STAN-CS-83-977.

Mittelbach/Schoepf:1990

[MS90] Frank Mittelbach and Rainer Schöpf. The New Font Selection — User Interface to Standard LAT_EX. *TUGboat*, 11(2):297–305, 1990.

Roth:postscript

[Rot88] Stephen E. Roth, editor. *Real World PostScript*. Addison-Wesley, Reading, Massachusetts, 1988. ISBN 0-201-06663-7.

EVH:Office

[vH88] Eric van Herwijnen. Future Office Systems Requirements. Technical report, CERN DD Internal Note, November 1988.

Wood:color

[Woo88] Pat Wood. *PostScript Color Separation*, pages 201–225. In Roth [Rot88], 1988. ISBN 0-201-06663-7.

1

Figure 13.15: List of entries in `bsample.bib` using `showtags` and `bibmods`

13.5   The General Format of the `.bib` File

(ℒ 140–47)
This section describes in greater detail the format of the entries in a BIBTEX data base. It updates the information in appendix B of the LATEX book with material about version 0.99c of BIBTEX [64] by Oren Patashnik, the author of the BIBTEX program.

13.5.1   The General Format of a BIBTEX Entry

(ℒ 140–41)
A BIBTEX entry consists of three main parts: a *type* specifier, followed by a *key*, and finally the *data* for the entry itself. The latter part consists of a series of *field entries*, which can have one of two forms as seen in the following generic format and example:

```
@type_specifier{key_identifier,        @book{lamport86,
   field_name_1 = "field_text_1",         author = "Leslie Lamport",
   field_name_2 = {field_text_2},         title  = "{\LaTeX{}} A Document
          . . .                                     Preparation system",
   field_name_n = {field_text_n}          publisher = {Addison-Wesley},
                   }                      year   = 1986             }
```

The comma is the field separator. Spaces surrounding the equals sign or the comma are ignored. Inside the text part of a field (enclosed in a pair of double quotes or a pair of braces) you can have any string of characters, but braces must be matched. The quotes or braces can be omitted for text consisting entirely of numbers (like the `year` field in the example above).

BIBTEX *ignores* the case of the letters for the entry type, key, and field names. You must, however, be careful with the key, since LATEX honors the case of the keys specified as the argument of a `\cite` command, so the key for a given bibliographic entry must match the one specified in the LATEX file (see section 13.1).

13.5.2   The Text Part of a Field Explained

The text part of a field in a BIBTEX entry is enclosed in a pair of double quotes or curly braces. Part of the text itself is said to be *enclosed in braces* if it lies inside a matching pair of braces other than the ones enclosing the entire entry.

The Structure of a Name

(ℒ 141–42)
The `author` and `editor` fields contain a list of names. The exact format in which these names are typeset is decided by the bibliography style. The entry in the `.bib` data base tells BIBTEX what the name is. You should always type names exactly as they appear in the cited work, even when they have slightly different forms in two works, for example:

```
author = "Donald E. Knuth"          author = "D. E. Knuth"
```

If you are sure that both authors are the same person, then you could list both in the form that the author prefers (say, Donald E. Knuth), yet you should always indicate (e.g., in our second case) that the original publication had a different form.

```
author = "D[onald] E. Knuth"
```

BIBTEX alphabetizes this as if the brackets were not there, so that no ambiguity arises as to the identity of the author.

Most names can be entered in the following two equivalent forms:

```
"John Chris Smith"                  "Smith, John Chris"
"Thomas von Neumann"                "von Neumann, Thomas"
```

The second form, with a comma, should always be used for people who have multiple last names that are capitalized, for example,

```
"Lopez Fernandez, Miguel"
```

If you enter "Miguel Lopez Fernandez," BIBTEX will take "Lopez" as the middle name, which is wrong in this case. When the other parts are not capitalized, no such problem occurs (e.g., Johann von Bergen or Pierre de la Porte).

If several words of a name have to be grouped, they should be enclosed in braces, since BIBTEX treats everything inside braces as a single name, as shown below.

```
{{Boss and Friends, Inc.} and {Snoozy and Boys, Ltd.}}
```

In this case, `Inc.` and `Ltd.` are not mistakenly considered as first names.

In general, BIBTEX names can have four distinct parts, denoted as `First`, `von`, `Last`, and `Jr`. Each part consists of a list of name tokens, and any list but `Last` can be empty.

Thus, the two entries below are different:

```
"von der Schmidt, Alex"        "{von der Schmidt}, Alex"
```

The first has a `von`, `Last` and `First` part, while the second has only a `First` and a `Last` part (`von der Schmidt`), resulting possibly in a different sorting order.

A "junior" part can pose a special problem. Most people with "Jr." in their name precede it with a comma, thus entering it as follows:

```
"Smith, Jr., Robert"
```

Certain people do not use the comma, and these cases are handled by considering the "Jr." as part of the last name:

```
"{Lincoln Jr.}, John P."          "John P. {Lincoln Jr.}"
```

Recall that in the case of "Miguel Lopez Fernandez," you should specify:

```
"Lopez Fernandez, Miguel"
```

The First part of his name has the single token "Miguel"; the Last part has two tokens, "Lopez" and "Fernandez"; and the von and Jr parts are empty.

A complex example is:

```
"Johannes Martinus Albertus van de Groene Heide"
```

This name has three tokens in the First part, two in the von, and two in the Last. BIBTEX knows where one part ends and the other begins because the tokens in the von part begin with lowercase letters (van de in this example).

In general, von tokens have the first letter at brace-level 0 in lowercase. As, technically speaking, everything in a "special character" is at brace-level 0 (see page 401), you can decide how BIBTEX treats a token by inserting a dummy special character whose first letter past the TEX control sequence is in the desired case, upper or lower. For example, in

```
Maria {\uppercase{d}e La} Cruz
```

BIBTEX will take the uppercase "De La" as the von part, since the first character following the control sequence is in lowercase. With the abbrev style you will get the correct abbreviation M. De La Cruz, instead of the incorrect M. D. L. Cruz if you did not use this trick.

BIBTEX handles hyphenated names correctly, for example an entry like:

```
author = "Maria-Victoria Delgrande",
```

with the abbrv style, results in "M.-V. Delgrande."

When multiple authors are present their names should be separated with the word "and" where the "and" must not be enclosed in braces.

```
author = "Frank Mittelbach and Rowley, Chris"
editor = "{Lion and Noble, Ltd.}"
```

There are two authors, Frank Mittelbach and Chris Rowley, but only one editor, since the "and" is enclosed in braces. If the number of authors or editors is too large to be typed *in extenso*, then the list of names can be ended with the string "and others," which is converted by the standard styles into the familiar *"et al."*

To summarize, you can specify names in BibTEX using three possible forms (the double quotes and curly braces can be used in all cases):

```
"First von Last"          e.g. {Johan van der Winden}
"von Last, First"         e.g. "von der Schmidt, Alexander"
"von Last, Jr, First"     e.g. {de la Porte, Fils, {\'Emile}}
```

The first form can almost always be used; it is however not suitable when there is a Jr part, or the Last part has multiple tokens and there is no von part.

The Format of the Title

The bibliography style decides whether a title is capitalized or not. Usually titles of books are capitalized, but those for articles are not. A title should always be typed as it appears in the original work, for example

    ($\mathcal{L}$ 142–43)

```
TITLE = "A Manual of Style"
TITLE = "Hyphenation patterns for ancient Greek and Latin"
```

Different languages and styles have their own capitalization rules. If you want to override the decisions of the bibliography style, then you should enclose the parts which should remain unchanged inside braces. The following titles are equivalent:

```
TITLE = "The Towns and Villages of {Belgium}"
TITLE = {The Towns and Villages of {B}elgium}
```

Accented and Special Characters

BibTEX accepts accented characters. If you have an entry with two fields

```
author = "Kurt G{\"o}del",
year = 1931,
```

then the alpha bibliography style will yield the label [Göd31], which is probably what you want. As shown in the example above, the entire accented character must be placed in braces; in this case either {\"o} or {\"{o}} will work. These braces must, however, not themselves be enclosed in braces (other than the ones that might delimit the entire field or the entire entry); and a backslash must be the very first character inside the braces. Thus, neither {G{\"{o}}del} nor {G\"{o}del} work here.

This feature handles accented characters and foreign symbols used with LaTEX. It also allows user-defined "accents." For purposes of counting letters in labels, BibTEX considers everything inside the braces as a single letter.

To BibTeX, an accented character is a special case of a "special character," which consists of everything from a left brace at the topmost level, immediately followed by a backslash, up through the matching right brace. For example, the field

```
author = {\OE{le} {\'{E}mile} {Ren\'{e}} van R{\i\j}den}
author = "\OE{le} {\'{E}mile} {Ren\'{e}} van R{\i\j}den"
```

has two special characters, "{\'{E}mile}" and "{\i\j}."

In general, BibTeX does not process TeX or LaTeX control sequences inside a special character, but it will process other characters. Thus, a style that converts all titles to lowercase transforms

```
"The {\TeX BOOK\NOOP} Saga" into "The {\TeX book\NOOP} saga"
```

where the article "The" remains capitalized because it is the first word in the title.

The special character scheme is useful for handling accented characters; to make BibTeX's alphabetizing do what you want, see the discussion of the \SortNoop command on page 404. Also, since BibTeX counts an entire special character as just one letter, you can force extra characters inside labels.

13.5.3   Abbreviations in BibTeX

(£ 143–44)
BibTeX text fields can be abbreviated. An abbreviation is a string of characters starting with a letter and not containing a space or any of the following ten characters:

```
"  #  %  '  (  )  ,  =  {  }
```

Abbreviations can be used in the text field of BibTeX entries, but they should not be enclosed in braces or quotation marks. If cacm stands for

```
Communications of the ACM
```

then the following two ways of specifying the journal field are equivalent:

```
journal = "Communications of the ACM"
journal = cacm
```

You can define your own abbreviations with the @STRING command in a .bib file, as shown below.

```
@string{AW         = "Addison--Wesley Publishing Company"}
@STRING{CACM       = "Communications of the ACM"}
```

```
@String{pub-AW     = {{Ad\-di\-son-Wes\-ley}}}
@String{pub-AW:adr = "Reading, MA, USA"}
@String{TUG        = "\TeX{} Users Group"}
@String{TUG:adr    = {Providence, RI, USA}}
```

The case of the name for an abbreviation is not important, thus CACM and cacm are considered identical, but BIBTEX produces a warning if you mix different cases. Also the @STRING command itself can be spelled as all lowercase, all uppercase, or a mixture. The @STRING commands can appear anywhere in the .bib style, but an abbreviation must be defined before it is used. It is good practice to group all @STRING commands at the beginning of a .bib style, or place them in a dedicated .bib style containing only a list of abbreviations. The @STRING commands defined in the .bib file take precedence over definitions in the style files.

You can concatenate several strings (or @STRING definitions) using the concatenation operator #. Given the following,

```
@STRING{TUB = {TUGboat }}
```

you can easily construct nearly identical journal fields for different entries:

```
@article(tub-86,
  journal = TUB # 1986,
  . . .
@article(tub-87
  journal = TUB # 1987,
  . . .
```

Most bibliography styles contain a series of predefined abbreviations. As a convention, there should always be three-letter abbreviations for the months: jan, feb, mar, etc. You should always use these three-letter abbreviations for the months, rather than spelling them explicitly. This assures consistency inside your bibliography. Information about the day of the month is usually best included in the month field, e.g., making use of the possibility of concatenation:

```
month = apr # "~1,"
```

Names of popular journals in a given application field are also made available as abbreviations in most styles, and you should consult the documentation associated with the bibliographic style in question. You can easily define your own set of journal abbreviations by putting them in @STRING commands in their own data base file and listing this data base file as an argument to LATEX's \bibliography command.

13.5.4   A B<small>IB</small>T<small>E</small>X Preamble

B<small>IB</small>T<small>E</small>X also offers a @PREAMBLE command with a syntax similar to the one for
@STRING except that there is no name or equals sign, just the string. For example:

```
@preamble{ "\newcommand{\SortNoop}[1]{} "
        # "\newcommand{\OneLetter}[1]{#1} "
        # "\newcommand{\SwapArgs}[2]{#2#1} " }
```

You can see how the different command definitions inside the @PREAMBLE
are concatenated using the # symbol. The standard styles output the argument
of the @PREAMBLE literally to the .bbl file, so that the command definitions are
available when L<small>A</small>T<small>E</small>X reads the file.

For instance, the \SortNoop command defined above can be used to guide
B<small>IB</small>T<small>E</small>X's sorting algorithm. The latter normally does an acceptable job, but sometimes you might want to override B<small>IB</small>T<small>E</small>X's decision by specifying your own sorting key. This trick can be used with foreign languages, which have different
sorting rules from English, or when you want to order the various volumes of a
book in a way given by their original date of publication and independently of
their re-edition dates.

Suppose that the first volume of a book was originally published in 1986,
with a second edition in 1991, and the second volume was published in 1990.
Then you could write:

```
volume=1, year = "{\SortNoop{86}}1991"
    .   .   .
volume=2, year = "{\SortNoop{90}}1990"
```

According to the definition of \SortNoop, L<small>A</small>T<small>E</small>X throws away its argument
and ends up printing only the true year for these fields. For B<small>IB</small>T<small>E</small>X \SortNoop
is an "accent" and it will sort the works according to the numbers 861991 and
901990, placing volume 1 before volume 2, just as you want.

13.5.5   Cross-References

B<small>IB</small>T<small>E</small>X entries can be cross-referenced. Suppose you specify \cite{Wood:color}
in your document, and you have the following two entries in the data base file:

```
@Inbook{Wood:color, author = {Pat Wood}, crossref={Roth:postscript},
        title = {PostScript Color Separation}, pages={201--225}}
@Book{Roth:postscript, editor = {Stephen E. Roth}, title=
        {{Real World PostScript}} , booktitle={{Real World PostScript}},
        publisher=AW , address=AW:adr , year=1988, ISBN={0-201-06663-7}}
```

The special `crossref` field tells BibTeX that the `Wood:color` entry should inherit missing fields from the entry it cross-references—`Roth:postscript`. BibTeX
automatically puts the `Roth:postscript` entry into the reference list if it is
cross-referenced by two or more entries on a `\cite` or `\nocite` command, even
if the `Roth:postscript` entry itself is never the argument of a `\cite` or `\nocite`
command. So `Roth:postscript` will automatically appear on the reference list
if one other entry besides `Wood:color` cross-references it.

A cross-referenced entry must occur later in the data base files than every
entry that cross-references it. Thus, all cross-referenced entries could be put
at the end of the data base. Cross-referenced entries cannot themselves cross-
reference another entry.

You can also use LaTeX's `\cite` command inside the fields of your BibTeX
entries. This can be useful if you want to reference some other relevant material
inside a note field:

```
note = "See Eijkhout~\cite{Eijkhout:1991} for more details"
```

However, you should be aware of the fact that such usage may mean that
you need additional LaTeX and BibTeX runs to compile your document properly.
This will happen if the citation put from BibTeX into the `.bbl` file refers to a key
that was not used in a citation in the main document. Thus, LaTeX is unable to
resolve this in the following run.

13.5.6   Some Further Remarks

Entries with identical sort keys will appear in citation order. The bibliography
styles construct these sort keys, which usually consist of the author information
followed by the year and title.

LaTeX's comment character % is not a comment character inside `.bib` data
base files.

In general, if you want to keep BibTeX from changing something to lowercase,
you should enclose it in braces. Note that this will not be sufficient when the
first character after the left brace is a backslash (see page 401).

13.6   Detailed Description of the Entries

As discussed in section 13.2, you must describe each bibliographic entry as
belonging to a certain class, with the information itself tagged by certain fields.

So the first thing you have to decide is what type of entry you are dealing
with. Although no fixed classification scheme can be complete, with a little
creativity you can make BibTeX cope reasonably well with even the more bizarre
types of publications. For nonstandard types, it is probably wise not to attach
too much importance to BibTeX's warning messages (see below).

(£ 144–46)   Most B<small>IB</small>T_EX styles have thirteen entry types, which are shown in table 13.2 on page 408. These different types of publications demand different kinds of information; a reference to a journal article might include the volume and number of the journal, which is usually not meaningful for a book. Therefore, different data base types have different fields. In fact, for each type of entry, the fields are divided into three classes:

required   Omission of the field will produce a warning message and, possibly, a badly formatted bibliography entry. If the required information is not meaningful, you are using the wrong entry type. However, if the required information is meaningful but, say, already included in some other field, simply ignore the warning.

optional   The field's information will be used if present, but you can omit it without causing formatting problems. Include the optional field if it can help the reader.

ignored   The field is ignored. B<small>IB</small>T_EX ignores any field that is not required or optional, so you can include any fields in a .bib file entry. It is a good idea to put all relevant information about a reference in its .bib file entry, even information that may never appear in the bibliography. For example, the abstract of a paper can be entered into an abstract field in its .bib file entry. The .bib file is probably as good a place as any for the abstract, and there exist bibliography styles for printing selected abstracts (see the abstract bibliography style mentioned in table 13.1 on page 377).

Table 13.2 on page 408 describes the standard entry types, along with their required and optional fields, as used by the standard bibliography styles. The fields within each class (required or optional) are listed in order of occurrence in the output. A few entry types, however, may perturb the alphabetic ordering slightly, depending on what fields are missing. The meaning of the individual fields is explained in table 13.3 on page 409. Nonstandard bibliography styles may ignore some optional fields in creating the reference. Remember that, when used in a .bib file, the entry-type name is preceded by an @ character (see also figure 13.4 on page 381).

In addition to the fields listed in table 13.2, each entry type also has an optional key field, used in some styles for alphabetizing, for cross-referencing, or for forming a \bibitem label. You should include a key field for any entry whose author information is missing. The author information is usually the author field, but some styles use the editor or organization field. A situation where a key field is useful is the following:

```
organization = "The Association for Computing Machinery",
key = "ACM"
```

Without the key field, the alpha style would construct a label from the first three letters of the information in the organization field; and although the style file will strip off the article "The," you would still get a rather uninformative label like "[Ass86]." The key field above yields a more acceptable "[ACM86]."

We now turn our attention to the fields recognized by the standard bibliography styles. These "standard" fields are shown in table 13.3 on page 409. Other fields, like abstract, can be required if you use one of the extended nonstandard styles shown in table 13.1 on page 377. As nonrecognized fields are ignored by the BibTeX styles, you can use this feature to include "comments" inside an entry: it is enough to put the information to be ignored inside brackets following a field that is not recognized by the BibTeX style.

(£ 146–47)

As with the names of the entry types in table 13.2 on the following page, the names of the fields should be interpreted in their widest sense to make them applicable in a maximum of situations. And you should never forget that a judicious use of the note field can solve even the more complicated cases.

13.7   Understanding BibTeX Styles

This section presents a condensed introduction to the language used in BibTeX style files. The information should suffice if you want to slightly modify an existing style file. For more details you should consult Oren Patashnik's original article: "Designing BibTeX Styles" [65].

13.7.1   A General Description of a BibTeX Style File

BibTeX styles use a postfix stack language (like PostScript) to tell BibTeX how to format the entries to go into the reference list. The language has ten commands, described in Table 13.4 on page 412, to manipulate the language's objects: constants, variables, functions, the stack, and the entry list.

BibTeX knows two types of functions: built-in functions, provided by BibTeX itself (see table 13.5 on page 413), and user functions, which are defined using either the MACRO or FUNCTION command.

You can use all printing characters inside the pair of double quotes delimiting string constants. Although BibTeX, in general, ignores case differences, it honors the case inside a string. Spaces are significant inside string constants, and a string constant cannot be split across lines.

Variable and function names cannot begin with a numeral and may not contain any of the ten restricted characters shown on page 402. BibTeX ignores case differences in the names of variables, functions, and macros.

Constants and variables can only be of type integers or string (Boolean true and false are represented by the integers 1 and 0 respectively).

article	An article from a journal or magazine.
	Required: author, title, journal, year.
	Optional: volume, number, pages, month, note.
book	A book with an explicit publisher.
	Required: author or editor, title, publisher, year.
	Optional: volume or number, series, address, edition, month, note.
booklet	A work that is printed and bound, but without a named publisher or sponsoring institution.
	Required: title.
	Optional: author, howpublished, address, month, year, note.
inbook	A part of a book, e.g., a chapter, section or whatever and/or a range of pages.
	Required: author or editor, title, chapter and/or pages, publisher, year.
	Optional: volume or number, series, type, address, edition, month, note.
incollection	A part of a book having its own title.
	Required: author, title, booktitle, publisher, year.
	Optional: editor, volume or number, series, type, chapter, pages, address, edition, month, note.
inproceedings	An article in a conference proceedings.
	Required: author, title, booktitle, year.
	Optional: editor, volume or number, series, pages, address, month, organization, publisher, note.
manual	Technical documentation.
	Required: title.
	Optional: author, organization, address, edition, month, year, note.
mastersthesis	A master's thesis.
	Required: author, title, school, year.
	Optional: type, address, month, note.
misc	Use this type when nothing else fits. A warning will only be issued if all optional fields are empty (i.e., the entire field is empty).
	Required: none.
	Optional: author, title, howpublished, month, year, note.
phdthesis	A PhD thesis.
	Required: author, title, school, year.
	Optional: type, address, month, note.
proceedings	Conference proceedings.
	Required: title, year.
	Optional: editor, volume or number, series, address, publisher, note, month, organization.
techreport	A report published by a school or other institution, usually numbered within a series.
	Required: author, title, institution, year.
	Optional: type, number, address, month, note.
unpublished	A document having an author and title, but not formally published.
	Required: author, title, note.
	Optional: month, year.

Table 13.2: List of BibTeX's entry types as defined in most styles

`address`	Usually the address of the `publisher` or other institution. For major publishing houses, just give the city. For small publishers, specifying the complete address might help the reader.
`annote`	An annotation. Not used by the standard bibliography styles, but used by others that produce an annotated bibliography (e.g., `annote`). The field starts a new sentence and hence the first word should be capitalized.
`author`	The name(s) of the author(s), in BIBTEX name format (section 13.5.2).
`booktitle`	Title of a book, part of which is being cited (section 13.5.2). For book entries use the `title` field.
`chapter`	A chapter (or section or whatever) number.
`crossref`	The data base key of the entry being cross-referenced (section 13.5.5).
`edition`	The edition of a book, e.g., "Second." This should be an ordinal, and should have the first letter capitalized, as shown above; the standard styles convert to lowercase when necessary.
`editor`	Name(s) of editor(s), in BIBTEX name format. If there is also an `author` field, then the `editor` field gives the editor of the book or collection in which the reference appears.
`howpublished`	How something strange has been published.
`institution`	Institution sponsoring a technical report.
`journal`	Journal name. Abbreviations are provided for many journals (section 13.5.3).
`key`	Used for alphabetizing, cross-referencing, and creating a label when the `author` and `editor` information are missing. This field should not be confused with the key that appears in the `\cite` command and at the beginning of the data base entry.
`month`	The month in which the work was published or, for an unpublished work, in which it was written. For reasons of consistency the standard three-letter abbreviations `jan`, `feb`, `mar`, etc. should be used (section 13.5.3).
`note`	Any additional information that can help the reader.
`number`	The number of a journal, magazine, technical report, or work in a series. An issue of a journal or magazine is usually identified by its volume and number; a technical report normally has a number; and sometimes books in a named series also carry numbers.
`organization`	The organization that sponsors a conference or that publishes a `manual`.
`pages`	One or more page numbers or range of numbers, e.g., `42--111` or `7,41,73--97` or `43+` (here the '+' indicates pages that do not form a simple range).
`publisher`	The publisher's name.
`school`	The name of the school where the thesis was written.
`series`	The name of a series or set of books. When citing an entire book, the `title` field gives its title and an optional `series` field gives the name of a series or multivolume set in which the book is published.
`title`	The work's title, typed as explained in section 13.5.2.
`type`	The type of a technical report, e.g., "Research Note." This name is used instead of the default "Technical Report." For the type `phdthesis` you could use the term "Ph.D. dissertation" by specifying: `type = "{Ph.D.} dissertation."` Similarly, for the `inbook` and `incollection` entry types you can get "section 1.2" instead of the default "chapter 1.2" with `chapter = "1.2,"` `type = "Section."`
`volume`	The volume of a journal or multivolume book.
`year`	The year of publication or, for an unpublished work, the year it was written. Generally it should consist of four numerals, such as 1984, although the standard styles can handle any `year` whose last four nonpunctuation characters are numerals, such as "about 1984."

Table 13.3: List of BIBTEX's standard entry fields

There are three kinds of variables:

Global variables   These are either integer- or string-valued, and are declared using an INTEGERS or STRINGS command.

Entry variables   These are integer- or string-valued variables, which are declared using the ENTRY command. Each of these variables will have a value for each entry on the list read in a BIBTEX data base.

Fields   These are string-valued, read-only variables that store the information from the data base file. Their values are set by the READ command. As with entry variables there is a value for each entry.

13.7.2   The BIBTEX Style File Commands

Table 13.4 on page 412 gives a short description of the ten BIBTEX commands. Although the command names appear in uppercase, BIBTEX ignores case differences.

It is recommended (but not essential) to leave at least one blank line between commands and to leave no blank lines within a command. This helps BIBTEX recover from syntax errors.

13.7.3   The Built-In Functions

Table 13.5 on page 413 gives a short overview of BIBTEX's 37 built-in functions (for more details, see [65]). You can see that every built-in function with a letter in its name ends with a $.

13.7.4   The Documentation Style btxbst.doc

Oren Patashnik based the standard BIBTEX style files abbrv, alpha, plain, and unsrt on a generic file, btxbst.doc, which is well documented and should be consulted for gaining a detailed insight into the workings of BIBTEX styles.

In the standard styles, labels have two basic formatting modes, *alphabetic*, like [Lam84], and *Numeric*, like [34].

References can be ordered in three ways.

Sorted, alphabetic labels   Alphabetically ordered, first by citation label, then by author(s) (or its replacement field), then by year and title.

Sorted, numeric labels   Alphabetically ordered, first by author(s) (or its replacement field), then by year and title.

Unsorted   Printed in the order in which they are cited in the text.

The basic flow of a style file is controlled by the following command lines, which are found at the end of the `btxbst.doc` file:

```
EXECUTE {begin.bib}          % Preamble and \begin{thebibliography}
EXECUTE {init.state.consts}  % Initialize the state constants
ITERATE {call.type$}         % Loop over entries producing output
EXECUTE {end.bib}            % Write \end{thebibliography} command
```

The meaning of these commands should be clear from tables 13.4 on the next page and 13.5 on page 413.

The code of a style file starts with the declaration of the available fields with the ENTRY declaration and the string variables to be used for the construction of the citation label.

Each entry function starts by calling `output.bibitem` to write the `\bibitem` and its arguments to the `.bbl` file. Then the various fields are formatted and printed by function `output` or `output.check`, which handles the writing of separators (commas, periods, `\newblock`'s) as needed. Finally, `fin.entry` is called to add the final period and finish the entry.

Then follow some functions for formatting chunks of an entry. And there are functions for each of the basic fields, such as `format.names`, which separates names into their "First Von Last, Junior" and separates them by commas and with an "and" before the last (but ending with "et al." if the last of multiple authors is `"others"`). There is `format.authors` for authors, and `format.editors` for editors (it appends the appropriate title: ", editor" or ", editors") and others.

The next part of the file contains all the functions defining the different types accepted in a `.bib` file, i.e., functions like `article` and `book`. These functions actually generate the output written to the `.bbl` file for a given entry. They must precede the READ command. In addition, a style designer should provide a function `default.type` for unknown types.

The next section of the `btxbst.doc` file contains definitions for the names of the months and for certain common journals. Depending on the style, the full or abbreviated names are used. It is followed by the READ command, which inputs the entries in the `.bib` file.

Then the labels for the bibliographic entries are constructed. Exactly which fields are used for the primary part of the label depends on the entry type.

The labels are next prepared for sorting. When sorting, the sort key is computed by executing the `presort` function on each entry. For alphabetic labels you might have to append additional "a"s, "b"s, and so forth to create a unique sorting order, which requires two more sorting passes. For numeric labels, either the sorted or original order can be used. In both cases, you need to keep track of the longest label for use with the `thebibliography` environment.

Finally, the `.bbl` file is written by looping over the entries and executing the `call.type$` function for each one.

ENTRY   *{field_list}*   *{integer_variable_list}*   *{string_variable_list}*

Declares the fields and entry variables. BibTeX declares automatically one supplementary field crossref, used for cross-referencing, and an additional string entry variable sort.key$, used by the SORT command. There should only be one ENTRY command per style file. For instance, for the styles alpha and plain you have respectively:

```
ENTRY   { address author booktitle ... } {} { label extra.label sort.label }
ENTRY   { address author booktitle ... } {} { label }
```

EXECUTE   *{function_name}*

Executes a single function.

```
EXECUTE {begin.bib}
```

FUNCTION   *{function_name}*   *{definition}*

Defines a new function. You cannot change the definition of a FUNCTION outside a style file.

```
FUNCTION {end.bib}
{ newline$  "\end{thebibliography}" write$ newline$ }
```

MACRO   *{macro_name}*   *{definition}*

Defines a string macro. You can change the definition of a MACRO outside a style file.

```
MACRO {feb} {"February"}
```

INTEGERS   *{global_integer_variable_list}*

Declares global integer variables.

```
INTEGERS { longest.label.width last.extra.num }
```

STRINGS   *{global_string_variable_list}*

Declares global string variables.

```
STRINGS { longest.label last.sort.label next.extra }
```

ITERATE   *{function_name}*

Executes a single function, once for each entry in the list, in the list's current order.

```
ITERATE {longest.label.pass}
```

REVERSE   *{function_name}*

Executes a single function, once for each entry in the list, in reverse order.

```
REVERSE {reverse.pass}
```

READ

Extracts from the data base file the field values for each entry in the list. There should only be one READ command per style file. The ENTRY and MACRO commands must precede READ.

SORT

Sorts the entry list using the values of the string entry variable sort.key$.

Table 13.4: List of BibTeX style file commands

$\mathcal{I}_1$ $\mathcal{I}_2$ >		($\mathcal{I}$)	1 (if $\mathcal{I}_1 > \mathcal{I}_2$) or 0 (otherwise)
$\mathcal{I}_1$ $\mathcal{I}_2$ <		($\mathcal{I}$)	1 (if $\mathcal{I}_1 < \mathcal{I}_2$) or 0 (otherwise)
$\mathcal{I}_1$ $\mathcal{I}_2$ =		($\mathcal{I}$)	1 (if $\mathcal{I}_1 = \mathcal{I}_2$) or 0 (otherwise)
S_1 S_2 =		($\mathcal{I}$)	1 (if $S_1 = S_2$) or 0 (otherwise)
$\mathcal{I}_1$ $\mathcal{I}_2$ +		($\mathcal{I}_1 + \mathcal{I}_2$)	add two integers
$\mathcal{I}_1$ $\mathcal{I}_2$ −		($\mathcal{I}_1 - \mathcal{I}_2$)	subtract two integers
S_1 S_2 ∗		($S_1 S_2$)	concatenate two strings
$\mathcal{L}$ $\mathcal{V}$:=			assign to $\mathcal{V}$ the value of $\mathcal{L}$
S	add.period$	(S.)	adds dot to string if not before '.', '?', or '!'
	call.type$		execute function whose name is the type of an entry, e.g., book
S "t"	change.case$	(S)	convert S to lowercase except at beginning
S "l"	change.case$	(S)	convert S completely to lowercase
S "u"	change.case$	(S)	convert S completely to uppercase
S	chr.to.int$	($\mathcal{I}$)	translate single string character to ASCII equivalent
	cite$	(*cite_string*)	push \cite command argument
$\mathcal{L}$	duplicate$	($\mathcal{L}$ $\mathcal{L}$)	duplicate entry
$\mathcal{L}$	empty$	($\mathcal{I}$)	1 (if $\mathcal{L}$ missing field or blank string) or 0 (otherwise)
S_1 $\mathcal{I}$ S_2	format.name$	(S)	format $\mathcal{I}$ names S_1 according to name specifications S_2
$\mathcal{I}$ $\mathcal{F}_1$ $\mathcal{F}_2$	if$		execute $\mathcal{F}_1$ if $\mathcal{I} > 0$, else execute $\mathcal{F}_2$
$\mathcal{I}$	int.to.chr$	(S)	translate integer into one ASCII character table
$\mathcal{I}$	int.to.str$	(S)	push string equivalent of integer
$\mathcal{L}$	missing$	($\mathcal{I}$)	1 (if $\mathcal{L}$ missing field) or 0 (otherwise)
	newline$		start a new line in the .bbl file
S	num.names$	($\mathcal{I}$)	number of names in S
$\mathcal{L}$	pop$		throw away top element on stack
	preamble$	(S)	push concatenation of all @PREAMBLE strings read in data base files
S	purify$	(S)	remove non-alphanumeric characters
	quote$	(S)	push double-quote character string
	skip$		do nothing
	stack$		pop and print whole stack
S $\mathcal{I}_1$ $\mathcal{I}_2$	substring$	(S)	substring of S starting at $\mathcal{I}_1$ and with a length of $\mathcal{I}_2$
$\mathcal{L}_1$ $\mathcal{L}_2$	swap$	($\mathcal{L}_2$ $\mathcal{L}_1$)	swap the literals
S	text.length$	($\mathcal{I}$)	number of "text" characters
S $\mathcal{I}$	text.prefix$	(S)	front $\mathcal{I}$ characters of S
$\mathcal{L}$	top$		pop and print top of stack
	type$	(S)	push current entry's type, e.g., book or "" if unknown
S	warning$		pop and print top (string) literal and a warning message
$\mathcal{F}_1$ $\mathcal{F}_2$ $\mathcal{I}$	while$		execute $\mathcal{F}_2$ while function value $\mathcal{I}$ of $\mathcal{F}_1$ has $\mathcal{I} > 0$
S	width$	($\mathcal{I}$)	push width of S (TEX units)
S	write$		write S to output buffer

Table 13.5: List of BIBTEX style file built-in functions

The built-in functions are preceded by the variable they consume on the stack. If they leave a result on the stack it is shown in parentheses. A "literal" $\mathcal{L}$ is an element on the stack. It can be an integer $\mathcal{I}$, a string S, a variable $\mathcal{V}$, a function $\mathcal{F}$, or a special value denoting a missing field. If the popped literal has an incorrect type, BIBTEX complains and pushes the integer 0 or the null string, depending on the function's resulting type.

13.8   Introducing Small Changes in a Style File

Often it is necessary to make slight changes to an existing style file to suit the particular needs of a publisher.

As a first example, we show you how to eliminate the (sometimes unpleasant) standard BIBTEX style feature that transforms titles to lowercase. In most cases, you will want the titles to remain in the same case as they are typed. Therefore, a variant of style unsrt can be made, and we shall call it myunsrt, since it is different from the original style. Similar methods can be used for other styles.

From table 13.5 on the page before you will probably have guessed that function `change.case$` is responsible for case changes. Therefore, with the help of an editor and looking for the above string, you will find that it is function `format.title` that must be changed. Below we show that function before and after the modification:

```
FUNCTION {format.title}                FUNCTION {format.title}
{ title empty$                         { title empty$
    { "" }                                 { "" }
    { title "t" change.case$ }             { title } % <== modified
  if$                                    if$
}                                      }
```
           Before modification   *After modification*

With the help of table 13.5 on the preceding page you can follow the logic of the function and the substitution performed. Another function that must be changed in a similar way is `format.edition`:

```
FUNCTION {format.edition}                FUNCTION {format.edition}
{ edition empty$                         { edition empty$
    { "" }                                   { "" }
    { output.state mid.sentence =            { output.state mid.sentence =
        { edition "l" change.case$ " edition" * }      { edition  " edition" * }%<== changed
        { edition "t" change.case$ " edition" * }      { edition  " edition" * }%<== changed
      if$                                      if$
    }                                        }
  if$                                      if$
}                                        }
```
           Before modification   *After modification*

In `format.chapter.pages`, `format.thesis.type` and `format.tr.number` similar changes must be made.

13.8.1   Adding a New Field

Sometimes you may want to add a new field to those already existing. As an example we could add an `annotation` field. Two approaches can be taken: either the one adopted in style annotate or the one in style annotation. Let us

look at the simpler solution first. The style annotation, based on plain, first adds
the field annote to the ENTRY definition list, and then the fin.entry function is
changed to treat the supplementary field. As seen in the example of the function
book, the function fin.entry is called at the end of each function defining an
entry type.

```
FUNCTION {fin.entry}                FUNCTION {fin.entry}
{ add.period$                       { add.period$
  write$                              write$
  newline$                            newline$
}                                     "\begin{quotation}\noindent{\sc Key:\ }" cite$ * write$
                                        annote missing$
                                        'skip$
                                        { "\\{\sc Annotation:\ }" write$  annote  write$ }
                                      if$
                                      "\end{quotation}" write$
                                      newline$
                                    }
```

| *Before modification* | *After modification* |

You see that after outputting the citation string inside a quotation environment, the annotation text is written following the text "Annotation," which
starts a separate line. If the field is absent, nothing is written (the test, annote
missing$, takes the skip$ branch of the if$ command).

The other style, annotate, based on alpha, takes a more complicated approach. After adding the element annotate to the ENTRY definition list, the
function format.annotate is created to format that supplementary field. The
function has a decision flow similar to the code shown above.

```
FUNCTION {format.annotate}
{ annotate empty$
  { "" }
  { " \begin{quotation}\noindent "
    annotate
    * " \end{quotation} " *
  }
      if$
}
```

Then, the formatting routine for each of the entry types of table 13.2 on page 408
has a supplementary line format.annotate write$ just following the call to
fin.entry.

Various style files have added other fields, like the isbn and issn number
of a publication (is-abbrv, is-alpha, is-plain, and is-unsrt). The abstract style has
three supplementary fields: abstract, keyword, and comment. They are treated
in a way similar to annotate above.

```
FUNCTION {format.editors}            FUNCTION {format.editors}
{ editor empty$                      { editor empty$
   { "" }                               { "" }
   { editor format.names                { editor format.names
     editor num.names$ #1 >               ", redactie" *
       { " (eds)" * }                  }
       { " (ed.)" * }                 if$
     if$                            }
   }
 if$
}
```
          Before modification   *After modification*

Figure 13.16: Adapting a BIBTEX style to Dutch

We can now turn our attention to the customization of the entries themselves. An interesting example is the chicago style, which was already mentioned
in section 13.1.1. This style is used with various new citation commands, and
the bibliography style was adapted to use the recommendations of *The Chicago
Manual of Style* [86]. Another interesting series of styles are authordate1 through
authordate4 by David Rhead. They implement many of the recommendations
of British Standards BS 1629 and BS 5605, Cambridge and Oxford University
Press, as well as of *The Chicago Manual of Style*. The files show clearly where
changes have been introduced, so they are worth studying to see how stylistic
modifications are made in general.

13.8.2 Foreign Language Support

If you want to adapt a BIBTEX style to languages other than English, you will, at
the very least, have to translate the hard-coded English strings in the BIBTEX style
files, like "edition" in the example at the beginning of this section.

First you should edit a style file and introduce the new terms in the necessary
places. As you are working with only one language, it is possible to introduce the
proper language-specific typographic conventions at the same time. An example
of this approach is the nederlands style by Werenfried Spit. It is a harvard based
style adapted to Dutch following the recommendations of Van Dale (1982).

We shall now look at a couple of examples of functions that were adapted.

As you can see in figure 13.16 in Dutch one does not make the distinction
between one or more editors. The generic Dutch word redactie replaces the
two possibilities.

Figure 13.17 on the next page shows how, for one particular language, you
can go rather far in the customization (in form and translation) of an entry,
in this case the format of the edition field. In this example, up to the third
edition, Dutch specific strings are used. Starting with the fourth edition the
generic string i^e is used, where i is the number of the edition. You can also see

```
FUNCTION {format.edition}           FUNCTION {format.edition}
{ edition empty$                    { edition empty$
  { "" }                              { "" }
  { output.state mid.sentence =       { edition "1" =
    { edition "l" change.case$ " edition" * }    { "Eerste" }
    { edition "t" change.case$ " edition" * }    { edition "2" =
    if$                                   { "Tweede" }
  }                                       { edition "3" =
  if$                                         { "Derde" }
}                                             { edition "$^{\mathrm{e}}$ " * }
                                              if$
                                          }
                                          if$
                                        }
                                        if$
                                        output.state mid.sentence =
                                          { "l" change.case$ " druk" * }
                                          { "t" change.case$ " druk" * }
                                          if$
                                      }
                                      if$
                                    }
```

Before modification   *After modification*

Figure 13.17: Customizing a BibTeX style file for a different language

the nesting of the `if$` statements and the use of the case changing command `change.case$`.

Of course, the strings for the names of the months should be changed and some other language specific strings can be defined.

```
MACRO {jan} {"januari"}
MACRO {feb} {"februari"}
MACRO {mar} {"maart"}
   . . .
MACRO {UvA} {"Universiteit van Amsterdam"}
MACRO {RUG} {"Rijksuniversiteit te Groningen"}
MACRO {RUL} {"Rijksuniversiteit te Leiden"}
MACRO {TUD} {"Technische Universiteit Delft"}
   . . .
MACRO {NTN} {"Nederlands tijdschrift voor natuurkunde"}
```

Then, of course, the sorting routine for the names, `sort.format.names`, must know about the specific language dependent rules for showing names in the right order.

Also, most languages have articles or other short words which should be ignored for sorting titles.

```
FUNCTION {sort.format.title}          FUNCTION {sort.format.title}
{ 't :=                               { 't :=
  "A " #2                               "De " #3
    "An " #3                             "Een " #4 t chop.word
      "The " #4 t chop.word            chop.word
    chop.word                          sortify
  chop.word                            #1 global.max$ substring$
  sortify                            }
  #1 global.max$ substring$
}
       Before modification                  After modification
```

Figure 13.18: Ignoring articles in BIBTEX sorting

Variables	ABBRV	ALPHA	PLAIN	UNSRT
ENGLISH	abbrv	alpha	plain	unsrt
FRENCH	fabbrv	falpha	fplain	funsrt
GERMAN	gabbrv	galpha	gplain	gunsrt

Table 13.6: The BIBTEX style files of the Delphi system

As seen in figure 13.18 it is the chop.word function that chops the word specified from the string presented on the stack—in this case the definite (De) and indefinite (Een) articles.

A more general approach was taken by the Delphi Group (Jörg Heitkoetter and colleagues) of the University of Dortmund (Germany). For their Delphi BibStyles collection, they have added in the generic btxbst.doc file conditional code, which is activated by supplementary preprocessor variables. They have versions for English, French, and German, from which they can generate the style files shown in table 13.6.

If you want to add more languages to this system, then the btxbst.doc file must be augmented with the necessary control variables and language-specific strings.

With his BIBTEX "adaptable" family, Hans-Hermann Bode of the University of Osnabrück has taken a road somewhat similar to the Babel system discussed in section 9.2. In his adaptation, he parameterizes the language dependent strings, so that the language dependent data can be kept in a file separate from the BIBTEX style [13].

He also takes the file btxbst.doc as a basis, and replaces the fixed English text strings by control sequences. The values for these command sequences can be defined for each supported language. Currently, only English and German are supported. Switching languages is not the same as with the Babel system, but it should not be difficult to provide such an interface.

Although both these systems do good jobs for specifying the language dependent strings, they do not go as far as the style nederlands, discussed above.

In particular, they do not pay any attention to problems of punctuation or to sorting specificities, but they do provide an automatic translation for foreign language terms.

13.9 `makebst`—Customizing Bibliographic Style Files

The makebst TeX program, written by Patrick W. Daly, together with a generic bibliographic style file, can produce custom-made `.bst` BibTeX files. The precise format of the bibliographic entities can be specified interactively, and the resulting output file can be processed by DOCSTRIP to generate the desired BibTeX style file (see section 14.3 for a description of the DOCSTRIP program). Technically speaking, a BibTeX bibliographic style file master contains alternative coding that depends on DOCSTRIP options. By choosing a given entry from the interactive menu (see the example below), some of this code is activated, thus providing the necessary customization.

13.9.1 Running `makebst`

The example shows the beginning and final part of a TeX run with the makebst system. After the DOCSTRIP run at the end you will obtain a BibTeX style file (`mytest.bst` in the example) that implements the style parameters you specified for your bibliography.

```
tex makebst
This is TeX, C Version 3.141
(makebst.tex
***********************************
* This is Make Bibliography Style *
***********************************
It makes up a docstrip batch job to produce
a customized .bst file for running with BibTeX.
Do you want a description of the usage? (NO)

\yn=y

Enter the FULL name of the MASTER file (def=genbst.mbs)

\mfile=genbst.mbs

Name of the final OUTPUT .bst file?

\ofile=mytest.bst

Give a comment line to include in the style file.
Something like for which journals it is applicable.
```

\ans=<u>Test of the generic bst making program makebst</u>
(genbst.mbs

STYLE OF CITATIONS:
(*) Numerical as in standard LaTeX
(a) Author-year with some non-standard interface
(c) Cite key (special for listing contents of bib file)
  Select:

\ans=<u>a</u>
  You have selected: Author-year

AUTHOR-YEAR SUPPORT SYSTEM:
(*) Natbib for use with natbib.sty
(l) Apalike for use with apalike.sty
(h) Harvard system with harvard.sty
(a) Astronomy system with astron.sty
(c) Chicago system with chicago.sty
(d) Author-date system with authordate1-4.sty
  Select:

\ans=<u>h</u>
  You have selected: Harvard

ORDERING OF REFERENCES:
(*) Alphabetical by all authors
(l) By label (Jones before Jones and James before Jones et al)
  Select:
                          ..... *Many more questions and answers* ....
Finished!!
Batch job written to file 'mytest.drv'
Shall I now run this batch job? (NO)

\yn=<u>y</u>
(a.drv (/usr/local/lib/tex/macros/docstrip.tex
Utility: 'docstrip' 2.0r <92/08/17>
English documentation <92/08/17>

****
* This program converts documented macro-files into fast *
* loadable files by stripping off (nearly) all comments! *
****

Generating file ./mytest.bst

Processing File genbst.mbs (ay,har,seq-lab,nm-rev,nmlm,x3,m3,nmft-sc,
dt-beg,yr-par,tit-it,atit-u,volp-com,edby,blk-com,pp) -> mytest.bst

CHAPTER 14

LaTeX Package File Documentation Tools

In this chapter we describe the doc package, which allows you to maintain your LaTeX packages in an easy way. The principle is that LaTeX code and comments are mixed in the same file and that the documentation or the stripped package file(s) are obtained from the latter in a standard way. We shall explain the structure that these files should have, and show how, together with the program DOCSTRIP, you can build self-installing procedures for distributing your LaTeX package(s) and generating the associated documentation.

14.1 · Documenting Package Files

The idea of integrated documentation was employed by Donald Knuth when he developed the TeX program using the WEB system, which combines Pascal-like meta source code and documentation. Thanks to this, it was particularly easy to port TeX and its companion programs to practically every computer platform in the world.

More recently, the authors of LaTeX packages have also started to realize the importance of documenting their LaTeX code, and many are now distributing their LaTeX macros using the framework defined with the doc package (by Frank Mittelbach) and its associated DOCSTRIP utility (by Johannes Braams, Denys Duchier, and Frank Mittelbach).

This system allows LaTeX code and documentation to be held in one and the same TeX source file. The obvious advantage is that a sequence of complex TeX

instructions become easier to understand with the help of comments inside the
file. In addition, updates are more straightforward as only a single source file
needs to be changed.

All you have to do is to run an "installation file" through L&TEX and all the
necessary files will be automatically generated and ready to use, including the
documentation.

By understanding the basics of the **doc** system, it will also be possible for you
to collect all files relating to one of your packages in a single file, including its
documentation. This packaged file, together with an accompanying installation
file, can then be sent easily to any destination.

14.2   The User Interface for the doc Package

14.2.1   General Conventions

A L&TEX file to be used with the **doc** system consists of *documentation parts*
intermixed with *definition parts*.

Every line of a documentation part starts with a percent sign (%) in the
first column. It can contain arbitrary TEX or L&TEX commands except that the %
character cannot be used as a comment character. User comments are possible
by using the ^^A character. Longer text blocks can also be turned into comments
by surrounding them with %␣\iffalse ... % \fi. All other parts of the file are
called definition parts. They contain (sections of) the macros described in the
documentation parts.

When reading the package file, L&TEX bypasses the documentation parts at
high speed, pasting the macro definitions together, even if they are split into
several definition parts.

On the other hand, if you want to produce the documentation of the macros,
then the definition parts should be typeset verbatim. This is achieved by surrounding these parts by the `macrocode` environment. More exactly, before a
definition part there should be a line containing:

```
%␣␣␣␣\begin{macrocode}
```

and after this part a line

```
%␣␣␣␣\end{macrocode}
```

It is mandatory that you put *exactly* four spaces between the % and
\end{macrocode}.

Inside a definition part all TEX commands are allowed; even the percent sign
can be used to suppress unwanted spaces at the end of lines.

Instead of the `macrocode` environment you can also use the `macrocode*` environment, which produces the same results except that spaces are printed as ␣ characters when the documentation is printed.

14.2.2   Describing New Macros and Environments

If you want to indicate at a given point in your document that you are explaining a new macro, you should use the command `\DescribeMacro`.

```
\DescribeMacro{macro name}
```

It takes one argument, which will be printed in the margin and which will also produce a special index entry, e.g.,:

```
% \DescribeMacro{\DocInput} \DescribeMacro{\IndexInput}
% Finally the \meta{input commands} part ...
```

```
\DescribeEnv{environment name}
```

A similar macro, `\DescribeEnv`, can be used to indicate that a LaTeX environment is being explained.

To describe the definition of a new macro, you use the `macro` environment.

```
\begin{macro}{macroname}
```

It has one argument: the name of the new macro. This argument is also used to print the name in the margin and to produce an index entry. Actually, the index entries for usage and definition are different to allow for easy reference.

```
% \begin{macro}{\MacroTopsep}
%    Here is the default value for the \verb+\MacroTopsep+
%    parameter used above.
%    \begin{macrocode}
\newlength{\MacroTopsep}
\setlength{\MacroTopsep}{7pt plus 2pt minus 2pt}
%    \end{macrocode}
% \end{macro}
```

For documenting environments that are defined with `\newenvironment` the environment `environment` can be used. This works like `macro` but expects the name of an environment as its argument.

14.2.3 Cross-Referencing All Macros Used

Inside a `macrocode` or `macrocode*` environment, index entries are produced for every command name. In this way you can easily find out where a specific macro is used. Since TEX is considerably slower when it has to produce such a bulk of index entries you can turn off this feature by using `\DisableCrossrefs` in the driver file. To turn it on again, just use `\EnableCrossrefs`.

Production (or not) of the index (via the *MakeIndex* program) is controlled by using or omitting the following declarations in the driver file preamble (if neither is used, no index is produced). Using `\PageIndex` makes all index entries refer to their page number; with `\CodelineIndex`, index entries produced by `\DescribeMacro` and `\DescribeEnv` refer to page number, but those produced by the `macro` and `macrocode` environments refer to the code lines, which will be numbered automatically.

14.2.4 Producing the Actual Index Entries

Several of the macros mentioned above will produce index entries. These entries have to be sorted by an external program, such as *MakeIndex* (see chapter 12). You need to run *MakeIndex* and specify its `-s` switch (see section 12.4.1 on page 358) with a suitable style, like `gind.ist`, which comes with the doc system.

To read and print the sorted index, you must put the `\PrintIndex` command at the end of your documented package file, possibly preceded by bibliography commands, as needed for your citations.

14.2.5 Additional Bells and Whistles

You can divide the documented file with your package into two parts, one containing a general description and a second giving a detailed description of the implementation of the macros. In general, you might want to give the user the ability to suppress this latter part.

`\StopEventually{`*final text*`}`

This is achieved by placing the command `\StopEventually` at the division point between the two parts discussed above. This macro has one argument in which you put all the information you want to see printed if your document ends at this point (for example, a bibliography which is normally printed at the very end). When the `\OnlyDescription` declaration is given in the driver file, LATEX will process the argument and then stop reading the file. Otherwise the `\StopEventually` macro saves its argument in a macro called `\Finale`, which can afterwards be used to get things back (usually at the very end). Using this scheme makes changes in two places unnecessary.

To document the change history, the `\changes` command can be placed amongst the description part of the changed code.

```
\changes{version}{date}{text}
```

The information in the `\changes` command may be used to produce an auxiliary file (LaTeX's `\glossary` mechanism is used for this), which can be printed after suitable formatting. To cause the change information to be written, include `\RecordChanges` in the driver file. To read and print the sorted change history, just put the `\PrintChanges` command at a suitable point in your package file. To generate the sorted file containing the changes, you should run the raw glossary file through *MakeIndex* using an adequate style (like `gglo.ist`, supplied with the doc distribution; see section 12.4.6 on page 364 for more information about how *MakeIndex* treats glossaries).

```
\MakeShortVerb{\character}
```

When you have to quote a lot of material verbatim, such as command names, it is awkward to always have to type `\verb+...+`. Therefore, the doc package provides an abbreviation mechanism that allows you to pick a character *c*, which you plan to use only very rarely inside your document, and use it to delimit your verbatim text (the character " is often chosen, but if that character is already used for another purpose, like for generating umlauts, then you may prefer "|"). Then, after including the command `\MakeShortVerb{\c}`, the sequence *c* text *c* becomes the equivalent of `\verb`*c* text *c*. If you later want to use *c* with its original meaning, just type `\DeleteShortVerb {\c}`. You can repeat this sequence using *c* as a shorthand for `\verb` and reverting to its original meaning as many times as needed. Note that the abbreviated *c*form, just like `\verb` itself, cannot appear in the argument of another command, but it may freely be used inside `verbatim` and `macrocode` environments.

Table 14.1 on page 429 gives an overview of all doc user commands.

14.2.6   The Driver File

To get the documentation for a set of macros with the doc system you have to prepare a driver file with the following characteristics:

```
\documentclass[options]{document-class}
\usepackage{doc}

    preamble
\begin{document}
    input commands
\end{document}
```

```
\documentclass{article}
\usepackage{doc}                    % Include doc package
\EnableCrossrefs                    % full index
\CodelineIndex                      % by line numbers
\RecordChanges                      % make change history
\setlength{\parindent}{0pt}        % no indents
\begin{document}
    \DocInput{docexam.dtx}   \PrintIndex   \PrintChanges
\end{document}
```

Figure 14.1: doc driver file example

The *document class* may be any legal class, e.g., article. In the *preamble*, you should place declarations that manipulate the behavior of the doc system like \DisableCrossrefs, \OnlyDescription, \CodelineIndex, and so on.

Finally, the *input commands* part should contain one or more \DocInput{*file name*} and/or \IndexInput{*file name*} commands. The \DocInput command is used for files prepared for the doc system, whereas \IndexInput can be used for all kinds of macro files. It takes a file name as argument and produces a verbatim listing of the file, indexing every command as it goes along. This might be handy if you want to learn something about macros without enough documentation. When used to cross-reference the file latex.tex, which contains the basic command definitions for LᴬTEX, you will get a verbatim copy of the approximately 8800 lines of code and comments, plus an index of about 15 pages.

It is also possible to use \PrintIndex and \PrintChanges (if the changes are recorded by \RecordChanges) commands. But they may also have already been issued in the file being processed.

14.2.7   A Simple Example of a File Documented with doc

To illustrate the use of the commands discussed in the previous sections, a driver file docexam.drv (figure 14.1) for generating the documentation of an input file docexam.doc (figure 14.2 on the next page), which is documented using the doc system, is shown. You should run the driver file thought LᴬTEX once, then generate the index and glossary with *MakeIndex* before running the file once more through LᴬTEX, to obtain the documentation shown in figure 14.3 on page 428.

```
latex docexam.drv
makeindex -s gind.ist docexam
makeindex -s gglo.ist -o docexam.gls docexam.glo
latex docexam.drv
```

```
\def\fileversion{2.1}
\def\filedate{1 Apr 93}
\def\docdate {15 Aug 93}
% \changes{v1.0}{1 Apr 93}{First release}
% \changes{v2.0}{3 Apr 93}{Documentation added}
% \changes{v2.1}{15 Aug 93}{Minor corrections and additions}
%
\MakeShortVerb{\|}
%
\title{Illustrating \texttt{doc} with \texttt{docexam}}
\author{All of us}
\maketitle
\begin{abstract}
% This is an example of a package documented
% using \LaTeX's \texttt{doc} system~\cite{Companion}.
\end{abstract}
%
\section{Introduction}
% This package does nothing useful, but serves as a simple
% example of how to document your packages using \LaTeX's
% \texttt{doc} system.
%
\section{The user interface}
%
% This section defines everything an average user should
% know. Note the use of the
% \DeleteShortVerb{\|}
% ''\texttt{|}'' character as shorthand for
% \MakeShortVerb{\|}
% |verb|, and how we switch back and forth between its
% two possible meanings.
%
% \DescribeMacro{\docsamplecmd}
% The command |\docsamplecmd| will print the text specified
% as argument in a small caps typeface, prepended by the
% string ''\texttt{doc:}''.
%
% \DescribeEnv{docsampleenv}
% The environment |docsampleenv| will print the text bracketed
% inside the environment as quoted and italicized text,
% preceded by a line containing \textbf{Nice, you are using doc}.
\StopEventually{
\begin{thebibliography}{9}
\bibitem{Companion} M.~Goossens, F.~Mittelbach, and A.~Samarin
\emph{The \LaTeX{} Companion}, 1994, Addison-Wesley.
\end{thebibliography}
%
}
%
\section{The code}
%
% We begin by identifying the version of this file on the
% terminal and in the transcript file.
% \begin{macrocode}
\typeout{Package 'docexam' \fileversion\space<\filedate>}
\typeout{English documentation\space\space<\docdate>}
% \end{macrocode}
%
% \begin{macro}{\docsamplecmd}
% We prepend the text \texttt{doc} and switch to a small caps font.
% \begin{macrocode}
\newcommand{\docsamplecmd}[1]{\texttt{doc}\textsc{#1}}
% \end{macrocode}
% \end{macro}
%
% \begin{macro}{\docsampleenv}
% We begin a line in bold, then specify a \texttt{quote}
% environment.
% \begin{macrocode}
\newenvironment{docsampleenv}{\begin{quote}\item
\textbf{Nice, you are using doc!}\par\itshape}{\end{quote}}
% \end{macrocode}
% \end{environment}
%
\Finale
\endinput
```

Figure 14.2: Example of a file documented with the doc system

Illustrating doc with docexam

All of us

November 28, 1993

Abstract

This is an example of a package documented using LaTeX's doc system [1].

1 Introduction

This package does nothing useful, but serves as a simple example of how to document your packages using LaTeX's doc system.

2 The user interface

This section defines everything an average user should know. Note the use of the "|" character as shorthand for \verb, and how we switch back and forth between its two possible meanings.

\docsamplecmd   The command \docsamplecmd will print the text specified as argument in a small caps typeface, prepended by the string "doc:".

docsampleenv   The environment docsampleenv will print the text bracketed inside the environment as quoted and italicized text, preceded by a line containing **Nice, you are using doc.**

3 The code

We begin by identifying the version of this file on the terminal and in the transcript file.

```
1 \typeout{Package 'docexam' \fileversion\space\filedate>}
2 \typeout{English documentation\space\space\docdate>}
```

\docsamplecmd   We prepend the text doc and switch to a small caps font.

```
3 \newcommand{\docsamplecmd}[1]{\texttt{doc}\textsc{#1}}
```

docsampleenv   We print a line in bold, then specify a quote environment.

```
4 \newenvironment{docsampleenv}{\begin{quote}\item
5     \textbf{Nice, you are using doc!}\par\itshape}{\end{quote}}
```

References

[1] M. Goossens, F. Mittelbach, and A. Samarin *The LaTeX Companion*, 1994, Addison-Wesley.

Index

The italic numbers denote the pages where the corresponding entry is described, numbers underlined point to the definition, all others indicate the places where it is used.

Change History

v1.0
    "General": First release 1

v2.0
    "General": Documentation added .. 1

v2.1
    "General": Minor corrections and additions 1

Figure 14.3: Documentation generated for the example showing the use of the doc system

Table 14.1: Overview of doc package commands

Preamble and input commands
\CharacterTable{*character table*}
User interface to character table checking. See example in figure 14.6 on page 437.
\CheckSum{*checksum*}
User interface to set the checksum of the document (number of backslashes in the code).
\CheckModules
Format module directives of DOCSTRIP specially (default).
\CodelineIndex
Index commands using code line numbers.
\CodelineNumbered
Number code lines but don't index commands.
\DisableCrossrefs
Don't produce index entries for commands within the code.
\DocInput{*file*}
Read in *file* assuming doc conventions.
\DontCheckModules
Don't format module directives of DOCSTRIP specially.
\EnableCrossrefs
Produce index entries for commands within the code.
\IndexInput{*file*}
Read in *file*, print it verbatim and produce a command cross-reference index.
\OnlyDescription
Don't format code; stop at \StopEventually.
\PageIndex
Index commands using page numbers.
\RecordChanges
Produce a history listing.
Document structure and validation support
\bslash
Command to print a backslash (\).
\DeleteShortVerb
Undoes the previous definition of \MakeshortVerb.
\DescribeEnv{*env*}
Flags point in text where environment *env* is described.
\DescribeMacro{*cmd*}
Flags point in text where macro *cmd* is described.
\begin{environment}{*env*} (environment)
Environment surrounding description of environment *env*.
continued on next page

continued from previous page
\Finale
Command executed at very end of document (see also \StopEventually).
\begin{macro}{*cmd*} (environment)
Environment surrounding description of macro *cmd*.
\begin{macrocode} (environment)
Environment surrounding the TeX code.
\begin{macrocode*} (environment)
Same as the macrocode environment, but spaces are printed as ␣ characters.
\MakeShortVerb{*char*}
Defines abbreviation character *char* for \verb.
\meta{*arg*}
Prints its argument as a meta sentence (default ⟨*arg*⟩).
\PrintChanges
Print the history listing here.
\PrintIndex
Print the index listing here.
\SpecialEscapechar{*char*}
Specifies new single escape character to be used instead of \.
\StopEventually{*cmds*}
The argument *cmds* specifies which commands should be executed at the end of the document (they are stored in \Finale).
\begin{verbatim} (environment)
Slightly altered version of LaTeX's standard verbatim environment to surround verbatim text ignoring percent characters in column one.
\begin{verbatim*} (environment)
Same as the verbatim environment, but spaces are printed as ␣ characters.
Index commands
\actualchar
Character used to separate "key" and actual index in an index entry (default =).
\DoNotIndex{*cmd*$_1$,...,*cmd*$_n$}
Names of commands which should not show up in the index.
\encapchar
Character used to separate the actual index and the command to format the page number in an index entry (default |).
\IndexMin
Length parameter (default 80pt) defining the minimal amount of space that should be left on a page to start an index.
\IndexParms
Macro controlling the formatting of the index columns.
\IndexPrologue{*text*}
Overwrites default text to be placed on top of index.
continued on next page

---

continued from previous page

`\levelchar`

Character used to separate different index levels in an index entry (default >).

`\main{`*number*`}`

Defines formatting style for page numbers or code line number of index entries for major references (default underlined digits).

`\quotechar`

Character used to suppress the special meaning of the following character in an index entry (default *).

`\SortIndex{`*key*`}{`*entry*`}`

Produce index entry for *entry*, sorting it using *key*.

`\SpecialEnvIndex{`*entry*`}`

Produce index entry for environment *entry*.

`\SpecialIndex{`*cmd*`}`

Produce a command index (printing the argument verbatim in the index).

`\SpecialMainIndex{`*cmd*`}`

Produce a command index with `\main` page encapsulator.

`\SpecialUsageIndex{`*cmd*`}`

Produce a command index with `\usage` page encapsulator.

`\usage{`*number*`}`

Defines formatting style for page numbers of index entries for usage descriptions (default italic digits).

`\verbatimchar`

Character used to delimit `\verb` constructs within an index entry (default +).

History information

`\changes{`*version*`}{`*date*`}{`*reason*`}`

Records history information for use in a history listing.

`\docdate`

By convention holds the date of the most recent documentation update.

`\filedate`

By convention holds the date of the most recent code update.

`\filename`

By convention holds the name of the source file.

`\fileversion`

By convention holds the version number of the source file.

`\GlossaryMin`

Length parameter (default 80pt) defining the minimal amount of space that should be left on a page to start the change history.

`\GlossaryParms`

Macro controlling the formatting of the change history columns.

`\GlossaryPrologue{`*text*`}`

Overwrites default text placed on top of history listing.

continued on next page

continued from previous page
Layout and typesetting parameters
`\*`
Symbol used in index entries to refer to a higher level entry (default '~').
`\@idxitem`
Macro specifying how index items should be typeset (by default they are set as a paragraph with a hanging indentation of 30pt for items requiring more than one line).
`\AltMacroFont`
Font used to typeset DOCSTRIP module code (default with NFSS is `\small\sl\tt`).
`\DocstyleParms`
Macro controlling the formatting of the TEX code.
`\MacroFont`
Font used to typeset the main part of the code (default `\small\tt`).
`\MacroIndent`
Width of the indentation for every code line.
`\MacroTopsep`
Vertical space above and below each `macro` environment.
`\MacrocodeTopsep`
Vertical space above and below each `macrocode` environment.
`\MakePrivateLetters`
Macro specifying symbols to be considered as letters (default only @).
`\Module`
Macro with one argument defining the formatting of DOCSTRIP module directives.
`\PrintDescribeEnv`
Macro with one argument defining the formatting of `\DescribeEnv`.
`\PrintDescribeMacro`
Macro with one argument defining the formatting of `\DescribeMacro`.
`\PrintMacroName`
Like `\PrintDescribeMacro` but for the argument of the `macro` environments.
`\ps@titlepage`
Macro specifying page style for the title page of articles bundled in a journal (default `\ps@plain`).
`StandardModuleDepth`
Counter holding the highest level of DOCSTRIP directives which are still formatted using `\MacroFont`. Deeper nested directives are formatted using `\AltMacroFont`.
`\theCodelineNo`
Controls the typesetting of the line numbers (default script-size arabic numerals).

14.3 The DOCSTRIP Utility

Basically the DOCSTRIP utility removes nearly all lines that begin with a percent sign, and supports conditional processing of code by including parts of the file only when some condition is true. It also lets you produce a single LATEX macro file from several files or split the source file into several smaller files. DOCSTRIP can be run interactively by processing `docstrip.tex` with LaTeX:

```
latex docstrip.tex
```

LaTeX will ask a few questions about how to process a given file. When the user has answered these questions, DOCSTRIP does its job and strips the comments from the source.

However, it is more convenient to create a "batch file," which contains all necessary instructions for the DOCSTRIP run. The default name for such a file is `docstrip.cmd`. If a file with such a name exists in the current directory, DOCSTRIP will process it; otherwise it starts an interactive session.

An even more user-friendly way is to prepare a driver file, which can be processed directly by LaTeX. In this case the user simply has to say:

```
latex batch-file
```

and then this automatically produces all "executables" from some source distribution.

The so-called Mainz distributions, i.e., files maintained by Frank Mittelbach and Rainer Schöpf, like doc itself, array, ftnright, multicol, theorem, and the NFSS2 system, are distributed in this form. An example of an installation procedure using a simple driver file is discussed in section 14.4.

In the next section we discuss input commands that can be used in such a DOCSTRIP batch file. We then explain how to make code fragments in a doc source that can be conditionally included.

14.3.1   Batch File Commands

It is possible to prefix the output of the DOCSTRIP program with some fixed text, such as a copyright notice or your standard disclaimer. The information you want to add to the start of DOCSTRIP's output file should be listed between the `\preamble` and `\endpreamble` commands. Lines that you want to add at the end should be listed between the `\postamble` and `\endpostamble` commands. Everything that DOCSTRIP finds for both the pre- and postamble is written to the output file, but preceded with two % characters. If you include a `^^J` character in one of these lines, everything that follows it on the same line is written to a new line in the output file without percent signs in front. This feature can be used to add a `\typeout` or `\message` to the file stripped by DOCSTRIP.

```
\generateFile{output}{ask}{\from{input}{optionlist}...}
```

The macro `\generateFile` instructs DOCSTRIP what to do. The arguments *output* and *input* are normal file specifications appropriate for your computer system. The *optionlist* parameter is a comma separated list of options, specifying which optional code fragments in the *input* file should be included in the file *output*. The argument *ask* instructs TeX either to silently overwrite a previously existing file (value f) or to issue a warning and ask if it should overwrite the existing file (value t). It is possible to specify multiple \from commands, i.e., multiple input files, each with its own *optionlist*.

To make a DOCSTRIP driver file that can be directly processed by LaTeX, you should start it with the following two lines:

```
\def\batchfile{<batch-file-name>}
\input docstrip.tex
```

\batchfile Batch file commands can be put into several batch files. The latter are then executed from a master driver file. This practice is useful, for example, when a distribution consists of several distinct parts that are kept in individual files. A master file then simply calls the batch files for the parts using the command \batchinput. You cannot use the command \input because the latter is reserved to call the DOCSTRIP utility only.

If you want to communicate with the receiver of your package the commands \Msg and \Ask can be used. \Msg will display its argument on the terminal. Using \keepsilent in the installation file will suppress most of the output generated by DOCSTRIP during processing, while \showprogress turns it on again. There are a few other commands available—look at the DOCSTRIP documentation for further details.

It is in principle possible to write installation files that communicate with the user and do arbitrary complex tasks; however they also might get arbitrarily difficult to write due to the way DOCSTRIP reads a batch file. Look at the installation files of larger packages if you are curious.

14.3.2 Conditional Inclusion of Code

Code fragments for conditional inclusion are marked in the source file with "tags." The simplest format is a <*tag> and </tag> pair surrounding the piece of the file to be included in *output* when option tag is present in the *optionlist* of the \generateFile command. Note that these tags must be preceded by a % at the beginning of the line, e.g.,

```
%<*style>
     text or code
%</style>
```

When a block of code is not included, all tags that occur within that block are not evaluated. In general these tags can be any combination or Boolean expression of the options. The | symbol is used for logical or, & for logical and, and ! for negation. An option is considered true if and only if it occurs in the *optionlist*.

```
\def\batchfile{fileerr.ins}
\input docstrip.tex
\preamble
    File to exit `missing file name' loop in TeX.
\endpreamble
\generateFile{x.tex}        {t}{\from{fileerr.dtx}{exit}}
\generateFile{e.tex}        {t}{\from{fileerr.dtx}{edit}}
\generateFile{h.tex}        {t}{\from{fileerr.dtx}{help}}
\generateFile{s.tex}        {t}{\from{fileerr.dtx}{scroll}}
\Msg{************************************************}
\Msg{* I'm now trying to generate a file called '.tex'}
\Msg{* This may fail on some operating systems}
\Msg{************************************************}
\generateFile{.tex}         {t}{\from{fileerr.dtx}{return}}
```

Figure 14.4: The batch file for the "file-error" system

14.4   An Example of an Installation Procedure

Many of the larger packages described in this book come in the form of an "installation kit" consisting of an installation batch file and one or more .dtx or .doc files that contain the code for all files and documentation.[1]

Such an installation kit enables you to run the batch file through LaTeX so that the system will automatically unpack all the files needed without further intervention. Installation procedures can easily be constructed to generate the needed files and documentation.

We shall now show the principle of how this works using a simple example, called the "file-error" system. It consists of the batch file fileerr.ins and the .dtx file fileerr.dtx. Using LaTeX and DOCSTRIP, the .dtx is read and several small files are generated. The presence of these little files on your system could prove useful in situations where your users are confused about how to exit the TeX loop when TeX keeps asking about a file it cannot find, etc. See the description of the file in figure 14.7 on page 438 for additional explanation.

First, in figure 14.4 we show the batch file fileerr.ins, which first inputs the file docstrip.tex and then generates the needed output file(s) from the file fileerr.dtx using the command \generateFile. The only thing you have to do is run the above file through LaTeX and watch how LaTeX reads the .dtx file fileerr.dtx and extracts from it all needed files. This sequence of events is shown in figure 14.5 on the next page. The input file itself (fileerr.dtx) is shown in figure 14.6 on page 437. Finally, to obtain the documentation shown in figure 14.7 on page 438 one has to run fileerr.dtx through LaTeX.

---

[1] By convention, documentation files that can be directly processed by LaTeX have the extension .dtx; those that need a driver file have the extension .doc.

```
This is TeX, Version 3.141 (C version d)
(fileerr.ins
LaTeX2e <1994/03/06> PRELIMINARY TEST RELEASE
(/usr2/users/latex3/distrib/inputs/docstrip.tex
Utility: 'docstrip' 2.2f <1994/02/26>
English documentation    <1994/02/26>
**************************************************
* This program converts documented macro-files into fast *
* loadable files by stripping off (nearly) all comments! *
**************************************************

Generating file ./x.tex
. . . . .
Processing File fileerr.dtx (exit) -> x.tex
% % % % % % % % % % % % % % % % % % % % % % % % % % % % % %
<*driver % % % > % % % % % % % % % % % % % <*help % % % % % % % % > % % % %
% % <+scroll|return % > <+scroll % > % % % % % % % % % % <+edit|exit . > % %
% % %
File fileerr.dtx ended by \endinput.
Lines  processed: 86
Comments removed: 71
Comments  passed: 0
Codelines passed: 1

Generating file ./e.tex
. . . . .
Processing File fileerr.dtx (edit) -> e.tex
% % % % % % % % % % % % % % % % % % % % % % % % % % % % % %
<*driver % % % > % % % % % % % % % % % % % <*help % % % % % % % % > % % % %
% % <+scroll|return % > <+scroll % > % % % % % % % % % % <+edit|exit . > % %
% % %
File fileerr.dtx ended by \endinput.
Lines  processed: 86
Comments removed: 71
Comments  passed: 0
Codelines passed: 1

Generating file ./h.tex
. . . . .
Processing File fileerr.dtx (help) -> h.tex
% % % % % % % % % % % % % % % % % % % % % % % % % % % % % %
<*driver % % % > % % % % % % % % % % % % % <*help % . . . . . > % % % %
% % <+scroll|return % > <+scroll % > % % % % % % % % % % <+edit|exit % > % %
% % %

File fileerr.dtx ended by \endinput.
Lines  processed: 86
Comments removed: 71
Comments  passed: 0
Codelines passed: 6

Generating file ./s.tex
. . . . .
Processing File fileerr.dtx (scroll) -> s.tex
% % % % % % % % % % % % % % % % % % % % % % % % % % % % % % % % %
<*driver % % % > % % % % % % % % % % % % % % <*help % % % % % % % % % > % % %
% % <+scroll|return . > <+scroll . > % % % % % % % % % % % % <+edit|exit % > % %
% % %
File fileerr.dtx ended by \endinput.
Lines  processed: 86
Comments removed: 71
Comments  passed: 0
Codelines passed: 2

**************************************************
* I'm now trying to generate a file called '.tex'
* This may fail on some operating systems
**************************************************

Generating file ./.tex
. . . . .
Processing File fileerr.dtx (return) -> .tex
% % % % % % % % % % % % % % % % % % % % % % % % % % % % % % % % %
<*driver % % % > % % % % % % % % % % % % % % <*help % % % % % % % % % > % % %
% % <+scroll|return . > <+scroll % . > % % % % % % % % % % % % <+edit|exit % > % %
% % %
File fileerr.dtx ended by \endinput.
Lines  processed: 86
Comments removed: 71
Comments  passed: 0
Codelines passed: 1

Overall statistics:
Files  processed: 5
Lines  processed: 430
Comments removed: 355
Comments  passed: 0
Codelines passed: 11
 ) )
No pages of output.
Transcript written on fileerr.log.
```

Figure 14.5: The transcript file when installing the "file-error" system

```
% \def\fileversion{v1.0c} \def\filedate{1994/04/06}
% \CheckSum{14}
% \iffalse    This is a METACOMMENT
% Doc-Source file to use with LaTeX2e
% Copyright (C) 1993-94 Frank Mittelbach, all rights reserved.
% \fi
% \title{File not found error\thanks{This file has version
% \fileversion\ last revised \filedate}}
% \author{Frank Mittelbach}
% \maketitle
%
% \section{Introduction}
% When \LaTeX{} is unable to find a file it will ask for an
% alternative file name. However, sometimes the problem is
% only noticed by \TeX{}, and in that case \TeX{} insists on
% getting a valid file name; any other attempt to leave this
% error loop will fail.\footnote{On some systems, \TeX{}
% accepts a special character denoting the end of file to
% return from this loop, e.g.\ Control-D on UNIX or Control-Z
% on DOS.} Many users try to respond in the same way as to
% normal error messages, e.g.\ by typing \meta{return}, or |s|
% or |x|, but \TeX{} will interpret this as a file name and
% will ask again.
% \par To provide a graceful exit out of this loop, we define
% a number of files which emulate the normal behavior of
% \TeX{} in the error loop as far as possible.
% \par After installing these files the user can respond with
% |h|, |s|, |e|, |x|, and on some systems also with
% \meta{return} to \TeX's missing file name question.
% \StopEventually{}
%
% \section{The documentation driver}
%    This code will generate the documentation. Since it is the
%    first piece of code in the file, the documentation can be
%    obtained by simply processing this file with \LaTeXe.
%    \begin{macrocode}
%<*driver>
\documentclass{ltxdoc}
\begin{document} \DocInput{fileerr.dtx}   \end{document}
%</driver>
%    \end{macrocode}
% \section{The files}
%
% \subsection{Asking for help with {\tt h}}
%    When the user types |h| in the file error loop \TeX{} will
%    look for the file |h.tex|. In this file we put a message
%    informing the user about the situation (we use |^^J| to
%    start new lines in the message) and then finish with a
%    normal |\errmessage| command thereby bringing up \TeX's
%    normal error mechanism.
%    \begin{macrocode}
%<*help>
\newlinechar='\^^J


\message{!The file name provided could not be found.^^J%
Use `<enter>' to continue processing,^^J%
`S' to scroll further errors^^J%
`X' to terminate TeX}
\errmessage{}
%</help>
%    \end{macrocode}
%
% \subsection{Scrolling this and further errors with {\tt s}}
%    For the response |s| we put a message into the file |s.tex|
%    and start \scrollmode| to scroll further error messages in
%    this run. On systems that allow |.tex| as a file name we
%    can also trap a single \meta{return} from the user.
%    \begin{macrocode}
%<*scroll|return> \message{File ignored}
%<+scroll>        \scrollmode
%    \end{macrocode}
%
% \subsection{Exiting the run with {\tt x} or {\tt e}}
%    If the user enters |x| or |e| to stop \TeX{}, we need to
%    put something into the corresponding file which will force
%    \TeX{} to give up. We achieve this by turning off terminal
%    output and then asking \TeX{} to stop: first by using the
%    internal \LaTeX{} name |\@@end|, and if that doesn't work
%    because something other than \LaTeX{} is used, by trying the
%    \TeX{} primitive |\end|.
%    \begin{macrocode}
%<*edit|exit>  \batchmode  \@@end \end
%    \end{macrocode}
%    We end every file with an explicit |\endinput| which prevents
%    the docstrip program from putting the character table into
%    the generated files.
%    \begin{macrocode}
\endinput
%    \end{macrocode}
%    \CharacterTable
%%  {Upper-case   \A\B\C\D\E\F\G\H\I\J\K\L\M\N\O\P\Q\R\S\T\U\V\W\X\Y\Z
%%   Lower-case   \a\b\c\d\e\f\g\h\i\j\k\l\m\n\o\p\q\r\s\t\u\v\w\x\y\z
%%   Digits       \0\1\2\3\4\5\6\7\8\9
%%   Exclamation  \!     Double quote  \"     Hash (number) \#
%%   Dollar       \$     Percent       \%     Ampersand     \&
%%   Acute accent \'     Left paren    \(     Right paren   \)
%%   Asterisk     \*     Plus          \+     Comma         \,
%%   Minus        \-     Point         \.     Solidus       \/
%%   Colon        \:     Semicolon     \;     Less than     \<
%%   Equals       \=     Greater than  \>     Question mark \?
%%   Commercial at \@    Left bracket  \[     Backslash     \\
%%   Right bracket \]    Circumflex    \^     Underscore    \_
%%   Grave accent \`     Left brace    \{     Vertical bar  \|
%%   Right brace  \}     Tilde         \~}
%%
% \Finale
```

Figure 14.6: The source of the doc file for the "file-error" system

File not found error*

Frank Mittelbach

April 7, 1994

1 Introduction

When LATEX 2ε is unable to find a file it will ask for an alternative file name. However, sometimes the problem is only noticed by TEX, and in that case TEX insists on getting a valid file name; any other attempt to leave this error loop will fail.[1] Many users try to respond in the same way as to normal error messages, e.g. by typing ⟨return⟩, or s or x, but TEX will interpret this as a file name and will ask again.

To provide a graceful exit out of this loop, we define a number of files which emulate the normal behavior of TEX in the error loop as far as possible.

After installing these files the user can respond with h, s, e, x, and on some systems also with ⟨return⟩ to TEX's missing file name question.

2 The documentation driver

This code will generate the documentation. Since it is the first piece of code in the file, the documentation can be obtained by simply processing this file with LATEX 2ε.

```
1 %<*driver>
2 \documentclass{ltxdoc}
3 \begin{document}   \DocInput{fileerr.dtx}   \end{document}
4 %</driver>
```

3 The files

3.1 Asking for help with h

When the user types h in the file error loop TEX will look for the file h.tex. In this file we put a message informing the user about the situation (we use ^^J to start new lines in the message) and then finish with a normal \errmessage command thereby bringing up TEX's normal error mechanism.

```
5 %<*help>
6 \newlinechar='\^^J
7 \message{!The file name provided could not be found.^^J%
8 Use '<enter>' to continue processing,^^J%
9 'S' to scroll further errors^^J%
10 or 'X' to terminate TeX}
11 \errmessage{}
12 %</help>
```

3.2 Scrolling this and further errors with s

For the response s we put a message into the file s.tex and start \scrollmode to scroll further error messages in this run. On systems that allow .tex as a file name we can also trap a single ⟨return⟩ from the user.

```
13 %<+scroll|return>  \message{File ignored}
14 %<+scroll>         \scrollmode
```

3.3 Exiting the run with x or e

If the user enters x or e to stop TEX, we need to put something into the corresponding file which will force TEX to give up. We achieve this by turning off terminal output and then asking TEX to stop: first by using the internal LATEX name \@@end, and if that doesn't work because something other than LATEX is used, by trying the TEX primitive \end.

```
15 %<+edit|exit>  \batchmode  \@@end \end
```

We end every file with an explicit \endinput which prevents the docstrip program from putting the character table into the generated files.

```
16 \endinput
```

---

*This file has version v1.0c last revised 1994/04/06

[1] On some systems, TEX accepts a special character denoting the end of file to return from this loop, e.g. Control-D on UNIX or Control-Z on DOS.

1

2

Figure 14.7: Output generated by running the file fileerr.dtx through LATEX

A LaTeX Overview for Package and Class Writers

This appendix gives an overview of the basic programming concepts underlying the LaTeX formatter. We explain how to define new commands and environments, including those with an optional argument. We discuss how LaTeX handles counters and their representation and introduce horizontal and vertical space parameters and how they are handled. The second section reviews the important subject of (LA)TeX boxes and their use. A good understanding of this topic is very important to fully appreciate and exploit the information presented in this book. We then describe in detail the LaTeX2ε interface that allows you to define your own options for packages and class files. The two package files calc and ifthen make calculations and building control structures with LaTeX easier. They are described in the last two sections and have been used in many examples of LaTeX code throughout this book.

A.1 Linking Markup and Formatting

This section reviews the syntax for defining commands and environments with LaTeX. It is important that you exclusively use the LaTeX constructs described below, rather than the lower level TeX commands. Then, not only will you be able to take advantage of LaTeX's consistency checking, but your commands will be portable, (probably) without modification, to future versions of LaTeX.

A.1.1   Defining New Commands

It is often advantageous to define new commands (e.g., for representing repetitive input strings or recurring combinations of commands). A new command is defined using the \newcommand command sequence, which can have one optional argument, defining the number of arguments of the new command.

(£ 55,173)

> \newcommand{\ *name*} [*narg*] {*command definition*}

The number of arguments is in the range $0 \leq narg \leq 9$. If your new command has no arguments, then the [0] can be omitted. Inside the *command definition* part, the arguments are referenced as #1 to #*narg*.

PostScript and its variant Encapsulated Post-Script are often used for including graphics information in LaTeX documents ...

```
\newcommand{\Ps}{Post\-Script}
\newcommand{\EPs}{Encapsulated \Ps}
\Ps{} and its variant \EPs{} are often used
for including graphics information in
\LaTeX{} documents \ldots
```

We can generalize the previous example and at the same time enter the relevant information in a consistent way into the index file.

```
\newcommand{\PsI}{PostScript\index{Postscript}}
\newcommand{\EPsI}{Encapsulated \Ps\index{Encapsulated \Ps}%
                   \index{\Ps!Encapsulated}}\index{EPS}}
```

If a command should work both in math and in text mode, special care should be taken in its definition. For example:

The series of $x_1, \ldots, x_n$ or $x_1, \ldots, x_n$ ...

```
\newcommand{\xvec}{\mbox{$x_1,\ldots,x_n$}}
The series of \xvec\ or $\xvec$ \ldots
```

This is better supported in LaTeX 2_ε, which offers the following command:

> \ensuremath{*math code*}

As the name implies \ensuremath ensures that its argument is always typeset in math mode by surrounding it if necessary with $ signs. Thus, the above example could be shortened to

The series of $x_1, \ldots, x_n$ or $x_1, \ldots, x_n + G_{x_1, \ldots, x_n}$

```
\newcommand{\xvec}{\ensuremath{x_1,\ldots,x_n}}
The series of \xvec\ or $\xvec+G_{\xvec}$
```

As you can see, this has the additional advantage of producing correctly sized symbols in subscript or superscripts, which is not the case if an \mbox is used in the definition.

A command like \xvec could also be defined with an *argument*:

The series of $y_1, \ldots, y_n$ or $z_1, \ldots, z_n$ ...

```
\newcommand{\avec}[1]{%    arg1: vector name
            \ensuremath{#1_1,\ldots,#1_n}}
The series of \avec{y} or $\avec{z}$ \ldots
```

The more complete example below defines commands implementing type-setting rules that state that elementary particle name abbreviations should always be in roman type.

The masses of the W^-, W^+ and Z^0 particles are m_W and m_{Z^0} respectively.
In general one has $m_W > m_{Z^0}$.

```
\newcommand{\PWm}{\ensuremath{\mathrm{W}^-}}
\newcommand{\PWp}{\ensuremath{\mathrm{W}^+}}
\newcommand{\PZz}{\ensuremath{\mathrm{Z}^0}}
\newcommand{\PMW}{\ensuremath{m_{\mathrm{W}}}}
\newcommand{\PMZ}{\ensuremath{m_{\mathrm{Z}^0}}}
The masses of the \PWm, \PWp\ and \PZz\
particles are \PMW\ and \PMZ\ respectively.
\par In general one has \(\PMW > \PMZ\).
```

Existing commands must be *redefined* with the command \renewcommand.   ($\mathcal{L}$ 57,173)
Note that you can redefine a command with a different number of arguments as
the original one. Therefore, you could redefine the \PMW command of the above
example, so that it now takes one argument:

In general one has $m_{W^+} = m_{W^-}$.

```
\renewcommand{\PMW}[1]{%
            \ensuremath{m_{\mathrm{W}^{#1}}}}
In general one has \(\PMW{+} = \PMW{-}\).
```

When redefining a command (or an environment, see below) you must, of
course, be cautious since commands which you are planning to redefine might
be used in the class or packages you have loaded (try redefining \uppercase in
a document that is formatted with the class book).

In LaTeX2_ε, you can also define commands so that their first argument is
optional. The syntax is:

> \newcommand{*mycom*} [*narg*] [*default*] {*command definition*}

Examples of such command definitions are:

```
\newcommand{\LB}[1][3]{\linebreak[#1]}
\newcommand{\PK}[1][0]{\ensuremath{\mathrm{K}^{#1}}}
```

The default for the optional argument is given between the second pair of
square brackets, "3" in the first case and "0" in the second. Inside the command
definition, the optional argument has the number #1, while the mandatory arguments (when present) are addressed #2 to #*narg*. Thus, typing \LB is a short

way of saying \linebreak[3], while \LB[2] uses the actual specified value. That is, you will obtain the same effect as when typing \linebreak[2]. The second command, \PK, is used in the example below.

Three K particles, K^0, K^+ and K^-.   `Three K particles, \PK, \PK[+] and \PK[-].`

In general, it is most practical to associate the case that occurs most often with the form of the command without parameters and to represent the cases used less often with longer command strings with an optional argument.

Another somewhat more complex example, with an optional and a mandatory argument, is the definition of a rule with a default width of 0.4pt and a height specified by the mandatory argument. Note the two uses of the \Rule command where the widths are specified explicitly. In the latter case an "invisible rule" (strut) makes the framed box higher than the natural height of its contents.

text text | text ▮ text ⬚xxx⬚ and ⬚xxx⬚.

```
\newcommand{\Rule}[2][.4pt]{\rule{#1}{#2}}
text text \Rule{4mm} text \Rule[1mm]{4mm}
text \fbox{xxx} and \fbox{\Rule[0mm]{4mm}xxx}.
```

LaTeX 2_ε offers you another possibility to define commands:

> \providecommand{*mycom*} [*narg*] [*default*] {*command definition*}

This works exactly like \newcommand, except that it is ignored if the command already exists. Such a feature is useful in sources that may get used in several documents, e.g., bibliography entries. For example, instead of using \newcommand in the @PREAMBLE of BibTeX for logos and other constructs used in the BibTeX entries, you can use \providecommand to avoid error messages in the case that such commands are already defined in the document.

A.1.2 Defining New Environments

(£ 57,173)   You can define or redefine an environment with the \newenvironment and \renewenvironment commands, respectively. You must specify, in each case, which actions should take place when you enter and leave an environment. For an environment called "myenv" this is signaled by the commands \begin{myenv} and \end{myenv} inside your document.

> \newenvironment{*name*}[*narg*]{*begdef*}{*enddef*}
> \renewenvironment{*name*}[*narg*]{*begdef*}{*enddef*}

As with \newcommand, the number of arguments is in the range $0 \leq narg \leq 9$; and, in the case of no parameters, you can omit [0]. Inside the definition part, *begdef*, these parameters are referenced as #1 to #*narg*. If arguments are present, then they are defined when *entering* the environment by specifying them on the command \begin{myenv} as shown below.

```
\begin{myenv}{arg_1}...{arg_k}
```

When *exiting* an environment with the command \end{myenv} no parameters can be specified. Moreover, the parameters specified with the \begin{myenv} command when entering the environment (see above) are no longer available in the definition part *enddef* where you define the actions which should take place when leaving the *myenv* environment. This means that it is your responsibility to store information needed at the end of an environment (see the Citation environment defined below).

Our first example defines an environment of type "Abstract," which is often used to give a short summary of the contents of an article or a book. It starts by typesetting a boldfaced and centered title, followed by the text of the abstract inside a quote environment.

Abstract

This abstract explains the approach used to develop the necessary tools to solve the problems at hand.

```
\newenvironment{Abstract}
  {\begin{center}\textbf{Abstract}%
   \end{center} \begin{quote}}
  {\end{quote}}
\begin{Abstract}
  This abstract explains the approach used
  to develop the necessary tools to solve
  the problems at hand.
\end{Abstract}
```

Our second example is somewhat more complex. It shows you how a Citation environment can be defined for quoting citations by famous people.

```
\newcounter{Citctr}\newsavebox{\Citname}
\newenvironment{Citation}[1]
   {\stepcounter{Citctr}%
    \sbox{\Citname}{\textit{#1}}
    \begin{description}\item[Citation \arabic{Citctr}]}
   {\hspace*{\fill}\nolinebreak[1]\hspace*{\fill}%
    \usebox{\Citname}\end{description}}
```

The LaTeX code shown above defines the counter Citctr, for numbering the citations, and a box \Citname to store the name of the person whom we are citing so that we can typeset it at the end of the citation, when the \end{Citation} command is encountered (remember that the value of the argument specified on the \begin{Citation} command is no longer available at that stage). When entering the environment, we increment our counter and save the value of the argument, typeset in italic, in the box \Citname. We then start a description environment. This environment will have a single \item containing the counter value preceded by the word "Citation." When exiting the Citation environment, we first twice issue a stretchable horizontal space separated by an allowed but discouraged line break. Then we typeset the contents of our box \Citname before leaving the description environment. This will put the author's name flush right and, if there is not enough space to place it on the same line as the citation, put the last line of the citation flush left, as you can see in the next example. Without this adjustment the text of the citation would always be fully justified, often with a lot of white space between the words.

Citation 1 Necessity is the plea for every infringement of human freedom.
William Pitt

This is some regular text in between two Citation environments.

Citation 2 Man is the measure of all things.
Protagoras

More regular text ...

Citation 3 On mourra seul.   *Blaise Pascal*

```
\begin{Citation}{William Pitt}
   Necessity is the plea for every infringement
   of human freedom.
\end{Citation}
This is some regular text in between two
Citation environments.
\begin{Citation}{Protagoras}
   Man is the measure of all things.
\end{Citation}
More regular text \ldots
\begin{Citation}{Blaise Pascal}
   On mourra seul.
\end{Citation}
```

For a discussion of the counter and box commands used in this example see section A.1.3 and section A.2. As with \newcommand LATEX 2ε lets you make the first argument of an environment optional, as follows:

```
\newenvironment{myenv}[narg][default]{begdef}{enddef}
```

The default for the optional argument is given between the second pair of square brackets [*default*]. Inside the *begdef* part, which is executed when the environment *myenv* is entered, the optional argument can be accessed with #1, while the mandatory arguments (when present) are addressed as #2 to #*narg*. When the *myenv* environment is used without an optional parameter, #1 will contain the string specified as [*default*].

As an example, we implement a variant called deflist [90] of the Ventry description list environment discussed in section 3.2.2. The deflist environment behaves like a standard description environment if it is specified without an optional argument. If an optional argument is specified, then the width of the description label will be put equal to the width of the argument. Thus, by specifying the widest entry as an optional argument, you will make sure that the description parts of all your entries line up nicely.

The example below first shows the (default) behavior of the `deflist` list and
then what it looks like when using the optional argument.

First This is a short term.

Long term This is a long term.

Even longer term A very long term.

First   This is a short term.

Long term   This is a long term.

Even longer term A very long term.

```
\newenvironment{deflist}[1][\quad]%
  {\begin{list}{}{%
    \renewcommand{\makelabel}[1]{\textbf{##1}\hfil}%
    \settowidth{\labelwidth}{\textbf{#1}}%
    \setlength{\leftmargin}{\labelwidth+\labelsep}}}
  {\end{list}}
\begin{deflist}
\item[First] This is a short term.
\item[Long term] This is a long term.
\item[Even longer term] A very long term.
\end{deflist}
\begin{deflist}[Even longer term]
\item[First] This is a short term.
\item[Long term] This is a long term.
\item[Even longer term] A very long term.
\end{deflist}
```

A.1.3   Defining and Changing Counters

Every number generated by LATEX has a *counter* associated with it. The name   (£ 91)
of the counter is usually identical to the name of the environment or command
where it is used except for the \. The following is the list of all counters used in
LATEX's standard document classes:

part	paragraph	figure	enumi
chapter	subparagraph	table	enumii
section	page	footnote	enumiii
subsection	equation	mpfootnote	enumiv
subsubsection			

An environment declared by `\newtheorem` can also have a counter with the
same name associated with it, unless the optional argument indicates that it is
to be numbered together with another environment.

The value of a counter is a single integer. Several counters can be combined
into a number, as is usually the case for numbering section headings. For example, in the book or report classes, 7.4.5 identifies the fifth subsection of the
fourth section in the seventh chapter.

Manipulating LATEX Counters

Below we list all the basic LATEX commands that define and modify counters.   (£ 92,175)

These commands are much more powerful if used in conjunction with the calc package, discussed in section A.4.

> `\newcounter{`*newctr*`}[`*oldctr*`]`

This globally defines a new counter, *newctr*, and initializes it to zero. If a counter with the name *newctr* is already defined, an error message is printed. When you specify the name of another counter as the optional argument, *oldctr*, then the newly defined *newctr* is reset when counter *oldctr* is incremented with the \stepcounter or \refstepcounter commands.

> `\setcounter{`*ctr*`}{`*val*`}`

The value of counter *ctr* is globally set equal to the value *val*.

> `\addtocounter{`*ctr*`}{`*val*`}`

This command globally increments the value of counter *ctr* by *val*.

> `\value{`*ctr*`}`

For use mainly in the *val* argument of the \setcounter or \addtocounter commands, this command produces the value of counter *ctr*.

> `\stepcounter{`*ctr*`}`

This globally increments the counter *ctr* and resets all subsidiary counters, i.e., those declared with the optional argument *oldctr* on the \newcounter command or with the first argument of \@addtoreset (see section 2.3.1).

> `\refstepcounter{`*ctr*`}`

This is the same as \stepcounter, but it also defines the current \ref value to be the text generated by the command \the*ctr*.

The visual representation of a counter is controlled by the following commands:

\arabic{*ctr*}	Represent counter *ctr* as an arabic numeral.
\roman{*ctr*}	Represent counter *ctr* as a lowercase roman numeral.
\Roman{*ctr*}	Represent counter *ctr* as an uppercase roman numeral.
\alph{*ctr*}	Represent counter *ctr* as a lowercase letter: a, b,..., z. The value of *ctr* must not be greater than 26.

`\Alph{`*ctr*`}`   Represent counter *ctr* as an uppercase letter: A, B,..., Z. The value of *ctr* must not be greater than 26.

`\fnsymbol{`*ctr*`}`   Represent counter *ctr* as a footnote symbol: *, †,... This command can only be used in math mode.

`\the`*ctr*   Command to print a representation of the value associated with counter *ctr*.

As an example, we shall look at the way counters are defined inside the standard class files.

For the sectioning commands we find definitions equivalent to the following:

```
\newcounter{part}
\newcounter{section}
\newcounter{subsection}[section]
\newcounter{subsubsection}[subsection]
\newcommand{\thepart}        {\Roman{part}}
\newcommand{\thesection}     {\arabic{section}}
\newcommand{\thesubsection}  {\thesection.\arabic{subsection}}
\newcommand{\thesubsubsection}{\thesubsection.\arabic{subsubsection}}
```

You see how lower level counters are reset when upper level counters are stepped, as well as how the representation of the counters (the `\the...` commands) are constructed from the current counter and the counters at a higher level. It is also seen that the `part` counter does not influence any of the lower levels.

Table 3.2 on page 57 shows the structure of the enumeration list counters. In fact, these counters are defined inside the file `latex.tex`, containing the basic code for LATEX. Only the representation and label field commands are defined in the standard class files as follows:

```
\newcommand{\theenumi}{\arabic{enumi}}
  \newcommand{\labelenumi}{\theenumi.}
\newcommand{\theenumii}{\alph{enumii}}
  \newcommand{\labelenumii}{(\theenumii)}
\newcommand{\theenumiii}{\roman{enumiii}}
  \newcommand{\labelenumi}{\theenumiii.}
\newcommand{\theenumiv}{\Alph{enumiv}}
  \newcommand{\labelenumi}{\theenumiv.}
```

A.1.4 Defining and Changing Space Parameters

As in TEX, basically two kinds of space parameters (lengths) exist, namely "rigid" lengths (called `<dimen>` in the TEX book), which are fixed, and "rubber" lengths (called `<skip>` in the TeX book), which have a natural length and a degree of positive and negative elasticity. New lengths in LaTeX are allocated as type `<skip>`, so that you always have the choice of initializing them as rigid or rubber lengths (by specifying `plus` and `minus` parts). All standard lengths in LaTeX are of type rigid, unless specifically declared in appendix C of the LaTeX book to be rubber. LaTeX defines the following commands for lengths.

(£ 149–205)
(£ 95,193)

> `\fill`

This is a rubber length with a natural length of zero. It can stretch to any positive value. Do not change its value!

> `\stretch{`*dec_num*`}`

This is perhaps a more useful rubber length. `\fill` is equivalent to `\stretch{1}`. More generally, `\stretch{`*dec_num*`}` has a stretchability of *dec_num* times `\fill`. It can be used to fine-tune the positioning of text horizontally or vertically.

> `\newlength{`*cmd*`}`

This defines a new length and associates the command name *cmd* with it. If a command *cmd* already exists, you will get an error message. The new length is preset to 0pt. This is a rubber length. In the examples below, the TeX command `\the` is used to show the actual contents of the length variable.

Mylen = 0.0pt

```
\newlength{\Mylen} % Declare new length \Mylen
Mylen = \the\Mylen % Show current value
```

> `\setlength{`*cmd*`}{`*len*`}`

This sets the value of the length command *cmd* equal to the length *len*.

Mylen = 28.45274pt
Mylen = 14.22636pt plus 2.84526pt minus 1.42262pt

```
\setlength{\Mylen}{10mm} % Set length to 10mm
Mylen = \the\Mylen       % Use a rubber length
\setlength{\Mylen}{5mm plus 1mm minus .5mm}
\par Mylen = \the\Mylen
```

Lengths can be specified in various units, as shown in table A.1 on the next page. Notice the difference between the typographic point (pt) which is normally used in TeX and the (big) point used by PostScript, for example. Thus, when reserving space for a PostScript picture you need to specify the bounding box dimension in bp to get the correct space.

sp Scaled point (65536 sp = 1 pt) TEX's smallest unit.
pt Point = $\frac{1}{72.27}$ in = 0.351 mm
bp Big point (72 bp = 1 in), also PostScript point
dd Didôt point = $\frac{1}{72}$ of a French inch, = 0.376 mm
mm Millimeter = 2.845 pt
pc Pica = 12 pt = 4.218 mm
cc Cicero = 12 dd = 4.531 mm
cm Centimeter = 10 mm = 2.371 pc
in Inch = 25.4 mm = 72.27 pt = 6.022 pc
ex Height of a small "x" for the current font
em Width of capital "M" in current font
mu Math unit (18 mu = 1 em) for positioning in math mode

Table A.1: (LA)TEX's units of length

\addtolength{*cmd*}{*len*}

This adds length *len* to the current value of the length command *cmd*.

Mylen = 8.19003pt
Mylen = 20.19003pt

```
\setlength{\Mylen}{1em}
Mylen = \the\Mylen
\addtolength{\Mylen}{1pc}   % Add a pica
\par Mylen = \the\Mylen
```

\settowidth{*cmd*}{*text*}

The value of the length command *cmd* is set equal to the natural width of the typeset version of *text*. This command is very useful for defining lengths that vary with the string contents or the type size.

Mylen = 23.0631pt
Mylen = 29.73709pt

```
% \Mylen is width of ABCD in current font
\settowidth{\Mylen}{ABCD}
Mylen = \the\Mylen
% Go to larger font and recalculate width
\settowidth{\Mylen}{\large ABCD}
\par Mylen = \the\Mylen
```

\settoheight{*cmd*}{*text*}   \settodepth{*cmd*}{*text*}

In LATEX2$_\varepsilon$ two additional commands have been added. They work like \settowidth but measure the height and the depth rather than the width of the typeset *text*.

\enspace	yields a space equal to half a quad
\quad	yields a space equal to the em value of the font
\qquad	twice a \quad
\hfill	horizontal rubber length which can stretch between 0 and ∞
\hrulefill	similar to \hfill, but draws a horizontal line
\dotfill	similar to \hfill, but draws a dotted line

Table A.2: Predefined horizontal spaces

Horizontal Space

($\mathcal{L}$ 95,96,193)   A horizontal space is produced by the \hspace command. The command \hspace* is the same as \hspace, but the space is never removed, not even at a line boundary. Table A.2 shows horizontal space commands known to LaTeX.

A space in front of or following the \hspace command is significant, as the following example shows:

This is a	0.5 in wide space.	`\par This is a\hspace{0.5in}0.5~in wide space.`
This is a	0.5 in wide space.	`\par This is a \hspace{0.5in}0.5~in wide space.`
This is a	0.5 in wide space.	`\par This is a \hspace{0.5in} 0.5~in wide space.`

The following example shows how the "rubber lengths" can be used to fine-tune the positioning of information on a line. Note that the \hfill command is in fact an abbreviation for \hspace{\fill}. To save typing, we also defined a command with an optional argument, \HS, which behaves like \hfill when used without an argument, but can be made to be less or more flexible than that command by specifying the stretchability (a value of one has the same effect as \hfill).

left		right	`\newcommand{\HS}[1][1.]{\hspace{\stretch{#1}}}`
left	$\frac{1}{3}$	right	`\begin{center}`
left	middle	right	`left \hfill                            right\\`
left ———— middle ———— right			`left \HS[.5]\fbox{$\frac{1}{3}$}\hfill right\\`
left .... right			`left \HS          middle \hfill        right\\`
left .... right			`left \hrulefill\ middle \hrulefill\    right\\`
left .... right			`left \dotfill\                         right\\`
left .... right			`left \dotfill\ \HS[.5] \dotfill\       right\\`
			`left \dotfill\ \HS       \dotfill\     right\\`
			`left \dotfill\ \HS[2.] \dotfill\      right`
			`\end{center}`

Vertical Space

($\mathcal{L}$ 95,96,193)   A vertical space is produced with the \vspace command, which works similarly to \hspace. In particular, a \vspace* command will generate vertical space that will never be eliminated, even when it falls on a page break where a \vspace

\smallskip	Vertical skip of \smallskipamount (default about one quarter of \baselineskip).
\medskip	Vertical skip of \medskipamount (default about one half of \baselineskip).
\bigskip	Vertical skip of \bigskipamount (default about one \baselineskip).
\vfill	Vertical rubber length which can stretch between 0 and ∞.

Table A.3: Predefined vertical spaces

command will be ignored. Table A.3 shows vertical space commands known to LaTeX that are common to all standard classes.

LaTeX users are often confused about the behavior of the \vspace command. When used inside a paragraph, the vertical space is added after the end of the line with the \vspace, while between paragraphs it behaves as you would expect.

The use of a \vspace command inside a

paragraph is considered somewhat odd. It could perhaps be used with a negative space value to get rid of redundant space.

Between paragraphs, adjusting the spacing is somewhat more useful, and it allows control of the white space before and after displayed material.

```
The \vspace{5mm}use of a \verb!\vspace! command
inside a paragraph is considered somewhat odd.
It could perhaps be used with a negative
space value to get rid of redundant space.

\vspace{\baselineskip}

Between paragraphs, adjusting the spacing
is somewhat more useful, and it allows
control of the white space before and
after displayed material.
```

Stretchable space can also be used for vertical material. The \vfill command is, in fact, an abbreviation for a blank line followed by \vspace{\fill}. More generally, you can use the \stretch command in combination with \vspace to control the layout of a complete page. This could be useful for designing a title page, like the one shown in figure A.1 on the next page, where we put the author and title about one-third down the page with the place and time of publication at the bottom.

A.2 Page Markup—Several Kinds of Boxes

The theory of composing pages out of boxes lies at the very heart of TeX and many LaTeX constructs are available to take advantage of this method of composition.

A *box* is an object that is treated by TeX as a single character. A box cannot be split and broken across lines or pages. Boxes can be moved up, down, left, and right. LaTeX has three types of boxes:

LR (left-right) The contents of this box are typeset from left to right. (£ 97,98)

```
\documentclass{article}
\usepackage{times}
\thispagestyle{empty}
\newcommand{\HRule}{\rule{\linewidth}{1mm}}
\setlength{\parindent}{0mm}
\setlength{\parskip}{0mm}
\begin{document}
  \vspace*{\stretch{1}}
  \HRule
  \begin{flushright}
    \Huge Geoffrey Chaucer\\[5mm]
          The Canterbury Tales
  \end{flushright}
  \HRule
  \vspace*{\stretch{2}}
  \begin{center}
    \Large\textsc{London 1400}
  \end{center}
\end{document}
```

Figure A.1: A title page example

(£ 98–100)   **Par** (paragraphs) This kind of box can contain several lines, which will be type-set in paragraph mode just like normal text. Paragraphs are put one on top of the other. Their widths are controlled by a user specified value.

(£ 100)   **Rule** A (thin or thick) line that is often used to separate various logical elements on the output page, such as between table rows and columns and between running titles and the main text.

A.2.1   LR Boxes

```
\mbox{text}                   \fbox{text}
\makebox[width][pos]{text}    \framebox[width][pos]{text}
```

(£ 97,194)   The first line considers the *text* inside the curly braces as a box, with-out or with a frame drawn around it. For example, \fbox{some words} gives some words . The two commands on the second line are a generalization of these commands. They allow the user to specify the width of the box and the positioning of the text inside.

```
\makebox[5cm]{some words}        \par
\framebox[5cm][r]{some words}
```

In addition to centering the text with positional argument [c] (the default), you can position the text flush left ([l]) or flush right ([r]). LATEX2ε also offers you an [s] specifier that will stretch your *text* from the left margin to the right margin of the box provided it contains some stretchable space, e.g., some \hspace or the predefined spaces given in table A.2 on page 450. The interword spaces are also stretchable (and shrinkable to a certain extent) as explained on page 201.

With LATEX2ε, the above box commands with arguments for specifying the dimension of the box allow you to make use of four special length parameters: \width, \height, \depth, and \totalheight. They specify the natural size of the *text*, where \totalheight is the sum of \height and \depth.

A few words of advice
A few words of advice
A few words of advice
	`\framebox{A few words of advice}          \par`
	`\framebox[\width + 4mm][s]{A few words of advice}`
	`\par \framebox[1.5\width]{A few words of advice}`

Zero width boxes are very handy if you want to put a marker on the page (e.g., for placement of figures) or to allow text to be put into the margins. The principle of operation is shown below, where a zero width box is used to tag text, without influencing the centering. Note that the optional parameter [l] ([r]) makes the material stick out to the right (left).

A centered sentence.[123]
Some more text in the middle.
[321]A centered sentence.
	`\begin{center}`
	`A centered sentence.\makebox[0cm][l]{$^{123}$}\\`
	`Some more text in the middle.              \\`
	`\makebox[0cm][r]{$^{321}$}A centered sentence.\\`
	`\end{center}`

⟺As seen in the margin of the current line, boxes with a vanishing width can also be used to make text stick out in the margin. This effect was produced by beginning the paragraph as follows

```
\noindent\makebox[0cm][r]{\(\Longleftrightarrow\)}%
As seen in the margin ...
```

These zero width boxes also come in handy for hiding material inside a tabular environment to allow placement across rows (see also the discussion of the \raisebox command below).

The appearance of frameboxes can be controlled by two style parameters: (*L* 195–6)

\fboxrule   The width of the lines comprising the box produced with the command \fbox or \framebox. The default value in all standard classes is 0.4pt.

\fboxsep   The space left between the edge of the box and its contents by \fbox or \framebox. The default value in all standard classes is 3pt.

Text in a box   **Text in a box**

```
\fbox{Text in a box}
\setlength{\fboxrule}{2pt}\setlength{\fboxsep}{2mm}
\fbox{Text in a box}
```

(£ 100,195)

An interesting possibility is to raise or lower boxes. This can be achieved by the very powerful \raisebox command, which has two obligatory and two optional parameters, defined as follows:

$$\boxed{\texttt{\raisebox}\{\textit{lift}\}\,\texttt{[}\textit{depth}\texttt{]}\,\texttt{[}\textit{height}\texttt{]}\,\{\textit{contents}\}}$$

x111x ^upward^ x222x _downward_ ^x333x^

```
x111x \raisebox{1ex}{upward} x222x
   \raisebox{-1ex}{downward} x333x
```

In this example, LATEX takes the added height and depth into account when calculating the distance between the lines. This distance can be manipulated by specifying a height and depth that the user wants LATEX to actually use when placing its material on the page. The second pair of lines below shows that LATEX does not realize that text has been moved upward and downward, and it composes the lines as though all the text was on the baseline.

x111x _downward_ ^x222x^
x333x ^upward^ _x444x_

x111x _downward_ ^x222x^
x333x ^upward^ _x444x_

```
\begin{flushleft}
x111x \raisebox{-1ex}{downward} x222x        \\
x333x \raisebox{1ex}{upward} x444x           \\[4mm]
x111x \raisebox{-1ex}[0cm][0cm]{downward} x222x\\
x333x \raisebox{1ex}[0cm]{upward} x444x
\end{flushleft}
```

Somewhat more useful applications are discussed in chapter 5 where the subject of tabular material is treated.

As with \makebox and \framebox the LATEX 2_ε implementation of \raisebox offers you the use of the lengths \height, \depth, \totalheight, and \width in the first three arguments. Thus, to pretend that a box extends only 90% of its actual height above the baseline you could write

```
\raisebox{0pt}[0.9\height]{text}
```

or to rotate a box around its lower left corner (instead of its reference point lying on the baseline), you could raise it by its \depth first, e.g.:

x1 _Bad Thing_   x2 _Good Thing_   x3 _Bad Thing_   x4

```
\newcommand{\DoT}[1]{\begin{turn}{-45}#1\end{turn}}
x1 \DoT{\fbox{Bad Thing}} x2
\DoT{\raisebox{\depth}{\fbox{Good Thing}}} x3
\DoT{\raisebox{-\height}{\fbox{Bad Thing}}} x4
```

A.2.2 Paragraph Boxes

Paragraph boxes are constructed using the \parbox command or minipage environment. The *text* material is typeset in paragraph mode inside a box of width *width*. The vertical positioning of the box with respect to the text baseline is controlled by the one-letter optional parameter *pos* ([c], [t], and [b]).

(£ 98,99,195)

\parbox[*pos*]{*width*}{*text*}	\begin{minipage}[*pos*]{*width*} *text* \end{minipage}

The center position is the default as shown by the next example. You can also observe that LaTeX might produce wide interword spaces if the measure is incredibly small.

This is the contents of the left-most parbox.

CURRENT LINE

This is the right-most parbox. Note that the typeset text looks sloppy because LaTeX cannot nicely balance the material in these narrow columns.

```
\parbox{.3\linewidth}{This is the
  contents of the left-most parbox.}
\hfill CURRENT LINE \hfill
\parbox{.3\linewidth}{This is the
  right-most parbox.
  Note that the typeset
  text looks sloppy because \LaTeX{}
  cannot nicely balance the material
  in these narrow columns.}
```

The minipage environment is very useful for the placement of material on the page. In effect, it is a complete miniversion of a page and can contain its own footnotes, paragraphs, and array, tabular, and multicols environments. Note, however, that it cannot contain floats or \marginpar's, but it can appear inside figure or table environments where it is often used for constructing a pleasing layout of the material inside the float. A simple example of a minipage environment at work is given below. The baseline is shown with an en dash generated by the command \HR. Note the use of the *pos* placement parameter ([c], [t], and [b]).

```
A A A A
A A A A B B B B B
A A A A B B B B B
_A A A  _B B B B B_C C C C_
        B B B B B C C C
        B B B B
```

```
\HR
\begin{minipage}[b]{12mm}    A A A A A A A A A A A A A A
\end{minipage}\HR
\begin{minipage}[c]{12mm}
             B B B B B B B B B B B B B B B B B B B B B
\end{minipage}\HR
\begin{minipage}[t]{12mm}  C C C C C C C \end{minipage}\HR
```

If you desire more complicated alignments, then you might have to stack the different `minipage` environments. Compare the behavior of the following examples. Below, we try to align the two leftmost blocks at their top and aligning the resulting block at the bottom with a third block by adding another level of minipages.

```
                    C C C C         \HR
_A A A A xx B B B B B _C C C   _    \begin{minipage}[b]{30mm}
  A A A A     B B B B B              \begin{minipage}[t]{12mm}
  A A A A     B B B B B                      A A A A A A A A A A A A A A
  A A A       B B B B B              \end{minipage} xx
              B B B B                \begin{minipage}[t]{12mm}
                                             B B B B B B B B B B B B B B B B B B B B B B B
                                     \end{minipage}
                                     \end{minipage}\HR
                                     \begin{minipage}[b]{12mm}  C C C C C C C \end{minipage}\HR
```

However, we do not get the expected result. The reason is the following: the two top-aligned `minipages` inside the bottom-aligned `minipage` form a paragraph with a single line (the `minipages` are considered to be large units in the line containing xx). Thus, the bottom line of the outer `minipage` is still the one containing the xx characters. To prevent this we need to add some invisible space after the paragraph.

```
A A A A xx B B B B B              \HR
A A A A     B B B B B             \begin{minipage}[b]{30mm}
A A A A     B B B B B              \begin{minipage}[t]{12mm}
A A A       B B B B B C C C C              A A A A A A A A A A A A A A
_           B B B B _C C C   _    \end{minipage} xx
                                  \begin{minipage}[t]{12mm}
                                          B B B B B B B B B B B B B B B B B B B B B B B
                                  \end{minipage}
                                  \par\vspace*{0mm}
                                  \end{minipage}\HR
                                  \begin{minipage}[b]{12mm}  C C C C C C C \end{minipage}\HR
```

In the case below, the two rightmost environments are aligned at their top inside another enclosing environment, which is aligned at its bottom with the first one. If you compare it with the previous case, then you see that you obtain a quite different result, although the sequence of alignment parameters is the same. Only the stacking order of the `minipage` environments is different.

```
      B B B B B xx C C C C
A A A A B B B B B    C C C
A A A A B B B B B
A A A A B B B B B
_A A A   _B B B B                    _
```

```
\HR
\begin{minipage}[b]{12mm}
              A A A A A A A A A A A A A A
\end{minipage}\HR
\begin{minipage}[b]{30mm}
  \begin{minipage}[t]{12mm}
              B B B B B B B B B B B B B B B B B B B B B B
  \end{minipage} xx
  \begin{minipage}[t]{12mm}  C C C C C C  \end{minipage}
  \par\vspace*{0mm}
\end{minipage}\HR
```

Again we had to add some vertical space to achieve alignment. This does, however, not always produce the desired result. If, for instance, there is a letter with a descender in the last line of the stacked minipage, as in the example below, then the alignment of the baselines is not perfect.

```
      B B B B xx C C C C
      B B B B B    C C C
A A A A B B B B B
A A A A B B B B B
A A A A B B B B B
_A A A   _gg jj                      _
```

```
\HR
\begin{minipage}[b]{12mm}
              A A A A A A A A A A A A A A
\end{minipage}\HR
\begin{minipage}[b]{30mm}
  \begin{minipage}[t]{12mm}
              B B B B B B B B B B B B B B B B B B B B B B gg jj
  \end{minipage} xx
  \begin{minipage}[t]{12mm}  C C C C C C  \end{minipage}
  \par\vspace*{0mm}
\end{minipage}\HR
```

To correct this, you have to add (negative) vertical space that compensates for the depth of the letters. In the next example this is achieved by explicitly measuring the depth of the letters in question using the \settodepth command provided by LaTeX 2_ε.

```
      B B B B xx C C C C
      B B B B B    C C C
A A A A B B B B B
A A A A B B B B B
A A A A B B B B B
_A A A   _gg jj                      _
```

```
\settodepth{\Mylen}{gj}
\HR
\begin{minipage}[b]{12mm}
              A A A A A A A A A A A A A A
\end{minipage}\HR
\begin{minipage}[b]{30mm}
  \begin{minipage}[t]{12mm}
              B B B B B B B B B B B B B B B B B B B B B B gg jj
  \end{minipage} xx
  \begin{minipage}[t]{12mm}  C C C C C C  \end{minipage}
  \par\vspace*{-\Mylen}
\end{minipage}\HR
```

Sometimes it is helpful to predefine the vertical dimension of a paragraph box. For this LaTeX 2ε offers you additional optional arguments for `minipage` and `\parbox`.

```
\parbox[pos][height][inner-pos]{width}{text}
\begin{minipage}[pos][height][inner-pos]{width}   text   \end{minipage}
```

The *inner-pos* determines the position of *text* within the box. It can be t, c, b, or s. If not specified, the value of *pos* will be used. You can think of *height* and *inner-pos* as the vertical equivalent of the *width* and *pos* arguments of a `\makebox`. If you use the s position the *text* will be vertically stretched to fill the given *height*. Thus, in this case you are responsible for providing vertically stretchable space if necessary using, for example, the `\vspace` command.

As with the other box commands you can use `\height`, `\totalheight`, and so on to refer to the natural dimensions of the box when specifying the optional argument.

Some text on top. And a few lines on the bottom of the	This time a few lines on the top of the box. But only one line
xx box.	down here. xx

```
xx \fbox{\parbox[b][\height+\baselineskip][s]
        {20mm}{Some text on top. \par\vfill
               And a few lines on the
               bottom of the box.}}
   \fbox{\parbox[b][\height+\baselineskip][s]
        {20mm}{This time a few lines on the
               top of the box. But only one
               line \par\vfill down here.}} xx
```

A.2.3 Rule Boxes

(£ 100,195)   Rule boxes are drawn with the `\rule` command, whose syntax is:

```
\rule[lift]{width}{total_height}
```

If we write `\rule{2cm}{2mm}` then we get a 2cm long rule that is 2mm thick ▆▆▆▆▆▆▆. The `\rule` command can also be used to construct rule boxes with zero width, i.e., invisible rules (also called *struts*). The latter are useful if you need to control the height or width of a given box (for example, to increase the height of a framed box with `\fbox` or `\framebox`, or to adjust locally the distance between rows in a table). Compare the following:

x111x ⟦some text⟧ x222x ⟦ more text ⟧ x333x

```
x111x
  \fbox{some text}
x222x
  \fbox{\rule[-5mm]{0cm}{15mm}more text}
x333x
```

A.2.4 Manipulating Boxed Material

Material can be typeset once and then stored inside a named box, so that its contents can later be retrieved.

(£ 101,194)

`\newsavebox{`*cmd*`}`	declare box
`\sbox{`*cmd*`}{`*text*`}`	fill box
`\savebox{`*cmd*`}[`*width*`] [`*pos*`]{`*text*`}`	fill box
`\usebox{`*cmd*`}`	use contents

The `\sbox` and `\savebox` commands are similar to `\mbox` and `\makebox`. The command `\newsavebox` globally declares a command *cmd*, for example, `\boxname`, which can be thought of as a named bin, where typeset material can be stored for later (multiple) retrieval. Be careful not to use the command name `\boxname` directly, since it only contains the TEX number of the box in question, i.e., `\boxname` will merely typeset the character at the position corresponding to the box number in the current font. Thus, you should manipulate boxes exclusively using the commands described above. The `\usebox` command allows the nondestructive use of the material stored inside box `\boxname`. You can reuse the same bin (`\boxname`) several times within the scope of the current environment or brace group. It will always contain what was last stored in it.

```
x111x inside box a x222x inside box b
x111x inside box a x222x    inside box b
```

```
\newsavebox{\myboxa}\newsavebox{\myboxb}
\sbox{\myboxa}{inside box a}
\savebox{\myboxb}[2cm][l]{inside box b}
    x111x \usebox{\myboxa} x222x \usebox{\myboxb}
    \par x111x \usebox{\myboxa}
\savebox{\myboxb}[2cm][r]{inside box b}
    x222x \usebox{\myboxb}
```

In addition to the above commands LATEX2ε also offers the environment `lrbox` with the following syntax:

`\begin{lrbox}{`*cmd*`}`   *text*   `\end{lrbox}`

cmd should be a box register previously allocated with `\newsavebox`. The environment `lrbox` will save *text* in this box for later use with `\usebox`. Leading and trailing spaces are ignored. Thus, `lrbox` is basically the environment form of `\sbox`. You can make good use of this environment if you want to save the body of some environment in a box for further processing. For example, the following code defines the environment `fminipage` that works like a `minipage` but surrounds its body with a frame.

```
\newsavebox{\fminibox}
\newlength{\fminilength}
```

```
\newenvironment{fminipage}[1][\linewidth]
  {\setlength{\fminilength}{#1-2\fboxsep-2\fboxrule}%
   \begin{lrbox}{\fminibox}\begin{minipage}{\fminilength}}
  {\end{minipage}\end{lrbox}\noindent\fbox{\usebox{\fminibox}}}
```

The above definition is interesting in several aspects. The environment is defined with one optional argument denoting the width of the resulting box (default is \linewidth). On the next line we calculate (using the **calc** package) the internal line length that we have to pass to the minipage environment. Here we have to subtract the extra space added by the \fbox command on both sides. Then the lrbox and minipage environments are started to typeset the body of the fminipage environment into the box \fminibox. When the end of the environment is reached those environments are closed. Then the \fminibox is typeset inside an \fbox command. The \noindent in front suppresses any indentation in case the environment is used at the beginning of a paragraph or forms a paragraph by itself.

In this environment verbatim text like \fminibox can be used.

```
\begin{fminipage}
  In this environment verbatim text like
  \verb=\fminibox= can be used.
\end{fminipage}
```

A.3   Package and Class File Structure

As described in section 2.1 the structure and handling of package and class files are enhanced and extended in the LATEX2ε release. In this section we discuss what commands are available for the authors of package or class files who want to make use of the new features.

Even if you do not intend to write your own package, this section will help you understand the structure and content of class and package files like **book** or **varioref**, and thus help you to make better use of them.

The general structure for class and package files is the same and consists of the following parts:

⟨*identification*⟩
⟨*initial code*⟩
⟨*declaration of options*⟩
⟨*execution of options*⟩
⟨*package loading*⟩
⟨*main code*⟩

All these parts are optional. We discuss the commands available in each of the individual parts below. Table A.4 on the next page gives a short overview.

Identification part
\NeedsTeXFormat{*format*}[*release*]
Needs to run under *format* (LaTeX2e) with a release date not older than *release*
\ProvidesClass{*name*}[*release info*]   \ProvidesPackage{*name*}[*release info*]
Identifies class or package *name* and specifies *release information*
\ProvidesFile{*name*}[*release info*]
Identifies other file *name* (with extension) and specifies *release information*
Declaration of options
\DeclareOption{*option*}{*code*}
Declares *code* to be executed for *option*
\PassOptionsToPackage{*option-list*}{*package-name*}
Passes *option-list* to *package-name*
\DeclareOption*{*code*}
Declares *code* to be executed for any unknown option
\CurrentOption
Refers to current option for use in \DeclareOption*
Execution of options
\ExecuteOptions{*option-list*}
Executes code for every option listed in *option-list*
\ProcessOptions   \ProcessOptions*
Processes specified options for current class or package; star form obeys the specified order
Package loading
\RequirePackage[*option-list*]{*package*}[*release*]
Loads *package* with given *option-list* and a release date not older than *release*
Special commands for package and class files
\AtEndOfPackage{*code*}   \AtEndOfClass{*code*}
Defers execution of *code* to end of current package or class
\AtBeginDocument{*code*}   \AtEndDocument{*code*}
Executes *code* at \begin{document} or \end{document}
\IfFileExists{*file*}{*then-code*}{*else-code*}
Executes *then-code* if *file* exists, *else-code* otherwise
\InputIfFileExists{*file*}{*then-code*}{*else-code*}
Executes *then-code* if *file* exists and input it, otherwise execute *else-code*
Special class file commands
\LoadClass[*option-list*]{*class*}[*release*]
Like \Requirepackage for class files, but does not see global options if not explicitly passed to it
\PassOptionsToClass{*option-list*}{*class*}
Passes *option-list* to *class*
\OptionNotUsed
For use in \DeclareOption* if necessary

Table A.4: Commands describing the structure of package and class files

A.3.1   The Identification Part

This part of a class or package file is used to define the nature of the file and also states the first LaTeX 2_ε distribution release for which the file was written.

```
\ProvidesClass{name}[release information]
```

A class file identifies itself with a \ProvidesClass command. The argument *name* corresponds to the name of the class as it will be used in the mandatory argument of the \documentclass command, i.e., the file name without extension. The optional argument *release information* should begin with a date in the form YYYY/MM/DD, followed by a string describing the release. For example, the class report contains something like

```
\ProvidesClass{report}[1994/01/01 LaTeX2e standard class]
```

In a document you can make use of the *release information* by specifying the date as a second optional argument to the \documentclass command in the following way:

```
\documentclass[twocolumn]{report}[1994/06/01]
```

This enables LaTeX to check that the report class used has at least a release date of 1994/06/01 or is newer. If the class file is older, a warning is issued. Thus, if you make use of a new release of a class file and send your document to another site, the people there will be informed if their LaTeX distribution is out of date.

```
\ProvidesPackage{name}[release information]
```

This command identifies a package file. The structure is the same as for the \ProvidesClass command. Again, the date in the *release information* can be used in a second optional argument to \usepackage to ensure that an up-to-date version of the package file is loaded, e.g., with

```
\usepackage[german]{varioref}[1994/01/01]
```

```
\ProvidesFile{filename}[release information]
```

This command identifies any other type of file. For this reason *filename* must contain the full file name including extension.

In addition to one of the above commands the ⟨*identification*⟩ part usually also contains a \NeedsTeXFormat command, as already mentioned in section 2.1.1, for example \NeedsTeXFormat{LaTeX2e}[1993/11/11].

All four declarations are optional. Nevertheless, their use in distributed class and package files will ease the maintenance of these files.

A.3.2   The Initial Code Part

You can specify any valid LaTeX code in the ⟨*initial code*⟩ part. This includes loading of packages with the \RequirePackage command (see section A.3.5) if their code is required in one of the option declarations later on. For example, you might want to load the calc package at this point, if you want to use it later on. However, normally this part is empty.

A.3.3   The Declaration of Options

In this part all options known to the package or class are declared using the \DeclareOption command. It is forbidden to load packages in this part.

\DeclareOption{*option*}{*code*}

The argument *option* is the name of the option being declared and *code* is the code to execute if this option is requested. For example, the paper size option a4paper normally has a definition of the form:

```
\DeclareOption{a4paper}{\setlength{\paperheight}{297mm}%
                        \setlength{\paperwidth}{210mm}}
```

In principle any action from setting a flag to some complex typesetting instruction is possible in the *code* argument of \DeclareOption.

An important function for use in \DeclareOption is the command \PassOptionsToPackage. It can be used to pass one or more options to some other package that is loaded later on.

\PassOptionsToPackage{*option-list*}{*package-name*}

The argument *option-list* is a comma-separated list of options that should be passed to the package with name *package-name* when it is loaded in the ⟨*package loading*⟩ part.[1] Suppose, for example, that you want to define a class file that makes use of two packages, say, A and B, both supporting the option infoshow. To support such an option in the class file as well, you could declare:

```
\DeclareOption{infoshow}{%
    \PassOptionsToPackage{infoshow}{A}%
    \PassOptionsToPackage{infoshow}{B}%
    ⟨code to support infoshow in the class⟩}
```

If a package or class file is loaded with an option that it does not recognize, it will issue a warning (in case of a package file) or silently ignore the option (in case

---

[1] It is the responsibility of the package writer to actually load such packages. LaTeX does not check that packages receiving options via \PassOptionsToPackage are actually loaded later on.

of a class file), assuming that it is a global option to be passed to other packages loaded with \usepackage later on. However, this behavior is not hard-wired and can be modified using a \DeclareOption* declaration.

> \DeclareOption*{*code*}

The argument *code* specifies the action to take if an unknown option is specified. Within this argument \CurrentOption refers to the name of the option in question. For example, to write a package that extends the functionality of some other package, you could declare:

```
\DeclareOption*{\PassOptionsToPackage{\CurrentOption}{A}}
```

This would pass all options not declared by your package to package A. If no \DeclareOption* declaration is given, the default action, as described above, will be used.

Combining \DeclareOption* with \InputIfFileExists (see below) you can even implement conditional option handling. For example, the following code tries to find files whose names are built up from the option name.

```
\DeclareOption*{\InputIfFileExists{g-\CurrentOption.xyz}{}{}}
```

If the file g-*option*.xyz can be found it will be loaded; otherwise the option is ignored.

A.3.4 The Execution of Options

Two types of actions are normally carried out after all options are declared. You might want to set some defaults, e.g., defining the default paper size. Then the list of options specified needs to be examined and the code for each such option needs to be executed.

> \ExecuteOptions{*option-list*}

\ExecuteOptions executes the code for every option listed in *option-list* in the order specified. This is just a convenient shorthand to set up defaults by executing code specified earlier with a \DeclareOption command. For example, the standard class **book** issues something similar to

```
\ExecuteOptions{letterpaper,twoside,10pt}
```

to set up the defaults. You can also use \ExecuteOptions when declaring other options, e.g., to define an option that automatically implies others. The \ExecuteOptions command can only be used prior to executing the

`\ProcessOptions` command because, as one of its last actions, the latter reclaims all the memory taken up by the code for all the declared options.

`\ProcessOptions`

When the `\ProcessOptions` command is encountered it examines the list of options specified for this class or package and executes the corresponding code. More exactly, when dealing with a package the global options (as specified on the `\documentclass` command) and the directly specified options (the optional argument to the `\usepackage` or `\RequirePackage` command) are tested. For every option declared by the package, the corresponding code is executed. This is done in the order in which the options were specified by the `\DeclareOption` declarations in the package, not in the order in which they appear on the `\usepackage` command. Global options which are not recognized are ignored. For all other unrecognized options the code specified by `\DeclareOption*` is executed, or, if this declaration is missing, an error is issued.

In the case of a class file, the action of `\ProcessOptions` is the same without the added complexity of the global options.

`\ProcessOptions*`

For some packages it might be more appropriate that they process their options in the order specified on the `\usepackage` command rather than using the order given through the sequence of `\DeclareOption` commands. For example, in the babel package, the last language option specified is supposed to determine the main document language. Such a package can execute the options in the order specified by using `\ProcessOptions*` instead of `\ProcessOptions`.

A.3.5   The Package Loading Part

Once the options are dealt with, it might be time to load some additional packages, for example, those to whom you have passed some options using `\PassOptionsToPackage`.

`\RequirePackage` [*option-list*] {*package*} [*release*]

This command is the package/class counterpart to the document command `\usepackage`. If *package* was not loaded before, it will be loaded now with the options specified in *option-list*, the global options from the `\documentclass` command, as well as all options passed to this package via `\PassOptionsToPackage`.

LaTeX 2_ε loads any package only once because in many cases it is dangerous to execute the code of a package several times. Thus, if you require a package with a certain set of options but this package was already loaded with a different set not including all options requested this time, then the user of your package has a problem. In this case LATEX issues an error message informing the users of your package about the conflict and suggesting to them to load the package with a \usepackage command and all the necessary options.

The optional *release* argument can be used to request a package version not older than a certain date as described above. For this to work, the required package must contain a \ProvidesPackage declaration specifying a release date.

A.3.6 The Main Code Part

This final part of the file defines the characteristics and implements the functions provided by the given class or package. It can contain any valid LATEX construct and usually defines new commands and structures. It is good style to use standard LATEX commands, as described in this appendix, such as \newlength, \newcommand, and so on, rather than relying on primitive TEX commands since the latter do not test for possible conflicts with other packages.

A.3.7 Special Commands for Package and Class Files

```
\AtEndOfPackage{code}      \AtEndOfClass{code}
```

Sometimes it is necessary to defer the execution of some code to the end of the current package or class file. The above declarations save their *code* argument and execute it when the end of the package or class is reached. If there is more than one such declaration present in a file the *code* is accumulated and finally executed in the order in which the declarations were given.

```
\AtBeginDocument{code}      \AtEndDocument{code}
```

Other important points at which you might want to execute deferred code are the beginning or the end of the document, or more exactly the points where the \begin{document} and \end{document} are processed. The above commands allow packages to add code to this environment without getting into conflicts with other packages trying to do the same.

```
\IfFileExists{file}{then-code}{else-code}
\InputIfFileExists{file}{then-code}{else-code}
```

If your package or class tries to \input a file which does not exist, the user ends up in TEX's file-error loop that can only be exited by supplying a valid file name. By using \IfFileExists your package or class can avoid this problem. The argument *file* is the file whose existence you want to check. If this *file* is found by LATEX the commands in *then-code* are executed; otherwise those in *else-code* are executed. The command \InputIfFileExists does not only test whether *file* exists but additionally inputs it immediately after executing *then-code*. It also adds the name *file* to the list of files to be displayed by \listfiles.

A.3.8   Special Commands for Class Files

It is sometimes helpful to build a class file as a customization of a given general class. To support this concept two commands are provided.

> \LoadClass [*option-list*] {*class*} [*release*]

The \LoadClass command works like the \RequirePackage command with the following three exceptions:

- The command can only be used in class files.

- There can be at most one \LoadClass command per class.

- The global options are not seen by the *class* unless explicitly passed to it via \PassOptionsToClass or specified in the *option-list*.

> \PassOptionsToClass{*option-list*}{*class*}

The command \PassOptionsToClass can be used to pass options to such a general class. An example of such a class file augmentation is shown in figure A.2 on the next page. It defines a class file myart accepting two extra options, cropmarks (making crop marks for trimming the pages) and bind (to shift the printed pages slightly to the outside to get a larger binding margin), as well as one additional environment, Notes.

The cropmarks option is implemented by setting a Boolean switch and re-defining various \pagestyles if this switch is true. The bind option modifies the values of \oddsidemargin and \evensidemargin. However, since these length registers do not have their final value at the time the bind option is encountered (they are set later when the article class is loaded by \LoadClass), the modification is deferred until the end of the myart class file using the \AtEndOfClass command.

> \OptionNotUsed

If your *code* for \DeclareOption* inside a class file is more complex—e.g., trying to handle some options but rejecting others—you might need to explicitly inform LaTeX 2$_\varepsilon$ that the option was not accepted using the \OptionNotUsed command. Otherwise, LaTeX 2$_\varepsilon$ will think that the option was used and will not produce a warning if the option was not picked up by a later package.

```
% --------------------------- identification --------------------------
\NeedsTeXFormat{LaTeX2e}
\ProvidesClass{myart}[1994/01/01]
% --------------------------- initial code --------------------------
\RequirePackage{ifthen}
\newboolean{cropmarks}
% ------------------------- declaration of options --
\DeclareOption{cropmarks}{\setboolean{cropmarks}{true}}
\DeclareOption{bind}
    {\AtEndOfClass{\addtolength\oddsidemargin{.5in}%
                  \addtolength\evensidemargin{-.5in}}%
                 }
\DeclareOption*{\PassOptionsToClass{\CurrentOption}{article}}
% ------------------------- execution of options ----------------------
\ProcessOptions
% ---------------------------package loading --------------------------
\LoadClass{article}                              % the real code
% --------------------------- main code ------------------------------
\newenvironment{Notes}{...}{...}                 % the new environment
\ifthenelse{\boolean{cropmarks}}                 % support for cropmarks
    {%
     \renewcommand{\ps@plain}{....}%
     ....
    }{}
```

Figure A.2: An example of a class file extending article

A.4 calc—Arithmetic Calculations

The package calc (by Kresten K. Thorup and Frank Jensen) contains a set of macros for enhanced arithmetic in LaTeX. Usual arithmetic in TeX is done by simple low-level operations like \advance and \multiply. This package defines an infix notation arithmetic for LaTeX. It, in fact, reimplements the LaTeX commands \setcounter, \addtocounter, \setlength, and \addtolength so that they can accept integer and length expressions rather than simple numbers and lengths.

(£ 175,193)

An integer expression can contain integer numbers, TeX's integer registers, LaTeX's counters (e.g., \value{ctr}), parentheses, and binary operators (-, +, *, /). For instance, to increment a counter:

The value is "3".

```
\newcounter{local}\setcounter{local}{2}
\setcounter{local}{\value{local}+1}
The value is ''\thelocal''.
```

An example is the definition of a command to print the time (note that the TeX register `\time` contains the number of minutes since midnight):

The time is 21h 29min.

```
\newcounter{hours}\newcounter{minutes}
\newcommand{\printtime}{%
  \setcounter{hours}{\time/60}%
  \setcounter{minutes}{\time-\value{hours}*60}%
  \thehours h \theminutes min}
The time is \printtime.
```

When dealing with lengths, the subexpressions that are added or subtracted must be of the same type. That is, you cannot have "2cm+4," but an expression like "2cm+4pt" is legal since both subexpressions have dimensions. You can only divide or multiply by integers, therefore "2cm*4" is a legal subexpression but "2cm*4pt" is forbidden. Also, the length part must come first in an expression, thus "4*2cm" is not allowed.

The commands described above allow you to calculate the width of one column in an *n*-column layout using the following single command (supposing that the variable *n* is stored as the first argument of a LaTeX macro):

```
\setlength{\linewidth}{(\textwidth-\columnsep*(#1-1))/#1}
```

The restriction that you can only multiply and divide by integers has been relaxed for calculations on lengths (dimensions), where those operations are allowed with real numbers. A real number can be represented in two forms:

`\real{`*decimal constant*`}`   `\ratio{`*length expression*`}{`*length expression*`}`

The first form just converts the text into a real value, and the second form denotes the number obtained by dividing the value of the first expression by the value of the second.

As an example, assume you want to scale a figure so that it occupies the full width of the page (`\textwidth`). If the original dimensions of the figure are given by the length variables `\Xsize` and `\Ysize`, then the height of the figure after scaling will be:

```
\setlength{\newYsize}{\Ysize*\ratio{\textwidth}{\Xsize}}
```

The calc package is used in many examples in this book. If you do not want to apply it, you need to express the code given in the examples in the form of primitive (LA)TeX constructs. For example, the setting of `\fminilength` on page 460 has to be translated from

```
\setlength{\fminilength}{#1-2\fboxsep-2\fboxrule}%
```

to the following statements:

```
\setlength{\fminilength}{#1}%
\addtolength{\fminilength}{-2\fboxsep}%
\addtolength{\fminilength}{-2\fboxrule}
```

Besides the fact that the infix notation provided by the calc package is certainly more readable (and much easier to modify), it contains constructs for division and multiplication that cannot be expressed with standard LATEX constructs. For example, to express the \topmargin calculation from page 88 the following code is necessary:

```
\setlength{\topmargin}{297mm}
\addtolength{\topmargin}{-\textheight}
\divide\topmargin by 3                    % TeX calculation
\addtolength{\topmargin}{-1in}
\addtolength{\topmargin}{-\headheight}
\addtolength{\topmargin}{-\headsep}
```

A.5 ifthen—Advanced Control Structures

Sometimes you may want to typeset different material depending upon the value of a logical expression. This is possible with the standard package ifthen (by Leslie Lamport, reimplemented for LATEX 2$_\varepsilon$ by David Carlisle), which defines commands for building control structures with LATEX.

| \ifthenelse{*test*}{*then-code*}{*else-code*} |

If the condition *test* is true, the commands in the *then-code* part are executed, otherwise the commands in the *else-code* part are executed.

A simple form of a condition is the comparison of two numbers (real or integer). For example, if you want to translate the chapter counter into English (not more that twenty chapters!):

This is the 1st appendix.

```
\newcommand{\toEng}[1]{%
  \the\value{#1}%
  \ifthenelse{\value{#1} = 1}{$^{\hbox{st}}$}{}%
  \ifthenelse{\value{#1} = 2}{$^{\hbox{nd}}$}{}%
  \ifthenelse{\value{#1} = 3}{$^{\hbox{rd}}$}{}%
  \ifthenelse{\value{#1} > 3}{$^{\hbox{th}}$}{}}

This is the \toEng{chapter} appendix.
```

The following example defines a command to print the time in short form. It shows how complex operations (using the calc package) can be combined with conditional control statements.

The current time is "21:29."

```
\newcommand{\Printtime}{\setcounter{hours}{\time/60}%
    \setcounter{minutes}{\time-\value{hours}*60}%
    \ifthenelse{\value{hours}<10}{0}{}\thehours:%
    \ifthenelse{\value{minutes}<10}{0}{}\theminutes}
The current time is ''\Printtime.''
```

> `\equal{`*string1*`}{`*string2*`}`

The `\equal` command evaluates to *true* if the two strings *string1* and *string2* are equal after they have been completely expanded. You should be careful when using fragile commands in one of the strings; they need protection with the `\protect` command.

False.
True.
True.

```
\newcommand{\BB}{\CC}\newcommand{\CC}{\DD}
\newcommand{\DD}{AA}\newcommand{\EE}{EE}
\ifthenelse{\equal{\BB}{\EE}}{True}{False}.\\
\ifthenelse{\equal{\BB}{\CC}}{True}{False}.\\
\ifthenelse{\equal{\DD}{\BB}}{True}{False}.
```

One application could be in the definition of a command for printing an item and for entering it in the index. In the case where it is defined, the index entry will be typeset in boldface; otherwise in a normal face. We use an optional argument for the least frequently occurring situation of the definition.

we define item `AAAA` ... we reference
item `AAAA`

```
\newcommand{\IX}[2][R]{\texttt{#2}%
    \ifthenelse{\equal{#1}{D}}%
        {\index{#2|textbf}}{\index{#2}}}
    we define item \IX[D]{AAAA}
    \ldots{}     we reference item \IX{AAAA}
```

This gives the required visual representation in the `.idx` file by specifying entries of the type:

```
\indexentry{AAAA|textbf}{471}     \indexentry{AAAA}{471}
```

A more complicated example, where you have complete control of what goes or does not go into the index or in the text, is the extended index command `\IXE`, defined as follows:

```
\newcommand{\IXE}[2][!*!,!]{%
  \ifthenelse{\equal{#1}{!*!,!}}{%
      \ifthenelse{\equal{#2}{}}{}{\textbf{#2}\index{#2}}}%
    {\ifthenelse{\equal{#1}{}}{}{\index{#1}}%
      \ifthenelse{\equal{#2}{}}{}{\textbf{#2}}}}
```

Its default optional argument "!*!,!" contains a string which you probably never want to use in the text. If you use the command \IXE with only one (normal) argument, then you will enter the same information into the index and the text. By specifying an optional argument, you can enter something in the index that is different from what is printed in the text. All possible combinations are shown below. The en dashes show that no unwanted spaces are generated.

Identical in text and index – **AAAA!both**-	`\par Identical in text and index` `--\IXE{AAAA!both}--`
Different in text and index – **textentry**-	`\par Different in text and index` `--\IXE[AAAA!indexentry]{textentry}--`
Only to index --	`\par Only to index --\IXE[AAAA!indexonly]{}--`
In text only -**textonly**-	`\par In text only --\IXE[]{textonly}--`
Nothing in text or index --.	`\par Nothing in text or index --\IXE[]{}--.`

The .idx file contains only three entries, since the case with the empty optional argument "[]" does not generate an index entry.

```
\indexentry{AAAA!both}{472}
\indexentry{AAAA!indexentrypage:AAAA1}{472}
\indexentry{AAAA!indexonlypage:AAAA1}{472}
```

Look in the index of this book and you will find the index entries generated by the last two examples.

For the LaTeX2ε release a few more tests have been added to the ifthen package, as suggested by Alexander Samarin.

`\boolean{`*string*`}`   `\newboolean{`*string*`}`   `\setboolean{`*string*`}{`*value*`}`

Basic TeX knows about some switches that can have the value true or false.[2] To define your own switch use \newboolean with *string* being a sequence of letters. This switch is initially set to false. To change its value use \setboolean with the *value* argument being either the string true or false. You can then test the value by using \boolean in the first argument of \ifthenelse. It is also possible to test all such internal flags of LaTeX with this command (the most common ones are shown in table A.5 on the next page). An example could be a test to see whether a document is using a one- or two-sided layout.

Two-sided printing.	`\ifthenelse{\boolean{@twoside}}{Two-sided}{One-sided}` `printing.`

---

[2]They are normally built using the \newif command.

TₑX switches	
hmode	true, if typesetting is done in a horizontal direction, e.g., inside a paragraph or an LR box.
vmode	true, if typesetting is done vertically, e.g., if TₑX is between paragraphs.
mmode	true, if TₑX is typesetting a formula.
LATₑX switches	
@twoside	true, if LATₑX is typesetting for double-sided printing.
@twocolumn	true, if LATₑX is typesetting in standard two-column mode (false inside `multicols` environments).
@firstcolumn	true, if @twocolumn is true and LATₑX is typesetting the first column.
@newlist	true, if LATₑX is at the beginning of a list environment (will be set to false when text *after* the first `\item` command is encountered).
@inlabel	true, after an `\item` command until the text following it is encountered.
@noskipsec	true, after a run-in heading until the text following it is encountered.

Table A.5: The important internal `\boolean` switches

`\lengthtest{`*test*`}`

To compare dimensions use `\lengthtest`. In its *test* argument you can compare two dimensions (either explicit values like 20cm or names defined by `\newlength`) using one of the operators <, =, or >.

As an example, let us consider a figure characterized by its dimensions `\Xsize` and `\Ysize`, and which should be made to fit into a rectangular area with dimensions `\Xarea` and `\Yarea`, but without changing the aspect ratio of the figure. The following code calculates the new sizes of the figure (`\newX` and `\newY`). The trick is to first calculate and compare the aspect ratios of both rectangle and figure, and from there obtain the magnification factor.

```
\newlength{\sizetmp}\newlength{\areatmp}
\setlength{\sizetmp}{1pt*\ratio{\Xsize}{\Ysize}}
\setlength{\areatmp}{1pt*\ratio{\Xarea}{\Yarea}}
\ifthenelse{\lengthtest{\sizetmp > \areatmp}}%
   {\setlength{\newX}{\Xarea}
    \setlength{\newY}{\newX*\ratio{\Ysize}{\Xsize}}}
   {\setlength{\newY}{\Yarea}
    \setlength{\newX}{\newY*\ratio{\Xsize}{\Ysize}}}
```

> `\isodd{`*number*`}`

With the `\isodd` command you can test if a given *number* is odd. If, for example, the string generated by a `\pageref` command is a valid number (as it normally is), then you can use the command in the following way:

This is an even numbered page.

```
This\label{testref} is an
\ifthenelse{\isodd{\pageref{testref}}}{odd}{even}
numbered page.
```

`\isodd` is specially tailored to support the above application even though the `\pageref` might be undefined in the first LaTeX run.

> `\whiledo{`*test*`}{`*do-clause*`}`

The `\whiledo` command is valuable for executing certain repetitive command sequences. The following simple example (using a counter from the examples above) shows how the command works:

The time is 1h.
The time is 2h.
The time is 3h.
The time is 4h.

```
\setcounter{hours}{1}
\whiledo{\value{hours}<5}{%
        The time is \thehours h.\\%
        \stepcounter{hours}}
```

> `\and        \or        \not        \(        \)`

Multiple conditions can be combined into logical expressions via the logical operators (`\or`, `\and`, and `\not`), using the commands `\(` and `\)` as parentheses. A simple example is seen below.

You agree "OK" or don't "not OK".

D'accord "OK" ou pas "not OK"?

```
\newcommand{\QU}[2]{%
 \ifthenelse{%
   \(\equal{#1}{ENG} \and \equal{#2}{yes}\)
      \or
   \(\equal{#1}{FRE} \and \equal{#2}{oui}\)}%
 {``OK''}{``not OK''}%
}
You agree \QU{ENG}{yes} or don't \QU{ENG}{no}.
\par\bigskip
D'accord \QU{FRE}{oui} ou pas \QU{FRE}{non}?
```

T_EX Archive Sites

If, after reading this book, you still have not found the file you need, you can consult the `TeX-index` file [36] maintained by David Jones (MIT). It is a catalogue of macros for T_EX, L^AT_EX, and others. Its scope includes all macros that are available via anonymous ftp or mail server on all sites mentioned below.

The file `TeX-index` itself, like all packages and files described in this book, is available via anonymous ftp on the Internet or through a mail server.

B.1 The Main T_EX Internet Sites

Presently, various T_EX user communities are coordinating their efforts to provide easy access to T_EX-related material for as many T_EX users as possible. A recent development is the "Comprehensive T_EX Archive Network" (CTAN), which has been set up [23]. At present, it includes the Aston, Sam Houston State University, and Dante Internet sites. These sites provide essentially the same T_EX-related software by mirroring each other.

Please bear in mind the geographical location of the site to which you intend to ftp. Choose a site as close to you as possible. Also, transfer rate will be drastically improved if you transfer large files outside normal (local!) working hours. The short list below shows the main T_EX archives in Europe and the United States of America. The directory where Jones' `TeX-index` can be found is shown right-adjusted on the first line of each applicable ftp address. The `CTAN` archives are marked with an asterisk (*).

America

`ftp.shsu.edu`*   `/tex-archive/help/TeX-index`
  A CTAN site.

`ftp.math.utah.edu`   `/pub/tex/tex-index`
  Nelson Beebe's server, which contains a lot of BIBTEX-related styles and
  data bases, especially in the field of text processing and mathematics. It
  has, for example, `tugboat.bib`, which lists all the articles published in
  TUGBoat.

`labrea.stanford.edu`
  The official repository for TEX, METAFONT, dvips, and related files.

Europe

`ftp.dante.de`*   `/pub/tex/help/TeX-index`
  A CTAN site. Also the primary source for emTeX, publicTeX, pub-
  licMF, and the "Mainz" packages by Frank Mittelbach and Rainer Schöpf
  (multicol, verbatim, theorem, NFSS, ftnright, and array).

`ftp.tex.ac.uk`*   `/pub/archive/help/TeX-index`
  A CTAN site. Home of the UKTeX electronic newsletter.

`ftp.cs.ruu.nl`   `/pub/TEX/DOC/TeX-index.gz`

For the location of one of the more well-known packages, you can search
archie for an archive site that carries the file. You can also find a lot
of information using the gopher, www, or wais service. Further information about (LA)TEX is also contained in the frequently asked questions file
`tex.faq`, maintained by Bobby Bodenheimer (Caltech, USA) (available from all
archives mentioned above and from the reference site `pit-manager.mit.edu` as
`/pub/usenet/news.answers/tex-faq`) and the "Supplementary TeX Information" file, maintained by Guoying Chen (NYU, USA) (reference site `cs.nyu.edu` in
the directory `ftp/pub/tex`).

Getting Files from an Archive

Figures B.1 and B.2 on pages 477–478 show an ftp session to the Aston CTAN
archive. The first command `cd ctan:` sets us in the top directory of the
"CTAN" tree. Then we issue the command `quote site index xspace.sty`,
which locates the file xspace.sty and shows its full file name in the CTAN
file hierarchy. We go to the directory where that file resides with the command `cd macros/latex/contrib/misc` and get the file in question using
`get xspace.sty`. We repeat the procedure for Jones's TeX-index file, going
to the relevant directory and retrieving it. In this case we specify the command
`get TeX-index.gz`, which compresses the file on the fly using the `gzip` utility
(which we chose by specifying the extension gz). These compressed files must be

transferred in binary mode, hence the command `binary` before the `get`. At any moment, you can issue the command `dir` or `ls` to see what is available, or `pwd` to see in which directory you are. As seen in the example, the CTAN archives support dynamic compression and uncompression of data sets, so that large files can be conveniently transferred (for instance, in the case of the `TeX-index` file, the compressed file is four times smaller—86,168 instead of 367,136 bytes—so the transfer time is reduced drastically). If your machine does not have uncompression tools, a compressed file can be uncompressed on the fly. The exact procedure of how these facilities work is explained in the online documentation at the CTAN sites. You can also get the listing of the contents of a (tar, zip, zoo) archive by appending the suffix `-1st` to the name of the archive, as shown in the command `get morebin.zip-1st` below. The command `!more` shows the contents of the `morebin` zoo archive on our local node.

```
$ ftp ftp.tex.ac.uk
Connected to ftp.tex.ac.uk.
220 ftp.tex.ac.uk FTP server (Version 2.0WU(11) Wed Apr 28 22:25:23 GMT 1993) ready.
Name (ftp.tex.ac.uk:goossens): anonymous
331 Guest login ok, send e-mail address as password.
Password: goossens@mysystem.cern.ch (use your email address)
230-Welcome, archive user!  This is an FTP server for the UK TeX Archive.
        .... several lines of information not shown ....
230 Guest login ok, access restrictions apply.
ftp> cd ctan:
250 CWD command successful.
ftp> quote site index xspace.sty
200-index xspace.sty
200-NOTE. This index shows at most 20 lines. for a full list of files,
200-retrieve /pub/archive/FILES.byname
200-1992/09/21 |      5494 | macros/latex/contrib/misc/xspace.sty
200  (end of 'index xspace.sty')
ftp> cd macros/latex/contrib/misc
200 CWD command successful.
ftp> get xspace.sty
200 PORT command successful.
150 Opening ASCII mode data connection for xspace.sty (5494 bytes).
226 Transfer complete.
5645 bytes received in 3.67 seconds (1.50 Kbytes/s)
```

Figure B.1: An example ftp session to the Aston CTAN TeX archive (part 1)

```
ftp> quote site index TeX-index
200-index tex-styles
200-NOTE. This index shows at most 20 lines. for a full list of files,
200-retrieve /pub/archive/FILES.byname
200-1993/01/04 |     367136 | help/TeX-index
200  (end of 'index tex-styles')
ftp> cd ctan:
250 CWD command successful.
ftp> cd help
250 CWD command successful.
ftp> binary
200 Type set to I.
ftp> get TeX-index.gz
200 PORT command successful.
150 Opening BINARY mode data connection for /bin/gzip.
226 Transfer complete.
86168 bytes received in 17.61 seconds (4.78 Kbytes/s)
ftp> cd ctan:
250 CWD command successful.
ftp> cd systems/msdos/emtex-contrib/bonus
250 CWD command successful.
ftp> get morebin.zip-lst
200 PORT command successful.
150 Opening BINARY mode data connection for /bin/LIST.
226 Transfer complete.
1595 bytes received in 0.68 seconds (2.28 Kbytes/s)
ftp> !more morebin.zip-lst
Listing of ./morebin.zip
Length  Method   Size  Ratio  Date    Time   CRC-32   Name ("^" ==> case
------  ------   ----  -----  ----    ----   ------   ----    conversion)
 36000  Implode  17648  51%  01-27-92  16:34  7a371924  ^emtex/wp2latex.exe
 23535  Implode  14583  38%  11-25-91  17:31  8dff2c94  ^emtex/dvi2tty.exe
 50422  Implode  27970  45%  12-12-91  21:04  7e2ac940  ^emtex/dviselec.exe
 26897  Implode  12942  52%  12-12-91  09:54  6f3a375e  ^emtex/dvidvi.exe
 48608  Implode  27219  44%  12-12-91  21:29  fd19e62a  ^emtex/dviconca.exe
            .... several lines of information not shown ....
------           ------  ---                            -------
407402           203175  50%                            16
ftp> quit
221 Goodbye.
```

Figure B.2: An example ftp session to the Aston CTAN TEX archive (part 2)

B.2 Mail Servers

Those who cannot connect directly to the Internet but who have access to electronic mail can also retrieve files and information by using mail servers, which have been set up by many sites carrying TEX-related information. Note, however, that each server tends to have its own syntax, which in each case must be carefully followed. More information can be found in the TEX supplementary information list maintained by Guoying Chen. Examples of mail servers and commands of how to contact them are shown in figure B.3.

address: `ftpmail@dante.de`
message: `help`
address: `fileserv@shsu.edu`
message: `help`
address: `mail-server@cs.ruu.nl`
message: `begin`
            `path user@machine.site` (**your** email address)
            `send help`
            `end`
address: `listserv@hearn.bitnet`
message: `get tex filelist` to get a list of files available
address: `listserv@vm.urz.uni-heidelberg.de`
message: `help`
            `get readme first tex`
            `get tex filelist`

Figure B.3: Example of TEX mail servers

B.3 TEX User Groups

TEX users in several countries have set up TEX user groups, mostly based on language affinities. If you need help, you are advised to contact your local user group first, since they might be able to come up with an answer that is most suited to your language-dependent working environment. Below we give the addresses of the groups known to us (fall 1993). Often they can help you obtain TEX-related material on diskettes or offer a mail service for those without access to the Internet.

TEX Users Group   (International)

TEX Users Group   Tel: 805-963-1338
P.O. Box 869   Fax: 805-963-8358
Santa Barbara, CA 93102-0869 USA   Email: `tug@tug.org`

CsTUG (Czech and Slovak Republics)
Dr. Karel Horák, President
Československé sdružení uživatelů TeXu
CsTeX Users Group, c/o MÚK UK
Sokolovská 83
CS-186 00 Praha 8, Czechoslovakia
Email: `horakk@earn.cvut.cz`

CyrTUG (Russia)
Irina Makhovaya, Executive Director
Associaciia Pol'zovateleĭ Kirillicheskogo
TeX'a
Mir Publishers
2, Pervyĭ Rizhskiĭ Pereulok
Moscow 129820, Russia
Tel: 095 286-0622, 286-1777
Fax: 095 288-9522
Email: `cyrtug@mir.msk.su`

DANTE e.V. (German-speaking)
Joachim Lammarsch, President
Deutschsprachige Anwendervereinigung
TeX e.V.
Postfach 101840
D-69008 Heidelberg, Germany
Tel: 06221/29766
Fax: 06221/167906
Email: `dante@dante.de`

Estonian User Group
Enn Saar, Tartu
Astrophysical Observatory, Tõravere
EE2444 Estonia
Email: `saar@aai.ee`

GUST (Poland)
Hanna Kołodziejska, President
Polska Grupa Użytkowników Systemu
TeX
Instytut Badań Systemowych PAN
ul. Newelska 6
PL-01-447 Warszawa, Poland
Email: `gust@camk.edu.pl`

GUTenberg (French-speaking)
Alain Cousquer, President
Groupe francophone des Utilisateurs de
TeX
GUTenberg, c/o IRISA
Campus de Beaulieu
F-35042 Rennes cedex, France
Email: `gut@irisa.fr`

ITALIC   Irish TeX And LaTeX Interest
Community (informal)
Discussions on mailing list `ITALIC-L`
hosted on the list server
`listserv@irlearn.ucd.ie`
(open for public subscription).

Japan TUG (Japan)
Nobuo Saitoh, Chairman
Japan TeX Users' Group
Faculty of Environmental Information
Keio University
5322 Endo, Fujisawa-shi
JP-252 Japan
Tel: +81 466 47 5111
Email: `ns@keio.ac.jp`

Nordic TeX Group (Scandinavia)
Roswitha Graham
KTH (Royal Institute of Technology)
TS DATA
S-100 44 Stockholm, Sweden
Email: `roswitha@admin.kth.se`

NTG (Dutch-speaking)
Kees van der Laan, Chair
Nederlandstalige TeX Gebruikersgroep
Postbus 394
NL-1740 AJ Schagen
The Netherlands
Email: `ntg@nic.surfnet.nl`

Spanish TUG (no formal group)
Electronic mail discussion list
`spanish-tex@eunet.es`
Send subscription requests to
Email: `listserv@eunet.es`
Julio Sanchez
GMV SA
Isaac Newton 11 PTM Tres Cantos
E-28760 Madrid, Spain
Email: `jsanchez@gmv.es`

UK TUG (United Kingdom)
Chris Rowley, Chair
UK TeX Users' Group
c/o Peter Abbott
1 Eymore Close
Selly Oak
Birmingham B29 4LB, United Kingdom
Email: `uktug-enquiries@tex.ac.uk`

Bibliography

[1] Adobe Systems Incorporated. *PostScript Language Tutorial and Cookbook.* Addison-Wesley, Reading, 1985.

This so-called "blue book" is the most common tutorial book on PostScript. It consists of two parts, an easy-to-follow tutorial introduction to the language and its graphics primitives and a cookbook, consisting of 21 programs that show how PostScript is used in real applications. The code of the examples covers most of the common applications that you will encounter and can be readily included in your own packages. The main drawback of this book is that it only describes PostScript Level 1. A more recent and very good introduction to PostScript Level 2 for PostScript users at all levels is *PostScript by Example*, by Henry McGilton and Mary Campione, Addison Wesley, 1992. The book also starts at novice level, but in later chapters it covers Level 2 features, such as composite fonts, patterns, forms, color and halftones. It has over 500 fragments of PostScript code and 750 illustrations.

[2] Adobe Systems Incorporated. *PostScript Language Reference Manual.* Addison-Wesley, Reading, second edition, 1990.

This so-called "red book" contains the complete definition of the PostScript language. It describes all PostScript Level 1 and Level 2 operators as well as the Display PostScript extensions. Appendices define the *Document Structuring Conventions* and the *Encapsulated PostScript File Format.*

[3] Adobe Systems Incorporated. *Adobe Type 1 Font Format.* Addison-Wesley, Reading, 1990.

This so-called "black book" contains the specifications for Adobe's Type 1 font format. It includes information on the structure of font programs, explains how computer outlines are specified and gives the contents of the various font dictionaries. It also covers encryption, subroutines, hints, and compatibility issues in the use of Adobe Type Manager.

[4] Jacques André and Jeanine Grimault. Emploi des capitales (première partie). *Cahiers GUTenberg*, 6:42–50, July 1990.

On the use of capitals in French.

[5] Jacques André and Philippe Louarn. Notes en bas de pages : comment les
     faire en LaTeX? *Cahiers GUTenberg*, 12:57-70, December 1991.
     Several special cases of using footnotes with LaTeX are discussed, for example, how to
     generate a footnote referring to information inside a tabular or minipage environment or
     how to reference the same footnote more than once.

[6] *Guide du typographe romand.* Association suisse des compositeurs à la
     machine, 4ᵉ édition, 1982.
     Typographic rules for French as used by the Roman Swiss typesetters.

[7] Richard Aurbach. IdxTeX and GloTeX—indexes and glossaries.
     TUGboat, 7(3):187, October 1986.
     A short description of two VAX/VMS specific processors for LaTeX indexes and glossaries.

[8] Richard Aurbach. Automated index generation for LaTeX.
     TUGboat, 8(2):201, July 1987.
     After a short introduction to the IdxTeX project, Richard Aurbach describes how the
     VAX/VMS program IdxTeX provides a full range of services for index generation. The input
     syntax is presented, and the internal data structures and various parts of the program are
     reviewed.

[9] Nelson H. F. Beebe. Bibliography Prettyprinting and Syntax Checking.
     TUGboat, 14(4):395-419, December 1993.
     Three software tools for BibTeX support are described. The first, bibclean, is a prettyprinter,
     syntax checker, and lexical analyzer for BibTeX files. The second is biblex, a lexical analyzer
     capable of tokenizing a BibTeX file. The third is bibparse, a parser that analyzes a lexical
     token stream from bibclean and biblex. bibclean is extensively customizable using
     initialization files, and run-time definable patterns for checking BibTeX value strings. A
     pattern-matching language is provided for this purpose.

[10] Karl Berry. Filenames for fonts. *TUGboat*, 11(4):517-520, November 1990.
     A consistent, rational naming scheme for font file names is proposed. Each name consists
     of up to eight characters that should identify each font file in a unique way.

[11] Neenie Billawala. Metamarks: Preliminary studies for a Pandora's Box of
     shapes. Technical Report STAN-CS-89-1256, Stanford University,
     Department of Computer Science, May 1989.
     A pleasing booklet describing studies of shapes for font production, like serifs, arches,
     bowls, etc. These studies eventually led to a typeface called Pandora.

[12] Neenie Billawala. Opening Pandora's Box. *TUGboat*, 10(4):481-489,
     December 1989.
     When creating the Pandora type family the author tried to use METAFONT as a design tool
     rather than a production tool. General descriptions of visual relationships between parts of
     characters, characters in a font, and fonts in a typeface were developed, so that one obtains
     the various fonts by changing the parameter settings of a single framework. This allows
     the designer to quickly study various possibilities.

[13] Hans-Hermann Bode. Neue BibTeX-Style-Files: Die *adaptable family*.
     Die TeXnische Komödie, 4(2):31-41, August 1992.
     A new family of BibTeX style files is introduced, in which the user can change the layout (fonts
     used for specific fields) and some words or phrases used by the style (such as the names

of months, edition, chapter, articles, and conjunctions). These strings are parameterized inside the BibTEX styles and are resolved when TEXing a document by reading a language-dependent external file that defines these terms for the chosen language.

[14] Francis Borceux. User's guide for the *Diagram* Macros. Electronic document distributed with the package, February 1993.

Commutative diagram package. Especially useful for the construction of diagrams in category theory. Uses LATEX picture mode as the underlying drawing mechanism.

[15] Johannes Braams. Babel, a multilingual style-option system for use with LATEX's standard document styles. *TUGboat*, 12(2):291-301, June 1991.

A description of a way to make LATEX adaptable to more than one language via the use of language-specific style options. An update was published in *TUGboat*, 14(1):60-62, April 1993.

[16] Pehong Chen and Michael A. Harrison. Index preparation and processing. *Software—Practice and Experience*, 19(9):897-915, September 1988. The LATEX text of this paper is included in the `makeindex` software distribution.

This paper shows how the tedious and time-consuming task of preparing an index can be automated in a way largely independent of the typesetting system and the specific format used. The ideas are illustrated with the help of the *MakeIndex* system, which transforms raw index data into an alphabetized version. A comparison of that system with other indexing facilities is made.

[17] Adrian F. Clark. Practical halftoning with TEX. *TUGboat*, 12(1):157-165, March 1991.

Reviews practical problems encountered when using TEX for typesetting halftone pictures and compares other techniques to include graphics material. Advantages and disadvantages of the various approaches are described and some attempts at producing color separations are discussed.

[18] Malcolm Clark. Portable graphics in TEX. *TUGboat*, 13(3):253-260, October 1992, and Chapter 17 of *A Plain TEX Primer*, by Malcolm Clark, Oxford University Press, 1992.

Discusses three major ways to include line graphics in TEX documents: special fonts, the `\special` command, and in-between solutions. Other reviews are *TEX and Graphics: The State of the Problem*, by Nelson Beebe, in: *Cahiers GUTenberg*, 2:13-53, May 1989, and *Including Pictures in TEX*, by Alois Heinz, in: *TEX applications, uses, methods*, Malcolm Clark (ed.), Ellis Horwood Publishers, Chichester, England, pp. 141-151, 1990.

[19] Dale Dougherty and Tim O'Reilly. *UNIX Text Processing*. Howard W. Sams & Company, Hayden Books, Indianapolis, 1988.

This book provides a complete description of UNIX's text processing tools. In particular, chapter 10, "Drawing Pictures," explains the syntax of the `pic` processor language with a lot of examples. Information about that language is also available in the UNIX man pages for the pic and gpic (GNU) processors.

[20] Lincoln Durst. Some tools for making indexes: Part I. *TUGboat*, 12(2):248-252, June 1991.

Reviews basic TEX coding tricks to generate indexes. You can also have a look at David Salomon's article *Macros for indexing and table-of-contents* in: *TUGboat*, 10(3):394-400, November 1989.

[21] Bernard Gaulle. Notice d'utilisation du style french (Version 3,25). Electronic document distributed with the package, November 1993.

A user guide to the french package (in French).

[22] Ronald L. Graham, Donald E. Knuth, and Oren Patashnik. *Concrete Mathematics: A Foundation for Computer Science.* Addison-Wesley, Reading, 1989.

A well typeset mathematics textbook, prepared with TEX, where the Concrete Roman typeface is used as main text font; see also [45].

[23] George D. Greenwade. The Comprehensive TEX Archive Network (CTAN). *TUGboat*, 14(3):342–351, October 1993.

An outline of the concept, development, and use of the CTAN archive, which makes all TEX-related files available on the network. CTAN relies on the close collaboration of the major TEX archives on various continents, which run synchronized mirror images of each other. CTAN provides a consistent way for identifying files and for retrieving them and thus should contribute to a reduction of overall network traffic and an increase of retrieval speed.

[24] Roswitha T. Haas and Kevin C. O'Kane. Typesetting Chemical Structure Formulas with the Text Formatter TEX/LATEX. *Computers and Chemistry*, 11(4):251–271, 1987.

The article gives an overview of the possibilities of the ChemTEX package. More information can be found in the various chapters of Haas's Ph.D. thesis that are distributed with the package. Other tools for typesetting chemical formulae are discussed in *Electronic Publishing and Chemical Text Processing*, by A.C. Norris and A.L. Oakley, in: *TEX applications, uses, methods*, Malcolm Clark (ed.), Ellis Horwood Publishers, Chichester, England, pp. 207–225, 1990, and in *Chemical Structure Formulae and x/y Diagrams with TEX*, by Michael Ramek, *ibidem*, pp. 227–258.

[25] Yannis Haralambous. Typesetting old german: Fraktur, Schwabacher, Gotisch and initials. *TUGboat*, 12(1):129–138, March 1991.

Shows how METAFONT can be used to recreate faithful copies of old style typefaces, which can be used with TEX. Rules for typesetting in the types are given and example output pages are shown.

[26] Doug Henderson. Outline fonts with METAFONT. *TUGboat*, 10(1):36–38, April 1989.

A description of the METAFONT code used to generate outlines from existing character descriptions.

[27] Eric van Herwijnen. *Practical SGML.* Wolters-Kluwer Academic Publishers, Boston, second edition, 1994.

An introduction to the use of SGML in real-life applications. Contains a lot of examples of areas where SGML has been successfully used and discusses various SGML implementations.

[28] Alan Hoenig. When TEX and Metafont Work Together. In *Proceedings of the 7th European TEX Conference, Prague*, pp. 1–19, September 1992.

A description of how TEX and METAFONT can communicate data to allow you to prepare diagrams and figures with METAFONT and labels with TEX. Conversely, METAFONT can generate special purpose fonts that can, for instance, be used to typeset text along a curved baseline.

[29] Thomas Hofmann. A LaTeX addition for formatting indexes. *TUGboat*, 7(3):186, October 1986.

The description of a Bourne Shell script, `latexindex`, to handle LaTeX indexes.

[30] IBM, International Business Machines Corporation. *Font Object Content Architecture: Reference*, New York, December 1988.

This manual describes the concepts of IBM digital font resources and their application. It gives general information on font storage, accessing, and referencing, and it explains concepts of character shape information. It gives a full reference of the font parameters used in IBM fonts including font-descriptive parameters, font-metric parameters, character-shape parameters, and code page parameters.

[31] IBM, International Business Machines Corporation. *Document Composition Facility—General Information Release 4.0 for DCF (GH20-9158-09)*, Boulder, 1990.

This manual contains general information about IBM's Document Composition Facility, which provides a text formatter, called SCRIPT/VS. It can process documents marked up with its own control words as well as documents marked up in the GML—Generalized Markup Language—a precursor of SGML. The system also has an (optional) Script Mathematical Formula Formatter—SMFF.

[32] *Lexique des règles typographiques en usage à l'Imprimerie nationale*. Imprimerie nationale, 3ᵉ édition, 1990.

Typographic rules for French as used by the "Imprimerie nationale," in Paris, the printing house that is responsible for printing all official government documents and all books edited by the French state.

[33] International Organization for Standardization. 8-bit single-byte coded graphics character sets, parts 1 to 10. ISO 8859, ISO Geneva, 1986–92.

A description of various alphabetic character sets. Parts 1 to 4, 9, and 10 correspond to character sets needed to encode different groups of languages using the Latin alphabet, while part 5 corresponds to Cyrillic, part 6 to Arabic, part 7 to Greek, and part 8 to Hebrew.

[34] International Organization for Standardization. Standard Generalised Markup Language (SGML). ISO 8879, ISO Geneva, 1986.

The—not always easy to read—ISO standard describing the SGML language in glorious technical detail. An easier to read review article, describing the role of SGML as first element in a chain of text processing standards, comprising also DSSSL (document formatting), SPDL (document presentation), and Unicode/ISO 10646 (character codes), is *Scientific Text Processing*, by Michel Goossens and Eric van Herwijnen, in *International Journal of Modern Physics C*, 3(3):479–546, June 1992.

[35] International Organization for Standardization. Universal Coded Character Set. ISO/IEC 10646, ISO Geneva, 1993.

This standard specifies the structure and defines the Universal Multiple-Octet Coded Character Set (UCS). It is a 32-bit character encoding standard, which can be used to encode all possible writing systems in the world. At present only the 16-bit base plane has been defined, and it is identical to the Unicode standard; see [85]. A short overview of this standard and its history can be found in *Untying tongues*, by Michael Y. Ksar, in *iso bulletin*, 24(6):2–8, June 1993.

[36] David M. Jones. A TeX macro index. *TUGboat*, 13(2):188–189, July 1992.

In this article David Jones officially announces his catalogue of TeX macros that are available via anonymous ftp or mailserver. A summary of archive locations where this catalogue is stored was published in *TeX and TUG NEWS*, 2(2):12-13, April 1993.

[37] Donald E. Knuth. *TeX and Metafont, New Directions in Typesetting*. The American Mathematical Society and Digital Press, Bedford, MA, 1979.

The first part of this book contains the reprint of an article by Donald Knuth called "Mathematical Typography," where the author discusses his motivation for starting to work on TeX and traces the early history of computer typesetting. The second and third parts of this book describe early (and now obsolete) versions of TeX and METAFONT, but they remain interesting reading for TeX *historians*.

[38] Donald E. Knuth. Remarks to Celebrate the Publication of Computers & Typesetting. *TUGboat*, 7(2):95–98, June 1986.

On May 21, 1986, the Computer Museum in Boston hosted a celebration in honor of the completion of TeX, Donald Knuth's computer typesetting system. This article summarizes the text of Knuth's speech on that occasion in which he retraced his nine years of work on the TeX and METAFONT systems.

[39] Donald E. Knuth. *The TeXbook*, volume A of *Computers and Typesetting*. Addison-Wesley, Reading, 1986.

The definitive user's guide and complete reference manual for TeX.

[40] Donald E. Knuth. *TeX: The Program*, volume B of *Computers and Typesetting*. Addison-Wesley, Reading, 1986.

The well typeset complete source code listing for the TeX program. The TeX program is written in the WEB language and the book is a (slightly edited) version of the source after running WEAVE and TeXing the output.

[41] Donald E. Knuth. *The METAFONTbook*, volume C of *Computers and Typesetting*. Addison-Wesley, Reading, 1986.

The user's guide and reference manual for METAFONT, the companion program to TeX for designing fonts.

[42] Donald E. Knuth. METAFONT: *The Program*, volume D of *Computers and Typesetting*. Addison-Wesley, Reading, 1986.

The complete source code listing of the METAFONT program.

[43] Donald E. Knuth. *Computer Modern Typefaces*, volume E of *Computers and Typesetting*. Addison-Wesley, Reading, 1986.

Over 500 Greek and Roman letterforms, together with punctuation marks, numerals, and many mathematical symbols, are graphically depicted. The METAFONT code to generate each glyph is given and it is explained how, by changing the parameters in the METAFONT code, all characters in the Computer Modern family of typefaces can be obtained.

[44] Donald E. Knuth. Fonts for digital halftones. *TUGboat*, 8(2):135–160, July 1987.

A discussion of some experiments in which METAFONT was used to create fonts to generate halftones on laser printers.

[45]   Donald E. Knuth. Typesetting *Concrete Mathematics.*
       TUGboat, 10(1):31–36, April 1989.
       Donald Knuth explains how he typeset the textbook *Concrete Mathematics.*

[46]   Donald E. Knuth. Virtual Fonts: More Fun for Grand Wizards.
       TUGboat, 11(1):13–23, April 1990.
       An explanation of what virtual fonts are and why they are needed. This information is
       followed by technical details of how these ideas are implemented.

[47]   Donald E. Knuth. The Future of TeX and Metafont.
       TUGboat, 11(4):489, November 1990.
       *My work on developing TeX, METAFONT, and Computer Modern has come to an end. I will
       make no further changes except to correct extremely serious bugs.* In the article starting
       with these words Donald Knuth announces that he wants to freeze the programs of the TeX
       system at their present versions.

[48]   Conrad Kwok. EEPIC: Extensions to EPIC and LaTeX picture environment.
       Unpublished machine-readable document, 1988.
       The user guide to the eepic package, which is distributed together with the software. Eepic
       is an extension of both LaTeX and epic.

[49]   Leslie Lamport. *LaTeX—A Document Preparation System—User's Guide
       and Reference Manual.* Addison-Wesley, Reading, 1985.
       The ultimate reference on LaTeX 2.09 by its author. A new edition covering LaTeX2ε is in
       preparation. It nicely complements the material presented in the present work.

[50]   Leslie Lamport. *MakeIndex*, An Index Processor For LaTeX. Electronic
       document coming with the *MakeIndex* distribution, 1987.
       This document explains the syntax that can be used inside LaTeX's \index command when
       using *MakeIndex* to generate your index. It also gives a list of the possible error messages.

[51]   John Lavagnino and Dominik Wujastyk. An Overview of EDMAC: A plain
       TeX format for critical editions. *TUGboat*, 11(4):623–643, November 1990.
       EDMAC lets you typeset critical editions of texts in a traditional way, i.e., similar to the Oxford
       Classical Texts, Shakespeare, and other series. The package adds marginal line numbering
       and multiple series of footnotes and endnotes keyed to line numbers. Users can control
       the exact format of their editions in a simple way.

[52]   Micheal J. S. Levine. A LaTeX Graphics Routine for drawing Feynman
       Diagrams. *Computer Physics Communications*, 58:181–198, 1990.
       A description of the Feynman package for drawing Feynman diagrams. More details can be
       found in Levine's Ph.D. thesis, which is distributed as a LaTeX file with the package.

[53]   Franklin Mark Liang. Word Hy-phen-a-tion by Com-pu-ter. Ph.D. thesis,
       Stanford University, Stanford, CA 94305, June 1983. Also available as
       Technical Report No. STAN-CS-83-977, Stanford University, Department
       of Computer Science.
       A detailed description of the word hyphenation algorithm used in TeX.

[54] Frank Mittelbach. An extension of the LaTeX theorem environment.
      TUGboat, 10(3):416–426, November 1989.

      The different mathematics journals often require different layouts for their theorems. When
      using the theorem package this layout can be customized with the help of a "style." The
      article describes the user interface and implementation.

[55] Frank Mittelbach. E-TeX: Guidelines for future TeX extensions.
      TUGboat, 11(3):337–345, September 1990.

      TeX started out originally as a system to typeset Donald Knuth's books. Nowadays it is
      used by tens of thousands of users. Is TeX still the right tool to address the typesetting
      requirements of the nineties? To answer this question, the output of TeX is compared with
      that of hand-typeset documents. Areas where TeX's algorithms are too limited in scope
      are discussed. It is shown that many important concepts of high quality typesetting are
      not supported and that further research to design a "successor" typesetting system to TeX
      should be undertaken.

[56] Frank Mittelbach. Comments on "Filenames for Fonts" (*TUGboat* 11#4).
      TUGboat, 13(1):51–53, April 1992.

      Some problems with K. Berry's naming scheme are discussed, especially from the point of
      view of defining certain font characteristics independently and the use of the scheme with
      NFSS.

[57] Frank Mittelbach and Chris Rowley. LaTeX 2.09 ↪ LaTeX3.
      TUGboat, 13(1):96–101, April 1992.

      A brief sketch of the LaTeX3 Project, retracing its history and describing the structure of
      the system. An update appeared in *TUGboat*, 13(3):390–391, October 1992. A call for
      volunteers to help in the development of LaTeX3 and a list of the various tasks appeared
      in *TUGboat*, 13(4):510–515, December 1992. The article also describes how you can obtain
      the current task list as well as various LaTeX3 working group documents via email or ftp
      and explains how you can subscribe to the LaTeX3 discussion list.

[58] Frank Mittelbach and Rainer Schöpf. A new font selection scheme for TeX
      macro packages — the basic macros. *TUGboat*, 10(2):222–238, July 1989.

      A description of the basic macros used to implement the first version of LaTeX's New Font
      Selection Scheme.

[59] Frank Mittelbach and Rainer Schöpf. With LaTeX into the Nineties.
      TUGboat, 10(4):681–690, December 1989.

      As LaTeX has spread into many different fields, many local changes and enhancements
      threaten the possibility of exchanging documents. Therefore this article proposes a reim-
      plementation of LaTeX that preserves the essential features of the current interface while
      taking into account the increasing needs of the various user communities. It also formulates
      some ideas for further developments.

[60] Frank Mittelbach and Rainer Schöpf. Reprint: The new font family
      selection — User interface to standard LaTeX.
      TUGboat, 11(2):297–305, June 1990.

      A complete description of the user interface of the first version of LaTeX's New Font Selection
      Scheme.

[61] Frank Mittelbach and Rainer Schöpf. Towards LaTeX3.0.
      TUGboat, 12(1):74–79, March 1991.

The objectives of the LaTeX3 project are described. The authors examine enhancements to LaTeX's user and style file interfaces that are necessary to keep pace with modern developments, such as SGML. They also review some internal concepts that need revision.

[62] Olivier Nicole, Jacques André, and Bernard Gaulle. Notes en bas de pages : commentaires. *Cahiers GUTenberg*, 15:46–52, April 1993.
Comments, clarifications, and additions to article [5].

[63] Hubert Partl. German TEX. *TUGboat*, 9(1):70–72, April 1988.
An early example of an attempt to use LaTeX with a language other than English, in this case German, and the problems that were encountered.

[64] Oren Patashnik. BibTEXing. Documentation for general BibTEX users, 8 February 1988. Electronic document coming with the BibTEX distribution.
This article describes, together with appendix B in Lamport's LaTeX manual, the user interface to BibTEX. It updates section B.2 in the manual and provides many useful hints for controlling the behavior of BibTEX.

[65] Oren Patashnik. Designing BibTEX styles. The part of BibTEX's documentation that's not meant for general users, 8 February 1988. Electronic document coming with the BibTEX distribution.
A detailed description for BibTEX style designers of the postfix stack language used inside BibTEX style files. After a general description of the language, all commands and built-in functions are reviewed. Finally BibTEX name formatting is explained in detail.

[66] Sunil Podar. Enhancements to the picture environment of LaTeX. (Version 1.2) Technical Report 86-17, Department of Computer Science, S.U.N.Y, 1986.
This document describes some new commands for the picture environment of LaTeX, especially higher-level commands that enhance its graphic capabilities by providing a friendlier and more powerful user interface. This should make it easier to create more sophisticated pictures with less effort than in basic LaTeX.

[67] Sebastian Rahtz. A survey of TEX and graphics. Technical Report CSTR 89-7, University of Southampton, Department of Electronics and Computer Science, Southampton SO9 5NH, England, October 1989.
A detailed review of various ways to include graphics material in LaTeX documents

[68] Sebastian Rahtz and Leonor Barroca. A style option for rotated objects in LaTeX. *TUGboat*, 13(2):156–180, July 1992.
A detailed description of the user interface and the implementation of the rotating package, which allows you to perform all the different sorts of rotation you might like, including complete figures, within the context of a whole series of PostScript drivers.

[69] Glenn C. Reid. *PostScript Language Program Design.* Addison-Wesley, Reading, 1988.
This so-called "green book" teaches you the programming fundamentals for designing efficient PostScript code, which is easy to understand and maintain. Some of the tasks discussed in the book are: setting text, dealing with graphics, and error-handling and debugging techniques.

[70] Glenn C. Reid. *Thinking in PostScript.* Addison-Wesley, Reading, 1990.

This book's aim is to teach you how to develop your PostScript programming skills by introducing you to some useful, though simple and elegant, programming techniques. Subject areas that are hardly covered anywhere else are discussed, for instance, how to optimize your loops, conditionals, and input/output, and how to deal with files, strings, and dictionaries.

[71] Thomas J. Reid. Floating figures at the right—and—Some random text for testing. *TUGboat,* 8(3):315, November 1987.

A description of the techniques used to implement the figure placements.

[72] Tomas Rokicki. DVIPS: A TEX Driver. Electronic document coming with the dvips distribution, January 1993.

The user guide to dvips and its accompanying programs and packages, in particular afm2tfm for generating tfm files from Adobe's afm font metrics and colordvi for using color.

[73] Kristoffer H. Rose. Typesetting Diagrams with XY-pic: User's Manual. In *Proceedings of the 7th European TEX Conference, Prague,* pp. 273–292, September 1992.

A detailed overview of the possibilities of the XY-pic package for drawing diagrams with TEX.

[74] Stephen E. Roth, editor. *Real World PostScript. Techniques from PostScript Professionals.* Addison-Wesley, Reading, 1988.

This so-called "orange book" contains a collection of articles written by professionals who have developed or used PostScript applications in their work. Subjects dealt with include sophisticated ways to use fonts and dictionaries, color issues, halftoning, precise kerning, tracking, and letterspacing.

[75] Richard Rubinstein. *Digital Typography—An Introduction to Type and Composition for Computer System Design.* Addison-Wesley, Reading, November 1988. Reprinted with corrections.

This book describes a technological approach to typography. It shows how computers can be used to design, create, and position the graphical elements used to present documents on a computer.

[76] Joachim Schrod. The Components of TEX. *TEXline,* 14:7–11, February 1992.

A short description of the supplementary programs and files, which, together with TEX, constitute a complete typesetting and authoring system.

[77] Ross Smith. *Learning PostScript—A Visual Approach.* Peachpit Press, 1085 Keith Avenue, Berkeley, CA 94708, 1990.

A very gradual and "visual" tutorial on the PostScript language. It introduces the main elements of the language with the help of examples, whose code is shown together with a short explanation on the left-hand pages, with the facing pages showing the resulting output.

[78] Friedhelm Sowa. Bitmaps and halftones with BM2FONT. *TUGboat,* 12(4):534–538, November 1991.

BM2FONT converts different kinds of bitmap files into TEX fonts and writes an input file for integrating these graphics into documents.

[79] *Code typographique.* Syndicat national des cadres et maîtrise du livre, de la presse et des industries graphiques, 13ᵉ édition, 1954.
Typographic rules for French as used by the French printing industry.

[80] Paul Taylor. Commutative Diagrams in TEX (version 4). Electronic document distributed with the package, January 1993.
A Commutative diagram package. Compatible with most TEX formats. It uses the LATEX line fonts for diagonal arrows, or optionally can use PostScript specials to produce rotated arrows.

[81] Philip Taylor. The future of TEX. In *Proceedings of the 7th European TEX Conference, Prague*, pp. 235–254, September 1992.
A discussion of options on how to perpetuate the TEX philosophy, after Donald Knuth decided to freeze the current implementation.

[82] TEXplorators Corporation, 1572 West Gray, #377, Houston, TX 77019-4948 *Mathtime, PostScript fonts for typesetting mathematics with TEX*, 1993.
A user's guide, distributed with the fonts, that explains how to install and use the *Mathtime* fonts.

[83] Harold Thimbleby. "See also" indexing with Makeindex. *TUGboat*, 12(2):290, June 1991.
Discusses how to code a "see also" entry for your indexes.

[84] Harold Thimbleby. Erratum: "See also" indexing with Makeindex, *TUGboat* 12, no. 2, p. 290. *TUGboat*, 13(1):95, April 1992.
An erratum and some comments on [83].

[85] The Unicode Consortium. Unicode 1.0—Draft Standard. Technical report, The Unicode Consortium, 1990.
A description of the 16-bit encoding standard adopted by most computer manufacturers. Unicode version 1.1 is identical to the 16-bit base plane of ISO-10646, see [35].

[86] *The Chicago Manual of Style.* University of Chicago Press, thirteenth edition, 1982.
Since 1906 the University of Chicago Press *Manual of Style* has been the standard reference tool for authors, editors, and proofreaders in the United States and elsewhere. Thanks to its clear presentation, its many examples, its extensive index, and its detailed treatment of its various subject areas, the *Chicago Manual* provides easy-to-understand and straightforward guidelines for preparing your texts for the great majority of American publishers.

[87] Peter Vollenmeider. *Encapsulated PostScript: Applications for the MacIntosh and PC.* Prentice-Hall and Carl Hanser, Hertfordshire, 1990.
This book focuses on how you can easily mix text, graphics, and images at the PostScript level by using the Encapsulated PostScript format as an interchange standard. It emphasizes practical issues such as how to import graphics produced by desktop publishing tools in your documents on personal computers, UNIX workstations, or mainframes.

[88] Michael Vulis. VTEX enhancements to the TEX language.
      TUGboat, 11(3):429–434, September 1990.

      The author describes his commercial VTEX system, which supports its own scalable font
      format. More details are given in Michael Vulis's book *Modern TEX and Its Application*, CRC
      Press, Ann Arbor, 1993

[89] Michael J. Wichura. PₗCTEX: Macros for drawing PₗCtures.
      TUGboat, 9(2):193–197, August 1988.

      PₗCTEX is a collection of TEX macros that make it easy to typeset complex pictures, especially
      mathematical figures. The PₗCTEX manual is available from TEX Users Group.

[90] Reinhard Wonneberger. *LATEX Kompaktführer*. Addison-Wesley Verlag,
      Bonn, Germany, third edition, April 1993.

      A handy overview (in German) of all aspects of LATEX that average users need in their daily
      work.

[91] Reinhard Wonneberger and Frank Mittelbach. BIBTEX reconsidered.
      TUGboat, 12(1):111–124, March 1991.

      After a general discussion of BIBTEX, several proposals for enhancements and changes are
      discussed.

[92] Haviland Wright. SGML frees information.
      Byte, 17(6):279–286, June 1992.

      Describes how SGML can help you avoid being overwhelmed by your data by emphasizing
      the definition of access structures for your information.

[93] Y&Y, 106 Indian Hill, Carlisle, MA 01741. *LucidaBright + LucidaNewMath*,
      1992.

      A user's guide, distributed with the fonts, that explains how to install and use the *Lu-
      cidaBright + LucidaNewMath* fonts.

[94] Maurizio Zocchi. LATEX's Index Processing. *TUGboat*, 8(1):62, April 1987.

      The description of INDTEX, a LATEX index processor running on VAX/VMS and on MS-DOS.

[added in the second printing]

[95] George Grätzer. *Math into TEX: A Simple Introduction to AMS -LATEX*.
      Birkhäuser, Boston, 1993.

      The first part of the book provides the novice user of AMS-LATEX with a simple approach,
      based on many examples, a formula gallery, sample files, and templates. The second part
      contains a systematic discussion with detailed examples and rules of all aspects of AMS-
      LATEX, while the final part looks at more advanced customization issues.

Index

Bold face page numbers are used to indicate pages with important information about the entry, e.g., the precise definition of a command or a detailed explanation, while page numbers in normal type indicate a textual reference.

Production Notes

This book was typeset by the authors on a Hewlett-Packard and a Sun workstation at CERN in Geneva and on a DEC Station in Mainz using an early version of LaTeX2_ε. Files were exchanged back and forth between the two sites via Internet electronic mail. Typeset chapters where translated into PostScript using dvips; proofs were printed on an Apple LaserWriter Pro and a Xerox Docutech. For copyediting and proofreading, PostScript files were also copied via ftp to Addison-Wesley's Sun computer in Reading, so that the chapters could be printed locally and the turn-around time for introducing changes was minimized.

The final version of the book—from front to back—was produced with a single huge LaTeX job. The index was generated from the LaTeX .idx file using *MakeIndex*; the bibliography was prepared with BibTeX. Four LaTeX runs were necessary to correctly resolve all references. The resulting PostScript file, 9.5 Mbytes in size, was then copied, in pieces, by ftp to Reading where camera-ready copy was produced on a Varityper 4300P at 1200 dpi.

The cover art of the *Companion* was rendered by Toni Saint-Regis, and the designer of the interior was Mark Ong of Side-by-Side Studios. Frank translated the designer's specifications into a LaTeX2_ε class file. The typeface used for the main text is Lucida Bright 9.5/12pt designed by Bigelow & Holmes, the sans serif font is Lucida Sans also by Bigelow & Holmes, and the typewriter font is Computer Modern Typewriter 10/12pt by Donald Knuth. Chapter heads are set in Lucida Bright bold 36/38pt; section heads in 14/15pt in the same typeface.

The production of the *Companion* was a challenge—both for the authors and for LaTeX. Indeed, several bugs were found in the packages when we tried to use them all together in a single LaTeX job.

In this book we advocate the separation of structure and form and suggest that you avoid visual markup whenever possible. Thus, after typesetting this book it is perhaps time to ask "How well does LaTeX do its job if it is given a design (a class file) and a document file?". For those of you who like data, here are some statistics using the *Companion* as a real-life example: the table below shows the amount of hand-formatting we found necessary to produce the final copy of this book.

To flag all visual formatting clearly (so that it can easily be identified and removed in case the text needs changing), we never used the standard LaTeX commands directly. Instead we defined our own set of commands, often simply by saying, for instance, \newcommand{\finalpagebreak}{\pagebreak}.

The table divides the commands used into three groups. The first deals with changes to the page length: \finallongpage and \finalshortpage run a page long or short, respectively, by one \baselineskip. The command \finalforcedpage is an application of \enlargethispage* and is therefore always followed by an explicit page break in the source. The techniques for defining such commands are explained in section 4.4. The second group contains the commands for "correcting" LaTeX's decision about when to start a new page, and the final group contains a single command for adding or substracting tiny bits of vertical space to improve the visual appearance.

The average number of corrections made with commands from the first group is slightly over 20%, or one out of five double spreads, since we applied such a change always to pairs of pages. If you look at the chapters with a large percentage of corrections, you will find that they contain either very large in-line examples or large tables that should stay within their sections.

Hard page breaks were inserted, on average, every tenth page, often in conjunction with a command from the first group. In most cases this was used to decrease the number of lines printed on the page.

Most uses of \finalfixedskip can be classified as "correcting shortcomings in the implementation of the design." With an average of about 16% this may seem high. But in fact such micro adjustments usually come in pairs, so this corresponds to approximately one correction every 12 pages.

As a conclusion, we think that LaTeX did a good job given the complex content. Even without any hand-formatting most pages were acceptable. It is for you to judge whether the additional effort was worth the trouble.

Chapter	2	3	4	5	6	7	8	9	10	11	12	13	14	A1
Number of pages	36	36	18	40	16	58	44	16	36	36	26	50	18	36
\finallongpage	0	3	1	0	3	10	4	2	3	0	4	9	7	4
\finalshortpage	0	5	4	4	0	2	10	0	0	8	6	0	0	2
\finalforcedpage	1	0	0	2	2	0	1	0	0	1	0	1	0	0
Page length change	1	8	5	6	5	12	15	2	3	9	10	10	7	6
Average per page	.03	.22	.29	.15	.33	.08	.34	.13	.08	.25	.38	.2	.39	.17
\finalpagebreak	4	5	2	4	3	7	12	1	0	6	4	5	3	6
\finalnewpage	0	1	0	0	0	0	0	0	0	0	0	1	0	0
Page break change	4	6	2	4	3	7	12	1	0	6	4	6	3	6
Average per page	.11	.17	.11	.1	.19	.12	.27	.06	0	.17	.15	.12	.17	.17
\finalfixedskip	4	3	4	11	0	8	2	2	0	14	6	10	7	3
Average per page	.11	.08	.22	.28	0	.14	.05	.13	0	.39	.23	.2	.38	.08
Sum	9	17	11	21	8	27	29	5	3	29	20	26	17	15
Average per page	.25	.47	.61	.53	.5	.47	.66	.31	.08	.81	.77	.52	.94	.42